CONFEDERATE GENERAL R. S. EWELL

CONFEDERATE

GENERAL

R. S. EWELL

ROBERT E. LEE'S HESITANT COMMANDER

PAUL D. CASDORPH

THE UNIVERSITY PRESS OF KENTUCKY

Publication of this volume was made possible in part by a grant
from the National Endowment for the Humanities.

Editorial and Sales Offices: The University Press of Kentucky
663 South Limestone Street, Lexington, Kentucky 40508-4008
www.kentuckypress.com

08 07 06 05 04   5 4 3 2 1

Library of Congress Cataloging-in-Publication Data

Casdorph, Paul D.
  Confederate general R.S. Ewell : Robert E. Lee's hesitant commander /
Paul D. Casdorph.
     p. cm.
Includes bibliographical references (p.) and index.
  ISBN 0-8131-2305-4 (hardcover : alk. paper)
  1. Ewell, Richard Stoddert, 1817-1872. 2. Generals—Confederate
States of America—Biography. 3. Confederate States of America.
Army—Biography. 4. United States—History—Civil War,
1861-1865—Campaigns. I. Title.
  E467.1.E86C37 2004
  973.7'3'092—dc22   2003024591

 Member of the Association of
American University Presses

To Homer Haskell Miller
1916–1996

CONTENTS

Illustrations follow page 212

MAPS

PREFACE

In the course of the fifty-two-month Confederate War for Independence, nineteen men attained the rank of lieutenant general, one of whom was Richard Stoddert Ewell, a forty-six-year-old Virginian and West Point graduate with more than twenty years' service in the Federal army. Upon the untimely death of Stonewall Jackson at Chancellorsville in May 1863, Ewell shot to prominence in the Confederate pantheon when he not only replaced the immortal commander but also attained corps command of his own in the fabled Army of Northern Virginia. Two years before the army reorganization of May 1863, Ewell had been one of the first experienced soldiers to join the Southern cause, and he remained active in the Virginia fighting from its beginning to the final Confederate collapse.

Although Ewell achieved a high station in the Southern war effort, he was a flawed commander in that he could not, or would not, act at the critical moment. Accordingly, a secondary consideration of this attempt to chronicle his life and career as first a cavalryman in the west and later as a Confederate leader is an examination of why Lee, with the acquiescence of President Jefferson Davis, should entrust to a seemingly impaired soldier one-third of the major force fighting for Southern independence. As early as the First Manassas in July 1861, many thought Ewell should have been charged with treason when he failed to seize the initiative by declining to move forward while holding the extreme right under P. G. T. Beauregard. Although he escaped censure on a technicality, his division was assigned to Jackson's Valley Army, where he did some hard trooping in the Shenandoah. Separated from Lee's direct charge, but serving under Stonewall's careful eye, Ewell developed into an able campaigner. He marched with Jackson to the defense of Richmond during the Seven Days battles, where he saw some good service in that memorable campaign.

When the army moved, with Lee in command, tragedy struck at Groveton on the eve of the Second Manassas; a severe wound resulted in

the battlefield amputation of Ewell's leg, leaving him to face a long recuperation in the mountains of western Virginia and in Richmond. Under
the supervision of his future wife, Mrs. Lizinka Brown, an early playmate
as well as his cousin, he slowly regained his strength. Nevertheless, some
officers thought the injury not only hindered his physical powers but also
further contorted his psyche. Ewell missed the Maryland campaign and
the bloodletting at Fredericksburg as well as the unparalleled Confederate
triumph at Chancellorsville, yet when Lee reshaped his army after Jackson's
passing, he chose to ignore Ewell's defects as an aggressive fighter. When
Lee undertook his invasion of Pennsylvania with Ewell leading the Second
Corps, he achieved a marked success at the Second Battle of Winchester
on the march north. At Gettysburg, however, the old Ewell returned when
his lack of aggressive action failed to secure the Confederate left at Cemetery Hill and Culp's Hill, ultimately leading to the loss of the great battle.
His lack of drive for whatever reason also earned him eternal damnation in
the eyes of most Civil War scholars to the present day.

Ewell, who was descended from families with long political, military, and professional ties to Virginia and Maryland, remained at Lee's
side as commander of the Second Corps for more than a year following
the debacle at Gettysburg. His wife—strong-willed, wealthy, and something of a social climber—played a prominent role in his career after
1863, which led to taunts of "petticoat government" among his staff and
senior officers. Finally, after a dismal showing in the Wilderness campaign and the murderous fighting at Spotsylvania, Lee had had enough.
Using the pretext of poor health, he entrusted the Second Corps to Jubal
Early, but, unable to abandon an old comrade, he placed Ewell in charge
of the Richmond defenses.

In spite of his well-known eccentricities, many thought him a lovable
old campaigner, who not only marshaled a polyglot assortment of clerks
and mechanics during the last months of the Confederate saga but also
oversaw enlistment of the first black companies into the army for a last-
ditch defense of the national capital. When the time arrived to abandon
the city, Ewell was again unable or unwilling to act on his own in the face
of a weeks-old charge from Lee and save Richmond from its terrible destruction by fire. After being captured at Sailor's Creek, three days before
Lee's surrender at Appomattox, he was incarcerated for several months in a
Massachusetts prison. Released from Federal custody in July 1865, Ewell
spent the remaining seven years of his life on a Tennessee farm owned by
his wife and on a leased Mississippi cotton plantation. Duty and circum-

stance had converged to produce an extraordinary life—a military life not only devoted to the Confederate cause but also one shaped by forces not fully appreciated by his contemporaries nor by the intervening years.

My serious interest in Ewell first surfaced while working on an earlier book about Robert E. Lee and Stonewall Jackson during the 1980s when I began to wonder why a man with such defects of character should reach a high station at a time of national crisis. From the beginning of my attempts to gather scholarly materials, I have enjoyed the enthusiastic support of numerous archivists around the country at historical societies as well as university libraries: Virginia Historical Society, Chicago Historical Society, Huntington Library, University of Missouri Library, Library of Congress, Maine Historical Society, Tennessee State Library and Archives, Perkins Library at Duke University, Preston Library at the Virginia Military Institute, Kanawha County Public Library, Swem Library at the College of William and Mary, West Virginia University Library, New York Historical Society, Massachusetts Historical Society, as well as many others. I can honestly say that I never received a negative or indifferent reply to my inquiries, and more times than not my requests for manuscript items brought tips about materials unknown to me.

Additionally, my appreciation is expressed to Celene Seymour and her staff—Lynn Edington, Lois McCarthy, and Beth Lewis—at the Marshall University Library for securing more library loans than any patron has a right to expect. Librarians at West Virginia State College—Shonnette Koontz, Diana Haberfield, Carol Machusak, and Nancy McClanahan—showed me every courtesy when I asked for their help. A former student of mine, Sherry Hodges Buchla, once more came to my aid by ferreting several items from the National Archives. Whitney Walker took my crude drawings and expertly fashioned the several maps that enliven the text. My wife, Patricia Barker Casdorph, found time to type the manuscript and to offer a congenial work environment; Ada Caruthers helped with the typing, and I give a note of thanks to Alex Cohen, Harvard Medical School, who offered excellent insights about Ewell's supposed psychological composure.

I want to thank several librarians who went beyond the "extra mile" in helping with the research. Richard Strader was unfailingly kind and helpful during my visits to the Southern Historical Collection at the University of North Carolina. John Coski at the Museum of the Confederacy, Richmond, alerted me to important items I had missed. Stuart Frazer, Old Dominion University, graciously secured several Civil War–era newspapers for me. Lynda Crist, Jefferson Davis Papers, again shared materials with me from the extensive collection of Confederate archives at Rice University, Houston. Suzanne Christoff and Debbie McKeon-Pogue, archivists at West Point, helped me sort out Ewell's career on the Hudson. Others who helped were Dick Gilbreath, University of Kentucky Cartography Lab, who gave unstintingly of his time and interest, as well as Monica Brooks, Marshall University, and Walter S. Griggs, Virginia Commonwealth University, who assisted in my unending search for materials.

In closing I must acknowledge two gentlemen in a special manner: Dennis R. Prisk, Distinguished Professor at Marshall University, who facilitated my work through a personal kindness, and the late Ronald Ross Wiley, librarian at West Virginia State College, who responded to my untold phone calls for detailed information.

Chapter 1

BEGINNINGS

The untimely death of Stonewall Jackson in May 1863 paved the way for Major General Richard Stoddert Ewell to join a select group of Confederate fighting men. "I agree with you in believing that our army would be invincible if it could be properly organized and officered," a shaken Robert E. Lee told a subordinate officer upon Jackson's misfortune at Chancellorsville. "But there is the difficulty—proper commanders—where can they be found?" As Lee cast about for Jackson's replacement in the interval between Chancellorsville and the ill-fated Pennsylvania campaign, it is puzzling in retrospect that he should have settled upon Ewell to marshal his reconstituted Second Corps. Although Ewell was a West Point graduate and had been a dutiful army officer on the Indian frontier for more than twenty years before the firing upon Fort Sumter, he was clearly a man with problems—problems that soon came to the fore in the Army of Northern Virginia. After marginal service at First Bull Run, his performance improved while tramping through the Shenandoah with Jackson and during the Seven Days around Richmond, where that stalwart fighter was able to direct his every move. At the Second Manassas Ewell had suffered a crippling wound that resulted in the amputation of his left leg, which no doubt compounded his existing tendency to hold back whenever forceful action was demanded.[1]

Brigadier General Eppa Hunton, who did not care for Ewell and who later became a Virginia congressman and U.S. senator, probably spoke for much of the army when he wrote after Appomattox that in the early part of the war "he was a splendid soldier until he lost his leg and married his wife. I don't think he was valuable afterwards." Apparently Lee himself

1

had misgivings about Ewell as he reshaped his army following the loss of "Mighty Stonewall." The two corps of Jackson and James "Old Pete" Longstreet were divided into three under Longstreet, Ewell, and Ambrose Powell Hill on the eve of Gettysburg, when all of Lee's commanders let him down. "We . . . talked of Gen. Ewell, of whom he spoke very kindly, said he had known him in the west & that he had long known his faults as a military leader," reports William Allan about a March 1868 conversation at Lexington, Virginia, where Lee served as president of Washington College (now Washington and Lee University). Although Ewell did not actually marry his first cousin Mrs. Lizinka Brown until after his appointment to corps command, which brought more than a little condemnation from his fellow officers, Lee was blunt when he spoke to Allan. Lee was obliged to confess that Ewell was afflicted with "quick alternations from elation to despondency" as well as "want of decision." Psychologists and medical men would later characterize such drawbacks as a manic-depressive disorder that was likely evident from Ewell's childhood; his loss of will and his lack of decision-making abilities at critical junctures could have resulted from either mania or depression separately, but the modern medic would be hard-put to identify it with an underlying manic-depressive syndrome. Ewell was hardly the kind of man to lead one-third of the Army of Northern Virginia into arguably the most critical campaign of the war. Stout men with strong purpose were needed, not psychological and physical cripples; yet Lee chose Ewell, and the result shaped the course of American history. The camaraderie of West Point and the old army coupled with an urgency to fill his command structure with seasoned officers, even if others would have done as well or better, unquestionably pointed Lee toward his fateful decision.[2]

Evidence abounds from the pens of creditable writers that Ewell not only let down the army but also proved a severe disappointment to Lee at Gettysburg and beyond. Even though he was removed from corps command one year after assuming charge of Stonewall's old berth, Ewell had his defenders. Soldiers besides his stepson, Major Campbell Brown, his aide during the war years and his constant apologist afterward, came to his support. "General Ewell as a soldier, was brave, frank, and generous, faithful to his country and true to every conviction of duty, and of such eminent and acknowledged military merit that, at the dying request of the immortal Jackson, succeeded to the command of his battle-scarred veterans," proclaimed a committee of Confederates headed by Generals E. Kirby Smith and Bushrod Johnson upon Ewell's premature death at age fifty-four. "That while his record is the highest meed of praise that can attach to his name, yet, as comrades and friends, we will by all proper means, perpetuate his name and fame to posterity."[3]

Ewell sprang from a long line of English forebears native to County Surrey near London, who had been in Virginia since the seventeenth century. Through the years, notes a family historian, the name has appeared in various old world instruments as "Awell, Etwell, Ewell, Yowell, Yewell, and Uel." From Danish origins we have it as "Berwell and Sewell." Exactly when the first Ewells made their way across the Atlantic to their home base in Prince William County, Virginia, is a matter of some dispute. Ewell's older brother, Benjamin Stoddert, sets 1670 for John Ewell's appearance in Prince William. Other family antiquarians, however, discount that finding and put the "first known Ewell" in America as one James Ewell found living at "Pungoteague in Accomack County on the Eastern Shore as early as 1668 who judging from his will and other records was a 'man of substance.'"[4]

One Charles Ewell migrated from the Delmarva Peninsula around 1710 to establish a branch of the family in Lancaster County on the Western Shore. Within a decade or so, two sons—Charles II and Bertrand—had departed the Lancaster Ewells near Richmond at the confluence of the Rappahannock and Chesapeake Bay for Prince William. Here, on the Occoquan River below its juncture with Bull Run, the brothers not only acquired extensive land holdings, but they also amassed fortunes of considerable merit while operating iron furnaces and cultivating tobacco. Bertrand Ewell derived his name from Jean de Bertrand, Count de Joli, who fled Catholic France upon Louis XIV's revocation of the Edict of Nantes for Protestant England, where he married into the Ewell clan before its migration to Accomack County; generations of Ewells in this country have since employed the name. The brothers had established themselves in Dettingen Parish of Prince William between 1739 and 1747 when Bertrand Ewell became county surveyor and founder of the town of Dumfries. Charles II, great-grandfather of General Richard S. Ewell, busied himself with establishing an iron furnace on the Occoquan. Considerable care was taken by both men to restrict their land acquisitions to areas beyond the pale of Lord Fairfax.[5]

Ewell's forebear Charles II married Sarah Ball, "a near relative of George Washington," in 1786. The Ewells were thus hurled into the first families of Virginia after a young widower named Augustine Washington took Sarah's twenty-three-year-old sister, Mary, as his second wife in 1731 and one year later became the father of the nation's first president. Charles II forged a closer link with the Washington clan when he organized and led a 120-man militia company to assist Colonel George Washington following Edward Braddock's defeat in the French and Indian War. Bertrand and Charles II carved a significant portion of their holdings in southern Prince William from a forty-thousand-acre tract owned by the Burwell family as both increased their fortunes after the county was created in 1731. On March 25 the legislature had set the boundaries for their new home: "all the lands on the head of said counties, above Chopawansick Creek on Potomac River, and Deep Run of Rappahannock River, and a southwest line to be made from the head of the north branch of the said creek, to the head of the Said Deep Run . . . To be made a distinct county, and shall be called and known by the name of Prince William County." The county, named for William, Duke of Cumberland, son of George II and Queen Caroline, is situated almost within sight of the Federal City; Alice M. Ewell says (1931) the lights of Washington were plainly visible from forty miles afield at Bel Air, the mansion built by Charles II for his growing family.

A staunch Episcopalian, Charles II and his brood became regular communicants of Dettingen Parish, created in the 1740s and named after Cumberland's great triumph during the War of the Austrian Succession. Situated south of Bull Run and extending to the Quantico River, Prince William is close to Mount Vernon on the Potomac and is nestled between Loudoun and Fauquier counties on the north and west as well as the Potomac estuary, which forms its easternmost boundary. Part of the famed Northern Neck, Prince William became home to generations of Ewells, including Lieutenant General Richard Stoddert Ewell.[6]

Three successive Jesse Ewells were born to Charles II and Sarah Ball; the first, Jesse I (1743–1805), became the grandfather of Richard Ewell after marrying a cousin, Charlotte Ewell, in October 1757. One of his younger brothers, James, who built a mansion at Greenville, Virginia, went him one better and successively wed two cousins. Charlotte Ewell, Jesse I's first cousin, was a daughter of Bertrand. Among the eighteen children born to this apparently happy union was Dr. Thomas Ewell, the father of Richard S. Ewell. "By the time Thomas Ewell was born in 1785, Ewell family estates were scattered over the length and breadth of Prince William County, and the Ewells had become a perfect example of the entangled cousinry so prevalent among Virginia's upper class in the eighteenth century," observes historian Anne Chapman. "Brothers of one family married sisters of another; a majority married his first cousin, sometimes successively." Richard

Ewell was no exception to the family tradition when he married his own first cousin on the eve of the Gettysburg campaign.[7]

A contemporary of Thomas Jefferson at the College of William and Mary, Jesse I remained a lifelong friend of the third president, and like his father in the French and Indian fracas, he served as a colonel of militia during the Revolution, thus maintaining family ties with the Washingtons. Percy Gatling Hamlin, an early biographer of Richard S. Ewell, labels Jesse I as an eccentric officer "who did some severe marching but who never seemed to have had the fortune to get up in time for battle." Although Jesse I learned that Cornwallis had surrendered before his troops could reach Yorktown, he afforded a generous hospitality to the great and near great at his Minnieville mansion, Bel Air, until his death at age seventy-two. The grand old home, still standing at a crossroads near the Quantico Marine Training facility, was a formidable place from the beginning: "The 5,600-square-foot homestead was built in 1741 by [Charles] Ewell . . . on a high hill to protect the family from malaria." Mrs. William Flory, a twentieth-century owner and occupant of Bel Air, continues: "The 14-room house boasts what has been called Virginia's largest chimney, 20 feet wide on the outside. The enormous state dining room has a fireplace that seats two people comfortably inside, with the burning fire set further inside. People sit in it to warm up." Local superstition holds that ghosts haunt Bel Air even though George Washington was entertained at its bountiful tables and Thomas Jefferson was a frequent overnight lodger as he traveled between the capital city and Monticello.[8]

Although Jesse I died twelve years before Richard Ewell's birth in 1817, Robert E. Lee's future lieutenant was surely an heir to the elite social and economic milieu of pre-1861 Virginia; Ewell's own father, Dr. Thomas Ewell, was born at Bel Air, May 2, 1785, before either Washington or Jefferson reached the presidency. Like his own son, Thomas Ewell was reared in the slaveholding environment of the Tidewater with all of its inbred advantages, even if he chose medicine rather than farming or the soldier's life as his chief endeavor. He would have been a mere fourteen years of age at Washington's death and twenty-four when Jefferson left the White House. Jesse I borrowed money and sold property to send his son Thomas to Philadelphia, where he studied under the renowned Benjamin Rush and other prominent physicians of the day. The precocious lad, who had already been apprenticed to a Virginia doctor before his university studies, was not unappreciative of his father's exertions. "[M]y intention in coming down [to Bel Air] was not to dance—but to try to add to your pleasure and happiness—which is among the first wishes of my heart," he informed the elder Ewell in December 1802. He also intended to call upon "Mrs. Washington," Thomas said, to pay his respects.[9]

Thomas Ewell, who received his medical diploma shortly before his twentieth birthday, was not an indolent young man. Something of a crank, who experienced lifelong difficulty with personal relationships, he developed an early literary flair as well as the cultivation of prominent men, including James Madison and Thomas Jefferson, to advance his career. In 1806, at age twenty-one he published a "469-page book entitled, 'Plain Discourses on the Laws of Matter,'" a tome on "modern chemistry." At least six books followed before his death at age forty, including a volume on the English philosopher David Hume. He also found time to send voluminous correspondence to fledgling medical journals in this country. An 1806 piece on "Generation" demonstrated his somewhat peculiar approach to things medical. In this piece, according to Dr. Jesse Ewell, Thomas wrote: "I am convinced that the presence of pure, vital or oxygen gas, is necessary to give the first animation to the embryo formed in the uterus; that is only after this union with a little oxygen, that the embryo is enabled to receive more oxygen and animation from its mother. . . . And that consequently, coition will always be unfruitful unless it be done in pure-air, so that some oxygen gas may be protruded into the uterus." On another occasion, while working in Washington Thomas Ewell was nearly lynched by irate relatives for dissecting the brain of a deceased patient without permission.[10]

While serving as a naval surgeon—a position obtained with the help of President James Madison—Thomas Ewell met and wooed twenty-four-year-old Elizabeth Stoddert, daughter of Benjamin Stoddert, who had served as first secretary of the navy under John Adams. Elizabeth had been born in 1784 to distinguished Maryland stock—a family that had been in America as long as the Ewells. The first Stoddert to cross the Atlantic, a Scotsman named James, arrived in the colony during the mid-seventeenth century; a surveyor, James Stoddert settled at La Plata, Charles County, across the Potomac estuary from Prince William County. His son, Thomas Stoddert, like Charles Ewell in Virginia, served as an officer in the Maryland militia during the French and Indian conflict. Thomas's marriage into the Marshall family, also from Maryland, produced the future politician, prominent businessman, and friend of presidents. Benjamin Stoddert (1751–1813), second in a line from the early Scottish surveyor, born near La Plata, became the grandfather of Richard Ewell as well as the founder of a sizeable economic empire in the Georgetown-Washington area.[11]

Apprenticed and schooled as a merchant, Benjamin Stoddert entered the Revolution as a captain in the Maryland militia at the outbreak of trouble with George III. "[H]e was wounded at the battle of Brandywine, so badly according to his granddaughter, that he was troubled until his death in 1813," notes his biographer. When his regiment was merged with a Pennsylvania outfit in 1779, he resigned after finding himself outranked by new officers. Although Stoddert had established himself in the army, his political contacts skyrocketed when he was appointed secretary to the war board, a high-priority post he held with distinction until February 1781. His rising governmental and business contacts were put on hold, however, as he courted Rebecca Lowndes, daughter of a well-to-do Bladensburg tobacco merchant, whom he married on June 17, 1781. Stoddert's grandson Benjamin Stoddert Ewell suggests that his grandmother also descended from the Bladen and Tasker families of Maryland.[12]

With the return of peace, Benjamin Stoddert moved his young family to Georgetown, Maryland, then a thriving port on the Potomac, where he quickly formed various partnerships to capitalize on the tobacco and mercantile trade. The young couple produced eight children between 1782 and 1798, including Elizabeth, born in 1784, who became the wife of Thomas Ewell and mother of General Richard S. Ewell; another daughter, Harriet, born five years after Elizabeth, married George Washington Campbell of Tennessee, onetime ambassador to Russia, and became the mother of Lizinka Campbell Brown (named after the Russian empress), Richard S. Ewell's childhood playmate and future wife. By 1783 Benjamin Stoddert had amassed sufficient wealth to build a new home for his growing family at the corner of Thirty-fourth and Prospect Streets in Georgetown. Located within a few blocks of Georgetown College overlooking the Potomac as well as the Chesapeake and Ohio Canal, the multistoried brick mansion known as Halcyon House not only played a significant role in the early lives of Benjamin and Richard Ewell, as well as in the life of their father, but it also became a meeting place for the Washington elite. Widely acknowledged as a "staunch Federalist," Stoddert was summoned by George Washington to conduct confidential negotiations for acquisition of land needed for the new national city following the famed pact between Alexander Hamilton and Thomas Jefferson to position the capital in the South. In time he became president of a specially chartered bank to handle these transactions, as he initially profited from these and other land dealings.

Stoddert eventually lost heavily from overspeculation, however, and saw much of his business empire unravel around him. As troubles with France escalated in the late 1790s, a hue and cry erupted from the "navalists" for creation of a navy department separate from the secretary of war; after heated debate, Congress sanctioned a new cabinet position, which President John Adams signed into law on April 3, 1798. Although the post was first offered to George Cabot of Massachusetts, who declined, Benjamin Stoddert joined Adams's cabinet in May as the first secretary of the navy. His connection with leading Federalists coupled with his wide business experience enabled him not only to weld the infant American navy into an effective war machine but also to successfully prosecute the "undeclared naval war" with France. At the conclusion of Adams's presidency in March 1801, Stoddert remained in office briefly under Thomas Jefferson. After the death of his wife in 1802 and the downward spiral of his financial enterprises, Stoddert turned Halcyon House over to Thomas and Elizabeth Ewell and retired to the Maryland countryside. Earlier, as John Adams left the White House, notes historian Michael A. Palmer, "he wrote Stoddert, who alone stood with the chief executive against the intraparty machinations of Alexander Hamilton, 'I am and ever shall be, I believe, world without end, your friend.'"[13]

Elizabeth Ewell, who lived to age seventy-five, never for a moment let her children forget their rich heritage as scions of the Federalist politician and financial guru. In addition to the uncompromising Federalism preached by Thomas Ewell himself amid his medical and literary excursions, young Richard Ewell and his siblings were related to another nationalist hero. "Parson" Mason Locke Weems, who became the master of Bel Air following his marriage to Fanny Ewell, daughter of Jesse I and a sister of Dr. Thomas Ewell, was a fixture in the early life of the Ewell children. After becoming one of the first Episcopal priests on this side of the Atlantic, if not the first, he not only traveled widely through Georgia and the South preaching and establishing congregations, but he also achieved lasting fame for his biographical writings on George Washington and other Americans of note. Weems was a regular visitor at Stony Lonesome, later home of Thomas and Elizabeth Ewell, before his death in 1825, where the entire family, including young Richard, became enamored with the gregarious clergyman. Although one modern student of Washington has labeled Weems a "persuasive fictionalizer," a story about the cherry tree did not appear until the fifth edition of his *History of the Life and Death, Virtues and Exploits of General George Washington, with Curious Anecdotes Equally Honorable to Himself and Exemplary to His Young Countrymen*; the book went through forty editions and attracted wide notoriety for Weems and his kinsmen. His upbeat writings did much to present Washington as a shining knight on a white charger coming out of the mists to lead America toward independence and nationhood—examples not lost on later generations, including Richard S. Ewell and Robert E. Lee. Lee's own childhood in nearby Alexandria had been heavily influenced by the precepts of Washington, and it is easy to fathom that years afterward he would want a kindred spirit at his side when he tapped Ewell to replace the indomitable Jackson.[14]

It is obvious that young Ewell sprang from an illustrious heritage that included his great-aunt Mariamne Ewell, a sister of Jesse I, "who married Dr. James Craik, the physician and intimate friend of General Washington." Also, when the marriage of Thomas Ewell and Elizabeth Stoddert had taken place at Halcyon House, the nation's first lady, Dolley Madison, was among the well-wishers. Even prior to her father's departure with his heavy debts, Elizabeth had been hostess/mistress at the great house with its swirl of gay and aristocratic soirees. With their enviable social connections, the young couple began their marriage and their family in Georgetown until 1818, when Thomas moved his brood to Philadelphia so that he could secure additional medical training. Six of the ten Ewell children were born in their grandfather Stoddert's mansion: Rebecca Lowndes (1807–1867); Benjamin Stoddert (1810–1894); Paul Hamilton (1812–1831); Elizabeth Stoddert (1813–1891); a girl (1815), and Richard Stoddert, born February 8, 1817, who lived at the home about one year before the family exodus. Two daughters, Charlotte (1818–1819) and Virginia (1820–1837), as well as two sons, Thomas (1822–1847) and William Stoddert (1824–1885), arrived after the family left the Georgetown house.[15]

Thomas Ewell's decision to leave Washington for Philadelphia had been several years in the making. His parting from the navy commenced in 1810–1811 when he worked with Secretary of the Navy Paul Hamilton to secure congressional acceptance of a bill to establish naval hospitals. Hamilton, a notorious inebriate, had been a rice planter and governor of South Carolina before President Madison named him to his first cabinet in 1809; but his heavy drinking—wags said he could only work half a day—and the approach of war with Great Britain prompted a heated confrontation in the presidential office that culminated in Hamilton's resignation and return to South Carolina. Because Thomas Ewell was close enough to Hamilton to name a second son in honor of his friend and associate, Madison's new secretary, a former Pennsylvania congressman named William Jones, immediately demanded Ewell's resignation from the Washington naval hospital. Suffering from alcoholism and depression himself, Thomas Ewell appealed to Madison in vain to save his position. Four years before his son Richard's birth, Thomas, still living at Halcyon House and deprived of his place with the navy, reentered private medical practice.[16]

His effort to find new patients came to an end in 1818, when Dr. Ewell moved the family, including the infant Richard, to Philadelphia for more schooling with his old mentor, Dr. Benjamin Rush. While pursuing his studies, Ewell had a new home built on Lafayette Square in Washington, where the family resettled from 1819 until early 1820. The residence located at 19 Jackson Place was immediately north of the White House. Some debate within the family suggests that Richard Ewell was born in the Jackson Place house, but his stepdaughter's memoir confirms that his birth occurred in the Georgetown home built by his grandfather. Although he was too young to observe the passing saga, his older siblings, Rebecca (Becca) and Benjamin, carried vivid memories of events around James Monroe's White House. Due to worsening health, Thomas Ewell abandoned Jackson Place for a six-hundred-acre farm in his native Prince William County. The Washington property, however, rented to Secretary of the Navy Smith Thompson, remained in Ewell ownership for several years and in fact became the only constant source of income for Mrs. Ewell and the children after her husband's death in 1826. In time the place "was occupied by three Secretaries of the Navy, also by Sir Charles Vaughan, Minister of Great Britain 1834; by John C. Spencer, Secretary of War; William C. Rives, father of Amelie Rives, the novelist, and by Vice President [Schuyler] Colfax," among others. While living in the house, General Daniel Edgar Sickles, then a New York lawyer and congressman, shot and killed Phillip Barton Key, son of Francis Scott Key, in February 1857 on the front sidewalk. He not only escaped a murder conviction by "pleading temporary insanity for the first time in history," but he also met Richard Ewell six years later on the field at Gettysburg. Mrs. Sickles and the younger Key were reputedly involved in a lover's tryst.[17]

All of that lay in the future when Dr. Thomas Ewell purchased the "Belleville" Estate near Nokesville, Virginia, from his cousin Solomon Ewell. Some years later, when Benjamin Ewell returned from West Point on vacation, he dubbed the place "Stony Lonesome" because of its isolation and barren soil. Situated south of Virginia Route 215, the "old brick home, now gone for many years [1941]," was home to Richard S. Ewell from age three until he left for the military academy in 1836. Attempts at farming were made with Ewell family slaves, the most noted being "Mammy," described by Harriet Turner as "a compactly built, stout, yellow woman of dignified presence. She wore a homespun dress, white turban, and white apron." Her sole fault, the account continues, was "a high temper" as she ruled over the younger children with a stern countenance while serving as nursemaid to the Ewell clan. Life at Stony Lonesome was difficult enough, but Thomas Ewell's premature death in 1826 placed a nearly unbearable strain on Elizabeth. With little ready cash beyond the Jackson Place income, the family soon experienced the discomforts of relative poverty.

An unidentified biography in the Ewell Papers at the College of William and Mary's Swem Library, written after the war to counter the notion that Ewell was "an eccentric, cynical mountebank," paints a trying boyhood for the nine-year-old lad after his father passed away. From age twelve, it says, the boy "knew the drudgery of farm labor" and that actual hunger was among "the trials of his boyhood," although with sufficient assets to afford slaves and a working farm, it is difficult to imagine the family in abject want. Hard work and his mother's steady influence, his anonymous biographer maintains, molded the young Richard into a "[warm-] hearted, earnest, and unaffected soldier and man." Elizabeth is presented as "a woman of extraordinary determination and uprightness of character and amid all the pressure of poverty she refused to incur debt or apply to her relatives for aid." She unhesitatingly launched a program to educate and guide her younger children; in order to obtain additional funds, his mother and Rebecca opened a school for neighborhood girls in nearby Centreville. Slowly, Elizabeth was able to salvage the family finances as Richard entered his teen years surrounded by women—Ben left for West Point in the summer of 1828, and Paul Hamilton, five years Richard's senior, was busily engaged in medical study with a local physician. His younger brothers, Thomas and William, were mere toddlers.

The toughness of approaching manhood inevitably shaped the boy into the man. While in early adolescence, Richard Ewell and his younger brother Tom, who was fated to die in the Mexican War, traveled alone into Washington from Stony Lonesome to peddle garden produce. "Darkness caught them on the road and they had to stay all night under a tree," relates his stepdaughter. "Richard was a hardy boy—Tom less so—so Dick with his usual unselfishness took off his coat to cover his younger brother. 'Tom was sickly,' he said, 'and mother would be uneasy.'" On another occasion, when he was sixteen, Richard Ewell attracted considerable local attention by killing a rabid dog that terrorized a "group of men" clustered about the village blacksmith shop.

It is likely that his sister Rebecca oversaw Ewell's early training, as he does not appear to have attended his mother's Fairfax County school; the older children had been schooled in some measure at private Georgetown and Washington academies before the exodus to Prince William. Rebecca, with Elizabeth's, and indeed Mammy's, urging, corralled the young Ewell long enough to instill in him the rudiments of an English education. "With but one year of regular schooling which was at Mr. Fitzhugh's—beside the teaching his mother and sister gave him," he was able to get over the preadmission hurdles at West Point in 1836. During the ten years from Dr. Thomas Ewell's death until he left Stony Lonesome, Richard also had the formidable library of his father near at hand. Since he entertained notions of a military life from an early age, Ben's departure for the Hudson led his older brother to join his Prince William schoolmasters with suggestions and admonitions.[18]

Ewell must have made formal application to West Point while attending "Mr. Fitzhugh's Academy" at seventeen years of age. When he did enter on July 1, 1836, at age nineteen, he was one of the oldest in his class, although several boys had already attained their twentieth birthday;[19] more than a few of his classmates had barely reached their sixteenth year. From the beginning, Elizabeth Ewell was instrumental in securing her son's acceptance to West Point as she enlisted the aid of her brother-in-law George Campbell, married to her sister Harriet since 1812. The Tennessee politician, onetime congressman, U.S. senator, secretary of the treasury, as well as ambassador to Russia, escorted Ewell to "Old Hickory's" office in the White House. The appointment became a reality when Andrew Jackson sent a memo to Lewis Cass, his secretary of war, 1831–1836, commenting favorably upon the young man's petition.[20]

Elizabeth proved an adept advocate for her son when she turned to Campbell, a Masonic brother of Jackson and his close ally in the rough and tumble of Tennessee politics. As a leading member of the "Nashville Central Committee," he had been a key player in securing the chief executive's 1828 Democratic nomination for the presidency. Family connections had long been employed to secure entry into West Point, and here we have one of the first links between Robert E. Lee and Ewell that led to the latter's appointment to corps command almost twenty years later. In the spring of 1824—twelve years earlier—Lee's aunt Nellie Lewis, known as the "Belle of Mount Vernon" and George Washington's favorite grandchild, had accompanied the seventeen-year-old Lee to Andrew Jackson in search of a cadetship. Jackson, who was U.S. senator from Tennessee and chairman of the military affairs committee, had been a longtime acquaintance of Mrs. Lewis. In spite of Lee's later enumeration of Ewell's defects as a soldier, it is easy to imagine a long-term tie between the two. Reminiscences around Civil War campfires during campaign lulls were powerful determinates of the close bonds among the men who led the Army of Northern Virginia—especially those who had weathered the rigors of West Point.[21]

Ewell's admission to the academy, however, did not sail smoothly; Congressman Joseph William Chinn, who gave up his seat on March 3, 1835, apparently at some juncture seconded the request, and Ewell's anonymous biographer at William and Mary says the appointment was "obtained after some difficulty." The difficulty led to his rejection for the class entering in July 1835. Soon an emboldened would-be cadet tracked down Cass in his war department office. "He placed himself where the secretary would see him in passing," for Cass, originator of the concept of popular, or "squatter," sovereignty, seemingly did not recognize Ewell from an earlier encounter. "'Who are you, my boy?' asked General Cass and 'What is your name?' 'I am Richard Ewell, Sir, to whom you promised the appointment to West Point which hasn't been given to me yet,' quietly answered the young Virginian." The appointment was quickly forthcoming for the new class entering in the summer of 1836.

Another Virginia lad, George Henry Thomas, who remained loyal to the Stars and Stripes in 1861 and became forever remembered as "The Rock of Chicamauga," entered the academy in the same class as Ewell. When he stopped in Washington to thank Congressman John Young Mason for his appointment, Thomas received a different, cooler reception than did Ewell. "None of the young men I secured appointments for to the military academy from my district ever succeed in graduating," Mason said. "If you fail, I do not want to see your face again." Both Virginia cadets were destined to achieve a high place in American military annals in spite of their less than happy beginnings.[22]

Richard Ewell's application papers in the National Archives are disappointingly shallow, although armed with a presidential commendation he was certain to receive a favorable response. When his official notification arrived at Stony Lonesome in the spring of 1836—as the followers of Sam Houston, another confidant of the president, were getting heated up for the fights at the Alamo and San Jacinto—the prospective West Point plebe composed a four-line response without hesitation: "I accept with pleasure the appointment of Cadet, as tendered by you. Should further instructions be sent, they will reach me, if directed to Greenwich, Prince William, Va., Respectfully, Richard S. Ewell." Since the letter was addressed to Cass, the appointment must have come directly from the war office. Elizabeth Ewell added a terse codicil that even to the untrained eye was penned by the same person, including her signature: "I consent to my son's signing articles by which he will bind himself to serve the United States, five years." Dated March 28, the missive set the course of Ewell's life, for better or worse: he would be a soldier. A note on the reverse, dated April 1, 1836, attests that "R. S. Ewell accepts his cadet appt."[23]

When Ewell arrived at the academy, he encountered an austere place with a no-nonsense regimen of hard work and discipline. Most plebes came upon West Point for the first time at the Hudson River dockside following a steamer ride from New York City. Once a boy eluded the fleshpots of Gotham—because few of them had ever been more than fifty miles from home—and proceeded to the wharf, wrote his classmate William Tecumseh Sherman, a sixteen-year-old redhead from Lancaster, Ohio, "the first thing he sees is a soldier with his dress and sword and a slate in hand." After his name had been duly noted, the young man confronted a winding pathway to the barracks and school buildings on the plain above; a band of potential porters usually clustered around hoping for a dollar or so to help the newcomer up the hill. Edward O. C. Ord, who entered with the class ahead of Ewell, toted his own trunk up the incline, and presumably the young Virginian did likewise.

About one hundred plebes entered with Ewell in the class of 1840, forty-two of whom survived the rigors of cadet life. Six of the forty-two registered during 1835—twenty-eight, including Ewell, on July 1, and eight on September 1, 1836. "The cadets roomed together regardless of class in two stone buildings," finds historian Stanley Hirshson. "Half lived in the North Barracks, a four-story rectangular structure with plain walls. The South Barracks was three stories and also contained offices and officers' quarters." Cadets slept on pallets on the floor of their rooms, and according to contemporary accounts, neither building had an overabundance of heat in wintertime.[24]

All incoming cadets were required to report early for the annual summer encampment, a fixture at the Point for more than a century before a superintendent named Douglas MacArthur abolished the practice, although it was shortly reinstituted. It exposed the newcomers to military regimens in the field, and it nearly drove Richard Ewell back to Prince William County. "In camp we have nothing to write on but the floor[,] not being allowed to keep a trunk or table in the tents," he apprised his sister Rebecca two months after his arrival. A somewhat disillusioned Ewell said his duties "were much more arduous than I had any idea of." He was mostly disturbed at having to walk incessantly while on guard duty; not only was he often mistaken for his brother Ben, a former mathematics instructor at the academy, but he felt out of place with the finely schooled Yankee boys who "take the lead in every class." When he wrote to Ben in November, his attitude had brightened substantially. "I have got along pretty well so far in my studies, the knowledge of algebra being of considerable service to me," he relayed. "At least I have not found it necessary to study hard, until within the last week or two. But during the last week I have found it no joke. I was obliged to sit up more than half the night several times, or go to the Section room without knowing anything of my lessons." The emphasis on engineering and mathematics, he continues, caused him to "like West Point much better than I did sometime ago," and he vowed to forgo the company of young ladies while at the academy "as I am rather apt to think of them rather than of algebra."[25]

Ewell finished his first year at West Point with fifty-six demerits and a standing of fifty-fifth among all cadets in conduct. Twenty-three members of the fourth class stood higher, but no members of his class had zero demerits. At West Point, then as now, first-year men constitute the fourth class, with the classes falling in descending order until the senior-year students or graduating cadets make up the first class. The conduct system had been worked out by Sylvanus Thayer, who stepped down as superintendent three years before Ewell's entry. During his long service from 1804–1833, Thayer influenced virtually every aspect of cadet life; he devised a method by which every man was measured in an impartial manner—both for his academic performance and his behavior as a soldier and gentleman. Demerits for infraction of academy regulations became critically important to the cadet, because his competency as a scholar was impacted by any defects of character. In other words, a cadet's ranking in any class and at graduation was determined by his academic ranking and his conduct. "When any cadet has a number expressing his demerits on the General Conduct Roll greater then 200," reads the official explanation, "for any one year, such Cadet is declared *deficient* in conduct, and recommended, by the Academic Board, to the War Department, for discharge." Although

Ewell was far below the limit for immediate expulsion, he was cited during 1836–1837 for such offenses as scuffling on the steps, visiting other members of the corps between ten and eleven o'clock at night, inattention at drill, and failure to keep his room swept.[26]

The academic scheme initiated by Thayer remained in use with little change until the twentieth century. It stressed, said Albert Ensign Church, a longtime math professor at the academy, "a course best fitted for an American military education—a course calculated to cultivate the powers of thought rather than store the memory." West Point accomplished these goals by teaching a few subjects well instead of bombarding the student with a smattering of many subjects. In addition to mathematics and engineering, an emphasis was placed on natural and experimental philosophy— a nineteenth-century term for physics—with a liberal offering of French. The French in Thayer's plan was intended to allow the fledging soldiers to read European military treatises in the original; to teach otherwise, academy authorities reasoned, would make their graduates into poets and philosophers rather than soldiers. Most of the actual teaching was done by advanced cadets or low-ranking officers, some of whom were not much older than their students. Richard Ewell told Ben that his first-year math instructor was a Lieutenant Bliss, and, he added: "I like him extremely, but he is not the most dignified person I have ever seen." Bliss, Ewell related, "sometimes sets the whole section to laughing with his grimaces." In Ewell's time at West Point, a number of distinguished professors guided their departments with a firm hand, including Dennis Hart Mahan (father of Alfred Thayer Mahan, the famed naval historian), who taught engineering and military tactics; William H. E. Bartlett, natural philosophy; and Claudius Berard, French.[27]

Ewell adjusted to the instructional routine without difficulty—at least he did not slip but one notch in position during his third-class year: In 1836–1837 he had finished twelfth in a class of seventy-six cadets who remained at year's end; during 1837–1838 he dropped to thirteenth in a class that had fallen to fifty-eight because of continued attrition that was not unique to Ewell's classmates. Ewell's demerits increased to seventy for shortcomings such as permitting disorder around his table at mess and scuffling in the ranks while on parade. At the end of his third-class year he stood eighty-fourth in conduct among a corps of 218 men. Throughout, Ewell drew a monthly pay of "$16 with two rations, in all $28." Like other members of the corps, he used the extra twelve dollars to eat at the mess hall, "a long two-story building," operated by the Cozzens family during much of the nineteenth century. Cozzens reportedly dished up a plain fare that was weak on meat but heavily laced with "bread, butter and potatoes." "At this time the vast majority of cadets lived no better at home, had not been accustomed to many cakes and sugar plums, and seldom complained," Albert Church writes. "Napkins, table cloths, except at dinner, three-tined forks, etc., were not heard of in the mess hall." Ewell's spartan environment extended to the recitation rooms, where the unadorned benches did not have backs, and "indoors lavatories did not appear until 1863."[28]

The Virginian appears to have taken little interest in girls, and years later, when he was on the staff of a school that became Louisiana State University, his chum William Tecumseh Sherman hinted that Richard Ewell was a dependent sort who could not be happy unless he was in the constant company of a select few—that he could not function, even at West Point, without the approval of people he could trust in difficult circumstances. Sherman, who went on to a spectacular Civil War career, finished seven places ahead of him in the 1837–1838 standings. As Ewell was struggling to maintain his position with the class of 1840, the number-one cadet in his forum was a Louisiana boy named Paul Octave Hebert, a future governor of the Pelican State and a Confederate brigadier general. Hebert likewise graduated first in Ewell's class two years later. Described as "a man of no military force or practical genius who preferred red-top boots, and a rat-tail moustache, with a fine equipage, and a fine suit of waiters, to the use of good, practical common sense," Hebert later commanded in Confederate Texas until he was replaced by John Bankhead Magruder from the class of 1830. Although it was customary for third-classmen to receive a lengthy furlough at the conclusion of term, Ewell passed up the opportunity to visit Stony Lonesome. "There is no possibility of my going home this June," he informed Becca on May 6, "but being considerably in debt and as it would be very expensive with little profit, I have thought it best to stay here." Ewell did not think two years away was enough time to break his familial bonds.[29]

Shortly after entering his second-class year, Ewell renewed his pledge to remain a bachelor. When his mother suggested that a Miss Mcrae might be a potential friend, he responded with force: "I made a vow many years ago that I would never marry, and my resolutions have been confirmed by my maturer deliberations," he told Elizabeth Ewell on October 3. Strong sentiments indeed for a twenty-one-year-old! "You know there are two kinds of people who never get married," he elaborated. "One kind includes those who never 'fall in love,' the other (to which I belong) are those whose hearts are very susceptible, yet owing to this quality are too tender to retain an impression long enough for it to lead to any dangerous consequences."

In a fit of youthful exuberance Ewell may have sworn off women, but nearly two years before graduation and a commission, he was mightily concerned about his future in the service. He had convinced himself that his education would be useless outside the army. The cavalry, or dragoons, appeared to attract him most because, as he told his mother, "being stationed in the west, I should have opportunities of resigning and entering upon some independent way of getting my living." Ewell even flirted with the notion of joining the marines, although he told Elizabeth the ordnance service was the best of all possible worlds. "The officers receive a third more pay, have nothing to do, and have more privileges than any others in the army."[30]

Ewell finished the 1838–1839 year with forty-one demerits and a class standing of fifteenth out of forty-six cadets. Among other infractions, he was penalized for being late on one occasion, absent for inspection on another, and failure to keep his shoes polished. In his second class, he was surrounded by future soldiers destined to fight the Confederate War two decades later as well as more than a few Federal officers in the same conflict. All of them, Ewell included, were exposed to the lectures and writings of Dennis Hart Mahan, and, notes Grady McWhiney, the biographer of Braxton Bragg, who graduated in the class of 1837: "In books written before the Civil War, three of Mahan's students—William J. Hardee, class of 1838, Henry W. Halleck, class of 1839, and George B. McClellan, class of 1846—emphasized the advantage of offensive over defensive operations." While Hardee and Halleck were at the academy in Ewell's time and McClellan arrived two years after his departure, Richard Ewell's Civil War performance and even his duty on the Indian frontier indicate that serious offensive campaigning on his own account was never a part of his military makeup. With few exceptions, such as an occasional Indian raid or the Battle of Winchester in 1863, Ewell was willing to stand back or find an excuse to interpret his orders in a defensive posture. Whether for psychological or neurotic causes, he simply did not become an aggressive campaigner during his later career.[31]

There can be little doubt that Mahan exerted a wide impact upon the American officer corps in the Mexican War as well as upon Confederate and Union officers in the Civil War. "He never commanded troops in action," and he invariably walked about the academy grounds carrying an umbrella in rain or shine during the years he taught Ewell and hundreds of other cadets. Mahan, a prolific writer on military tactics, who lived until 1871, when he died at age sixty-seven, even published a book on Confederate military practice. The present (2002) West Point library catalog lists thirty-eight volumes with his imprint, and none have "the science of war" in the title, although he termed his major course "Engineering and the Science of War." Mahan was officially designated the Professor of Military and Civil Engineering and the Science of War from 1832. Many of his books are revised editions of earlier volumes, and McWhiney relates that one cadet remembered that Mahan's lectures "were restricted almost entirely to short descriptions of campaigns and battles with criticisms upon the tactical positions involved." "Celerity on the battlefield" was at the heart of Mahan's teaching, and his charges were admonished to forgo feelings of big-headedness and to employ "good common sense" just like ordinary people.[32]

A careful search of the West Point library lending records for the 1836–1840 period reflects that Ewell checked out only one book during his four years on the Hudson; and when he did so, he ignored Mahan, who had published two titles prior to Ewell's graduation: *A Complete Treatise on Field Fortification: With the General Outlines of the Principles Regulating the Arrangement, the Attacks, and the Defense of Permanent Works* (1836) and *An Elementary Course of Civil Engineering for Use of the Cadets at the United States Military Academy* (1837). Ewell was no doubt familiar with these works during his studies even if he did not borrow them from the library. What he did take out was a two-volume work by the French writer Baron Simon François Gay de Vernon titled *A Treatise on the Science of War and Fortification* . . . . In 1816–1817 the war department had contracted with Captain John Michael O'Connor, an early instructor at the academy, to translate Gay de Vernon's book, which was intended as a work "for the use of the Imperial Polytechnick School, and Military Schools . . . To which is added a summary of the Principles and Maxims of Grand Tactics and Operations."[33] Volume 2 of O'Connor's treatment was an atlas accompanying the main text. Abner Doubleday, class of 1842, the subsequent inventor of baseball, and W. T. Sherman likewise borrowed the Gay de Vernon text within weeks of Ewell.[34]

Although he was obviously not a bookworm and complained to his mother that he had no dictionary to verify his spelling in his letters to her, Ewell told Ben in March 1840—one month after pursuing Gay de

Vernon—that he had been in the library searching for books on integral and differential calculus. There is no indication, however, that he left the building with either work. Ewell was also exposed to the writings of Baron Antoine Henri de Jomini, a Swiss scholar from the Napoleonic period, who thought a general should have "physical courage, which takes no account of danger." Jomini, who had been translated into English by Captain O'Connor, also based his findings on Gay de Vernon's *Fortification and the Science of War*, to argue that Bonaparte was the master of all things military. Both Mahan and Henry Wager Halleck, his favorite student, "drew deeply upon Jomini in their later books," finds Professor Stephen E. Ambrose, to emphasize "the importance of speed, maneuver, and a strong base of operations, not the attack." When Ewell chose the O'Connor translation of Gay de Vernon, which includes a synopsis of many European theorists, he may well have been pursuing a class assignment, since some of his contemporaries were also reading the same text, although Mahan consistently touted the notion that a study of military history was the avenue to campaign success. Like other pre-1861 West Point men, including Robert E. Lee, who graduated eleven years ahead of him, Richard Ewell left the academy with a strong dose of Napoleonic history and strategy.[35]

When Ewell received his commission on July 1, 1840, forty-two members of his class remained. At number thirteen he was well above the average mark, although he had been incapacitated and even hospitalized during the spring with a severe throat infection. Paul O. Hebert, the future governor, was number one, and the last was a Maine boy, John D. Bacon, destined to die in Mexico City during 1847 from wounds suffered at Churubusco. Eventually, eight of the forty-two, including Ewell himself, gained entry into the prestigious *Dictionary of American Biography*; and the longest surviving member of the class, Robert Plunkett Maclay, from Pennsylvania, lived until 1903, when he died at age eighty-three. Maclay later moved to Mississippi, where he became a cotton planter as well as a Confederate brigadier general during the Civil War.[36]

Class members living in 1861 appear to have divided about evenly in the war between the North and South, with W. T. Sherman, who finished six places behind Hebert, becoming far and away the most prominent Union officer. Ewell without question became the most distinguished Confederate. He made valuable acquaintances with men in his own class, as well as those in other classes, who later fought on both sides of the Civil War. During his first year at the academy he associated with men who had entered as early as 1832, and when he finished in the summer of 1840 fourthclassmen who had entered in 1839 would be there until graduation day in 1843. This ten-year spread afforded him an opportunity to know and observe a wide spectrum of future Civil War officers at close quarters—observations that would stand himself and his Confederate compatriots in good stead on the killing fields of northern Virginia.

"The Order of Merit . . . As determined at the General examination, in June 1840" indicates that Ewell did not score above tenth in any field while attaining his upper-half ranking. His best performance was tenth in Mineralogy and Geology followed by Artillery, eleventh; Engineering, twelfth; Ethics, sixteenth; and Infantry Tactics, twentieth, which was his worst subject. Apparently he had abandoned the boyish exercise of scuffling in the ranks, although he still amassed forty-six demerits during the 1839–1840 year, for a ranking of 126th out of 192 cadets in the entire corps; among other infractions, he was cited for "neglecting his drawing." Several cadets were routinely expelled nearly every term for acquiring more than 200 demerits, yet Ewell accumulated just 213 spread over four years, which may have affected his overall standing in a slight manner. In the weeks leading to his graduation, he informed Ben, who had stayed on at West Point for a short time as an instructor of mathematics, that he would never consider remaining unless it was with the chemistry faculty. Albert E. Church explained that the poorly equipped "Chemical Laboratory, with some apparatus and means of making experiments" was located in the library along with the mineralogy recitation rooms. "My standing in Chemistry was quite respectable and should have been better," he advised his brother. And in a fit of bravado, Ewell said he did not want to teach anything, because: "I have no particular wish to stay in the army but a positive antipathy to starving or to doing anything for a living that requires any exertion of mind or body." For the time being, Ewell added, he had accepted a commission in the United States dragoons.[37]

When Richard Stoddert Ewell left West Point as a second lieutenant in the cavalry, he was fated to spend the next twenty-one years in a moribund army with little or no prospect for speedy promotion. Even fighting in the Mexican conflict and hard service in the Indian wars did not bring advancement beyond the rank of captain. As a West Point graduate he held membership in a select group that many thought were the best-educated men on this side of the Atlantic. In time he would join 303 other West Point–trained officers, including seven from the class of 1840 besides himself, who abandoned the old flag to cast their fortunes with the infant Confederacy. After that, advancement under the Stars and Bars came with startling quickness; within two years, from 1861–1863, he had risen to corps command in the fabled Army of Northern Virginia with the rank of lieutenant general. And it happened because Elizabeth Ewell made certain that her third son found a place on the Hudson.[38]

Chapter 2

DRAGOON

While spending the customary leave upon graduation from West Point with friends and relatives in Prince William County, Richard S. Ewell received orders in late July directing him to Carlisle Barracks in Pennsylvania. His sister Rebecca accompanied him to Washington on his way north, and according to post returns, he "reported for instruction" on September 28, 1840. As he awaited his first regimental berth, Ewell was subjected to a rigorous training regimen designed to turn the academy graduate into an accomplished cavalryman. "I am working harder than I ever did in my life having to be in the stable from Reveille to Breakfast, then drilling and reciting tactics until Dinner & Stable duty until Retreat," he wrote his brother Ben on October 21. "So far from disliking the duties, I would not care if they were increased as I spend the time more agreeably." A few weeks later, however, he told Becca: "Duties here are more constant and laborious than I believe they are at my Post." And, he continued, the drills never ceased because of cold or rainy weather: "Thus far I thank my stars I have been able to stand as much cold as others and think that I can continue to do so."

The post commander was Captain Edwin Vose Sumner, an officer he would encounter again in Mexico as well as in Virginia during the Civil War. Although he admired Sumner in Pennsylvania—even bragging that he was a good drillmaster—both Ewell and his brother Thomas developed a dislike for him during the fighting in Mexico. A leave during October found Ewell in York, Pennsylvania, where he visited several relatives of his mother and "waltzed" with the local girls, proclaiming one in particular "the most strikingly pretty creature" he had ever encountered. But when Sumner gave "a

party" for several officers awaiting new posts, he observed: "The young ladies here are too puritanical to dance, though they have no objection every
now and then to a little flirtation and gossip." Then, after telling his sister
that he would be assigned to a fort in the west, Ewell was posted to Fort
Wayne in "the Cherokee Nation." Unable to call at Stony Lonesome, he left
Carlisle Barracks on November 23, traveling to Oklahoma through Pittsburgh and from there down the Ohio and Mississippi rivers.[1]

Originally known as Camp Illinois and situated on the Illinois River
near present Watts in Adair County, the post subsequently moved thirty-
five miles northward to Delaware County, both in present Oklahoma.
Named for "Mad Anthony" Wayne, Revolutionary War hero and Indian
fighter, the encampment had been moved to its new location in June 1840.
Although an outbreak of sickness prompted the change, Fort Wayne, which
existed until May 1842, was designed to be one of several outposts "extending north and south for a planned military road from Fort Snelling in
Minnesota to Fort Towson" near the Red River. "The post was moved to
Beatties (also Baries, Beaties, etc.) Prairie within the state of Arkansas,"
reads a government document; in actuality, however, it was positioned "near
a big spring in a bend of Spavinaw Creek" immediately across the Arkan-
sas-Oklahoma border from Maysville, the "northwestest town in northwest Arkansas." "Indeed the spring is still running—very much so," writes
Mrs. James Edmondson, a local historian. Spavinaw Creek is a tributary of
the Neosho River before it joins the Arkansas a few miles south of Fort
Gibson. The young lieutenant told his brother Professor Benjamin S. Ewell,
later a Civil War officer and the longtime president of the College of William and Mary, that the post was "a collection of huts" when he got there
from the east. A more healthy location or not, the lonely garrison func-
tioned as an outpost for Fort Gibson, seventy miles to the southwest in
present Muskogee County, Oklahoma.[2]

Ewell, who found the place tiresome, remained at Fort Wayne until
its dissolution and the removal of his company to first Fort Leavenworth
and then Fort Scott. Never very far from home, he reached northeastern
Oklahoma after a journey from Carlisle Barracks through Pittsburgh, where
he attended a theater, "the most blackguard hole I ever saw of the kind."
His boat trip down the Ohio and Mississippi was "agreeable," but when he
disembarked at Montgomery Point—where the White River strikes the
Mississippi—he was obliged to wait several days before finding a boat to
carry him up the White and into the Arkansas. "I was forced to take a
wagon when I steam boated within a few miles of Fort Gibson, making a

two days journey across the country, thereby acquiring a very good idea of Western traveling as we had to swim a stream and were forced to leave a wagon and baggage behind and ride on horses, going into the Fort in style." Ewell apparently thought he would be stationed at Fort Gibson but proceeded to Fort Wayne upon learning that his company had been reposted shortly before his arrival.[3]

About thirty men and three officers besides himself manned the post, including Captain Isaac Prince Simonton, an Ohio-born graduate of the military academy, who died in February 1842. Also present was Lieutenant Robert H. Chilton, three years ahead of Ewell at West Point and a man he would know well in the years ahead; during much of the Civil War Chilton served as Robert E. Lee's chief of staff, and he fought at Ewell's side as commander of the Fifty-seventh Virginia Infantry through the Wilderness and Spotsylvania combat. The post surgeon was Dr. Richard F. French, another Virginian, who had been at Fort Wayne just a short while before Ewell got there. Simonton immediately appointed Ewell quartermaster and commissary, who later told his family in Virginia that he "was half time commanding the post." Even so, Ewell had difficulty occupying himself. "I like the duty very well except my time hangs on my hands," he told Ben in his letter of February 2, 1841. Although many Cherokees owned slaves, his letter expressed a low opinion of the local tribes, and, he continued: "Many of the officers have Cherokee mistresses, a scrape I intend to keep out of, both on account of my purse and taste." By twenty-first-century correctness Ewell's view of native women was blatantly racist, even though the twenty-three-year-old officer confessed that "occasionally a good looking half breed may be seen."[4]

Although he had sworn off women during his years at West Point, like all energetic bachelors, the fair sex was never far from Ewell's mind during the Fort Wayne sojourn. Throughout his stay on the frontier Ewell seemed more concerned with finding a wife than with military matters, or at least equally so. After telling Becca in November that Simonton had borrowed his dictionary, he requested that she have some of her lady friends write to him at Fort Wayne. He also related a brief visit to Fayetteville, Arkansas, "thirty-five miles distant," in which he attended a Campbellite service. A spin-off from the Baptists, the religious group, also known as the Disciples of Christ, had been founded by the Reverend Alexander Campbell in the 1820s and was particularly zealous at proselytizing along the frontier. Although the staunchly antislavery denomination that originated in western Pennsylvania and northwestern Virginia had no allure for Ewell, he told his sister: "I had a great mind to join the brothering and sistering just for the sake of shaking hands with the girls, which is the first ceremony, but was deterred because some of them had been crying and I believe wiping their noses without their handkerchiefs which is considered quite the thing here."

Ewell had an equally poor estimation of the citizenry of Bentonville, Arkansas, whom he proclaimed more ignorant than the Cherokees; as post quartermaster at Fort Wayne and required to purchase supplies in the town, he found their "impertinence at times unbearable." "The good people of Bentonville," he told Becca, treated all army officers with contempt unless they were anxious to land a government contract. He was forced to stay in the Arkansas town during November 1841 while attending the trial of several Fort Wayne troopers accused of "killing an Indian in a drunken brawl, at a miserable assemblage of grog shops" outside the post. And to his disgust, he informed Becca, all were set free. Moreover, Ewell's well-known baldness, an identifying characteristic that followed him for the remainder of his life, showed itself while he served at Fort Wayne. "As there are no wigs to be had, I am obliged to wear a skull cap. It would have made you laugh to have seen the people in the courthouse when I took off my hat," he commented while describing his Bentonville visit. "I really believe they thought I had been shaved for some misdemeanor or other." He had indeed shaved his head in a vain attempt to preserve what hair he had left.[5]

Regimental returns for the First Dragoons report Ewell at Fort Wayne through May 1842, but he surely knew that his days on the Oklahoma-Arkansas border were coming to a close. "Orders are to select a site about 100 miles south of Fort Leavenworth inside the Indian country," he told Becca on April 10, including that Captain Benjamin D. Moore was absent from the post in search of a new location for its garrison. He would write again, he said, when Moore returned "in a few days" with definite word of his new address. A site had been espied by Colonel Stephen W. Kearny, commanding officer of the First Dragoons, several months earlier, and it was confirmed by Moore and Jacob Rhett Motte, an army surgeon, one day before Ewell's letter. The new post, Fort Scott—also known at various times as Camp Scott, Fort Blair, Fort Hemming, and Fort Isley—was officially opened on May 30, 1842, "on the Marmaton River, a tributary of the Osage . . . about eight miles west of the Missouri line in Bourbon County." Ewell marched out of his Fort Wayne bivouac with Simonton and his Company A companions on May 21 and, after a brief detour to Fort Gibson, proceeded northward to his posting in Kansas.[6]

Although he would remain on station at Fort Scott until 1844, he was not pleased with the move. The Osages are "a flock of sheep stealing vagabonds," he told his sister as he prepared to join a caravan of forty wagons toward the Kansas Territory; and he emphasized his displeasure that "we must set to work building log cabins and [the] government must be put to an expense of $4000 on acct of transportation instead of shooting the Indians like the beasts they are." Ewell remained upset at local whites who found "a godsend" at hiring out their wagons and teams to the army for the move: "The chance of getting their teams employed seems to run them almost crazy, scarcely a day passes but they are in to see me 'about a chance for hauling' & this is just the season too that farmers ought to be employed about their corn." One of Ewell's last personal acts at Fort Wayne was the purchase of a fourteen-year-old "negro boy to cook and take care of my horses for me." Presumably the lad accompanied Ewell on his northward trek.[7]

Ewell was attached to the First Dragoons until the outbreak of Civil War, when he resigned to join the Confederacy. The unit—the oldest cavalry regiment in the United States Army—had been formed by an act of Congress in 1832, eight years before Ewell's graduation from West Point. Although it was first activated in 1833 at Jefferson Barracks, Missouri, under the command of Colonel Henry Dodge, the war department had foreseen the need for cavalry units on the frontier during the Black Hawk troubles of 1832. As early as 1833–1834, parts of the regiment, including Company A, marched overland from the Mississippi River to a new posting at Fort Gibson. The satellite outpost at Fort Wayne was established about the time Ewell arrived to assume his first military duties as second lieutenant in Company A. Fort Wayne's abandonment occurred when Ewell and his compeers left the place in May 1842, even though it had another life during the Civil War years. Reactivated by the Confederacy, it served as a training center for the Cherokee officer Stand Watie, who commanded his Indian troops throughout fighting along the frontier. Made a brigadier general in the Confederate army in 1864, Watie had previously marched his cavalrymen out of Fort Wayne to play a pivotal role in the Battle of Pea Ridge during March 1862 at the same time Ewell, an officer in Stonewall Jackson's command, struggled to secure the Shenandoah Valley from Yankee control. Following the Confederate collapse, Fort Wayne lay idle until March 26, 1871, writes a post chronicler, when its "land and property were turned over to the Interior Department for disposition."[8]

Fort Scott became an anchor point on the Western Military Road as a replacement for Ewell's old post. The roadway, authorized under a July 1836 act, stretching from present Minnesota to the Gulf of Mexico was designed for rapid deployment of troops engaged in the protection of frontier settlements from Indian incursions. A northern section ran from Fort Snelling—made famous as a temporary home for Dred Scott in free territory—across Iowa and Missouri to Fort Leavenworth on the Missouri; the middle portion, dominated by Fort Scott, connected Leavenworth with Fort Gibson; and a southern leg followed a zigzag path through Forts Washita, Towson, and Jesup (Louisiana) to the Louisiana coast. Ewell had accurately forecast that his troops would be put to work constructing temporary log structures after their arrival from Oklahoma. The encampment was built on lands belonging to a small New York tribe, while more permanent buildings were erected before year's end. "Magnificent Headquarters House, where commanding officers up to generals resided, was the first major structure completed," finds a post historian. The three-story Headquarters House, completed in 1843 and still standing today, overshadowed the fifty or so structures built of lumber sawed from "the deep forest almost surrounding the fort site alive day and night with anxious, watchful Indians." Although dragoon companies were regularly sent from Fort Scott on frontier duty, the nearby tribes remained remarkably calm throughout the 1840s, and conditions were surely better for Ewell, who, despite his earlier grumbling about the Kansas assignment, was comfortably ensconced in one of "four palatial officers structures." His available letters are uncharacteristically silent regarding living arrangements during the sixteen months' stay at Fort Scott.[9]

The Fort Scott interlude was another monotonous posting for Ewell, although he was sent "on escort duty to Springfield, Mo.," during October 1842. When he returned to Fort Scott from the 160-mile jaunt across southwestern Missouri, he was placed in command of Company A to replace Simonton, who had been assigned elsewhere. But Ewell escaped the garrison routine one month later when he returned to Oklahoma on detached assignment at Fort Gibson. Although his promotion to first lieutenant did not come for another two years—in September 1845, when he was stationed at Jefferson Barracks—he occasionally found himself in charge at Fort Scott until his departure in May 1844. And with few Indians to restrain around the post, Ewell and his fellow officers were obliged to oversee completion of the building program. "At Fort Scott, the works are in progress; they have been delayed in consequence of the troops being necessarily called off to other duty," reads the quartermaster general's report for

December 1844. "Two blocks of officers' quarters, with three sets of soldiers' barracks, are nearly completed and materials are ready for another set of officers' quarters. If laborers can be obtained, the whole may be completed in a few months." By that time Ewell had left Fort Scott for good.[10]

A terse entry in the regimental log says that Ewell, in command of his company, was sent from Fort Scott "for [the] protection of the Santa Fe Trail"; Companies A and C left May 27 and did not return until July 23 on what became a memorable scout through virtually uninhabited sections of western Kansas. Ewell traveled 150 miles northward along the Neosho River until he rendezvoused at Council Grove with Captain Philip St. George Cooke and two additional companies from Fort Leavenworth. Other than Bent's Fort, near present La Junta, Colorado, Council Grove was the most distinctive spot on the famed pathway to Santa Fe, then located in the Republic of Mexico. Situated 110 miles west of the Missouri border, Council Grove "was a beautiful motte or copse of oak . . . on a branch of the Neosho River, surrounded by excellent pasturage of the tall prairie grasses." An oasis upon the vast prairies that reached to the Rockies, it was regularly used as an assembly place for frontiersmen and wagoners. "I was so full of Santa Fe that the buffaloe etc., of the wilderness did not make an impression on me as it would otherwise," he told Ben in November. "Though at the time I was more astonished with the novelty and grandeur of the sight than I conceived possible for a person of my phlegmatic disposition." Ewell's anticipation of spending a month or so "in Santa Fe, dancing the Spanish dances with the loveliest and kindest (so those who pretend to know say) of the human race [and] visit all the villages there" notwithstanding, he did not reach his destination but returned to Fort Scott disappointed that he had not whirled the senoritas of northern Mexico.[11]

Cooke led his column of two hundred troopers as a guard for a train of Mexican traders bound from Missouri to New Mexico. Two earlier caravans had been set upon by Texas raiders who sought to repay the wealthy Mexican merchants for previous troubles along the Rio Grande. Mirabeau B. Lamar, president of the Republic of Texas, had dispatched military units to attack the Santa Fe Trail where it crossed lands claimed by his government before the Compromise of 1850 fixed the present-day boundaries of Texas. When Mexican traders became frightened at the prospect of additional difficulties, Washington was forced to act and began ordering army escorts along the trail. The famed Santa Fe Trail, established by American adventurers twenty years before, originated at present Independence, Missouri, and reached across Kansas to Pawnee Rock, where it followed the northern shore of the Arkansas River into Colorado and Bent's Fort; then it veered southward along the Purgatoire River and through Raton Pass into New Mexico and Santa Fe. The roadway was later shortened by the Cimarron cutoff, "which crossed the Arkansas River in western Kansas and proceeded in a more nearly southwesterly direction to Lower Spring on the Cimarron, up and across the Cimarron to the eastern New Mexican settlements and on to Santa Fe." This route, however, lay entirely within the boundaries of land claimed by Texas after 1836.[12]

Ewell told his brother that while escorting wagons under American protection southward toward Santa Fe, Cooke's force met "about fifty Mexican troops" at a crossing of the Arkansas River. Apparently the confrontation was in western Kansas, because Ewell plainly states that "the main body was positioned at the Siminone [Cimarron] seventy miles distant." Cooke had strict orders not to cross the Arkansas but to remain firmly planted on American soil, and upon his return toward Fort Leavenworth he encountered the remnants of Jacob Snively's Santa Fe expedition. Snively, a Pennsylvania-born frontiersman, had been sent along the trail by President Lamar to divert some of its trade to Texas. Shortly before his encounter with Cooke, he had made quick work of a squad of Mexican cavalry on June 19, 1842, when he reputedly killed eighteen and "cut the throats of his prisoners." The renowned Kit Carson took part in the melee of June 19, but when his force met Cooke, "the Americans were on the north side of the Arkansas, and the Texans under Snively, fewer than a hundred men remaining, on the south side. Both sides raised flags of truce. After a parley Snively crossed over to confer with Cooke." Then, continues historian Seymour Conner, "he was forced to surrender his arms, and then Cooke and his men crossed to the Texas side and demanded that the Texans give up their weapons." Cooke allowed Snively's men to keep enough guns for hunting purposes and defense against the Indians. Although Cooke may well have been beyond the international boundary, the incident had no further repercussions except that the Mexican authorities in Santa Fe closed the border to further trade until 1850.[13]

While Cooke continued his eastward trek toward Fort Leavenworth, Ewell and Company A veered off at Council Grove and reached Fort Scott on July 23. In late August Ewell was assigned once more for service on the Santa Fe Trail. Upon his return, however, he briefly took charge of the entire post until November 18, when he relinquished command to Captain Burdette A. Terrett, another Virginia-born officer. Ewell continued in charge of Company A until he left Fort Scott for good on May 3, 1844, but Terrett died a few months later in a tragic accident. Colonel Kearny, regimental commander, described the incident in an official report of March 25, 1845: "As reported to me he [Terrett] had just returned from a drill on the morning of that day [March 17], and having dismounted in front of his quarters, holding his pistol in his hand, his horse started which caused it to be discharged, when the ball passed through his right lung, which caused his death in twenty minutes."[14]

Had Ewell stayed at Fort Scott a few weeks longer, he would have accompanied Company A on an even longer march when the company was merged with four other dragoon companies that covered twenty-two hundred miles through the west in ninety days of hard trooping. Prior to giving up his company on April 25, 1844, because of illness, he told Becca that he wanted to study Spanish and Italian but did not have the books to do so. When Ewell and another officer traveled to Fort Leavenworth for the Christmas holidays, he was once more the lovesick bachelor. "I went across the Missouri River while there to a ball, a pretty unique sort of affair it would be in Virginia but elegant out here. There was hardly a single girl over thirteen years old, so fast do they get married," he informed his sister. "I did not feel in a good humor that night. Somebody asked me to let them introduce me to a partner." When the lady in question proved to be an "excessively heavy" widow, he "got so mad that he sat down."[15]

Ewell's correspondence from Fort Scott suggests that he was in regular contact with his brother Thomas, who had become a resident of Jackson, Tennessee, as well as with Benjamin, then a professor at Hampden-Sydney College in Virginia; and he was chagrined that William, his youngest brother, a recent graduate of Richmond's Union Theological Seminary, had become a Presbyterian missionary. Ewell called them "the sour Presbyterians," telling Becca that he had "seen so much done to the Indians here by them, that [he was] skeptical as to their utility." Thomas Ewell, born in 1826, had become actively engaged in Tennessee Democratic politics; no less a figure than James K. Polk, former congressman and governor, implored him to remain in the Volunteer State when he flirted with the idea of taking up residence in Arkansas. In the early months of 1844, as Polk was diligently seeking the Democratic vice-presidential nomination, he wrote from his home in Columbia: "You are already favorably known, and have been singled out by our leading Democratic friends in this Division of the State—as one of the electoral candi-

dates, in the great political contest upon which we are about to enter."
Nonetheless, Polk added, he would address a letter to his "friend" Arkansas
governor Arnold Yell asking him to assist young Thomas in any way possible; Polk thought the aspiring politico would "become a stranger in a
new country" if he moved to Little Rock.[16]

Ewell found his new assignment at Jefferson Barracks both uncertain
and unappealing when he reported for duty in late April 1844; the biographer of 150 or more years later who reads his correspondence to his family
during this period in the west indeed wonders why he kept his commission. Although informed upon his arrival from Kansas that he would stay
for at least one year, Ewell told Becca in July: "I recv'd rather an unwel-
come piece of news a few days since to-wit, that I might expect orders to
rejoin my company, at Fort Scott or wherever it might be within a week."
Shortly afterward, he told Ben that he was definitely returning to his former
post but that he would rather stay at Jefferson Barracks until Company A
returned from its trek across Kansas, Colorado, and Wyoming. Finally,
Colonel Kearny, who had left command of the regimental scout to others,
apprised Ewell that he would keep his berth in Missouri through the winter of 1844–1845.[17]

Ewell found Jefferson Barracks not only "disagreeable" but also "cal-
culated at present, to cure an officer of any matrimonial disposition." As
usual, he thought the single ladies at the post and in St. Louis unattractive,
except for the "devilishly pretty" Garland sisters, daughters of General John
Garland; but he soon learned that the two women were about to marry
Lieutenant Edward Deas and another young officer, Lieutenant James
Longstreet, his former acquaintance from West Point. Yet his closeness to
St. Louis had some compensation. "I have now the first chance, I may say,
since graduation, for entering civilized society, and if possible I shall take
advantage of it," he told Becca in October. When Kearny invited him to a
soiree in the city, he found the conversation exciting, but "the ladies present
did not give me a very exalted idea of the beauty of St. Louis, for I did not
think I ever saw a more homely set together."[18]

Situated on the Mississippi "about ten miles" south of St. Louis,
Jefferson Barracks was originally tagged "Camp Adams" in honor of the
second president. Established in 1826 by Brigadier General Henry Atkinson
and Major General Edmund P. Gaines, the post was intended as a supply
garrison for small installations throughout the midsection of the country.
Upon Thomas Jefferson's death on July 4, 1826, the place was renamed,
and it remained constantly manned by the U.S. Army troops until 1946

when the war department relinquished ownership. Ewell remained at Jefferson Barracks until December 1844 and his transfer to Louisville, Kentucky, "by order of Colonel Kearny." With little to occupy him at the post, he spent considerable time in the city, where army engineers were busy trying to divert the river. "I have seen a good deal of Capt. [Thomas Jefferson] Cram of the Topog's [topographical engineers] since last August; he is in St. Louis on duty connected with the harbor of the Town which is in some danger of being left by the Mississippi above instead of underneath the water," he told Ben during mid-October. "The Capt. is engaged in a most important work here & one that requires a[n] entirely different plan from any operation in the water that I have heard of before."

According to Robert E. Lee's biographer Emory Thomas, from 1837 through 1840, before he went east to work on the harbor at Fort Hamilton, New York, Lee had been in charge of "coaxing the current of the Mississippi back to the St. Louis shore." But Lee and Ewell must have crossed paths during the latter's stint along the Mississippi. He boasted to his brother Ben that he had made "many pleasant acquaintances, chiefly among the officers families" in St. Louis and Jefferson Barracks. Whether it was the first encounter with the future Confederate commander or not, Ewell added: "Always Lee has treated me with as much kindness as any person that I have met, out of my own corps.[19]

Life surely brightened when Ewell took up his recruiting station at the important Ohio River town of Louisville. He had been there a scant two months before he began "sparking a rich widow." Louisville delighted the twenty-seven-year-old bachelor, who told his brother that his only displeasure was a nagging fear that he would be sent back to the frontier. "There are a number of beautiful women in this place, and as unsophisticated a personage as myself would certainly fall victim were it not that one heals the wounds left by another." When he was not pursuing the girls, Ewell encountered several old acquaintances who came through Louisville in search of a steamboat berth to Cincinnati and Pittsburgh, including his brother Tom, who arrived from western Tennessee, and Henry Clay Jr. Young Clay, who graduated second in the West Point class of 1827 and who resigned from the army four years later, wanted to know about Ben, his classmate at the academy. Shortly after he joined the service upon the outbreak of war with Mexico, Clay was killed at Buena Vista while serving under Zachary Taylor.[20]

Louisville, on the edge of the Kentucky Bluegrass, with all of its charm and Anglo-Saxon decorum, was indeed an appealing location. Positioned "on a level plain that curves for eight miles along the Ohio," it had been visited by the French adventurer LaSalle in the 1680s. Its geography was amplified by the only falls on the "mighty river in its 1,000 mile sweep from western Pennsylvania to its meeting with the Mississippi at Cairo, Illinois, some 100 miles below St. Louis." When great swells of immigrants began rushing down the Ohio in quest of new homesteads following the Revolution, Louisville grew rapidly as flatboats and other river craft were forced to portage around the falls. Although the obstruction—actually a series of chutes in the river created by rock formations—never completely hampered navigation, the opening of a canal fifteen years before Ewell's arrival enabled traffic to pass unimpeded. At the instigation of Governor Thomas Jefferson, when Kentucky was still part of Virginia, George Rogers Clark had planted a permanent American presence at Louisville in the 1780s, and by the 1830s a flourishing steamboat construction industry had developed. Ewell had passed through the place in 1840 on his way to Fort Wayne, but now the merging of energetic enterprise and Southern gentility made the place an inviting respite from the frontier regimen of "fried bacon and Indians."[21]

After a two- or three-week stay in Kentucky, Ewell told Becca he had called upon "a local Belle." Apparently not the "rich widow" he met later, the young lady in question had another suitor present, and she entertained the party by reading extracts from "Desdemona." Ewell related that she wore excessive amounts of rouge as he repeated his earlier views about ladies in general: "There are some beautiful girls in this place & nothing but honesty prevents my falling deeply in love." But much of his time was taken by a visit from Tom, who arrived by steamboat. His brother had no sooner reached Louisville than he fell violently ill with the "black tongue." A private physician was summoned for the "swelling & inflammation of the face & scalp" (Ewell's words). "Tom's face was swelled so much that he could not see & from the constant application of diluted lunar caustic, was black as Othello," he continued. "The attack was accompanied by delirium & for several days while at its worst he was in great danger of his life."[22]

Although Tom had partially gotten over his sickness before his return to Tennessee, Ewell was saddened that his brother "did not recover sufficiently for him to visit some of the ladies as his wit would have delighted them." When they parted at the Louisville landings, the brothers would not meet until several months later on the battlefields of Mexico. Ewell's pleasant sojourn in pursuit of genteel Southern belles came to a halt when the war in Mexico took him further afield in search of men for the armies

of Zachary Taylor and Winfield Scott. Younger officers not actively attached to Taylor's Army of Occupation were given a virtual free hand to
roam around the countryside seeking recruits. William Tecumseh Sherman
writes in his memoirs that he found it "intolerable" to be on recruiting
duty "when my comrades were actually fighting." Lieutenant John Bankhead
Magruder, who became a major general in the Confederate army, even
returned to the United States from the initial engagements at Palo Alto
and Resaca de La Parma under orders to seek new enrollees for the expand-
ing armies that would march through the Mexican heartland. Upon leaving Louisville, Ewell traveled into Ohio gathering new men at Cincinnati,
Zanesville, and Columbus. In Zanesville, while seeking cavalrymen, he
encountered his West Point pal "Cump" Sherman doing the same for the
infantry and promptly beat a hasty retreat.[23]

Earlier in the year Ewell had been granted an extended leave until
April 20, which he spent at home in Prince William County. He immedi-
ately reported for duty with the Coastal Survey "by order of the Adjutant
General until September 9." A subsequent order dated May 19, however,
assigned him to Company F, Second Dragoons, commanded by Captain
Philip Kearny, nephew of his old chief on the frontier, Colonel Stephen
Watts Kearny, who was raising several cavalry/dragoon units throughout
the Midwest. Although obsessed with a military career from an early age,
Philip Kearny, scion of a wealthy New York family, did not attend West
Point but graduated from Columbia College in 1833. "[W]hen his grandfather died in 1836, leaving him a fortune of about a million, he at once
applied for a commission in the army. Keenly fond of horses and a fearless
rider from boyhood, he naturally turned to the cavalry and secured (March
8, 1837), a second lieutenancy in the 1st United States Dragoons, commanded by his uncle."

Kearny saw vigorous service in the Indian Wars and was sent to France
by the secretary of war to observe European cavalry maneuvers before his
resignation from the service in 1846. At the outbreak of war with Mexico,
he immediately rejoined the Second Dragoons, which became, says one
account, "mounted on uniform dapple gray horses, selected by Kearny at
his expense, 'the hoofs all striking the ground simultaneously . . . as if they
were galloping to set music.'" Official documents for September-Decem-
ber 1846 indicate Ewell was on detached service and had not reported for
duty with his newly gathered company. When Company F did reach Palo
Alto in extreme south Texas during the last weeks of 1846, Ewell and Kearny
had joined Zachary Taylor's army on the Rio Grande.[24]

Ewell and his fellow officers gathered their recruits with generous offers of bounty money—"each private serving a year or more was to receive 100 acres of government land or $100 in treasury script." Some of the dragoon regiments, however, were not included in the arrangement. Captain William E. Eustis, Ewell's later commander, got a severe reprimand: "It is seen by the Muster Rolls of your company just received that you have paid the first bounty to your recruits," the adjutant general wrote on September 4, 1847, after the fighting was under way. "As the 1st and 2nd Dragoons are not by law entitled to bounty money, you will please report how it happened that you overlooked this provision in the law." Irregularities aside, the men were needed for an expanded army in the aftermath of a congressional declaration that was signed into law by President James K. Polk on May 13, 1846, within days of Ewell's recall from the Coastal Survey. And by April 1847, when Winfield Scott began his inland march from Vera Cruz, his cavalry chief, Colonel William S. Harney, led volunteer units from the First, Second, and Third Dragoons under Phil Kearny, Edwin Vose Sumner, and Andrew T. McReynolds. Although Ewell later trekked with Kearny into the Mexican interior, he was now a part of an army that the United States sent against a civilized enemy for the first time since the War of 1812, more than thirty years earlier. He was no longer bogged down in a stagnant force with little chance of quick promotion but found himself, like thousands of others, caught up in a vibrant engine about to storm the very citadel of the enemy.[25]

"The war had its origins in events that occurred years before its inception that not only involved the United States and Mexico but also certain European nations," writes historian T. Harry Williams. Texas, of course, was the sticking point through the 1830s and '40s when Anglo-Saxon Americans began spreading across the Sabine and Red River boundaries. The authorities in Mexico City had granted settlement rights to "impresarios" and had encouraged the newcomers to occupy its virgin northern reaches. As Ewell wrestled with his studies on the Hudson and immediately afterward, a veritable clash of cultures took place in that vast borderland between the Red River and the Rio Grande. A mere three life spans separated the Spanish Armada of 1588 from the 1830s, and the distrust between Roman Catholic Spaniards and Protestant Englishmen continued to play itself out on the Texas frontier. The religious and cultural hatreds spawned by Reformation Europe found expression on the American continent in the form of "Manifest Destiny," or the notion that the Almighty himself had preserved the new Eden for the white races. Put another way, the dark-skinned peoples of Mexico, with their pervasive Roman Catholicism, stood in the way of divine ordinance. Although Northern politicians and their abolitionist allies, men like Abraham Lincoln and David Wilmot, branded the new expansionism as "the Great Slave Plot" to annex additional slave-holding territory to the United States, the "Texicans" would not be denied.[26]

Once they found themselves under Mexican rule, the seething resentments they had carried across the Atlantic a century and a half earlier soon reached the boiling point. The Texas Revolution was spawned by a revulsion against everything Spanish and Roman Catholic, because the North American conscience was nettled by such things as being compelled to marry under the rites of the Roman church or to be buried in consecrated ground. After Sam Houston led the Texans to victory over the forces of Generalissimo Santa Anna at the Battle of San Jacinto to establish the Republic of Texas, 1836–1845, the old animosities persisted. What amounted to constant warfare occurred along the Rio Grande border during the Republic, as Mexico City never recognized Texas nationhood but maintained that it was merely a "province" in revolt. Although Washington kept an outward neutrality throughout the cross-border confrontations, large segments of the American people enthusiastically sympathized with their coreligionists on the Texas prairies. Understandably when Congress rammed through its joint resolution of February 1845 that made Texas a part of the Federal union, Mexican rage at the detested "gringos" literally exploded.[27]

The immediate point of contention between the two governments after the admission of Texas to statehood was the new international boundary—whether it was the Rio Grande or the Nueces River, which strikes the Gulf of Mexico 130 miles to the north at present Corpus Christi. When Mexico severed relations with the United States on May 28, Secretary of War William L. Marcy ordered General Zachary Taylor to maneuver his "Army of Observation" into position to protect the new frontier. And by July 31, less than a month after Texas had adopted the instrument of annexation, Taylor had marched his forces to Corpus Christi from Fort Jesup on the Louisiana border. Several months were spent in camp along the Nueces before the renamed "Army of Occupation" moved southward through the no-man's-land of prickly pears and barren sand dunes to the Rio Grande. Taylor reached the border on March 28, 1848, and settled into a near constant skirmishing with his Mexican counterparts beyond the river. Then, as Ewell left Louisville for the Coastal Survey and joined

Captain Kearny on the recruiting circuit, Lieutenant William Thornton and a force of American dragoons got themselves cut off and surrounded by a superior force of enemy cavalry. More than sixty American horsemen were killed in the melee, and when word of the debacle reached Washington, President Polk urged an immediate war declaration: "Whereas the Congress of the United States by virtue of the Constitutional authority vested in them, have declared by their act, bearing this date, by the act of the Republic of Mexico, that a state of war exists between that government and the United States."[28]

While Zachary Taylor awaited further orders on the Rio Grande, Mexican General Mariano Arista crossed the river on the night of May 7—before the war declaration—to block the pathway between Point Isabel on the coast and Matamoros. The first serious scrap of the war took place the following morning at a water hole along the road called Palo Alto when twenty-three hundred Americans easily bested six thousand enemy troops with their superior cannon fire. Taylor gained the undying admiration of his men when he rode onto the field "in a blue-checkered gingham coat, blue trousers without any braid, a linen waistcoat and a broad-brimmed straw hat. Neither his horse nor his saddle had any ornament." When he crushed Arista again the following day, May 9, 1846, at Resca de la Parma, a ravine crossing a few miles up the road toward Matamoros, Taylor became an instant national hero, to the considerable discomfort of President Polk and his Democratic cronies. The Mexicans under Arista withdrew southward, followed by the Americans before they gave up the chase after sixty miles or so. Taylor remained in Matamoros several weeks before descending upon Monterrey by way of Camargo and Mier. Monterrey, the major city of northern Mexico, fell in mid-September after a prolonged battle in which Brigadier General William J. Worth carried the day with a heroic flanking movement. Worth, Taylor's second in command and Ewell's first commander in Mexico, was described by another young officer named Ambrose Powell Hill as a "weak headed, vain glorious, but brave man perfectly reckless of the lives of his soldiers and his own." Although crippled from a wound sustained in the War of 1812, Worth was a fighting man whom some felt should be given credit for the Battle of Monterrey.[29]

As Ewell and Kearny headed for the battle zone, which they reached in late November, Taylor consented to an armistice that allowed the enemy to gather his forces for a counterattack. No additional fighting took place in the north until February 23, 1847, when Taylor trounced the forces of Santa Anna at Buena Vista. By that time Lieutenant Richard Ewell had been assigned to another sector as a result of Polk's conviction that Mexico City could never be reduced by Taylor's small army clustered around Matamoros and Monterrey. A presidential decision was made to split the army and place one wing—the most important—under Winfield Scott for a proposed invasion of the Mexican heartland from Vera Cruz. Worth's division, including Ewell and Company F, was immediately assigned to Scott, although there is no suggestion that the close association between Thomas Ewell and the president played any part in the new arrangement. By early February, Worth had not only been promoted to major general but had also moved his command nearer the coast for the descent on Vera Cruz. When Ewell encountered Tom in northern Mexico, it was their first meeting since Louisville. The younger Ewell, who reached the Rio Grande after a five-day voyage from New Orleans in charge of several hundred horses, had joined the army in Tennessee. In a long letter home he told his mother that the brothers were bivouacked eighteen miles apart. "General Worth with 3,000 men is encamped near Palo Alto. I was sent up there the other day, of which I was very glad as I wished to see the country, the battle ground, and Dick, who is with Worth," he wrote on February 12. "I came to Worth's camp, where I found Dick, looking rather badly, for he has been quite sick this winter." Without mentioning the nature of his brother's illness, Tom continued, "the prospect of getting knocked on the head at Vera Cruz cheers him up." Like all soldiers, both Ewells fussed about the lack of letters from Stony Lonesome.[30]

By early March an armada of two hundred ships laden with men and supplies had been assembled for the Vera Cruz operation. Company F sailed aboard the transport *Rufus* for Tampico, which had already been occupied by the navy. At Lobos Island near Tampico, Scott put the final touches on his "Little Cabinet," which included Colonel William Harney, who had charge of the cavalry. He also decided "to keep the engineers, artillery and cavalry under his immediate orders." After the capitulation of Vera Cruz, Harney was instructed to assign several dragoon squadrons for service with the infantry. Although Kearny and Ewell would be attached to others later in the campaign, Scott's plan to retain direct control of the cavalry gave them a special place in the army.[31]

The fleet did not sail directly for Vera Cruz—the City of the True Cross—but called first at Anton Lizardo, an island within sight of the city walls, and its fortified castle of San Juan de Ulloa. Tom had been correct about the fierce wave of anticipation and excitement that gripped not only Richard Ewell but the entire army as well. "On the decks of the various ships the regimental bands played such favorites as 'Love Not,' 'Some Love to Roam,' 'Alice Gray,' 'Oft in the Stilly Night,'" writes Alfred Hoyt Bill. "Ammunition and three days rations were issued, swift boats sped from ship to ship with orders for the landing." While the troops awaited the go-ahead, which came on March 7, Scott and the officers who surrounded him—Robert E. Lee, Pierre Gustav Toutant Beauregard, Joseph E. Johnston, George Gordon Meade—aboard his flagship, USS *Massachusetts*, worked with Commodore David Conner to find a suitable beachhead. "Northers slowed the debarkation, hurling high waves up the beach to wreck havoc among the wagon loads of shells, the tentage, the mess-bags and the barrels of bread that were stacked at the foot of the sand hills," continues historian Bill. "Transports were driven ashore with crews and soldiers clinging to the shrouds." It was the foremost amphibious operation in modern warfare to that time, and the ships of several European nations watched intently as the United States flexed its muscle upon the world stage. When the landings were complete, Lieutenants Richard and Tom Ewell spent "an agreeable" month together before the army began its inland trek on April 8. The capture of Vera Cruz was primarily an artillery bombardment that left the dragoon regiments under Kearny, Sumner, and McReynolds with little to do. Company F, say the regimental returns, suffered no casualties during January, February, and March 1847.[32]

Since the cavalry remained inactive except for one or two minor forays throughout the army's stay on the coast, First Lieutenant Richard Ewell played an insignificant part in the capture and occupation of Vera Cruz; but the dreaded "vomito," with its potential to kill thousands, caused Scott to move without delay from the disease-laden lowlands. The inland march commenced along the National Road, used by Hernando Cortez in 1519, stretching more than two hundred miles to Mexico City. From Vera Cruz the ancient roadbed veered northwestward across a sandy waste to Jalapa, sixty miles from the coast. When Scott's lead units under General David E. Twiggs—to whom Harney and the Ewell brothers had been assigned—reached the Rio del Plan, a small river flowing seaward through a deep chasm from the Sierra Madre, they encountered two cone-shaped hills blocking their advance. Known as Atalaya and Cerro Gordo—or El Telegrafo, from an old relay station used to signal between Mexico City and Vera Cruz—the two hills had been heavily fortified with enemy cannon. Santa Anna himself, newly returned to power after his defeats in the north, was on hand to oversee the defenses that had to be eliminated before the American advance could continue. Robert E. Lee, Richard Ewell's future warlord, was summoned to locate a path around the guns, and following several reconnaissances with P. G. T. Beauregard and others, the hoped-for route was found. When the army led by Robert Patterson, James Shields, and William S. Harney was ordered forward on April 17, a young officer named Ulysses S. Grant later wrote: "Perhaps there was not a battle of the Mexican War, or any other, where orders issued before an engagement were nearer being a correct report of what afterward took place." The attacking columns, which sent the enemy reeling, surged forward along a series of roads and paths constructed by Lee's engineers.[33]

The following day, however, disaster struck as Harney's dragoons again charged the fleeing enemy, who were desperately seeking safety in flight. "Down Atalaya's slopes they dashed across the intervening hollow, up the slopes of Cerro Gordo, firing as they went," writes Robert Selph Henry. "Seventy yards short of the crest, being much blown by the climb, the men halted, lay down for a few moments to catch their breath, and then red-headed Harney calling them on, they rushed the breastworks, and were over the crest." Richard Ewell himself was never under fire, but Tom fell with a mortal wound when he "took the head of the regiment and led the first line." As Santa Anna retreated toward the capital, the Americans occupied Jalapa on April 19 about twelve miles up the National Road from Cerro Gordo. One officer after another fired off detailed battle reports from the city, the provincial seat of Vera Cruz, that Lieutenant George Brinton McClellan found "delightful." "The white faces of the ladies," he commented, "struck us as being exceedingly beautiful—they formed so pleasing a contrast to the black and brown complexions of the Indians and Negroes who had for so long been the only human beings to greet our sight." Others, including young A. P. Hill, commented upon the attractiveness of the Mexican ladies, but Ewell was too taken with his brother's death to pay them heed. He sped an April 23 letter to his mother at Stony Lonesome detailing Tom's stomach wound as well as his last agonizing hours, which, he added in another letter, "were too painful to reflect upon without great exertion." Forced to move forward with Harney and Kearny, he returned as quickly as he could to comfort Tom after the doctors told him that he could not recover. Richard Ewell was able to secure some "rough boards" for a crude coffin.[34]

"The ball entered on the left side between the navel and the point of the hip, about an inch from the navel, and was taken from under the skin just above the extremity of the spine without depriving him of the use of his limbs," he apprised Elizabeth Ewell. Winfield Scott came to the death room in person to encourage the stricken lieutenant. "In the short term of service that he was here, by his good conduct, activity, & gallantry he gained a great reputation," Richard wrote to Benjamin Ewell on May 3, also from Jalapa. "His gallantry, coolness & zeal place him beyond any person (I do not refer to Generals) who has figured in this war. He found the road to the top of Cerro Gordo & led the way." When the official reports were filed, Scott included notice of Tom's death without comment in his lengthy account of the battle to Secretary Marcy. William W. Loring, who took command of Sumner's brigade after that soldier was "wounded in the head by an escopette ball," said that Tom "fell in desperate combat." Although Twigg's battle summary says nothing about Thomas Ewell, Colonel Harney singled out the fallen hero for praise: "I lament to refer to the death of Lieutenant Ewell, whose gallant demeanor, throughout the several engagements of the enemy, attracted my special notice, and who fell in the breastworks, notably leading his men to victory."[35]

After the Cerro Gordo imbroglio, Scott advanced the army through Jalapa and Perote to the ancient city of Puebla. Ewell, however, relayed to Ben on May 7 that he was returning to Vera Cruz "with a train of wagons." The dragoons under Harney were in constant demand as escorts for the thousands of new troops and war materials arriving daily from the coast. While his compeers in the infantry and artillery were enjoying the delights of central Mexico, Ewell was off with the cavalry bringing additional manpower to the front. "There is no prospect of a move from here [Jalapa] for ten days to come as we require so much transportation, although there will be no resistance between this and the City of Mexico provided we move speedily," he wrote. "This country is to all intents and purposes conquered. No army or anything else. Santa Anna is a wanderer & though he may raise 1 or 2 [troops] to attack a baggage train [he] cannot raise another formidable Army unless he receives the most extraordinary assistance from our bad management." Although a mere first lieutenant, Ewell's assessment was correct: one-third of the Mexican army had been lost at Cerro Gordo, forcing Santa Anna into a massive retreat toward the safety of Mexico City.[36]

Ewell was reported sick and unfit for duty during June and July, although the army as a whole had a grand time when the invasion was delayed for another three months. At Perote men and officers alike "watched the inviting glances of any Indio or Mozo maiden." And, continues Scott biographer Arthur D. H. Smith: "There would be many blond babies born in Central Mexico in the early months of 1848." When the army biv-

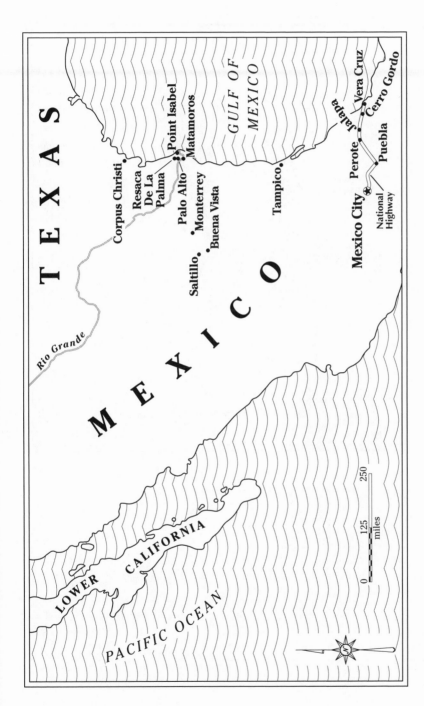

Mexico 1846–1848

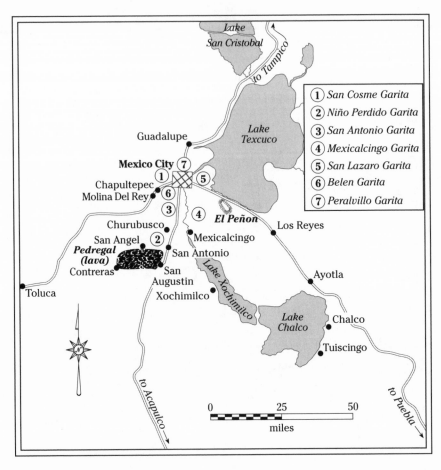

Mexico City

ouacked at Puebla, a city of some dimension, before the descent into the Valley of Mexico, the entertainments flared anew. Ladies of every station sought the attention of Scott's troopers as promiscuity and venereal complaints sped through the ranks. While they "enjoyed the novelty of *neverias,* where ice cream and sherbets, cooled with snow from the mountains, were served," and waltzed to the music of regimental bands, Scott's benevolent occupation established a feeling of mutual respect between conqueror and conquered. "Puebla was a center of religious culture, and its streets abounded with priests and nuns. And since the Catholic Church was tilted against Santa Anna, its discipline kept the atmosphere quiet," writes John Eisenhower. "As an indication that not all Mexicans were hostile was that [Ethan Allen] Hitchcock was able to recruit a band of irregulars as spies." Winfield Scott also reorganized his command before proceeding toward the prize; the cavalry, including Kearny and Ewell, continued under Harney, while the infantry was parceled into four divisions under Twiggs, Worth, Gideon Pillow, and John A. Quitman. Each division contained units of Rifles, Voltiguers, and Volunteers. A battalion of marines also accompanied the army—"This last is the reason why the Marines, who as usual, were an infinitesimal portion of the whole force, were able to build up the delusion that they had fought 'from the Halls of Montezuma to the shores of Tripoli'; that they had carried the burden of Uncle Sam's warfare."

General Franklin Pierce, the future president, brought up the last three thousand troopers to round out the invasion force, and immediately word was handed down to advance on August 6. When Scott terminated the three-month interlude at Puebla, the famed Duke of Wellington proclaimed his army doomed as it prepared to move on the Mexican citadel without reinforcements. No enemy forces were encountered until the Americans reached Ayotla, a village within a few miles of the San Lazaro *garita* that guarded the easternmost entrance into the capital. Mexico City, situated in the great central depression of the country, was surrounded on the east and south by a series of lakes and their attendant swamplands: Zumpango, San Cristobal, Texcuco, Xochimilco, and Chalco. The only approaches were a number of causeways—some of them built by the *conquistadores* more than two centuries earlier—that in turn were surmounted by a *garita,* or customs station, garrisoned by troops in more peaceful times. At the road junction near Ayotla, the Americans learned that Santa Anna, resourceful as ever, had fortified El Peñon, a nearby prominence, with enough artillery to make an assault through the San Lazaro *garita* out of the question. Unable to proceed by the most direct route into the city,

Robert E. Lee and P. G. T. Beauregard were again called upon to find an alternate route. Several reconnaissances revealed that a suitable path lay south of Lake Chalco, easternmost of the lakes to San Augustin, within seven or eight miles of the capital. Scott and his commanders quickly determined a new plan of attack. The approach to Mexico City would not come from the east but from the south and west.[37]

Winfield Scott established army headquarters at San Augustin on August 17 after advancing south of Lakes Chalco and Xochimilco over the route suggested by Lee. The most direct avenue into the capital lay along the road through San Antonio and Churubusco to the San Antonio causeway and *garita*. West of San Augustin was an immense lava bed of jagged mounds known as the Pedregal, which the Mexicans thought impassable to the invaders. As the highway leading south from Mexico City neared the Pedregal it divided into two branches: the easternmost passed through Churubusco, San Antonio, and San Augustin, while the western fork ran through the small villages of San Angel and Contreras. Although Santa Anna had withdrawn the main army toward the capital, his General Gabriel Valencia had taken up a position on the plain surrounding Contreras and Padierna. With Valencia on his flank beyond the lava fields from San Augustin, Scott found it impossible to advance directly north until this formidable enemy contingent had been destroyed. On August 18, one day after his arrival at San Augustin, Scott ordered Worth's division, with Harney and the dragoons in the van, to probe northward toward San Antonio and the San Antonio causeway. The foray ended in failure when the cavalry "ran into heavy cannon fire from a strong position . . . some three miles south of Churubusco." Kearny and Ewell did not take part in this action, which resulted in the death of Captain Seth Thornton, the dragoon who had precipitated the fighting some months earlier on the Rio Grande.[38]

When Worth brought word that the route through San Antonio was blocked, Scott, knowing that Valencia posed a threat to any advance in force, recalled the cavalry and ordered a sortie into the Pedregal under Lee's direction, still on the eighteenth. "[B]y the partial reconnaissance of yesterday, Captain Lee discovered a large corps of observation in that direction, with a detachment of which his supports of cavalry and foot under Captain Kearney [*sic*] and Lieutenant Graham, respectively, had a successful skirmish," reads Scott's August 19 report to Secretary Marcy. Lee not only found a path through the treacherous lava, but Ewell, who accompanied the scout himself, was under fire for the first time. His "conduct in our previous affair of the squadron on the 18th instant, was most conspicuous," Phil Kearny wrote in his official report of operations in front of the capital. Two weeks after the event, Ewell, who remained intensely proud of his exploits in Mexico, wrote to his mother: "My company was in another fight/skirmish on the 18th when we were reconnoitering a road on the very spot where the battle afterwards took place. . . . Some 900 [Mexicans] fired upon us from the crevices of the rocks, etc., but we dismounted & soon convinced them it was no place for [a fight.]"[39]

When the artillery under Captain John Bankhead Magruder and Lieutenant Thomas Jackson (the future "Stonewall") was brought on the field under Lee's direction, the Americans were able to hold Valencia in check. The Contreras fight was renewed on August 20 but ended in an astounding seventeen minutes as the infantry regiments overran Valencia's entrenchments. "Twenty-five men under Lieutenant Ewell, myself attending, accompanied the general-in-chief to the redoubt at Contreras, captured a short time previously," Kearny wrote later. After the Contreras set-to, which saw the death of Lieutenant J. P. Johnstone, nephew of Joseph E. Johnston, the army quickly overtook a fleeing Santa Anna at Churubusco the same afternoon. Colonel Harney had returned to San Augustin through the Pedregal but received a hurried summons to speed his cavalrymen to the renewed fighting at Churubusco. Here, on the banks of the Churubusco River that flows through steep banks into Lake Xochimilco, the combined armies of Santa Anna and Valencia turned to face their pursuers. When the enemy lines commenced to falter within sight of the Piedad gates—there were two of them—into Mexico City, Harney wrote in his battle summary:

> At this moment, perceiving that the enemy were retreating in disorder on one of the main causeways leading into the City of Mexico, I collected all cavalry within my reach, consisting of Captain Ker's company of 2nd dragoons, Captain Kearney's [sic] company 1st dragoons and Captains McReynolds and Dupreu's companies 3rd dragoons, and pursued them vigorously until we were halted by the discharge of the batteries at their gate. Many of the enemy were overtaken in the pursuit, and cut down by our sabres. . . . My only difficulty was restraining the impetuosity of my men and officers, who seemed to vie with each other who should be foremost in pursuit. Captain Kearney [sic] gallantly led his squadron into the very entrenchments of the enemy, and had the misfortune to lose an arm from a grape-shot fired from a gun at one of the main gates of the Capital.

Captain McReynolds and Lieutenant Graham were also wounded, and Lieutenant Ewell had two horses shot under him.[40]

Winfield Scott's official report indicates not only that "Lieutenant Ewell had two horses killed under him" but also that he assumed command of the squadron when Kearny was wounded. Company F, according to Phil Kearny, "was the leading one on the causeway, which explain[ed] its severe loss." Five privates under Ewell were killed—roughly 20 percent of the men under his charge; the company also lost five horses. There can be no question that he had "seen the elephant" at Contreras and Churubusco, an experience that garnered official recognition. "The charge that we made to the city gates was so exposed to fire that I lost my horse & had another shot under me," the young lieutenant matter-of-factly wrote in his September 1 letter to Elizabeth Ewell. Eight years later, in response to an inquiry from Congressman William Smith, a future governor of Virginia as well as Confederate major general, Secretary of War Jefferson Davis replied that Ewell had been cited by Scott and Harney, including page numbers, in congressional documents about the war. Although Smith acted on behalf of the family, who sought a new assignment for him, it is interesting to note that Davis omitted Philip Kearny's report of August 24, 1847, in the Senate *Appendix,* which mentioned Ewell no less than three times.[41]

In the days following Churubusco, a former president of Mexico, Jose Joaquin Herrera, headed a commission to open talks with the Americans. A temporary break in the fighting, known as the Truce of Tacubaya, took effect on August 24, four days after Kearny and Ewell had pummeled the enemy at the very gates of Mexico City. It was designed to give Nicholas P. Trist, chief clerk in the state department and Polk's personal envoy, an opportunity to open talks that would end the war. Although Scott, increasingly estranged from the administration, viewed the armistice as an unwarranted intrusion into military matters, he had no choice but to oblige by calling a halt to his advance. His men were hotted up in the aftermath of recent fighting, and now they had to cool their heels while the negotiations proceeded. "In the meantime," Ewell told his mother, "we are left waiting around the suburbs of the City in the most disagreeable state imaginable not permitted to enter & very much annoyed with insects and fleas." As Santa Anna used the lull to replenish his command, and as Ewell and the rest itched to renew the fight, Winfield Scott made a momentous decision: the Americans would not renew their hammering across the Piedad causeways but would shift the attack to the westernmost entrances through the San Belen and San Cosme *garitas*. Scott spurned the counsel of Lee and other advisers with the decision to drive through the formidable obstacles at Molino del Rey and Chapultepec. When the Truce of Tacubaya halted abruptly on September 6 with Mexican rejection of Trist's demands, the commanding general roared out orders to renew the advance.[42]

Ewell had never liked Mexico, and now a new tragedy struck with the death of his cousin Levi Gantt. On September 8, lead units under Worth reached the fortified position at Molina del Rey, where it was believed that church bells were being recast into cannon. The two-hour battle to capture the foundry—the Mill of the King—was primarily an artillery and infantry engagement that became a disaster. One hundred seventeen men were killed, 653 were wounded, and 18 were missing, nearly 25 percent of Worth's attacking force, including young Gantt. Ethan Allen Hitchcock later compared Molino del Rey to Pyrrhus's fight with Fabricius: "A few more such victories and the army would have been destroyed." Ewell was not the only future Confederate to witness the costly triumph; Robert E. Lee, George E. Pickett, James Longstreet, and Lewis A. Armistead, among others, saw the disastrous consequence of an assault upon an entrenched foe, a lesson they might have remembered sixteen years afterward at Gettysburg.[43]

A few hundred yards beyond Molino del Rey sat the ancient citadel of Chapultepec atop a prominence rising 150 feet above the surrounding terrain. Although Lee continued to urge other routes into the city, Scott said no, the army would reduce the fortress once used by Aztec chieftains and Spanish viceroys. After a heavy artillery bombardment in which none other than Lee oversaw placement of Scott's guns, the infantry was ordered to cross an old stand of cypress trees and scale the heights. Chapultepec had been used as the Mexican equivalent of West Point since 1833, and to the present day animosities persist south of the Rio Grande over the deaths of "los niños," one hundred or so youthful cadets who defended the place. Ewell and the cavalry took no direct part in the assault, although he encountered his kinsman Gantt during the opening preparations. Gantt had graduated with West Point's class of 1842; his mother, Nancy Stoddert, was the younger sister of Elizabeth Stoddert Ewell and had married Thomas Gantt in 1811. "He formed a portion of one of the storming parties for Chapultepec, and the place whence he started being a rather central one, the cavalry were moved to be ready at any point," Richard Ewell wrote to Ben on September 25, two weeks after the battle. Following a conversation between the two cousins—both were first lieutenants—in which Gantt asked him to see after his watch, "the Dragoons were ordered into the saddle and his party advanced to the attack." Then, continues Ewell, "within ten minutes he was a corpse, being shot by a musket ball in the center of the chest. . . . I have been informed that he stepped forward to lead the Marines, who did not that day get any credit worth having."[44]

Lee's cannonade commenced at 5:30 in the morning of September 13, and the first infantrymen swept up the slopes at 8:00 A.M. Ewell's later comrades in the Army of Northern Virginia, James Longstreet and George E. Pickett, were among the young officers who spearheaded the attack that often found scaling ladders in the wrong place at the wrong time. "Reaching the top in a breathless rush, he shot down at least one defender who sought to bar his path, hauled down the Mexican flag, and ran up the banner of the Eighth Infantry," writes Pickett biographer Edward Longacre. "Moments later other Americans clustered around him; one planted the national standard beside the regimental colors." By 9:30 A.M., Chapultepec was solidly in American hands as Scott's rejuvenated army raced through the San Belen and San Cosme gateways. Mexico City, with a population of two hundred thousand, had fallen to an invading army of less than six thousand effectives.[45]

After the infantry battered through the city walls with "pick and crowbars," at noon on September 14 Scott rode into the central plaza with his entourage and raised the Stars and Stripes above the National Palace. Ewell at first remained in Tacubaya with the dragoons, while the army moved quickly to halt what amounted to guerrilla activities throughout the city. Sniping was rampant from rooftops in every part of Mexico City, and on a single night "nine Americans, most of them dead, were found on the streets." After a declaration of martial law and the execution of several troublemakers, including those Americans who had joined the Battalion San Patricio to fight their comrades, calm and tranquility was established. The National Theater was opened almost immediately, catering to the victors, and by September 22 "the Eagle Café was offering, in addition to food and drink, such other drugstore items as patent medicines, soap, tooth wash, and oil which would make the hair grow." It is unknown if Ewell bought any of the last commodity, but, continues Robert S. Henry, "more significant than these and other signs of American business activity was that nearly all stores and tiendas of the city were 'open for business.'"

Less than a month after the occupation, the famed Aztec Club was "quietly established in the City of Mexico on October 13." Ewell, who had moved up from Tacubaya, is listed as number 43 on the alphabetized roster of 160 officers who joined the premier social organization. When the group adopted a formal constitution on January 13, each candidate was assessed "$10, payable in advance." General John A. Quitman, also military governor, was made president and other officers were named. From its inception the Aztec Club maintained a clubhouse for the entertainment of its members and their guests while in Mexico. "The original home of the club was the handsome residence of Senor Boca Negra, who had been formerly minister to the United States, and was located on one of the streets leading out of Calle Plateros, and was not far from the headquarters of General Scott." When he was not busy with escort duty to and from Vera Cruz, Ewell presumably joined the festivities, although other officers, including Robert E. Lee and Stonewall Jackson, did not attend the often raucous meetings held on the stage of the National Theater. Captain John Bankhead Magruder frequently acted as master of ceremonies before the officer corps left Mexico City during the summer of 1848, but even then the club's organization remained intact; and, indeed, it exists to the present day for descendants of the original members.[46]

Ewell was back in Vera Cruz during November before he was transferred from the commands of Harney and Kearny the following January. He was assigned to Company K, First Dragoons, captained by James Henry Carleton, a Maine officer whom he would encounter later in New Mexico. His new company was ordered out of Mexico City and bivouacked at Toluca, a few miles southeast of the capital, as part of General George Cadwalader's regiment. Although he was within easy riding distance of the Aztec Club and other entertainments, Ewell was again busy with escort duty and court-martial trials until the army sailed for home later in the year. As he lingered in Toluca with his regiment, negotiations were racing to a climax over implementation of the Treaty of Guadalupe-Hidalgo that had been ongoing since January between Nicholas Trist and representatives of the Mexican government. "To use a common expression, peace talk is very high," Ewell wrote home in April. And he was once more in direct contact with the commanding general, which was a remarkable feat for a lowly first lieutenant: "Gen Scott told me he had very little doubt that the Mexican Congress would immediately agree to the treaty as the modifications were agreeable to all parties."

On May 25, roughly one month after Ewell's conversation with Scott, the Mexicans ratified the document that added a vast new domain to the

United States extending from Texas to the Pacific. Ironically, until the outbreak of the Civil War Ewell's army life was spent almost totally in those lands annexed to the country after the Mexican War. Before President Polk used July 4, 1848, to proclaim the treaty in effect, Ewell and Company K had moved to Jalapa on their way to the coast and debarkation for home. Although the last American trooper did not leave Vera Cruz until August 2, he had already taken a transport for New Orleans in July. Ewell's Mexican experiences would earn him a captaincy just twelve years after he left Stony Lonesome for West Point. First on the frontier and then south of the Rio Grande, though a subaltern, he had associated with Winfield Scott as well as a host of other officers destined to lead the Confederate war machine in a great Civil War. Ewell had not only seen men die in combat, including members of his own family, but, like the rest, his experiences under fire at Contreras, Chapultepec, and later at remote locations in New Mexico and Arizona, taught him the essentials of nineteenth-century warfare—essentials that steeled him for command on the battlefields of northern Virginia.[47]

Chapter 3

INDIAN FIGHTER

Although Ewell returned from Mexico a first lieutenant, he was soon promoted to captain and placed in command of Company G, First Dragoons, detailed to New Mexico. The thirteen-year period between the Treaty of Guadalupe-Hidalgo and outbreak of Civil War found him almost constantly in the saddle chasing Apaches and other Indians across the Southwest. He remained a bachelor throughout the 1850s, but his correspondence suggests that a relationship developed with his cousin Mrs. Lizinka Brown while he served on the frontier. Besides his distinguishing baldness, "Ewell was full of eccentricities, chief of which was the fancy that he suffered from a curious internal malady," writes Ewell biographer James S. Hutchins. "His associates found highly amusing his mournful way of talking of his ailments as if he were someone else." Afterward, during the Shenandoah campaigning with Stonewall Jackson, a North Carolina Confederate was induced to write: "Gen. Ewell is a man of very poor appearance and is very shabbily dressed." Yet his fellows in the frontier army thought him a likeable, even lovable comrade, in spite of his tendency to use foul language while addressing his troops. Ewell's reputation spread far and wide through the ranks during the 1850s, with an army post in LaSalle County, Texas, as well as both an Arizona town and county being named in his honor. By 1861 "an energetic and conscientious performance of his duty" had made Ewell well known before he resigned his Federal commission to accept command with the Confederacy.[1]

Upon his arrival in New Orleans during the summer of 1848 with Company K, he traveled up the Mississippi to Jefferson Barracks—that great collection depot for units serving on the frontier. Within weeks his new company was posted to Fort Leavenworth, while Company G, which he would eventually rejoin, was returned to Fort Scott and later to Taos and Albuquerque, New Mexico. Early 1849 found Ewell listed in regimental returns as "Capt. By Bvt" as well as "absent, place and date unknown." Although headquarters clerks may have been uninformed about his movements, he was placed on recruiting duty in October, and following a leave he reported to Boston with Captain William E. Eustis. For the next fourteen months, until July 1850 when he was ordered to assume command of Company G on the frontier, he was on detached service. A majority of his time was spent in Baltimore, where he was able to partake of the city's vigorous social life.[2]

In the first months of 1849, however, Ewell spent six months at Carlisle Barracks, where his army career had started nearly a decade earlier. When a former officer in the First Dragoons, James W. Schaumburgh of Louisiana, applied for reinstatement, Ewell set out to have it blocked. Schaumburgh had been commissioned a second lieutenant in the marine corps during March 1829 but got himself cashiered three years later. In July 1833 he joined the "Mounted Rangers" and transferred to Ewell's dragoon regiment in 1836—while the latter studied at West Point—but resigned from the army in 1843. The sometime cavalry officer regained his commission in 1844 only to be "dropped" in March 1845. When Ewell read a newspaper notice that Schaumburgh had petitioned to resume his commission, he not only thought an injustice would be done to other officers in the regiment, but he also set out on a one-man crusade to thwart senate confirmation.

A good part of Ewell's stay at Carlisle Barracks was taken with a letter-writing campaign to keep Schaumburgh out of the regiment, as his reappointment would interfere with Ewell's own seniority. "I write to you as Senior Officer of the Regiment to consult as to what steps should be taken in this case," he wrote to Major Phil Kearny on March 7 at his New York home. He also sought the help of his brother Ben, who had recently joined Professor Joseph Henry, the early electrical experimenter, in a fundraising campaign for the fledgling Smithsonian Institution in Washington. "As those officers of who will suffer by the loss of rank attendant upon his return had no opportunity of showing a counter statement it is evident that untill they be heard action upon the case may cause injustice." When he learned that Ben was leaving Prince William County for Williamsburg, Ewell implored him further: "I would request you, if in your opinion it could do any good, to stop in Washington and through Col. [William W. S.]

Bliss or by personal application to the Pres have action upon this matter suspended or a Board of Officers convened to end the matter forever." Not content with intermediaries, Ewell made a trip to Washington, where he stayed at Willard's Hotel before traveling on to Virginia. He called on both the adjutant general and Secretary of War G. W. Crawford, who informed him that Schaumburgh's petition had not been received by the new administration. Ewell even gained an interview with President Zachary Taylor, who told him: "The subject had not been brought before him by Schaumburgh and that he considered him out of the service by his own act." First in Mexico with Winfield Scott and now in Washington with Taylor, one thing is clear: Ewell was developing a forward, even forcible manner in dealing with superiors.[3]

Whether Ewell's actions had influenced the outcome, Schaumburgh's bid to reenter the army failed. He was not given his old rank in the First Dragoons, although he briefly entered the Federal army during the Civil War and served a few months before the senate once more negated his commission. While in Washington, Ewell, who thought Schaumburgh an accomplished "pugilist," nonetheless tried to see him at his lodgings but was unsuccessful. "I felt very uneasy," he told Ben, "from the want of some sensible friend in case I should meet with insult etc from him to assist me in steering between the dangers of caution on the one and rashness on the other side." His business finished in Washington, Ewell visited Prince William County, where he found an absent Ben, Stony Lonesome, and Williamsburg. The soiree to Washington and Virginia may not have been entirely business to protect his place in the First Dragoons; he was once more the anxious swain and told his brother: "I am beginning to feel very much interested in Miss Tucker whom I thought the prettiest girl in Williamsburg." Like his other attempts at courtship, however, the new relationship failed to develop.[4]

Ewell reported to Baltimore for recruiting duty from Carlisle Barracks in June 1849; although he remained until August 1850 upon receiving his captaincy dated July 13 and a posting to New Mexico, he appears to have done little recruiting. The official notice of promotion from Adjutant General Lorenzo Thomas backdated his commission to August 4, 1849. Interspersed with his drive to assure his rank by thwarting Schaumburgh, Ewell kept his eye on various investments throughout the 1850s as a means to augment his meager army pay. He was not the only young officer to seek financial opportunity in a moribund army with few promotions. In the far northwest, Lieutenant Ulysses S. Grant tried his hand at potato farming in the Columbia River bottoms around Fort Vancouver, and Captain John Bankhead Magruder undertook extensive land speculations while stationed at San Diego. Ewell himself later engaged in a silver-mining operation near Fort Buchanan in southern Arizona. A chance encounter with Thomas Jordan, his classmate at West Point, induced him to invest in insurance companies; several letters in the Library of Congress exchanged between Ewell and brothers Ben and William spell out the details. Although it is unclear if his efforts turned a profit, Jordan, who served as P. G. T. Beauregard's chief of staff at Shiloh, advised him "to put his money in state securities." William, who had officially changed his name from Ewell to Stoddert, ignored his fiscal pleadings in spite of Ewell's attempts to help him.[5]

Ewell was far from the hesitant bachelor as he took in the sights of Baltimore with a set of shiny captain's bars firmly attached to his uniform. A June 7 letter revealed that he squired one of his McIlwain cousins to the museum for an operatic performance by an "Italian troupe." But he was in the east to recruit dragoons whom he could command in the west. If he relied upon bounty money during 1846–1847 as he prompted young Ohioans to enlist for the Mexican War, he may have resorted to outright chicanery as he looked for new recruits in Maryland. With little regard for army regulations, Ewell approached a young man named David Johnson on one of his trips from the city. He attempted to have the boy join the dragoons while returning home from college, but Johnson, two weeks under the legal age, declined. "After a night in Baltimore, Ewell offered him a drink before breakfast. After two glasses of what he thought was wine, the next thing the student knew he was headed for Carlisle Barracks." Then, continues an army historian: "When he complained, Ewell showed him his signature on the enlistment page." Johnson not only deserted within a few weeks, but Congress also passed a law in September 1850 mandating the release of enlisted men who had signed up while they were under age.[6]

George Campbell, brother of Lizinka Campbell Brown, who had recently sold his Nashville property, was also in contact with Ewell during his stay in Baltimore, but Ewell told Becca that Campbell's correspondence did "not amount to much." Ewell's on-again, off-again contact with Lizinka Brown, whose husband, James Percy Brown, had died a few years earlier, did not keep Ewell from socializing in the home of Robert E. Lee. In February he referred to Lee's family as "a most agreeable set." Lee had been in Baltimore since September 1848 directing renovation work on historic Fort Carroll in the city's Patapsco River. His considerable engineering skills coupled with his services at Winfield Scott's side in the Mexican War were already making Lee one of the nation's foremost military men; and his house on "Madison Street, three doors above Biddle," with its jovial hospitality, became a welcome harbor for the bachelor Ewell. The new captain of dragoons may have retained a longing for his childhood friend and playmate in Tennessee, but when he encountered a "Miss Peters from New York" at one of Lee's levees, he told Becca that he had "not seen so agreeable and interesting personage." On the eve of his departure for the west Ewell retained his fascination for the ladies.[7]

Ewell reached Fort Leavenworth on August 6, although he had called at Jefferson Barracks a few weeks earlier. "[T]he 228 recruits expected to be found here were reduced by sickness & desertions to 160—the young gentlemen in charge let them glide like water in a steam boiler," he wrote Ben on August 10. "I hope they will not credit me with mismanagement in Wash as I am the last in command." Concerned though he was, Ewell announced proudly that no additional desertions had taken place since his arrival. He was obliged to wait for horses to be brought into camp—located three miles from the fort—before he left on the fifteenth. The weather was as "hot as possible on the Missouri River," but he managed to kill several grouse while on a hunting expedition into the Kansas countryside. It was so warm, he said, that he and two other dragoon officers "lay in bed untill 7 & remain under the shelter of their arbor all day." Amid the heat, Ewell applied to the paymaster general for two months of advanced pay to be used during his journey across the prairies. His request was marked "approved" in September, although he had not received the funds before his departure. The available documentation does not verify his route to the west, but he unquestionably traveled over the well-defined Santa Fe Trail, and by September 5 he was receiving official communiqués from Washington posted to Taos, New Mexico.[8]

After 1836 and termination of the Texas Revolution, the infant Republic of Texas claimed all of New Mexico to the eastern shore of the Rio Grande, which nearly bisects the territory from north to south, while its tributary, the Pecos, drains the southeasternmost sections. When Ewell arrived in the early autumn of 1850, New Mexico had been firmly under the American flag since 1846; General Stephen Watts Kearny had marched into the Mexican provincial capital at Santa Fe during the first days of the Mexican War and raised the Stars and Stripes over the entire territory. Several days later, on August 22, he issued a formal proclamation to the civilian population that guaranteed civil and religious freedom—he even attended mass, but he went further. In a prearranged action from Washington, Kearny defined the limits of his conquest: "He announced his intention 'to hold the department, with its original boundaries (on both sides of Del Norte) as part of the United States, under the name of the Territory of New Mexico.'" And, continues Paul Horgan, "there went, at one stroke of the pen, the old fiction about the Texas boundary at the east bank of the Rio Grande." The Treaty of Guadalupe-Hidalgo in 1848 merely confirmed what was already an accomplished fact when the United States agreed to hand over fifteen million dollars for New Mexico, Arizona, and California.[9]

Although Kearny received embassies from Utes, Navajos, and Apaches upon his "bloodless possession," of later concern to Ewell, Guadalupe-Hidalgo obligated the United States to restrain Indians in the Southwest from cross-border raids into Mexico. While admitting that the figures may be "too high," state historian Warren A. Beck sets the number of Indians in New Mexico during the 1850s at: "10,000 Navahos, 5,000 Apaches, and 2,000 Utes." Twelve to fifteen army posts were scattered across the territory, most of them with very small garrisons. Never more than 1,400 to 1,800 troopers were available to man these often remote outposts before 1861, although it cost Washington three million dollars annually to maintain them. "This meant that frequently the troops would be doing very well if they protected themselves, let alone punishing the Indians or even overawing them by their strength," Beck continues. Ewell became concerned with the Apaches of southeastern New Mexico, but it was the Navajos who raised the greatest turmoil throughout the 1850s. "That tribe particularly viewed the white man with contempt, looked upon his numerous treaties as a measure of weakness, and it was not until the Civil War years that the Navahos were brought under control."[10]

Because of their remoteness the various posts frequented by Ewell were nearly impossible to supply. "In New Mexico great difficulty was experienced in securing forage for the trains and horses of mounted troops, the shortage being accentuated by California-bound emigrants who managed to secure whatever surplus there was." Many parts of the Southwest did not possess sufficient wood for construction of forts, to say nothing of such trivial things as furniture for the troops or shelter for animals. The necessity of feeding docile tribesmen who had subscribed to the relocation programs of two early governors, James S. Calhoun and William Carr Lane, taxed army quartermasters already overburdened with problems of supply. In August 1853, however, a get-tough policy initiated by Governor David

Meriwether reversed previous pacification plans and induced some New Mexico tribes to become unruly. With government programs designed to feed the Indians out of the question, "the southwestern commanders mounted a dozen offensives between 1854 and 1861." And, continues Robert Utley, "two netted positive results, but the rest turned out to be inconclusive." Captain Richard Stoddert Ewell played a pivotal role in at least two of the major campaigns.[11]

Later, according to Richard Taylor, as Ewell sat around Civil War bivouacs, he repeatedly asserted that on the frontier "he had learned all about commanding fifty United States dragoons, and had forgotten everything else." Nor was he the only West Point man to suffer from his experiences in the west; it was said that Philip St. George Cooke, father-in-law of the renowned J. E. B. "Jeb" Stuart, knew everything about handling a troop of cavalry and nothing about regimental command. Unlike Cooke, who fell by the wayside during the upheavals of 1861–1865, Ewell was destined for high command in an army not yet dreamed about when he took charge at Rayado, New Mexico, in the spring of 1851. Located in present Colfax County, north of the Santa Fe Trail and not far from the Colorado border, Rayado Post had been established in May 1850 by Companies K and G, First Dragoons. Near the landmark Point of Rocks, eagerly anticipated by hundreds of wagon trains, the post was created "to safeguard the travel routes across northern New Mexico." Ewell remained at Rayado, "which occupied a large mansion belonging to affluent landowner Lucien B. Maxwell," until the army abandoned the place in August 1851. The outpost positioned on Rayado Creek, a tributary of the Canadian River, was reactivated two years later, but by then Ewell had been assigned elsewhere.[12]

Before his tenure at Los Lunas, another new post, twenty-two miles south of Albuquerque on the Rio Grande, Company G was ordered to Fort Defiance in Arizona prior to division of the two territories. Fort Defiance, the first U.S. Army post in what is now Arizona, was established on September 18, 1851, by Colonel Edwin Vose Sumner of Mexican and Civil War fame, adjacent to the New Mexico line. Ewell and his dragoons were present from the beginning, although he was never commanding officer at the post, which consisted of a parade ground surrounded by "a number of structures including barracks, officers' quarters, and a stable. Most of them of pine-construction with dirt roofs but a few adobe." The founding of "Fort Defiance in the heart of Navajo country almost at once had a profound effect," writes Frank McNitt, a historian of the Navajo wars. "Ill chosen as the site was, the presence of the fort and its small

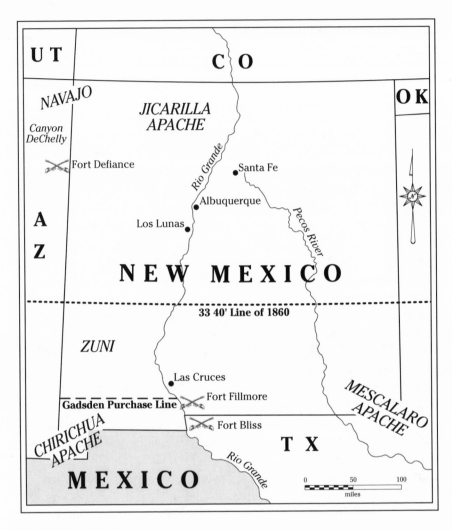

Ewell's New Mexico

garrison unquestionably in the months ahead had a restraining influence upon elements of the Navajo nation."

But pacification of Indians along the New Mexico-Colorado border would have to await more favorable conditions, as the post commander, Major Electus Backus, was forced to abandon the site in December because of food shortages for men and animals. Ewell himself chaperoned the horses of Companies G and K for forage in the Red Lake region a few miles north of Defiance; and he led an escort toward Albuquerque to meet a supply train led by Lieutenant Colonel Daniel T. Chandler that was unsuccessful in bringing succor from the Rio Grande settlements. Finally, confronted with actual starvation of his command and an unseasonable snowstorm, Backus ordered Company K to another post. Ewell and Company G were directed to accompany Chandler and his wagons to Laguna and "then proceed to Los Lunas to seek winter shelter."[13]

With minor diversions Ewell remained at Los Lunas until the summer of 1854. He had no sooner arrived from Arizona when he sent a January 1, 1852, communiqué to Colonel H. K. Craig, chief of army ordnance, indicating that he was returning several pieces used by Company G at Fort Defiance. When Backus directed Ewell to the small trading community at Los Lunas, it was without an army presence, as the records indicate the subsequent post was established by Company G on January 3. The garrison, "intended to curb the marauding and depredations by bands of Apaches and Navajo," was abandoned entirely within a short time. Although Ewell did not officially take charge until almost a year afterward, he was clearly contented at first with the assignment: "I am delightfully fixed now, cows, chickens, etc., and I make my own butter and all that sort of thing, as comfortable as any farmer," he wrote Ben on July 21. "My garden, though late, is coming on finely, with a good prospect of onions and cabbage." He was fearful that Sumner, now commanding the First Dragoons, would learn about his easy lifestyle and recall him. The only drawback, he said, was the absence of any officer but himself so that he had to do everything around the post. Ewell, who "scarcely spent 30 dollars a month" at Los Lunas, was able "to invite several ladies to tea lately, and give them a quite respectable table."[14]

His "respectable table" resulted from an extensive farming operation undertaken during the summer of 1853. Although Ewell had a poor knowledge of the "soils" along the Rio Grande, he put his troopers to work planting forage crops and "a large kitchen garden." By midsummer he informed Washington that Company G under his supervision had sown "twenty-four bushels of Wheat, ten bushels of Barley, three bushels and twenty-seven quarts of Beans, and twelve quarts of Clover seed." He planted an additional "ten to twenty acres in Corn." While the enterprise was designed to augment the poor food supply at Los Lunas, Ewell said that during his absence from the post on scouting duty for nearly two months in June, July, and August, some of his men kept the farm going under direction of his first sergeant. "It may be relevant to state . . . that I have found the labor to be beneficial in the most decided manner to discipline & therefore to the health of my company," he wrote in a May report to the divisional adjutant. "With abundance of liquor of every kind for sale there have been few cases of intoxication & none of serious sickness during the last four or five months." In spite of his best efforts, Ewell confessed his clover crop had been "a complete failure."[15]

A short time later he entertained his West Point chum Captain John Buford at Los Lunas and described his future enemy at Gettysburg as a gambler who "won $1,800 on a single horse race." "Here the natives call him 'hell-roaring Buford.' He is over six feet and out of proportion, large in other respects." Ewell's letters to Ben and Becca, however, became less exuberant as the year progressed. In December he told his brother: "There is nothing new out here—Things are going on in the same old style." With Becca he was concerned about money previously borrowed from her, at one point sending four hundred dollars to square an outstanding debt. And when Ben offered to select "a finer specimen of the genus woman that can be found in New Mexico," Ewell told him, "But as you have not seen the latter, I doubt your capability of judging—Yet awhile these are good enough for me."[16]

Ewell's "same old style" at Los Lunas in the summer and fall of 1853 came to a head when the Navajos of northern New Mexico became restive. A Mexican sheepherder named Ramon Martin was killed in a raid by five Indians near Vallecitos on May 3. Although the incident north of Santa Fe was far removed from Ewell, another incident occurred within a few miles of Los Lunas. One month later, a Navajo raiding party seized two thousand sheep belonging to Anastacio Garcia at Valverde about thirty miles from Socorro on the Rio Grande. The Martin and Garcia attacks combined to incite the entire territory, and Ewell set out on a chase to recover Garcia's stolen sheep. He traveled north through Albuquerque and Santa Fe to the Chuska Mountains near the famed four corners—the common point of Arizona, New Mexico, Utah, and Colorado. Accompanied by Henry L. Dodge, a frontiersman from Wisconsin, who was not only proficient in the difficult Navajo language but who also later became a government agent to the tribe, Ewell joined forces with Major Henry L. Kendrick, the commandant at Fort Defiance. In the region later designated as a huge tribal reservation, Kendrick took an unflinching line with the Navajo, warning their chiefs that he would unleash "the last war ever necessary upon them."

Kendrick, Ewell's superior officer, went further and drafted a document signifying: "That the New Mexicans, Pueblos, Dine Ana'aii [a dissident Navajo faction], and the Americans would loose upon them, their flocks seized, their men killed, their women and children taken captive, and ultimately the [Chuska] mountain [range] made their eastern limit." More peaceful Navajos attempted to replace Garcia's sheep and to give assurances that Martin's murderers would be handed over to the Americans in an effort to placate Governor Lane as well as Kendrick. Ewell was given the task of carrying the ultimatum to the San Juan River in the very heart of Navajo country. The San Juan, a tributary of the Colorado, originates along the New Mexico-Colorado border and flows almost exactly past the four corners before it joins the mighty river in southern Utah. Ewell and Dodge reached Santa Fe on June 21 after a grueling gallop across the semibarren New Mexico countryside.[17]

Following Kendrick's campaign and a shakeup in territorial politics as well as in army command structures, Ewell was once more called upon to venture among the Navajos. E. V. Sumner left for the east never to visit the frontier again; he was replaced by Lieutenant Colonel Dixon Stansbury Miles, who admitted that he knew nothing of the Navajo and that he had no stomach for a renewed campaign. A graduate of the West Point class of 1824 and a veteran of the Seminole and Mexican Wars, Miles had seen heavy duty on the frontier and was known for his heavy drinking and impetuousness; Governor Lane branded him "a walking sponge, martinet, & _____, the governor leaving the last judgement blank." A colonel at the outbreak of the Civil War, Miles was charged with drunkenness during the First Manassas, although a special tribunal found insufficient grounds to try him by court-martial. In the summer of 1853, however, Governor Lane, who awaited the arrival of a new territorial governor, David Meriwether of Kentucky, an appointee of the Pierce administration, wanted to try anew at subduing the Navajos in northern New Mexico. Miles had little option but to comply with Lane's wishes, and, declares historian McNitt: "It was not his purpose, Miles emphasized, for the troops to make war on the Navajos, but he directed the officers to impress on the Indians once more that stringent measures would be taken against them unless restitution were made for stolen livestock and the thieves among them handed over for punishment." The plan of attack required Ewell to march from Los Lunas with fifty horsemen for Fort Defiance, a post he had left a few weeks earlier. He once more joined Henry L. Kendrick, post commander at the Arizona garrison, who led one prong of a converging column into the heart of Navajo country. The troops under Kendrick and Ewell set out on July 19 and reached the San Juan four days later, where they joined another detachment of dragoons under Lieutenant Robert Ransom. On July 26 Ransom was ordered back to his post at Abiquiu, while Kendrick and Ewell marched westward along the south bank of the San Juan after delivery of Lane's message to several Navajo chieftains. "After parting with Lieutenant Ransom," continues McNitt, Kendrick's column traveled "eighty miles in five days until it reached the mouth of the Rio de Cheille or Chinle Wash." That part of the march took Ewell into southern Utah before he turned south into present Arizona. When the company reached the Canyon de Chelly, now a national monument, and a tributary of the Rio de Cheille, Ewell and his compeers turned eastward. Dodge once more rode at Ewell's side, and the soon-to-be Indian agent noted in his diary, "they were doubtless the first Americans that passed entirely through the canyon." Throughout the summer of 1853, Ewell, as captain of his own company, was almost constantly in the saddle as he rode into the remote four-corners regions at least twice. Although he was one of a handful of determined men who brought Anglo-Saxon law to the Southwest, he had yet to lead a major expedition on his own.[18]

Upon his return to Los Lunas, Ewell was preoccupied with schemes to augment his meager salary and with additional Indian scouts. Following an interlude at Santa Fe, he told Becca in January 1854: "Since the 16th of Dec I have been leading a very active life marching several hundred miles through the mountains travelling on horseback at more than the usual rates." Unfortunately, he did not elaborate on his itinerary, but he spent several weeks in the New Year at Fort Union in eastern New Mexico, where the Jicarilla Apaches had become warlike, even attacking the fort shortly before Ewell's arrival. Fort Union, commanded by Philip St. George Cooke, was considerably larger than the customary western outpost because of its position on the Santa Fe Trail to guard westward-bound pioneers and to serve as an army supply depot. Here Ewell linked up with Major J. H. Carleton in charge of the First Dragoons, on a chase after the tribesmen "tracking them through forests of pine and aspen where snow had fallen to a depth of two feet." Carried out in retaliation for a brutal attack upon a detachment of the Second Dragoons "about seventy miles east of Fort Union near the Cimarron," the march ended when the Apaches "fanned out into twenty-two separate trails."[19]

Ewell developed a sudden interest in California through a renewed contact with Kit Carson, who made Bent's Fort and Fort Union his home when not scouring the countryside for Indians or moneymaking ventures. Carson returned to his wife and family near Fort Union with a partner on Christmas Day 1853, and, comments his biographer, "they had driven 12 to 14000 sheep from New Mexico to California where they made an enormous profit." Little wonder that Ewell told his sister in January that he wanted to do the same thing: "I think of buying sheep to take them to California obtaining a leave for the necessary time. They are said to be worth a good deal there." Less than a month later, his personal talks with Carson led him to badger Ben about joining him in a financial undertaking. "Large dray horses," he said, "are worth $800 to $1,200 in San Francisco." Ewell planned to borrow $6,000 from his classmate W. T. Sherman, then working for a St. Louis bank, but he wanted Ben to cough up another $2,000 for the enterprise. With $8,000, he reasoned, they could obtain "30 to 90 horses, 10 men, and 5 ambulances." It was never clear how his professor brother would leave the lecture room to join him in New Mexico. The anticipated expedition never materialized, although Ben vowed to take a leave in order to accompany his kinsman. "The danger of stampeding is the drawback," Ewell allowed.[20]

Nor did Ewell's interest in Lizinka Brown falter during 1853–1854. In more than half of his January 1854 letter to Becca he talked about his cousin without mentioning any fondness on his part, although it was surely implied. "There has been a failure of the mails this month as all that came to me was one letter from Aunt Rebecca in Nashville." Rebecca Stoddert Hubbard, younger sister of his mother and likewise the aunt of Lizinka, was another family member who helped the budding romance. Ewell learned from Mrs. Hubbard that Lizinka's property in Nashville was "estimated at $500,000," a tidy sum in the antebellum South. "I believe from what I have seen of her that in the end she will be a happier person than ever before not of course because she has the property but because of the duties it will entail, will keep her mind employed." But he was obviously concerned about the thirty-three-year-old widow and how he might approach her after the 1853 death of her brother. "I have not written to her since hearing of George['s] death, partly because her residence has been constantly changing & partly because her pain I thought, must be so great that sympathy would appear like mockery." George W. Campbell, born in 1819, and Ewell were likewise first cousins through their mothers.[21]

When Ewell learned that legislation was pending before Congress to expand the army, he immediately seized upon a scheme to win promotion: "If you go to Washington and lobby a little for me, I will come down very handsomely, paying all expenses if you fail, say one thousand dollars for the grade of Major," he implored Ben on February 25. "Wonders are sometimes done by spending a little money among the proper agents." Supposedly because of the time delay for letters to reach Virginia from the territory, his brother did not call upon Secretary of War Jefferson Davis until later in the year. First, he secured a letter of recommendation from Winfield Scott, dated December 16, in which Ewell's old mentor was full of praise. In Mexico, Scott said, "Captain Ewell, although suffering with ague & fever, was never out of the saddle when an enterprise was to be undertaken or deeds of daring performed." When Benjamin Ewell called at the war department on January 11, Davis was unavailable and thus had to content himself with a letter. After touting Ewell's devotion to duty on the frontier, he called the future Confederate president's "attention to General Scott's opinion of him." Next he approached Virginia senator James M. Mason to inform R. M. T. Hunter, Virginia's other senator, about Ewell's "fitness as an officer." In spite of their efforts, as well as the outlay of time and money, the army appropriation bill never became law, and Richard Stoddert Ewell remained a captain of dragoons until his resignation to join the Confederate service.[22]

While Ben was working for him in Washington, Ewell began wending his way down the Rio Grande in late 1854 after hearing reports that the Mescalero Apaches were becoming restive. He traveled initially from Los Lunas to Fort Craig located on the river eighty miles to the south, near the present Elephant Butte Reservoir; and by November he was in command at Fort Thorn, where the Rio Grande veers sharply to the southeast on its run to El Paso. Both were small garrisons established in Apache country as a counter to their marauding and sheep-stealing forays among the Mexican population. Ewell was posted at Thorn, a mere eighty miles northwest of El Paso, when he received instructions to march against a band of Mescalero accused of raiding ranches and settlements two hundred miles to the east in uncharted territory near the Texas border.[23]

After David Meriwether took over as territorial governor and Indian agent in the summer of 1853, he sought to follow the carrot-and-stick policies of his predecessors, with little success. Described as "a widely experienced administrator and politician" with an annual salary "of $1,500 as governor and $1,000 as Superintendent of Indian Affairs," Meriwether had inherited an intolerable situation. A native of Louisa County, Virginia, he removed to the area around Louisville, Kentucky, at an early age. Following a stint in the Missouri fur trade, Meriwether, whom Ewell would come to know intimately, entered the rough and tumble of Kentucky politics. After thirteen terms in the state legislature, including service as speaker of the lower house, he was appointed to the United States Senate to fill the unexpired term of Henry Clay upon the Great Compromiser's death in 1850. When Meriwether left the senate in September 1853 and traveled to New Mexico, he learned that in a futile attempt to pacify the Jicarilla Apaches, Governor Lane had "contracted to furnish them with brood mares, corn, beef, salt, and other supplies." Lane's pact was contingent upon approval from Washington, and when that approval was not forthcoming, "because no funds were available for the purpose," not only the Jicarillas but also the Utes and Mescalero Apaches faced with starvation resumed their attacks upon isolated sheep ranches.[24]

When others marched against their kindred tribesmen, Ewell was given the job of corralling the Mescalero. Known as the "mescal eaters," the Mescalero called the lands astride the Pecos home. They were primarily wanderers with little interest in agricultural pursuits, as they ranged over a vast area that extended "from the White Mountains in southern New Mexico into west Texas and southward into the north Mexican states." The tribe ventured as far east as San Antonio and south to the Mexican hamlets around Chihuahua from their home territory in the White Mountains. "This will cover a space of about fifteen thousand square miles," Meriwether wrote in his 1853 report to the commissioner of Indian Affairs. "And as they number about seven hundred and fifty souls, the country occupied by them will average, say twenty square miles to each Indian." The Mescalero had almost no connection with other groups, and, commented another Indian agent: "They are unquestionably the most indigent Indians in the Territory, which is the result of their lazy and indolent habits. . . . While they are a cowardly band, they are nevertheless cruel and revengeful, never forgetting an injury, nor letting an opportunity for retaliation escape them if the chances of success are greatly in their favor."

The Spanish had not only fought the Mescalero from the sixteenth century, but they also established the Mission of San Saba de la Cruz in a lost effort to civilize and subdue them. The California-bound '49ers from the Texas ports had incurred their wrath, and, always hostile to the white man's way of life, Meriwether said that they "have committed many depredations upon the citizens of the Territory during the last and present year." Hungry and unable to secure food from Uncle Sam, the Mescalero began stealing livestock during 1854 throughout the Pecos settlements. When one party raided a ranch within ten miles of Santa Fe, both citizens and the army became aroused. Ewell set out in late December, because "this time the military leaders were not going to be satisfied with punitive expeditions," writes C. L Sonnichsen. "Already a full scale invasion of the Mescalero country was in motion."[25]

Ewell left Fort Thorn on December 28 with sixty-one men from Company G and twenty from Company K, both First Dragoons, as well as Lieutenants Isaiah N. Moore, John W. Davidson, and an army surgeon. Among his eighty or so troopers was a newly reinstated private in his own company named James Augustus Bennett from Rochester, New York. Bennett had enlisted in the First Dragoons hoping that it would ultimately open a way for him to reach California. Although he never got to the promised land, Bennett was important to the campaign because he was one of the few enlisted men to keep a diary—probably written later but helpful for a colorful glimpse into the hardships endured by the expedition. When Ewell filed his report from Los Lunas on February 10, his dates vary slightly from those of Private Bennett, but he reported later that the detachment covered thirty miles on the first day. "In fording the Rio Grande, lost 3 horses and 2 mules by drowning. We lost 2 boxes of ammunition and some provisions also." After that inauspicious beginning, a swirl of events seemed to engulf the entire enterprise, even though it was eventually successful.

After reaching Albuquerque the column turned eastward across the Rio Grande watershed to the Pecos and the hamlet of Anton Chico, a collection of five hundred souls living in dwellings "built of adobes or unburnt blocks of clay." It was a "miserable, dirty little town," according to Bennett, where Ewell got word for the first time that a contingent under Captain Henry W. Stanton would rendezvous with him on the Rio Bonito. With or without Ewell's approval, a Mexican was given "50 lashes on his bare back" for stealing a rifle from his men. The expedition acquired a guide named Gleason at Anton Chico and headed south along the Pecos. After trooping through a sheep-grazing region until January 13, Ewell led his command westward up the Bonito to the vicinity of El Capitan, a ten-thousand-foot peak near Lincoln, a town William Bonney would make famous several decades later. Here in the shadow of the mountain he was joined by Stanton, with 29 dragoons and 50 infantrymen, which raised his available manpower to more than 160 men. Stanton had been dispatched by General John Garland from Fort Fillmore on the Rio Grande near Las Cruces, New Mexico. "Upon combining the two commands, I moved south toward the Guadalupe and Sacramento Mountains and the 17th of Jany, encamped on the Penasco, a fine stream running toward the Pecos," reads Ewell's account. His troops camped under a rock ledge above the eastward-flowing Penasco—about forty miles south of the Bonito—and though they had not seen an Indian until now, the bivouac was beset, in Ewell's words, "with arrows and firearms, at the same time they tried to burn us out." Ewell admits that food for men and animals was in short supply and that Lieutenant Moore found his horses so enfeebled that he was unable to mount a spirited counterattack. At daybreak on the eighteenth about one hundred warriors renewed the fight: "They were dancing around a fire, 'hollering,' and seemed to be daring us," recounts Private Bennett. "We saddled our horses, took no breakfast, mounted in pursuit. . . . The main body of troops moved up the stream and small parties of Dragoons kept charging out after parties of Indians." Ewell reported fifteen Indians shot but carried off to avoid capture during a running fight in which the Mescalero "gave the impression that they were trying to keep us from their families and hoping to bring on a close fight."

The enemy's lodges were found the following afternoon, which turned out to be "a miserable collection of tipis on a snow-powdered slope, abandoned and empty." When Ewell spotted a side valley or draw, he summoned Stanton and twelve men after a body of fleeing Apaches; but the pursued soon turned on the pursuers with what amounted to an ambush. Ewell's account has Stanton "firing his Sharps carbine" until he was "instantly killed [with] a shot in the head." Bennett, however, is more poetic: "He fell, a ball having passed through his forehead, one private soldier was killed. The horse of one man fell wounded. The Indians gathered around him and filled the rider's body with arrows. Those in camp heard the firing, ran to the rescue, met the Indians, had a hard fight of 20 minutes, when the red men fled."

When night fell over the gruesome scene, Ewell ordered the bodies buried and campfires built over the graves to disguise their locations. The Mescalero, Ewell continues, scattered once more so that "my guides were incapable of tracking them." With no forage the horses became so weak they had to be led back to Los Lunas; nor was food available for Ewell's men, because his remaining beeves had been slaughtered a day or so earlier. Ewell gave the word to march across the divide between the Penasco and the Rio Grande on January 20, and it was a bedraggled company that found its way home. A small group turned back long enough to check the graves of Stanton and the enlisted men. "Found the bodies turned from the grave; their blankets stolen; bodies half eaten by wolves, their eyes picked out by ravens; their bones picked clean by ravens and turkey buzzards." And, continues Bennett, "Revolting sight. We built a large pile of pine wood; put on the bodies; burned the flesh; took the bones away."

Stanton's remains were returned to his wife at Fort Fillmore, although it is unclear if Ewell made the extra journey. In an attempt to put a good face on a poor situation—Bennett says the men pronounced one campsite on the return march "Camp Starvation"—Ewell reported that "within five miles of my camp the day of the fight were over 300 newly abandoned lodges. And, he added, "the Signal Smokes of the Indians on my return satisfied me that they had retreated towards the lower range of the Guadalupe Mountains."[26]

"The campaign was a terrible blow to the Apaches," writes C. L. Sonnichsen. "It was the first time the heartland of their domain had been penetrated by a hostile enemy of such force and effectiveness . . . Never before had the entire tribe been driven from its tipis and turned out in the wilderness with neither food nor shelter." Although a small band of warriors sought to raid a "grazing camp" on February 23, they were not only driven off, but dragoons from Fort Bliss, Texas, also joined the chase to disperse them. The chastened Mescalero had had the fight taken from them and petitioned Governor Meriwether to grant a treaty ending their tribulations. Ewell's superiors in Santa Fe were obviously pleased with his performance in spite of Stanton's death as well as the loss of two enlisted men and the severe privations of Ewell's men. When Garland forwarded his report to Washington, he offered his own explanation for Stanton's loss: "But for the impatience of one of his officers, under smarting disappointment in the Mexican War, it is believed that not a man of his command would have been killed." Furthermore, Garland called Ewell a "well-tried, gallant, and valuable officer" who "whether on the field or in the Barracks . . . was looked upon by his comrades as the very pattern of an officer and gentleman."[27]

Although the regimental returns list Ewell in command at Los Lunas until his departure for Fort Leavenworth on September 27, he was seemingly in constant motion after the Mescalero campaign. If Bennett is to be believed (this part of his diary is frequently misdated), Company G traveled from Los Lunas to Fort Fillmore and then farther south to Franklin (present El Paso) and Fort Bliss. Ewell's troops spent four days looking over El Paso del Norte, "a city of 10,000 inhabitants," and, continues the dragoon diarist: "It is a rendezvous for rascals, cut throats and knaves. Murders are committed almost nightly on the streets." At Doña Ana, close by Las Cruces, on the return Company G captured and hanged four Mexicans whom it said "forced" the wife of an American trader during a bungled robbery attempt. From Los Lunas Ewell's company left the river and marched eastward across the Sacramento Range to the Rio Bonito (today's Rio Hondo), where it had been three months earlier in pursuit of the Mescalero. Three hundred men were there under Colonel Dixon S. Miles to build a new outpost, Fort Stanton, in the heart of Apache country. Private Bennett reported "all of the officers" getting drunk at the gathering. Fort Stanton's location had been personally selected by Garland, although he had earlier labeled the fallen officer's conduct less than honorable when Ewell ordered the attack on the Penasco. The incessant trooping in the vicinity of Alamogordo, a place made famous in another American war, was not all bad as the dragoons "saw thousands of wild game: deer, elk, bear, and turkey." They even "caught some trout" in a mountain stream.[28]

Back on the Rio Grande, Ewell resumed his command at Los Lunas until July 1855, when he joined Meriwether and Garland on a troop northward into Navajo country. On July 1 he told Becca that he had been in contact with Lizinka Brown. Apparently his Nashville cousin had made an overture for him to oversee her large landholding and business enterprises throughout central Tennessee. Ewell informed his sister that he had answered in a manner that "was neither obsequious or submissive." Although he indicated no desire "to resign my commission," he was already keeping the door ajar for both a personal and financial alliance with Mrs. Brown. "The disposition that I might have to accept Cousin L's offer would spring more from the admiration that I always had for her than from any idea of getting rich & philosophically speaking this very admiration would be the best reason for not accepting." In a pensive mood Ewell said, "money is to be made with labor and capital," and if he had pursued several business ventures during his three years in New Mexico he would now be independently rich. While lamenting his lost opportunities in the California sheep trade, he mentioned that he had "business in the East and was expecting to see L."[29]

Ewell's visit to Virginia would have to wait when word arrived two weeks later for him to march from Los Lunas. The new assignment stemmed from Meriwether's notification from Washington that he had been designated—and money appropriated—to negotiate treaties with the Mescalero and Mimbre Apaches as well as the Utes and Navajos. Meriwether was told to arrange boundaries between the tribes and to keep them as far as possible from the settlements; in short, he was ordered to oversee the beginnings of the reservation system. After completion of his treaties with the Mescalero, Meriwether resolved to meet with the Navajos at Fort Defiance in mid-July. Although the Navajos were badgered constantly by the Utes to join them in warfare along the Colorado border, they had refused to cooperate. And when word spread about Meriwether's impending council, Navajos commenced gathering around Fort Defiance in large numbers. Major Kendrick, however, thought it best not to meet at the fort proper for fear of alarming the Indians—already frightened of the army—with an overt display of military might; thus the decision was made to meet at Laguna Negra, a "beautiful, clear lake 12 to 14 miles north of the fort."

Meriwether left Santa Fe on July 13 with his son Raymond and W. H. H. Davis, his private secretary, but when Garland and Ewell failed to join him "at a junction of the Los Lunas road west of Albuquerque," the governor proceeded alone. Ewell and Company G finally caught up with the party on July 15 at the fort. When Meriwether went north to Laguna Negra, Ewell accompanied his party as an escort, although Garland and Kendrick stayed behind at Defiance. "The place swarmed with Navajos, their numbers ranging from Meriwether's estimated fifteen hundred warriors to a figure of two thousand reported by Davis and Henry Dodge," writes historian McNitt. "The governor observed that few women and children were present but 'every man was mounted and armed.'" At one point several Navajos boldly occupied Meriwether's tent, but the near proximity of Ewell's dragoons averted serious trouble. Bennett sets the number of Indians at three thousand and says they were threatening enough for Ewell to have a man mounted ready to ride hell-for-leather to Fort Defiance with an urgent appeal: "Go as soon as God will let you, and tell the Commanding Officer to send me some help or we will all be killed in the morning." Fortunately, additional troops were not needed even though seventy-five men arrived at the council site without summons from Ewell or Meriwether.

After the Navajos disposed one chieftain and selected a new spokesman, the Treaty of Laguna Negra—never ratified by the United States Senate—was

concluded on July 17, 1855. The document "set apart a reservation estimated by the governor to be about seven thousand square miles," although
it was not surveyed when Congress failed to act. "In return for taking more
than two thirds of their country, or an area corresponding in size to Massachusetts, Connecticut, and Rhode Island, Meriwether proposed to pay the
tribe a total of $102,000 in graduated annuities through 1876." Twenty-
seven Navajo "headmen" signed the abortive treaty as did six representatives of the United States government: Brigadier General John Garland;
Governor Meriwether; Major Kendrick; W. H. H. Davis; Captain O. L.
Shepherd, Third Infantry; and Captain Richard S. Ewell. Clearly, Ewell
was associating with the civil and military elite of the territory as he returned to his berth at Los Lunas for another two months. First the Mescalero
campaign and now treaty making at the governor's right arm and the stream
of correspondence to and from Washington marked the cavalryman for
recognition. Yet no promotions or duty postings in the east were forthcoming in spite of brother Ben and other family members' continued efforts on his behalf.[30]

It is unknown if Ewell knew that Governor Meriwether was heading
for the States when he applied for a leave following the Laguna episode,
but when he left Los Lunas in late September he had been assigned a troop
of cavalry to escort him to Fort Leavenworth. Subsequent letters in the
Brown Archive suggest that Ewell called upon Lizinka in Nashville before
proceeding to Ben's home in Williamsburg. On November 21 he applied
for a six-month extension, which Winfield Scott "affirmed and respectfully forwarded" to the secretary of war. Although Jefferson Davis would
actively solicit Ewell's help later in accompanying Meriwether back to Santa
Fe, he was not enthusiastic about his leave. Colonel Samuel Cooper, assistant adjutant general, attached a note to Ewell's request that appears to
have soured Davis: "None of the officers of Company [G] were serving
with it at the date of the last return (September 30), and it was commanded
by Lt. Moore of Co. C." When Davis responded with a hand-written memo
on December 7, he was not complimentary: "The Capt. [Ewell] should
not have been permitted to leave his company when no officer belonging
to it was present to take command. Being now however so remote from his
Company . . . the leave granted will be extended so as to make the whole
time of absence six months."[31]

Undeterred by bureaucratic wrangling, Ewell proceeded to enjoy his
visit with his "widowed mother" at Stony Lonesome and with Ben at the
College of William and Mary. A subsequent letter to Elizabeth hints that he

saw something of a "Miss Scolley" while taking in the sights of Williamsburg, but nothing developed between the two—the lady in question married another at the same time Ewell made his way to the frontier. Much of his time was taken with attempting to arrange business and investment possibilities with brothers Ben and William. He wrote in January from Williamsburg asking his sister to purchase several parcels of seed—cabbages, nutmeg, melons, turnips, cauliflower, spinach, and so forth—and mail them to Santa Fe. In early March he made two visits to her Georgetown lodgings but did not find her at home. "I wanted to say to you that my fiscal affairs being more straightened than I had expected prevented my making the bargain we were speaking of," he informed Elizabeth by mail. "I have to spend a good deal of money & prefer letting our affairs remain in status quo." Ewell was short of cash because he had joined Ben in a scheme to purchase a tract of land on Hog Island located off the coast of Northampton County. He owed his sister $140.[32]

Chapter 4

FORT BUCHANAN

The warmth of home and the allure of eligible belles as well as the prospect of profitable land purchases came to a halt in the first weeks of March 1856. The thirty-nine-year-old Ewell was reassigned to further frontier duty when Governor David Meriwether specifically asked that he be detailed to accompany him from Fort Leavenworth to Santa Fe. "The Secretary of War has accepted his request and you will accordingly repair to Carlisle Barracks, Pa, on or before the 25th instant and take charge and conduct to Fort Leavenworth a detachment of mounted service recruits," the adjutant general wrote on March 6. Another directive five days later told Ewell to forget about Carlisle Barracks and report directly to the war office in Washington for "further orders," where he was informed: "On arrival at Fort Leavenworth you will as soon as practicable complete the equipment of your party and hold yourself in readiness to proceed across the plains with Governor Meriwether at such time as he may indicate." Additional orders assigned the new recruits permanently to Ewell for subsequent duty in New Mexico and Arizona.[1]

Ewell obviously had little desire for the rigors of service with the frontier dragoons. As he prepared to decamp for Fort Buchanan in the fall of 1856, his aunt, Mrs. David Hubbard, pleaded with Jefferson Davis: "My nephew Capt. R. S. Ewell's company I understand is ordered to 'Tucson on the Gila river in the extreme South most border joining Cal.' He is pained at the change." Mrs. Hubbard, youngest sister of Ewell's mother and then living at Kinlock, Alabama, was one of several relatives who embarked upon a campaign to have him named paymaster general of the army, although in a February 12 missive to the secretary of war Ewell de-

75

nied any personal involvement. Several letters found their way to Washington urging his appointment, from Campbell and Aaron Brown, Major David Hubbard, and his brother Ben. Jefferson Davis himself responded on February 16 that no appointment would be forthcoming and that he would be reassigned to the "frontier service." As a consolation Davis added Ewell's name to a "list of applicants" for paymaster. Unable to keep him in the east, his Brown and Hubbard relatives renewed the campaign on his behalf after his return to New Mexico. Lizinka's letter of October 2 demonstrated a remarkable ignorance about his early career in the army—she had him serving in Oregon prior to the Mexican war. And in conclusion, she told Secretary Davis: "I can offer no apology for the liberty I take in troubling you about this matter other than my earnest desire to get the strongest possible influence with the government in Washington and my conviction that should the appointment be made the conduct of Capt. Ewell will never give you cause to regret its recommendation." Even though she had enthusiastically joined the cabal to keep him in the east, which extended into the winter of 1856-1857, Ewell remained on the far frontier.[2]

By the last weeks of March, Ewell had made his way to the Planter's Hotel in St. Louis. Thomas T. Gantt, who managed Lizinka's business affairs in the city, wrote her on March 14: "Dick Ewell will be here the 20th or 25th March on his way to N.M. and thinking it might be pleasant for you to meet him before he goes off to the Indians, I suggest that you do not put off your visit to us longer than then." Although Ewell informed Ben on March 26 that he had been detained longer than expected, there is no evidence that Lizinka made the journey from Nashville for a renewed encounter with her cousin. When she did strike up an ongoing correspondence after his return to the west, she recalled his visit to Nashville with nostalgic fondness. William, his younger brother, who intended to open a school in New Mexico or California, accompanied him first to Fort Leavenworth and then Santa Fe.[3]

Ewell had no sooner arrived during early May at his old Los Lunas billet than orders came directing the First Dragoons to California and to Tucson in the newly acquired Gadsden Territory. Although he did not move to Camp Moore—later named Fort Buchanan, after the new president took office in March 1857—for several weeks he was ambivalent about his new assignment in southern New Mexico while his comrades trooped farther west. Since Arizona Territory was not organized until 1863, he was still in New Mexico and subject to the commanders at Santa Fe. After telling his sister Elizabeth about Tucson's location, Ewell said Company G was one of four dragoon units posted to the adobe-studded hamlet. "I prefer this to Cal. as [it] is in some parts sickly & as much isolated." Mostly he worried that mail from the east would have difficulty finding him. "I don't care much about the move, except that my garden is just beginning to yield & I don't like to leave its benefit. It is more however for the sake of testing different products than for my own use." Amid his agricultural pursuits Ewell traveled to Santa Fe and several other posts throughout the summer and fall as he waited to go farther west; mostly he worked at his garden, telling Elizabeth: "Unless one drinks or gambles it is necessary to keep from absolute stagnation that interest should be taken in something."[4]

Actually, even though Ewell got his mail from the Tuscon post office, Fort Buchanan—the first United States military encampment in the Gadsden Purchase—was not situated in Tucson but was several miles to the south. The Treaty of Guadalupe-Hidalgo ending the Mexican war had not ended this country's dispute with Mexico; but the document "recognized the American view of the Rio Grande River as the boundary of Texas and ceded to the U.S. Upper California and New Mexico with the Gila River and an arbitrary line along the 32' parallel as the boundary of the [Mexican] cession." The 32nd parallel is the northern boundary of the western protrusion of Texas as it passes north of El Paso on its way to California, but the location proved unsatisfactory when railroad men began searching for a southern route to the Pacific. James Gadsden, an agent of the pro-Southern Pierce administration, was able to negotiate "an agreement with Mexican president Santa Anna that added 29,142,000 acres of land in return for $10 million and other considerations which included United States assistance in suppressing Indian depredations." The new treaty immediately became embroiled in the ongoing controversy over slavery that was threatening to tear the country apart. Although it met strong opposition from abolitionist forces, the senate ratified the document on April 25, 1854, thereby adding the southernmost portions of New Mexico, and later Arizona, to the country—territory that was "considered essential for a railroad route." Long before the transcontinental lines, Ewell would spend the remainder of his time in the Federal army fighting Indians in the hot, semiarid region of present Arizona acquired by the Gadsden Treaty.[5]

Ewell became one of the first officers to enter the Gadsden region. Along with Colonel J. V. C. Blake and Major Enoch Steen, he arrived at his new station on November 17 to begin construction of the future Fort Buchanan. It was built east of the old settlement at Tubac along Sonoita Creek, a tributary of the Santa Cruz River that empties into the Gila near

Phoenix. From the beginning the fort was intended as an outpost to restrain the westernmost Apaches and to offer protection for the overland routes across southern Arizona. The dragoons used "trees, brush, and other materials available from [the] surrounding countryside." Despite their efforts, Fort Buchanan remained a miserable duty station. A post historian writes: "It consisted of a series of temporary jackals. The quarters lacked neatness and comfort, and the houses were built of upright posts of decaying timber coated with mud. The floors and roofs were covered with dirt and grass, and the rooms were low, narrow, and lacked any ventilation."

The post was not only the first American presence in the new territory, but it was also one of four maintained in Arizona by the army during the decade before Fort Sumter. Besides Fort Defiance, where Ewell had served previously, Uncle Sam kept Fort Yuma, far to the west on the Colorado, as well as Fort Mohave, also on the Colorado but in northern Arizona. Buchanan was likewise established to protect several mining ventures around Tubac and Patagonia as well as a number of Mexican ranchers newly placed under the Stars and Stripes, although the territory was relatively free of Indian troubles except for isolated incidents. Nor did army commanders have a high opinion of its value. "Fort Buchanan is entirely out of position, it being southeast from Tucson forty-five miles in a direct line, thirty-five to forty miles from the mail route, and from eighty to one hundred and twenty miles from Tucson by the traveled road, on the opposite side of the mountain," reported Colonel B. L. E. Bonneville three years after Ewell's initial arrival. It was too far from the Apache homeland, he said, to be of any use in a major campaign. Bonneville and "the officers of Fort Buchanan," which presumably included Ewell, recommended that it be abandoned and the garrison moved eastward to the San Pedro. In 1856, however, when Ewell dispatched a Christmas letter to Elizabeth, he complained about the cold weather and having to live in a tent, which he "expected to occupy for some time."[6]

Ewell reportedly raised the first American flag over the new lands purchased from Mexico when he arrived on the Sonoita. Although he spent the winter at Fort Buchanan, he mailed reports from a "Camp at Taos" in January 1857. But his company had returned by February and stayed until May, when he was summoned to join the well-known Gila Expedition against the western Apaches. Two incidents, the murder of Henry L. Dodge and rampant sheep-stealing along the Rio Grande, prompted army suspicions to fall upon the Mogollon tribe—inhabitants of the Mogollon Mountains of southern Arizona. The Mogollon Apaches lived near the trail to

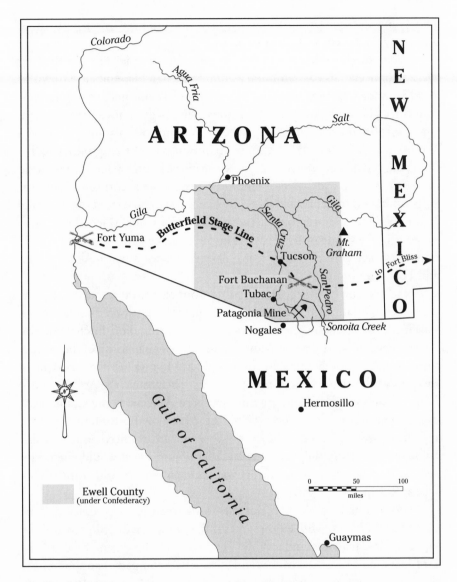

Ewell's Arizona

Fort Yuma and California, and when they failed to heed official warnings, a foray against them was initiated in early 1857.

The Gila Expedition was the brainchild of Bonneville, who had replaced John Garland as temporary commander in September. Known as "Old Bonney Clabber," the sixty-one-year-old Bonneville, with a reputation throughout the army as a garrulous "windbag," enjoyed an extensive career on the frontier dating from the 1820s. French-born in 1796, and a West Point graduate, 1815, he sold a manuscript to Washington Irving for one thousand dollars, which "the author fashioned [into] an enduring classic of the fur trade." It detailed Bonneville's adventures scouring the west for pelts, where among other activities he became the discoverer of the Yosemite Valley while temporarily out of the army. When Garland left for the east on leave in the spring of 1857, writes historian Robert M. Utley, Bonneville began "to concentrate troops from all over the territory at Albuquerque and Fort Fillmore."[7]

He not only planned the expedition but also led it in person. A rendezvous was established west of Albuquerque on a headwater branch of the Gila immediately across the New Mexico border from Fort Buchanan. The "Gila Depot" was situated in Grant County "three miles south of the present town of Clift." Originating in the Mimbres Mountains of New Mexico, the westward-flowing Gila joins the San Francisco across the Arizona–New Mexico line to start its course across southern Arizona to the Colorado at Fort Yuma; it also flows through the heartland of the western Apaches. Here Bonneville divided his force between two experienced commanders: William W. Loring, the one-armed soldier whom Ewell would encounter later in the Shenandoah with Stonewall Jackson, and his old commander, Dixon S. Miles.

While Loring took charge of the northern contingent, Ewell was ordered to join Miles, who led the other—the group fated to do most of the fighting. The troopers under Miles "consisted of three companies of the 1st Dragoons, two of the Mounted Rifles, a two-company battalion of the 3rd Infantry, and another of the 8th Infantry." It was in turn divided into two wings for Bonneville's sweep down the Gila. The commander himself rode with Miles. Ewell left Fort Buchanan on May 13 with Lieutenant Chapman and sixty-five dragoons over the Chiricahua Range and past Mount Graham. Ten days afterward, Major Steen was incapacitated because of illness, which placed Ewell in charge of "103 men, besides herders, packers, etc." Ewell spent "seven days exploring rather than scouting" before crossing the Buro Mountains in eastern Arizona. Everywhere, he reported, signs of Indians on the move were found as he neared the gathering point. Finally, on June 4 he left the horses and twenty men with his trusted sergeant major at the base of Mount Graham and proceeded to the depot.[8]

Although the force under Loring began chasing Apaches north of the Gila almost immediately, the men commanded by Miles and Ewell remained at Bonneville's bivouac for another two weeks. Clearly put out with the delay, Ewell complained to his mother: "I am very tired of chasing a parcel of Indians about at the orders of men who don't know what to do or how to do it if they knew what they wanted." Ewell said he would rather be tending his "potatoes and cabbages." The June 10 letter from "Gila River, New Mexico," mentioned that Lizinka had not written for some time, and he asked his mother to tell her he was "on a scout" in the event she did write while he was in the field. "We now are about starting in a 'solumn' (solid column) of 600 men," he told Elizabeth Ewell; "we will *not* be apt to see Indians, and mules and horses will be the only sufferers."[9]

Ewell could not have been further from the mark when Bonneville's "solumn" swept westward along the Gila. Although the expedition was searching for Mogollons, Ewell and Miles ran smack into the Coyotero tribe when it crossed the Arizona boundary, to the instant surprise of both Apache and dragoon. "[T]he White Mountain Coyoteros is that portion of the Apache living north of the Gila, upon the San Francisco and head waters of the Salinas. They occupy a fine country with many mountain streams and rich fertile valleys for cultivation," Dr. Michael Steck, Indian agent for the southern Apaches, commented two years later. "This division numbers two thousand five hundred souls, of whom six hundred are warriors." In the summer of 1857, however, they had the unquestioned misfortune to be camped not only in "the very shadow of Mt. Graham" but also in the path of Ewell's horsemen. Both Bonneville and Miles were on hand to urge him forward for the June 27 fight, which was "short and sweet," with Ewell walking away with the lion's share of honors. "Victory was total," writes a historian of the fracas. "Scarcely an Apache escaped. Nearly 40 warriors were killed or wounded and 45 women and children taken captive." Ewell lost two officers and seven troopers were wounded.[10]

When Bonneville and Ewell sent in their reports, Ewell was "freely acknowledged as the hero of the day"; his unhesitating leap to action crushed the western Apaches and forced them to sue for peace. Ewell's aggressiveness in the Gila River fight was yet another laurel that attracted notice in Santa Fe and Washington. Some years after the Civil War, when a debate raged over army treatment of the Indians, Colonel C. D. Piston recalled that Ewell had been a proponent of unrestrained combat with the Apaches. "How the Devil can a soldier stop in the midst of battle and summon a jury of matrons to decide whether a redskin pouring bullets into the soldier is a woman or not," Piston says Ewell yelled out. "Take aim boys: Steady now. Fire. And the boys mowed down all combatants, both great and small, regardless of color, sex, or the mistaken pity of false humanity." Ewell, Piston recalled in 1891, held that "an armed squaw is worse than an armed buck, as she will shoot the wounded and helpless, being apparently inspired with the ferocity of a wild beast." Although Ewell modified his attitude about Indians and bondsmen when the occasion demanded, after nearly twenty years on the frontier engaged in constant Indian hostilities, his views had changed little if any since his first station at Fort Wayne.[11]

About the time Ewell returned from the Gila campaign, Lizinka Brown wrote a letter from her farm near Spring Hill, Tennessee. Addressed to "My dear Cousin," the missive acknowledged his letter of May 29 but suggested nothing about an intimate relationship. Yet it is easy to imagine the lonely bachelor at Fort Buchanan poring over every sentence with fervent interest. In considerable detail, Lizinka expressed her "nervousness" over the possibility of slave unrest across Tennessee and Mississippi: "I am told that in Bolivar County [Mississippi]—containing 5 to 10,000 blacks & 171 voters—there is great apprehension of insurrection. Judge [unnamed] made several speeches on the importance of strict discipline on every plantation & abolitionists are suspected to be amongst them in the disguise of teachers." More slaves than ever had escaped from the Nashville region during 1857, she proffered, before switching to a more personal vein: "How I wish you and William were here and we could talk to 12 o'clock—I would take some interest in housekeeping if there was some body to appreciate it," Lizinka chided. "Well, never mind, I shall try for political influence some of these days & when I get it you shall be stationed where you please."[12]

Later in the summer Ewell invested one hundred dollars with a Mexican sheepherder for controlling interest in a silver mine near Fort Buchanan. It was situated a few miles south and very near the international boundary. As early as 1539 Spanish priests and adventurers had been in the Patagonia Mountains; they gave the region its name while searching for the legendary Cities of Cibola. At one point in the 1700s Philip V had taken part of the area under his direct control because of its mineral deposits. "But neither royal decree nor fierce Apache could quell rumors of the fabulous wealth of the mountain ridges which lay in the vicinity of Arizonac," writes a historian of the mines. After all, a prime reason for establishing Fort Buchanan had been the use of U.S. troops for protection of American mining companies in the Gadsden Purchase lands. Although Ewell was superintendent and a major stockholder in the venture, he was never outright owner of the Patagonia mine. The operators drew upon eastern banking houses for venture capital, set up a reduction plant, and began refining silver in 1858. Most of the workers were Mexican nationals from south of the border in Sonora.[13]

There were a number of nearby mines, including one operated by Major Samuel P. Heintzelman, also of the U.S. Army. A San Francisco newspaper reported that Ewell's facility was one of the richest in the Patagonia area; but Apaches were a constant menace, with several parties raiding the silver operations themselves. The *San Francisco Daily Bulletin* said that Ewell's mine, "almost fifteen miles from the Fort produc[ed] $75 dollars per day at an expense of only $15." In August 1858 Ewell told his niece Lizzie that he had been offered $1,000 for his share but had refused to sell: "The Patagonia mine (so they call the one in which I am interested) is sinking fast toward the center of the earth," he informed her. "It is the darkest, gloomiest looking cavern you can imagine, about 50 feet deep, with prospects looking bright." One year later he wanted four thousand dollars for his share, yet by 1860 he had divested himself entirely from the enterprise. Ewell had changed his tune completely when Elias Brevoort, "a former sutler at Fort Buchanan," bought into the operation. "A man disagreeable to me in every respect, managed to become interested to such an extent in the mine as to influence its management," he avowed in 1859. Unable to abide Brevoort and no longer in charge of things, Ewell closed his share on the eve of his final departure for the east.[14]

In the last months of 1857, however, he was concerned with more than budding business undertakings. "In order to relieve myself of the tedium of nothing to do, I went down to the river on a hunting excursion and was quite successful, obtaining something like one hundred birds, including snipe, ducks, geese, crane, all of which I have been distributing among the officers' families, here," he wrote to Lizzie while he sat on a court-martial proceeding in Santa Fe. "The greatest acquisition I made was a lot of potatoes, an article in great demand in New Mexico and which are more welcome to the ladies than compliments ever would be." Some weeks earlier Ewell was hardly bored when the renowned Butterfield Overland Mail carried news of his exploits to the larger world. Although the line had been in operation for several years, in March 1857 Congress authorized it to deliver the mail twice weekly between St. Louis and San Francisco. Almost immediately happenings across the territory were relayed to West Coast newspapers by the overland express, which ran through Texas to El Paso and from there to Tucson, Fort Yuma, and the Pacific. "A party of Apaches having killed a couple of immigrants, at Apache Cañon, Captain Newell [they got his name wrong], with two companies of dragoons, started in pursuit, and came up with a tribe of those Indians near Mount Graham about 150 miles from the Cañon," said the *San Francisco Golden Era* during mid-October. "These he attacked with such force that the day after the fight the chief came into camp, and stated that out of 90 warriors he could only muster 20 men." While those numbers appear uncommonly high for a frontier skirmish, Ewell reportedly took "30 or 40 prisoners." He also brought two Mexican lads from Sonora into Fort Buchanan to await a return to their families. In a letter of October 31 to Lizzie, Ewell complained that the same raiding party had stolen "twenty-five or thirty" head of his own cattle pastured near Tucson.[15]

Following the Indian upheavals of 1856–1857, the Arizona frontier settled down in the vicinity of Fort Buchanan. "With the exception of the Navajos, the Indians of this department have been unusually quiet," Garland informed Washington on September 5, but the tranquility among the Apaches was brought about in great measure by Garland's reticence to press them for minor infractions. "The Indians around us are sobbing all the time, but without any prospect of arousing the Fabius who commands us," a still-irritated Ewell told Lizzie a few months earlier. He had developed a special rapport with his nineteen-year-old niece, who was the only child of his brother Ben and his wife, Julia McIlvain; born the year following his graduation from West Point, Elizabeth Stoddert Ewell, or Lizzie, later married Beverly S. Scott. For the remainder of his stay in the Federal army she became his faithful correspondent. The absence of Indian troubles through much of 1858 prompted him to tell her in May: "This place is dull beyond any thing I ever imagined—nothing going on. I try to work myself tired in the company garden so as to sleep away some of the time but it wont do." Ewell sold his "ranch" near Tucson and informed Lizzie that he would have to rely upon the Patagonia mine to make his fortune. "I am puzzled to know what I shall do with so much money—whether to make the Pacific rail road—buy New York City or what."[16]

Some of the boredom stemmed from "the withdrawal of two companies from Fort Buchanan for service in California." Garland told Washington the "move was embarrassing" to him personally because he had planned to abandon the post and relocate the garrison "to a point near the San Pedro River which would be in striking distance of Tucson and the great western mail route, besides the advantage of being nearer the proximity to the marauding Indians of the Gila." The reduced manpower made the change impractical; for the time being in late 1858 Ewell would stay put on the Sonoita and with fewer companions in arms. However, his routine picked up in the fall when he had the first of several encounters with the legendary Cochise, who had recently emerged as undisputed chieftain of the Chiricahua Apaches. The near-mythical leader has been described "as a tall, dignified-looking Indian." Another American contemporary, John H. Tevis, recorded that Cochise was "as fine a looking Indian as one ever saw. He was about six feet tall and as straight as an arrow, built from the ground up, as perfect as any man could be."[17]

Although his days of fierce, unrelenting warfare to check penetration of his homeland lay in the future, throughout the 1850s Cochise and his tribesmen remained quiet north of the border. "He kept his people at peace with the Anglos and there were no clashes of any consequence until 1861 though minor depredations and stock thefts occurred, whether by Cochise's people or with his assent can never be known," asserts Dan Thrapp. "Indian agent Michael Steck conferred with him in 1859 and found him peaceful and guiltless of hostilities." The reasons for this serenity were twofold: Cochise and his warriors had declared war to the death upon the ranchers of Sonora, and he could not sustain a two-front siege from Mexican and United States forces. Likewise, he managed to provide his charges with food and provender by catering wood to the isolated way stations of the Butterfield line between Tucson and Stein's Peak. This tacit understanding between Cochise and the army began to weaken "with a growing American presence in southern Arizona" after 1858 around the mining operations at Tubac and Patagonia. Also, records his chief biographer, "Sonora strengthened its northern presidios in the late summer and early fall of 1858, partly to protect itself from American expansion and partly to forestall Apache raiding." Prior to his official confrontation with the Chiricahua leader, Ewell had two minor brushes with him in June 1857 when he retrieved several stolen horses from the Indians.[18]

Also during the summer of 1858 "the Apaches captured and drove off a large herd of horses and horned cattle near the town of Altar in the Mexican state of Sonora." A running fight through Fronteras, not far from the border crossing at Nogales, developed as the Chiricahua headed for the

United States with their plunder. Once across the border the Mexican ranchers persuaded a group of Americans living at the Canoa Crossing near Fort Buchanan to join them in exchange for one-half of any livestock recaptured. In the fight that ensued near Tumacacori, several Apaches were killed as Cochise and his warriors retreated toward their haunts in the vicinity of Stein's Peak. Situated in the Peloncillo Mountains astride the New Mexico-Arizona boundary, Stein's Peak (sometimes referred to as Steen's Peak) was also the site of a way station on the Butterfield line at the point where it crossed into New Mexico. "The stations after leaving Tucson are large square enclosures, with adobe walls," said the *San Francisco Daily Bulletin*. "Rifles, shot guns, revolvers, and muskets, heavily charged, at convenient places, are the objects that first strike attention, upon first entering them; and four or five men who are in attendance, appear always on the alert against the attack of Indians."

Although he remained outwardly friendly with the army, the old understanding with Cochise was clearly coming apart. The Apaches were licking their wounds after the Tumacacori set-to when they had lost their limited supply of firearms as well as several warriors and their Mexican cattle. The Arizonians were understandably disturbed when Ewell was summoned to visit the Chiricahua encampment. After informing its readers that New Mexico territory, including modern Arizona, had nearly 3,000 voters and "10,000 Indians at least," a San Francisco newspaper continued: "The only means of defense provided by the Government against the outbreak of these tribes, is about 100 soldiers, located at Fort Buchanan, about 65 miles from this place [Tucson], under Capt. Ewell—an efficient officer but rendered powerless to act for want of sufficient force. He has started to Steen's Peak, 125 miles from here on the mail route, to have a 'talk' with the Apache hanging around the Peak, and to ascertain what is the object of their remaining there." The *Bulletin* did not have any hope that Ewell would meet with success in advance of the soiree because of his small force. "I have been campaigning (peacefully) for the last two weeks," he relayed to Lizzie on November 14 after his return to Fort Buchanan. For the time being, at least, Cochise had forsaken the warpath north of the border. "There is nothing stirring out here of particular interest—the Indians scaring one man last week & and stealing a beef the week before."[19]

A pattern had developed for Ewell at Fort Buchanan; when little was "stirring" he would complain about his boredom when writing to his family in Virginia—after all, if a bachelor cannot gain sympathy from his female relatives, to whom does he turn? Things began to change in early

1859 when he took the campaign trail, this time against the Pinal tribe, characterized as "the most powerful and mischievous of the whole Apache nation." The Pinal, relates historian Frank C. Lockwood, "occupied the country watered by the Salinas and other tributaries of the Gila. They take their name from the Pinal Mountain [elevation 7,850 feet] in and around the base of which they reside[d]." Numbering an estimated "three thousand souls, of which seven hundred [were] warriors," the *Tubac Weekly Arizonian* proclaimed: "Their depredations are incessant, and they deserve a severe whipping." As Ewell was readying a foray into their homeland in February, two Pinal chiefs suddenly appeared at Fort Buchanan professing friendship for the Americans and seeking assurances of peace. Ewell immediately agreed to a rendezvous northeast of Tucson on May 20 at Cañon del Oro. Although the Apaches attempted to move the meeting to another site, Ewell would not comply with their request and was successful in implementing a treaty in which, continued the *Arizonian*: "The Pinals agreed not to molest Americans and their property; and the government promised, if they kept their word, to distribute goods and provisions to them."[20]

By actual count 288 tribesmen "fit to bear arms" met with Ewell and Michael Steck, territorial Indian agent, along with a smattering of Tonto Apaches; roughly 600 women and children were also present. They were "a dangerous, thievish, wolfish, looking set as we ever happened to meet," said a newspaper correspondent, "but very shrewd." Ewell, it seems, allowed a number of trading goods to be transported to Cañon del Oro in his personal ambulance. And when word spread among the Pinals that "blankets and butcher knives" were being sold at Ewell's wagon, the correspondent's account continues:

> Among the purchasers was a blanketed [Indian] who evidently "had a secret to impart" so he waited his opportunity and slyly slid into the trader's willing palm an eagle quill full of gold. It was a round washed, all placer production, and as the banker viewed it with pleasure he mechanically ventured: "cuanto?" as he returned it to the owner. A trade was eventually made and a cotton blanket and a cast iron butcher knife went to the Indian and the quill of gold back to the trader, who paid no further attention to it at the time, but later in the day he called the attention of Hon. Grant Oury to his proceeds, among other things to his big quill of placer gold. No sooner, however, did Oury see it than he roared with laughter, as he said: "Brass fil-

ings by _____." "What!" said Ewell, who was sitting near, "Have you been encouraging these fellows to steal and file up my soldiers' spurs? By _____ if that is all you wanted for your goods I could have you plenty nearer home."[21]

Although the "cheap treaty" would not last with the Pinals—more campaigning against them was in the offing—Ewell returned to Fort Buchanan, where he served as post commander for several months. Soon to be relieved by Lieutenant Colonel Isaac V. D. Reeve, he learned about the death of his mother in April. The mother of ten children, seventy-four-year-old Elizabeth Stoddert Ewell, daughter of George Washington's secretary of the navy, had remained the Ewell family matriarch since the death of her husband more than twenty years earlier. Besides Captain Richard S. Ewell, only four of her children were living in 1858: Rebecca, Benjamin, Elizabeth, and William. Lizzie, who Ewell sometimes addressed as "Bettie" had been her only grandchild. "Your concern at the loss of your grandmother has good reason, for in all of her letters she showed constant interest in your welfare," Ewell assured her. "One advantage about youth is that these losses do not make a lasting impression compared with the grief of greater age & it is a law of nature that at your time of life gayety is soon resumed." For himself Ewell told his niece that he was managing his own emptiness by occupying his mind "with my usual business."[22]

Ewell simply did not have enough men to hold the Apaches in check as the tribesmen grew bolder on the eve of Civil War, which forced him to stay near Fort Buchanan for the remainder of the year. While attempting to improve the post's water supply with a detail of men, he was set upon by a band of warriors within sight of the fort. "In order to make a decent fight, Ewell in a stentorian voice, cried, 'Halt, repeating Halt Boys! Let us retreat in good order,'" writes a local historian. "They formed in line and marched to the post at rather a quick pace, but they were pricked occasionally by the Indian arrows as they left the place." In the autumn of 1859 Ewell was trooping with his company from Tucson to Dragoon Springs, about sixty miles to the east, when another band of Apaches swooped down upon them. The war party had raided a nearby ranch and made off with thirteen mules and nine oxen as Ewell unsuccessfully gave chase. When he renewed his pursuit the following day, the Apaches turned on Ewell's twenty-five-man contingent, killing two of his troopers, Wilbur Craver and Charles Tucker. At nightfall the Indians stampeded Ewell's horses, which were never recovered. "A week later," the account continues, "the captain met a party of Apaches at Puerto del Curcucouco near the Buseni Ranch in the Santa Rita mountains, and left sixteen of them dead on the field." Other Indian episodes occurred during the summer and fall as Ewell awaited the arrival of Reeve to take command.[23]

There were the customary letters to Lizzie that "nothing was stirring" when he was not out "campaigning"; Ewell either did not wish to worry his family with his hostile encounters—after all, he was chasing men who would kill him if they could—or he considered the expeditions part of his normal routine. And he had the ability to dissociate himself from the killings; a September letter to Lizzie said that he had been reading Lord Chesterfield but had given his copy to the governor: "You will not lose time to read [Chesterfield's work], as it is a remarkable instance of patience, long suffering, and forgiveness in one not a professed Christian." He even found time to pursue the Swiss theologian Johann Lavater, who wrote good advice, in Ewell's words, that "indulgence of feeling or thoughts produces their impress upon the countenance." In other words, he told Lizzie to defer the pleasures of the moment for some greater fulfillment in the future. But an October letter conveyed news of a rude interruption to his tranquil literary pastimes when two members of his company deserted with "two of my best horses." After a chase southward across the border with several troopers, Ewell caught up with the culprits only to find that one had been killed by Sonoran highwaymen. He did not tarry beyond the border but made a speedy return to Fort Buchanan because of "the dangers of interference by Mexican authorities and outlaws."[24]

While still engaged with his mine at Patagonia—he told Lizzie it was "commencing the work of reducing lead ore to silver"—Ewell was sent on an international mission. The obvious regard of his superiors led to his embassy to Governor Pesquiera of Sonora to iron out a nasty border incident. The trouble started when Captain Charles F. Stone and a party of surveyors working on the new international boundary were forcibly ejected from Mexican territory. After word reached Washington, Secretary of War John B. Floyd, working through Adjutant General Samuel Cooper, ordered Ewell south of the border on October 10: "Captain Ewell is elected for this delicate duty from his known intelligence and discretion." Simultaneously, the administration dispatched the sloop *St. Mary's*, skippered by Captain William David Porter, into the Gulf of California. Even the press joined in a chorus of approval of Ewell for the task at hand. "No better man could have been selected for this duty," said the *San Francisco Evening Bulletin*. "His long residence on the Mexican frontier, knowledge of the people and firmness of character, particularly adapts him for so important a [mission]."[25]

Ewell was instructed "to proceed to Sonora and call upon the Governor and protest against the expulsion of Captain Stone and his party, not only as a wrong done them but also as a gross violation of treaty obligations existing between Mexico and the United States." A subsequent communiqué from Washington said that he could take an escort only as far as the "Boundary Line," and if he found it unsafe to enter Mexican jurisdiction alone, he was empowered to communicate with Pesquiera by letter. After departing Fort Buchanan on November 2, Ewell reached the provincial capital at Hermosillo a few days later, where he found the authorities indifferent to his arrival. Pesquiera denied that he had sanctioned the expulsion of "Stone and his party—that it was done without his authority and that they were at liberty to return whenever they please, but they will not be permitted to continue the survey." Newspaper reports touted that Ewell was received with a warm outpouring by the populace but that Sonoran officialdom was pointedly cool.

While he was in Hermosillo, a Mexican citizen spotted a U.S. Army mule with what he claimed was his brand upon it. Although the animal had been under the quartermaster's charge for "several years," Ewell was required to give a heavy bond that he would not travel northward until the matter was resolved. He was held a "virtual prisoner" for eight days but somehow managed to get off a message to the *St. Mary's* at Guaymas on the coast. Porter thereupon "demanded of Governor Pesquiera an immediate apology for the insult offered Capt. Ewell and an escort to protect him on his journey from the country." And he positioned his guns at point-blank range toward the town, threatening to open fire if Ewell was not released. During a three-hour extension to Porter's deadline, several foreign consuls repaired to the *St. Mary's* in hopes of avoiding a bombardment. Pesquiera finally relented and even offered the requested escort to accompany him homeward, which Ewell declined. After a thirty-day adventure south of the border, Ewell reached Fort Buchanan on November 30. In the aftermath of his official report to Washington, Secretary Floyd sent an endorsement via Adjutant General Cooper: "Although the object of the mission seems not to have been fully accomplished by Captain Ewell's visit, yet it is understood to have been done by other means and no further action under the orders to him is therefore necessary."[26]

Ewell was no sooner back at his post than he joined Reeve as second in command of another campaign against the Pinal Apaches. Following a period of renewed agitation by the Arizonians, Colonel Bonneville approved a second campaign to check supposed raiding on both sides of the border. Many others did not think the tribe was at fault and counseled against any action that would upset the delicate status quo. Indian agent Steck, for instance, protested vociferously that a campaign could well "throw all of the western Apache into open hostility without really punishing any." But Ewell's treaty of Cañon del Oro had been breached, said the civilian agitators, and Bonneville ordered Reeve to proceed from Fort Buchanan and a supply depot on the San Pedro that later became Fort Breckinridge. The resultant campaign, which included Ewell's Company G, marched over "a very rough country 140 miles to the Mescal Mountains, and was in the field fifteen days." Reeve managed to capture one man, two women, and a number of children.

Another effort to subdue the elusive Pinal left Fort Buchanan on December 14 with Ewell again in a subordinate position. Lasting twenty-one days, this move netted "eight Indians killed, one wounded, and twenty-three prisoners, all but one of the latter being women and children," reads the report of Colonel Thomas T. Fauntleroy, who had replaced Bonneville at Santa Fe. "One hundred and eleven head of horses and cattle, four guns and numerous bows and arrows, and other property of much value to the Indians was captured." This troop, also under Reeve, covered 350 miles and suffered only one injury, Ewell receiving a slight wound to the hand. "Colonel Reeve states that the exposure to cold, mud, rain, and snow, and the excessive fatigue of marching over very rough country, were borne by the troops with cheerfulness, and their arduous duties performed with alacrity." In spite of the words of support for his men, Fauntleroy became disenchanted with the questionable results and called off the affair in January 1860.[27]

"Since early November I have been away from here almost the whole time in one or the other sort of duty and very little time for correspondence," Ewell told his sister Rebecca on January 10 from Fort Buchanan. Following the return from Sonora, he added, "I have been on Indian campaign suffering from cold and fatigue and heartily anxious to be somewhere else." He said nothing about his wound, nor did he mention that he was now in command at Buchanan. Colonel Reeve had been granted an extended leave upon his return from the Pinal campaigns, which placed Ewell in charge. Although he was almost constantly at the head of his dragoons, Ewell ran the post until September 15, when he was ordered to El Paso's Fort Bliss on detached duty. At the start of 1860, however, he was mightily concerned over the worsening sectional controversy that governed national politics as well as his financial dealings with Rebecca, Ben, and William. He was busy settling a number of debts left over from his mining venture and therefore declined to enter into a scheme to pay three thousand dollars for his share in a Ewell farm "south of the Brentsville Road" in faraway Prince William County. And there must have been a strain among his brothers and sisters over their mother's estate. "It is [illegible] that legal title should be made as I don't want to pay twice for the same thing and relinquishment on parts of Elizabeth or Ben without legal forms would not be considered by me as I have had enough wrangling out of the family without running the risk of the same thing in it."[28]

In early February Ewell was once more called to the "Indian campaigns" when an Apache war party raided the Arivaca Ranch on the roadway from Sopori to Sonora; it made off with an estimated thirty head of cattle, which the owners demanded the army find and return. "Captain Ewell, (now in command at Fort Buchanan), who has the reputation of being a most efficient and meritorious officer, was at Tubac, preparing to go to the mines when the news arrived," reported the *San Francisco Evening Bulletin*. Although he took the trail with "25 picked men" from the fort, that venture, like most excursions to hunt down warlike Indians, became an exercise in futility; typically, the Apaches dispersed in several paths at once, making an effective retaliation next to impossible. But the pursuits reinforced his standing with the Arizonians. Not only was a county about to be named for him, but also a stop on the Butterfield Mail Route dubbed "Ewell Station" had been established the year before; it was located "between Apache Pass and Dragoon Springs, fifteen miles west of the pass. Water was hauled here from Apache Pass and Dragoon Springs, which was also known as Ewell Springs." The well-known Ewell's Depot, north of Fort Defiance and close by the Arizona-New Mexico boundary, continued to service cavalry horses until well after the Civil War. The March 26 edition of a San Francisco newspaper graciously acknowledged that his February "expedition was unsuccessful, owing to the unusually high state of the rivers, and information conveyed to the enemy by a woman who swam them."[29]

Three weeks after the expedition, on March 16, Ewell was plunged into a frontier drama that has attracted the attention of writers and historians from that day to this: the capture of Larcena Page and Mercedes Sais Quiroz by a band of Tonto Apaches. Born Larcena Pennington, the twenty-two-year-old Mrs. Page had arrived in the Tucson vicinity during 1858 from Texas with her parents and several brothers and sisters. Following her marriage in December 1859 to John Hempstead Page, she joined her husband and his partner, William Randall, at a logging camp in the Santa Rita Mountains not far from Canoa Crossing. Situated between Tucson and Tubac, "the pinery" was about thirty miles west of Fort Buchanan. The family made its living by "felling trees and sawing them into lumber sorely needed by settlers in this remote Gadsden Purchase region of the New Mexico Territory." But Mrs. Page, several weeks pregnant at the time of her abduction, had been engaged by Tucson's William H. Kirkland as tutor to his young ward, Mercedes Quiroz. Kirkland, an Arizona lumberman who enjoyed a business relationship with Page and Randall, thought the "bright, promising" eleven-year-old Mexican girl deserved an education.[30]

Without warning, the Indians burst into the tent of Mrs. Page, who reached in vain for a secreted pistol, dragging the mother-to-be and young Mercedes into the wilderness. For the next two weeks the woman experienced the most brutal savagery, including exposure to the elements, hair pulling, and repeated piercing by Tonto lances, as her captors had no firearms. Pursued by her husband and several of his axe men, who had been at the cuttings when the raid occurred, the Apaches continued their flight. "Mrs. Page having overcome the first fright, now rallied her courage and began to fight her captors with tooth and nail, trying her best to scream," writes Captain John A. Spring. "She was a very strongly-built young woman, and fought desperately for her liberty, thus retarding the progress of the Indian who had her in charge, while others with the little girl were pushing ahead." As her husband and his companions closed on the fleeing band, the Indians, fearing capture themselves, removed her clothing—one confiscating her shoes for his own, and after stabbing her several times with a lance, hurled her over a cliff, "which according to exact measurement taken later, proved to have been a sheer descent of sixty-two feet." Although one or two Indians looked over the incline and thought her surely dead, others pushed on with the "wailing child." Meanwhile, John Page passed within a few yards of the stricken woman—close enough, she said later, to hear his voice as she lay helpless in the rocky abyss.[31]

Thinking her lost, Page returned to his timbering camp and then to Tucson with news of the capture, which set the entire Santa Cruz River Valley, and indeed all of Arizona, ablaze with agitation. No fewer than six rescue parties were organized to chase down the marauders. When word reached Fort Buchanan, Ewell immediately joined the search with his dragoons. Mrs. Page had landed in a snow-shrouded clump of elderberry bushes that checked her fall, while the snow served to congeal her wounds. For the next two weeks—until Saturday, March 30, when she stumbled into her husband's logging operation—she clawed her way back to civilization. "My feet gave out the first night and I was compelled to crawl most of the distance," she related afterward:

> I did not dare go down to the foot of the mountain for I could find no water, and was therefore compelled to keep on the rocky and steep. Sometimes after climbing up a steep ledge, laboring hard for half a day, I would loose my footing and slide down lower than the place from which I started. As I had no fire and no clothing, I suffered much from the cold. I was at a point said to be six thousand feet above the sea, and the only wonder that I did not freeze. I scratched holes in the sand at night in which to sleep, and before I could travel was obliged every day to wait for the sun to warm me up.

Mrs. Page, who first asked for a "chew of tobacco" upon her return, later gave birth to a healthy baby girl. After her husband was killed by Indians a year or so afterward, she remarried and even reared another family.[32]

While the drama of Larcena Page was unfolding, Ewell trailed the fleeing Tontos, who had divided into several groups, to the Cañon del Oro a few miles north of Tucson. When he encountered several Pinal Apaches, he attempted a negotiation to secure the Quiroz girl's release. The Pinals "promised to find and obtain the girl for a consideration consisting of blankets, flour, and two mules, the meat of which the Apache consider[ed] the greatest delicacy." From his previous associations with these Indians, who pledged anew their friendship with the Americans, Ewell thought he could rely upon their help and even "loaned" them a cavalry horse for the ride into Tonto country. The Pinal were successful in regaining the girl, and on April 2 she was handed over at his new bivouac on Arivaipa Creek. He had waited four days when a Tonto rode into camp "with Mercedes Sais on the saddle in front of him," relates Captain Spring. "She threw herself from the horse at Ewell's feet, clasping his knees, besought him to take her away from her captors, of whom, however, she said the present Indian was not one. The food that was placed before her she ate ravenously."

Ewell started immediately for Tucson with the girl, and he was clearly "the man of the hour" among the Arizonians. The *San Francisco Bulletin* and *Tucson Arizonian* praised him for the negotiated release, loudly proclaiming that he had been "unceasing" in his efforts. "The Indians assembled in large numbers, but were peaceful and gave up the child, with apparent good feeling." Two days later, on April 4, five days after the return of Mrs. Page, Ewell reached Tucson with his charge. "The church bells were rung, the populace assembled in the Plaza and the little girl, now a heroine indeed, passed from one to another to receive their embraces, congratulations and welcome," recounts historian Constance Wynn Altshuler. "Such a scene of hugging and kissing! Capt. Ewell too was not forgotten, and blessings were showered on his head for the active part he had taken in the rescue."[33]

"The people made a great fuss about the child and not knowing how to thank providence for the safe recovery vented their gratitude in making a fuss over me," he told Lizzie shortly afterward. Ewell's other letters during the summer did not mention the incident nor did he elaborate on the "fuss." "I was marched into a convention hall, had a county named after me and a public hall, all of which, under a different description, would appear very ridiculous." And in an attempt at modesty: "The fact is, they had not time to think over the matter, being taken, as it were by surprise." But "the three dozen men" who convened in Tucson to form a constitutional convention were deadly serious. Repeated overtures to form a separate Arizona Territory had fallen on deaf ears in Washington and Santa Fe, and, convinced that the governors of New Mexico paid scant attention to the concerns of Arizona, they resolved to act until such time as Congress responded to their needs. Spearheaded by William Oury, Tucson's overland mail agent, the gathering proceeded to draft a constitution, designate Lewis S. Owings governor, and make provision for a court system as well as a militia. "Just how seriously Arizonians viewed the new government is not clear," observes L. Boyd Finch. "Both the *Arizonian* and the Mesilla *Times* which began publication in October [1859], reported on its activities, and editors in the east and in California copied the items. Whatever else it may have been, Arizona's provisional government served up, propaganda."[34]

One thing is certain: the conventioneers assumed a decidedly pro-Southern stance from the beginning. When the Democratic National Convention met in Charleston, South Carolina, on April 22, at the start of the momentous presidential campaign of 1860 that most scholars agree plunged the country into civil war, several delegates were convinced the new regime in Arizona would "help our cause." William Need, a pro-Union man from Fort Fauntleroy in Arizona, thought Ewell and other Southern-born officers were in on the plan to create a Confederate government in the territory, although their military commissions precluded any active participation, and believed the whole movement had been orchestrated by Jefferson Davis before and after he "swayed the councils of President Pierce" as secretary of war, 1853-1857. Furthermore, Need informed Lincoln's secretary of war, Simon Cameron, that Arizona "was terra incognita of a grand scheme of intercommunication and territorial expansion more vast and complicated than ever dreamed of by Napoleon Bonaparte in his palmiest days of pride and power." All appointments in the Southwest under Presidents Fillmore, Pierce, and Buchanan, he maintained, "were made solely and exclusively with reference to future operations in this quarter of the Union." Ewell was not the only pro-Southern soldier branded as one of Davis's minions: Fauntleroy, Steen, Loring, Longstreet, Crittenden, and Grayson, among others, were included in Need's sweeping indictment. Even John Bankhead Magruder, stationed at San Diego and Fort Yuma for a brief spell in the early fifties, was made into a pro-Southern plotter "to make the region safe for the Confederacy."[35]

Whether Ewell was part of an ongoing scheme to secure Arizona for the South is open to question, but it is worthy of note that the compilers of the *Official Records* of the Civil War saw fit to include Need's letter. Yet a more plausible explanation is that his arrival in Tucson with Mercedes Quiroz occurred at an auspicious moment—that his own assessment for Lizzie had been the correct one. Although his Southern birth and affiliations were well known, his standing on the Southwestern frontier had been keenly established long before the constitutional convention. Ewell must have gotten to town on April 4, the day of the constitutional gathering, because when it reconvened at 2:00 P.M., the official minutes record: "Mr. [Frederick W.] Cozzens stated that Capt. R. S. Ewell, U.S.A., was present and moved that he be invited to a seat within the bar of the House. Carried." Later in the afternoon, "Mr. Alden moved to amend by inserting the name of 'Ewell,' to the county comprising the territory between the Chirricahua [*sic*] Mountains and the longitudinal line proposed as the western boundary of the county in place of 'Santa Rita,' as called for in the report." The proceedings say nothing about a demur from Ewell when Alden's motion carried by unanimous action.

The boundaries of the new territory had already been set at Texas on the east, California on the west, Sonora on the south, and an arbitrary 33'40" line on the north. From east to west, four counties were formally organized: Doña Ana (land east of the Rio Grande), Mesilla, Ewell (which lay entirely within present Arizona), and Castle Dome, extending from the latter to the Colorado River. Repeated efforts to gain congressional sanction for the new scheme went unheeded until February 1863 when the Arizona Territory was formally separated from New Mexico, thereby completely ignoring the pro-Southern conventioneers of 1860. By this time Ewell was a major general in the Army of Northern Virginia, which meant that Ewell County was never legitimized except for a brief interval in 1861 when Colonel John Baylor took formal possession of the "Territory of Arizona" for the Confederacy. Although the name appeared on several maps of the Civil War period, Ewell himself took an off-the-cuff approach to the whole affair.[36]

Still in command at Fort Buchanan, Ewell once more took the trail in search of the elusive Cochise during the first weeks of June. Although the wily chieftain led his warriors on a raid across northern Sonora in the winter of 1859–1860, he was back in Arizona by mid-May. After a "friendly Indian" warned the Butterfield station agent at Apache Pass that a new round of troubles was at hand, writes his biographer, Cochise's band "ran off the entire herd of the Santa Rita Mining Company near Tubac." Without a moment's hesitation, Ewell charged once more into the Chiricahua Range, where Cochise handed over a number of animals and confessed that the tribe had eaten several more. After the Indians agreed to provide the remaining mules if Ewell would allow them to return to their haunts in June, they were let off with a stern warning. He was still trying to maintain peace north of the border by not pressing Cochise if a confrontation could be avoided. "Capt. Ewell," said the normally favorable *San Francisco Evening Bulletin,* was on "an Apache scout, and it is expected he will bring [them] to their senses, for the Apache will steal any mule and horse as the meat is a delicacy to them."[37]

Once back at Fort Buchanan, Ewell received a visit from Andrew Talcott, a former army officer and well-known engineer in the United States and Mexico, where he had recently completed construction of a railroad from Vera Cruz to Mexico City. The Connecticut-born Talcott, a West Point man, class of 1818, who had resigned his commission in 1836 to pursue a civilian career, was a great friend of Robert E. Lee. Lee's own engineering skills had been honed during 1835 when the two of them had surveyed the Ohio-Michigan boundary. In the thirties Talcott had devised a procedure he dubbed the "Talcott Method" of determining "terrestrial latitudes through the observation of stars near the zenith, adapting the zenith telescope to the purpose." Although Talcott left the fort for Tubac and points west, he was soon a key player in the initial defense of Virginia from Yankee invasion, and his brief visit presented Ewell with one more entrée with the men about to mastermind the Confederate war machine.[38]

Four days after Talcott's departure Ewell led "a detachment of seventy-five" dragoons from Buchanan for another rendezvous with Cochise. "[I]t is believed that he will severely punish [the Apaches] of their many depredations on the settlements in the way of stealing stock, etc.," said the *San Francisco Evening Bulletin*. By the time he returned to Cochise's stronghold, additional mules had been stolen from Tubac; again the animals that had survived Apache cooking pots were given up, and Ewell promptly returned them to their owners. "Letters written to the *Alta Californian* and *Missouri Republican* were scathingly critical of 'Old Baldy' for holding a parley instead of attacking the Chiricahua," writes historian Edwin R. Sweeney. But Ewell responded to his critics in a lengthy, detailed report and vindication of his tête-à-tête with Cochise. "After all, he had received some of the stolen animals, and any attack would have been in violation of a truce." He concluded by pledging that in the event of another theft he would not ask for restitution but would leave the fort "at night, and attack them when unprepared and try to make an effective blow." A powerful argument can be made that the very traits that induced him to avoid head-to-head warfare whenever possible while on the frontier were carried over into the Virginia fighting—that his inclination to hold back in spite of years in command cost the Confederate cause dearly at Gettysburg and finally prompted Lee to terminate his active participation with the Army of Northern Virginia following the Wilderness bloodbath. In 1860, however, with the red-hot presidential campaign hurtling to a climax that provoked the American people into a bloody Civil War, Ewell was denied the opportunity to again tackle Cochise. Just as he was on the verge of a new military career, albeit of marginal value, Cochise too was about to enter national prominence with his struggle to drive all white men from the Southwest.[39]

There were additional minor expeditions during the late summer of 1860, although Ewell's days in Arizona were rapidly coming to a close. He was ordered to Fort Bliss at El Paso on September 20 for court-martial duty; and in November the regimental returns reported him sick in Tucson. From there he traveled to Albuquerque, where the El Paso trial had been reconvened, and in a January 22 letter from New Mexico he uncharacteristically complained about his health: "Since writing from Fort Bliss," he said, "I have been very ill with vertigo, nausea, etc., and now am excessively debilitated, having occasional attacks of the ague. Chills and fever were not the form taken by my disease but violent pain in the head with sick stomach." An army surgeon recommended that he leave the Southwest "as soon as possible" because of health, and on January 15, 1861, a week after his letter to Elizabeth, he was granted a six-month leave of absence. By the time Ewell received word of his return to "the states," Abraham Lincoln had been elected president, and South Carolina as well as three other "cotton states" had already left the Union, precipitating a rupture between North and South. Sick and worried about his future as well as that of Lizinka Brown, whom he learned was experiencing health difficulties of her own, Ewell's Indian fighting ceased on January 31, when he left Albuquerque "in a wagon for San Antonio, Texas."[40]

Chapter 5

THE LOST ORDER

The entire country, even faraway New Mexico Territory, was in an uproar as Ewell made his way from Albuquerque to Virginia. "Everyone here is on tenterhooks of impatience to know what the Southern States will do," he had written to his sister Elizabeth before leaving. Even on the frontier, talk of national disruption and eventual war was already in the air in the aftermath of Lincoln's election to the presidency. "I look to business with particular dread because every cent I have in the world may be lost in the distress and trouble of civil war and disunion," Ewell added. "From this point of view no one doubts but that the one will turn into the other. They say here that war cannot be postponed for sixty days." Although most historians agree that the Civil War commenced in Charleston Harbor on April 12 when the first Confederate cannonballs rained down on Fort Sumter, trouble was brewing across the whole South as Ewell made his way toward the ease of family.

The great convulsion that gripped the South stemmed from the presidential canvass of 1860; throughout Ewell's last months at Fort Buchanan every part of the nation had been mesmerized by that momentous, four-cornered contest that had the abolition or continuation of slavery as its chief focus. "A house divided against itself cannot stand" and "I believe the government cannot endure half slave and half free. . . . Whether this shall be an entire slave nation is the issue," Lincoln had roared out in his famed debates with Stephen A. Douglas two years earlier. Before the contest ended in November, every citizen, North and South, understood the overpowering gravity of the sectional resolve—that North and South could not agree on the vital question. And each camp had powerful advocates as Southern apologists sought to counter the Northern onslaught exemplified by Lincoln's ringing dicta. But the Democrats, unable to agree upon a common response to this Republican attack from north of the Mason-Dixon Line, had split at their national convention in Charleston, South Carolina. Although Southerners with their pro-slavery positions had dominated the party for more than two decades as the sectional debates unfolded, the Democrats named two candidates in 1860: John C. Breckinridge of Kentucky, who ran on a pro-slavery platform, and Stephen A. Douglas of Illinois, the country's chief proponent of popular sovereignty, or the proposition that the slavery question could be settled in the voting booth, who became the candidate for the Northern wing of the party. A new party, the Constitutional Unionists, who wanted to maintain the status quo, emerged on the scene and agreed upon John Bell, a U.S. senator from Tennessee, as their candidate. It was Abraham Lincoln and the Republicans, a free-soil party created in the wake of the notorious Kansas-Nebraska law of 1854, who carried the day. They were dedicated to the proposition that slavery should be barred from the western territories, though Lincoln announced grandly that the institution should not be molested where it then existed, which did nothing to soothe the Southern psyche. Southerners realized from the start that defeat of their pro-slavery candidate was a possibility, but when the electioneering was complete, with Lincoln not receiving a single vote in seven "cotton states," diehard slavery men proclaimed they could not remain in the Union with that "black Republican" in the White House.[1]

Seven weeks after the election, and before Ewell left Albuquerque, South Carolina led the way by withdrawing from the Union. No wonder that he was on "tenterhooks" as one Southern state after the other followed the lead: Mississippi, January 9; Florida, January 10; Alabama, January 11; Georgia, January 19; Louisiana, January 26; and Texas, February 1. Texas was the last to leave in the initial wave of anti-Unionist euphoria; and the state's delegates to Montgomery, Alabama, where other secessionist delegations had gathered, were making their way east when a provisional Confederate government was established on February 8 with Jefferson Davis as president and Alexander H. Stephens as vice president. Governor Sam Houston—that quintessential Texan—recent German immigrants, and other pro-Unionist factions had fought long and hard to keep the Lone Star loyal to the Union before secessionists won the day on a close tally in their breakaway convention at Austin. Even Robert E. Lee had encountered difficulties in leaving the state a few weeks before Ewell when summoned to Washington by General in Chief of the Army Winfield Scott. Virginia, after all, was still in the Union, and officers like Lee and Ewell were guarded in their demeanor until the Old Dominion resolved upon a course of action. "En route [to Virginia] from New Mexico in 1861, I volunteered to fight the Texans, threatening a United States post, and was careful to do nothing against the United States before resigning," Ewell recalled after the war. Circumspect though they were, Lee and Ewell were not the only Southern-born officers to experience hostility from Texas hotheads who demanded their loyalty before they had resigned from the Federal army. James Longstreet even requested an official escort for his wife and himself on his way to San Antonio from a duty station in northern New Mexico. Ewell and his fellow officers encountered a whirlwind as they passed through Texas on their way to Indianola—located on the Gulf Coast—to book passage on steamers bound for New Orleans and home.[2]

Two months after the surrender at Appomattox, while he was imprisoned at Fort Warren in Massachusetts, Ewell set down the reasons for his resigning from the United States Army and why he chose to cast his lot with the Confederacy. Upon learning of Ewell's confinement, a onetime dragoon living in St. Paul, Minnesota, wrote "to tell you if there is anything I can do to add to your comfort or ease your situation, I would be proud to do it." The man, who identified himself as "a high private in the rear," had served under Ewell when he had first appeared in the west fresh out of West Point. Whether he remembered his correspondent or not, Ewell seized the opportunity to respond in depth; and the former cavalryman was so captivated with the response that he offered it to the *St. Paul Pioneer.* The piece was picked up by the *New Orleans Times* as well as other newspapers.

After reading press accounts that several Northern politicians had urged armed resistance to Southern secession, Ewell told the "high private" that he decided to act in the spring of 1861: "I found myself forced to fight against my brothers and all my nearest and dearest relatives—against my own state, when many abler men than myself contended that she was right." And, he continued: "It is hard to account for my course, except for a painful sense of duty—I say painful because few were more devoted to the old country than myself; and the greatest objection I had to it was my predilection for a strong one." Ewell may not have been totally pleased with his actions and seemingly harbored some resentment toward Jefferson Davis, although there is surely no evidence that the Confederate president was prejudiced against him during the war years. "By taking the side of the South I forfeited position, fine pay, and the earnings of twenty years hard service. All the pay I drew in four years in the South was not as one year's pay in the old army. The greatest political favoritism against me was from Mr. Jefferson Davis after the Mexican War." Nowhere in his letter of June 13, 1865, does Ewell say that he was proud of his service in the Army of Northern Virginia. Still suffering the ill effects of his leg amputation during the Second Manassas three years earlier and chagrined over his continued confinement as well as his dismissal from corps command by Lee during the last year of the war, Ewell may well have felt ill-used. And, as we shall see, he was particularly upset about the arrest of his wife on questionable charges during Reconstruction.[3]

After Ewell reached home in the early months of 1861, he was still sick with the fever contracted in New Mexico, and, by his own words: "Staid in the country in Virginia, my state, trying to get well, and found that the war to my bitter regret, was being started." Not only Ewell but other professional soldiers who were Virginia-rooted watched with anticipation to see what course the Old Dominion would take once the new government had been formed. Like the rest, Ewell was dedicated to his home state, which failed to rush headlong into the new experiment in self-government. From the standpoint of time, many were waiting to see which way "the cat would jump" before resigning their commissions.

Governor "Honest John" Letcher, who opposed secession, had first resisted a November 7 demand by several legislators that he call the legislature into session to debate Lincoln's victory; but the regular convocation of the legislature in January 1861 resulted in a formal call for action. The general assembly promptly dispatched an embassy to President Buchanan asking for moderation in the worsening crisis, and a call was sent out for a state secession convention to assemble in Richmond. The Virginians even sponsored the famed Washington Peace Conference, chaired by former president John Tyler, in a failed attempt to find a common ground between North and South. Meanwhile, the gathering at Richmond debated the pros and cons of secession as Ewell and his fellow Virginians looked on. As late as April 4 the convention voted forty-five to eighty-five to remain under the old flag. Unionist sentiment was powerful in every part of the state, particularly in the western mountainous regions, despite the violent rhetoric of former Governor Henry A. Wise and the secessionist faction. But the events at Fort Sumter in South Carolina when aged Edmund Ruffin was permitted to fire the first shot at Captain Robert Anderson's helpless garrison had an instant impact upon the Richmond conventioneers. The Civil War had not only commenced, but Abraham Lincoln also sent out a call for seventy-five thousand men to put down the rebellion, and Virginia—still in the Union—was expected to supply her quota. Letcher immediately denied the presidential request, saying that Virginia would not act to suppress a sister slave state. In a fit of indignation the Richmond convention rammed through an ordinance of secession by a vote of eighty-five to fifty-five.[4]

The secession of Virginia was not complete until results of a state-wide referendum on May 23 were known, yet with the support of the convention and a newly formed committee on public safety, Governor Letcher moved quickly to secure her borders beforehand. Everyone knew from the outset that the state's location and internal geography would make it difficult, if not impossible, to defend over the long haul. Even before Robert E. Lee was placed in command of Virginia's military forces on April 23, Letcher sent officers to strategic positions, although many of the first appointees were shortly replaced with more aggressive soldiers. While Ewell waited, ostensibly to recoup his health, Virginia Military Institute (VMI) professor Thomas J. Jackson was sent into the Shenandoah to organize the defenses at Harpers Ferry and to replace Major General Kenton Harper; Philip St. George Cooke was hurried off to the Potomac line opposite Washington; General Daniel Ruggles was placed at Fredericksburg, while William B. Taliaferro took charge at Norfolk to oversee fortifications along the lower Chesapeake; and lastly, Ewell's visitor at Fort Buchanan less than a year before, Andrew Talcott, was dispatched to the Virginia peninsula between the York and James Rivers to begin fortifications that would pro-tect Richmond from the sea.[5]

When Ewell's resignation from the Federal army was accepted on May 7, his brother Ben was already in charge of an infantry regiment at Williamsburg. Events were unfolding with mind-boggling quickness as he accepted a lieutenant colonelcy in the provisional army of Virginia. Militia companies, former army officers, and men from every station nearly over-whelmed induction centers and hastily organized camps throughout cis-montane Virginia. "Our people did not stop half way and try to maintain a neutral position, but Virginia with a unanimity almost entire, east of the Allegheny mountains, took her stand in front of her Southern sisters to resist the invader," notes William T. Poague. He goes on to describe his own artillery outfit: "We had the very best material . . . Men who could take care of the horses and educated high spirited men for the guns. Farm-ers, mechanics, laborers, lawyers, university students and theological stu-dents made up the bulk of the company."[6]

Poague's experience was not unusual, as Virginia boys by the thousands rushed to the standard. War fever was in the air, and hardly an able-bodied man, it seemed, wanted to be left behind. As Major General Lee oversaw the organization and provisioning of the mass influx of men, almost without exception the West Point–trained officers flocking to the Confederate cause were initially pressed into service for the training and disciplining of individual units. Lieutenant Colonel Ewell, who was no exception, was ordered to Ashland, a few miles north of Richmond in Hanover County, to take charge of a training facility for cavalrymen. With help from several VMI cadets, he was able to employ his long experience with the frontier dragoons. Ewell had been at Ashland less than a month when on May 25 orders were cut in Richmond for him to join Brigadier General Milledge L. Bonham, in command of the "Alexandria Line," at Fairfax Court House. Captain William P. Snow, a participant in the Confederate effort from the beginning, was moved to write that "his services were invaluable at Ashland." Ewell did not hesitate to use strong language as he whipped the young cavalrymen into fighting shape, and, continues Snow: "His discipline was stern and rigid, but humane, and, out of raw mounted militia, he soon formed a most efficient body of troops."[7]

While Ewell went about his training duties in Hanover County, the infant government at Montgomery voted to relocate its capital at Richmond, which, after all, was the jewel of the Southland; from that moment until the final collapse of the Southern war effort, "On to Richmond" became the overpowering obsession of Abraham Lincoln and his advisers. Almost instantly a huge Federal army began to collect across the Potomac from Washington headed by Brigadier General Irvin McDowell, an 1838 graduate of West Point and veteran of the Mexican War. From its headquarters around Alexandria and Centreville, the Yankee behemoth readied for a plunge southwestward along the Warrenton Pike, through Fairfax Court House, across a sluggish stream called Bull Run, toward a rail junction at Manassas where two Virginia railroads converged: the Manassas Gap, running almost due west into the Shenandoah Valley, and the Orange and Alexandria, leading through Culpeper and Gordonsville to the prize at Richmond. The Federal capture of Manassas Junction was deemed crucial to Lincoln's invasion strategy. Like Lee and the Southern war engine at Richmond, who were busy with war preparation and equipage, McDowell was forced to wait until June 16 before opening his grand offensive as anxious politicians streamed in and out of his headquarters. Vice President Hamlin joined the parade to the front "to see how a rebel picket looked at close range."[8]

Meanwhile, Robert E. Lee, who served as military adviser to President Davis, rushed to the front during mid-May for a personal inspection that set the stage for the Battle of First Manassas and indeed for all subsequent fighting in northern Virginia; thus Lee, and not P. G. T. Beauregard nor Joseph Eggleston Johnston, orchestrated the first major victory of the war. "I made the following arrangements for the light troops," he telegraphed on May 30 to Johnston, who had replaced Jackson at Harpers Ferry:

> A corps of observation, of cavalry and infantry, has been established under Colonel Ewell, in advance of Fairfax Court House, the right extending towards Occoquan, the left to the Leesburg road. Col. Eppa Hunton, commanding at Leesburg, has been ordered to have an advance post at Dranesville, and to extend his scouts down the Alexandria and Leesburg roads, to communicate with Colonel Ewell. He is to inform you of any movement of the U.S. troops, in the direction of Leesburg, tending to threaten your rear, through Captain Ashby, at Point of Rocks. In the event of such a movement, should you deem it advisable, and should you be unable to hold your position, I would suggest a joint attack by you and General Bonham, commanding at Manassas, for the purpose of cutting them off.

The masterstroke to unite Johnston and the Valley Army with the troops at Manassas was born in the fertile mind of Lee during those first crucial weeks of war preparation. And it is clear that Ewell, who had joined Bonham in the Manassas sector, was intended to be a major player in the effort to keep McDowell at bay.[9]

"Not long before his appointment as Lt. Colonel of State Troops, Ewell was sent to command at Fairfax C. H. Here he found Capt. (Now Col.) J. S. Shackleford, Green's Cav. Comp. F. from Rappahannock & Capt. Wm. Thornton's 'Prince William Cavalry.' The former were armed with double-barreled shotguns[,] many of both had nothing at all," reads a delightful memoir, "From Fairfax C. H. to Richmond," among the Polk, Brown, Ewell Papers in the Southern Historical Collection at the University of North Carolina. For the scholar conversant with Ewell letters and manuscripts, it is clear that the unsigned, undated piece was penned by George Campbell Brown, with detailed corrections by Ewell himself. Campbell Brown, born in 1840, was the eldest child of Elizabeth McKay Brown (or Lizinka), Ewell's childhood playmate and future wife; since

Lizinka Brown and Ewell were first cousins, Campbell Brown was also his kinsman. He was likewise Ewell's stepson after 1863. The memoirs as well as his massive handwritten "Reminiscences," which surprisingly were not issued in printed form until 2002, contain a trove of personal and military information about not only Ewell and Brown but also the people around them in the Army of Northern Virginia, 1861–1865.

Brown had been in Europe with his mother and sister Harriet Stoddert Brown, four years younger than himself, as the secession crisis raced to a climax. Fearing for their safety as well as their extensive financial holdings, the family sailed from Liverpool and reached New York before the assault on Fort Sumter. Following a tour of Washington, the twenty-two-year-old Tennessean stopped in Richmond, where he attended several meetings of the secession convention. He was impressed, he wrote later, "with stormy debates of old H. A. Wise." Although the documented evidence is not clear, Brown and his mother also called on Ewell and other family members while in the Old Dominion. After a speedy trip to Nashville and a survey of the Brown properties with his mother, he returned to Virginia, where he joined Ewell at Union Mills (on Bull Run) as aide-de-camp with the rank of captain. Brown remained at Ewell's side through much of the war, not only writing his dispatches but also collecting material for his own postwar writings. Until Brown's death in 1893, he was an unstinting defender of Ewell's war record and legacy.[10]

Once he arrived at the front, Ewell "hardly took off his clothes" until he was summoned to hold the keep at Fairfax Court House barely fifteen miles from the crossings into Washington itself. Nestled between the Potomac and Ewell's own Prince William County—he was, after all, within shouting distance of Stony Lonesome—Fairfax County was awash with anxiety in the spring and summer of 1861. "Almost every night we were snatched from our blankets and thrown into our saddles by false alarms," wrote a lieutenant in the Prince William cavalry. "We are almost in the enemy's country and are keeping a sharp lookout for them, and don't intend to be trapped if such a thing can be avoided." Twenty-four hours later, on the night of May 31, the real thing occurred when Lieutenant Charles H. Tompkins, commanding fifty men from Company B, Second United States Cavalry, left Arlington to scout down the Warrenton roadway.[11] Between two and three o'clock in the morning Tompkins's outriders made contact with Ewell's advance pickets east of the Court House Square, where a good many of his troops were tented, including the newly arrived Warrenton Rifles under Captain John Q. Marr.[12]

When the advanced guard galloped into Fairfax yelling "The Yankees are coming," a half-aroused Ewell rushed to the sound of gunfire. Captain Marr was killed at the first rush of Tompkins's men, which left no one in charge until Ewell reached the town square. The Warrenton Road forks at Fairfax—one branch leading southward through Centreville, while the other strikes almost due west toward Germantown. The bluecoats rode straight through the town on the Germantown branch, firing at the confused and hapless defenders, but soon regrouped for a renewed charge.[13]

When Tompkins filed his report of the assault, he claimed being "fired upon by the rebel troops from windows and house tops." Even so, Ewell was ready for the second foray. "He [had] hurried out but on reaching the street partially clad found a Federal soldier standing between him and his men," reads Brown's account. "Slipping past him he reached the Court House and found everything in confusion. . . . As they came back down the road, he ordered his men to fire," although some refused, announcing that the approaching horsemen were their own compeers, who had fled down the Centreville Pike before the attackers. When things sorted out and when Tompkins did appear, his troops were driven back by the Confederates now under Ewell's direction. Actually the Yankees made two attempts to reenter the town but were thwarted on both occasions.

"Having reformed, the enemy again advanced, and more firing took place on both sides," reads Ewell's own retelling. "They again retreated and made their way through the fields by pulling down the fences." A cavalry troop under Captain George F. Harrison went after them, but Tompkins made good his escape, although he reported "nine horses lost and four wounded." Ewell's official report said the Federals "left no dead on the ground, but carbines, pistols, sabers, were lying around"; three prisoners and four horses were taken by the Southerners. Although the fight was nothing more than a skirmish—and an insignificant one at that when compared to later engagements—when Irvin McDowell sent his own report to Washington, he noted: "Tompkins . . . reached Fairfax Court House about 3 A.M. where he found several hundred men were stationed—Captain Ewell, late of the U.S. Dragoons, said to be in command."[14]

The Yankee high command now knew that Ewell was an enemy to be reckoned with, and despite the successful repulse at Fairfax, he managed to get himself shot during the affray. Captain Snow relates that Ewell ran into the street wearing a white undergarment that made him an easy mark, even though Ewell himself admitted to a mere "flesh wound." Brown as usual finds merit in this, as he does with everything concerning his kinsman and superior officer: "The Fairfax Court House fight was the first of the war where blood was shed on our side & Col. Ewell was the first man wounded." Despite the fight at Philippi in western Virginia on June 3 as well as John Bankhead Magruder's triumph at Big Bethel a week later, Brown insisted on making this minor engagement into the first battle of the war. "In that little affair at the C House, 45 Rifles on foot and poorly armed wakened out of their sleep with no leader, he having been shot when the action commenced. . . . Col. Ewell rushing out without his coat & then not even knowing who [the enemy] was until told by a gentleman present," Mrs. Robert E. Lee noted. She thought he would have escaped unharmed, "according to eye witnesses," had he been wearing his coat. Perhaps the worst effect was the injury itself on the heels of Ewell's several wounds in New Mexico and Arizona. The lacerations, admittedly of little importance in themselves, coupled with a general weakness from his recent bout of fever unquestionably had a cumulative effect upon his health and state of mind. Even before the traumatic impact of his leg amputation more than a year later, Ewell had undergone enough bodily discomfort to interfere with his ability to rest.[15]

The "gentleman" mentioned by Mary Lee was a former governor of Virginia, William Smith. Known as "Extra Billy," Smith, who gained his enduring sobriquet through an uncanny ability to wrangle "extra" money from the government while transporting the U.S. mail over his privately owned stage line, was visiting in Fairfax when the early morning raid took place. Sixty-four years old in 1861, the onetime congressman, who would become governor again in 1864, was awakened like everyone else; he immediately grabbed a rifle and took his place on the firing line. During the melee, Brown says, Smith noted the blood from Ewell's wound and cried out: "Col., I am sorry to hear that you are wounded——hope you aren't hurt much." Ewell, testy and profane as ever, replied: "I should like to know if it is any of your d——d business." The rough language of the frontier had followed him into the Confederate army.

Samuel Wragg Ferguson, himself a Confederate brigadier general, tells a slightly different version of the story—that a "trooper" asked after the wound, to which Ewell answered, "none of your damned business." An 1857 graduate of West Point, Ferguson was a South Carolinian who fought through the entire war, eventually becoming an escort to President Davis on his southern escape attempt after the Confederate collapse of 1865. "I have often pictured to myself the old soldier, mad as a hornet at being taken by surprise and his command thrown into confusion and smarting too with a wound, having a raw recruit interrupting him with his sympathy," a charitable Ferguson added.[16]

Although P. G. T. Beauregard, who replaced Milledge L. Bonham on June 3 in command of the Manassas sector, would later order Ewell and other advance units to fall back toward the protective barrier of Bull Run as the Yankee onslaught developed, Colonel Maxey Gregg sent word from Vienna that he was rushing reinforcements to Fairfax immediately after the skirmish. Although Gregg implored him "to take care that no mistake is made & the [fresh] troops not be fired on as an enemy," Ewell received word four days before the big fight at First Manassas that the Confederate congress had approved his promotion to brigadier general. He had been in the Federal army from 1836 until 1861 and had advanced from West Point plebe to captain; now he had been in the Confederate service for three months and had risen from lieutenant colonel to general. The surprise at Fairfax had obviously not damaged his standing with the Confederate chieftains, and he had the good fortune to be in the right place at the right time. Nor was Ewell singled out for promotion. At least ten other officers were elevated to general rank by the same congressional mandate, including John Bankhead Magruder, William J. Hardee, D. R. Jones, Benjamin Huger, Bernard E. Bee, James Longstreet, E. Kirby Smith, John Clifford Pemberton, Henry H. Sibley, and Thomas J. Jackson—all of them West Point graduates. "I wonder if you were as astonished as I was at my promotion," a humbled Ewell wrote to General Bonham on June 21. His physical condition remained a concern, as he added: "I assure you it is a matter that gives me no rejoicing as the responsibility is painful—particularly in my present state of health."[17]

One day after his promotion, a telegram addressed to "Genl. R. S. Ewell" from P. G. T. Beauregard ordered him to assume a new position behind the Union Mills Ford over Bull Run. The Louisiana-born Beauregard, forty-three years old in 1861, had graduated from West Point in the class of 1838. After a respectable duty in Mexico, where he served on the staff of Winfield Scott and as the engineer "in charge of draining New Orleans," he had been superintendent at West Point when the secession storm broke. An early devotee to the Confederate cause, Beauregard was already known as "the hero of Fort Sumter" for his role in its capture before he arrived at Manassas on June 3. Even though Lee had formulated a defensive plan for the "Alexandria Line," Beauregard, like all fired-up commanders, lost no time in developing his own scheme. "Old Borey" wanted Joseph E. Johnston to march immediately from the Shenandoah with a combined force to charge the Federals gathering in northern Virginia. He hoped to cross the Potomac and envelop Washington itself once McDowell was on the run. When Beauregard enlisted the aid of James Chesnut, a former U.S. senator from South Carolina and a Confederate congressman, to carry the plan to Richmond, President Davis, with Lee at his side, said, "No!"[18]

Davis considered the idea impractical for reasons of supply and logistics. Still, Bonham, among others, thought Beauregard's scheme had merit: "I have always believed that had your plan been adopted we would have taken Maryland forcing the enemy out of Washington & have ended the war then and there," he wrote afterward. In the summer of 1861, however, Beauregard had no choice but to conform to the president's wishes. In early July he called his brigadiers together and laid down a revised scheme to meet the sure-to-come onslaught. The army would stand on the defensive behind a creek known as Bull Run and not initiate a thrust toward the Potomac. Although Ewell became a vital part of the new troop alignment, he had not yet received his brigadier's star and thus probably did not attend the meeting. Writing from Bull Run on July 21, the very day of the battle, Ewell told his friend Bonham: "I don't know how things stand here but I hope if I am left at this place that you will continue to have the direction. I don't think I need tell you how much pleasure it will give me to carry out your views."

Although he was clearly a member of the Beauregard team at this point, Ewell fell back through Centreville with the rest of the army to the south bank of Bull Run, a tributary of the Occoquan before it flows into the Potomac estuary. Beauregard ordered a new concentration of his force at several fords to the right of the soon-to-be-famous Stone Bridge that carried the Warrenton Pike across the stream. When complete, the new Confederate line ran approximately eight miles from northwest to southeast, with Nathan G. Evans, otherwise known as "Shanks" from the construction of his legs, west and at the bridge itself; Philip St. George Cooke at Lewis, Ball's, and Island Fords; Milledge L. Bonham at Mitchell's Ford; James Longstreet at Blackburn's Ford; D. R. Jones on Ewell's immediate left at McLean's Ford; and, finally, Ewell at Union Mills Ford, where the Orange and Alexandria Railroad crossed Bull Run on its way northward toward Washington. With Jubal Anderson Early in support, Ewell thus held the extreme right flank extending from the railroad to the Occoquan; and before the opening shots, Theophilus H. Holmes was ordered north from Fredericksburg and Aquia Landing to bolster his position.[19]

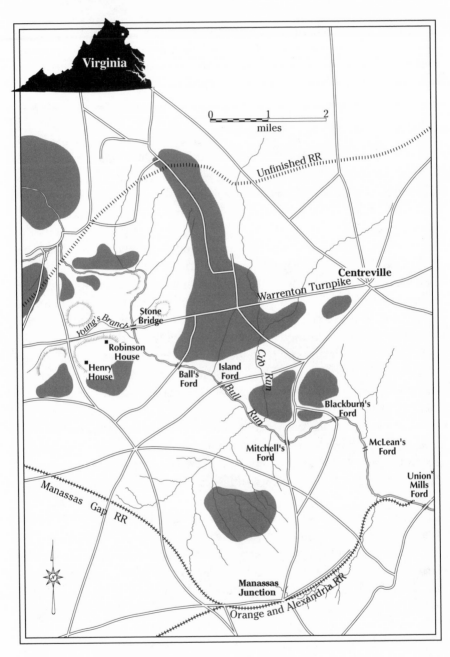

The Manassas Battlefield, July 1861

"At 2 p.m., July 16, the march began," as McDowell started his columns toward Manassas to open the campaign. When reliable information from Beauregard's spy in Washington, the venerable Mrs. Rose O'Neale Greenhow, reached Bonham at Fairfax, Beauregard not only knew the Yankees were coming but also issued orders for the retreat. McDowell's march proceeded smoothly enough on the first day as fresh, eager troopers tramped across the north Virginia plain with enthusiasm, although green units under Oliver Otis Howard reported several men wounded from the careless handling of their own firearms. The retreating Confederates set fire to Fairfax as they sped southward; and three Federal columns under Daniel Tyler, David Hunter, and Ambrose E. Burnside that converged on the town finished its near destruction. Out on his far left McDowell directed a column under Samuel P. Heintzelman to travel east of the Orange and Alexandria Railroad through Fairfax and Sangster's stations. Heintzelman was told to cross Bull Run at the Union Mills Ford, proceed southward, and then storm Beauregard's line from the rear, thereby cutting his communications to the south. This Yankee scheme failed, but eager bluecoats boasted they would hang Jeff Davis from a sour apple tree as they set out on what they thought to be an easy romp into Richmond.[20]

Ewell reached his assigned spot on July 17 with instructions "to stand fast at Union Mills Ford and to communicate closely with Jones and Early on his flanks." Three regiments, the Fifth and Sixth Alabama as well as the Sixth Louisiana, made up Ewell's Second Brigade on the trek from Fairfax Court House. A battery from New Orleans' Washington Artillery and four infantry companies were also added to Ewell's command prior to the main battle. As he traveled down the roads parallel to the Warrenton Pike from Centreville to Union Mills, one of his infantry regiments became the first to engage the enemy. The Fifth Alabama, led by Robert Emmett Rodes, which remained behind with several extended pickets to watch for advancing Yankees, got into a nasty little affray along the "Old Braddock's Road" with McDowell's lead units.

"The skirmish took place four hundred yards in advance of our breastworks, which [were] three-quarters of a mile east of our encampment, and which were by this time occupied by the main body of my command," Rodes said later. "Our skirmishers, being completely outflanked, retired in good order to their station in the barricades . . . [although the enemy did not follow], they had outflanked my position to the right during the skirmish for they could be seen crossing the clearing along the edge of which we were posted in large numbers." Rodes had received no orders to fall back when Bonham intervened and commanded him to rejoin Ewell as soon as possible, which he accomplished via McLean's Ford later in the evening. According to Rodes, his casualties "were two men slightly wounded—one in the leg, the other in the ear; on the side of the enemy, one prisoner and at least twenty wounded and killed." When Ewell filed a summary of his movements at Bull Run, he gave Rodes credit for "checking the enemy owing to the non-reception of orders to fall back upon their appearance."[21]

Beauregard complimented "Generals Bonham, Ewell, and Colonel Cooke, and the officers under them for the ability shown in conducting and executing the retrograde movements on Bull Run—movements on which hung the fortunes of the Army." Once he reached Union Mills on the seventeenth, Ewell stayed in place throughout the evening, although he did send a troop of cavalry north of the stream to check on Heintzelman's wagon trains before dark. The next day, however, the campaign heated up when McDowell ordered Tyler to probe the lower fords. Colonel I. B. Richardson, with four infantry regiments, immediately made contact with Longstreet's brigade, and the struggle for Blackburn's Ford was on. Not only did Longstreet hand the Yankees "a sharp repulse" in close combat reaching right down to the water's edge, but he also won wide commendation for his victory over Richardson on the eighteenth. After an artillery barrage, which Private James Franklin of the Eleventh Virginia Infantry pronounced the loudest he experienced during the war, the Federal commander launched three separate assaults on the ford, but Longstreet, reinforced by Jubal A. Early's troops after the initial foray, was able to carry the day.

Although Ewell was close by at the Union Mills crossing, he took no active part in the engagement. Lieutenant Thomas Rosser brought "four 12-pound howitzers" from the Washington Artillery, which Ewell placed on a rise overlooking the enemy's positions beyond the stream. When Rosser, with Ewell at his side, looked out and observed Heintzelman's men deployed near the railroad, the cavalryman wanted to open fire. But Ewell would not allow it, saying they would await further orders. His legalistic posture instead of an aggressive stance with Rosser's cannon meant they were "constantly in position during the day, in momentary expectation of an attack on that point (Union Mills) from the enemy, who had been seen the evening before and during the day reconnoitering our position, small squads frequently emerging from the woods on the other side of the ford near the railroad," wrote Major J. B. Walton, commanding officer of the

Washington Artillery. "This battery, however, had no opportunity of firing a gun, thus disappointing as brave and efficient a command as any command on that memorable day." It would not be the last time Ewell found an excuse to avoid a fight. After the Blackburn's Ford rebuff, McDowell decided to shift his main attack away from the lower crossings and to concentrate on Beauregard's left near the Stone Bridge. When he sent his engineers to search for an alternative route that would bypass Evans and Cooke along the Warrenton Pike, the center of action shifted away from Ewell and the Union Mills garrison.[22]

When McDowell discovered the landscape itself was ill-suited for his preconceived plans, he not only sought a new attack route, but he also spent the nineteenth and twentieth in reconnoitering operations, which, according to Edward Porter Alexander, "gave time for a good part of Johnston's force to arrive." President Davis, who had rushed to the front by special train, sanctioned the call for Joseph E. Johnston to bring the Valley Army over the Blue Ridge at the first notice of the Federal advance. When Johnston received the command at one o'clock on the morning of July 18, one of those remarkable episodes in American military annals was set in motion. The Confederates gave the slip to aged Robert Patterson, a veteran of the War of 1812 whom Lincoln and the Northern war machine had expected to keep Johnston from Manassas. While Longstreet fought for control of Beauregard's left flank, with Thomas J. Jackson in the van, the valley brigades began pouring through Ashby's Gap from Winchester heading for Piedmont Station on the Manassas Gap Railroad. "It was feared that many men from the valley would not cross the Blue Ridge, leaving their homes unprotected, and to obviate this difficulty we were told for the first and last time where we were going," observed Captain Samuel D. Buck; it was the only time that the secretive Jackson ever confided in his men while on the March. Once aboard "the cars," Jackson's lead units of Johnston's twelve thousand fresh troops began filtering onto the field at Manassas by July 19, although some later arrivals under E. Kirby Smith did not get there until the twenty-first, after the great battle had begun.[23]

After the Yankee commander had fixed upon a revised attack plan, he ordered a force under Tyler and David Hunter to move northwestward from the Warrenton Pike and strike Beauregard's left flank west of the famed Stone Bridge. Though "Shanks" Evans turned to meet the onslaught on July 21, Beauregard "was inadequately prepared for it," and disaster threatened until Jackson and the other brigadiers arrived to tip the balance. "Their orders were of the vaguest, but they plainly saw an overmastering Federal force pressing the Confederates very hard in their immediate presence," writes G. C. Eggleston. "So, following the Napoleonic instruction to go to the point of heaviest firing the officers commanding the arriving Confederates went at once to the thick of the fight." The valley troops had experienced irritating delays when overworked, poorly constructed railroad equipment failed. But the tracks from the Blue Ridge to Manassas had delivered them a mile or so east and south of the field around the Stone Bridge. While Ewell was stationary four miles away, the combined brigades of Jackson, Bernard E. Bee, Francis S. Bartow, and Evans formed a new line extending from the famed Henry House to the commands of Arnold Elzey and Jubal A. Early. The cavalryman Jeb Stuart held Beauregard's extreme left.

Along with his "obstinate Virginians," Jackson was a particularly prominent player in the struggle to hold the Confederate left and simply would not give ground. When Bernard Bee, one of his fellow brigadiers, looked over and saw Jackson's fighting prowess, he yelled out the immortal words, "There is Jackson standing like a stone wall," words that became embedded in the national lexicon. Untold thousands of words have been expended on the incident, and whether Bee, who died the following day from battle wounds on the twenty-first, was referring to Jackson the man or to the "Stonewall Brigade." "His name of Stonewall indicated only his tenacity & determination but gives no idea of the motives & dash & courage of the man," wrote Major General William H. C. Whiting, who served as Jackson's adjutant early in the war. Jackson's "intense faith" in the Southern cause as well as his subsequent career, Whiting added, "is part & a glorious part of our country's history." In less than a year, Ewell would establish his own place in the Confederate saga at the side of "Mighty Stonewall" as the two soldiers fought throughout the Valley, Seven Days, and Second Manassas campaigns.[24]

Ewell's movements during the twenty-first are open to various interpretations. When he finally marched his command to the main battle, neither he nor his men saw actual combat, although Beauregard reported that he came under heavy artillery fire as he pulled back from an earlier advance across Bull Run. Beauregard's finely reasoned report of August 26 refrains from labeling Ewell a malingerer, but it is nonetheless critical. In at least four instances he refers to "a miscarriage of my orders" before coming out with it: "In connection with the unfortunate casualty of the day, that is the miscarriage of my orders sent by courier to Generals Holmes and Ewell to attack the enemy in flank and reverse at Centreville, through which the triumph of our arms was prevented from being more decisive . . ." Clearly Beauregard regarded Ewell's hesitancy on the morning of July 21 as cause for the Confederate inability to crush McDowell totally.

In 1884, when Ewell had been dead for twelve years, Beauregard published a surprisingly ordered account of the battle in the widely circulated *Century Magazine*. The difficulty arose from a misunderstanding purveyed by Beauregard before the main fighting. On the night of July 20, he had called his subordinates together and laid out his plan for the next day. Ironically, just as McDowell hoped Heintzelman would cross Bull Run from the north and assault Beauregard's rear at the Stone Bridge, Beauregard developed a similar plan for Ewell to cross at Union Mills and accost the Federal rear after it had passed through Centreville via the Warrenton Pike on its march toward the bridge. In other words, the Confederates schemed to sever McDowell's communications with Washington at the same time Heintzelman sought to cut Beauregard's with Richmond. "Centreville was the apex of a triangle—its short side running by the Warrenton turnpike to Stone Bridge, its base Bull Run, its long side a road that ran from Union Mills along the front of my other Bull Run positions and trended off to the rear of Centreville where McDowell had massed his main forces," Beauregard wrote. "Branch roads led up to this one from fords between Union Mills and Mitchell's. My forces to the right of the latter ford were to advance, pivoting on that position. Bonham was to advance from Mitchell's ford, Longstreet from Blackburn's, D. R. Jones from McLean's, and Ewell from Union Mills by the Centreville road. Ewell having the longest march, was to begin the movement, and each brigade was to be followed by its reserve." At Beauregard's evening confab, which Ewell presumably attended (see D. R. Jones's report in the *Official Records*), the subordinate commanders—Longstreet, Jones, Bonham, and Ewell— were instructed to establish close communication with each other before making the attack. All but Ewell appeared to understand Beauregard's instructions.[25]

On the morning of July 21 Beauregard joined Joe Johnston at a "convenient position—a hill in the rear of Mitchell's Ford" to oversee the battle. Although in nominal command, Johnston entrusted direction of the engagement to Beauregard because of the latter's familiarity with what had been accomplished thus far. Beauregard, he said, waited in vain for Ewell to commence the attack, and D. R. Jones relates that he told Ewell that he was starting as ordered. When Ewell did not respond, Jones informed Longstreet he was moving across Bull Run—that he was starting the pivot.

Ewell and Campbell Brown maintained throughout that no order ever arrived from headquarters for the Second Brigade to attack. Beauregard was patently perturbed by Ewell's failure to move as anticipated: "The commander of the front line on my right [Ewell], who failed to move because he received no immediate order, was instructed in the plan of attack, and should have gone forward the moment General Jones, upon whose right he was to form, exhibited his own order, which mentioned one as having been already sent to that commander," Beauregard wrote in his 1884 memoir. "I exonerated him after the battle, as he was technically not in the wrong; but one could not help recalling Desaix, who even moved in a direction opposite his technical orders when facts plainly showed him the service he ought to perform, whence the glorious result of Marengo—or help believing had Jackson been [there], the movement would not have balked." For the armchair historian writing more than 130 years after the fact, it is difficult to fathom Ewell's blindness to both McDowell's intentions and his own obligation to advance. With or without specific orders, battle circumstances dictated that he should have joined the fray. His official exoneration notwithstanding, Ewell's failure to act at the vital juncture at the First Manassas no doubt presaged the disaster of July 1, 1863, when he failed to implement Lee's "suggestion" that he capture Cemetery Hill on the first day at Gettysburg "if practicable."[26]

Ewell had his apologists from the beginning in spite of rampant talk in Richmond that he was in trouble. One week after the battle, the diarist Mary Boykin Chesnut wrote that Eugenius Aristides Nisbet, a Georgia congressman, had asked her "if it be true that Ewell was to be court martialed [because] he did not obey orders." But "it seems he did not receive them," she entered in her journal for July 28. When Ewell wrote to Lizzie on July 31, he was distressed at not having been under fire but confirmed Beauregard's order: "I was directed to do so, at the critical moment to take the road to Centreville to attack the enemy in flank, and the various other brigades, between this and the point of attack of the enemy, were also to cross the run and do likewise." While he said nothing about a court-martial, he admitted that D. R. Jones had communicated with him before he moved out alone. He told his niece that he had advanced across Bull Run though he was recalled to his position south of Union Mills Ford. "The reason I had not received the order was that it had not been sent, but the time lost was so short that it made no difference."[27]

Campbell Brown, who was present at headquarters, later stated that Ewell waited for the attack order in vain and finally sent a runner to

Beauregard asking what was awry. "I have inserted the correspondence bearing on this affair, so misunderstood at the time & by at least one person wantonly misrepresented—viz. the correspondent of the Columbus (Ga.) Sun—who insinuated a charge of treason against Genl. Ewell—but apologized & retracted when called on to give authority of his statements," Brown included in his postwar memoir. "Genl. Beauregard gave Genl. Ewell full permission to publish his (Genl. B's) letter in his own defense—but presently wrote to him, begging him to wait for [Beauregard's] official report, which would fully & satisfactorily explain the matter." However, when the report appeared over a month later, Brown's wrath, and by inference that of Ewell, knew no bounds. Beauregard's treatment of Ewell—who refrained from a public response, although he encouraged others to offer a defense—"was so vague and unsatisfactory that he was greatly disgusted seeing the probability that nine out of ten who read it would still impute blame to him when in fact it belonged to Beauregard." If his stepson, with whom he had constant contact, was derogatory, Ewell himself was circumspect toward his superior. His handwritten report as well as the *Official Records* version, both very brief, emphasized the absence of an attack order—that he had marched only after D. R. Jones showed him his directive to advance, and, Ewell added, "I deem it proper to state the courier said he had been accompanied by an aide-de-camp, whose horse gave out before reaching me."[28]

There matters rested until 1884 when Beauregard's rendition appeared in *Century Magazine*. "I have read General Beauregard's fooling article on the Battle of Manassas, and realize the fact that he has done himself more harm than any [one] else," Jubal A. Early commented upon its appearance. Besides his "Reminiscences," Brown published a lengthy retort in a later edition of the same journal, which cited a recently composed assessment of the affair by General Fitz Lee. Robert E. Lee's nephew, who served as Beauregard's adjutant at First Manassas, joined the hassle by verifying that Ewell had acted in concert with Jones as soon as possible upon learning about the latter's order.

And Brown cited Beauregard's later communication with Ewell: "I do not attach the slightest blame to you for the failure of the movement on Centreville, but to the guide who did not deliver the order to move forward sent at about eight A.M. to General [Theophilus H.] Holmes and then to you. . . . Unfortunately no copy, in the hurry of the moment, was kept of said order, and so many guides, a dozen or more, were sent off in different directions, that it is next to impossible to find out who was the bearer of the orders referred to." Despite Beauregard's change of heart, Captain George F. Harrison, a cavalryman under Ewell, upon publication of Brown's 1885 defense, wrote that Ewell was in a state of "intense anxiety while awaiting the order to march. I cannot conceive how General Beauregard could utter such a reflection—even entertain such a thought—as he put on record in the *Century Magazine* in regard to General Ewell damning him with faint praise of obedience to 'technical orders,' and plainly imputing to him blame for not moving *without* orders—more especially right in the teeth of his own letter of unqualified exoneration."[29]

When Ewell was sent to serve under Jackson during the Valley campaign, apparently that intrepid warrior did not hold the Manassas incident against him—and Jackson was a man who forgave very little. Stonewall too had been in the thick of the fighting at the Stone Bridge and the home of the tragic Mrs. Henry before a hard-pressed McDowell broke off the engagement. Joe Johnston had sped to the front upon hearing heavy gunfire east of his temporary headquarters with Beauregard at Mitchell's Ford. Sensing that reinforcements would become necessary, Johnston issued a new directive for Ewell to bring his brigade toward the Confederate left. "My feelings were terrible then, as such an order could only mean that we were defeated and I was to cover the retreat," Ewell told Lizzie on July 31. But the South was not beaten—far from it—as Federal troopers and visiting politicians alike, with their ladies who had come to see the rebel drubbing, broke in a mad scramble for the safety of Washington and the Potomac crossings. As a hotted-up Jackson pleaded with President Davis to give him five thousand men so that he could take Washington itself on the very evening of the battle, Ewell had arrived in time to witness the first great triumph of the war. "I countermarched and marched at once to headquarters in the field, remained in reserve at that point until ordered back to Union Mills, which I reached after a long and fatiguing march the same night," he included in his official report.[30]

"I never saw so many dead & wounded before. There are not one half of them buried yet & they have quit burying them," J. A. Gardner, a Tarheel Confederate, wrote from Union Mills six days after the battle. "There are hundreds of them not a half a mile from here & in places the road is almost blocked with dead men and horses." Amid the carnage, Ewell remained at Union Mills for several days before he was ordered forward a mile or so to Sangster's Crossroads on the way to Centreville, where he stayed until the fall back to the Rappahannock in late September. Two weeks after the Confederate victory, Ewell rode out from his new bivouac for a personal inspection of the field, accompanied by Brown and several officers. Besides one of Beauregard's aides, the party included "two or three Colonels, namely Col. [Harry T.] Hays of Louisiana, brother of Jack Hays, Col. [Richard] Griffith of Mississippi, who was adjutant of Jeff Davis's Regt. in Mexico & Col. [Robert E.] Rodes of Alabama, whom Gen. Ewell thinks very highly of, as an able man & efficient officer."[31] Although they found a desolate landscape, where grass trampled by contending armies refused to grow, "the wounded had been taken away and buried," Brown recounted in a letter to his aunt, Mrs. G. C. Hubbard, who had worked to have Ewell appointed army paymaster a few years earlier. "While the broken pieces of guns, &c. & the accouterments of the killed which strewed the field so thickly had been seized upon & carried away as relics, so that the only signs of a great battle having been fought upon the spot were the skeletons of horses which lay here and there around us. The trees and houses which we approached—shattered by cannon & rifle-balls, & the tainted breeze that swept over the field, reminded one of the atmosphere of a vault." Upon their return to Sangster's Crossing, Brown describes a peaceful, settled camp with Ewell "lying listlessly on his couch studying tactics," while his aides idly passed the time reading novels and writing letters.[32]

Ewell experienced several command changes in late 1861–early 1862 while he remained in northern Virginia. On November 2 he was summoned to turn over the Second Brigade to Rodes and report to General Gustavus W. Smith for reassignment. Four days later he was formally relieved of duty with the First Corps and assigned to Smith's Second Corps. Two days after that he was ordered to return to Beauregard for a new posting, where he remained until February 1862 when he assumed command of the Third Division, Army of the Potomac, replacing E. Kirby Smith, who was dispatched to take charge in the trans-Mississippi; and for a short time he was placed under James Longstreet.[33] These assignments were paper changes, however, that kept him in Sangster's Crossroads and Centreville, and on the Rappahannock until April 1862, when he was linked to Jackson's command. Except for sporadic contact between his cavalry outriders and those of the enemy, including a troop of Heintzelman's horsemen that found Ewell's brigade "in force between Long Branch and Accotink Run, above the Telegraph Road," things remained relatively quiet through the winter of 1861–1862.[34]

At Sangster's Crossroads and the camps around Centreville and Manassas before Ewell was ordered to a new position south of the Rappahannock, his brigade was caught up in a great wave of religious intensity that swept the Confederate ranks. Ewell's twenty-five hundred men were no exception as a near-constant round of prayer meetings and fervent preaching engulfed their bivouacs. For nearly "half a year" the Reverend Beverly Tucker Lacy stayed at Ewell's headquarters before he joined Jackson as chaplain of the Valley Army. But Ewell, as well as Dr. Hunter McGuire, the ubiquitous army surgeon, could not abide the man and went to considerable lengths to "get rid of him." Although Jackson put great store in the Presbyterian minister, Brown, who always speaks for his chief in his writings, shared their contempt: "He was very fond of eating & jokes—some of them not very clerical—a lazy, good-natured, talkative man well able to preach eloquent sermons—but did not advance the cause of religion much at our Hd.qrs while he staid there—nor did those who knew him best have much reverence for his character." While Brown hoped he had not misjudged him, Lacy, born in Prince Edward County in 1819, was minister of a Presbyterian congregation at Frankfort, Kentucky, before the war. Ewell would encounter him again at Jackson's headquarters, as Stonewall had confidence in Lacy, even entrusting his wife and infant daughter to his care when he went off to conduct the great Confederate triumph at Chancellorsville. While Ewell lay recuperating from his own wounds incurred at the Second Manassas, Lacy ministered to Jackson until the moment of his death in 1863 at Guiney Station.[35]

While the generals plotted their strategies in the face of a renewed Federal thrust, officers and men settled into a fixed regimen as autumn melded into winter. Besides the perpetual prayer meetings, the possession and consumption of spirits was closely regulated, and one North Carolinian wrote home: "We can stay here all winter if necessary, and if the relative status of the two parties remains as it is until spring, the enemy will have been whipped without another blow. The winter will whip him for us more effectively than we can." Until the onset of foul weather, Ewell's stay on the Alexandria Line was enlivened by the presence of Lizinka Brown, who was staying with his family at Stony Lonesome. And in spite of the flap with Beauregard, his star was rising in the Confederate command structure; on January 24, 1862, Congress named him major general. Although the rank had been authorized previously, Ewell was the fifteenth brigadier to receive the honor. Unlike his former promotion, when an omnibus bill had elevated several men at once, Congress approved his new rank in a separate action.

In spite of his promotion and a rejuvenated romance, Ewell's health was still a concern and the wounds from Arizona and Virginia continued to be a problem. Brown describes an informal get-together in Ewell's tent at Sangster's with G.W. Smith and Joe Johnston in which Ewell complained about the pain in his shoulder from the Fairfax wound eight months earlier. Since both guests had experienced battlefield wounds, their response was not encouraging. Smith told him that he had "to expect it" before relating his own problems: "Do you know it was only a few years since my wound in Mexico ceased troubling me?" Johnston, who had replaced Beauregard, was asked by Ewell about his sensations upon being shot during the Seminole Wars. "He observed," Brown recounts, "that in his experience a man is liable to suffer seven years, more or less, from pains & then generally get over it entirely."[36]

Across the mountains in western Virginia, Robert E. Lee and Union General George Brinton McClellan had been contesting trans-Allegheny Virginia as Ewell lay with the army around Manassas. In that memorable campaign, which ultimately led to creation of the new state of West Virginia, Lee returned to his desk as military adviser to President Davis, a beaten man, while McClellan emerged as the man of the hour. At Beverly in the Tygart River Valley, McClellan received a July 22 telegram from the White House summoning him to Washington, where Lincoln handed him command of the Federal army five days later. From the very inception, delays and differences with the president and his war council plagued McClellan's ability to crush the infant Confederate army. Lincoln wanted him to act, and "Little Mac," a future presidential candidate as well as governor of New Jersey, wanted to attack Richmond not by the direct overland route from Manassas but by a seaborne landing on the peninsula formed by the York and James Rivers and then assault the Southern citadel from the Chesapeake. The prolonged shilly-shallying prompted Lincoln's famous quip: "If McClellan is not going to use the army anytime soon I want to borrow it."

Johnston too had been watching the Federal buildup and, being a man who avoided every possible fight, fell back from the Alexandria Line. Johnston also had a cancer eating at his soul over rankings in the Confederate service, and he held the president personally responsible when aging Samuel Cooper, Albert Sidney Johnston, and Robert E. Lee were listed ahead of him; after all, he had been the only Southern officer to attain general rank as quartermaster general of the old army, and he was obsessed that it should be honored by the Richmond authorities. The Davis-Johnston tiff, which persisted until the death of both men, did irreparable harm to the Confederate cause. Although Johnston gave the order to abandon the

Manassas defenses, his divisions—including that of newly minted Major General Richard Stoddert Ewell—were gone by the time Lincoln at last prodded McClellan to move. "The Manassas march soon concluded on a note of anticlimax," writes McClellan's major biographer; "the Confederates had abandoned their fortifications without detection and with a twenty-four hour lead slipped away southward to new positions behind the Rappahannock River." Great quantities of "property, private and regimental" had been destroyed by Johnston's units upon the withdrawal, although McClellan found himself embarrassed by "Quaker guns" or logs painted to look like cannon left behind to deceive his march. "[G. W.] Smith's and Longstreet's divisions followed the Warrenton Turnpike," Johnston wrote in his terse report of March 12 from the Rappahannock Bridge. "Ewell's and Early's the railroad and a route through Brentsville. The first named is now near Culpeper Court-House. The last two have this morning completed passage of the river here."[37]

At last the Army of Northern Virginia had a major geographical barrier between it and the Yankees—the Rappahannock and its tributary, the Rapidan. Once south of the stream Ewell worked feverishly to establish a defensive line. His Third Division, also designated the "Reserve Division," was given the task of holding the Rappahannock line as a cover for Johnston's movements about the Peninsula when McClellan opened his notable campaign two weeks later. Besides the cavalry under Jeb Stuart, Ewell's division had three brigades commanded by Arnold Elzey, Isaac Trimble, and Richard Taylor. The entire force was clustered around the Orange and Alexandria Railroad bridge, or "Rappahannock Bridge," over the river about fifteen miles above its confluence with the Rapidan, which also flows south and east. Taylor was on the left—east of the bridge—and, finds Brown, he was "rather in reserve." But the "Louisiana Tigers," as his brigade became known—composed of three regiments: the Sixth Louisiana, under Colonel Isaac E. Seymour; Seventh Louisiana, Colonel Harry T. Hays; and the Eighth Louisiana, Colonel Henry B. Kelly—was a "rough and rowdy bunch" throughout the Virginia fighting. E. Kirby Smith had ordered two of the men shot by firing squad the previous December. The outrageous antics persisted under Ewell's command, and, says Brown, their battery "gave Taylor infinite trouble & caused much swearing." Yet the Tigers did some of the heaviest combat of the war, particularly after Harry Hays assumed command following Taylor's departure for the western theater.

Richard Taylor, who remained with Ewell through August 1862 when he was promoted to major general and sent to command in Louisiana, became a pivotal figure for his subsequent reputation. It is his classic memoir of the war, *Deconstruction and Reconstruction*, published in 1879, that paints Ewell as an eccentric with its comments about his birdlike mannerisms. Taylor also sets forth the vignette that he introduced Mrs. Ewell as "My wife, Mrs. Brown," although he had left to spearhead the Red River campaign under Kirby Smith before Ewell's May 1863 marriage. He no doubt encountered the two of them in the autumn of 1861 at Centreville when Lizinka Brown visited Ewell's camp with her daughter two years before their marriage; Ewell may well have announced her as "the widow Brown" or simply as Mrs. Brown.[38]

Isaac Ridgeway Trimble, whom Ewell had inherited from Kirby Smith along with Taylor and Elzey, was posted west of the bridge. His guns under Captain A. R. Courtney were "positioned on two knolls," giving the Richmond battery a sweeping view of the roadway from Warrenton as it approached the Rappahannock. Trimble's four regiments—Fifteenth Alabama, Colonel James Cantey; Sixteenth Mississippi, Colonel Carnot Posey; Twenty-first North Carolina, Colonel William W. Kirkland; and the Twenty-first Georgia, Colonel John T. Mercer—were picketed in front of the bridge itself. An 1822 graduate of West Point, the sixty-year-old Trimble "was regarded as the most prominent soldier contributed by Maryland to the Southern cause." The regiments of Arnold Elzey, including the Thirteenth Virginia, Colonel James A. Walker, who survived the war to become lieutenant governor of Virginia as well as a Republican congressman during the 1890s, held Ewell's right flank below the railroad crossing.[39] Also serving under Elzey, a West Point man in the class of 1837 from Maryland, was the Tenth Virginia, Colonel Samuel Gibbons, killed a few months later while fighting under Jackson at McDowell during the Shenandoah campaign. Elzey likewise commanded the First Maryland Infantry, or the "Maryland Line," under Colonel George H. "Maryland" Steuart. The Brockenbrough or "Baltimore Artillery of four guns" was also a part of his command as well as the Third Tennessee Infantry, which was added later.[40]

During his first days on the Rappahannock, Ewell made his headquarters in the "Cunningham Mansion" that was later destroyed by Pope's army. Jubal A. Early's division marched on to the south bank of the Rapidan, while those of G. W. Smith and Longstreet concentrated in the vicinity of Orange Court House. Ewell was left behind, Early writes, "to guard the crossing of the Rappahannock," thereby holding the northernmost keep of the Confederacy. While the Army of Northern Virginia could not sustain itself against the Yankee colossus gathering in front of Manassas, the Confederates were intent upon concealing their own numbers from the enemy. Thus, when a Federal cavalry thrust drove Jeb Stuart across the Rappahannock with Ewell's advance pickets, which kept a watch north of the stream, a hurried decision was made to withdraw "out of sight of the river." Although Stuart "burned the bridge as he crossed," Ewell took up a new defensive position extending about three miles from Kelly's Ford to the Orange and Alexandria Railroad. "But the troops camped two miles back and Hd.Qrs. were [established] at the Barbour House near Brandy Station," reads Brown's account. "Here we remained pretty quiet for the rest of the winter & until April."[41]

Chapter 6

"ALL RUNNING—ALL YELLING"

While Ewell remained at Sangster's Crossroads and Centreville, numerous visitors called at his bivouac, including Mary Lee, youngest daughter of Robert E. Lee. Lizinka Brown, who stayed with her Ewell relations at nearby Stony Lonesome through the fall of 1861, continued to call at Ewell's headquarters with her eighteen-year-old daughter, Harriet. "Just before my mother left Stony Lonesome to return to Nashville she told me of her engagement to Genl. Ewell," Campbell Brown relates. Although he was "very glad" to hear the news, Brown added: "I do not believe they would have married, had it not been for his wound." The injury and leg amputation at the Second Manassas lay several months ahead as the forty-five-year-old bachelor launched into an energetic correspondence with his childhood playmate and fiancée. The fact that Lizinka's son paints her as a reluctant partner did not deter an enthusiastic Ewell while he kept a watchful eye on the gathering Yankee army under Irvin McDowell. Although his several letters from northern Virginia are concerned for her welfare after her return to Tennessee, they are surprisingly free of endearments. "I merely write to get rid [of] as far as possible my dismal thoughts & forebodings," he penned on February 20; "I have been probably more anxious about you than you are yourself as we are entirely in the dark here." When Lizinka was later obliged to flee Nashville, he blamed Albert Sidney Johnston (whom he insisted on calling "Johnson") for not only her troubles but for those of the country as well. "Of course the move is consequent upon the terrible disasters caused by Johnson's generalship in Tennessee," he relayed on March 7. "Our whole position being more untenable—we will be stronger when more concentrated—but much of the state of Va. will be given up to the Yankees and great consternation prevails among the people."[1]

War in the west had affected his beloved Lizinka in a personal way, even though Ewell had sent Campbell Brown to see after his mother. General Don Carlos Buell—ironically, a messmate of Ewell at West Point—upon succeeding William T. Sherman as commander of the Department of Ohio in November 1861, had occupied Bowling Green, Kentucky, a short time afterward and immediately prepared to move south. And when Grant reduced Forts Henry and Donelson during February 1862, Buell was on hand to give the future general in chief a helping hand. The collapse of Donelson not only opened the Cumberland Valley and central Tennessee to Federal occupation, it also took the Volunteer State out of the Confederacy for the remainder of the war. While Confederate forces concentrated around Corinth, Mississippi, Buell strode into the Tennessee capital on February 25 to establish control. Before the mayor formally surrendered the city, "Nashville which had been proudly confident, went into a panic," observes Robert S. Henry. "Everyone who could, left the city; mobs took possession of the streets and pillaged the government storehouses before opportunity was had to remove the stores south." Lizinka had made her way to the Alabama home of her aunt (and Ewell's) Rebecca Hubbard before the tumult that engulfed the city, although Ewell admonished her to return, because he considered Yankee officers gentlemen who would quickly reestablish law and order.[2]

At first he thought she should stay out of Nashville, but the new order of affairs after Lincoln appointed Andrew Johnson military governor prompted his change of heart. An east Tennessee Unionist, Johnson was a United States senator when the secession storm broke and was the only Southern senator to retain his seat. He subsequently caught the attention of Lincoln, who summoned him to head a loyal state government until he became the Republican vice presidential candidate in 1864. After Appomattox, Mrs. Lizinka Ewell called upon then President Johnson for help in regaining her Tennessee property in spite of his famous antipathy for the Confederate upper class.

Although he refused to sign some of his letters lest he betray military information if seized by the enemy, Ewell wrote incessantly after the army's withdrawal from Manassas. "You must not dream of remaining in the country, either in the immediate vicinity of our army, or in the enemy's lines," he told Lizinka on March 16. "The houses in the country cannot have a guard at each one and they are prey of any marauding party of 4 or 5 men of either side who choose to plunder." All the while, he was as concerned for her financial as much as her physical security. In Virginia, Ewell told his fiancée, rogue bands "destroy everything and impoverish helpless females killing their stock and running off their negroes." At the same time he oversaw the return of escaped slaves to their masters around Gordonsville, he thought Lizinka should move "your negroes" out of Tennessee and away from Buell's invaders. Slave labor was the essential component of any large-scale agricultural endeavor. And, like many Confederates, he wanted that force protected—especially for his wife-to-be.[3]

As the grand drama to capture Richmond began to unfold, Ewell was forced to put aside thoughts of Lizinka and her problems in Tennessee. The strategy developed by McClellan and reluctantly approved by Lincoln to drive an army toward the Confederate capital was about to propel Robert E. Lee and Thomas J. Jackson into the first ranks of military commanders. And Major General Richard Stoddert Ewell was expected to play his own role in the developing campaign to thwart the Yankee invasion. His orders from Joe Johnston—then occupied with defenses east of Richmond—had been somewhat discretionary, authorizing him to cooperate with either Charles W. Field on the Rappahannock or Jackson in the Shenandoah Valley. "Charley" Field, Kentucky-born and an 1849 graduate of West Point, had been assigned to the Aquia sector since March 27 as part of A. P. Hill's command. Although he told Lee on April 23 that all was quiet on his front, Field later reestablished his headquarters "13 miles from Fredericksburg" when Ewell began his move toward Gordonsville. Ewell's couriers traveled northward across the Rapidan at Germanna Ford and then down the north bank of the Rappahannock to Field's old headquarters at Falmouth before both were forced to withdraw. At one point Ewell uncharacteristically suggested that Field and his brigade join him for a thrust at the Federal force concentrated around Warrenton and perhaps march on Washington itself. But Lee wanted him to keep his meager force of twenty-five hundred Virginians—composed of the Fortieth, Forty-seventh, and Fifty-fifth regiments plus the First brigade of artillery—on the Rappahannock to deter Nathaniel P. Banks from joining McDowell in the vicinity of Fredericksburg. When Field was obliged to give ground before McDowell's renewed posturing, Ewell abandoned any notion of a linkup, although he was not anxious to join Jackson in the valley.[4]

Ewell had been around Gordonsville since April 18, when he reached the Orange County town after a tormented march from Brandy Station. Jackson had considered him as part of his command from the beginning, his discretionary orders from Johnston notwithstanding. Ewell, however, had heard stories circulating through the ranks about Jackson's secretive ways and odd mannerisms—he would later label him "mad as a March hare"—and he clearly did not relish a trek into Stonewall's bailiwick. While he still remained on the Rappahannock, Ewell informed Johnston: "There is a rumor that the President has avowed his intention of going to Tenn since the death of Genl. A. S. Johnson [sic]. If so, he will undoubtedly take Taylor and the La. Brigade. If so, I will have too many or too few, here & if events make it possible for me to be of use in the Peninsula, I hope you will not forget me," he wrote on April 8. His appeal to Johnston fell on deaf ears, because within the week he was headed for the Shenandoah Valley.[5]

Yet, despite his own well-documented oddities, Ewell, like Jackson, had ingratiated himself with his men while he guarded the Rappahannock crossings. Before the march to Gordonsville, Ewell decided to do a little scavenging himself and on one occasion "paraded back into camp with a single bull." When he confronted his subordinate General Richard Taylor, the Louisianan pointed out that a single animal would hardly feed a division of eight thousand men. "'Ah!' Exclaimed Ewell. 'I was thinking of my fifty dragoons.'" Such good-natured bonhomie, notes Taylor biographer T. Michael Parrish, "enlivened Ewell's popularity with his troops." That he was a committed soldier, at least in the glory days before his amputation, was never in doubt. He got into trouble only when faced with difficult command decisions. "I saw a good deal of Ewell, who was a queer character, very eccentric, but brave, upright, and devoted," noted John C. Haskell, a North Carolina officer. "He had no very high talent but did all a brave man of moderate capacity could."[6]

When Ewell wrote to Johnston on April 16, he announced that "I hear regularly from Jackson" and accounted for "8,000 men with 14 pieces of artillery," which did not include "500 effective cavalrymen." As early as April 4, Jackson had asked a pertinent question: "What instructions did General Johnston give you?" Over the next several days a torrent of letters from Jackson—now preserved in the Tennessee state archive—bombarded Brandy Station. The modern scholar sifting through this correspondence must question the popular notion that Stonewall was inordinately secretive about his military stratagems. Jackson surely passed many of his ideas to Ewell by "a daily courier service" that Campbell Brown describes in some depth: "by a line established by him [Jackson] & running through Chester Gap at first. Then through one that he always spoke of as well known & designated Milam's Gap north of Swift Run Gap." Jackson sent a remarkable missive on April 13 in which he discusses their options for a linkage:

> If I fall back we should effect a junction on the road lead-ing from Madison C. H. to New Market. This will prevent our missing each other. My impression is Genl. Johnston was of the opinion that this road crossed the Blue Ridge at Swift Run Gap, but which is not the case. Its name is Fisher's Gap, and we should meet the enemy this side of Fisher's Gap a short distance. Swift Run Gap is where the road from Harrisonburg to Gordonsville crosses the Blue Ridge. Until yesterday I was under the impres-sion that Swift Run Gap was at this Gap. We will have a strong position this side of Fisher's Gap, and at the Gap. I do not much expect that Banks will follow me to them.[7]

Jackson clearly meant for Ewell to join him at the Blue Ridge, but when the time came to move, Ewell jumped at the opportunity to once more approach Johnston. Not wishing to alienate his nominal commander, Ewell suggested that he would attack McDowell from Brandy Station in-stead of joining Jackson. Johnston replied that he was too far from Ewell's front and that the decision to attack would have to be made by him in the field. "It would be well to drive him [the enemy] away. You would be freer to aid Jackson & it might make a diversion in his favor," Johnston wrote at 9:30 on the morning of April 17 from Richmond. And, he added, "should you [attack] apply your whole, instruct every brigade to press forward with the utmost vigor." However, with his customary reticence, Ewell failed to seize the moment.[8]

Although Joe Johnston was vying mightily to retain control over all Confederate forces in northern Virginia, including Jackson's and Ewell's, decisions at the highest level had fated Ewell to reinforce Stonewall. Rob-ert E. Lee, now chief military adviser to President Davis, had resolved that the best way to handle McClellan was to worry Lincoln into withholding troops for the defense of Washington. In 1964 Confederate historian Clifford Dowdey coined an apt phrase, "intuitive collaboration," to ex-plain the unique relationship between Lee and Jackson to accomplish this great purpose. Lee won out because he knew how to manipulate the some-times-difficult Davis from his sparse office in Richmond's Mechanics Hall. And the festering canker between Davis and Johnston meant that Ewell should have been courting Lee instead of Johnston if he had no desire to join the Valley Army. Jackson needed troops, needed Ewell's eighty-five hundred infantry and cavalry in his campaign to clear the Shenandoah of enemy invaders, and Lee saw to it that they were assigned to him. The worsening military situation eventually made it clear that Ewell was required in the valley, and he wrote to Johnston on April 18 indicating that he was "expecting an hourly summons to Jackson's aid."[9]

The word came when twenty-two-year-old Henry Kyd Douglas rode up to Ewell's headquarters tent later the same day. "About the time of the setting sun and before we reached Harrisonburg, General Jackson called for me," Douglas writes in his classic memoir, *I Rode with Stonewall.* "The general handed me a paper from under his rubber cape and requested me to take it to General Richard S. Ewell. And proceeded to tell me that he was on the other side of the Blue Ridge Mountains, somewhere near Culpeper Court House." Born in Shepherdstown (now West Virginia), young Douglas, a lawyer who was soon to become a trusted member of Jackson's staff and attorney general of Maryland after the war, immediately set off on one of the memorable exploits of the war. Using a borrowed horse, he rode around the southern tip of the Massanutten—a forty-mile-long mountain that runs northeast to southwest through the valley—to Swift Run Gap and Conrad's Store on the South Fork of the Shenandoah River.

With night approaching and totally unfamiliar with the landscape, Douglas climbed the western slope of the Blue Ridge and passed over Swift Run Gap. It was from this summit that colonial Governor Alexander Spotswood had first looked out on the lands of western Virginia with his Knights of the Golden Horseshoe more than 150 years earlier. "Vision was impossible, but fortunately the road was solid and fairly good and my horse could keep to it. I could reach out and feel her neck and ears, but could not see them," Douglas writes. "At times I heard water rush under and cross the road and tumble in torrents so far down below that I knew we were travelling on perilous edges." Although he met one of Ewell's couriers in the pitch-black night, Douglas pressed on through Standardsville and Madison Court House. Then, drawing upon fresh mounts, he sped through James City and Culpeper until he arrived at Brandy Station; he had covered 105 miles "in less than twenty hours" only to reach his destination in near collapse. "You don't say," Ewell called out when he read Jackson's urgent summon to combine forces. "The sentence was not finished. Seeing me totter and about to fall, he caught me, laid me there; and then the dear, rough old soldier made the air blue with orders for brandy and coffee and breakfast—not for himself but for me."[10]

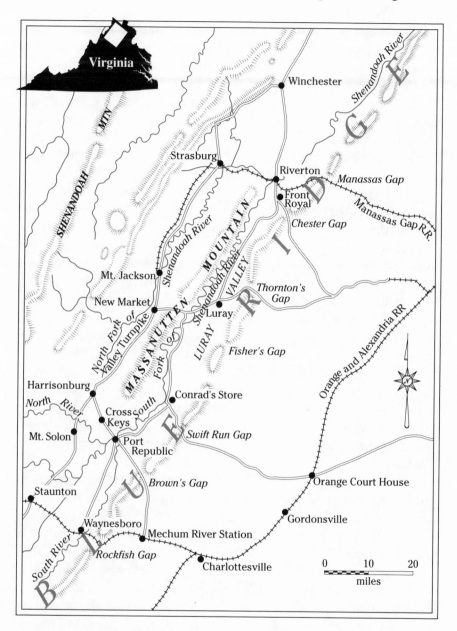

Ewell and Jackson in the Valley, 1862

Jackson kept changing his mind about a rendezvous point with Ewell as his own cat-and-mouse game with Nathaniel P. Banks fluctuated. While it is true that Jackson sent an April 17 communiqué urging Ewell to Swift Run Gap, a rash of subsequent messages preserved in the *Official Records* and in various archival repositories render it difficult to ascertain Jackson's reasoning at any given moment. Professor Frank E. Vandiver in his unsurpassed biography of Jackson says the *Official Records* communication dated April 18 from Harrisonburg is the one relayed by Douglas: "Circumstances have so changed since Mr. Boswell left that I will be prevented from joining you at Fisher's Gap.[11] You will therefore come on the direct road to this point (Harrisonburg) via Standardsville."[12] Campbell Brown seems to concur with this sequence: "Finally about the 17th of April, [Jackson] directed us to move to Standardsville en route for Swift Run Gap. Before we got there marching by Gordonsville & to the right of it, he halted us near Liberty Mills, or Somerset, as it was sometimes called." The two dispatches of April 17 mention Swift Run Gap but say nothing about Standardsville, while the one mentioned by Vandiver on the eighteenth does.[13]

With Elzey's brigade in the van, Ewell lost no time in complying with Jackson's mandate. Richard Taylor says winter had "returned" to the Virginia Piedmont with "renewed energy," and even after reaching Gordonsville "we had for several days snow, sleet, rain, and all possible abominations in the way of weather." The movement south and toward the Blue Ridge took Ewell's command through Culpeper, where the "stores and baggage" as well as some troops boarded the Orange and Alexandria Railroad into Gordonsville. "Reached Gordonsville after midnight, supperless and wet," reads Brown's account. The next morning, April 19, a renewed march began through Standardsville and Liberty Mills for those who had disembarked at Orange Court House before a courier from Jackson called a halt to both columns. Ewell established his headquarters "at the house of a queer fish named Ruhl . . . an inventor of two or three patent ploughs & rollers, harrows, etc., really an ingenious man & the vainest creature I ever saw (Brown again)." While Ewell amused himself looking at Ruhl's three hundred or more specimens, an urgent appeal reached his new bivouac. It was dated April 29: "Please let me see you as early as practicable as I wish to consult with you upon important business."[14]

When Jackson sent the renewed summons, the Valley Army was gathered around Elk Run, a stream flowing westward from Swift Run Gap into the South Fork of the Shenandoah at Conrad's Store. He had been in the valley since November, applying what pressure he could at the same time

Ewell held the flank for Joe Johnston on the Rappahannock. In late December President Davis had approved a brainchild of Jackson, the ill-fated Romney expedition. Located on the South Branch of the Potomac, beyond the Appalachian Front in present West Virginia, Jackson was certain the small hamlet held the key for control of the Little Kanawha and Monongahela/Tygart/West Fork valleys.

Anxious to keep his native area loyal to the Confederacy, Stonewall's soiree became a fiasco when he encountered rough winter travel over nearly impassable roads. The Valley Army, which remained at Romney for about two weeks or less, had returned to Winchester by January 24. Although Jackson accomplished little or nothing, he became embroiled in a nasty confrontation with Brigadier General William W. Loring, an old Indian fighter as well as veteran of the Mexican War, and Secretary of War Judah P. Benjamin. When Loring and his command protested to Richmond politicians about being left behind at Romney in hard weather with scant provisions, Benjamin issued an order for Jackson to withdraw him. Stonewall promptly resigned from the army over having his orders countermanded, but the forceful intervention of Virginia Governor John Letcher and others saved him for his subsequent contributions to Confederate greatness.[15]

While Jackson reestablished himself at Winchester, Lincoln directed General Nathaniel P. Banks, former governor of Massachusetts and onetime speaker of the national House of Representatives, to drive him out of the Shenandoah and thus relieve the pressure on Washington as part of McClellan's campaign on the Peninsula.

Pursued by James Shields, an Irish-born soldier, Jackson commenced a retreat up the valley only to learn from cavalryman Turner Ashby that Banks, believing he had departed the Shenandoah, had withdrawn over the Blue Ridge himself. Jackson thereupon pointed his meager command north again, where he clashed with Shields at Kernstown, a few miles south of Winchester. The March 23 set-to resulted in a Confederate defeat, with Shields crowing ever afterward that "he had defeated Stonewall Jackson in battle." By an ironic twist, Jackson accomplished in defeat what he could not in victory. Shields and Banks convinced themselves that Jackson would hardly have attacked had he not been expecting reinforcements, and the latter did not join McClellan as planned but returned to the valley immediately. Accordingly, Lincoln not only ordered McDowell's forty thousand bluecoats to stay in front of Washington, but he also detached General Louis Blenker and his Germans from McClellan and sent them to John C. Fremont in western Virginia.

Following the Kernstown debacle, Jackson had retreated up the valley first to Newtown, or Stephens City, and then Mount Jackson (where the railroad from Manassas Junction terminated), and still farther to an elevated section of the Valley Pike called Rude's Hill. Although he was fearful lest Banks would send a portion of his troops up the Luray Valley and cut him off, Jackson continued to fall back before his adversary. Unable to confront Banks in pitched battle, Old Jack withdrew through Harrisonburg (occupied by Banks on April 24) to Conrad's Store and Elk Run to establish contact with Ewell. It was during his withdrawal up the Shenandoah that Jackson was in near-constant communication with not only Ewell but also Lee. "Dutifully, Ewell made all of the starts and stops, and he voiced no complaints in writing," observes a recent Jackson biographer. "Still he must have thought at this early point that the new general to whom he was about to report was a bit unstable." A careful reading of Jackson's numerous letters to Ewell shows his own movements were governed by those of Banks. With Jackson on the western slope of Swift Run Gap and Ewell around Standardsville not thirty miles to the east, a linkup was near at hand. Stonewall "now occupied a classic flanking position" in his chess match with Banks and Shields; "that is, if Banks moved south of Harrisonville [and the Massanutten] it would be easy for Jackson to advance and cut him off from his communications whereas Jackson's own communications remained secure."[16]

Jackson needed Ewell's contingent along with a troop under General Edward "Allegheny" Johnson to shift the balance even further. (The sobriquet came from Johnson's early service in present West Virginia, where he established a reputation for hard fighting.) No sooner had Jackson camped at Elk Run than he fired off a letter to Lee suggesting that he was about to adopt one of three scenarios:

> either to leave General Ewell here [Swift Run Gap] to threaten Banks' rear in the advent of his advancing on Staunton, and move rapidly on the force in front of General Edward Johnson, or else, co-operating with General Ewell, to attack the enemy's detached force between New Market and the Shenandoah, and, if successful in this, then to press forward and get in Banks' rear at New Market, and thus induce him to fall back; the third is to pass down the Shenandoah to Sperryville and thus threaten Winchester via Front Royal. . . . . Of the three plans, I give preference to attacking the force west of Staunton, for, if suc-

cessful, I would afterwards be re-enforced by General Edward Johnson, and by that time you might be able to give me re-enforcements, which, united with the troops now under my control, would enable me to defeat Banks.

As it turned out, Jackson had not only decided upon a course of action, but Ewell was also summoned to Conrad's Store. Ewell must have spent a considerable time in the saddle as he rode the twenty-five miles (Brown's figure) to Jackson's headquarters and then returned to Standardsville. The day after, April 30, he sent a late-evening letter to Lee that confirmed his "interview" with Jackson. From the conversation, he relayed: "I inferred that he [Jackson] considered the force of General Banks too strong to be attacked with confidence contrary with our combined commands." In a midnight postscript, Ewell added: "I have just returned from my interview with General Jackson. He moves toward Staunton and I take his position." Jackson had undeniably taken Ewell into his confidence, contrary to the assertions of others that he was left in the dark. Jackson likewise sent a late-night dispatch from Swift Run Gap on April 30: "Please bring your command to this side of the Blue Ridge at once." Jackson had already resolved upon a foray into the west with Ewell's aid and to avoid Banks for the time being.[17]

Ewell's correspondence with Lee on the thirtieth indicates the letter was carried to Richmond by General Richard Taylor. Even at this late date, following his tête-à-tête with Jackson, according to Major David French Boyd, a staff officer under Taylor and a future president of Louisiana State University, Ewell was yet maneuvering to avoid service under Jackson. Since Jefferson Davis had been married briefly during 1835 to Sarah Knox Taylor, daughter of President Zachary Taylor, Richard Taylor and the president were onetime brothers-in law. Given Davis's well-known propensity to favor relatives and cronies, the two comrades-in-arms anticipated relief in Richmond. But his willing subordinate returned empty-handed. When Taylor found his way back to Ewell's old campgrounds around Gordonsville, he had already marched for Swift Run Gap, and those remaining, including Boyd, could tell him little else. "I again had to confess my ignorance and could only say that [Jackson] had broken camp on a certain morning, going with his own division southwest, no one seemed to know where, and that General Ewell occupied his camp that night, and had been there ever since," Boyd recounts in his memoir of the war. "'Well,' said Taylor, 'this is strange. Nobody at Richmond knows anything about it. But,' he added, 'there is one consolation: We won't be under this damned old crazy fool long. General Longstreet is coming here to take command.'"[18]

Ewell had indeed proceeded over the Blue Ridge at the same time Old Jack "joined Ed. Johnson & defeated Milroy," says Brown, "while we took his place at Conrad's Store and lay idle for two weeks." And it was soon apparent to everyone that Longstreet was not coming to the Shenandoah—that Ewell would remain under Jackson's charge until the tragedy at Groveton. Taylor had spoken to the wrong people at the capital; he should have talked to Lee, who shared the "old crazy fool's" confidence. Notwithstanding Jackson's well-documented aversion to discussing his strategic operations, Ewell certainly had been apprised of the incursion into western Virginia. When he saw a general order stating that one of his regiments—the Maryland Line, commanded by Brigadier General George H. "Maryland" Steuart—had been assigned to Jackson, Ewell was quick to vent his anger. "I wish to bring this to your notice to prevent any mistake—as though I was placed under orders of Maj. Gen. Jackson—it was for a temporary purpose & specific object," he told Adjutant General Samuel Cooper on May 14. "It ought to be expressed therefore whether it is intended to transfer [Steuart's] Regt. to his division as otherwise there may be some misunderstanding in the matter." He viewed his association with Jackson as a transitory one that would end shortly, although Lee and Jackson considered it permanent.[19]

Ewell was unquestionably miffed when he marched into Conrad's Store and found Jackson gone, although his chagrin has been overdone by some writers. Jackson had already informed him that he was heading west, and by May 2 he had traveled through Port Republic and gained entrance to Brown's Gap through the Blue Ridge. Jackson was heading for the Virginia Piedmont in an effort to lull Banks into thinking that he was abandoning the valley for Johnston's army east of Richmond. "The bad roads have greatly impeded my progress. . . . The proposition to turn Banks by New Market has received much attention by me and we both consulted about it previous to my leaving," he told Ewell on the third. "I am of the opinion that the attempt is too hazardous so long as Banks keeps a strong force near New Market." Although Ewell would eventually move a few miles down the Luray Valley before Jackson's return, he now had another excuse not to seize the initiative. He had failed to act when Joe Johnston gave him the go-ahead on the Rappahannock, and now he remained in place, fixed in spite of repeated proddings from Jackson to pursue Banks.[20]

The next day, May 4, found Jackson nearing Staunton, where he made contact with Allegheny Johnson, who reported an enemy force sixteen miles to the west. "Do what you can consistent with the safety of your command to prevent Banks from giving assistance to the forces in front of Johnson," he implored Ewell. Again on the fifth Jackson advised that cavalry reports indicated Banks was withdrawing from New Market and that he should do all in his power to draw him back. With part of his command still at Gordonsville, Ewell remained in place around Conrad's Store.[21]

Meanwhile, it was an army of hungry troopers that trekked into Mechum's River Station on the Virginia Central Railroad, where they "took the cars" through Rockfish Gap to Staunton. Already the near-spartan conditions of a fast-moving march were earning his men an immortal sobriquet: "Jackson's Foot Cavalry." Jackson took rooms in Staunton's Virginia Hotel and immediately renewed his correspondence with Ewell. With the Valley Army headed for the west, he had become mightily concerned that Ewell keep a tight watch on the Yankees at New Market. When he learned from spies that Banks was about to move toward Strasburg, he told Ewell to follow "as may be consistent with your safety." And later the same day, May 6: "Should you follow the enemy and have to fall back before I join you, circumstances may render it desirable for you to cross the Shenandoah via Columbia Bridge to Fisher's Gap or via Port Republic by Brown's Gap.[22] But this must be judged by you." Once more Ewell did nothing.[23]

Then, as he made several troop dispositions within his own command at Gordonsville as well as in the valley, Ewell received a May 8 communiqué from Robert E. Lee. On his own Ewell had informed Lee that Jackson was still in the west and that he would remain at Conrad's Store for the time being. When Lee corresponded with Jackson on the eighth—the very day of McDowell—he said that Ewell would "not leave his position at Swift Run Gap, until the enemy [has] entirely left the Valley or he had orders to that effect from you." It is clear from an examination of their correspondence that Lee and Ewell at this point were unaware that Jackson was closing in on Robert H. Milroy. At 5:10 in the morning of May 8, as Jackson was preparing to open his attack, he was concerned enough about Banks to forward a last-minute instruction: "If the enemy are in the vicinity of New Market, I hope he will remain there," he told Ewell. "All I desire you to do is to keep near enough to Banks to let him know that if he goes down the Valley you will follow him and that you are all the time in stricking [sic] distance of him. I can only give general instructions, you must conform to circumstances, but try to avoid bringing on a general engagement with Banks' present force, unless he attempts to cross the Blue Ridge where you can meet him in a strong position."[24]

Although Stonewall apprised Ewell about the May 7 skirmish between Allegheny Johnson's troops and the Federals, Ewell remained ignorant that a larger fracas was in the offing. When Campbell Brown wrote to his mother on May 9, he did not mention Ewell, saying only that "we are all well" and commenting that he had "heard no news, except for Longstreet's brilliant skirmish on the Peninsula." While he added that Ewell's force remained ensconced around Conrad's Store "in an exceedingly healthy country & a very bad place for Yankees to get at us," he told Lizinka that Banks had withdrawn in haste: "I suppose from all indications he is going to Fredericksburg to help in the attack on Richmond from that side." Banks, however, did not leave the Shenandoah but withdrew toward Strasburg at the northernmost tip of the Massanutten at the same time Jackson opened the fight at McDowell. The Federals may have withdrawn from Ewell's haven along Elk Run, but they surely knew he had crossed the Blue Ridge. Cavalry patrols sent out by Banks had spotted the encampment as early as May 5, and one day later he informed Secretary of War Edwin M. Stanton that Ewell had 12,750 men to reinforce Jackson. Banks had overestimated Ewell's bivouac, which received its mail twice a week from Gordonsville, by more than 40 percent.[25]

Before that, Jackson had "marched 92 miles in four marching days (not including the 25-mile train ride)" to reach the Highland County town of McDowell, where Milroy had been reinforced by Robert C. Schenk following the initial set-to on May 7. After the Confederates took a position on Sitlington's Hill south of the Bull Pasture River, a tributary of the James, the combined Union force, now commanded by Schenk, launched a direct attack. After a mean little fight that Jackson labeled "fierce and sanguinary," the Yankees were driven back after losing fewer men than the Confederates. The affray ended when Schenk and Milroy withdrew northward toward Franklin—now West Virginia—by setting the woods on fire to thwart Jackson's pursuit. "To carry out my design against Milroy General Ewell was directed to march his division to the position which I had occupied, in the Elk Run Valley, with a view to holding Banks in check, while I pushed on with my division to Staunton," Old Jack noted in his official summary. Ewell's eight thousand (more or less) at Conrad's Store may have pushed Banks away from the railroad through Rockfish Gap and Staunton, but Stonewall took the precaution of posting a troop under topographer Jed Hotchkiss at several gaps in the Allegheny foothills to block a direct western march by the Federal commander.[26]

Ewell was in a state of frustration and anxiousness and heard nothing of Jackson's triumph until cavalryman Turner Ashby rode up to Conrad's Store a few days later. According to Franklin M. Myers, an officer in White's Thirty-fifth Battalion, Virginia Cavalry, Ashby encountered a mightily agitated Ewell. "He saluted and inquired how he did, to which Ewell replied, 'I've been in hell for three days, Gen. Ashby. What's the news from Jackson?'" Upon hearing a firsthand account of the victory over Milroy and Schenk, Myers relates, Ewell's disposition improved on the spot. "The boys began to think there might be a warm place somewhere down in his rugged, iceberg of a heart, and they decided that he wasn't such a savage after all, but the change didn't amount to much." The swearing and rough talk returned soon enough as Myers makes one of the few contemporary references to an Apache boy dubbed "Friday," "the ugliest, dirtiest, and most aggravating and thievish little wretch of an Indian boy in the country." The lad, who had accompanied Ewell from the west in 1861, remained his constant companion during the Virginia fighting. It was common talk throughout the ranks "that 'Old Ewell' didn't love but one thing on earth, and that one thing was Friday."[27]

The suspense of waiting and uncertainty over a course of action prompted Ewell to lash out on at least two occasions as he sought word from Jackson—outbursts that can be easily overblown. Although Campbell Brown says "not much happened" while Ewell remained at Elk Run, Colonel (later General) Thomas T. Munford encountered a riled-up commander when he arrived with his own cavalry outfit. As Jackson chased down Milroy's wagon train in the aftermath of McDowell, Munford says, Ewell "thought him a 'crazy wagon hunter' and 'an old fool.'" And it is Munford who relates the oft-quoted diatribe against Isaac R. Trimble, who was stationed on the Blue Ridge "behind Ewell." Cavalryman Munford stumbled into Ewell's headquarters immediately after a request to send additional couriers up the mountain to Trimble and found the camp in an uproar. "'Look here! *Send that old man* [Trimble was sixty, Ewell forty-five] a mounted man or two,' Ewell exploded. 'Nobody is going to hurt him way behind me, yet he wants some cavalry to keep him posted; and he has a fellow over on the mountain named [William W.] Kirkland, on picket, who wants horsemen. I expect if a fellow in the woods would say boo, the whole crew would get away.'"[28]

In the interval before Ashby's coming Colonel James A. Walker also found a steamed-up Ewell when he arrived on "important business." Walker, known throughout the army as "Stonewall Jim," a noted firebrand and a Republican congressman after the war, later assumed command of Jackson's own Stonewall Brigade. While a student at VMI, he had once challenged Professor Thomas J. Jackson to a duel. Although Jackson spurned the offer, Walker was not promoted to general until May 1863. A year earlier, however, when he confronted Ewell at Conrad's Store, he found him in such a rage that others advised him to be quiet and not divulge the nature of his visit. "But as he was about to leave Ewell called to him abruptly and asked, 'Colonel Walker, did it ever occur to you that General Jackson is crazy,'" writes Armistead L. Long, an early biographer of Robert E. Lee. "'I don't know, General,' was the reply. 'We used to call him Fool Tom Jackson at the Virginia Military Institute, but I do not suppose that he is really crazy.'"

"'I tell you sir,' rejoined the irate Ewell, 'he is crazy as a March Hare. He has gone away, I don't know where, and left me here with instructions to remain until he returns. But Banks' whole army is advancing on me, and I do not have the most remote idea where to communicate with General Jackson. I tell you, sir, he is crazy, and I will just march my division away from here. I do not mean to have it cut to pieces at the behest of a crazy man.'" Some weeks afterward, in the aftermath of the culminating battles in the Valley campaign at Cross Keys and Port Republic, Ewell had adopted a decidedly pensive stance. "'I take it all back and will never prejudge another man,' he told Tom Munford. 'Old Jackson is no fool; he knows how to keep his own counsel; and does curious things; but he has method in his madness.'" Ewell even called Trimble "an old trump," and he praised the later fighting of Kirkland, who "behaved as handsomely near Winchester as any man in our army."[29]

Ewell's presence in the Shenandoah to watch Banks had insured Jackson's mastery of Milroy, but once Old Jack had his victory in western Virginia, Ewell, still at Conrad's Store, was subjected to even greater pressures. And the question remained: Was he under the immediate orders of Jackson, or Johnston? Put another way—did Johnston really have control of the valley, or was Stonewall adhering to Lee and his effort to relieve the threat to Richmond by using the Valley Army to threaten Washington? Ewell pretty well outlined his dilemma in a May 13 letter to Lizzie:

> I have spent two weeks of the most unhappy that I ever remember. I was ordered here to support General Jackson, pressed by

Banks. But he [Jackson], immediately upon my arrival, started on a long chase after a body of the enemy far above Staunton. I have been keeping one eye on Banks, one on Jackson, all the time jogged up from Richmond, until I am sick and worn down. Jackson wants me to watch Banks. At Richmond, they want me elsewhere and call me off, when at the same time, I am compelled to remain until that enthusiastic fanatic comes to some conclusion. Now I ought to be en route to Gordonsville, at this place, and going to Jackson, all at the same time.

The uncertainty of conflicting demands was unmistakably affecting a wrought-up Ewell as he awaited orders. "I have a bad headache, what with the bother and folly of things," he wrote to his niece. "I have never suffered as much from dyspepsia in my life. As an Irishman would say, 'I'm kilt entirely.'" Yet Ewell must have spent much of May 13 writing and receiving letters, although several probably reached him a day or so later.[30]

First, Jackson sent word he was returning to the valley and suggested that Ewell keep a tight watch on Banks: "I wish you to follow him so that he may feel that if he leaves the valley that not only will we reoccupy it, but that he will also be liable to be attacked as soon as he shall have sufficiently weakened his force this side [of] the Shenandoah." At the same time, he received an order from Joseph E. Johnston telling him the same thing—to combine with Jackson for a thrust at Banks if he and Stonewall felt they had adequate manpower to carry it off. In accordance with Johnston's instruction, Ewell telegraphed Lawrence O'B. Branch, at Gordonsville east of the Blue Ridge, that Banks had abandoned his positions around Columbia Bridge and that he should proceed to the Peninsula fighting. Another missive alerted Jackson that the Unionists were heading north.

From his perch on the Blue Ridge, Colonel Kirkland also confirmed that Banks was on the prowl. Finally, in exasperation he wrote to Lee in Richmond saying that he had "dispatched couriers" informing Jackson about developments on his front. Ewell not only seized the opportunity to correspond directly with Lee, but he also played upon the special collaboration existing between Jackson and Lee when he added a postscript that he would abide by Jackson's admonition to "remain in the valley untill Banks leaves it."[31]

Faithful to his instructions, Ewell stayed at Elkton for four days until Jackson led the Valley Army into Mount Solon, a few miles southwest of Harrisonburg; that was after Old Jack had spent the sixteenth in prayer and fasting at Lebanon White Sulphur Springs. Although Jackson reached the valley on May 17, thunder struck on the same day when Ewell received a direct order from Johnston: Jackson can observe Banks, "and you come eastward. . . . We want troops here; none, therefore, must be kept away." Johnston, facing a renewed threat from McClellan on the Peninsula, added that Ewell should forward the communiqué to Jackson, "for whom it is intended as well as yourself." When Jackson saw Johnston's missive, relayed by mounted horsemen from Elk Run, he sent an immediate reply to Ewell: "Suspend the execution for returning eastward until I receive an answer to my telegram" to Richmond. More letters followed in both directions, but the time had come for action, and a nervous Ewell could wait no longer. He set out for Mount Solon and a meeting with Jackson.[32]

The two met in an "old mill" aside the Shenandoah to hash out their options. Both soldiers were of a mind to ignore Johnston as far as they could without an overt act of insubordination. "The enemy had committed a classic blunder: The Federals in central Virginia were divided into four parts (Fremont, Banks, Shields, and McDowell) over a wide arc—just at the moment when the forces of Jackson, [Edward] Johnson, Ewell and Branch, a total of 20,000 men, were within three days march of each other by interior lines within the arc of Union troops," writes Robert G. Tanner. Each man instinctively grasped what was at stake—that a combined Jackson-Ewell contingent had an opportunity to strike a decisive blow at Banks before James Shields at Fredericksburg could come to his aid. "Both were sorely perplexed as to what was their duty under the circumstances," notes Jackson's wife. "But Ewell proposed that if Jackson, as the ranking officer, would take responsibility, he would remain until the condition of affairs could be represented to General Johnston, which was decided upon." Ewell's unhesitating resolution to forget Joe Johnston earned him the undying gratitude of Jackson—"his willingness to combine forces with the Valley Army virtually insured the eventual outcome of Stonewall's immortal campaign in the Shenandoah."[33]

The linkup took place on May 20 at New Market after Ewell had marched his division around the southernmost shank of the Massanutten. In the meantime, Jackson had learned from Ashby's outriders that Banks was encamped around Strasburg with a detached force under Colonel John R. Kenly at Front Royal; in other words, the Federals had positioned themselves astride the north and south forks of the Shenandoah with the crests of the Massanutten between them. Without pause Jackson resolved to cross the mountain from New Market to the Luray Valley and march north for the weakest, most exposed units under Kenly. Campbell Brown is insistent that Ewell's men were in the van as Jackson drove his "foot cavalry" toward the prize. Composed of brigades under Arnold Elzey, W. C. Scott, Richard Taylor, Isaac Trimble, the Maryland Line commanded by George H. Steuart, and several artillery batteries, his division camped the first night immediately north of Luray.[34]

Jackson, observes James Robertson, "knew that Front Royal was indefensible" before Ewell reached the Warren County town on a hot, clear Friday. Aware that Kenly's force contained several Maryland units, Jackson summoned Bradley T. Johnson from the Maryland Line to spearhead the assault, which commenced "about one or two p.m." One of the most famous incidents of the entire war occurred as Jackson and Ewell sat with their aides watching Johnson push to the fore. All present saw the well-known Confederate spy Belle Boyd waving her bonnet and running at full speed down an adjacent hillside, signaling to Jackson about Kenly's troops. Although Richard Taylor maintains that Jackson already knew the facts but had said nothing because of his innate secrecy, he listened intently as Boyd told him "there was only one reg't in the town—the Fed'l 1st Maryland & 2 cos. of a Penna Reg't," according to Brown, who was also present. Kenly nonetheless put up a fight of sorts with his men arrayed before the town and a few artillery pieces on a hill beyond the confluence of the two main branches of the Shenandoah.[35]

The Yanks left in such haste that Johnson's men encountered still-standing tents and food cooking over numerous campfires when they swept through the place. "I shall never forget the style in which Wheat's Battalion passed us as we stood in the road," Brown writes. "He was riding full gallop, yelling at the top of his voice—his big sergeant major running at speed behind him, calling to the men to come on & they strung out according to their speed or stomach for the fight, following after—all running—all yelling—all looking like fight." When the melee ended Jackson had seven hundred prisoners, including twenty officers, and a trove of supplies. Lieutenant Charles A. Atwell, Pennsylvania Light Artillery, left little doubt about whose men had been responsible for Jackson's triumph. In a May 27 report he wrote: "On Friday, May 23, at about 2 p.m., the rebel forces reported to be under the command of General Ewell, made a sudden descent upon the town of Front Royal, Va." That Ewell had undergone a complete metamorphosis was evident, since he paced and stewed at Conrad's Store when he filed his own battle summary on June 4: "The attack and decided results at Front Royal, though this division alone par-

ticipated, were the fruits of Major General Jackson's personal superinten-
dence and planning." And despite the exhilaration of battle, Ewell found
time to dash off a letter to his sister on May 23 telling her to stop sending
"so much Madeira until I call for more."[36]

Jackson and Ewell immediately began a triangular race with Banks
toward Winchester—twenty miles north of Front Royal—as the Yankees
sped toward the town, while the two chieftains pursued Kenly along the
Front Royal-Winchester roadway. Upon reaching the Valley Pike at
Middletown, they soon had the retreating Federals trapped between a series of stone walls that lined their escape route. Amid the resultant slaughter, Jackson, anxious to press the pursuit, became miffed when Ashby's
men and some of Ewell's division stopped the chase to plunder the enemy's
discarded wagons. "But in the midst of these hopes I was pained to see
both cavalry and infantry, forgetful of their high trust as the advance of the
pursuing army, desert their colors and abandon themselves to pillage to
such an extent as to make it necessary for that gallant officer [Ashby] to
discontinue further pursuit," he put in his official report.

"The gentle Tigers [of Wheat's command] were looting right merrily,
diving in and out of wagons with the activity of rabbits in a warren," noted
Richard Taylor, who thought Jackson misunderstood his men because he
was "oblivious" to their personal comforts. "But this occupation was abandoned on my approach, and in a moment they were in line, looking as
solemn and virtuous as deacons at a funeral." Ewell, however, said nothing
about the delayed pilfering but commended his brigades for "capturing
some hundreds of prisoners, many wagons, etc." Throughout May 24,
Ewell continually urged his division, spearheaded by the Louisianans under Taylor and Steuart's Marylanders, toward the prize. "The Twenty-first
North Carolina, under Colonel Kirkland, drove the enemy's pickets that
evening and held the position 2 miles from Winchester during the night,"
he said later. "The rest of the command slept on their arms about three
miles from Winchester."[37]

The affray at Winchester on May 25, in which seventeen thousand
Confederates under Jackson and Ewell simply overwhelmed Banks's force
of seventy-five hundred, was a continuation of the Front Royal fight. Ewell
was in the forefront of the engagement that commenced at "5:40 a.m., in
a heavy mist and ended between 8 and 9 o'clock." When Jackson arrived
on the scene, he quickly ordered Richard Taylor to gain the high ground
southwest of the Valley Pike. The Louisianans fought throughout under
the direction of Stonewall himself, while Ewell personally accompanied

Isaac Trimble and the Twenty-first North Carolina Infantry as well as Branch's brigade to the Confederate center south of Winchester. Bradley T. Johnson and the Marylanders held the extreme left. "[A]s soon as the balance of my command [Fifteenth Alabama under Colonel James Cantey, and the Sixteenth Mississippi, under Carnot Posey] came on the field I joined them to the Twenty-first Georgia, and, the mist then admitting of a better view, I adopted the suggestion of Brigadier General Trimble and marched them to the right," Ewell said. "This movement was immediately followed by a retrograde one by the enemy; soon converted into flight, as the attack, conducted by General Jackson in person on the south side of town, was driving them on."[38]

Banks fled Winchester for the Potomac with Jackson in close pursuit; in a sense that part of the campaign was an extension of the running fight that started when Jackson and Ewell left New Market on May 20. A nasty little set-to developed on the northern outskirts of Winchester when George H. Steuart refused an order to send his cavalry after the scampering Federals. The bullheaded Marylander said he would take orders from no one but Ewell—his immediate commanding officer—when Jackson sent his adjutant, Lieutenant A. S. "Sandie" Pendleton, to summon him forward. Steuart's delay, said Jackson, enabled Banks to make good his retreat, although he finally went into action after an hour's dillydallying before Pendleton sought out Ewell and relayed his command for him to advance. "General Ewell seemed surprised that General Steuart had not gone immediately upon receipt of the order," Pendleton later told Jackson. After a wild extravaganza of celebration and unrestrained hoopla as the Winchester populace welcomed their deliverers, the Valley Army pressed northward after Banks. With Campbell Brown at his side, Ewell and several new staff members turned east toward Charlestown and Harpers Ferry. "At Bolivar Heights. . . . The Maryland regiment had a brilliant affair . . . drew three Yankee regiments off the Heights, took and held them." But Ewell's stay on the Potomac was short-lived, because he was back in Winchester by May 31 after outriders brought word to Stonewall Jackson that several enemy columns were closing on the Valley Army.[39]

If the Valley campaign was a ploy to goad Lincoln into withholding manpower from McClellan's march up the Peninsula, when Jackson plunged into the lower Shenandoah, it was a success. It also elicited a quick response from the Republican president. "I think the evidence now preponderates that Ewell and Jackson are still about Winchester," Abe Lincoln telegraphed Irvin McDowell on May 25 at Manassas Junction. "Assuming this, it is for you, a question of legs. Put on all the speed you can." One day earlier the president had summoned John Fremont to head for Harrisonburg from the west as well as McDowell from northern Virginia. Jackson and Ewell were also confronted with a question of legs as they began a head-long march up the valley to avoid the Fremont-McDowell vise. As he passed through Strasburg on June 1, Ewell traveled with Taylor's brigade a few miles up the Wardensville (present West Virginia) road to confront Fre-mont, who had been diverted from Harrisonburg by the White House. "With the enemy not availing himself of the opportunity of attacking our forces," Ewell said the engagement broke off after a brief skirmish in which neither side incurred losses.[40]

Although heavy rains and mired roads prompted Fremont to disen-gage, Ewell did not force the issue after Jackson admonished him to keep free of a general engagement during the retreat; but it also reinforced his innate pattern of seeking excuses not to commit when left on his own. Moreover, the lead units of McDowell's contingents from the east, headed by Shields, marched into Front Royal on May 31 and made ready to push up the Luray Valley. Once Jackson collected Charles Sydney Winder and the Stonewall Brigade, the Valley Army sped along the pike toward Harrisonburg at the southwesternmost tip of the Massanutten, with Fre-mont in tight pursuit. Ewell later told Joseph E. Johnston that his division "moved up the valley without further incident." With Fremont and Shields unable to unite quickly because of destroyed bridges east of the Massanutten, Jackson and Ewell were south of Harrisonburg by June 7 after a grinding march from the Potomac one hundred miles to the north. The trek had taken a toll on men and horses, even if uneventful—the foot cavalry, which included Ewell's brigades, had earned its laurels on the valley thoroughfare.[41]

As Jackson swung the army around the Massanutten for the sanctu-ary of the Blue Ridge, Ewell became entangled in a hot affair a few miles east of Harrisonburg. Although he brought up the rear, his Fifty-eighth Virginia Infantry, part of W.C. Scott's brigade—then led by George H. Steuart, who had been relieved of his cavalry command—"got entangled with the Pennsylvania 'Buck-Tail Rifles,' and had their hands full until the First Maryland came to their help," writes General James H. Lane. "The fight lasted only half an hour. Our loss was seventy-five, that of the enemy nearer one hundred and fifty. Ashby was killed ten steps in front of the Fifty-eighth Virginia trying to induce them to charge. His horse was killed under him, and he had scarcely disengaged himself and started forward when he too was killed, shot directly through the body—some insisted from behind, but I think not, from what I could learn." Captain Turner Ashby, who was promoted brigadier general without Jackson's second, with his "sad eyes, jet-black hair and flowing beard, his lithe and graceful form mounted upon a superb steed, he was a typical knight of the Golden Horseshoe," Jackson's wife was moved to note. "His daring and intrepid exploits soon shed a romance around his name." When his much-loved brother died early in the war, Ashby became a one-man killing machine with one purpose: to dispatch as many Yankees as humanly possible. And his inordinate hatred of all bluecoats soon became legend throughout the army. Although Jackson did not care for Ashby because of his insistence upon an independent command in the valley, Ewell, like many others, had the highest regard for him as a soldier and a man. "Ewell was deeply moved when Ashby fell, and remained on the field with me untill all the prisoners and wounded men were taken back," General Tom Munford records. "He assisted many of the wounded to mount behind the cavalry, who carried them from the field, and I saw him give what money he had to some of the Maryland troops who were too badly wounded to be carried from the field on horseback." Ewell's well-known compassion certainly extended to his fellow officer: "Unfortunately the gallant Ashby leading as usual the advance was killed he & his horse lying side by side & we had the painful duty of bearing back all that was mortal of as knightly a man as ever bestrode a horse," he told Joseph E. Johnston after the war.[42]

Ashby's stubborn defense on the Harrisonburg road no doubt led to Jackson's successful positioning of the army on the South Fork of Shenandoah during the night of June 7. In two stiff encounters at Cross Keys (June 8) and Port Republic (June 9) Ewell's division played a key, if not vital, role as the historic Valley campaign raced to a climax. The small hamlet of Port Republic at the southern extremity of the Massanutten was situated at the confluence of South and North Rivers that form the easternmost branch of the Shenandoah, while the battle site at the Cross Keys settlement was six miles (according to Ewell) nearer Harrisonburg. Since Jackson concentrated most of his attention on Shields, he left Ewell to face Fremont, who had dogged him for days, from the Valley Pike. On the evening of June 7, Ewell put his second in command, Arnold Elzey, in charge of the division encampment south of Mill Creek—a tributary of North River—as he rode forward to confer with Jackson. But he soon returned to learn that Fremont was pressing his new position and that Elzey had deployed Steuart to the left, himself in the center, and Trimble "at some considerable distance" on the right "across the crest of a long ridge rising from the south bank of Mill Creek." Richard Taylor's brigade had gone forward with Jackson but had been recalled as reserve for the main fight that opened on June 8.[43]

"The enemy opened a heavy art, fire on our centre & marched a strong inf. column to attack Trimble," Ewell told Joe Johnston in his 1866 letter.

> This attack was handsomely repulsed as were several lesser ones on our left centre & Taylor was ordered to report to Trimble with his Brigade to attack and turn the enemy's left (Blenker). Lt. Heindricks top. Eng. had reported a column of the enemy moving to our right that he had seen four reg'l flags and the column was still moving. This caused a little delay but as soon as examined Trimble was directed through my chief of staff Maj. James Barbour to attack with his own & Taylor's Brig & at the same time carrying to the enemy's left—a portion of our troops which pushed forward driving the enemy's skirmishers.

The heaviest Yankee casualties were among a contingent of German recruits from New York led by Louis Blenker, with Julius Stahel's brigade alone losing 427 men in the fight with Trimble. Although nightfall was fast approaching, Trimble, ever the gamecock, wanted to press his rout, but Ewell refused, saying the division would rest in place after repulsing Fremont "so decisively on one wing as to paralyze his army and to secure all the advantages of victory." The resounding triumph at Cross Keys was entirely Ewell's work, and Campbell Brown later told Lizinka that Ewell really wanted a second go at Fremont while he had him "in the hollow of his hand," but it was Jackson himself who restrained him. Ewell had not only sent the luckless Fremont fleeing from the field, but he had also inflicted nearly three times as many killed, wounded, and missing upon the enemy as he suffered himself. In spite of his reticence on other fields, Ewell could act when the occasion demanded.[44]

On June 8, while Ewell was contesting Fremont, Shields had hurled a troop of cavalry from the Luray Valley at Jackson himself; before the ensuing melee ended, Stonewall was nearly captured along with several of his artillery pieces. The untoward incident convinced Old Jack that Shields, not Fremont, was the real threat, and thus he sent word to Ewell not to pursue Fremont from the Cross Keys battlefield but to hold himself in readiness to support operations at Port Republic. Actually, the enemy, under Samuel S. Carroll and Erastus B. Tyler (Shields himself never got beyond Luray) had arrayed themselves around a coaling, or charcoal manufactory, operated by the Lewis family at Lewiston three miles from town on the Port Republic-Luray thoroughfare. The Federal artillery composed of seven guns had been positioned on a small hillock (actually the coaling) that swept the entire field from "a spur of the Blue Ridge to the South Fork of the Shenandoah." Carroll and Tyler had their infantry brigades entrenched behind a country lane that stretched along Still House Run to a gristmill owned by the Lewis clan and situated on the river.[45]

When Jackson opened the fight on June 9 by advancing across a wheat field in front of the Federals, Tyler's guns atop the coaling soon found their range as well as the Yankee riflemen in front at the foot of the hill. The famed Stonewall Brigade under "Charlie" Winder in particular was nearly cut to pieces before Ewell came up from Cross Keys; "but Jackson," finds historian James I. Robertson, "seemingly oblivious to the plight of his old brigade, sent Taylor's men double-timing to the right to turn the Federal battery." Although he had left two brigades behind as a foil to Fremont beyond the river, other units from Ewell's division quickly went into action in support of Jackson's hard-pressed troopers. Campbell Brown told his mother that events "hung on a thread & finally decided in our favor by two Regiments [the 58th & 44th], which had been previously repulsed, but were met by Genl. Ewell as they retired from the field, reformed by his personal exertions & thrown upon the enemy's flank at the critical moment." Taylor's Tigers had a hard fight on the coaling and were nearly driven from the hillock, but, he writes, "at this moment our batteries in my rear opened fire and re-enforcements coming up, led by Major-General Ewell, the battle [was] decided in our favor, and the enemy precipitately fled." Not only had Ewell's division tipped the balance at Port Republic, but Ewell himself had also been highly visible on the field, directing his men and even firing one of the captured Federal pieces at the hightailing enemy. But it was Stonewall who had called the shots, not Ewell.[46]

As the Yankees scurried up the valley toward Luray with Jackson in hot pursuit, the Valley campaign of 1862 came to a close. Although Ewell made an obvious contribution to Jackson's success, starting with the decision to ignore Johnston's demand that he come east with his division, the two may not have parted the campaign amicably. Neither man mentioned the other in their several battle reports on Cross Keys and Port Republic— gone were Ewell's flowery references to Jackson in his assessment of Winchester. Robert K. Krick, an exacting student of the campaign, relates an episode in which Ewell watched "a gallant Federal officer" on a white horse race back and forth in front of the Confederate lines, and at some risk to himself he did likewise, asking his men to spare the daring Yankee: "A day or so later, when General Jackson learned of the incident, he sent for General Ewell and told him not to do such a thing again; this was no ordinary war and the gallant Federal officers were the very kind that must be killed."

Ewell had little choice but hold his counsel when dealing with the irate "major general, commanding." And perhaps the confrontation explains an outburst by Campbell Brown when he complained about Ewell's timidity to Lizinka:

> I wish that one defect in the temper of our chief could be remedied, but it is one common to all his family, & I suppose is past all cure. He sees very plainly the good that might be done by a little more common sense in the control of our movements, but having formed an idea that his advice will be ungraciously received & perhaps his interference rebuked; he refuses to interpose in any way. Don't you say a word to him about my having written you any such thing as this, for it is after all only my own conclusion from what I see & know.

A dressing down by a superior officer would irk almost any soldier, but by looking the other way Ewell was admittedly able to cooperate in two future campaigns with Jackson. His success in the valley resulted from his close proximity to Jackson after May 20 when the two had combined forces at New Market, and, of equal importance, he was learning the art of graceful subservience when confronted with higher authority. In short, he had become a yes-man, who found great difficulty in making decisions beyond the reach of his immediate superiors.[47]

Chapter 7

IN FRONT OF RICHMOND

After the round of fighting with Shields and Fremont, the Valley Army, including Ewell's division, lay encamped around Weyer's Cave—an old-time watering place for Virginia aristocrats, near the Port Republic battle-field. Although this bivouac was short-lived, Richard Taylor emphasizes that he renewed many pleasant chats with his old comrade but says Ewell was eccentric as ever. It was time to talk around the campfire, Taylor continues, because his brigade and indeed the division "in twenty days marched over two hundred miles, fought in five actions, of which three were severe, and several skirmishes, and, though it had suffered heavy loss in officers and men, was yet strong, hard as nails, and full of confidence." But there was little time for rest, because by Sunday, June 15, Ewell and his men had moved to Staunton and the Virginia Central Railroad on the first leg of a notable tramp to unite with Lee's army in front of Richmond. During a two-day stopover in the Augusta County town, Campbell Brown told his mother that he had spent twenty-five dollars on a new pair of boots for Ewell. Unquestionably the Confederates under Ewell and Jackson had achieved a great success in the heavy campaigning along the Shenandoah, and more glory days lay ahead in the marshy, low country beyond the capital, but all was not well with the Southern war effort. "I am writing this with a pen without any point to it, consequently my hand is not exactly the same as usual, I being obliged to adapt myself to the caprices of the case & to write any way the pen will," noted Campbell Brown from Staunton. Civilian scarcities must have been invading the chief town of the upper valley when a divisional staff officer could not obtain a simple writing tool.[1]

153

By June 17 the army was on its way toward the Blue Ridge crossings and the fighting around Richmond to what became known as the Seven Days campaign. And though the common soldier remained full of vigor, Ewell's outward composure may have masked a lingering antipathy for Jackson. Just three days after Jackson's reprimand over the gallant Yankee incident, Old Jack, secretive as ever, suddenly left his command and headed east. Before his departure he told Ewell only to keep his division going toward Charlottesville. Ewell, who was nominally second in command, no doubt dredging up old hurts, blew his stack when he learned that Jackson had not only confided in John Harman, his commissary officer, but also placed the Reverend Robert Lewis Dabney in charge of the eastward trek.[2]

Although evidence is lacking that Ewell was jealous of Dabney, a Presbyterian clergyman who later conducted Jackson's funeral, he was a strange choice to conduct the march. The divine possessed no military training, yet Jackson placed great confidence in Dabney, whom he regarded as a kindred spirit. The two had met in the early 1850s when Old Jack first arrived in Lexington as professor of natural history in the Virginia Military Institute and Dabney was a prominent Presbyterian theologian. Highly educated at Hampden-Sydney, the University of Virginia, and the Union Theological Seminary, Dabney had taught at the latter academy after 1853. Dr. Hunter McGuire, who removed Ewell's leg two years later, however, thought the forty-two-year-old preacher/scholar should never have been named to Jackson's staff. Not only was he ill-suited for the rigors of camp life, but his dress and manner evoked guffaws among the ranks. "The doctor wore the Prince Albert coat to which he had become accustomed, and he also carried an umbrella of a dull brown or bluish color." When Dabney shortly resigned to resume his seminary duties, Jackson replaced him with young A. S. "Sandie" Pendleton, son of Lee's artillery chief, William Nelson Pendleton. After the war Dabney left Virginia to join the new University of Texas, where he continued his writing of religious and philosophical books. He also published an 1866 biography of Jackson that to the present day has remained the bedrock source of all biographical material on Stonewall Jackson.[3]

When the army crossed into the Piedmont, Ewell's division was in the van with instructions to follow country roads parallel to the railroad through Charlottesville and Gordonsville. Dabney, who survived until 1898, told Harvey Hill after the war that he traveled with Ewell when Jackson suddenly departed, saying he would return in due time. "I dined that day [June 19] with General Ewell, and I remember that he complained to me with some bitterness of General Jackson's reserve." Then, continues Dabney's account: "'How, now, the general has gone off on the railroad without entrusting to me, his senior major-general, any order, or other hint whither we are going; but Harman, the quartermaster enjoys his full confidence, I suppose, for I hear that he is telling the troops that we are going to Richmond to fight McClellan.'" As for the ultimate destination of their march, everyone, including the lowest private in the ranks, could guess that the Valley Army was needed to help Lee on the Peninsula. Edward A. Moore, who crossed the Blue Ridge at Rockfish Gap with the Rockbridge Artillery, says flat out that their destination "was now evident." Still, Dabney sought to reassure Ewell by commenting that Harman was only guessing and did not have information beyond camp scuttlebutt. And, he told Hill, "'You may be certain General Ewell . . . that you stand higher in General Jackson's confidence than any one else.'"[4]

Although Campbell Brown allows Ewell and the army did not know with certainty they were going to Richmond until they reached Gordonsville on the twentieth, a linkup of the Valley Army and Lee's force in front of the capital had been in the works for some weeks. As early as April 29, more than a month earlier, Jackson had mentioned to Lee that "if necessary [he could] cross the Blue Ridge to Warrenton, Fredericksburg, or any other threatened point."[5] Then, in late May, following his victory over Banks at Winchester, while the army was in the lower Shenandoah, Jackson had hurried his confidant A. R. Boteler to Richmond with a scheme to cross the Potomac into Pennsylvania. However, his idea to launch a northern invasion with forty thousand men brought the retort from Lee, according to Dabney: "First you must help me drive these people away from Richmond." Lee, who had been in command of the army since June 1 and the wounding of Joseph E. Johnston at Seven Pines, began to act in mid-June. Although they did not reach Staunton until the fifteenth, Lee ordered units under Alexander R. Lawton, William H. C. Whiting, and John Bell Hood to the valley as reinforcements for Jackson. The troops that left Richmond on June 11 were intended as a boisterous ruse to deceive the Federals and were immediately returned without stepping down from the railroad.[6]

"Leave your enfeebled troops to watch the country and guard the passes covered by your cavalry and artillery, and with your main body, including Ewell's division and Whiting's and Lawton's commands, move rapidly to Ashland by rail or otherwise," Lee's communiqué of June 11 informed Jackson. Throughout the Shenandoah fighting Jackson had co-operated intuitively with Lee—acting as adviser to President Davis—to worry Lincoln into withholding additional troops from McClellan's drive up the Peninsula. Now Lee needed his active participation to defeat the national enemy, and, Jackson, as close-mouthed as ever, had not bothered to confide his plans—certainly not to Ewell. On June 18, while Dabney employed his best ministerial charm to reassure Ewell, Jackson was in Waynesboro perfecting his plans for the eastward move; and when he rejoined the army on June 20 he was as secretive as ever. Although the fresh troops sent by Lee rode "the cars" from Staunton, Ewell's brigades and the remainder of the valley command tramped across the Blue Ridge. "No general knew better than he [Jackson] how to employ the transportation of a railroad in combination with the marching of an army," Dabney relates. "While the burthen trains forwarded his stores, he caused the passenger trains to proceed to the rear of his line of march, and take up the hindmost of his brigades. These were forwarded in a couple of hours, a whole's day march, when they were sat down, and the trains returned again to take up the hindmost, and give them a like assistance."[7]

The journey to Richmond was not without its lighter moments. At Walker's Church, between Charlottesville and Gordonsville, the locals turned out to prepare a feast for the passing Confederates. Pressed though he was, Ewell "compromised by halting each regiment for a short time" so that his "tired and dirty" troopers could partake of the largess. In order to prevent a stampede, Ewell insisted that a bevy of "pretty girls" who had gathered around the church remain behind a picket fence to dispense their food and "buttermilk." Another young lady, Miss Louisa H. K. Minor, recounted a great excitement when part of the army passed her Albemarle County home, "Pant Ops." She even had to give up her bed to several of Jackson's officers during their brief stay. When Ewell, accompanied by Arnold Elzey, spent an evening visiting in the family parlor, Miss Minor noted in her diary that she "enjoyed his company because he had the heart and simplicity of a child." But pleasant diversions along the way soon terminated as Ewell's overriding orders remained marching at the double-quick. By June 22 the army had reached Fredericks Hall, a few miles beyond Louisa, where Jackson called a halt for rest and divine services led by the Reverend Dabney and his fellow chaplains.[8]

Jackson again disappeared and made his way to Lee's headquarters in the Widow Dabbs House on the Nine Mile Road east of Richmond to plot the campaign. Also, on the twenty-second, Dabney addressed a letter to Ewell ordering him "to move your command to Beaver Dam, with

Cunningham's, if cars enough." Lieutenant Colonel Richard H. Cunningham had taken charge of John R. Jones's brigade composed of the Twenty-first, Forty-second, and Forty-eighth Virginia as well as the First Virginia Irish Brigade and two artillery batteries under W. E. Cutshaw and William H. Caskie. Although Cunningham shortly relinquished command when Jones recovered from a brief illness, Ewell was told further: "Your baggage train must reach Beaver Dam by tomorrow night."

A mile or so south of the South Anna, a tributary of the Pamunkey River, Beaver Dam was a mere way station on the Virginia Central Railroad before its junction with the Richmond and Fredericksburg from the north. Ewell's division with the remainder of Jackson's command traveled south by rail until it reached Ashland, immediately north of Richmond, on the twenty-fifth. Here, the army was on the Chickahominy northwest of Mechanicsville, and though Jackson was yet silent, its movements under Dabney were in keeping with Lee's communiqué of June 11 ordering it from the Shenandoah. Upon reaching Ashland, Old Jack had been told to "sweep down between the Chickahominy and Pamunkey, cutting up the enemy's communications, etc., while this army [Lee's] attacks General McClellan through the front." Although Ewell remained in the dark because of Jackson's secretiveness, Lee, with surprising foresight, had already formulated his basic strategy for driving the abolitionist hordes from the capital.[9]

The Valley Army, accustomed to the well-defined Valley Pike, with the Allegheny Front and Blue Ridge for constant reference points, soon encountered difficulty when it entered the swampy lowlands of the Peninsula. Bounded by the estuaries of the James and Pamunkey/York Rivers, the Peninsula of Virginia is dissected by the Chickahominy, a sluggish, marshy stream that originates northwest of Richmond and makes its way to the James about ten miles east of Williamsburg. Its chief feeder is White Oak Swamp Creek, another boggy waterway flowing eastward until it strikes the Chickahominy southeast of the Richmond and York Railroad, which makes its way to White House at the meeting of the Mattapony and Pamunkey. Together the two streams dominate the Peninsula landscape. South of the Chickahominy the Peninsula is transversed by several pathways: the Nine Mile Road, where Lee made his headquarters, from Richmond to Fair Oaks; the Williamsburg Pike, running through Seven Pines and crossing the Chickahominy at Bottom's Bridge; the Charles City Road, south of White Oak Swamp; and the New Market Road, which hugged the James and ran past a rise known as Malvern Hill. The Mechanicsville

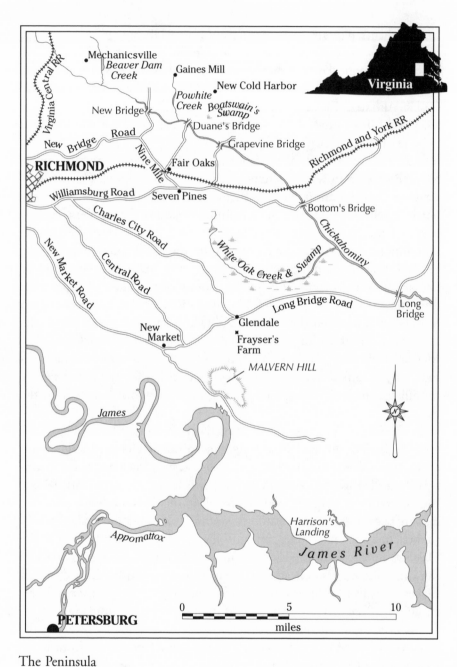

The Peninsula

Pike was north of the river. From northwest to southeast in the Richmond area, the Chickahominy was spanned by six bridges—New, Duane's, Grapevine, Lower, Bottom's, and Long—and most, if not all, played a key role for both armies in the ensuing campaign.

After landing on April 2 at Fortress Monroe at the tip of the Peninsula, McClellan had first chased John Bankhead Magruder and then Joe Johnston eastward until the fight at Fair Oaks/Seven Pines on May 31. Although Little Mac later shifted his base of operations to White House and tramped along the Richmond and York toward the capital, Lee was not ready for a confrontation until Jeb Stuart found that Fitz-John Porter was isolated north of the Chickahominy from the main Yankee force. While Ewell led his division east from Ashland, Lee called his chief lieutenants, including Jackson, to his Dabbs House headquarters for a session on how best to concentrate against the hapless Porter. The Valley Army under Jackson and Ewell was soon handed the crucial task of attacking Porter from the north while A. P. Hill crossed the Chickahominy from the south. Daniel Harvey Hill and James Longstreet were summoned to cross the river in support of A. P. Hill and Jackson once the upper bridges were firmly in Confederate hands. As the fight with Porter developed, the remainder of McClellan's army in front of Richmond would be held in check by Benjamin Huger and Magruder.[10]

Lee's initial scheme, which devolved upon the precise movement of disparate units, went awry from the beginning when Jackson failed to reach his designated position at the appointed hour. At the Dabbs House conference, largely at the suggestion of Longstreet, it was agreed that Jackson would open the engagement "during the morning of the 26th" and that A. P. Hill would press Porter upon hearing the roar of Old Jack's guns. Although Jackson assured Lee and his fellow commanders that he anticipated no difficulty, the Valley Army did not reach the field until 5:00 P.M.[11]

"Near Ashland we again saw Genl. Jackson & found ourselves in communication with Lee's army," writes Brown. "The march thro the 'Slashes of Hanover' began before day & was a strange & dreary one—simply on account of the flat, swampy, dense nature of the country with no extended views, almost no population." Further complicating the drive forward was an encounter with Branch's brigade of A. P. Hill's division. "Near Crenshaw's the road on which the column commanded by Major-General Ewell (of Jackson's) was advancing and that on which I was advancing, approached within one fourth of a mile of each other," noted Branch, who had been ordered across the Chickahominy to invest the

Mechanicsville road. "The heads of our columns reached the point simultaneously, and after a short personal interview between General Ewell and myself, we proceeded on our respective routes." As Brown tells the story, Ewell and "Major Nelson" had an amusing "adventure with a belligerent wagon driver whose team they stumbled across in the dark" during the march.[12]

Meanwhile, A. P. Hill, miffed at Jackson's late arrival, crossed the Chickahominy on his own initiative to open the fight with Porter. After a raging battle that included reinforcements from south of the river, the resultant Battle of Mechanicsville became an indecisive contest before Porter withdrew behind his fortifications beyond a local stream called Beaver Dam Creek. Then, strangely, as Jackson approached from the north past the Green Pole Church, he ordered the Valley Army to set up camp around a crossroads intersection called Hundley's Corner. Captain William T. Poague, in charge of the Rockbridge Artillery, and others in Jackson's force reported musketry and heavy firing toward the southwest, where A. P. Hill's men were finishing the affair at Mechanicsville. Hundley's Corner was about "two and a half miles as the crow flies from [Joseph R.] Anderson's brigade at the end of Hill's line across Old Church Road." It was also roughly five miles north of a soon-to-be notorious gristmill owned by Dr. William G. Gaines located on Powhite Creek, a stream parallel to and east of Beaver Dam Creek. Although a nearly exhausted Jackson, who had covered more than fifty miles in two days, was in no mood to hurl his men into battle, he ordered Ewell to send several detachments forward when Yankee outriders were discovered on his front.[13]

Ewell says in his battle report that the ensuing action was initiated "by the major general commanding," and that he responded by sending the First Maryland and Thirteenth Virginia against the intruding horsemen. While Brown reported "heavy fighting" about dark, Dabney insists the Hundley's Corner set-to flared up when the Federals came up to Jackson's bivouac. According to Bradley Tyler Johnson, the Marylanders under him "immediately drove them in, and upon their receiving re-enforcements and making a stand, I took Companies A and D and drove them over Beaver Dam Creek" on direct orders from Ewell. "[H]aving thus gained a hill commanding the other side of the creek," Johnson continues, "I was ordered by Major-General Jackson to hold it and take two pieces of artillery under my command and disperse the enemy, who appeared in some force beyond it. This was done and I bivouacked on the hill in reach of their guns." The skirmish developed, relates Colonel John F. Farnsworth,

Eighth Illinois Cavalry, because the enemy was afraid that Ewell's men advancing down the Green Pole Road "would inevitably have cutoff the rear of the forces under General [John F.] Reynolds," who made up Porter's extreme right or northernmost flank. Yet Jackson, who remained well away from the two armies that confronted each other across Beaver Dam Creek, was in clear charge with the onset of darkness; it was Jackson, not Ewell, who parceled out troop positions for the night.[14]

After the Hundley's Corner/Mechanicsville scrap on the twenty-sixth, McClellan made two fateful decisions: He resolved to shift his base of op- erations at White House on the York to the James, and, gripped with fear that Jackson was bearing down on him from the north, he directed Porter to withdraw eastward to a new position on Powhite Creek. Actually, Porter established himself along a broad arc between the Powhite and Boatswain's Swamp, another southern-flowing tributary of the Chickahominy. On the morning of June 27 the Yankee line extended along a plateau called Turkey Hill overlooking the swamp, extending from near the Chickahominy to Cold Harbor—a distance approaching two thousand yards. At their clos- est point, matching Federal and Confederate lines were about fifteen hun- dred yards southeast of Dr. Gaines's house and mill, thus the name of the battle.[15]

With the order to march on the morning of Gaines Mill neither Jack- son nor Ewell had a fixed idea of the terrain ahead, and if Ewell was con- fused and slow to action it was because Jackson himself had a similar mindset. "Vine-draped woods obscured the right side of the road and dust rose in thick clouds over the columns," notes Clifford Dowdey. It was a trying march, which frightened officers and men alike in a strange country infested with lurking enemy snipers. As Jackson plunged farther south— guided by two troopers from Jeb Stuart's cavalry who were native to the area—Ewell's division led the way, followed by those of Whiting and Winder.[16] The group was spearheaded by Bradley T. Johnson, who put the Thirteenth Virginia and Sixth Louisiana "out in front as Skirmishers" un- til it reached an intersection at the Walnut Grove Church. Lee too had arrived at the church, and after a hurried conference with Jackson it was determined that Ewell and the Valley Army "would turn Powhite Creek" after changing their direction from south to east. But a detour of a mile or so to the millpond of Dr. Gaines revealed that Porter was not on the Powhite but farther east on the Boatswain, which necessitated a time-consuming reverse march.

Although Ewell's formal report is silent about the trek, his brigades soon made contact with D. H. Hill's division near Old Cold Harbor. "We passed thro various Federal camps, and after a long tramp, made more trying by our frequent halts and the suspense of our situation . . . we came upon D. H. Hill's divs," Brown confirms. "When we did so, heavy firing was going on ahead and I suppose we had marched ten miles or more [from Hundley's Corner] and that it was two o'clock." Dowdey, a careful student of the campaign, allows that Jackson arrived at three in the afternoon and that he "looked tired and ill-humored"—and that he was lethargic. As Ewell prepared to enter the fray with Fitz-John Porter, it is very likely that he was influenced by Jackson's frame of mind, though he was only one of three divisional chiefs under his direction.[17]

When he marched to the west at Cold Harbor, Ewell became enmeshed in Lee's order of battle to confront Porter. When finalized it called for Longstreet to hold the extreme right nearest the Chickahominy. A. P. Hill and the Light Division held the center or a position to the left of Longstreet. The Valley Army, which did not come on the field until nearly four o'clock, occupied Lee's left, with D. H. Hill—later under Jackson's command—holding the easternmost flank. Since Ewell and B. T. Johnson once more led Jackson's columns from the Walnut Grove Church and arrived first, he was "met by Colonel [Walter] Taylor of General Lee's staff, sent to bring up re-enforcements, and received directions for the march of [his] division." As Ewell "moved in the direction of heavy firing" because A. P. Hill and Longstreet had already engaged the foe, he deployed his brigades between those of D. H. Hill on his left and William H. C. Whiting of A. P. Hill's division on his right.[18]

Arnold Elzey's brigade—all Virginians except the Twelfth Georgia—went into line first on Ewell's extreme left next to Roswell S. Ripley's brigade of D. H. Hill's division. Ewell accordingly directed Bradley Johnson's Maryland Line to remain in support of Elzey, which it did "until between 5 and 6 p.m., when Major-General Jackson ordered me to take my regiment into action." Again Jackson intervened directly to position Ewell's troops, and Johnson elaborates: "I went in about the central point of fire." Yet Ewell was not above bypassing Jackson when the opportunity presented itself. When Elzey was slow getting into place, he later reported, "I took advantage of the interval to report to General Lee, who ordered me to hurry up my division as rapidly as possible, indicating where it was to take part in the action."

Ewell thereupon placed Trimble and his five regiments to the right of Elzey; Isaac G. Seymour, who had taken charge of the Louisiana troops from Richard Taylor, occupied the extreme right. Interestingly, when the main fight developed, all of Ewell's men were removed from Boatswain's Creek while the units of Gouverneur K. Warren and Charles S. Lovell of Sykes division faced them on the other side of the stream at the foot of Turkey Hill. All three of his brigades—Elzey, Trimble, and Seymour—were placed between Charles S. Winder and the brigade of Maxey Gregg under A. P. Hill. Ewell's brigades, however, would join the fray in short order.[19]

In the late afternoon, as Longstreet, the two Hills, and Jackson threw their legions against Porter, Ewell played a significant role in handing Robert E. Lee his first concrete victory. Although A. P. Hill and Longstreet had already engaged the enemy, Jackson and Ewell were needed to cave in Porter's right flank. But the Confederate thrusts were piecemeal until an all-out assault by the Texans under John Bell Hood of William H. C. Whiting's command tipped the scale in Lee's favor. "Having crossed the branch and commenced the ascent of the hill, my division became warmly engaged with the enemy," Ewell noted in his skimpy report. "The density of the woods and the nature of the ground were such as to prevent any extended view; and this fact together with the importance of holding the position occupied by the Louisiana Brigade, and that portion of Trimble's which was on its left, now severely pressed by the enemy, made it necessary to confine my exertions mainly to that locality." Despite Ewell's claims, most scholars agree with historian Emory M. Thomas that "the break came first where it was least expected, in the center of Porter's line. . . . Credit for the breakthrough is given usually to Brigadier General John Bell Hood's brigade. They held their fire as they approached and suffered their losses without responding. But they continued to advance. The Southern troops were on the verge of using bayonets when the first rank of Federals fled. Then Hood's men commenced firing, moving forward, and firing again. At last they crashed through and saw before them a steady retreat by blue coated soldiers from many sections of the front."

Ewell later recorded that Hood, assisted by Wade Hampton, "came to my assistance, and rendered valuable assistance in keeping back the enemy, until the arrival of General Lawton enabled our forces to take the initiative." Although the Federal cavalry, led by Philip St. George Cooke, Ewell's old superior from the frontier, mounted a futile countercharge to thwart the oncoming Texans, the Battle of Gaines Mill was over when Hood's men reached the plateau atop Turkey Hill at the onset of darkness. Ewell's brigades suffered badly in the fight, including two of Trimble's regiments that "lost one of every five men" on the twenty-seventh. Arnold Elzey was shot in the face but recovered to fight another day after a long convalescence. Also among Ewell's officers killed was Colonel Seymour, the Louisiana editor whose son was jailed by Benjamin F. Butler for running a memorial piece about his father in a New Orleans newspaper. Lee lost eighty-seven hundred men to Porter's sixty-eight hundred in the daylong struggle as the sorely chastened Unionists fled across the Chickahominy. "[T]he enemy in overpowering numbers forced our troops to retire and took possession of our former ground," wrote Major Lovell, Tenth United States Infantry, in his own battle summary.[20]

Both Ewell and Brown leave little doubt that Ewell was active on the battleground. He "seemed to be everywhere," an early biographer posits, and as they sought to clear the woods along Boatswain Creek, Ewell yelled out, "Hurrah for Georgia!" with sword raised when Lawton's three thousand Confederates rushed to his aid at a critical moment. "I remained on the ground myself until after dark, in order that the troops which came up later might profit by what I had learned of the ground and the position of the enemy," Ewell later said. And his praise for others under his command who fought mightily throughout the day knew no bounds. When he rode across the field urging his comrades forward with enemy bullets whizzing around his head, John F. Trentlen, lieutenant colonel of Trimble's Fifteenth Alabama, later wrote that Ewell "displayed the most indomitable courage." And later in the evening, Ewell sent Brown to locate and fetch Private Frank Champion, also of the Fifteenth Alabama. During the melee near Boatswain Creek, when Ewell threw caution to the wind and rode among his lines trying "to instill a similar courage in his men," "young Champion"—Brown's words—had grabbed an abandoned horse and galloped into the fray, Ewell said, "very conspicuous[ly] rallying the troops." Nor was Ewell disturbed that Private Champion had impersonated an officer during his outburst.

Finally, as Brown relates the tale, Ewell did not escape unscathed. After a return from some errand of command, "I met Genl. Ewell on foot, his splendid chestnut sorrel mare 'Maggie' having just been killed under him," Brown writes. "He was limping slightly from a spent ball which had entered his boot & glanced around his leg." While sitting by the roadway, Ewell removed the flattened bullet that had apparently struck a tree before ricocheting against his boot. He was none the worse for his injury, however, because he immediately dispatched Brown to find Champion and to locate Lee and Jackson for additional instructions as the evening wore down.

Just as he sat down with several staff officers to eat his first meal of the day, the Georgian Roswell Ripley rode into his bivouac and was invited to share his meager fare. As a result, Brown became the odd man out and had to wait until the next day for his own food.[21]

When Saturday, June 28, arrived troops involved in the Gaines Mill fight enjoyed a day of rest and sorting out, with the exception of Ewell's division. Until Sunday, Confederate forces were still clustered about the same field, although McClellan had pulled his forces south of the Chickahominy. President Davis was on hand to confer with Lee, but both men remained unaware that the Unionists were in the process of shifting their supply base to the James. Lee's entire strategy changed from the instant he learned that McClellan was wending his way through White Oak Swamp toward the protection of his gunboats at Harrison's Landing. The campaign to save Richmond thereupon became a southwestward race or maneuver to crush the Yankee war machine while it remained on the Peninsula. Before the great swing in Confederate movement, Lee, intent upon severing McClellan's link with the York, summoned Jackson to his headquarters and ordered him to send the cavalry under Jeb Stuart to burn the railhead at Despatch Station.

Ewell, already on Lee's northern flank, was told to accompany Stuart: "I advanced, preceded by a cavalry force, down the north bank of the Chickahominy to Dispatch [sic] Station, and destroyed a portion of the railroad," reads Ewell's report on the operation. "The station and stores had, unfortunately, been burned by the cavalry advance guard before my arrival." Ewell was correct; Jeb Stuart's horsemen occupied Despatch Station before noon and promptly set about wrecking the railroad with abandon. Retreating Federals had already destroyed the middle section of the railroad span. When his division left Cold Harbor before daybreak for the eight-mile trek, W. H. F. "Rooney" Lee, second eldest son of Robert E. Lee, was ordered to spearhead Ewell's march. Bradley T. Johnson and the Maryland Line once more took the van, this time behind Rooney Lee and the Ninth Virginia Cavalry. Other than ripping up additional parts of the Richmond and York, Ewell had little to do. The cavalry, however, upon learning that Generals George Stoneman and William H. Emory had sped toward White House on the Pamunkey, tore after the scampering enemy with gusto.[22]

Although Jeb Stuart was perplexed to find the railroad bridge so lightly defended, he quickly relayed information to Lee that McClellan's planned withdrawal was in operation. "Yankee wagons to the number of five thousand, loaded with everything that could be carried, was set on their way across White Oak Swamp," writes Alexander Webb. "Twenty-five hundred head of cattle on the hoof were added to this long column. . . . Lines of fire marked the camps and depots of the Union troops. Millions of rations, hundreds of tons of fixed ammunition and shells for the siege guns were thus lost." Not everything could be carried away, so Ewell's men, as Percy Gatling Hamlin puts it, "for many days dined in luxury on dessicated [*sic*] vegetables washed down by the coffee of Java." While destruction of the railroad proceeded, a troop of Union cavalry appeared, and though chased by a squad under William W. Goldsborough, Ewell decided it was not worth an all-out fight and halted the intrepid Marylander.[23]

A remarkable episode of the war occurred at Despatch Station—Richard Taylor called it "a queer event"—about dark while Ewell was gathering his brigades for the march to Bottom's Bridge, a mile or so down the Chickahominy. At Savage Station, closer to Richmond, where John Bankhead Magruder confronted the enemy south of the river, the Federals packed a train with all manner of guns and ammunition—everything they could not use on their march to the James—and launched it at full throttle. Indeed, men and officers of both armies stood transfixed at the fireworks. Although many have written about the errant locomotives, none surpasses the account left by General Taylor, who watched the convulsion with Ewell: "[G]athering speed [the train] came rushing on, two engines drawing a long string of carriages. Reaching the bridge, the engines exploded with terrific noise, followed in succession by explosions of the carriages, laden with ammunition. Shells burst in all directions, the river lashed with foam, trees torn for acres around." Taylor adds that several of his Louisiana boys were wounded during the upheaval.[24]

Ewell intuitively knew that a wrecked train laden with munitions indicated the enemy was abandoning its positions north of the river; and according to several sources, he too called for a withdrawal in pursuit. After spending the night of June 28 near Despatch Station, Ewell noted: "About noon on Sunday [June 29] I was ordered to prevent the enemy from crossing Bottom's Bridge and took position accordingly until about 6 p.m., when I received directions to return to Grapevine Bridge and follow General Jackson's [Winder's] division." Bottom's Bridge, across the Chickahominy, was less than a mile east of the famed railroad crossing of the Richmond and York, but it was directly north and connected by road to White Oak Swamp on the pathway to Harrison's Landing. Grapevine Bridge was roughly four miles east (upstream) and very near the Gaines

Mill battleground. It was situated on the road through Savage Station and White Oak Swamp but had been destroyed during Porter's retreat the previous night. Although Ewell's terse entry in the *Official Records* is silent about his movements on the thirtieth, Richard Taylor, traveling in an ambulance "to husband [his] little strength," maintains the division moved upstream about sunset and tramped over Grapevine Bridge, which had been rebuilt under Jackson's guidance during the twenty-ninth. Taylor adds that Ewell's men bivouacked just south of the Chickahominy in a heavy downpour that "converted the ground into a lake."[25]

Ewell had waited the entire day at Despatch Station and Bottom's Bridge, because a lackadaisical Jackson chose to take his time rebuilding the Grapevine Bridge. Although he was not summoned until late in the day, Ewell had no part in spanning the fifteen-foot Chickahominy, but men in his division reported hearing the roar of battle from the east throughout the day. What Ewell's brigades heard was John Bankhead Magruder fighting Edwin V. Sumner and Samuel P. Heintzelman at Savage Station on the railroad nearer Richmond. Earlier strategy sessions involving Lee, Jackson, Longstreet, and A. P. Hill called for a concerted attack designed to pound the Federal right before it reached the swamp. Longstreet and A. P. Hill were to cross by New Bridge upriver from Grapevine and loop behind Magruder to halt the retreat. General A. L. Long, later biographer of Lee and his aide during the war, says flat out that "Jackson was directed to cross the Chickahominy and relieve Magruder in pursuit." When the flash point arrived, however, Jackson left Magruder to face the fury alone. Poor Magruder—nervous, highly agitated, and probably intoxicated after his retreat up the Peninsula following his earlier triumph at Big Bethel—fought alone until the Federal withdrawal with the onset of darkness. Even though Jackson had Whiting and Winder with him in plain sight of Magruder's uneven struggle and Ewell was nearby at Bottom's Bridge, Stonewall made no effort to span the river until late in the evening.[26]

When Magruder had advanced along the railroad to open the Savage Station fight, he was accompanied by a "monster cannon" mounted on a flat car that "blasted holes in Sumner's ranks." Most of the fighting was done by Joseph B. Kershaw's brigade of South Carolinians. Ewell, like others, could hear Magruder's raging fight but could do nothing as long as Jackson maintained his hard-to-explain indolence. "The commander of [Magruder's] left [D. R. Jones] realizing the importance of action and the necessity of additional troops, called upon General Jackson to co-operate on his left, but Jackson reported that he had other important duties to perform," Longstreet wrote in his postwar account. "The affair, therefore, against odds too strong for Magruder, so that he was forced back without important results for the Confederates, the Federals making safe passage of the crossing and gaining position to defend against pursuit in that quarter." And Kenneth B. Williams, a conscientious student of the Northern war machine concludes: "If Jackson had repaired the Grapevine Bridge . . . as early as Lee expected and joined forces with General Magruder, Sumner and Franklin would have been in difficulty. But the danger passed and during the night the Second and Sixth Corps crossed the swamp and destroyed the bridges." Ewell showed no inclination to assist Magruder on his own, and it was probably just as well that he avoided the Savage Station fight. When his division did resume its southward trek on Monday, June 30, it encountered not only dead comrades and mangled horses but also great confusion and disorientation among Magruder's ranks.[27]

After McClellan withdrew across White Oak Swamp and wrecked its passageways, he arrayed his forces in an inverted "L" formation extending from a rise called Malvern Hill northward through Frayser's Farm (or Glendale) to the very edge of the swamp itself.[28] With Erasmus D. Keyes and Porter on the extreme southern flank at Malvern Hill, Heintzelman and Franklin held the line to White Oak Creek; W. E. Smith and Israel B. Richardson occupied the short arm of the "L" opposite Jackson and Ewell's line of approach from the north. Many historians agree that Lee had a marvelous opportunity to crush the Federal army on June 30, but inadequate commanders again cost him a stunning victory. In a show of concentrated attack, Longstreet and A. P. Hill opened the contest by ramming John Sedgwick and George A. McCall of Heintzelman's corps, who held the Federal line about the middle of McClellan's upside down "L." At no time did Lee get more than twenty thousand of the hoped-for seventy thousand effectives into the fray when Magruder, Benjamin Huger, and especially Jackson, who went to sleep with a biscuit in his mouth, did not come to his aid because of various reasons.[29]

Although William Swinton argues that Jackson (with Ewell at his side) "was impotent to help" from his position north of the swamp, he did open with his artillery—if somewhat blindly—against Smith's and Richardson's divisions. Upon approaching the swamp, Colonel Stapleton Crutchfield, Jackson's artillery chief, had called up twenty-three cannon from the outfits of William H. C. Whiting and Daniel H. Hill. "[A]bout 1:45 p.m., we opened upon the enemy who had no previous intimation of our position and intention," he said. "The [bluecoats] only fired four shots in reply and then abandoned their position in extreme confusion." Others, however, had an entirely different assessment of Jackson's cannonade, which did not involve Ewell's batteries. Crusty Isaac Trimble wrote that the Valley Army did not reach the swamp until four in the afternoon, more than two hours after Crutchfield's account, "where after an hour's engagement with artillery, General Jackson's army bivouacked for the night, including General Whiting's division." But it was Longstreet's artilleryman Colonel Edward Porter Alexander who recorded the most scathing condemnation of Jackson and, by implication, Ewell. When Crutchfield's guns roared at the unseen foe, "that absurd farce of war was played, our guns firing at the enemy's sound & their guns firing at ours." What is worse, Alexander continued, "all four divisions of infantry laid there all day in the roads & never fired a shot." He then says bluntly that "never before or after, did the fates put such a prize within our reach," at the same time Jackson had his men fashion a crude footbridge across White Oak Swamp Creek.[30]

Jackson's bombardment may have kept Smith and Richardson from the Yankee center as it was being driven by Longstreet and Hill. Later, when Jackson was subjected to severe criticism by factions within the army, Dr. Hunter McGuire defended him with the observation that he was merely carrying out Lee's orders. Old Jack himself even advanced the proposition that "if General Lee had wanted me at Frayser's Farm he would have sent for me." Although Porter Alexander hints that Jackson's infantry, including Ewell's division, sat there and did nothing, what could Ewell have done under the circumstances? He could hardly have crossed White Oak Swamp on his own and without a directive from Jackson. Longstreet and A. P. Hill "fought magnificently"—Southall Freeman's words—but without the weight of Jackson's divisions, the enemy was allowed to escape once more, this time to the infamous Malvern Hill. In spite of Ewell's inability to reach the field, Frayser's Farm had been a bloodbath. According to James E. Phillips, who struggled under Longstreet: "The next morning we moved down to Malvern Hill and in going down the road we saw in all directions scattered along the road drums, horses, guns, ammunition, knapsacks, clothes & all sorts & kinds of goods in untold quantities. All appearances of a general stampeed." The Yankee "stampeed" notwithstanding, James I Robertson offers that Jackson had no specific orders to reinforce Longstreet and Hill but that "the Confederates lost thirty-three hundred men in the vain effort to trap part of McClellan's army at Glendale."[31]

During the morning of July 1, before the Battle of Malvern Hill, the Ewell–Jubal Early nexus was initiated, which had a profound impact upon both soldiers to the end of their lives. They had known each other since 1836–1837 when Ewell was a plebe at West Point and Early was a first-classman who graduated eighteenth in a class of fifty cadets in 1837. While Ewell remained in the army, Early had devoted himself to the law and a stint in the Virginia legislature. Three months older than Ewell, he had opposed taking Virginia out of the Union while a member of the 1861 Secession Convention. Later he was given command of the Twenty-fourth Virginia Infantry, now a part of James L. Kemper's brigade in Longstreet's division. Promoted to brigadier general in July 1861, Early was part of D. H. Hill's command on the Peninsula until a wound he received in the fighting at Williamsburg removed him from active service. Destined to become a major player in the Confederate pantheon, Early eventually rose to lieutenant general and led Ewell's and A. P. Hill's corps later in the war.[32]

When Early had recovered sufficiently from his injury, he called upon Secretary of War George W. Randolph, "who gave [him] a letter to General Lee, suggesting that [he] be assigned the temporary command of Elzey's brigade of Ewell's division, as General Elzey had been severely wounded." Armed with Randolph's letter, Early rode to the front, conferring first with Lee, who sent him to Jackson, who in turn promptly ordered the Reverend Dabney to execute the paperwork giving him Elzey's men. There is absolutely nothing in Early's accounts in his memoirs or reports in the *Official Records* to suggest that Ewell was consulted in the matter. Thus on the morning of Malvern Hill he took charge of Elzey's brigade, numbering 1,025 officers and men, roughly one-fourth of Ewell's divisional strength. Without ever serving a single day with Ewell in combat, Early went into battle with the "remnants of seven regiments, to-wit: The 13th Virginia, 25th Virginia, 31st Virginia, 44th Virginia, 52nd Virginia, 58th Virginia, and the 12th Georgia Regiments," he observed afterward. Other than James A. Walker, Early had no colonels present to lead his brigades and only two lieutenant colonels for the Twenty-fifth and Fifty-second Virginia; the remaining four brigades were led by captains.[33]

The night before Early's arrival, McClellan had withdrawn from Frayser's Farm and aligned his legions around the crest of a gentle swell known locally as Malvern Hill near the James, with swampland between it and the flotilla of gunboats on the river. What proved a murderous wall of cannon positioned to sweep the open fields leading to the plateau had been executed by McClellan's artillerist Colonel Henry J. Hunt. Several of Lee's lieutenants, including Jackson and D. H. Hill, looked up at those cannon and counseled against any notion of a frontal assault. Apparently only Longstreet thought an attack could succeed, while the others were concerned that the lay of the land presented two sharp ravines on each side of the northern face, which meant the Confederates would have to charge uphill and across open country. Ever anxious to destroy McClellan's war machine, the undeterred Lee began organizing his forces as a hot July 1 wore on. When finally in place, his battle line had Jackson on the far left, with D. H. Hill and Huger—reinforced by Magruder—in the center, and Theophilus H. Holmes, newly arrived from the Suffolk area, holding the extreme right.[34]

Northern historian Alexander Webb says it with blunt force: when McClellan was allowed to leave Frayser's Farm on June 30, his "whole army was put in position on Malvern Hill." With Ewell in the lead, as Jackson advanced south on the famed Quaker Road past the Willis Methodist Church, they faced a still-vigorous enemy ready and poised for battle. "The Union left rested on a bluff crowned with guns and as the line curved toward the center a gentle decline dropped away toward the Confederates," observes Frank Vandiver, Old Jack's most perceptive biographer. "Facing Jackson's men, the center and right of McClellan's line rested on the same rise of open ground, offering magnificent opportunities for killing to his formidable batteries on the crest of the hill." Jackson halted the Valley Army in a wooded area short of the plain stretching south and upward toward Hunt's guns, and they soon found that D. H. Hill had been "posted on the right of the road leading to the enemy," with Whiting's division on the left. Ewell arranged his brigades along a lane going east to Dr. Poindexter's house from the Quaker or Willis Church Road. The Louisiana brigade, now commanded by Colonel Leroy A. Stafford and supported by Early, was posted in front of Whiting; Trimble "was formed in the rear of Whiting's left, which constituted the extreme left of [his] line." Jackson did not "develop his line until 10 a.m.," and his divisions lay in reserve until nearly dark, with his men subjected to a grueling cannonade. Although some disjointed fighting by D. H. Hill and Magruder was raging to Ewell's right, there was little to do but take what the guns atop Malvern's plateau had to offer.[35]

Captain William W. Goldsborough confirms that the First Maryland was held in reserve until the battle ended, "though during all that time under one of the most terrible artillery fires it had ever encountered." He adds, "nothing is so demoralizing to a soldier as to have to take an enemy's fire without being able to return it." Stafford and the Louisiana brigade were detached for service under Whiting and saw some hard combat as a result; near sunset Trimble's brigade was summoned to the Confederate right, "where the battle raged," Trimble wrote later. "I moved quickly guided by an officer of General D. H. Hill's staff, through a dense woods, in the dark, exposed for 1 1/2 miles to a continuous and rapid fire of the enemy's artillery, and took up a position on that part of the field where General Magruder had made his disastrous charge across an open field, every yard of which could be swept by adverse artillery." Although Trimble reported to both D. H. Hill and Ewell from his new vantage point, he was told to remain in place. Later in the evening he rode forward very close to several of the Union batteries, so near that he could hear their normal conversations; and though Hill dissuaded him from charging McClellan's guns, it took a direct order from Stonewall himself to prompt Trimble to give up the fight. He and his men, like others under Ewell's command, lay on their arms until midnight when the firing stopped. "[A]s Generals Ewell and Hill had both been absent during this time," Trimble said, "I retired the brigade into the woods to bivouac for the night, as the men were completely worn out and no further action expected."[36]

Ewell was absent from the extreme right, because nearer his original position around the Poindexter farm, Early, with Elzey's brigade, had been sent into the fracas to bolster D. H. Hill's piecemeal attack on the Federal center. Hill had followed an earlier advance by Lewis A. Armistead, of Huger's division, without meaningful support from Lee's artillery, which ended in abysmal failure. "Just about sunset I was ordered to move my brigade towards the right to support General D. H. Hill," Early relates. "General Ewell accompanied me, and we had to move through the woods in a circle in the rear of the position Hill had first assumed. . . . We were still within range of the shells from the enemy's numerous batteries, and they were constantly bursting in the tops of the trees over our heads, literally strewing the ground with leaves." The two middle-aged bachelors—Early was forty-six and Ewell a year younger—must have formed an immediate affinity for each other, as Ewell was constantly at Early's side helping direct his brigade and riding forward to reconnoiter the enemy. Finally, while subjected to an unrelenting fire, Ewell had his new commander form a line with Kershaw's South Carolinians "in a clover field in view of the flashes from the enemy's guns." This line was in front of Trimble's bivouac, and, says Early: "Generals Hill and Ewell remained with us until after the firing had ceased, and then retired after giving me orders to remain where I was until morning and await further orders."[37]

Elements of Ewell's division under Early, and to a lesser extent Trimble and Stafford, had seen action in this the last battle of the Seven Days, but Ewell's troops had not advanced until such a time that it was too late to alter the outcome. The lateness of the hour and exhaustion of the men on both sides put an end to the killing—Lee had lost over five thousand men to McClellan's less than three thousand; and, Captain Goldsborough writes, "except for an occasional shell from the gunboats there was nothing to disturb the night but the cries and moans of the thousands of wounded." After the lopsided affray at Malvern Hill, McClellan gave up his overload campaign to capture Richmond and withdrew to the safety of the Yankee navy clustered about Harrison's Landing. With the help of Jackson and Ewell, Lee had saved the Confederate capital, but, tellingly, he had not destroyed the abolitionist crusade threatening the Southland.[38]

Captain Brown relates that Ewell, like others, including D. H. Hill, was fearful lest McClellan would renew the fight on July 2. Accordingly, he ordered several wagonloads of ammunition captured at Gaines Mill repositioned for a quick retreat toward Richmond, but Jackson vetoed the order, saying the fight was over—McClellan would not bother Lee's army again. Ewell's division and the rest of Jackson's men "lay still most of the 2nd, resting and getting rations" until an order arrived summoning them to Westover. The crossroad church and village was east of Malvern Hill and about one mile north of the James. Although Ewell got his brigades in line to launch another attack, men in both armies had had enough fighting. James A. Walker of the Thirteenth Virginia soon encountered Brown with a message for divisional headquarters: "Well, said he, I don't like to say it, but you must tell Genl. Ewell the men *won't fight* much—they are too tired & they don't like those gunboats that we hear."

Fitz-John Porter noted much the same sentiments among McClellan's men when he walked over the Malvern Hill battleground after the fight of July 1. Ewell had lost a total of 985 men killed and wounded since June 26, and his troops were in no condition to face another pitched confrontation. Mercifully, Lee called off the new offensive but not before Ewell was nearly killed by random firing from the Yankees' fortifications around Harrison's Landing: "Genl. Ewell took advantage of the leisure to ride out to our skirmishers [to] reconnoiter the ground in front. We came to a small house on a knoll some 150 yards behind the skirmish line, which was here considerably thrown forward—and as it commanded a wide view of our front got off our horses & sat down in the shade to await events," Brown says.

An occasional shot was whistling by but no danger expected, so Genl. E. presently sat down on a large box with his feet drawn up on it, his back against a tree & his head on his hands & went to sleep. I sat on the ground with my back against the same tree. . . . All at once four or five shots whisked past us & Genl. E got up with his hat in hand and began examining the box where a ball had struck within an inch of his heel & passed between his foot & thigh. As he was doing so, he found a couple of holes in his cap—which it was barely possible could have been made while on his head, without killing him.

When Brown wrote to his mother from Malvern Hill on July 3, he told Lizinka that both he and Ewell had come through the campaign unhurt, although he did relay an account of Ewell's horse "Maggie" as well as the incident when Ewell was shot through the boot at Gaines Mill. Without mentioning Ewell in any way, Brown told his mother that he "would like to get out of Genl. J_____'s command." And, he added, "I don't see exactly so much chance of that."[39]

Unquestionably, Ewell had been overshadowed by Jackson, although he had done his part to insure Lee's mastery of the Peninsula. He demonstrated plenty of gumption at Gaines Mill as well as at Bottom's Bridge, when he wanted to lunge across the Chickahominy and engulf Porter's northern flank. "'Dick' Ewell was to be reckoned with those who had contributed unmistakably to the defeat of the Federals," writes premier Confederate historian Douglas Southall Freeman. "He had been denied full play of his abilities because of the circumstances of the field, but in every essential, to the limits allowed, he had met the test." Although some writers, anxious to make reputations for themselves, have made a career of demeaning his assessment of men and events, Freeman's evaluation of Ewell after the Seven Days is essentially correct: "At Malvern Hill he had been held in reserve until late in the action. Then he had advanced valiantly. As at Gaines Mill, he seemed to be everywhere on his part of the field. No officer was mentioned more often or more gratefully by others. The picture of him that takes form, in a score of reports, is that of an intelligent, trained, self-contained and daring man, unique in personality, who had cheer and help for every fellow soldier who needed either." New battles and challenges lay on the horizon for Major General Richard Stoddert Ewell, but he had acquitted himself as well as any divisional commander on the Peninsula, even while serving under a sleepy-headed and domineering Jackson.[40]

Chapter 8

JACKSON'S MAN

On the very day that Robert E. Lee opened the Seven Days campaign at Mechanicsville, Abraham Lincoln, always searching for a suitable commander—or at least one who would fight—lifted the notorious John Pope to command. While McClellan waited and fumed at Harrison's Landing, the Yankee president not only found a new general, but he also created a new Army of Virginia composed of disparate forces under Major Generals Franz Sigel, Nathaniel P. Banks, and Irvin McDowell—altogether nearly forty thousand men. Lincoln's earlier choices of an army generalissimo, McDowell and McClellan, had ended in failure. Now the forty-year-old Pope emerged as the great hope for victory over Lee and company. After graduating from West Point in 1842, the Kentucky-born officer had seen service in the west as well as the conflict in Mexico. Upon the outbreak of civil strife, then-Captain (since 1856) Pope was promoted to brigadier general and sent to command in Missouri. His military notice came from leading the Army of Mississippi "at Island No. 10, and the advance upon and siege of Corinth."

Pope was handed a heavy responsibility from the outset: "The Army of Virginia shall operate in such manner as, while protecting western Virginia and the national Capital from danger or insult, it shall in the speediest manner attack and overcome the rebel forces under Jackson and Ewell, threaten the enemy in the direction of Charlottesville, and render the most effective aid to relieve General McClellan and capture Richmond." Although he was yet a divisional commander, Lincoln apparently continued under the misapprehension that Ewell and Jackson were equals in the conference scheme; the president must also have thought the two had commands separate from that of Lee.[1]

175

Immediately following Pope's June 26 appointment, the new commander, emboldened by his position, began to alienate soldiers on both
sides of the conflict with his self-enhancing proclamations. McClellan was
beside himself when Pope met defeat at Cedar Mountain and Second
Manassas. Accordingly, John C. Fremont, the 1856 Republican candidate
for president, refused to serve under him and thus the foreign-born Franz
Sigel was elevated to command in Fremont's place. In a famous outburst
an unnamed Union general at Washington said that he did not care for
"John Pope one pinch of owl dung." But it was his orders establishing "the
strictest kind of martial law" across northern Virginia that aroused and
angered Confederates. Among other things, Pope declared that Yankee forces
could confiscate what they required from disloyal Southerners and issue
vouchers for later payment. Any persons within his lines suspected of Confederate sympathies were liable to immediate seizure; "if a soldier or legiti-
mate follower of the army be fired upon from any house, the house shall be
razed to the ground, and its inhabitants sent to the headquarters of the
army." On it went—his forces were handed life-and-death power over not
only Confederate soldiers captured in battle but also common citizens living in the war zone.[2]

An unintended consequence of Pope's actions was that deserters, already bereft of morale and normal military discipline, took his mandates
as a license to ravage the countryside. "Straggling soldiers have been known
to rob farms and even small cottages, the homes of the poor, of every ounce
of food or forage found in them," Lieutenant James Gillette, one of Sigel's
commissaries, told his mother. "Families have been left without the means
of preparing a meal of victuals." Nor did the well-to-do escape. The stately
mansions of more than one plantation owner in the region met similar
fates. As reports of continued atrocities rolled into Richmond and Lee's
headquarters, Jefferson Davis countered with an order to treat all Union
prisoners, including officers, as felons. The payback policy soon reached
Lee, who dispatched a direct order to Jackson preparing to march north
with Ewell in his van to confront Pope on the Rappahannock. "I want
Pope suppressed," Lee told Stonewall in no uncertain terms on July 27.
"The course indicated in his orders, if the newspapers report them correctly, cannot be permitted, and will lead to retaliation on our part. You
had better notify him the first opportunity."[3]

A widely circulated announcement by Pope that he meant to make
his headquarters in the saddle as he energetically pursued the Confederates
prompted a sour response: almost to the man Lee's troopers cried that his

headquarters were where his hindquarters ought to be. Always the brag-gart, Pope crowed on July 14 that in the west his men had ever faced their foes and that he had been summoned to Virginia to implement the same strategy. "Let us look before us and not behind," he told the army. "I come from the west where we have been accustomed to see only the backs of our enemies." Ewell, like everyone else in the Southern armies, absorbed Pope's bombasts, and though the two soldiers had been messmates during 1838–1839 and 1839–1840 on the Hudson, he took no notice of George Pickett's observation that West Point had created "an extreme cordiale entente be-tween us old fellows." "He'll never see the backs of my troops," Ewell re-portedly shouted upon learning of Pope's self-proclaimed exploits.[4]

Lee, Jackson, Longstreet, and Jeb Stuart had already watched McClellan's camp at Harrison's Landing and decided that Little Mac had no intention of renewing the fight in front of Richmond. The "Gallant Pelham," Stuart's twenty-four-year-old cavalryman in charge of his horse artillery, lobbed a few cannon shot into the Union encampment, which had little effect other than to provoke an abortive cavalry charge. Although Stuart looked on with unrestrained glee as the startled bluecoats ran helter-skelter, it was time to move. "Lee wanted to fight," observes historian Emory Thomas, and correctly reasoned that he had to prevent the combination of two Union armies (Pope's and McClellan's) whose total strength would overwhelm him. With McClellan showing no hostile intent, Lee resolved to march toward the Rappahannock, where Pope was posturing with vigor. Jackson's force around "the old Mansion Westover, that William Byrd built under grant from the English king," began to withdraw on July 9. With Jackson's departure, Ewell marched his troops, in the words of Brown, "back to the vicinity of Richmond & encamped near the Chickahominy, with hqtrs of our division at Strawberry Hill."[5]

Although Brown avows he cannot remember how long they remained on the Chickahominy, it was probably from July tenth through the thir-teenth, when Lee gave the order to head northward. Strawberry Hill, situ-ated on a bluff overlooking the river a hundred yards or so south of the stream, was directly north of Richmond. Captain Goldsborough reports that the Maryland Line bivouacked three miles from the capital. Ewell's new headquarters was between the Meadow and Mechanicsville bridges on the Virginia Central Railroad. Jackson, reports Henry Kyd Douglas, was nearby on the road from Mechanicsville to Richmond.[6]

The division remained "long enough, I know, for me to make one or two visits to Richmond & get two pairs of capital boots for General E. &

myself," Brown records. Ewell also made at least one and perhaps more trips into the city to call at the war department. Apparently Campbell Brown was not the only dissatisfied officer in his division who wanted to be separated from Jackson, because an unidentified brigadier had gone directly to Adjutant General Samuel Cooper asking that Ewell's division be assigned elsewhere. Ewell, who realized that advancement in rank comes from acquiescence in the face of higher authority, also went to Cooper urging that his command be left where it was. If Stonewall knew about the episode, he said nothing, but his continued high estimation of Ewell may well have resulted from the latter's willingness to remain a part of the Valley Army in spite of his frequent comments to Dick Taylor that Jackson was a "crazy fool" or worse. There had been a long-simmering discontent among the Louisianans, and at least one brigade was removed from Ewell and attached to the Light Division of A. P. Hill while his command tarried at Strawberry Hill.[7]

Other organizational changes occurred during the trek to confront Pope when Jefferson Davis ordered disbandment of the Maryland Line without consulting Jackson or Ewell. Washington Hands, a Maryland officer, is insistent that the breakup resulted when "two or three politicians from Maryland," hoping to gain "military fame," persuaded Davis that a larger contingent of Confederate Marylanders would be raised to replace the tired and worn outfit. Although the new unit was never organized, the Baltimore Light Artillery was attached to William E. Starke's Louisiana brigade of William B. Taliaferro's division and thus remained under Jackson's command but not Ewell's. Colonel Bradley T. Johnson, who had led the Marylanders under Ewell in the Shenandoah and during the Seven Days, was also removed and given a brigade of Virginians in Taliaferro's division. Ewell, however, had every reason to be proud of the service rendered by the troopers under Johnson and Captain John Bowyer Brockenbrough, who not only commanded the Baltimore battery but also became Taliaferro's chief of artillery later in the year. "It was the 1st of August 1862, if I mistake not, that Colonel Johnson drew the little remnant of heroes up in line for the last time, and after a few appropriate and touching remarks, read the order disbanding them," reads Washington Hands's account. "Not a man but felt his humiliation, for as the order was being read the troops of Longstreet were flying by on their way to new fields of adventure and glory. 'Come on Marylanders, we can't get along without you,' they exclaimed in their ignorance of what was transpiring, and not dreaming that they had seen the last of us as a body for the last time."[8]

Prior to the July 19 order to move north from Strawberry Hill, Lieutenant Colonel John M. Jones, son of Lee's biographer J. William Jones, joined Ewell's staff as assistant adjutant general to assist Campbell Brown and Tom Turner. At Jackson's headquarters Ewell met additional staff changes after the Reverend Dabney returned to his clerical duties in private life and Major (later General) Elisha F. Paxton replaced the genial "Sandie" Pendleton as chief of staff. Shortly after Lee's directive to Jackson, an order signed by Paxton arrived at Ewell's headquarters, in Brown's words, "to pack everything, let the troops go to Richmond & take the cars & to send the wagons off towards Louisa Court C.H." Ewell set out to confront Pope's army with three brigades under Early, Trimble, and Leroy A. Stafford—a total of 399 officers and 4,628 enlisted men reported present and fit for duty. Roughly one-half of his division was carried on the rolls as sick, primarily with malaria.[9]

Jubal A. Early, now a solid part of Ewell's command, says the division left the Chickahominy on the fifteenth, while others set the departure as the sixteenth. Two of Ewell's six batteries traveled on the railroad transporting his infantry, while the remainder trudged along with the wagon trains.[10] "We rode on horseback & as there had been some delay in getting the troops aboard the Cars, or rather furnishing enough Cars, we waited till all had started & leaving Strawberry Hill about 9 a.m., reached a delightful house belonging to a widow [Mrs. Nelson] . . . about 9 p.m.," reads Brown's account. Ewell and his staff, who followed the railroad north in a drenching rain while his troops "rode the cars," arrived at the Hanover home, where they not only "enjoyed greatly the intercourse with a family of such refinement and gentleness" but were also treated to a sumptuous table.

The next day Ewell reached Gordonsville on the Orange and Alexandria Railroad at the end of his second day in the saddle. Along the march his entourage stopped briefly at a farmhouse during a renewed storm and encountered a crusty "old gentleman." As the assemblage looked on in disbelief, a flash of lightning that "nearly blinded" his party ignited the man's haystack and adjacent barn. Although their host thought his barn was destroyed beyond saving, "Gen'l E called his couriers, got the old man's two or three negroes, we of the staff went hard at work, we checked the fire & after nearly an hour's very hard work put it out & saved the old fellow's barn," Brown recounts. "He was very grateful, fed us all like fighting cocks & gave us some capital liquor." Then, upon reaching Gordonsville, Ewell found other brigades already bivouacked around the town, which obliged him to create his own encampment a mile or so from "the village." Ewell also learned that a troop of Pope's cavalry was threatening along the Rapidan at Orange Court House. Before settling himself, he took "some cav'y just arrived from the Valley & one or two Inf'y reg'ts" and set out in hot pursuit, but the bluecoated horsemen had already fled northward.[11]

Even though he remained at Gordonsville for a mere day and a half, Ewell found time to dash off an insightful letter to his niece. He indicated that he had visited his brothers Ben and William in Richmond, but he told Lizzie nothing about his visits to the war department. William, he said, had signed on with the Fifty-eighth Virginia in Early's brigade and thus had come into his division. After Lizzie had chided him in an earlier letter about his having actually seen a battle, Ewell let his feelings come to the fore: "Since March I have been almost constantly within hearing of skirmishing, cannon, etc., and would give almost anything to get away for a time as to have a little quiet," he wrote. "I don't know that I ever lived as hardily or so much exposed to everything disagreeable as during the last few weeks." And Ewell told her that he had "been sick with the exposure and malaria of the Chickahominy swamps." With much of the army on sick call, including his brother William, who had not reported for duty with the division, a prudish Ewell did not tell Lizzie that he had contracted body lice during the Seven Days. Henri J. Mugler, a bugler with a Confederate battery, noted that upon crossing the Grapevine Bridge a few weeks earlier, his brigade "suddenly came upon General Richard Ewell in an open field, with his pants partly down 'skirmishing for greybacks' which had become a source of great discomfort in both armies."[12]

From Gordonsville Ewell moved farther north to Liberty Mills, or present Somerset, on the Rapidan, where he established a headquarters until August 7. In the three-week interval before the army set out anew to confront Pope's Army of Virginia, he was busy reorganizing parts of his division. As other troops arrived on the Rapidan, Ewell was given command of six Georgia regiments under Alexander R. Lawton. The Maryland Line along with the Baltimore Artillery, before their disbandment, was shunted to Charlottesville in an attempt at recruitment of replacement troops for their depleted ranks. When that effort fell short, Ewell wrote a warm letter supporting not only Bradley T. Johnson's retention in the army but also his elevation to brigadier general. "I have witnessed during the campaign in the Valley of the Shenandoah as well as the Peninsula and on other occasions that officer's ability, zeal and bravery and, wish to state that the interests of the service would suffer if he went out of commission," Ewell said after the fight at Cedar Mountain. Two years later, in June 1864, Johnson, who survived the war by almost forty years, was handed a brigadier's star.[13]

Ewell met an uncertain response when he approached the war department about lesser promotions in his division. "I am instructed by the Sec of War to inform you that the Department is not issuing Commissions to Company officers at present," V. D. Groner, assistant adjutant general in Richmond, informed him. "But if those recommended are competent to receive promotion, they can be assigned by your (special) order, and will be borne on the rolls from the date on which Captains Strong & McArthur were elected Lt. Col. and Major." Ewell's intervention must have worked, because Charles W. McArthur was promoted to major in November 1862 and to lieutenant colonel in early 1863 before his death at Spotsylvania. Likewise, Henry B. Strong, a peacetime clerk in New Orleans, was named colonel prior to his death at Antietam a few weeks later. While at Liberty Mills, Ewell maintained a rigid inspection of his brigades, including that of Isaac Trimble, who unsuccessfully sought to invoke Jackson's intervention to afford his batteries more time to prepare for the divisional inspector general.[14]

At the same time Ewell was realigning his command to meet the coming fury, Pope commenced his advance on August 1 with thirty-eight thousand men. Although he did not cross the Rappahannock until the sixth, a combination of Confederate spies and sightings by Jeb Stuart's cavalry had already alerted Jackson that his Northern foes were on the move. Jackson had been augmented by the arrival of A. P. Hill's Light Division at Lee's command to bolster Charles S. Winder, who led Jackson's old division, and Ewell. John Pope's loud talk had turned to aggressive action so that the first clash at Slaughter, or Cedar, Mountain—about half the distance from Liberty Mills to Culpeper—"was fought between the corps of General Banks (Nathaniel P.), and the advancing confederate forces under Generals Jackson (Thomas J.), Ewell (Richard S.) and Hill (Ambrose P.)." And the Reverend Frederic Denison, chaplain of the First Rhode Island Cavalry, continues: "Our army was advancing to a demonstration upon Richmond, by way of Culpeper and Orange Court House, to relieve the heavy pressure then on the heroic Army of the Potomac, under General McClellan (George B.), by drawing off from his front a portion of General Lee's army." Lee and the boys could hardly allow this to happen as they prepared to confront the aggressor before the combined forces of Pope and McClellan could unite against them. Titans were about to clash in the rolling piedmont of Virginia, and though the Confederates managed to manhandle Pope, the Reverend Denison also noted: "This object we certainly accomplished, as well we knew when the challenged enemy poured down on us from the banks of the Rapidan."[15]

When the first word reached Liberty Mills that Banks was on the move, Ewell, along with several other officers, was busy hearing the notorious court-martial of Brigadier General Richard Brooke Garnett. In addition to his well-documented secrecy, Stonewall Jackson, for all of his contributions to Confederate arms, could be equally petty—if not downright vindictive—when dealing with subordinates. Jackson's chief difficulty arose from his psychological reticence to discuss strategy and marching destinations or battle maneuvers with anyone—not even his divisional commanders or his personal staff. Although Ewell, if not his staff, had learned to abide his ploy of "saying nothing to anybody" and therefore enjoyed Jackson's trust and respect, others, such as Winder and the hot-tempered A. P. Hill, were not. Like others, Garnett, whose personal transcript of the charges against him had "lie" scribbled before almost every entry, had developed a dislike for the soldier when he was accused of withdrawing his troops from the Kernstown fight in April 1862 without Jackson's approval. When word arrived that Pope's army was crossing the Rappahannock, the trial that no one but Jackson wanted, after having commenced on August 6, disbanded the following day, never to resume. Ewell and the panel were saved from having to pass judgment on a fellow officer.[16]

Steadfast in his determination to strike Pope and to forget about McClellan for the moment, Robert E. Lee issued orders to Jeb Stuart and Jackson on the seventh. Stuart was told to give Old Jack "all information and cooperation," and the general commanding added: "The greatest thing you can do is to do what you are now doing, cutting up their communication, trains, etc." Jackson, on the other hand, had his command—except that of A. P. Hill, who was advancing through Gordonsville—south of the Rapidan in a triangular configuration extending from Ewell at Liberty Mills to Winder at Orange Court House. Although Lee was at New Market near Richmond, he gave Jackson all the discretion of maneuver that an army commander can offer. "I would rather you should have easy fighting and heavy victories," he told him on the seventh; "I must now leave the matter to your reflection and good judgment." Beyond the Rapidan lay Madison and Culpeper counties, where Pope and Banks were thought to be concentrating, and the next morning, August 8, Lee sent an additional communiqué: he felt a move into Culpeper would be judicious and urged Jackson to attack while the Yankees were on the prowl.

By that time, however, Jackson had his entire corps on the march, including Ewell's division. With the breakup of Garnett's court-martial, orders had been cut during the evening of August 7 "to move at dawn the next morning in the following order, viz, Ewell's, Hill's, and Jackson's [Winder's] divisions," relates A. P. Hill in his battle report. A close inspection of Jackson's intent demanded that Ewell follow the south bank of the Rapidan to Orange Court House and then merge with Hill and Winder. But in order to avoid an unnecessary clogging of the roads, Ewell, with Jackson's blessing, had crossed into Madison County and followed a circuitous route across Beautiful Run to the Rapidan at Barnett's Ford—the latter in Orange County north of Orange and a primary crossing of the roadway to Culpeper. Campbell Brown, who had been away from Liberty Mills attending the funeral of Captain Hugh Nelson, one of Ewell's staff officers, caught up with the division at sunrise on August 8. "It had crossed at Somerset, turned right by a farm road, or no road at all, down the Rapidan till nearly dawn, then slept." When Ewell established a makeshift camp for the night at Barnett's Ford, he was approximately three miles north of Orange.[17]

The ever-secretive Jackson had not bothered to apprise Hill of Ewell's altered route. A. P. Hill has left a detailed account of his conception of ensuing events in the *Official Records,* although it is tempting to speculate that a hurried discussion between Ewell and Jackson had taken place at the former's headquarters after the adjournment of the court-martial proceeding, at which Ewell's new route was approved. Jackson himself could have suggested the change, as Ewell was not the kind of man to march off into the dark on his own. Be that as it may, Hill waited at his assigned place on the streets of Orange for Ewell's division to pass so that the Light Division might fall in behind it. When Ewell did not appear, Hill supposedly vented his frustrations on the Reverend J. William Jones, who happened to be at hand: "I tell you, I do not know whether we march north, south, east or west, or whether we march at all. General Jackson ordered me to have my division ready to move at dawn." Hill told Jones he had been ready to move at the appointed time, but when he saw that the passing regiments belonged to Winder, he knew that something was not right.

Collecting his wits, Hill rode to the Rapidan at Barnett's Ford, where he found sheer pandemonium. Not only did he learn for the first time that Ewell had bypassed Orange Court House, but he also found "that a portion of Jackson's [Winder's] division had not crossed, and all were delayed by the passing of Ewell's troops and trains." Back in Orange, Hill had joined the march behind Winder before riding ahead to determine what snafu blocked the northward trek. "Between 4 and 5—the wagons of Ewell still passing and a portion of Jackson's still not having crossed the river—I received an order from General Jackson to go back to Orange Court House and encamp for the night," Hill wrote in his campaign summary. "The head of my column having only made about a mile, I bivouacked the brigades where they were."[18]

The colossal bottleneck at Barnett's Ford ended any chance Jackson had to launch a surprise attack on Nathaniel P. Banks, then stationing his forces along the north branch of Cedar Run—a tributary of the Rapidan—where it crossed the Culpeper Road. When Jackson was forced to cancel his advance, he blamed Hill for the mix-up, and although he was fresh from the Richard Garnett imbroglio, Old Jack immediately initiated a running feud with another of his subordinates that continued until his death. The aborted plans of August 8, writes Hill biographer James I. Robertson, produced a convulsion: "Winder was ill; Ewell was swearing in exasperation; Hill was angry; Jackson was livid." If Ewell was indeed cursing, as was his wont, it must have been one of his last profane outbursts, as two or three nights later he encountered Jackson at prayer, which in turn led to his own religious conversion. Yet, two years later he erupted into a well-documented explosion that contributed mightily to Lee's loss of confidence in his command abilities. Ewell, moreover, does not mention the Jackson-Hill flap in his account of the campaign nor does Brown in a later handwritten summary. "At Barrett's Ford A. P. Hill coming from Gordonsville direct fell in our rear," Brown commented without elaboration, when the march resumed.[19]

Lee had chosen Stonewall Jackson to take the lead due to his supreme confidence in Old Jack's tenacity and eagerness to carry out his wishes while detached from the main army; and Jackson once more tapped Ewell to take the van for the same reasons. Whatever his command drawbacks, Ewell would implement his chief's desires—if he knew what they were—and Jackson may have confided in his divisional head a bit more than is commonly suspected. Although an attack was out of the question on August 8, and in spite of his abysmal showing on the march, Jackson continued to push ahead. When night closed—Brown says they marched until nearly midnight—Early's brigade was encamped on the north side of Robertson's River, another feeder of the Rapidan that runs south of but

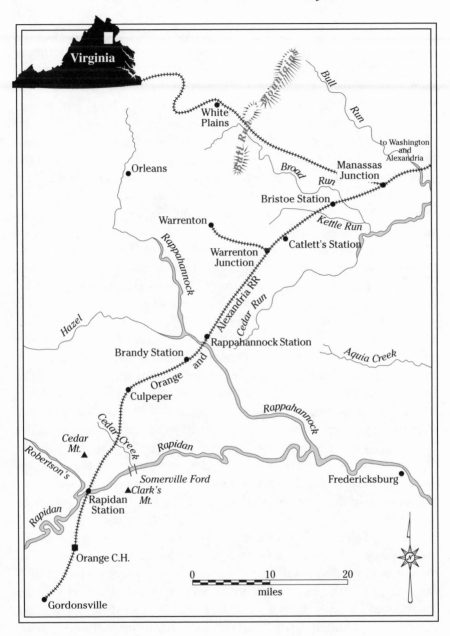

Cedar Mountain and Kettle Run

parallel to the celebrated Cedar Run. A scorching heat wave, with the thermometer well above ninety, contributed to the misery of men and animals. John O. Casler, who tramped with the Thirty-third Virginia, wrote that a number of troopers fell dead from sunstroke during the day. If that were not enough, cavalry units under Beverly H. Robertson and John Buford jousted with each other throughout the day as Ewell led the army forward.[20]

"In the forenoon of the 9th we came to Cedar Run Mountain where the troops halted for some time," notes Brown. "This appeared to be the place chosen by Gen'l Jackson to receive the enemy's advance." As the Confederates moved northward on the Culpeper Road (present U.S. 15), every officer and man could see Cedar Mountain, an inselberg, or isolated mountain, looming on their right. The mountain is still a prominent landmark on the eastern horizon as the motorist of today travels along the Orange-Culpeper roadway. It is a tree-covered eminence jutting about two hundred feet above the surrounding piedmont. Also called Slaughter Mountain, it took its name from the home of the Reverend D. F. Slaughter, which was situated on its northern slope. "The bitter fighting that was soon to take place in its vicinity would serve to confirm the name, but history would call it the Battle of Cedar Run as a more euphonious title and in deference to the twin-forked creek whose branches, originating on either side of the Gordonsville-Culpeper Road, meandered east and south to join at Hudson's Mills, about a mile from the Slaughter home and, thence flow on to the Rapidan." Actually the fight took place almost exclusively in the Cedar Run Valley, although Ewell initially amassed his artillery on the slopes to rake the lowlands to the north. The field of conflict, writes the Reverend Denison, "was an open valley, in the main, of plantation grounds and fields, about two miles in length and a half in width, running southeast and northwest, lying to the north and northwest of Cedar Mountain."[21]

In his unbelievably brief battle account, Ewell commented: "My division followed the cavalry advance, and when we reached the south end of the valley the enemy's cavalry were seen in strong force in our front. . . . It was evident that the enemy intended to make a stand at this place." When Ewell got to Crooked Run Creek at the southern tip of the mountain, his division split with Early, whose brigade had been in the van since leaving Barnett's Ford, proceeding north toward Culpeper. The brigades of Trimble and Forno veered to the right around the southern end of the mountain to another road that ran from Rapidan Station to the main Culpeper route. After halting at a stand of pine trees, Trimble moved forward to a second position on the north flank of the mountain. "We kept on and by pushing the guns by hand up a steep place, got them into position a hundred yards to S.W. of Mr. Slaughter's house," observes Brown. "A reg't was sent around the point of the Mt. to protect our right, & the guns were soon opened on the enemy, who by this time got fairly in our front & were firing from a low ridge at the north end of the valley at our troops advancing thro the open and along the road in the woods." At Ewell's command, Forno's Louisiana brigade was held in reserve behind Trimble through the subsequent melee.[22]

The guns near Slaughter's home were served by a colorful nineteen-year-old captain of artillery named Joseph White Latimer; Brown calls him the "pet" of Ewell's division. After leaving his studies at the Virginia Military Institute upon the outbreak of war, Latimer joined Courtney's Richmond Artillery as lieutenant. He quickly rose to command, and his steadfast performance in front of the Reverend Slaughter's home earned him a niche in the Confederate saga comparable to that of the "Gallant" John Pelham, another boyish gunner, a few months later at Fredericksburg. The steady roar of Latimer's cannon across the Cedar Run Valley did much to dissuade Banks's brigades in their headlong thrust at Jackson, Ewell, Early, and Winder. Guns from another battery under Lieutenant Nathaniel Terry were rushed forward to assist Latimer. But it was Latimer whom Ewell singled out for his coolness and judgment. A year later, the twenty-year-old gunner fell "mortally wounded while withdrawing his battalion from an unequal artillery duel supporting the attack on Culp's and Cemetery Hills."[23]

Meanwhile, at Ewell's insistence Jubal Early had pushed ahead to the juncture with the road from Madison Court House; but when Winder brought his division into place to form the Confederate left, he crossed to the east side of the Orange-Culpeper pike on the north of Cedar Run. When Banks unleashed his attack, Early was in the center behind the brigade of Lawrence O'B. Branch. Still, "there was a gap of half a mile between our wing [Trimble and Forno] & the nearest troops of the center, not even filled by skirmishers, being every foot of it clean & commanded by our guns," notes Brown. "This circumstance prevented that sort of magnetic sympathy with the main body and having that instant knowledge of difficulty elsewhere so often instantly experienced by any part of a connected line." Even Brown was disturbed by the gap in Ewell's line. Winder, who was succeeded by Taliaferro, was killed in the assault at the moment of his success as he sought to rally the flagging left and center. When Jackson galloped to the scene and found "the Confederates giving ground and fighting with clubbed guns, stones, and anything they could get," he was able to embolden the troops by his mere presence.[24]

Old Jack, who proclaimed on another occasion that he "would go where they send me—under Ewell, or any one, if ordered—but Lee I would follow blindfolded," was able to reverse the field after a last effort by Winder, who called one of his brigades from the extreme flank. The reserves were called, with Stonewall losing no time in summoning A. P. Hill, whose Light Division was spread along the Orange Court House road. Hill did not enter the fray a moment too soon when he hurled his brigades to strengthen the disintegrating lines of Early and Winder. Ironically, Hill, who was to have taken Winder's place on the march until the misunderstanding at Orange, became the man of the hour as he tipped the balance in Jackson's favor. The guns under Latimer and Terry, with their murderous crossfire into the melee below, were Ewell's only contribution to Jackson's initial rout except for Early's fight along Cedar Run. And, strangely, neither Ewell nor Brown mentioned Hill in their accounts of Cedar Mountain.[25]

As Ewell watched the deadly combat along the Orange-Culpeper thoroughfare and the south branch of Cedar Run, Banks and George D. Bayard, in a futile attempt to check the rebel tide, threw "the 164-man battalion of the 1st Pennsylvania Cavalry" into the fight. "They charged in a column of fours, parallel to the pike and into the spearhead of a Confederate counterattack," writes historian Edward J. Stackpole. "Crossfire from Branch's brigade and the remnants of Taliaferro's division emptied many saddles, but the impetus of the charge carried the enemy inside the Confederate lines." It did little good, however, as only seventy-one horsemen returned to safety. Once a general stampede sat in with Yankees scampering in every direction, Ewell led Trimble's and Forno's brigades down from Slaughter's house to join in mopping-up operations. Upon attaining the roadway at the base of the mountain, he was forced to veer west toward the Culpeper Pike, because "a mill pond" in dammed-up Cedar Run blocked his advance. But Ewell was able to use his batteries once more during the Yankee retreat. "A member of the Twelfth Georgia," offers Robert K. Krick, "overheard his command to a gunnery officer. "A little more grape, Captain, if you please, for they travel too fast for our boys."[26]

Although Ewell declares that darkness halted his part in the battle, historian Krick, the foremost authority on the Cedar Mountain affray, finds: "Desultory enemy contact notwithstanding, Ewell did not accomplish much with Trimble's and Forno's brigades once he reached the main intersection and turned eastward." Ewell had acted on a personal instruction from Jackson, but in reality there was little for him to do with the entire Federal army in a headlong withdrawal. When Isaac Trimble filed his report, he praised Ewell's conduct in placing his brigade in secure positions shielded from the enemy's return fire: "Latimer's battery was also protected from loss under a several hours incessant fire from three batteries of the enemy by the judicious positions in which it was placed by you [Ewell], preventing entirely the enemy's shot from the effects of ricochet shot." Jackson likewise lauded his handling of Latimer's guns two hundred feet above the valley below: "For two hours a rapid and continuous fire of artillery was kept up on both sides," Old Jack said. "Our batteries were well served and damaged the enemy seriously." And Ewell himself was unstinting in his recommendations that Early and Colonel James A. Walker of the Thirteenth Virginia receive special recognition for their part in the fighting.[27]

Following a truce to carry off the dead, both sides remained quiet in the aftermath of Banks's cavalry charge. Private John Blue, who rode over the field the next day with General James J. Archer, has left a graphic description of the carnage inflicted by Ewell's men. "We rode down to the road where the Yankee cavalry had made their gallant but foolish charge," he wrote. "The lane for two hundred yards was a sight. It was jammed by dead men and horses. This was the work principally of the 13th Virginia commanded by Col. J. A. Walker." Little wonder that Ewell recommended Walker so heartily for promotion. After the battlefield tour, Archer, a Marylander who commanded a brigade in A. P. Hill's division, led young Blue back to Jackson's headquarters "about a mile and a half to the rear." Here they found "Generals Jackson, Ewell, Hill, and [Stuart] sitting on a log a little distance from the road holding a consultation." Ewell, who would take the van once more for the Rappahannock, was in near constant contact with Jackson in the weeks leading to the next clash on the Manassas plain. Jackson had found a killing man and kindred spirit, willing to act under his supervision, if not on his own, and he intended to make maximum use of him.[28]

"After Cedar Run we returned to our former camps at Liberty Mills where we lay until Gen'l Lee began the Manassas campaign," reads Brown's account. According to Early, Ewell occupied his former encampment on August 10—the day following Cedar Mountain—after Jackson ordered him to send his wagon trains to Gordonsville and to keep his campfires lit in order to confuse the enemy. The stay at Liberty Mills was short-lived when Ewell was told to "move your command towards Orange C.H. at dusk" on the eleventh. It was initiated by Lee's anticipated arrival, which occurred on August 15 when he reached Gordonsville from Richmond. Following a jaunt to the crest of Clark's Mountain with Jackson, and probably Ewell, the commanding general summoned a concentration behind the rise in order to shield the army from the prying eyes of enemy cavalry. Clark's Mountain, five miles or so southeast of Cedar Run Mountain is another (or companion) inselberg rising about two hundred feet above the surrounding countryside. Situated at the end of present Virginia Route 697, the summit still offers a stunning view of north central Virginia as it did in 1862.[29]

Upon his coming to Gordonsville and Orange, Lee began to formulate a scheme to strike his enemies before Henry W. Halleck, Lincoln's new army chief and principal adviser, could effect a linkage between Pope and McClellan from the Peninsula. While he prepared to join the march toward the Rappahannock, Ewell, although he was a frequent participant in the ongoing strategy sessions, found time to recoup himself and to correspond with loved ones. Once Lee and Jackson gave the order to advance, there would be scant opportunity for letter writing until the tragedy at Groveton on the twenty-eighth. But that lay on the unknown horizon as he jotted a note to his niece on the fourteenth; he also sent her "a needle case" found in a captured Yankee writing packet during the Seven Days campaign. "I fully console with you over the gloomy prospect in regard to the war," he told Lizzie. And he poured forth one of his rarely offered political discourses: "Some 100,000 human beings have been massacred in every conceivable form of horror, with three times as many wounded all because of a set of fanatical abolitionists and unprincipled politicians backed by women in petticoats and pants and children." If Ewell were critical of Northern antislavery factions and the politicos who capitalized on their vote-getting potential, he likewise felt they had opened "a series of events that no one can see the end." On a more practical level he complained to Lizzie that his brother William, who had yet to join the division from Richmond, had his bathtub, "which puts me to a great deal of inconvenience."[30]

Ewell also wrote to his beloved Lizinka, still residing with their Hubbard relatives in Alabama. Although the missive—once more free of endearments—is dated from Orange Court House, it was no doubt written as the army marched to its bivouac at nearby Clark's Mountain. Both Ewell and Campbell Brown were "shivering" from colds they had contracted during the Cedar Mountain campaign. After all, if a fellow cannot elicit a bit of sympathy from a fiancée, to whom can he turn? The letter was written on Sunday, August 17, when Ewell was not well enough to care about attending church. Jubal Early, he told Lizinka, "is an excellent officer and ought to be a major general." The relationship between the two soldiers was obviously developing into a strong personal and professional bond, and it spilled over into his letter. "He is dissatisfied, as well he may be, and talks sometimes of going to join Bragg. He is very brave and would be an acquisition to your part of the world."

On the eve of the Second Manassas Ewell took time to mention "the possibility or probability that in a day or two we shall be engaged on a grand scale." "Only the god of Battles" knew what the outcome would be, as he sought to reassure Lizinka about her son—Ewell did so by calling upon his newly found commitment to Christ. "I hope and pray your child may be spared," he continued. "If God sees fit that it be otherwise you should remember his virtues, his religion, his merits as reasons which, besides Revelation, make you hope it is for the best should he be taken." Maudlin though Ewell could become, Campbell Brown survived his mother and stepfather by more than twenty years.[31]

As soon as Pope decided to pull his army behind the defensive barrier of the Rappahannock, Lee ordered his own forces to advance from their camp at Clark's Mountain; and John Hennessy, foremost chronicler of the Second Manassas, posits that "Cedar Mountain had taken the aggressive edge off" the Yankee leader. The fight, however, had only served to spur Lee and his cadre to greater exertions, with Ewell drawn into the argument over a proper name for the battle of August 9. As early as August 12 Jackson wanted Ewell to submit his account accompanied by a list of his killed, wounded, and missing. Although his official report was not completed until six months later because of his wounding on the twenty-eighth, he referred to the fight at "Cedar Run" and reported 17 men killed with 178 wounded. He was apparently able to account for all of his men, but a majority of his casualties had been in Early's brigade.

Jackson had admonished Ewell five days after the fight, while the army lay about the Rapidan, that he thought it best not to change the name of the battle. He was most concerned that proper names of engagements be inscribed on regimental banners and therefore did not want changes inserted into official reports. Ewell wanted to call it "Slaughter Mountain" but altered his completed official summary; Isaac Trimble's report of August 14 called it "Slaughter Mountain" with "Cedar Run" in parentheses; modern historians Hennessy and Krick name it "Cedar Mountain"; and Campbell Brown, ever Ewell's alter ego, has it "Cedar Run Mountain" in his handwritten account.[32]

From Clark's Mountain, where Ewell remained for "one or two days," he moved his division across the Rapidan "just too late to strike Pope in flank, he having retreated up to the Rappahannock the day before." Brown continues: "We crossed at Somerfield Ford, moved by way of Stevensburg & Brandy Station, & encamped on Mr. Cunningham's splendid farm near the Rappahannock and Hazel Rivers." Somerfield Ford across the Rapidan was below the confluence of Cedar Run after the latter made its way around Cedar Mountain, and it was immediately north of Clark's Mountain. Hazel River is another feeder into the Rappahannock that flows northeastward from the Blue Ridge and joins the stream some two miles above Brandy Station. The march of Jackson and Ewell paralleled the Orange and Alexandria Railroad from Culpeper to Brandy Station, where the line crossed the river with Rappahannock Station on the opposite or north bank; put another way, Hazel River flows into the Rappahannock two miles above the railroad crossing between Brandy and Rappahannock stations.

Ewell made his camp on the first night of the northward trek south of Hazel River and adjacent to the Rappahannock on the Cunningham farm. He covered not more than ten miles on the last day, although the march started early, with some regiments eating breakfast before daybreak. While units under Jeb Stuart, A. P. Hill, and James Longstreet crossed the Rappahannock at other points, "Jackson's men jumped in at Somerfield Ford 'yelling like a lot of school boys,'" and one of Ewell's troopers took time to record: "The water was pretty deep but very pleasant to our bodies." The high jinks and frolicking at the crossing aside, Ewell had his division alongside Jackson's other contingents between Stevensburg and Brandy Station by the evening of August 20.[33]

Ewell remained about Brandy Station from the evening of the twentieth until the early morning of August 25, while both armies "waltzed for position." On the twenty-second, Jeb Stuart made a daring raid into Pope's headquarters at Catlett's Station on the Orange and Alexandria, some twenty miles north of the Rappahannock. Among other items, the cavalryman retrieved Pope's dispatch book that included recent correspondence between Washington and the Federal army. Now for the first time Lee had positive proof that McClellan's troops were coming ashore at Aquia Creek near Fredericksburg. The time for action had arrived, or the Confederates would be overwhelmed by Pope's seventy thousand abetted by much of McClellan's command. Lee conceived an audacious scheme to send Jackson, reinforced by James Longstreet's corps, on a flanking maneuver to get between Pope and the Yankee capital before help arrived. If it worked Pope would be forced to fight in the open. "The Confederate commander was gambling that Jackson and Longstreet would be able to unite in time for the showdown," writes historian Emory Thomas. "Otherwise Pope would have a wonderful opportunity to destroy Jackson's and Longstreet's fragments separately." Daring though the plan might have been, Lee had his detractors, with John Esten Cooke even labeling it "reckless."[34]

When Lee gave the nod to advance on the twenty-fifth, Jackson once more tapped Ewell to continue the lead in separating from his immediate command and signaled Ewell's division to take the van. This time Colonel Forno and the Louisianans were chosen by Ewell to march out first. This confidence of Lee and Jackson could not have helped but swell Ewell's self-esteem as he issued his own orders on the night of August 24. Each man was handed three days' cooked rations of beef and flour. The sick were ordered left behind, and to emphasize the impending swiftness of the movement, Ewell directed further: "The troops that march will carry their blankets and provisions. Only the Ambulances and Regiment Ordnance Wagons and one wagon from Divisional H'dquarters will move." For all of his preparations, Banks and Pope knew about the flanking movement from its inception. "The march of this column could not of course be kept a secret," notes John Codman Ropes. "Everyone saw it—the clouds of dust were plainly visible, the signal officers reported its strength." Pope's only problem was one of interpretation; he totally misread Jackson's destination, and even thought he was going to the Shenandoah.[35]

Ewell had no sooner forded the Hazel River and headed for the upper fords across the Rappahannock than he ran into trouble. "A half mile beyond the Hazel our route led behind the crest of a high hill on which Stuart's Horse Artillery was placed engaged with a superior number of guns," Brown recounts. "The shells and solid shot passed just over the heads of our men, & at one place the troops had to go fast, stooping half bent. Near this as I came along the column Gen'ls Jackson and Ewell sat studying a map." Although two men were killed from Yankee fire, Ewell pushed on through Jeffersonton and Amissville. After some difficulty with rising water, he got his brigades across the Rappahannock and into Orleans. The first day's march of twenty-four miles—thwarted much of the way by Sigel's hastily arrayed artillery—halted at Salem, a small village on the Manassas Gap Railroad. According to Brown, Ewell rode through the campsite until late into the night, checking on his troops. The general and his aide fashioned a crude shelter in a fence corner, covered themselves with straw, and went to sleep in a thunderstorm. Their saddles served as pillows.[36]

The next day, August 26, Ewell and Forno again spearheaded Jackson's corps on its eastward trek through White Plains, Thoroughfare Gap in the Bull Run Mountains, Gainesville, and finally Bristoe Station. Robert E. Lee himself followed one day behind with Longstreet's corps. According to Jubal Early, at about sunset, "After a long and fatiguing march that paralleled the Manassas Gap Railroad, Ewell reached his destination." Bristoe Station was another depot on the Orange and Alexandria two or three miles southwest of Manassas Junction where the Manassas Gap linked up with the mainline into Alexandria and Washington; it was likewise five miles northeast of Catlett's Station and eight or so miles from Warrenton Junction. Cedar Run (not to be confused with the stream of the same name around Cedar or Slaughter Mountain), a tributary of the Occoquan, ran north and parallel to the Orange and Alexandria Railroad. Although the famed Bull Run empties into the Occoquan from the north, several rivulets struck Cedar Run from the northwest, including Broad and Kettle Runs, the latter streams being about a mile and a half apart.[37]

Upon reaching Bristoe, Jackson again interfered with Ewell's command by calling Isaac Trimble to take two of his regiments—the Twenty-first North Carolina under Lieutenant Colonel Saunders F. Fulton and the Twenty-first Georgia commanded by Major Thomas C. Glover, six hundred men in all—to seize Manassas Junction. Just as Early had been detached at Cedar Mountain, Jackson once more bypassed a compliant Ewell. Trimble and Jeb Stuart, who was present with the cavalry, both subsequently claimed credit for overwhelming the contingent of bluecoats guarding the vital rail junction. "Over 300 prisoners were taken, an immense quantity of commissary and quartermaster's stores, a large train loaded with precious army supplies, just arrived from Alexandria, and about 200 horses independent of those belonging to the cavalry," Trimble later wrote. "In this successful issue of the night's work I had no assistance from artillery or from any part of General Stuart's cavalry, a regiment of which arrived some hours after the attack was made and commenced an indiscriminate plunder of the horses." Trimble reported his losses at none killed and fifteen wounded. Major Glover, who filed a separate report, was even more pointed that Ewell's men had won the victory: "We attacked and captured Manassas Junction about 12 o'clock, this regiment charging and capturing a battery of artillery (four pieces) and about 70 prisoners, including a lieutenant colonel and several commissioned officers," he commented. About daylight "Stuart's cavalry arrived in town."[38]

While two of his regiments under Trimble were mastering the enemy at Manassas Junction, Ewell posted the remainder of his division across the railroad to guard against any surprise incursion from Pope. The forlorn Yankee generalissimo by this time had come to the stark realization that Jackson was between his own army and the Potomac—that he would have to fight his way to safety and that it was Major General Richard Stoddert Ewell who blocked his escape. Early, who filed a lengthy detailed divisional report after Ewell was wounded, tells what happened: "As soon as it was light next morning [August 27] the three brigades of the division left at Bristoe were placed in position as follows: Lawton's brigade was posted on the left of the railroad, Hays' [Forno's] brigade on the right of it, and my own brigade to the right of Hays' in a pine wood, our line of battle being fronted toward Warrenton Junction and occupying a ridge a short distance from Bristoe in the direction of that junction." What Early did not mention was that Ewell not only oversaw the new battle formation, but he also ordered four Louisiana regiments and one of Lawton's Georgia outfits forward to destroy the railroad bridge and adjacent track across Kettle Run— all under the command of Colonel Forno. More importantly, for the task at hand, it was Ewell, intent upon carrying out Jackson's implicit instruction to avoid a general engagement, who engineered a withdrawal when the enemy responded to Forno's advance. Colonel H. B. Strong (Sixth Louisiana) was stationed at Kettle Run, and Major T. B. Lewis (Eighth Louisiana) was at Broad Run when the Yankee fury struck.

Acting on Ewell's wishes, "the two regiments successfully [repulsed] two brigades of the enemy until their ammunition was expended until I ordered up the Fifth Regiment (Major B. Menger, commanding) to support them, when, after a few discharges from the latter regiment, the whole retired in as good order as if on parade," Forno said later. "One regiment from General Lawton's brigade, with one piece of artillery, supported the left of my line, and did good service in repelling an attempt of the enemy to flank us." Ewell was able to execute the withdrawal with textbook precision, and the successful maneuver was most important for its resultant impact upon the thinking of his antagonists. As a recent scholar put it, Pope believed "that elements of Jackson's force had been beaten at Kettle Run and that he was falling back on Manassas Junction in disarray." Although Joseph "Fighting Joe" Hooker had taken personal command of New Jersey troops fighting opposite Forno and Ewell, the drawback continued unhindered. Unaware that Longstreet was closing on the scene from gaps in the Bull Run Mountains, "Pope ordered the three columns of his army moving northeastward to divert from their original line of march and head towards Manassas Junction with the intent of crushing Jackson." But Pope's eagerness to annihilate the Confederates proved his undoing. When he turned his back on the pathways leading to the west, he unknowingly chose to ignore almost half of Lee's army that was approaching along the Manassas Gap Railroad. The arrival of Longstreet's division enabled Lee to complete a stunning victory a few days later after Jackson subsequently fell back to a defensive position behind an unfinished railroad near the old Manassas battlefield.

Although Ewell lay recovering from the surgeon's blade when the great fight took place, his masterful stand at Kettle Run contributed to Pope's discomfort, which eventually led to his defeat and dismissal from the Army of Virginia. Ewell's staged withdrawal at the critical moment made Pope think that Hooker had gained a tactical victory. It mostly blinded him to the impending harshness of Lee's plan to drive his forces beyond the Potomac. And Ewell had done it with minimal losses, although thirty-five of his men were reported killed during the twenty-sixth and twenty-seventh. On the eve of the Second Manassas, one day before suffering a great personal tragedy, Ewell had again proven himself an able lieutenant ever willing to effectuate "Stonewall's" every command. But a nagging question lay on the horizon that no one, not even Ewell himself, could have foreseen: Would he return to the army nine months later with an amputated leg and a new, but domineering wife, as the soldier he had been in the west and in the Confederate service under Jackson's tutelage? Or would he be an even more hesitant fighter when confronted with his own command decisions?[39]

Chapter 9

"WHAT! OLD EWELL GOING TO MARRY THAT PRETTY WOMAN"

Following Kettle Run, Ewell withdrew his division between Broad Run and Manassas Junction on the night of August 27, as Jackson, who knew that Lee and Longstreet were closing fast through Thoroughfare Gap with the rest of the army, prepared to spring the trap on Pope. The resultant battle, known as the Second Manassas, or Bull Run, had little to do with the set-to of July 1861 other than its near proximity to the latter. "The stream itself, Bull Run, played a minor role . . . except as a terrain feature for reference purposes," writes historian Edward J. Stackpole. "The 1862 battle was fought six or eight miles west of Centreville and three miles east of Gainesville, astride the Warrenton turnpike in an area about Groveton, where the opening engagement between Jackson and [Rufus] King occurred on the evening of August 28." Although Pope mistakenly determined that Jackson was withdrawing in the direction of Lee and Longstreet, Old Jack correctly perceived that the Federals were moving northward toward Centreville. In anticipation, he summoned William B. Taliaferro and A. P. Hill to begin a concentration east of the turnpike so that he might strike Pope's southernmost flank as it marched past. By the morning of August 28 he had his corps positioned along a partially completed railroad grade and extending from Sudley on Bull Run itself southeast to the hamlet of Groveton. Campbell Brown suggests that when Ewell's command reached Jackson's new line, the division could not see the turnpike but that it could hear King's wagon trains heaving toward the safety of the Washington defenses.[1]

Isaac Trimble, who had no direct order to move, held up the column for several hours until he could be persuaded to join the rest of the division when Ewell's men arose before daybreak for the trek north. Then, after a night spent pilfering and burning Federal supplies at Manassas Junction, Ewell commenced his march toward Mitchell's Ford across Bull Run. A. P. Hill also crossed at the same place but proceeded on to Centreville before backtracking over the famed Stone Bridge and then across Henry House Hill to the railroad cut. Taliaferro's division, on the other hand, marched directly from the junction to the rendezvous point. After crossing Bull Run, Ewell made a sharp turn to his left and tramped parallel to the notorious stream until he too reached the Stone Bridge.

Upon recrossing Bull Run and entering a road leading north to Sudley Springs, Ewell's division "halted & remained for sometime listening to the cannonading going on near Warrenton where our cavalry were slowly falling back on us," writes Brown. "After two or three hours, Gen'l Jackson and Gen'l Ewell (who had first held a rather lengthy consultation & then gone to sleep in a fence corner) ordered us into a wood near Sudley & south of the road." Ewell did not march into Sudley but followed the route taken by A. P. Hill to reach the railroad cut. Once in position between Taliaferro on his left and Hill to his east, he lay on the ground for a second nap before telling Brown that his horse "was used up" and sending him to acquire another. Brown crossed Bull Run to find "a powerful sorel" in Loudoun County, but when he could not locate a suitable ford and the horse would not swim the stream, he returned with Ewell's old mount. "Just then," he continues, "up came Captain E. V. White & lent the Gen'l a fine mare just captured."[2]

After some juggling of his brigades as well as those of Taliaferro and Hill, Ewell's four contingents were aligned so that part of Early's and all five of Trimble's regiments as well as Lawton's six were south of the unfinished railroad, while Forno was north of it and away from the turnpike. When Jackson gave the order to move on the Warrenton roadway about 7:00 P.M., he instructed Ewell to take charge of Taliaferro's men in addition to his own—the entire Confederate right flank. In spite of the late hour, Jackson acted when he learned "that a large body of the enemy, approaching from the direction of Warrenton, was moving down the turnpike towards Centreville." Then, continues Walter H. Taylor, one of Lee's aides, "this proved to be King's division of McDowell's corps." Early and Forno were left in reserve when Ewell ordered the brigades of Lawton and Trimble to attack. "We were ready & Taliaferro moved forward. As he did so a sharp fire was opened by our guns & as sharply answered," Brown re-counts. "The field over which we advanced was gently undulating—quite open, except on our left, where a ravine ran down toward the pike full of small trees & old-field pines. As we advanced a heavy fire was opened by the enemy's infantry which had been laying down in a slight depression of the ground (a dry ditch probably) & now, when they rose, only exposed the upper parts of their bodies." The Groveton imbroglio soon developed into point-blank mayhem, with neither side able to find shelter from the murderous hail of lead. In a classic piece of historical summary, Taliaferro wrote later: "It was a question of endurance and both sides endured."[3]

Lawton and Trimble had run into John Gibbon's command com-posed of the Nineteenth Indiana as well as the Second, Sixth, and Seventh Wisconsin regiments, known as the Black Hat Brigade because of its dis-tinctive headwear. Dubbed the Iron Brigade—a name that stuck for the rest of the war—by a zealous reporter at Antietam three weeks later, the outfit bore the Federal brunt at Groveton when "it suffered 33 per cent casualties while fighting a part of Stonewall Jackson's Corps." Although some of Gibbon's troops were interlaced with Abner Doubleday's brigade, the Sixth Wisconsin held the extreme right near the infamous ravine and pine trees mentioned by Campbell Brown. During the Confederate ad-vance, Ewell had joined one of Lawton's Georgia regiments in his zeal to drive the enemy from the ravine and open a path to the turnpike. As he squatted under a pine branch to get a better view of the field opposite the Sixth Wisconsin, led by Major Rufus R. Dawes, disaster struck when a Yankee bullet suddenly penetrated his left kneecap. The instantly disabling wound and his subsequent amputation removed him from active service for the next nine months and ultimately led to a changed Ewell.[4]

When Ewell was carried from the field at Groveton, Robert E. Lee and Stonewall Jackson had a half-won battle to complete. Although the main fight with Pope would come the next day, both commanders noted that tragedy had befallen their comrade. When Lee dashed off a brief communiqué to President Davis five days later, he took time to say that Ewell, as well as William B. Taliaferro, Isaac Trimble, Charles W. Field, and William Mahone, had been wounded during the fray. "The loss on both sides was heavy," read Lee's formal report dated June 8, "and among our wounded were Major-General Ewell and Brigadier-General Taliaferro, the former severely." Jackson likewise noted the loss of Ewell and Taliaferro at Groveton: "The former I regret to say, is still disabled by his wound, and the army deprived of his valuable service," he wrote a few days be-

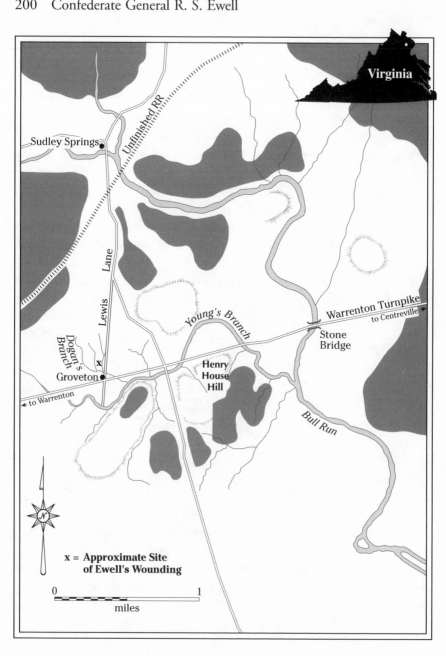

Groveton, August 28, 1862

fore his own fatal wounding as Ewell struggled to regain his strength in Richmond.[5]

Jeb Stuart told his wife on September 4 about Ewell's wounds and subsequent amputation, with the hope that "he will soon get well." Nine months earlier, however, the cavalryman had had a somewhat different view of his fellow officer when both men struggled for recognition in the new Confederate service. "It is whispered in the street that I was to be a Major General," he informed his beloved Flora. "I have no such expectations, but I do know I would make better than some. [George B.] Crittenden and Ewell for instance." Stuart's battle summaries for the twenty-eighth mention Ewell on various occasions but say nothing about his wounds, even though an addendum filed by Jed Hotchkiss, who acted as his stenographer on occasion, indicates that Stuart "spent the night on Thursday, June 28, with General Jackson near Sudley Mills."[6]

Jackson had plenty to occupy his mind through the night of August 28 with the wounding of Ewell and Taliaferro. When the battle reopened, he had assigned the Georgian Alexander R. Lawton to command Ewell's division and William E. Starke that of Taliaferro. After Ewell was shot on his extreme left at Groveton, Campbell Brown says nothing about Jackson's role in securing help for his fallen lieutenant. Yet Dr. Hunter McGuire, who examined him shortly afterward and performed his leg amputation, clearly avows that Jackson sent one of his aides to summon McGuire from another part of the field. The actual wounding occurred near or in a ravine that separated Ewell's left from the extreme right of A. P. Hill. Both Robert H. Fowler and Robert E. L. Krick, in carefully reasoned studies, fix the spot on Dogan's Branch of Bull Run just north of the Warrenton Pike and a nearly equal distance west of Lewis Lane.

Ewell was stricken but a few yards in front of the Twelfth Georgia Infantry, a part of Isaac Trimble's brigade, and, as Brown points out, he was surrounded by other Confederates. Amid the battlefield confusion, with wounded and dying comrades at every turn, no one apparently thought it necessary to summon immediate help. When Ewell sought a decisive action, he attempted to maneuver additional troops in support of Trimble's position. In other words, he wanted to reinforce the Confederate left west or along the depression that separated Trimble and Powell Hill. "Ewell was leading the 31st Georgia around or perhaps through the 12th Georgia in his push down the ravine," reads Krick's account. "The unit he was leading virtually *had* to be one of Lawton's, as all other regiments are accounted for. William Oates of the 15th Alabama asserted that men of Lawton's

Brigade cried, 'Here is General Ewell, boys,' which prompted the Federal fusillade that hit Ewell." John Hennessy says it "was probably the 12th Georgia."

When Brown lost sight of Ewell, he rode forward with Captain Tom Turner to locate him. Brown writes: "We came upon Gen. Trimble [in command of Ewell's left flank], who made us dismount and eat something with him." The din of battle must have subsided, because otherwise it would have been difficult to explain the repast. "I then left Turner and rode a little farther to try to find the Genl," Brown continues. "Very soon, in answer to my calls, somebody ran out and called that Genl. Ewell was there." Brown is emphatic that he discovered Ewell among some pine trees and, though he was in pain, set out "to find a surgeon—letting Trimble know on the way, what had happened and that he was in command." It must have been at this point that Jackson learned Ewell was injured and hurried his aide to find Dr. McGuire.[7]

Isaac Ridgeway Trimble's tenure in charge of Ewell's division must have been short-lived if it occurred at all. The sixty-year-old soldier says nothing about it in his autobiography/diary, nor does he mention Ewell's misfortune. In a twist of fate, Trimble was wounded on the twenty-ninth [one day after Ewell] in the leg by an "explosive ball which broke the bone & inflicted a bad wound." An 1822 graduate of West Point, he had served ten years in the prewar artillery before entering private life as a successful railroad engineer.

Although Trimble's limb was not amputated, he spent a long convalescence in Richmond when it failed to heal properly. Promoted to major general in January 1863, Trimble was given command of Jackson's "Old Division," but he was too weakened for active field command. After a period of recuperation in North Carolina, Lee placed him in charge of the Shenandoah Valley, but when he arrived at Staunton in June 1863, he discovered the area denuded of troops because of the Pennsylvania invasion. Immediately proceeding north in search of the army, Trimble served as a "volunteer aide" to Ewell until July 3, and it is his subsequent writing about the fighting for Culp's Hill and Cemetery Ridge that presents Ewell in such a negative light for latter-day historians. Trimble did in fact lose a leg when he suffered a wound on July 3, 1863, while leading Dorsey Pender's brigade in Pickett's ill-fated charge.[8]

Meanwhile, Jubal Early, by his own account, came on the scene "and had him [Ewell] carried to the hospital, after having difficulty persuading him to go, as he insisted upon having his leg amputated before he left the ground." Captain Brown avows that Ewell was being removed by litter bearers when he returned with an unnamed surgeon. He was in such a weakened condition from several days' constant exertion that he actually "slept on the litter." Apparently the physician accompanying Brown or other medical men on the field suggested that the limb might be saved. Hunter McGuire, who performed the operation, however, convinced him that the leg had to come off. Upon being transported to a makeshift field hospital "& after resting there a short time [he] was taken by a road thro the woods to Sudley's across the Run to a house just below the Ford where there was a field hospital," Brown asserts. "Here he remained until about 8 a.m., when the engagement on the opposite bank having begun shortly after daylight, became heavy & our left was driven a short distance, bringing the hospital under fire. We then removed him to 'Buckner's House' four miles off—where about 2 p.m. the amputation was performed." John Hennessy, a meticulous student of the Second Manassas, confirms that Ewell lay in two facilities before he was taken to the Buckner home. Ewell's own stepdaughter verifies his route to the place owned by Ariss Buckner, known locally as Auburn.[9]

There can be no question that the exigencies of battle coupled with the tortuous journey to Auburn had taken their toll on Ewell. According to Dr. McGuire: "The general's health, naturally not very good, was unusually bad at this time. He had also lost a great deal of sleep, and the night he was hurt, was compelled to drink a large quantity of tea to keep awake." McGuire continued in his 1866 remarks: "Tuesday night [August 26] his troops were engaged at Bristoe Station, and all day Wednesday [27th] they were fighting the advance of Gen. Pope's army. The whole of that night was occupied in marching to join the main body. Thursday [28th] they were fighting, marching and counter-marching all day, during a heavy engagement the General was wounded."

Born in 1835, the twenty-seven-year-old McGuire had been a valued member of Jackson's staff for several months. Characterized by Frank Vandiver as "blunt, good humored & full of honest life," he had not only finished medical school at age twenty but also enjoyed a wide professional reputation that reached beyond Virginia. The Winchester native's subsequent writing, including *The Confederate Cause and Conduct of the War,* contains meaningful insights into the men who forged the Southern war machine. A few months after his experience with Ewell, McGuire gained a lasting Confederate fame by tending Stonewall Jackson during his own amputation and last illness.[10]

Brown, McGuire, Harriet Turner, and others have left detailed, even graphic descriptions of Ewell's wounds. McGuire asserts the entry scar did not appear serious to the untrained eye—that only "a drop or two of blood" was trickling from the opening. But Brown and McGuire agree that Ewell was near collapse from trauma or shock when carried into the field hospital. Because he was kneeling under the pines to get a better view of the enemy, "he was hit upon being flexed, the ball passed down the tibia, and splitting it into several fragments." McGuire adds that the ball "came to rest in the leg muscles." He told Ewell, by his own account, that in all of his experience he had never encountered a successful outcome for such a wound without amputation. Although some writers ascribe the subsequent operation to others, and though he was assisted by several surgeons, McGuire is adamant: "I amputated the thigh just above the knee, performing the operation as rapidly and with as little loss of blood as I could."

The surgery took place in the early afternoon of August 29 at Auburn.[11] Ewell's stepdaughter called it "an amputation of the upper third" and added that his lean physical build made such an operation necessary to obtain sufficient "flaps" to cover the stump. Interestingly, the accounts by McGuire and Brown are strikingly similar. "While under the influence of chloroform," Brown relates, "he gave several orders to troops, spoke hurriedly of their movements, & only appearing to feel conscious of pain when the Doctor . . . began to saw the bone—at which he stretched both arms abroad & said: 'Oh! My God!'" Presumably Brown either witnessed the cutting or remained close by during the surgery, and, according to his account, Ewell was probably not completely desensitized to pain during the procedure. Before the limb was buried in a corner of the Buckner family garden, it was dissected and examined by another physician to satisfy Brown and the family that the amputation had been necessary. The ball had traveled six inches down the marrow of the leg bone before shattering it and entering the muscle. Brown pocketed several fragments for his mother but did not show them to Ewell. A severe reaction developed some hours following the amputation; McGuire told Brown that Ewell had become so weak that a real possibility of death from exhaustion was evident. When the doctor left for the front, other medicos, including Dr. S. B. Morrison—an in-law of Stonewall Jackson—stayed behind to oversee his care. Whiskey mixed with water was administered at frequent intervals until Ewell's pulse quickened and a semblance of recovery became manifest. "After remaining at Buckner's a week or more, during which the Gen'l progressed pretty well, we removed him to his cousin's Dr. Ewell's at the foot of Bull

Run Mtn.," Harriet Turner writes. She suggests that the move was necessitated by an outbreak of erysipelas among other convalescents in the temporary hospital nearby.[12]

Fortunately, for posterity, we have a fairly complete account of Ewell's stay in Dunblane, the home of Dr. Jesse Ewell, written by his daughter Eleanor M. B. Ewell: her memoir, "War Time Memories," which is included in the delightful little study *A Virginia Scene; or, Life in Old Prince William*, written by her niece, Alice Maude Ewell, in 1931.[13]

Some family wags referred to the place as "Dumblane," but the name was actually Dunblane, taken from a McGregor (his wife's family) place name in Maryland and before that Scotland. The home was south and west of Auburn and, says Miss Ewell, "it was a retired place, sheltered by woods at the back and by shade trees and much shrubbery on the other three points of the compass." Nearby, "within sight and call," was Edge Hill, the residence of John Smith Ewell, a son of Dr. Jesse Ewell. The homes were situated along present Virginia Route 15 "five miles from Aldie, Loudoun County, on the north and eight miles from Haymarket on the south in [the] County of Prince William." At the entrance to Dunblane "along the Carolina Road" was a small church "then called Ewell's Chapel, now [1931] Grace Episcopal Church." Although it has been dismantled, the chapel housed soldiers assigned to guard Ewell during his stay in Loudoun County.[14]

At Dunblane, in Brown's words, Ewell was "treated as kindly as possible & remained unmolested for several weeks until at length a raid of the enemy's cavalry was planned to capture him." As Eleanor Ewell points out, he was surely among friends who catered to his every need. Dr. Jesse Ewell (known as Jesse III) shared a common grandfather with Richard Stoddert Ewell in Colonel Jesse Ewell (1743–1805), or Jesse I. Jesse II, his father, became a successful planter in northern Virginia, but his son, Jesse III (1802–1897), not only became a respected physician but also received much of his early training from Dr. Thomas Ewell. James Ewell, a brother of Thomas and Jesse II, also a practicing doctor, had "commenced the study of medicine under the direction of his uncle, Dr. James Craik of Alexandria, family physician to General Washington."

It was a fortuitous circumstance that the injured Ewell found himself amid a congenial atmosphere permeated with medicos as well as Dr. S. B. Morrison and other army doctors who accompanied him to Dunblane. His host had visited him at the Buckner home and inspected his stump, but his family was hardly prepared for the wounded invalid whom litter bearers deposited on their doorstep. "I remember well the maimed figure on the litter, covered with a sheet, and the pale haggard face upon the pillow," Eleanor Ewell wrote. "The keen blue eyes were, however, wide open, and seemed to note everything. He spoke not a word, but one had the impression that nothing said or done escaped him." Edward Carter Turner, who visited Ewell on September 10, confirms that he seemed "quite feeble but [did] not complain of pain."[15]

Ewell remained at Dunblane for "about a fortnight," and though Dr. Ewell at one time thought that he might not pull through, he slowly began to gain strength. His brothers Benjamin and William came to the home immediately and kept him company to the last of his stay. "[F]or the first time these three brothers were at our house," writes Eleanor Ewell. "My father was several years their senior, but the four had lived in one household when he was a youth and they children. All took pleasure of being again a family party." Ewell was also attended by his servant John France, "a dignified personage," who helped with his meals, which were personally prepared by the lady of the house. The Apache lad, Friday, whom Ewell had "purchased" in the west, likewise accompanied him to Dunblane. "His daring feats of horsemanship, riding without saddle or bridle with arms extended and sometimes standing upright, were the marvel of our colored people," comments Miss Ewell.[16]

Several prominent men called to chat and pay their respects, including Alfred Randolph, later Episcopal Bishop of Virginia, Congressman Jackson Morton, and Arrel Marsteller, Ewell's neighbor at Stony Lonesome, who would later plead for a preferred place for his son after Ewell's promotion to corps command the following year.[17] In spite of his callers, and constant attention from his brothers, who took turns with Brown reading novels to him, it is clear that Ewell was not a well man. Although Brown told his mother on September 18 that "Gen'l Ewell's, steadily & pretty well progressing towards recovery," he also pointed out: "Three of the ligatures on the arteries have already come away, and the other three will in a few days. We have delayed in moving by the unusual amount of pain which follows any movement of the leg—consequent on his high state of excitement at the time he was shot, but not interfering in any way with his recovery." While Brown makes no mention of enemy raiding parties, the groups at Dunblane soon had reports that Lieutenant Colonel Joseph H. Brinton and the Yankee cavalry were scouring the countryside for him. According to Harriet Turner, Ewell was sought as a bargaining chip for a number—she set the figure at sixty—of Northern soldiers. Finally, in order to thwart their designs, Ben Ewell decided that his brother could not fall into enemy hands, and following hurried preparations, his attendants began a westward trek that eventually carried him to an early resort on the Cowpasture River.[18]

From his sickbed at Dunblane, Ewell could detect the unmistakable sound of cannon fire rumbling across the Manassas plain. It came from the Antietam battlefield, where the armies of Robert E. Lee and George B. McClellan were locked in the deadliest single day of the entire war. Lee had ordered Jackson toward the Potomac on September 9—a mere twelve days after the Second Manassas. The invasion of Maryland had been undertaken with no small Confederate trepidation, but the "Indomitable Jackson" obligingly led the van of Lee's invasion, and Ewell would surely have been at his side had he not fallen at Groveton. Alexander Lawton now had charge of Ewell's division and remained very near Jackson as the dreadful contest unfolded around the famed Dunker Church on September 17— one day before Brown's appraisal of Ewell's condition for Lizinka. Weak though he was, Ewell knew Jackson's fighting tenacity firsthand and feared for his safety. At Dunblane he told Ben that if Jackson fell, "the Confederacy might fall with him—he might be 'crazy as a March Hare,' but method surely lurked in Old Jack's madness." In a sense, he lived to see his premonitions fulfilled. Eight months later he joined a number of Confederate luminaries as honorary pallbearer for Jackson's Richmond funeral after the fighting at Chancellorsville. It is worthy of mention that Lee—even with Ewell at his side commanding Jackson's old Second Corps—never won another major engagement after May 1863.[19]

The Antietam fight took place within forty miles of Dr. Ewell's home, and not only Brinton but other Yankee cavalry patrols swept the surrounding countryside nearly at will. It was time to move, and, shaded by men who held an umbrella to shield him from the September sun, Ewell, accompanied by Brown and relays of soldiers to carry his litter, set out for the west along an obscure pathway across Bull Run Mountain. Although the Reverend William Stoddert left Dunblane by an alternate route to confuse their pursuers in the event of capture, he shortly rejoined his brother to serve as companion and stenographer. "We just crossed the top of the mountain when it was found something had been forgotten & Private Fox was sent after it on a horse or mule," Brown recounts. "He got to Dr E's safely but in coming away met a body of Federal Cavalry, who took him prisoner & questioned him closely as to Gen'l E's whereabouts." Although Fox pleaded ignorance, Dunblane was searched thoroughly by the Yankees both on the evening of Ewell's departure and afterward. One Federal officer even scoured the bedchambers of Dr. Ewell's daughter, but, says Eleanor Ewell, "'this Yankee,' at least acted like a gentleman." Dr. Ewell himself was incarcerated briefly after "five or six searches of his home."[20]

Meanwhile, Ewell's party made its way southward into Fauquier County and Kinloch, the home of Edward Turner. Then it was into Culpeper County across the Rappahannock and Hazel rivers to Rixeyville, where the fugitives rested briefly before renewing their journey to Culpeper Court House and the Orange and Alexandria Railroad. Ewell had now traveled upward of fifty miles, and the constant swaying of his litter caused the bone to protrude through the slowly healing stump. Another operation resulted in the removal of an inch of bone before he was "put in a baggage car" for the train ride to Charlottesville. After a respite in the home of Mrs. Thomas Farish, where "he was very well cared for," he boarded the Virginia Central Railroad for the sixty-five-mile jaunt to Millsboro Springs. The entire company landed at a hotel owned by "Old Captain" John U. Dickinson. "Opened a few years before the war of 1861," Dickinson's establishment was situated three miles west of the rail stop at Millsboro. The Bath County hotel and spa, which served as Ewell's home for the next two months, was one of several popular watering places in the Bath-Greenbrier region that encompassed the more renowned Greenbrier Resort beyond the Allegheny Front in present West Virginia.[21]

Ewell was met shortly by his brothers Ben and William; his niece Lizzie also arrived with her father from Pittsylvania Court House to console her favorite uncle. As early as September 4 she had received word that Uncle Dick had undergone an amputation, but "so far as [his] sinking under the operation he bore it well, and that he [was] not to be considered dangerously wounded." But perhaps the best gift of all was the coming of Lizinka with her daughter, Harriet Brown, from her home in Tennessee. Brown's letter of September 18 to his mother from Dunblane hinted that she should make preparation to come east. The biographer of 140 years later can only speculate, but it seems plausible that the forty-two-year-old Lizinka Brown not only took charge of the convalescent's sickroom, but she also encouraged the courtship that led to her marriage the following May. Captain Thomas Turner, who courted and shortly married Harriet Brown, also joined the "secure" coterie at Captain Dickinson's after serving under Jeb Stuart in the recapture of Harpers Ferry. The near-idyllic setting of Bath County among the sweeping valleys of the Cowpasture and Jackson rivers, with their numerous resorts astride the chief roadway to the

Kanawha Valley, proved a good place for recuperation and for courtship. "Gen'l E. steadily recovered," Brown notes, "& sometime in November was well enough to get to Dr. Hancock's in Richmond."[22]

Unlike the bone-jostling journey to Bath County, Ewell's passage to the capital was relatively uneventful. After a buggy ride from the hotel to the depot at Millsboro, he once more boarded the Virginia Central train that carried him through Staunton, Charlottesville—where he did not have to change trains as before—and Hanover Junction to Richmond. Ewell and his companions settled into the residence of Dr. F. W. Hancock, a regimental surgeon, on East Main Street. The house, which served as his home until he resumed active service in late May, was situated within a few blocks of the Confederate capitol on Franklin Street. It was also very near St. Paul's Episcopal Church, where his wedding ceremony was performed six months later. The grand old church—still an active congregation—had Jefferson Davis as a communicant in April 1865 when Lee sent an urgent message to the president: "My lines have broken around Petersburg, I can no longer defend the capital." In November 1862 the final Confederate collapse lay three years on the horizon as Ewell moved into the tranquil home of Dr. Hancock and his family.[23]

The period from his wounding, particularly after November, until he assumed command of Lee's Second Corps, found Ewell writing few letters. He had no active command, and his customary correspondents, Lizinka and Lizzie, were at his side. And since Brown had gone from Virginia to join Joseph E. Johnston in the west, we are obliged to draw upon others for insights into Ewell's progress. An informative, even interesting letter tucked among the Ewell correspondence in the Library of Congress, dated January 22, from Ben to his own daughter Lizzie, freely discusses "your Uncle Dick" and his health. Written from Chattanooga, where he too had joined the staff of Joe Johnston, it calls attention to an accident on Christmas Day 1862 in which Ewell fell on an icy pavement while hobbling about on crutches. The incident must have gained a wide notice, because Ben learned about it from a Tennessee newspaper. Although he immediately telegraphed the Reverend Stoddert, who had joined the Richmond cortege, for information, Ben received an indifferent answer: "From your Uncle William's reply," he told Lizzie, "I thought he received little or no injury." Whether William was fearful lest the Yankees might intercept his telegraphic response is unknown, but, as Dr. McGuire points out, the fall probably set Ewell's recovery back by several weeks. He had knocked off another piece of bone, which then led to severe hemorrhaging of the reopened wound.

Ewell's reluctance to have outside assistance caused Dr. Hancock to warn that a similar incident could happen at any time. "It is strange how an indisposition to have people stirring around you or helping you in case of sickness, over those unable to help one's self, runs in families." Notwithstanding a strong Ewell appetite for personal independence, Ben admonished his daughter that Uncle Dick needed a strong-willed nurse. "He ought to have his choice of following the instructions of Dr. Hancock or of being under the care of a strapping Negro of the female sex."[24]

Dr. McGuire attests Ewell had a difficult time because due to "the shape of the stump and the ill-contrived wooden leg he wore, he was frequently troubled with abrasions of the skin, small abscesses, and so on." After he was fitted with a suitable prosthesis, Ewell made a modicum of progress before his death in 1872, ten years after the amputation. During the war he was not a well man, as his stepdaughter points out, when he resumed active field service in May 1863. "His physical condition was greatly impaired by the loss of his leg," observed Thomas H. Carter. "I recall most vividly his pale and anemic face at Gettysburg and Spotsylvania battles." Carter, an artillery officer under Robert E. Rodes, generously added that Ewell's "courage was of the most undying character; nothing could demoralize it." Other Confederate fighting men, including John H. Claiborne, were more direct in their assessments: "Ewell has never been able to command troops since he lost his leg though they gave him Jackson's immortal corps—nor can any man who has lost a leg high up," Claiborne conjectured in July 1864.[25]

Although criticism of Ewell in Confederate ranks became nearly universal following his dismal performance at Gettysburg, there can be no question that the amputation not only affected him physically but psychologically and emotionally as well. It is probably impossible to separate these vital components of the human psyche, but the loss of a limb is traumatic by any measure. Military surgeons from antiquity have wrestled with the need for quick amputations after battlefield injuries, and a substantial medical literature has developed over the centuries on how best to treat the wounded soldier. Until the development of gunpowder and firearms in fourteenth-century Europe, wounds made by slow-velocity projectiles left an easily discernable and relatively clean aperture that could be easily treated. All manner of techniques were attempted from ligation of damaged arteries to drawing horsetails through wounds of the legs and arms to remove poisons. But injuries from gunshot with the need to remove bone fragments and to cleanse larger areas of collapsed tissue changed the old practices. "The nineteenth century saw a resurgence in the use of amputation for gunshot wounds of the extremities," says one scholarly study. "In the context of large battles and massive casualties of the Napoleonic Wars, primary amputation within a few hours of injury became the most important surgical operation." One of Napoleon's surgeons reported performing two hundred amputations on a single day during the Little Corporal's Russian campaign.[26]

Ewell clearly fit into the prevailing nineteenth-century practice of quick amputations after a battlefield event. What was less well-appreciated by Civil War medicos was the psychological impact, both short- and long-term, of his injuries. The famed phantom pain syndrome—not fully understood to this day—in which the brain imprints the feelings of hurt in the lost limb, is nearly always experienced by amputees. And importantly, a measured loss of self-esteem or the fundamental way in which a man views himself occurs in such cases. A soldier of Ewell's cast of mind accustomed to leading his troops on horseback—the epitome of nineteenth-century manhood—who afterward had to be helped from his carriage would experience an understandable impact upon the psyche. Yet "those who suffer amputation by reason of war-incurred disability are, in one sense, more fortunate," proffers a modern authority. "Under ordinary circumstances, they can point to the amputation with justifiable pride; the result of an honorable wound incurred in the defense of one's country."[27]

There is no indication that Ewell was proud of his misfortune; if anything, the opposite may have been true. As late as March 1863 he appeared more concerned about its negative impact upon his career. "Should General Jackson or Lee in your presence make any inquiries as regards my health, you will oblige me if you will say that my leg is not yet healed," he appraised Jubal A. Early as the Chancellorsville operation began to unfold. "I am sitting up to write, though it is not pleasant, and I have to lie down occasionally to rest." If they needed someone in his "fix," Ewell said, he was ready to serve.[28]

But was he ready to serve psychologically and emotionally as well? "Setting aside all attempts at psychology, a simple fact becomes very clear indeed," notes a modern doctor. "There is absolutely nothing to be gained (and the risk of increased disability can result) if amputees dwell upon the reasons for having become an amputee." Besides the written comments of John Claiborne, Harriet Turner, Dr. McGuire, and others, Ewell himself spoke about his injury in his several letters to Jubal A. Early and P. G. T. Beauregard during his stay with Dr. Hancock. In addition to the letter of

March 8 cited earlier, another, dated January 7, says, "I'm still on my back"; and he complained about his fall on Christmas Day. A letter to Beauregard, commanding at Charleston, South Carolina, was a bit more optimistic: "I have been in the saddle several times since my leg has healed, and find that I have so little trouble keeping my seat that I have offered my services in the field, proferring my willingness to take a small division in view of my shortcomings in the way of legs." If the notion is correct that commenting or "harping" about an amputation is detrimental, then from the available evidence it appears Ewell fell into that pattern.[29]

Ewell's early biographer Percy Gatling Hamlin, himself a military physician, comments that Ewell "was debilitated and anemic from his previous medical history"—that "he was forty-six years-old, and the twenty years spent under the semi-tropical sun of the Southwest made him look twenty more." Hamlin also argues that after the amputation Ewell became a changed man spiritually through the admonitions of Lizzie and the Reverend Moses Hoge, a family confidant, to curb his cursing and profane outbursts. Although good surgical results are essential to any satisfactory recovery, modern medical thinking suggests that resolution of "psychosocial issues is equally important." Working in Ewell's favor was the concept that older amputees are able to accept their fate more readily than younger ones. Another physician, Paul E. Steiner, who studied Ewell in depth, offers a similar evaluation. Upon a lengthy overview of Ewell's medical and military background as well as his family tree, Steiner concludes: "It would seem that Richard Ewell's troubles were probably acquired"—that his indecisiveness on later battlefields resulted not from his misfortune at Groveton but had long been a part of his makeup. "It is important that his insecurity existed in 1862, and did not follow his wound as had been alleged." And, he adds, "it is possible that the loss of vigor that followed the wound increased the indecision."[30]

Curiously, John Bell Hood, another high-profile Confederate, suffered an amputation comparable to Ewell, with a different yet similar outcome. Hood, an 1853 graduate of West Point, like Ewell, had served in the Indian Wars prior to secession and rushed to the Stars and Bars at the outbreak of Civil War. After receiving an arm wound at Gettysburg that rendered the limb useless for the rest of his life, he suffered a leg wound at Chickamauga that led to an amputation above the knee. "During the convalescence from both wounds spent in Richmond, he wooed and was kept dangling by a beautiful young woman, but won the personal interest and military support of Jefferson Davis." Unlike Ewell, he did not win the

Robert E. Lee. The sculptor Valentine called this Lee's "most accurate likeness" (West Virginia State Archives).

Jeb Stuart. The cavalry-man who thought himself a better officer than Ewell (U.S. Army Military History Institute).

Stonewall Jackson, who kept a tight rein on Ewell until his wounding at Groveton. Ewell called him mad but not to his face (National Archives).

Joseph E. Johnston, who told Ewell it took seven years to recover from a wound (Massachusetts Commandery of the Loyal Legion and the U.S. Army Military History Institute).

Robert E. Rodes. Ewell's faithful subordinate before he fell in the fighting under Jubal Early (Massachusetts Commandery of the Loyal Legion and the U.S. Army Military History Institute).

Richard Taylor. Son of President Zachary Taylor. Served under Ewell until assuming command in Louisiana. His 1879 memoir did much to present Ewell in an unfavorable light to subsequent generations (U.S. Army Military History Institute).

Richard Stoddert Ewell (Massachusetts Commandery of the Loyal Legion and the U.S. Army Military History Institute).

Lizinka Brown Ewell. A cousin, she was the only woman Ewell ever loved and was his wife from 1863 until his death in 1872 (Tennessee State Archives and Library).

Above left, G. Campbell Brown. Ewell's stepson, wartime aide, and lifelong defender (Tennessee State Archives and Library). *Above right,* Susan Polk Brown. Mrs. Campbell Brown (Tennessee State Archives and Library).

Above left, A. S. "Sandie" Pendleton. Ewell's aide, who took a dim view of officers' wives staying with the army (West Virginia State Archives). *Above right,* Dr. Hunter McGuire. Ewell's surgeon at Groveton (West Virginia State Archives).

Above left, Ambrose Powell Hill. Ewell's fellow corps commander in the Army of Northern Virginia (West Virginia State Archives). *Above right,* James Longstreet. Commander of the First Corps who sought to influence Ewell during the Pennsylvania campaign (Massachusetts Commandery of the Loyal Legion and the U.S. Army Military History Institute).

Isaac Ridgeway Trimble. A Marylander who pleaded with Ewell to attack at Gettysburg (The Huntington Library and Art Gallery).

Above, Hetty Cary. The beautiful
Baltimore performer who be-
friended Ewell and his wife in
Richmond (Enoch Pratt Free
Library). *Right,* Benjamin Stoddert
Ewell. Ewell's older brother and
lifelong supporter (Swem Library,
College of William and Mary).

Jubal Anderson Early. Ewell's friend who led the Second Corps into the Shenandoah after Ewell was "laid on the shelf" (Massachusetts Commandery of the Loyal Legion and the U.S. Army Military History Institute).

woman of his dreams, although he was promoted to lieutenant general and placed in command of the Army of Tennessee when Joe Johnston was shunted aside during the ill-fated Georgia campaign. Ewell's promotion to lieutenant general and assignment to Jackson's old command came first, but the question arises: Did President Davis have a fondness for wartime generals who recuperated in Richmond? Whereas Ewell continued to find every opportunity for evading headlong contact with the enemy, when Hood returned to the field he was often the rash, bold commander who threw caution to the wind. Even though his chief biographer registers a strong demur, Dr. Steiner contends Hood's wounds caused a psychological change that "bordered on an obsessive-psychoneurotic reaction." Hood became the overly aggressive generalissimo, while Ewell became an overly reticent one—in both instances, it might be argued, amputations led to disaster for the Confederacy.[31]

In addition to the physical agitation of his slowly healing stump as well as his associated mental readjustments, Ewell's religious transformation unquestionably affected his later persona. The Civil War was permeated with a rampant evangelism that raced not only through the Army of Northern Virginia but through Confederate forces in the west as well. It was founded upon an Anglo-Saxon homogeneity encompassing the larger Southern society that marshaled the great field armies of 1861–1865. This widespread adherence to "a fundamental emphasis upon sin and salvation" contributed in a real manner to the creation of a Confederate nationalism that sustained those forces—it provided a Southern cohesiveness. And, writes, Emory Thomas, "however much southerners railed against the Puritan origins of their New England brethren, they themselves had incorporated much of the Puritan heritage into Southern style evangelical Protestantism."

Colportage, tractarianism, and energetic revival meetings conducted by a host of protestant chaplains attached to the army characterized the Southern war effort; many, if not most, soldiers and officers alike "yoked duty to God and country" as the war progressed. One of Ewell's division commanders after 1863, Brigadier General Stephen Dodson Ramseur, writes Gary Gallagher, implored a family member not to become discouraged with the Confederate cause—that "the God of Justice will order all things for good." Although Ewell frequently exploded with a soldier's profanity—all uttered with a noticeable lisp made worse by agitation—he had been reared in a Christian environment at Stony Lonesome, had exhibited a keen interest in things religious while a young officer on the frontier, and watched his own brother become an ordained Presbyterian minister. A man with that background could not be totally oblivious to the ubiquitous camp meetings, officially sanctioned fasting days, and evangelical fervor sweeping the ranks. And perhaps most telling of all was the consuming devoutness of Jackson, with whom he had an intimate association through the Valley campaign, Seven Days, and Cedar Mountain—the same commander's safety that alarmed him as an invalid at Auburn.[32]

Ewell could not have been unaware that his own troops were ablaze with religious intensity. As he rode about the avenues of Richmond with Lizinka and Lizzie at his side, the men who had followed him for the past year—now commanded by Jubal A. Early—were in a state of decided excitement. After the Maryland fight, as the army lay encamped around Winchester, "the great body of soldiers" in some regiments under Alexander Lawton met "for prayer and exhortation every night, [while] exhibiting the deepest solemnity, and presented themselves numerously for the prayers of the chaplains and the church." Then, continues the Reverend W. W. Bennett, a Confederate chaplain as well as superintendent of the Soldiers' Tract Association, "quite a pleasant number express hope in Christ." An identical phenomenon developed in Trimble's brigade, where "the most glorious revival ever witnessed by the Rev. D. Joseph Stiles, also took place at Winchester." These were Ewell's men, who would soon rejoin his command in the newly constituted Second Corps—men who exerted a quiet influence and who would not appreciate profane utterances even in the turmoil of battle.[33]

Richard Stoddert Ewell's religious conversion, by his own admission, developed from his close connection with Jackson, although the cursing continued, if Dr. Hamlin can be believed, until Lizzie and the Presbyterian divine, Dr. Moses D. Hoge, urged him to give up the habit. As related by the Reverend Beverly Tucker Lacy, a confidant of Jackson:

[A]t a council of war, one night, Jackson had listened very attentively to the view of his subordinates, and asked to wait until the next morning to present his own. As they came away, A. P. Hill laughingly said to Ewell, "Well! I suppose Jackson wants time to pray over it." Having occasion to return to his quarters again a short time after, Ewell found Jackson on his knees and heard his ejaculatory prayers for God's guidance in the perplexing movements then before him. The sturdy veteran Ewell was so deeply impressed by this incident and by Jackson's general religious character, that he said: "If that is religion I must have it;" and in making a profession of faith not long afterwards he attributed his conversion to the influence of Jackson's piety.

The episode must have taken place during the Seven Days or Cedar Mountain (June-August 1862), as A. P. Hill, active on the Peninsula, did not take part in Jackson's Shenandoah campaign. The Reverend J. William Jones, a Baptist minister and later biographer of Robert E. Lee, includes a full-page lithograph titled "Stonewall Jackson Preparing for Battle," depicting Jackson in consuming prayer inside an army tent, with Ewell (wearing a campaign hat) looking through the open flaps, in his account of Ewell's experience. "Gen'l Ewell—'If this is religion, I must have it,'" reads the drawing caption—the same words used by Lacy.

Ewell, Jones relates, "was ready to stand up for Jesus" throughout the remainder of his life. After Gettysburg, when Ewell was castigated within army circles, the religious activity continued unabated within the Second Corps "while it lay on the Upper Rappahannock." Dr. Leo Rosser, a representative of the Methodist Episcopal Church, South, announced his intention "to visit and preach [to Ewell's men] division by division, brigade by brigade—stopping longest where I can do the most good, noting vacancies in the chaplaincy, circulating religious reading as it reaches me, and sympathizing with the sick and wounded soldiers." The swirling revival among the Second Corps surely had Ewell's active encouragement—it could hardly have been otherwise. Jackson was the most overtly pious commander in the Southern cause, and he had never flinched when it was time to send his troopers into harm's way. While Stonewall Jackson could send his legions to their deaths with sure knowledge in the rightness of the Confederacy, Ewell was never able to act decisively except in rare instances. It is difficult, if not impossible, to assert whether his religious transformation or psychological trauma accompanying the amputation led to Ewell's hesitancy on later battlefields. But his newly acquired religiosity did not end his irrationality under stress, as Robert E. Lee and other Southern strategists soon learned.[34]

Two months after Ewell told Early that the doctors had ordered him not "to ride on horseback," word reached Richmond from Guiney Station that the lamented Jackson was dead. Wounded by his own men on May 2 at Chancellorsville, Stonewall had lingered until the tenth at the home of Thomas D. Chandler on the Richmond, Fredericksburg, and Potomac Railroad. The impact of the intrepid warrior's loss was immediate and far-reaching—like a thunderclap across the Southland. Although Ewell had missed the greatest Confederate triumph of the war when Jackson had spearheaded a march to Joe Hooker's rear at Chancellorsville, his old division was once more in the forefront of the fight. And he could hardly have missed a piece in the *Richmond Enquirer* for May 13, three days after the tragedy: "During his delirium [Jackson's] mind reverted to the field of battle, and he sent orders to Gen. A. P. Hill to prepare for action and to Maj. Hawks, his commissary, and to the surgeons," the paper reported. "He frequently expressed to his aides his wish that Major General Ewell should be ordered to the command of his corps; his confidence in General Ewell was very great, and the manner in which he spoke of him showed that he had duly considered the matter." The Ewell-Jackson association had clearly been a success from the Shenandoah to Kettle Run, and though Ewell's stepdaughter declared him a sick man, the upheaval surrounding Jackson's death induced public support for his elevation to corps command.[35]

A national hero had been taken from the Confederate pantheon, and the question rapidly became: Was Ewell the soldier to replace him? Even Harriet Turner had to admit that no one could take Jackson's place. Ewell, who had his supporters from the beginning, also had a number of detractors, but propriety demanded that he say nothing in his own behalf. There was little for the invalided soldier to do but await events. Although dismal performances at Gettysburg and in the Overland campaign lay on the horizon, once Lee and the president decided to raise him to corps command, several of his fellow commanders voiced reservations. "As the senior major-general of the army, and by reason of distinguished services and ability General Ewell was entitled to command the Second Corps," James Longstreet observed. "But there were other major generals of rank below Ewell whose services were such as to give them claims next after Ewell's, so that when they found themselves neglected there was no little discontent, and the fact that both the new lieutenant generals [A. P. Hill was the other] were Virginians made the trouble more grievous." He all but said Ewell's appointment would not have materialized had he been from another state. Daniel H. Hill, a North Carolinian, who was next in line behind Ewell, became extremely critical of Lee's subsequent Pennsylvania campaign with Ewell in the forefront of the Northern invasion.[36]

Meanwhile, Jackson's body was transported by rail to the capital and preparations set in motion for a state funeral. Although Ewell was named honorary pallbearer, it is unclear if he was fit enough to attend the funeral or take part in the grand procession from the Governor's Mansion to the capitol.[37] As the sorrowful cortege passed Dr. Hancock's house on Grace Street, a Richmond paper noted that Jackson's hearse, "with corpse, was followed by the war steed of the dead hero, caparisoned, and led by a groom, members of the old Stonewall Brigade, composed of invalids and others, not now in the ranks, (these attracted much sympathic notice as they moved with slow tread and downcast look, as though each was following the corpse of a father). . . . Major General Elzey and staff mounted; Generals officiating as pallbearers, etc, among them [Lieutenant] General Longstreet, Brigadier Generals Winder, Garnett, Kemper, and Corse, Commodore Forrest, all in full uniform and mounted." Following the generals and Forrest came a carriage bearing President and Mrs. Davis as well as carriages transporting a number of invalids. If Ewell was among them in his own carriage, as was his custom, local reporters failed to notice it. Similarly, when the body was taken by train and canal boat to Lexington for burial, there is no mention of Ewell in press accounts of Jackson's interment in the Shenandoah Valley that he loved so much. Like his compeers throughout the army, Ewell was unquestionably heartbroken and bereaved at the deceased soldier's removal from the scene. The ceremonies in Lexington were a VMI affair throughout, with the corps of cadets, General F. H. Smith, school commandant, and local ministers overseeing the last rites.[38]

In the weeks following Jackson's death, events quickened for Ewell; immediately after his promotion to lieutenant general, his fiancée of more than a year consented to marriage before he departed Richmond to join the army for the march into Pennsylvania. Whether Lizinka Brown was impressed with his new position as Robert E. Lee's immediate subordinate or she agreed to consummate the union before he once again went in harm's way, she at last gave in to his suit. Constance Cary, the actress/writer who attended the wedding, wrote later that "Mrs. Brown and her pretty, bright-eyed daughter Harriot" were in complete charge of Ewell's sickroom whenever she and her cousins Hetty and Jeannie Cary had called at the Hancock home. She straightforwardly says the Ewell-Brown marriage "was the outcome of his convalescence from his wound."

The remarkable Cary sisters, Hetty and Jeannie, as well as Constance, were in the forefront of Richmond's wartime society, and their visits indicate that Richard Ewell was abreast of the latest goings-on. According to Mary Boykin Chesnut, Hetty was a favorite of Lee—he once held her hand in public—and she enjoyed a wide reputation among the young blades in his army. Henry Kyd Douglas adjudged her "the handsomest woman in the Southland—with her classic face, her pure complexion, her auburn hair, her perfect figure, and carriage, altogether the most beautiful woman I ever saw in any land." Known as the "Belle of Richmond" after her flight from Baltimore, Hetty later became the bride of General John Pegram, who was killed at Petersburg during the last phases of the war and after only three weeks of marriage. Her sister Jeannie is generally credited with using a poem by James Ryder Randall, a fellow Baltimore Confederate, to fashion the popular wartime song "Maryland, My Maryland," which the Carys frequently performed on the Richmond stage; they often entertained the Maryland Line in the field while it was part of Ewell's command. Their Virginia cousin Constance, an intimate of the Ewell family, later married Burton Harrison, personal secretary to Jefferson Davis, and became a noted writer after the war; her *Reflections, Grave and Gay* is considered by many to be "one of the fine social records of the war."[39]

Ewell and Lizinka, who had been a widow for nineteen years, were obviously hobnobbing with the Confederate elite during the last part of their engagement—with politicians, soldiers, and socialites who would and did help him. As had been the case with Jackson's funeral, it is unclear precisely when their marriage vows were exchanged. Although the marriage records at St. Paul's indicate May 26, three days after his promotion to lieutenant general, Harriet Turner is insistent that the two were quietly "married at our lodgings at Mrs. Hancock Lee's, on Grace Street, Richmond." Presumably Mrs. Brown and her daughter had rooms near Dr. Hancock's home, also on Grace Street, during Ewell's recovery. The Reverend Charles Minningrode, a nationally known divine, who had come from St. Paul's to officiate, in all probability recorded the event the following day in the church registry. A former professor at the College of William and Mary, Minningrode remained at the church for thirty-three years (1847-1880) and became the cleric who conducted burial ceremonies for numerous Confederate heroes.

Ewell's stepdaughter is correct that it was a quiet affair, because even my own close examination of several Richmond newspapers failed to uncover the merest contemporary mention of the marriage. That in itself is strange since the President and Mrs. Davis were in attendance. Also present, Harriet Turner records, were: "General A. R. Lawton, Colonel B. S. Ewell and Miss [Lizzie] Ewell, Dr. Moses Hoge's family, and Miss Constance Cary, . . . Dr. Hancock and his family, and other members of Ewell's staff." Ewell announced at the ceremony that he had waited longer than Jacob "to marry the only woman he had ever loved," that his constancy had extended over twenty-five years, since 1837 when he first fell in love with his cousin while a plebe at West Point. "Their union was a singularly happy one," Mrs. Turner offers. "Many years after this, Miss Emily Mason, then at the head of one of the large hospitals in Richmond, since known on both sides of the Atlantic for her great charm of manner, literary cultivation, and inexhaustible benevolence told me that General Lee told [her] when he heard of this marriage—'What! Old Ewell going to marry that pretty woman.'"[40]

Lizinka Ewell held extensive landholdings in Tennessee, Mississippi, and Missouri that had been inherited from her father, George Washington Campbell (1769–1848); her brother, George Washington Campbell Jr. (1819-1853); and her husband, James Percy Brown, who died in 1844 at age thirty-two. Fearful that her marriage to a high-ranking Confederate might lead to some or all of these properties already in Union hands being confiscated by Federal authority, Ewell sought out Judge James Lyons, a famed Richmond attorney, on May 25. An intimate of Robert E. Lee and President Davis as well as a member of the Confederate congress, Lyons, who later defended Davis against charges of treason, counseled restraint. As it turned out, the quest for legal help in 1863 profited little.[41]

Actually, Ewell had every reason to be concerned about his wife, as subsequent events proved. Two years later her property in St. Louis and Nashville was indeed not only seized by the Johnson government, but she was also put under arrest briefly when Andrew Johnson became convinced that she was not a redeemed Confederate. Although Mrs. Ewell had known the new president personally for several years prior to secession and made repeated appeals to him during 1865, Johnson apparently harbored an intense dislike for the Ewells. After extensive legal and indeed political maneuvering, her properties were returned to her control after the war, but that lay in the future as Ewell prepared to lead his Second Corps northward to a place called Gettysburg. "President Johnson restored my mother's property to her because the government had ascertained that it had no legal right to retain it," writes Harriet Turner. "In other words, her appeal had no effect on Andrew Johnson." He did, however, ask her a blunt question during an 1865 session at the White House: "Couldn't you find somebody better to marry than a one-legged man?"[42]

Chapter 10

THE MARCH NORTH

As Ewell lay recuperating from his wounds and pursued his beloved Lizinka, Robert E. Lee, always the supreme offensive tactician, was quietly hatching a scheme to take the Army of Northern Virginia into Federal territory. Even today some scholars contend it was a logical extension of a stratagem to force the war upon the enemy developed by Lee and Jackson during 1862. Although the Pennsylvania campaign was approved by Jefferson Davis and the Confederate cabinet before Ewell's promotion to lieutenant general, the Northern invasion was nearly thwarted by critics in both army and governmental circles before its inception. Once Lee concluded that a defensive posture would never bring victory, he began to foment a plan for marching the army north—even before the astounding Confederate triumph at Chancellorsville.[1]

Jefferson Davis lent support to the scheme on May 16 following a daylong and often heated cabinet session. While Lee never intended to remain north of the Mason-Dixon Line for an extended time, the plan aroused a vocal opposition. General James Longstreet, perhaps Lee's worst enemy at Gettysburg and who never wanted to march on Pennsylvania, argued for a transfer of Virginia troops to bolster the war against Ulysses S. Grant in the west. Another outspoken critic was John Henninger Reagan, a Texan and the only cabinet member from the west; he wanted to use western troops to maintain a viable connection between Virginia and the trans-Mississippi as the Federal noose tightened around Vicksburg. Even President Davis, with his strong ties to Mississippi, initially favored a renewed offensive in the western theater.[1]

However, with his quiet persuasion, Lee carried the day, because an incursion into the heart of the enemy's country held obvious advantages. The field of battle would be shifted from the Southland, which it was hoped would give farmers in the Shenandoah Valley an opportunity to tend their crops and livestock without the ravages of war. A Confederate thrust onto Yankee soil coming on the heels of Chancellorsville might well bring diplomatic recognition. "A great offensive victory," notes Robert Selph Henry, "was all that was needed to secure an alliance with imperial France, ran the thought of southern statesmen—and it was an alliance with royalist France, they remembered, which had secured the independence of the United States of America." While Lincoln's envoy at the Court of Saint James, Charles Francis Adams, remained at this post, there was little hope that Great Britain would accept the new government in Richmond—a Northern triumph or no! And the move toward Pennsylvania "could influence operations as far west as the Mississippi River by drawing Union troops eastward." Similarly, any attempt to march north would surely goad Lincoln into withdrawing men from the Army of the Potomac to shield Washington, Baltimore, Philadelphia, and other urban centers. The same ploy had struck terror at the hearts of Federal warlords during the Seven Days campaign a year before, and Lee had no doubt that it would accomplish the same result in 1863.[2]

As he prepared to march, Lee unquestionably entertained an inflated confidence in his army—and himself—after experiencing the twin victories at Fredericksburg and Chancellorsville (the latter scarcely a month earlier) when he had Jackson at his side and Longstreet was absent in the west. Ewell not only became a vital part of these war preparations, but he also found himself in a swirl of personal activity, which included a complete restructuring of the Army of Northern Virginia. The biographer of 135 years after can only speculate upon Ewell's state of mind before the army headed out from Hamilton's Crossing. His wedding had taken place before the cabinet session that resulted in approval of Lee's plans. A day or two earlier, on May 23, his promotion to lieutenant general had been confirmed by the Confederate congress. With his head reeling from the delights of the honeymoon as well as his elevation to a coveted rank, Ewell received word on May 30 that he had been designated to command under Lee's reorganization scheme.

Upon Jackson's death, Lee found it incumbent to find a replacement for his foremost lieutenant before undertaking a new campaign. The two corps of Longstreet and Jackson that had served the Confederate nation with unbelievable distinction were recast into three, led by Longstreet, A.

P. Hill, and Ewell. Given Ewell's penchant for a hesitant approach to command, it is difficult to fathom his appointment at perhaps the most critical juncture of the war. Yes, he had more than thirty-five years of service in the Federal and Confederate armies, and he was unquestionably a seasoned fighter, but his selection stemmed from his days at Jackson's side during the Shenandoah campaign, the Seven Days, and Groveton. He had performed satisfactorily under the careful eye of the ever-vigilant Stonewall, but now he would have to carry his own weight. By assuming Jackson's old command Ewell was placed in a nearly impossible situation from the beginning. Professional soldiers and the general public alike began to scrutinize his every command decision. The one-legged Ewell—still suffering from the effects of his injury and amputation, both psychological and physical—soon joined Hill and Longstreet, neither of whom served Lee particularly well during the ensuing campaign. A. P. Hill's men fought valiantly in the first clash of armies at Gettysburg, but when Lee asked Hill to attack Cemetery Ridge on the evening of July 1, he balked. As the subsequent battle raged to a Confederate disaster, concluded Hill's biographer, he was unable "to provide personal and inspiring leadership." Entire books have been written on James Longstreet's less than admirable conduct throughout the entire Pennsylvania operation. In addition to his failure to move at the appointed hour on July 2 and 3, Longstreet, a South Carolinian who had spent most of his life in Georgia, and who fancied himself the man of the hour upon Jackson's death, did not like the new army reorganization: "Too much Virginia," he wrote in his postwar memoir.[3]

According to his own words, Longstreet sought to influence Ewell with the assertion that the Southern cause would be better served by engaging the enemy once more in Virginia, where the army could fight on the defensive. "A few days before we were ready . . . General Lee sent for General Ewell to receive his orders," he declared later. "I was present at the time and remarked if we were ever going to make an offensive battle it should be done south of the Potomac. . . . I made this suggestion in order to bring about a discussion which I thought would give General Ewell a better idea of the plan of operations." Although Ewell took part in the talks with Lee, Hill, and Longstreet about ensuing strategy, he also threw himself into a vigorous preparation for Lee's plans. "I only spent one or two days in Richmond & hurried on to Hamilton's Crossing, where I found everything in the bristle & exhilaration of an expected move, on an unrevealed but brilliant campaign," noted Campbell Brown upon his return to Virginia. He had been in Alabama as aide to Joseph E. Johnston and Colonel Benjamin Ewell while his stepfather recovered from Groveton. Brown had been unable to attend the wedding as he sped north in response to a telegram from Richard Ewell that he was taking charge of the Second Corps. "Never was our army in finer fighting trim than at this time. . . . The health & physical condition of the troops were excellent & the prestige of a recent victory & a full knowledge of the depressed condition of the Federals contributed to inspire confidence."[4]

Lee, who had consulted with President Davis about personnel for the reorganized army, summoned Ewell to report for duty at Fredericksburg/Hamilton's Crossing on May 25: "In part, the appointment was made because of sentimental association of his name with Jackson, and in part because of admiration for his unique, picturesque and wholly lovable personality," writes historian Douglas Southall Freeman. "Of his ability to lead a Corps nothing was known. Everything was a gamble." Ewell may indeed have been an eccentric with wide appeal through the ranks, but he was also on the verge of military disaster. The army was preparing to move with two sickly warriors (Ewell and Hill) who were completely untried beyond divisional command. Five days later, after Ewell had arrived in the Fredericksburg sector from Richmond, Lee's Special Order Number 146 announced: "The divisions of Major Generals Early, Johnson, and Rodes will constitute the Second Corps, and be under the command of Lieut. Gen. R. S. Ewell." In retrospect, there can be little doubt that Lee, who had depended upon the strong arm of Jackson, was now putting his confidence in mediocre subordinates.[5]

All three of Ewell's immediate subordinates had served with distinction under Jackson in the Valley or subsequent campaigns. In addition to his division chiefs for the Second Corps, Ewell received four artillery contingents under Lieutenant Colonels H. P. Jones (assigned to Early's division), Thomas H. Carter (Rodes), Richard Snowden Andrews (Johnson), as well as two reserve artillery groups under Lt. Col. William Nelson and Col. J. Thompson Brown. "General Lee, having determined to improve the efficiency of his artillery, directed a plan to be drafted for its more perfect organization," comments A. L. Long. Although artillery of the line was parceled among various corps commanders, William Nelson Pendleton, the Virginia clergyman-turned-soldier, was kept under the direct authority of the commander-in-chief. "This organization proved entirely successful, and the Confederate artillery became famous in the later campaigns," Long continues, but much to Lee's later discomfort, Jeb Stuart was left in control of the unified cavalry.[6]

The army, including Ewell's Second Corps, was organized and ready to march by June 1, within days of his arrival on the Rappahannock. Jubal Early and Robert E. Rodes had been in the murderous fighting with Jackson at Antietam and Chancellorsville, while Allegheny Johnson, wounded at McDowell, like Ewell, had been away. Any of them could have risen to corps command without difficulty, yet Lee informed President Davis on March 30 that Ewell was "an honest, brave soldier, who has always done his duty well." But it is clear that he harbored a modicum of misgiving. "If, therefore, you think Ewell is able to do field work, I submit to your better judgment whether the most advantageous arrangement would not be to put him in command of three divisions of Jackson's corps." Lee was asking the president, who would see Ewell a few days later at his wedding, to assume partial responsibility for putting the three soldiers and their troops under his direct charge. Although he was preoccupied with word that John Pemberton was "bottled up" at Vicksburg, Davis gave the nod for Lee to proceed.[7]

Early's division was composed of units under Harry Thompson Hays, John Brown Gordon, William "Extra Billy" Smith, and Isaac E. Avery—all seasoned campaigners—but all was not well. "The brigade inspection reports in my division show that about one-third of the men were without bayonets, and this deficiency existed in the rest of the army, owing in great measure to the fact that nearly all of our small arms had been taken from the enemy on the various battlefields," Early wrote. "There was a very great deficiency in shoes for the infantry, a large number of the men being indifferently shod, and some barefooted. A like deficiency existed in regard to the equipment of the men in other respects, the supply of clothing, blankets, etc., being very limited." And, he added, "the largest guns we had were a very few twenty pounder Parrotts." Perhaps worst of all, Ewell allowed himself to be dominated by Early throughout July 1–3 in addition to his failure to implement Lee's discretionary orders. The two soldiers had enjoyed a long personal relationship, and one scholar says that Early "acted much of the time as the Corps spokesman."[8]

In fairness, it should be pointed out that Ewell was not given an opportunity to select his division and brigade commanders but inherited Jackson's organization almost intact, although his brigadiers generally served him well during the ensuing campaign. Harry T. Hays, who served under Early, was a New Orleans lawyer who led his Louisiana brigade through the campaigns from First Manassas to Chancellorsville. He missed the Seven Days and Second Manassas campaigns after he was wounded at Port Republic in June 1862, when he had been replaced by Henry Forno. The forty-three-year-old Hays, again wounded at Spotsylvania, survived the war to resume his law practice until his death in 1875. The Georgia brigade of Alexander R. Lawton that fought under Ewell at Groveton was assigned to John B. Gordon, a onetime entrepreneur in the Georgia coal industry. Although Henry Kyd Douglas, one of Ewell's aides at Gettysburg, labeled him "a picture for the sculptor," Gordon fought throughout the Virginia campaigns before being shot at Antietam. After Chancellorsville and Gettysburg he became Lee's trusted corps commander during the last phases of the war. Gordon then served as United States senator and governor of his native Georgia before his death at age seventy-two.[9]

Brigadier General William Smith was a fighter who "despised West Point and its tactics," believing that "common sense was all that was needed in battle." Although a two-term congressman in the 1850s and a member of the Confederate congress, he fought at the side of Ewell and Early throughout the early fighting in Virginia. Smith, newly elected governor of Virginia, commanded his brigade of Virginians at Gettysburg. Already sixty-six years of age in 1863, he took office on January 1, 1864. Early's remaining brigade captain was Isaac E. Avery, who took over from Robert F. Hoke after the latter's wounds at Chancellorsville. A North Carolinian like Hoke, Avery had been in uniform since the Seven Days campaign. Unfortunately, the "farmer and railroader" was shot dead while leading his troops on July 1 during Ewell's abortive attempt to take Cemetery Hill.[10]

Appointed a brigadier general four months after Ewell, Robert E. Rodes nonetheless served with him "on the quiet far right" at First Manassas after service under John Bankhead Magruder and Joseph E. Johnston on the Peninsula. He was shot at Seven Pines but recovered in time to take part in the Seven Days battles. New injuries, however, kept him out of the scrap at Second Manassas when Ewell had fallen. Rodes rejoined the army during the Maryland campaign, and he saw limited action at Fredericksburg. After the fighting at Chancellorsville he was promoted to major general on the eve of his joining Ewell's new corps in charge of the division formerly commanded by Daniel H. Hill.

Although he became one of Lee's valued lieutenants in the campaigns of 1864—before his death at the third battle at Winchester—Rodes commanded a division for the first time at Gettysburg, that command resulting from his brilliant performance at Chancellorsville less than two months earlier, when he crashed down the Orange Plank Road into the unsuspecting forces of Fighting Joe Hooker. Rodes's Confederate career turned on his association with the Virginia Military Institute, first as a student and later as professor of physics. And it was partly from recognition by his onetime colleague among seventeen VMI-trained officers that Stonewall Jackson uttered his famous words, "The Institute will be heard from to-day," as the May 3 assault on Hooker commenced.[11]

Fresh from his laurels at Chancellorsville and a new insignia on his shoulders, Rodes was assigned five brigade commanders: Junius Daniel, George Doles, Alfred Iverson, Stephen D. Ramseur, and Colonel E. A. O'Neal. A North Carolinian and West Pointer, class of 1851, Junius Daniel had commanded a brigade in Virginia before the reorganization of May 1863. Although he had seen earlier service on the Peninsula and in the Seven Days campaign, where he headed a brigade at Malvern Hill, he had been transferred to North Carolina until the Pennsylvania campaign. Daniel was killed at the Bloody Angle the following summer. Another of Rodes's men killed in the Overland campaign of 1864 was Brigadier General George Pierce Doles. A Georgia businessman before the war, who was named colonel of the (Milledgeville) Baldwin Blues in April 1861, Doles had been wounded at Malvern Hill but returned to the army in time to see action at South Mountain. As Ewell prepared to advance with the Second Corps, Doles had recently survived the Chancellorsville bloodletting, where he took part in the Jackson-Rodes advance that crumbled the enemy. At Fredericksburg D. H. Hill had labeled him a "tried veteran and brigade commander whose men always do well."[12]

Alfred Iverson and Stephen D. Ramseur were likewise fresh from the melee at Chancellorsville. Iverson, another Georgia businessman before the war, who had fought in the Mexican conflict, first saw duty along the North Carolina coast under Theophilus Holmes upon joining the Confederacy. Besides Chancellorsville he had seen combat at South Mountain and Fredericksburg after taking a wound in the Seven Days. At Gettysburg, when Ewell ordered Iverson and Edward O'Neal into the fray against Cemetery Hill, Iverson's brigade lost 766 men killed, wounded, or missing out of 820 engaged. Iverson later took part in the Atlanta campaign with Joseph E. Johnston and John Bell Hood. He survived the war by forty-six years until his death in 1911 at age eighty-two.[13]

Stephen Dodson Ramseur, West Point class of 1860, another North Carolinian, born in 1837, was the youngest brigadier with Ewell and Rodes. His initial Confederate action was under John B. Magruder on the Peninsula followed by duty with Stonewall Jackson and D. H. Hill in the Seven Days, Second Manassas, and Chancellorsville campaigns. At Second Manassas

Ramseur's name was often invoked to emphasize the camaraderie of West Pointers, North and South, when a dying Federal officer, Lieutenant W. W. Chamberlain, wanted to know if Ramseur were nearby. When asked why he wanted Ramseur, Chamberlain replied that they were friends from the academy. Ironically, Ramseur, promoted to major general in June 1864, was carried into the headquarters tent of General Phil Sheridan, another West Point man, to die from wounds suffered at Cedar Creek the following October.[14] Colonel Edward Asbury O'Neal, an Alabama politician and businessman before 1861, was given command of Rodes's old brigade at Chancellorsville. Although he was elevated to brigadier general on June 8 as the army marched for Pennsylvania, his poor performance at Gettysburg caused President Davis to rescind the commission after he made the mistake of failing to lead his troops in person. O'Neal had been on the Peninsula and had taken a wound at Seven Pines as well as Chancellorsville; but his Alabama troops apparently held nothing against him, because he served two terms as governor of the state before his death in 1890 at Florence, Alabama.[15]

Of all his new commanders, Edward Johnson, who took command of Stonewall Jackson's old division, was probably least known to Ewell. Although he finished at West Point in 1838, when Ewell was completing his second year, their paths had not really crossed until 1862 after Ewell joined Jackson's command in the Shenandoah. It was "Old Allegheny" Johnson who marched off with Stonewall in May 1862 while Ewell kept the watch at Conrad's Store. Shot through the ankle at the Battle of McDowell, Johnson was forced to sit out the year in Richmond, where he became something of a lady's man. Promoted to major general on April 22, 1863, he barely rejoined the army in time for the Pennsylvania fray. "[W]hile under my command, General Johnson was uniformly distinguished for hard and successful fighting," Ewell wrote after Gettysburg and Spotsylvania. Captured at Spotsylvania, Johnson was subsequently exchanged and sent to division command in the Atlanta campaign. Taken prisoner a second time at Nashville, he was obliged to sit out the war in Washington's Old Capitol Prison until his release in July 1865.[16]

Always known as "Maryland Steuart" to distinguish him from Jeb Stuart, George H. Steuart commanded a brigade of Virginians and North Carolinians under Johnson. Although Ewell had known him since the Valley campaign, where he had to be reprimanded in the field for refusing to charge the enemy without a direct order, he spelled Steuart's name incorrectly in his Gettysburg report. Fortunately "Stewart" was changed to "Steuart" in the printed version of the *Official Records*. Steuart fought throughout 1861–1865 in Virginia, was taken prisoner at Spotsylvania, but exchanged in time to serve under Pickett at Petersburg.[17] James A. Walker, who survived the war to become active in the Virginia Republican Party during Reconstruction, was handed command of the Stonewall Brigade under Johnson. Something of a firebrand, he once challenged Professor Thomas J. Jackson to a duel while a student at VMI, where he graduated in 1851. "Walrus-like in appearance," observes James I. Robertson, "with profanity and short temper in keeping with his fighting prowess, Walker participated in more than fifty engagements during the war." Often called "Stonewall Jim," he not only led his brigade until wounded during the Wilderness campaign, but he also served as lieutenant governor of Virginia as well as a two-term Republican congressman before his death in 1901.[18]

Another casualty at Spotsylvania was Brigadier General John Marshall Jones, a West Point man who commanded a brigade of Virginians under Allegheny Johnson. A former instructor at the academy, who also saw duty in the west before 1861, Jones had taken over as Ewell's adjutant general during the Valley campaign. He received a nasty wound at Antietam but returned to the army for the fights at Fredericksburg and Chancellorsville. A brigadier's star came on May 15 in time for Lee's reorganization, and along with the rest of Johnson's command, his men suffered heavily in the ill-conceived fight at Cemetery Hill.[19]

After Brigadier General Francis T. Nicholls lost his foot, his brigade of Louisianans was handed to Colonel Jesse Milton Williams and assigned to Allegheny Johnson's command. Although he enlisted in a Louisiana outfit at the beginning of the war, Williams was never promoted to general rank. He had served on the Peninsula and in the Seven Days as a company officer; and, promoted to colonel, he commanded the Second Louisiana at Cedar Mountain and Second Manassas. After being wounded at Antietam he was briefly out of action but returned to lead a brigade at Chancellorsville. At Gettysburg his men suffered 44 dead, 309 wounded, and 36 missing. One year later, while leading the Second Louisiana, Williams was killed at Spotsylvania.[20]

Ewell remained on the Rappahannock from May 29 until June 4, when the Second Corps headed toward Yankee territory. Although the officers under Ewell were experienced soldiers, it is worthy to note that two of his immediate subordinates—Rodes and Johnson—had only recently been promoted to major general and given divisional command. Of his thirteen brigade commanders, five—John B. Gordon, Edward A. O'Neal,

Extra Billy Smith, "Stonewall Jim" Walker, and John M. Jones—were made brigadiers after Chancellorsville and two, Isaac Avery and Jesse M. Williams, never attained general rank. Ewell outwardly kept his counsel about the men who commanded his corps, but his arrival at Lee's headquarters in the Yerby House south of Fredericksburg with his bride of three days, her daughter, Harriet Brown, and Lizzie Ewell aroused feelings of resentment almost immediately. Jed Hotchkiss, who stayed on as a member of Ewell's staff, noted the marriage "made the old fellow look young again, having taken away much of his former toughness of manner." And young Alexander "Sandie" Pendleton, soon named a member of Ewell's personal staff, told his mother on June 4, "the old hero, friend, and fellow sufferer, comrade in battle, and fellow mourner [for Jackson]" was his new chief, but the enthusiasm of both men changed soon enough.

Mrs. Ewell, whom Ewell insisted on parading before his fellow officers, was initially well received. When several prominent families in the Fredericksburg area put on a gala feast to honor their marriage, one of the participants, Marietta Andrews, was moved to write later: "The elegance of the entertainments was hard to associate with war. Plenty of music, beaux galore, luxuriant plants . . . and a delicious repast." Somehow amid the perils and hardships of civil strife, their hosts had managed to lay a table that included "ham, turkey, fried chicken, roaster pig, oysters, saddles of mutton, stuffed mangoes, spiced pears, beaten biscuits, hot rolls and cakes, all of which were consumed with potations of wine, mint juleps, punch and coffee." Despite Ewell's delight in his marriage and newfound family, resentments among officers and staff began to develop over Lizinka's pride in her husband and her subsequent efforts to advance not only his career but also that of her son. Derogatory remarks abound in letters and postwar memoirs referring to her supposed or actual influence upon Ewell and his battlefield performance. The short interval before June 4 was not sufficient time for a hostile environment to surface, but when Ewell returned following the Cemetery Hill/Culps Hill fiasco and resumed his living arrangement with his wife and stepdaughter, the fireworks began in earnest.[21]

One of Ewell's severest detractors was Colonel (later General) James Conner, a South Carolina lawyer, who was eventually attached to his staff. In February 1864, seven months after Gettysburg, Conner received an invitation to visit the Ewells and came away with a low opinion of the household. "I was presented to Miss Brown, Mrs. Ewell's daughter, a dark-eyed, clever girl, but not very pretty; a very large head, and a stout, roll-about figure," he told his mother. "Mrs. Ewell is very agreeable and clever, decidedly smart, and must have been very handsome when she was young." If the forty-three-year-old Lizinka had lost her appeal to young officers, Ewell himself came in for considerable criticism. "The general is not what he was. The loss of his limb has seriously affected his usefulness and even impaired his mind," Conner noted. "His artificial leg is as poor a concern as I ever saw."[22]

Members of Ewell's staff, most of whom had served under Jackson, became increasingly critical of Mrs. Ewell throughout 1864. Many considered it poor form for women to remain constantly in camp, because it was thought a nuisance and a detriment to military discipline. Dr. Hunter McGuire, now a member of Ewell's inner circle, voiced the opinion that Lizinka "was not very good for the old gent." And when Ewell asked Sandie Pendleton to bring his bride to live with Mrs. Ewell and himself at headquarters, Pendleton told his mother that he not only declined the invitation but also that he "did not approve of such schemes of having male servants waiting upon ladies." Mrs. Ewell's attempts to gain an enhanced rank for her son and to advance her husband's standing with Richmond as his health began to decline soon evoked talk of "petticoat government." More than twenty-five years after Appomattox, the Reverend B. T. Lacy, chaplain on the staffs of both Jackson and Ewell, related an incident to Jed Hotchkiss: "One day [during 1864] I went out to Rodes' head-quarters when General Rodes asked me who commanded the Second Corps, whether it was Mrs. Ewell, General Ewell or Sandie Pendleton hoping it was the last." The love-smitten commander was blissfully unaware that his own division chiefs had begun to poke fun at his new bride.[23]

In May-June 1863, as Ewell put the final touches on his headquarters staff in anticipation of the thrust into Pennsylvania, he discovered what others elevated to high position already knew: old friends and acquaintances began to demand favors. Samuel A. Marsteller, for instance, addressed a letter to "Dear Richard" asking that his youngest son be given a place near Ewell; the boy was not "afraid of the battlefield" but only wanted to serve in a headquarters position. "[The son], for the sake of being near you, and your command, and further feeling that beggars are not choosers, will take a humble position." The father lived near the Ewell homestead in Prince William County and took the opportunity of passing along a bit of good news in spite of Yankee depredations in the vicinity: "I must say something about Stoneylonsome [sic], it is pretty much status quo. The house standing, the fense tho' in bad order, not burning, and how could we have expected this when . . . sometimes occupied by Yankees. The movable furniture is Safe here and elsewhere, the stock principally saved, except the sheep."[24]

Although young Marsteller was seemingly ignored by Ewell, his personal staff, with one or two exceptions, like his divisional and brigade commanders, were holdovers from Jackson's command. For the first three weeks or so Colonel Charles J. Faulkner served as his chief of staff. A few months after the war ended, Faulkner wrote a defense of his Confederate career in which he invoked the name of Dr. Hunter McGuire. In a scathing rebuttal, which may or may not have been mailed, McGuire took him to task for saying that he had fought under Jackson out of consideration for the man and because he enjoyed watching "battles and skirmishes." "You joined the army under Ewell for the sole purpose of getting home and seeing your family," McGuire asserted. "[And] during the whole of the war you had no sympathy for the south. . . ." Little wonder Ewell replaced him with Sandie Pendleton before the big fight at Gettysburg, although Faulkner had a new career after the war as a Democratic congressman from West Virginia before his death in 1884.[25]

Stonewall's old staff, including Faulkner, offered to resign in a body, but Lee and Ewell would have none of it. Ewell did, however, designate Pendleton as his chief of staff upon Faulkner's departure; and he summoned his stepson, Campbell Brown, as assistant adjutant general as well as Lieutenants Thomas T. Turner (who shortly married his stepdaughter, Harriet) and James Power Smith as aides-de-camp. Others at headquarters were: Colonel A. Smead and Major Benjamin H. Green (assistant inspectors general); Major J. A. Harman (chief quartermaster); Wells J. Hawks (chief commissary); William Allan (chief of ordnance); R. E. Wilbourn (chief signal officer); H. B. Richardson (chief engineer); and Jed Hotchkiss (topographical engineer). Several volunteer aides accompanied the corps, including Colonel John E. Johnson and Lieutenants Elliot Johnston and R. W. Elliot.[26]

With his staff, divisional, and brigade organizations in place, Ewell and the Second Corps set out for the Shenandoah Valley on June 4. Although numbers vary depending upon the authority consulted, Lee marched for Pennsylvania with an army of sixty thousand infantry distributed almost equally among the commands of Longstreet, A. P. Hill, and Ewell. Lee himself rode with Longstreet as was his wont from the early campaigns. A close reading of Brown suggests that Ewell traveled with Rodes once he said good-bye to his wife and stepdaughter, who waited in

Charlottesville for his return. From Hamilton's Crossing the Second Corps traveled west through Old Verdierville, where it turned north across the Rapidan at Raccoon, or Somerfield, Ford very near the Chancellorsville fighting ground. By the seventh, Ewell's official report reads, he had reached Culpeper. He also says that he thereupon "moved my corps, by the direction of the general commanding to General Stuart's support."

On the ninth, as Ewell and Rodes headed north from Culpeper on the Rixeyville Road, the latter was detached in the direction of Brandy Station, a depot on the Orange and Alexandria Railroad, where Stuart had gotten himself embroiled in the biggest cavalry fight of the war. Something called the fight at Fleetwood Heights—a hill within sight of Brandy Station—developed when Joe Hooker, still in command of the Federal army, sent a cavalry force under Alfred Pleasanton to ascertain Lee's whereabouts. Although Stuart stoutly maintained otherwise, he was caught by surprise when Yankee horsemen appeared in force south of the Rappahannock northwest of its juncture with the Rapidan. The prolonged melee cost both sides dearly—the Federals losing 936 officers and men, Confederates 532—before Stuart finally reestablished order. It was "a day of fighting, in which there were cavalry charges, lines of mounted men, boot to boot, using the shock and weight of the horse and the swordsmanship of the trooper in combat," writes Robert S. Henry. Pleasanton broke off the combat when strange infantry was seen approaching across the Culpeper County countryside even though he was unable to identify it. What he saw was Rodes's division rushing to Stuart's rescue.

Stuart says nothing about Ewell's help, and Rodes's terse entry in his Gettysburg report mentions only that under orders he marched toward Brandy Station "but did not get in reach of the enemy, he having apparently been repulsed by the cavalry." Ewell confirms Rodes's assertion that Pleasanton was "already retiring" when they arrived. Campbell Brown offers a somewhat different version of the Brandy Station affair: "This fight of Stuart's not only delayed our march for a day, but as it was a surprise to the enemy & in some degree a success, they joined the object of the demonstration by developing our infantry in force, & showing what they were hardly certain of before—that we were really withdrawing from the lower Rappahannock." Stuart had been caught off guard, so some scholars are quick to draw the inference that his infamous ride around the enemy in Pennsylvania that "virtually paralysed the entire army" was an ill-conceived effort to redeem himself.[28]

While diverted to Brandy Station, Ewell and Rodes not only stopped by the Barbour House, where Ewell had quartered during the winter and spring of 1862, but they encountered the colorful and pugnacious John Minor Botts. "I have often heard that that old lunatic individual came out in great rage, inquiring for the commanding officer of the force, & informed Rodes with copious oaths that he must move his men off," comments Brown. In strong words, Botts warned that he wanted no fighting around his house and fields endangering his family and property. He was particularly upset that Ewell's troops would destroy his fences. A former Whig congressman during the 1840s, Botts was a strong Union man, who had opposed Virginia secession in 1861; at one time there was even a move to make him governor of Unionist Virginia instead of Francis H. Pierpont. In June 1863, however, Rodes told "some of his staff to make that old fool go back into his house & behave himself—which cooled him down."[29]

When the northward trek resumed on the tenth, the Second Corps, with Rodes and Allegheny Johnson in the lead, headed for the Shenandoah Valley via Chester Gap. Johnson says, "nothing occurred worthy of particular note on the march" until his division bivouacked at Cedarville, north of Front Royal, on the thirteenth. Rodes's division had already reached the Warren County hamlet with Early's bringing up the rear. Richard Ewell also arrived at Cedarville on the thirteenth, where he learned that Robert H. Milroy had six thousand to eight thousand men blocking the Valley Pike at Winchester, several miles to the north. When he ascertained further that more Federals were positioned at Berryville, ten miles east of Winchester, Rodes, accompanied by the cavalry of Albert Gallatin Jenkins, was detached to secure the Confederate right. The artillerist Captain John Hampden "Ham" Chamberlayne told his mother that Rodes's men reached Berryville after "seven days of incessant marching"—that he had no time for writing.

Ewell and the Second Corps were clearly on the move, and the Stonewall Brigade under James A. Walker of Johnson's division, composed almost entirely of valley boys, was ecstatic to be once more on familiar ground. "As they passed through the villages, it was hailed with cheers by the people who flocked in from the countryside," notes W. G. Bean. "All kinds of dainties were dispensed by the hands of 'pretty pink-cheeked mountain maidens'" as they crossed the Blue Ridge. With Rodes's departure from the main body, Ewell rode along with Allegheny Johnson's division, and he was understandably charged up by the corps' reception in the lower Shenandoah. Also on the thirteenth, Milroy's pickets began skirmishing with lead units under Early and Johnson on the road to Winchester. "Milroy occupied the town," writes Early, "with a considerable force in strong fortifications, and my orders were to move along the pike to Kernstown, and then to the left, so as to get a position northwest of Winchester from which the main work of the enemy could be attacked with advantage."[30]

Actually Milroy had been sending reconnaissance vedettes toward the south for a day or two in an attempt to learn Ewell's whereabouts. A captured trooper from Harry T. Hays's Louisiana brigade convinced the unfortunate commander to pull in his outriders, including Colonel Andrew T. McReynolds, commanding Union troops at Berryville, who was pursued by Rodes. As had been the case at Brandy Station, the Federals at Berryville departed before Rodes arrived on the scene. He did manage to capture a few stores before speeding Jenkins and his cavalry toward Martinsburg to thwart McReynolds's retreat. Although his superiors Henry W. Halleck and Robert C. Schenk as well as President Lincoln had ordered him to withdraw, Milroy found himself cut off by Ewell's advance on June 13.

Ewell and Early held a conference on the roadway leading into Winchester late on the thirteenth and resolved to concentrate on Milroy's fortifications northwest of town. It was decided to send Early around the western outskirts, while Johnson was told to make a demonstration on the south. Without a moment's hesitation Ewell made the troop dispositions that insured not only a Confederate victory but also opened a path for Lee to speed his northward thrust. Ewell had not been in battle for ten months, since the Second Manassas, and he was anxious to prove himself under fire; and Lee was interested to see if his one-legged corps commander could measure up against a hostile enemy. The moment of truth had arrived— far in the advance of Lee, A. P. Hill, and Longstreet, Ewell ascertained the necessity for immediate action, and in no doubt his finest hour as a corps commander he plunged headlong into Milroy's regiments. Although he acted resolutely at Winchester, his deteriorating physical condition induced by the amputation was producing a different Ewell—a Ewell who suffered from a diminution of determination. Two weeks later, "the changes were tragically revealed. . . . Where formally the great division commander— accustomed to operating under Jackson's iron control—suffered a paralysis of will when confronted with the necessity for initiative in the lonely sphere of high command," opines historian Clifford Dowdey. "From then on [Gettysburg] his course went downhill militarily, though he continued personally high in the esteem of Lee and brother officers." His unacceptable dalliance during the Pennsylvania campaign also caused many "fellow officers" to decry his actions. At Winchester, however, on the night of June 13, not even a heavy rainfall that caused him to spend a fitful night under his carriage parked alongside the Valley Pike could deter his fighting elan.[31]

Jubal A. Early spent much of Sunday, June 14, getting his cannon in position to bombard Milroy's forts. Twenty-year-old Joseph W. Latimer, dubbed the "pet of the 2nd Corps" by Major Brown, arrayed another twenty or so pieces south of Winchester near Ewell's vantage point atop Camp Hill, close by the road to Millwood. After a cannonade lasting nearly three-quarters of an hour that effectively disabled both Union emplacements, Early sent Hays and his Louisianans scampering down a hill—later designated Louisiana Ridge by Ewell in honor of their feat—with Extra Billy Smith's brigade in reserve. Smith's Virginians were not needed in this remarkable display of Southern manhood. "When Hays' yelping men reached the abatis protecting the fort, Early's artillery fell silent and the five hundred Union defenders sprang to the wall. In closing the gap to the fort, James Stewart, the 9th Louisiana color-bearer fell dead from a ball through his head. 'Hoist those colors in the Ninth!' roared Hays, and the flag was grabbed up again," writes Terry L. Jones. "Stunned by the barrage and with only two guns still in operation, the Yankee defenders were barely able to fire a volley before the Confederates scaled the wall and jumped in on top of them."[32]

From his hillock perch south of town, Ewell used his binoculars to watch the unfolding drama. A number of writers, including Douglas Southall Freeman, Percy G. Hamlin, and Terry L. Jones, among others, have Ewell's vision obscured by "dust and smoke." At one momentary break he thought that Early could be seen "among the first to mount the parapet" and cried out for his safety. Although Early has a detailed account of the Winchester fighting, he says only: "Riding on myself in advance of the supports ordered to Hays I discovered him in secure possession of the captured works, and ascertained that the attempt against him had been abandoned." And when Ewell saw that Hays had reached his objective, he instantly yelled out: "Hurrah for the Louisiana boys!" Battlefield tragedy nearly struck a second time when a spent bullet hit him "squarely in the chest." Fortunately, Ewell escaped with nothing more than a severe bruise.[33]

The Early/Hays capture of Fort Milroy effectively ended the action, although Ewell sealed his victory by speeding Allegheny Johnson's division north of Winchester to block any Federal retreat toward Martinsburg and Harpers Ferry. When Johnson himself got tangled up with "Milroy's whole division in retreat," James A. Walker spurred the Stonewall Brigade into the fray with a renewed vengeance. There, a few miles north of Winchester in a heavy fog on the morning of June 15, Johnson's troopers "pushed the Federals into the woods," capturing entire regiments of the hapless Yankees. "Over 800 Federals surrendered to the [Stonewall] brigade; more than 2,000 fell into Johnson's hands," writes a brigade historian. "All this was accomplished . . . at a loss of 3 killed, 16 wounded, and 19 missing." One Confederate wrote that his outfit captured more Northern prisoners than men in his own brigade, although Milroy himself managed to ride away with an escort of 300 horsemen. Brown called Winchester "a complete victory," and a pleased Ewell commented in his official report: "The fruits of this victory were 23 pieces of artillery (nearly all rifled), 4,000 prisoners, 300 loaded wagons, more than 300 horses, and quite a large amount of commissary and quartermaster stores." Ewell and his men had done all of this with a loss of 269 men. Captain Charles M. Blackford, Second Virginia Cavalry, thought the victory at Winchester "would give the corps more confidence in Ewell."[34]

Following Milroy's destruction on June 15 and the removal of Federal opposition in the lower Shenandoah, Ewell and the Second Corps— far in advance of Hill and Longstreet—were preoccupied with spearheading the march into Maryland. Four days earlier Ewell had invoked the memory of Jackson as he admonished his men to "remember that discipline to orders is the means to secure success." He not only used the occasion to invite divine intervention, but he also did so again in a June 15 directive to his men concerning the triumph: "The Lieutenant General Commanding asks the men and officers of the corps to unite in returning thanks to our Heavenly Father for the signal success which has crowned the valor of this command." Because of the blessing, he said, brigade chaplains were obliged to hold special services throughout the corps. Ewell further suggested that divine sanction of the Confederacy at Winchester had "strengthened the reliance of our cause, which has inspired every effort of our troops." The new corps commander had progressed from his profane, irreverent days as a subaltern on the frontier.[35]

When Lee issued his General Order Number 72 on June 21 after the army had entered Maryland, he said nothing about the divine but spelled out how his troops were expected to conduct themselves in the enemy's homeland. His lengthy edict opened with a stern admonition: "No private property shall be injured or destroyed by any person belonging to or connected with the army." Although many in the South urged Lee to retaliate for Yankee excesses in Virginia and elsewhere, he clearly wanted to refrain from acts of overt destruction. Once in Pennsylvania, Ewell's confidence in his men must have slipped, because he posted orders on his own, which, among other prohibitions, prevented the purchase or consumption of intoxicating liquors. Moreover, local saloonkeepers were enjoined from selling any spirits whatsoever to his men without a written order from a major general. Only Rodes, Johnson, and Early were thus permitted to grant relief from Ewell's strictures.[36]

In mid-June, after Winchester, however, all three division commanders raced toward the Potomac. Allegheny Johnson was the first to cross by Boteler's Ford "below Shepherdstown," on the eighteenth, and immediately encamped on the old battlefield near Sharpsburg. Ewell, who had missed the Antietam fight because of his wound, no doubt enjoyed looking over the field where Jackson and Lee had tangled with George B. McClellan. For the first time since September 1862, nine months earlier, Southern troops had left their homeland. Edmund Stephens, marching with Hays's Louisianans, told his parents that a short halt was called at Sharpsburg after the brigade had been "averaging 25 miles per day [with] rest at night." Another Louisiana soldier, Lieutenant Charles Batchelor, wrote that Ewell and Johnson ordered a two-day halt so that men could rest and also allow time for other units to close up.[37]

When Johnson and Ewell took the road north, an amusing incident occurred at Tilghmanton, a village about half the distance to Hagerstown, after lead units approached an elderly toll collector named John Bloom. Henry Kyd Douglas, riding in the van with Johnson and his staff, tells what happened next: "'Who is going to pay for all the horses and wagons I see coming[?]' 'I am[,] Mr. Bloom,' I replied, 'I'll give you an order on President Davis—take it to Richmond and get the money.' 'Jeff Davis! I'll see him in hell. But look here! I'll swear! (recognizing me) you're running with this crowd are you. Go along (throwing open the gate). I wonder how long I could stop your army, with this old toll gate.'" Years later when Douglas, who became attorney general of Maryland and a critic of Ewell after the war, encountered Bloom, the old gent informed him: "'The army had better taken my advice and gone back into Virginny.'"[38]

Meanwhile, on the nineteenth, Rodes, who had marched his division cross-country from Berryville, forded the Potomac a short way above Williamsport. The brigades of Ramseur, Iverson, and Doles were hurried toward Hagerstown, and Rodes himself, with O'Neal's brigade, halted two miles south of town to await Ewell's arrival from Sharpsburg. Rodes sent Jenkins's cavalry to Chambersburg, where it initiated a systematic raiding along the Maryland-Pennsylvania border. Jubal Early brought up the rear and did not reach the Potomac at Shepherdstown until June 19. After crossing by Boteler's Ford three days later, he encamped a mile south of Rodes near Hagerstown. Although A. P. Hill and Longstreet did not cross the river until June 23, one day after the last of Ewell's men, Longstreet in particular was appreciative of the Second Corps as it went farther north: "As General Ewell marched he sent us three thousand head of beef cattle and information of five thousand more head of cattle." Confederate instructions to treat Yankee property with respect apparently did not include sustenance for the army. "At a big horseshoe bend in the Shenandoah River near Mount Jackson, Virginia, [one of Ewell's men] remembered having seen two or three thousand acres of bottomland filled with cattle and sheep," comments Edwin Coddington. "Upon inquiry one of the herdsmen told him that approximately 26,000 head of cattle and 22,000 head of sheep taken in Maryland and Pennsylvania were gathered there."[39]

Even a cursory reading of the *Official Records* and numerous manuscript collections suggests that the major participants in Lee's plans were engaged in heavy letter writing from the moment they entered Maryland. As early as June 17, two days after Winchester, a directive from Daniel Butterfield, Hooker's chief of staff, to the cavalry of Alfred Pleasanton makes certain that Federal units were searching for Ewell as he moved down the Shenandoah. Pleasanton was told to send patrols through gaps in the Blue Ridge to determine his whereabouts if necessary. Although the Second Corps had escaped unscathed from Virginia, and as Ewell waited at Sharpsburg, Lee became concerned about his progress without cavalry support. Throughout June 21–23, Lee did two things from his temporary headquarters at Berryville: he directed Ewell to move on the Susquehanna, and he ordered Jeb Stuart to support him. After telling his cavalryman his fears that Hooker might catch the army unawares, Lee continued: "If you find that he is moving northward, and that two brigades can guard the Blue Ridge and guard your rear, you can move with the three others into Maryland, and take position on General Ewell's right, place yourself in communication with him, guard his flank and keep him informed of the enemy's movements, and collect all supplies for use of the army." Lee clearly intended that Stuart act as Ewell's eyes and ears during his march into Pennsylvania.[40]

Stuart left his two brigades to monitor Ashby's and Snicker's Gaps according to Lee's instructions and promptly ignored the rest. After skirmishing with Federal cavalry across northern Virginia, he forded the

Potomac "twenty miles above Washington" and rode into Rockville, Maryland, on June 28. Here, writes Emory Thomas, "he discovered two delights—women and wagons." The agreeable young lasses were found at a local female academy, but the wagons—150 in number, stretching eight miles toward Washington—proved his undoing. Taking them in tow without sufficient forage for the mules and horses that pulled them, Stuart was soon laden with an unintended burden as he sought out the main army. He crossed into Pennsylvania during June 29–30 and reached Carlisle on July 2, after Ewell was long gone, although he found time to burn the old Federal barracks at the edge of town. By that time the fight was raging on the slopes of Cemetery Hill, twenty-six miles to the south. Even though his biographers struggle valiantly to find loopholes in Lee's discretionary orders, Stuart's unauthorized jaunt did no one any good. Certainly he had not aided Ewell's march, to say nothing of Hill and Longstreet, by failing to feed them with "information and supplies." "So our plans, adopted after deep study," Longstreet noted after the war, "were suddenly given over to gratify the youthful cavalryman's wish for a nomadic ride."[41]

While Stuart galloped around Maryland and Pennsylvania with his wagons, Ewell trekked with Johnson and Rodes through Hagerstown and Greencastle to Chambersburg, where he rested for one day. Jubal Early pursued a somewhat parallel route through Waynesboro, Pennsylvania, to Greenwood, ten miles east of Chambersburg, where he too went into camp. "I visited General Ewell at Chambersburg, and received from him instructions to cross the South Mountain to Gettysburg, and then proceed to York, and cut the Northern Central Railroad, running from Baltimore to Harrisburg, and also destroy the bridge across the Susquehanna at Wrightsville and Columbia, on the branch road from York to Philadelphia . . . and rejoin him at Carlisle by way of Dillsburg." Thus Ewell split the Second Corps on instructions from Lee, with Early making straight for York while the divisions of Johnson and Rodes accompanied him to Carlisle.[42]

During the temporary lull, in which frightened blacks fled Chambersburg for safer domains, both Ewell and Brown found time to dash off letters to loved ones. At Sharpsburg Brown had informed his sister and mother in Charlottesville that he was carrying a list of items that they wanted in a commodity-starved South. Later he purchased five dresses, because thus far "Confederate money [was] normally taken, getting 62 1/2 cents on the dollar." And the stark difference between the Northern and Southern home fronts was inadvertently noted in his letters. "All these little Yankee towns are full of things," he told his mother, but added that Ewell would not permit his men to force Confederate money upon local shopkeepers.

While Brown was buying additional dresses for Lizinka and Harriet, Ewell made his headquarters in Chambersburg's Franklin Hotel after Rodes's division marched into town "preceded by a band of musicians playing 'The Bonnie Blue Flag.'" Jacob Hoke, a Chambersburg native, has left a telling portrait of Ewell as he stepped from his carriage:

> One of the occupants . . . was a thin, sallow-faced man, with strongly-marked southern features, and a head and physiognomy which strongly indicated culture, refinement and genius. When he emerged from the carriage, which he did only with the assistance of others, it was discovered that he had an artificial limb, and used a crutch. After making his way into the hotel, he at once took possession of a large front parlor, and, surrounded by six or eight gentlemanly-looking men, he was prepared for business. A Confederate flag was run out a window, and head-quarters established. This intellectual-looking man was Lieutenant-General R. S. Ewell.[43]

After making his requisition for all manner of supplies through his quartermaster, Major John Harman, Ewell wrote a personal note to Lizzie before advancing on Carlisle to continue what one local paper called "a few days of Rebel Rule." "It's like a renewal of Mexican times to enter a captured town," he said. "The people look as sour as vinegar, and I have no doubt would gladly send us to kingdom come if they could." The women of Chambersburg, Carlisle, and York were uniform in their disdain for all Confederates and made it a practice to turn their backs when approached. Brown told Lizinka their frowns made Northern ladies uglier than usual, and John Brown Gordon, still riding with Early, told his wife one young lady with whom he initiated a conversation sped from "me like I was a demon." However, a Carlisle editor told his readers they had nothing to fear from men without shoes or sufficient tents to sleep in and such "ragtale appearances" if only Hooker would rally his command to drive them out.[44]

Two days after the stopover in Chambersburg, Ewell reached Carlisle. "At five o'clock in the afternoon the sound of music announced the entrance of Ewell's corps," a paper recorded. "It came by way of the Walnut Bottom Road, down Pitt Street, thence to Bedford Street, and thence to the Garrison. The band at the head of the column playing 'Dixie' as it passed down the streets." Ewell knew how to proceed with flair! Carlisle Barracks, where he had served briefly during the 1840s, quickly became the focal point for his occupation, although all of the town's hotels "filled up with rebel officers." On Sunday, June 28, reads the diary of Jed Hotchkiss, "we spent the day at the Barracks—Rev. Lacy preached there twice. . . . We raised the Confederate flag on the staff of the Barracks in the P.M. and remarks were made by Gens. Rodes, Trimble, Daniels, [sic] Ewell." Ewell made additional requisitions upon the Pennsylvanians, which they had difficulty meeting to his satisfaction; and Johnson's men reportedly burned some materials turned in at the courthouse that could not be used by the army. One "scoundrel" from Johnson's division supposedly "outraged a Miss Wolf," but even the *Carlisle Herald* had to admit, "the rebels conducted themselves, generally speaking, with decorum."

When the Second Corps departed Carlisle, where the "citizens were not as sullen as in Chambersburg," on the twenty-ninth, with Allegheny Johnson in the van, followed by Rodes, Ewell saw fit to comment in his official report that he had not torched Carlisle Barracks. Still, countered the *Herald,* "it was his intention on his arrival here to destroy the Barracks, but at the earnest solicitation of some ladies who were formerly his friends, he agreed to spare them, and with the exception of the unavoidable litter and filth that attended his occupation of the position no other destruction occurred." Jeb Stuart and the wayward cavalry had no compunction to save the old station when they arrived there two days after Ewell's departure. Interestingly, the same edition of the paper that praised Ewell for sparing the barracks came down hard on Johnson and Rodes. Johnson's men committed acts of violence, it said, and "what was left by Rhodes [sic]. . . not through mercy, but from want of information, was swept away by this horde. . . . Every barnyard was visited, and poultry, and in fact everything which would furnish a mouthful of food, was taken."[45]

While Ewell tarried at Carlisle, Early crossed South Mountain from Greenwood and made his way through Gettysburg to York. Twelve miles east of York is Wrightsville, hard by the Susquehanna opposite Columbia and twelve miles from Harrisburg, the capital of a major Northern state and transportation hub, which after all was the prize sought by Lee and Ewell. When Early raced forward to the river, he found that twelve hundred Pennsylvania militiamen had set fire to the bridge linking Wrightsville with Columbia and the eastern part of the state. Although his division sought to save the span, it was unable to quench the flames. "The bridge [which Ewell termed "magnificent"] was one mile and a quarter in length, the superstructure being of wood, on stone pillars, and it included in one structure a railroad bridge, a pass-way for wagons, and also a tow path for the canal, which here crosses the Susquehanna," Early noted. "The bridge was entirely consumed, and from it the town of Wrightsville caught fire and several buildings were consumed, but the further progress of the flames was arrested by the exertions of Gordon's men."

Meanwhile, cavalryman Albert Jenkins had discovered Harrisburg completely undefended and galloped to Ewell at Carlisle with the news. Although orders were cut for a concentration on the Pennsylvania capital by Early, Johnson, and Rodes for June 30, nothing more drastic took place than a sporadic exchange of artillery rounds between Jenkins and militiamen beyond the river. Even so, Ewell had readied himself to accompany Rodes and Johnson toward the "eagerly sought place" when word came from Lee that with all due haste the Second Corps was needed at a small college town called Gettysburg. One day earlier Abraham Lincoln had replaced Fighting Joe Hooker with another seasoned general, George Gordon Meade, which altered the entire campaign for the Confederates. And though the deciding battle of the entire war was in the offing a mere twenty-seven miles to the south, it is easy to speculate that Ewell could have easily carried out his mission to engulf Harrisburg as well as destroy its rail connections with Baltimore and Philadelphia.[46]

Chapter 11

PARALYZED WITH INDECISION

In late June 1863 Ewell had driven his men farther into enemy territory—
at least in the Virginia sector—than any other Confederate commander.
Here, a good thirty-five miles north of the Mason-Dixon Line, within
sight of the Pennsylvania capital, he sought to govern a hostile foe and to
keep his troopers from the wanton destruction of Yankee property. At
the same time, a Harrisburg newspaper reported "twenty-nine rebel deserters . . . mostly from Ewell's division" had surrendered to the Federal
provost marshal as the Second Corps remained about Carlisle and York. In
spite of the headaches that result from commanding an army of occupation, it was not a position that Ewell wanted to relinquish when Lee quickly
summoned him to march south on the twenty-eighth. "I desire you to
move in the direction of Gettysburg, via Heidlersburg, where you will have
turnpike most of the way, and you can join your other divisions to Early's
which is east of the mountains," reads the 7:30 A.M. communiqué from
Lee, who made his headquarters at Chambersburg. "When you come to
Heidlersburg, you can either move directly on Gettysburg or turn to
Cashtown. Your trains and heavy artillery you can send, if you think proper,
on the road to Chambersburg."[1]

Lee's order came in response to his June 27 intelligence from Longstreet
that Joe Hooker, still in command of the Federal juggernaut, had crossed
the Potomac in pursuit of the invaders. Ewell's summons to proceed south
was an integral part of Lee's plan to concentrate his army east of the mountains and to provide a convenient rendezvous point with A. P. Hill and
Longstreet. The Confederates were spread out like a triangle in Pennsylvania, notes Jacob Hoke: "The vertex of this triangle was at Chambersburg,

the left extended to near Harrisburg—fifty-two miles distant; the right side to York, fifty-three miles and the Susquehanna River formed the third side. The distance from York to Harrisburg is twenty-eight miles; by way of Columbia, along the eastern bank of the Susquehanna, it is forty miles." Ewell had Rodes's and Johnson's divisions encamped with him at Carlisle, while Early was thirty miles southeast at York; the Second Corps thus occupied the base of the triangle from Carlisle, fifteen miles west of Harrisburg, to Columbia/York.[2]

Also east of South Mountain, a northern extension of the Blue Ridge, was the cavalry of Brigadier General Albert Jenkins on the Susquehanna opposite Harrisburg and John B. Gordon's brigade of Georgians at Wrightsville on the roadway to Lancaster. In other words, Rodes and Johnson were west of South Mountain, while Early was east of it. As Ewell set out for Cashtown, riding in his carriage with Rodes's division, he sent an order for Early to abandon York and follow the rest of the corps. Also traveling with Ewell were "two brigades of cavalry belonging to Stuart's Corps commanded respectively by Generals William E. Jones and Beverly Robertson, which did not accompany their chief in his erratic course around the Federal army, but accompanied Lee's infantry up the valley." "About three o'clock on Tuesday [June 30] morning the rumbling of wagons announced the movement of the enemy. At that hour the trains of Rhodes' [sic] Division commenced to move and a continuous stream of men poured out of town," reported the *Carlisle Herald*. "Brigade after brigade passed until about eight o'clock the main army had disappeared. It took the Baltimore Pike, leading to Gettysburg, and the last of the column passed Mount Holley about 11 o'clock."[3]

Ewell left two hundred cavalry behind for provost duty as the corps headed across South Mountain toward Cashtown on the path from Chambersburg to Gettysburg. Six miles from Carlisle at Mount Holley the Baltimore Pike forked, with one leg passing through Hanover, and the other—taken by Rodes and Ewell—leading through Biglerville directly into Gettysburg from the north. "We encamped five miles [from Gettysburg] that night [June 30]—Early some four or five miles from us—& next morning moved in accordance with instructions from Gen'l Lee to rejoin Hill at Cashtown." Then, continues Campbell Brown, now Major Brown, "but when at Middletown [a few miles northwest of Gettysburg], word came from A. P. Hill that he would move directly on Gettysburg, where he asked us to join him." Hill was closing the eight-mile gap between Cashtown and Gettysburg when James J. Pettigrew's brigade ran head-on into units of John Buford's cavalry. As Pettigrew reported his first encounter with the enemy on June 30 near the famed Lutheran seminary, Hill dispatched couriers to both Lee and Ewell, informing them that "I intended to advance the next morning and discover what was in my front."

Upon receipt of Hill's call for help, Ewell abruptly altered his line of march, which put Rodes on an intercept course with his fellow corps commander nearing Gettysburg from the west. Ewell also hurried Brown to locate Early near Hunterstown on the pike from York, with word to come as quickly as possible and to prepare himself for immediate action. When Ewell had ordered his change of direction, Brown was sent to inform Lee that he had shifted his destination from Cashtown to Gettysburg; but Lee, whom Brown describes as distant and "querulous," was more concerned to know if Ewell had established contact with the errant Stuart. Lee instructed him to send vedettes to the east in search of the cavalryman. Quick action by Ewell, who turned his men "sharply to the left" at Middletown—present Biglerville—meant that Rodes soon established contact with Hill's left astride the Cashtown Pike. And by the afternoon of July 1 the nine brigades under Rodes and Early were deployed in an arching semicircle around Gettysburg's northern reaches. Allegheny Johnson did not reach the northern outskirts of Gettysburg until nearly dusk after an arduous march and therefore did not see action on the first day.[4]

When the blond-headed Rodes and the maimed Ewell approached Gettysburg in mid-morning of July 1, they were taken aback to find a full-scale fight under way between A. P. Hill's forces as well as a reinforced Federal presence under Oliver Otis Howard and Abner Doubleday. George Gordon Meade, now in charge of the Army of the Potomac as a replacement for Joe Hooker, had responded quickly to the Confederate threat and in doing so forced Ewell into making a decision. At Heidlersburg the evening before, he held a discussion with Rodes, Early, and Isaac Trimble, the latter with no official command and acting only as a volunteer. According to Trimble's account, Ewell kept poring over his instructions from Lee and asking repeatedly what he should do. Ever inclined to interpret his orders literally and to avert the need for decisive action, Ewell could not decide if he should march for Cashtown or for Gettysburg, as per Lee's instructions. "General Early especially commented in severe terms of its ambiguity with reference to Cashtown or Gettysburg as the objective point," Trimble relates. "When my opinion was asked, I said I could interpret it but one way after hearing from General Lee a few days before of his plan to attack the advance of the enemy and throw it back in confusion on the

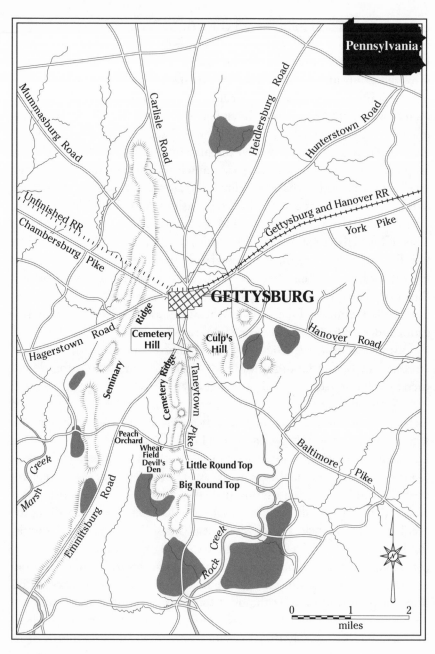

Gettysburg, July 1863

main body, and that as this advance was in Gettysburg, we should march to that place and notify General Lee immediately." Whether Ewell was irked at Trimble's outspokenness or found himself gripped with indecision, the advice was rejected.

Without Jackson's exacting commands to guide him, Ewell made no determination, but his dilemma about the renewed march was solved when one of A. P. Hill's riders arrived with urgent word that Ewell's corps was needed at Gettysburg. Upon nearing the town, Rodes, with Ewell's acquiescence, sent O'Neal's and Iverson's brigades scampering up Oak Hill, while he personally directed Thomas H. Carter to open on the enemy with his battery. Events rapidly took on a life of their own, as Ewell confessed in his official report: "It was too late to avoid an engagement without abandoning the position already taken up, and I determined to push the attack vigorously." In spite of his determination to avoid a heavy fight, Rodes was drawn into the melee because there was no other option. "When within four miles of the town," Ewell wrote, "the presence of the enemy there in force was announced by the sound of a sharp cannonade, and instant preparations for battle were made."[5]

Rodes, a major general since May 7, led his division into the fracas along the wooded ridge known as Oak Hill northwest of town. Oak Hill, which reached almost to Gettysburg itself, was situated between the Mummasburg and Carlisle Roads. Two or three miles southwest of the former was the famous cut for an unfinished railroad, which ran parallel to the Cashtown-to-Chambersburg Pike that approached from the west. A. P. Hill had taken this route when he made first contact with Buford's horsemen. South of the Chambersburg Pike was the seminary used to train Lutheran ministers in more tranquil times that gave its name to the ridgeline where Lee would array his two hundred cannon two days later. Opposite Seminary Ridge, beyond the road leading south toward Emmittsburg, lay the Peach Orchard, Devil's Den, and the Wheat Field—places soon to be immortalized in the American conscience. And rising precipitously east of the Emmitsburg Road came the Round Tops, soon to become Federal bastions, which gave way to the northward-running Cemetery Ridge that extends nearly into Gettysburg from the south. At its northernmost extreme lay two formations—Cemetery Hill and its companion, Culp's Hill—that in many eyes proved the undoing of Lieutenant General Richard Stoddert Ewell.

By the evening of July 1, the notorious Federal "fishhook" had been formed in a line from the Round Tops to Cemetery Ridge to the barb or "hook" on first Cemetery and then Culp's Hill. When Old Jube came on the scene from York with fifty-five hundred men, he rapidly deployed his four brigades across the Heidlersburg Road north of town and opposite the latter formations. Early was in position by 2:30 P.M., which means the initial arrangement of the Second Corps—at least Rodes's and Early's brigades—was accomplished largely without Ewell's direction. "I immediately ordered the artillery [under Henry Pollard Jones] forward and the brigades into line," Early wrote later. "Gordon's brigade being in front formed first in line on the right side of the road, then Hays,' with Smith's in the rear of Hoke's and thrown back so as to present a line toward the York pike. Jones' battalion was posted in a field immediately in front of Hoke's brigade, so as to open on the enemy's flank, which it did at once with effect, attracting the fire of the enemy's artillery on Cemetery Hill and that in front of the town." As reinforcements poured into the sector west and north of Gettysburg throughout the morning and early afternoon, it was the overpowering punch of Rodes's left augmented by Early's timely arrival that caused the Federal lines to crumble "slowly and stubbornly in most places, but more and more rapidly on the right as Early's attack gathered momentum."[6]

Before that, Rodes fought alone atop Oak Hill as well as toward the Chambersburg Pike perpendicular to Henry Heth's division of A. P. Hill's corps. While Ramseur's and Daniel's brigades were held in reserve, O'Neal, commanding the Third, Fifth, Sixth, and Twenty-sixth Alabama regiments plus W. A. Owens's artillery battalion, led the way, although Rodes kept the Fifth Alabama in reserve with him. And close behind was Alfred Iverson's brigade, comprising the Fifth, Twelfth, Twentieth, and Twenty-third North Carolina Infantry, which followed along the crest toward the division of James S. Wadsworth of Abner Doubleday's First Corps. If Jubal Early, a confirmed bachelor known throughout the ranks for his never-ending chew of tobacco, had problems, Rodes also had a bit of personal baggage as the campaign unfolded.[7] At Carlisle "somebody of Rodes' staff had found a keg of lager beer—and Rodes, his A.A.G. [Moses G.] Peyton, and A.C.S. Ben Greene were all somewhat affected by the liquor," offers Brown. "I never saw Rodes intoxicated before or since—& it was an accident this time." Apparently a veritable debauchery had taken place when the lager, laced with whiskey, was passed around, but Brown is adamant that Ewell, suffering from "a severe headache," had retired for the evening before the revelry commenced.[8]

Although a sober Rodes had rushed into the fray without a moment's hesitation, he was obliged to look on in horror as first O'Neal and then Iverson ran into a slaughterhouse. As he watched with the Fifth Alabama, which he had joined personally, O'Neal launched a premature assault with but three of his regiments "and at the wrong point." The Alabamians were shortly repulsed by Henry Baxter's brigade of Massachusetts, New York, and Pennsylvania boys and suffered heavy losses. "When Iverson saw what had taken place, he, too, decided to rush the enemy." Baxter thereupon "went forward and took shelter behind a stone fence on the Mummasburg Road which protected his flank, while an angle in the fence which turned in a southwesterly direction covered his front," reported Abner Doubleday. "As his men lay down behind the barrier, Iverson's brigade came up close behind not knowing our troops were there. Baxter's men sprang to their feet and delivered a most deadly volley at very short range, which left 500 of Iverson's men dead and wounded, and so demoralized them, that all gave themselves up as prisoners." By any measure it was not a good time for Rodes or Ewell, although they later drove the enemy through Gettysburg itself with help from A. P. Hill and Jubal Early. When he filed his report, Rodes castigated O'Neal for not moving forward, although he informed him beforehand that Baxter "was not mounted." As for Iverson, Rodes said his men "fought and died like heroes"—that his dead "lay in a distinctly line of battle."[9]

Rodes's problems had been compounded when Iverson displayed what Brown called cowardly behavior; and since Brown always spoke for his stepfather, who was still living in Tennessee when he wrote, it is reasonable to assume that Ewell concurred with his assessment. Abner Doubleday says that some of Iverson's men raised the white flag and used the opportunity to flee the field. However, sympathetic Confederate writers argue that Iverson was seized with what today could be called battle fatigue or panic in a difficult situation when O'Neal folded on his front during Baxter's counterattack. "Some of Iverson's men realizing they were about to be surrounded and slaughtered waved their handkerchiefs in surrender," notes Douglas Southall Freeman. "Iverson saw this and thought the dead men in line were alive and were yielding." He became so unnerved that one of his officers, Captain D. P. Halsey, had to assume command as Iverson was led from the field. Interestingly, neither Ewell nor Rodes faulted the North Carolinian, even though he was removed from command; he later took part in the Georgia fighting and became a "Florida orange grower until his death in 1911."[10]

Meanwhile, units under Junius Daniel and George P. Doles engaged the enemy in front of Gettysburg. On the right between Oak Hill and the railroad cut, Daniel, with the help of Stephen D. Ramseur, joined Dorsey Pender's division (of A. P. Hill's corps) to charge down the Chambersburg Pike. "My command continued to move forward until it reached the out-skirts of the town, where, agreeably to instructions received from Major H. A. Whiting, I halted," Daniel commented. Doles, who had been sta-tioned near the Carlisle Road, held Rodes's extreme left east of Oak Hill. Although he found himself unsupported, he became engaged with Carl Schurz's division, now commanded by Alexander Schimmelfennig. With the Fourth, Twelfth, Twenty-first, and Forty-fourth Georgia regiments, he managed to force the Germans back in confusion. It was an uneven con-test, with fifteen hundred Confederates against five thousand Yankees, as Doles's brigade "found an attack on its front, flank and rear." Then, at about 3:00 P.M. Early arrived via the Harrisburg Road and immediately ordered John B. Gordon into action on Doles's left flank. Doles, Rodes said, renewed his assault with Gordon's help and drove the enemy into Gettysburg itself. With Early's assistance the contest shifted rapidly, and Ewell, anxious to put a good face on the day's fighting, pronounced that Doles achieved on the left "a success no less brilliant than that of Ramseur in the center, and Daniel, on the right."[11]

When Early came up on the Harrisburg Road, Gordon's brigade was on the right; Hoke's, now commanded by Colonel Isaac Avery, was on the left, with Extra Billy Smith in reserve. Harry T. Hays's brigade, still com-posed entirely of Louisiana regiments, kept to the road as Early's entire division advanced toward Gettysburg from the east. Although Early—with-out immediate instruction from Ewell—ordered his artillery to open on the enemy's left to relieve the pressure on A. P. Hill, Gordon's men rushed Francis C. Barlow's division of Howard's Eleventh Corps with a penetrat-ing yell. "The musketry was very severe and we feared that Gordon would be borne back, but after a few minutes the firing ceased, & the smoke lifting from the field, revealed to our sight the defeated Federals in disor-derly flight, hotly pursued by the gallant Georgians," said Captain Will-iam J. Seymour, one of Hays's men, who looked on from behind. "Though this little engagement did not last fifteen minutes, our pioneers buried two hundred and twenty-nine of the enemy's dead. Gordon's loss was seventy-six in killed and wounded." While Gordon was spurring his men to vic-tory "mounted upon a magnificent black stallion," Hoke's and Hays's brigades swept aside the last Federal force north of Gettysburg, driving "the enemy pell-mell through and beyond the town."[12]

Not only Ewell but practically the entire Second Corps as well as A. P. Hill's command could plainly see two prominent elevations rising some eighty feet above the town and immediately south of Gettysburg—Cemetery and Culp's Hills. Just about every officer and man except Ewell himself recognized the importance of these hills to Lee's army—that both needed to be seized before they were taken in force by the enemy. Shortly after the battle north of Gettysburg, Gordon found Ewell and stressed that Cemetery Hill at least should be occupied. Although Gordon possessed the momentum to move ahead, the commander simply would not or could not free himself from Lee's admonition to avoid a general engagement. "At this time, about three o'clock, the firing had ceased entirely save occasional discharges of artillery from the hill above the town," noted Trimble, still tagging along as a volunteer. As one of the great imponderables of the entire war started to unfold, Ewell galloped into Gettysburg in the company of Gordon, who kept pressing for authority to charge ahead and take possession of Cemetery Hill.

But Ewell continued in his steadfast refusal to use any part of the Second Corps for an assault. As he rode along town streets at Gordon's side, sniping and random small arms fire played havoc with the occupying force even though the main battle had faded away. "A number of Confederates were killed or wounded, and I heard the ominous thud of a minie ball as it struck General Ewell at my side," Gordon noted in an oft-repeated scenario:

"I Quickly asked: 'Are you hurt, Sir.'
'No, no' he replied.
'I'm not hurt.'
'But suppose that ball had struck you.'
'We would have had the trouble of carrying you off the field, Sir.'
'You see how much better fixed for a fight I am than you are.'
'It don't hurt a bit to be shot in a wooden leg.'"[13]

Edward J. Stackpole, who probably knows as much about the Gettysburg fiasco as anyone, allows that Ewell was "suffering from the heat, fatigue, and the pain in his infested stump of a leg" and wanted to give his men a rest. As he was being implored to act, to send an attacking force up Cemetery Hill, Trimble observed that Ewell "moved uneasily, a good deal excited and seemed to me undecided want to do next." Clifford Dowdey, author of numerous studies on the Confederacy, maintains bluntly that he was "marked by a paralysis of will, like a fatal disease"; and Douglas Southall Freeman titled his chapter on July 1 "Ewell Cannot Reach a Decision." Campbell Brown, who was on the field with Ewell, offers that he "comes to dangerous ground" when attempting to explain Ewell's actions on the evening of July 1, "which is believed to have lost us the battle already half-won."[14]

Actually Ewell's failure or inability to act for whatever reason when the Second Corps emerged victorious south of Gettysburg allowed Meade and his generals sufficient time to fortify the two hills, therefore enabling the Federals to carry the entire battle. The argument in most camps is that the unexplained inaction not only cost Lee a triumph in Pennsylvania, but it also cost the war for the Confederacy. Gettysburg, after all, was the point of greatest penetration for the South—it was high noon for the effort to establish Southern independence. Writing in 1869, six years after the battle, Brown assessed the situation as Ewell rode in front of the town, with Early attempting to determine what he should do, or, as many Civil War soldiers and a preponderance of modern scholars would say, trying to determine what not to do. After it was learned that A. P. Hill pointedly refused to help and that Longstreet was not in position, "Gen'l Ewell finally decided to make no direct attack—but wait for [Allegheny] Johnson's coming with his fresh troops and hold the high peak to the left of Cemetery Hill." Brown continues: "The discovery that this lost us the battle is one of those frequently-recurring but tardy strokes of military genius, of which one hears of long after the minute circumstances that rendered them at the time impracticable, are forgotten—at least I heard nothing of it for months & months—& it was several years before any claim was put in by Early or his friends that his advice had been in favor of an attack and had been neglected."[15] Alan T. Nolan, a modern scholar devoted to questioning Lee's handling of the Army of Northern Virginia, has broken with a majority of historians to agree with Brown: "It is unhistorical to conclude that Ewell was necessarily wrong in his judgment. His decision was reasonable in the circumstances, and that responds to the only historically appropriate question concerning Ewell's conduct."[16]

Still, the historical record is exceedingly clear—it rings down through the intervening years. Those present on July 1 were universally agreed that in the flush of victory, Brown's "half-won battle," Ewell's subordinates wanted to attack Cemetery Hill in the time remaining before nightfall. Lieutenant Randolph H. McKim, as aide-de-camp under Allegheny Johnson, has written a compelling account of a late-afternoon session between Ewell and Trimble with "at least three hours of daylight remaining." On his own initiative, Trimble had ridden out from Gettysburg to observe the two hills. When he returned, Trimble told him: "General, there (pointing to Culp's Hill) is an eminence of commanding position and not now occupied, as it ought to be by us or the enemy soon." Trimble thought it could be carried with a brigade, but try as he might he could not persuade Ewell to act, even though the rise was plainly visible from Gettysburg streets. "General Ewell made some impatient reply, and the conversation dropped," Trimble relates. He kept falling back on the canard that Lee did not want a full-fledged battle.[17]

McKim, however, describes a much more heated confrontation, at least on Trimble's part: "'Give me a division,' he said, 'and I will engage to take that hill.' When this was declined he said: 'Give me a brigade and I will do it.' When this, too, was declined he said: 'Give me a good regiment and I will engage to take that hill.' When this was declined the gallant Trimble threw down his sword and left General Ewell's headquarters, saying he would no longer serve under such an officer!" Although this account has appeared in every history of the battle for nearly 140 years, McKim confesses that Trimble got away with his seeming insubordination because he was yet a volunteer officer without any official position in the Second Corps.[18]

Gordon and Trimble were not the only Confederates to condemn Ewell for inaction; Robert E. Rodes in his battle summary says merely that "to have attacked [Cemetery Hill] with my division alone, diminished as it had been by a loss of 2,500 men, would have been absurd. . . . I concluded that the order not to bring on a general engagement was still in force, and hence placed my lines, and skirmishers in a defensive attitude to await orders." While his immediate superior may have been diplomatic, George Doles, who held the point of Rodes's line, was not. Colonel E. A. O'Neal, commanding the Twenty-sixth Alabama, wanted to charge ahead with Doles's help, but Doles was forced to reject his request. Although O'Neal was adamant that he would have no difficulty in carrying the heights, "Doles realized the fact, but would not act without further orders." Thereupon, continues C. D. Grace, who was present with Doles's brigade: "It was a fatal mistake. The delay enabled the Federals to reform and hold the position until reinforcements came up in the night." He had been restrained, Doles later said, because Rodes and Ewell bade him halt on the outer limit of Gettysburg "and to form a line of battle in the street running east and west through the town."[19]

O'Neal was correct, wrote Yankee General Winfield S. Hancock, who maintained that there were no fortifications on Cemetery Hill when he arrived on the scene about four in the afternoon. "[T]here can be no question that a combined attack," by Doles, Hoke, and O'Neal "made within an hour, would have been successful," said John B. Bachelder. If O'Neal and Doles were miffed, Harry T. Hays, who arrived with Early's division, was livid with Ewell's procrastination. Hays and the Louisiana brigade had been actively engaged throughout July 1 and by his own reckoning had taken more prisoners than he had men in his brigade. He cleared the streets of Gettysburg with a loss of "1 officer and 6 men killed, 4 officers and 37 men wounded, and 25 men missing." Like others at brigade level, Hays held his counsel in his official reports, but he too was stymied after moving through the town, although he advanced to the very base of Cemetery Hill without orders to go farther.

"As the afternoon slowly passed, the [Louisiana] Tigers watched more and more Union troops arrive on the hill to their front. Oaths and curses were muttered along the line and many openly exclaimed their wish 'that Jackson were here,'" finds their chief chronicler. "The 15th Louisiana's Colonel David Zable remembered that when Johnson's men finally arrived on the field late in the day, and still no advance was made 'the troops realized there was something wanting somewhere. There was an evident feeling of dissatisfaction among our men [that] we were not doing [it] Stonewall Jackson's way.'" According to John F. Gruber, by a "unanimous vote" Hays was requested to seek a transfer of his brigade from the Second Corps. This spontaneous outcry, Gruber affirms, "caused General Ewell much regret."[20]

Ewell's mule-headed reticence prompted an instant and inevitable comparison to Stonewall Jackson's propensity for aggressive action without orders from Lee. Where most believed Jackson, who had been gone a mere fifty-four days, would have rushed to capture the hill or exhausted himself in the effort, Ewell demurred, and many a soldier at every rank yearned for former days. Henry Kyd Douglas, who served under both Jackson and Ewell, is responsible for at least some of the pro-Jackson legend that came out of July 1, and it was soon apparent that Ewell had not been the man to replace Stonewall Jackson as Lee's right arm. Although his well-known *I Rode with Stonewall* posits that Ewell's adjutant, Alexander "Sandie" Pendleton, exclaimed at the time, "Oh, for the presence and inspiration of Old Jack for just one more hour!" Douglas had joined the controversy long before its 1940 publication. He gave a slightly different version in an undated newspaper article, as he went on to elaborate what both he and Pendleton meant by the quip. "Ewell did not attack and it was that which caused me to make the remark I did to the Count de Paris: 'General Lee had not yet realized that Stonewall Jackson was dead,' which of course meant that Ewell was not a Jackson or to be trusted to the same extent. We all know what Jackson would have done. He would have needed no suggestion to attack a demoralized enemy without an order from Lee," Douglas wrote. "The remark I made to the Count de Paris, repeated by him in England, had been very much quoted."[21]

Sandie Pendleton, on the other hand, seemingly did not fault Ewell alone for the Gettysburg fiasco. After the retreat into Virginia, he offered a lengthy summary of the battle and concluded: "There has been some mismanagement in this affair & while the fault may be with others, the blame must and should fall on Gen. Lee." Earlier Pendleton makes no mention of Ewell in the main body of his discourse other than saying Lee had recalled him from Harrisburg when the battle opened. A more sensible evaluation of his remark about Jackson is that it was a passing quip in the heat of the moment.[22]

Whatever the arguments advanced by others, Ewell had it in his power to take Cemetery Hill on July 1, and David French Boyd, commissary officer in Hays's brigade, presents perhaps the best explanation of why he failed to issue the attack order. Boyd in effect offers a plausible evaluation of Ewell's psyche without ever mentioning the words *psychology* or *psychiatry*:

> This peculiarity of Ewell's in the army, of never liking to be alone or in independent command—never to do anything by himself—appeared at West Point. He liked to depend in everything on someone else, and especially on some certain one, whom he respected and loved. Like the vine, he must have someone to cling to and intertwine around. This trait made him the best and most loyal of subordinates. He was of Sherman's class at West Point, and took a great fancy to him there, as he did afterwards to Dick Taylor in the Confederate army, and loved to be with him. Sherman was his chum. Ewell was fond of fishing while a cadet, but would never go unless his friend Sherman went along.

Although Lee told William Preston Johnston after Appomattox that Ewell "showed vacilation that prevented him from getting all out of his troops he might," Boyd, a onetime faculty member with Sherman at a Louisiana military school, was more direct: "General Lee seems not to have understood Ewell's peculiarities; else he would never have made him a Lieutenant General and put him in Jackson's place after his death." And Boyd was equally caustic about the consequences: "It was Ewell's want of decision and aversion to act on his own judgment and responsibility that lost the battle of Gettysburg the first evening."[23]

Ewell's inability to confront difficult military alternatives was evident when California and Missouri newspapers chastised him for not tearing into the Chiricahua Apaches, saying that he avoided aggressive warfare whenever possible while in command at Fort Buchanan. Afterward, during the First Manassas, when Thomas Rosser brought up several Howitzers on the Confederate right at Union Mills, Ewell would not let him open on the enemy without a direct command. Even here, in the first major confrontation of the war, he had adopted a legalistic approach to interpreting his orders. Although Ewell had been summoned to attack on the right flank at Manassas, he failed to implement Beauregard's commands, because he had no orders to do so—and Beauregard condemned him for not taking the plainly called-for initiative at the critical juncture. In the Shenandoah Valley, where he had the meticulous Stonewall for a superior, Ewell had remained ensconced at Conrad's Store in spite of repeated urgings from Jackson that he move down the Luray Valley in pursuit of Nathaniel P. Banks. Joseph E. Johnston had given him an opportunity to move when he was encamped on the Rappahannock, which Ewell declined. Significantly, Boyd and other contemporaries said nothing about his physical discomfort from the amputation or any emotional upheavals from his marriage to explain his behavior as a reticent soldier. Despite the contention of various modern writers that Ewell wanted to attack Cemetery Hill on July 1 but hesitated when A. P. Hill refused to help, the man was clearly possessed by a long-standing dependency need.

Surely a man of Lee's alacrity and perception of the human condition must have grasped Ewell's deficiency as he looked out from his vantage point on Seminary Ridge. With his field glasses Lee could plainly see across the mile or so of open ground that the Second Corps had stalled after its victorious sweep through Gettysburg. Like everyone else in the army, he realized that the high ground should be secured immediately and dispatched an aide, Major Walter Taylor, to find Ewell. Lee did not employ the term "practicable" with respect to Ewell and Cemetery Hill until his official report, written in January of the following year, but on the afternoon of

July 1 Taylor was instructed to tell Ewell "it was only necessary to press those people in order to secure possession of the heights, and that, if possible he wished him to do this." Then, continues the account by Harry W. Pfanz, "Taylor recalled also that Ewell had expressed no objection to Lee's request or indicated any impediment to it." But Ewell also claimed later that Lee's instruction through Taylor said, "attack this hill if I could do so to advantage."[24]

Lieutenant James P. Smith from Ewell's own staff had already been dispatched to inform Lee that he was awaiting the arrival of Allegheny Johnson before proceeding. As the two aides crossed paths, Ewell was fixed in his determination to remain in place. Regardless of Taylor's intelligence to Lee, he showed no inclination to move. Campbell Brown vehemently denied that any such visit had taken place when Taylor's account appeared in 1877. Still, in his memoir entry for December 1869 he includes the following: "But a staff officer sent by him [Ewell] (I forget whom, but have an idea it was Pendleton or Jos. Smith) brought word that Hill had not advanced & that Gen'l Lee who was with him, left to Gen'l Ewell's discretion whether to advance or not." Brown was apparently referring to the word conveyed by Smith on the return from his encounter with Lee. Brown's sister, Harriet Turner, writing in 1878, asserted that Brown refrained from openly challenging Taylor's assessment because he felt others had already risen to Ewell's defense, including Early.[25]

Lee's judgment as to giving Ewell an option to remain in place or advance can certainly be questioned; Ewell's whole persona as military leader dictated that he would not move until ordered by the general commanding. In fact, Joseph Smith had been instructed to tell Lee that not only was he waiting for Johnson, but also reports from Extra Billy Smith indicated Federal troops were marching on his rear. Ewell, who thought Lee was still in Cashtown, was in an obvious quandary when he sought to rationalize his failure to advance. Later, according to historian Gallagher, when Ewell was a prisoner in Boston Harbor, he told Eppa Hunton: "[I]t took a dozen blunders to lose the Battle of Gettysburg and he had committed a good many of them. . . . When speaking to a group of former Confederates a few months later, he took a different stance." Ewell said if Johnson had been on the field sooner, "there would have been no second day at Gettysburg."[26]

Be that as it may, Lee decided to visit his recalcitrant commander at Second Corps headquarters located in the Adams County almshouse north of town. As Lee and Ewell sat on an outside porch at dusk in the company of Rodes, a courier was dispatched to fetch Early for the meeting. According to Early's recent biographer, Ewell again deferred to his subordinate and let him do the talking. Early made the argument that the Second Corps was used up from the day's campaigning and that any attack should be made on the Confederate left—in other words, let someone else do the fighting. "But on July 1, a new caution had been manifest," writes Charles Osborne, with the normally aggressive Early now counseling restraint, to Lee's chagrin. Lee had come expecting to find another Jackson and encountered a pervasive defeatism. Osborne adds that Early "was eloquent in erecting obstacles to Lee's will." Since Ewell was present throughout, he surely concurred with Early as did Rodes.

"Perhaps that victory might have been decisive, so far as Gettysburg was concerned, by a prompt advance of all the troops that had been employed on our side against the hill upon and behind which the enemy had taken refuge," Early wrote in his postwar memoir. He appeared to place the blame on Lee, adding that "a common superior was not present, and the opportunity was lost." Strange indeed, because Early spent much of his later life defending Lee's performance at Gettysburg while castigating others. Although he wrote after Ewell's death, he used the old argument to defend what Lee had been told that July evening: "The only troops engaged on our side were Hill's two divisions and Ewell's two divisions, the rest of the army not being up."[27]

Tom Turner, however, told a different tale in his own memoir, resurrected by his wife (Ewell's stepdaughter), to refute Walter Taylor's later accusations. Prior to Lee's appearance, Ewell had sent Turner and Early's nephew, Lieutenant John Early, to the crest of Culp's Hill to reconnoiter adjacent Cemetery Hill. When the two staffers came back with news that the area was free of bluecoats (in the late afternoon), they found Ewell sitting in a fence corner with Rodes and Early. "Upon hearing our report Gen'l Ewell asked Rodes what he thought of sending Gen'l Johnson upon Round Top 'tonight'—he (Rodes) replied that the men were tired & footsore & he did not think it would do any thing 'one way or the other,'" Turner recalled. "Upon putting the same question of Gen'l Early the latter replied (I remember his words distinctly) 'if you do not go up there tonight, it will cost you ten thousand to get up there to-morrow.'" All of this was certainly on the minds of both Early and Ewell as they sought to justify their position to Lee, who rode away from Ewell's headquarters after informing all present that an attack would be made along the line at daybreak.[28]

About 10:00 P.M., says Turner, Ewell mounted his horse for a conference at Lee's headquarters on the Confederate left near Seminary Ridge. After the late-night session, Lee had fixed upon his ruinous strategy for July 2. Young George Peterkin, future Episcopalian bishop of West Virginia and an aide to artillerist William Nelson Pendleton, rode to the same meeting with his boss. "Of course I did not hear their conversation, but my recollection is perfectly clear as to this, that as we rode away, your father said to me that General Longstreet was to attack very early in the morning—this coming from General Lee," Peterkin afterward told Pendleton's daughter. Lee had made his decision—Longstreet would move against the ensconced Federals on the Confederate right while Ewell and the Second Corps made a thrust on the left. Upon returning to his almshouse bivouac around 2:00 A.M., Ewell summoned Turner from his bed with an urgent communiqué for Allegheny Johnson, who was encamped along the base of Culp's Hill. The message from Ewell told Johnson "to maintain the status quo" while preparing to scale the height in the morning. For the time being Ewell and Early had their way—the Second Corps could rest easy for the night without further action.[29]

If the adage about the best laid plans of mice and men has any meaning, Lee must have been aghast when most of July 2 wasted away without any forward movement from his legions. Despite Peterkin's recollections that Longstreet was to open the fight in the early morning, the advance did not take place until four o'clock in the afternoon. Longstreet "allowed his disagreement with Lee's decision to affect his conduct," writes his biographer Jeffry D. Wert. "Once the commanding general determined to assail the enemy, duty required Longstreet to comply with the vigor and thoroughness that had characterized his generalship." After a dalliance that bordered on insubordination—what Moxley Sorrell labeled "apathy in his movements"—the First Corps ran headlong into the command of General Daniel E. Sickles; and in quick succession fights etched in the national psyche—Peach Orchard, Wheat Field, and Devil's Den—unfolded before a hopelessly outgunned Longstreet ordered a withdrawal to the security of Seminary Ridge. Had the attack come earlier in the day, coordinated with an assault by Ewell on Cemetery Hill to hinder Meade from reinforcing his position on the Round Tops, there may have been some prospect of success. But that scenario falls into the realm of "what if." "The long and short of the matter seems to me as follows," notes E. P. Alexander, Longstreet's artillerist and expert chronicler of the war. "Longstreet did not wish to take the offensive. His objection to it was not based at all upon the peculiar strength of the enemy's position . . . but solely on general principles—perhaps the same referred to implied in Gen. Lee's report where he says that he 'had not designed to give battle so far from his base unless attacked.'"[30]

Although there is probably no answer, an interesting question presents itself: Longstreet had attempted to influence Ewell before the thrust across the Mason-Dixon Line, and was he now influenced by Old Pete's desultory inaction? During Longstreet's long preparations to advance on July 2 and the bloodbath that followed, writes Edward Stackpole, the movements of Ewell and A. P. Hill are "a mystery." Ewell did move his headquarters from the almshouse to the vicinity of the "Culp buildings" between Gettysburg and Rock Creek, which flows past Cemetery and Culp's Hills, to be nearer his men. The Second Corps was supposed to advance on Lee's left at the sound of Longstreet's cannon, which could well have influenced the outcome by occupying a good portion of Meade's men. What Ewell did do was order his artillery to open against the Federals atop Culp's Hill; but he aroused a firestorm when the Yankees returned a blistering cannonade of their own. The result was disastrous, with "most of his artillery silenced and his gun crews crippled," observes historian Glenn Tucker. "Among the mortally wounded was the competent young commander, Major [Joseph White] Latimer, who had been a sophomore at the Virginia Military Institute when the war broke and was not yet twenty-one when he fell." During the bombardment, Ewell said, Latimer was forced to withdraw his guns.[31]

After it was too late to matter—after Longstreet led "the best three hours' fighting ever done on any battle-field" and lost six thousand men in the bargain—Ewell decided to "do his duty" and order a move against Cemetery Hill. The task was given to Early, who marched around 7:00 P.M., with the brigades of Harry Hays and Isaac Avery; Gordon was held in reserve and Extra Billy Smith had been temporarily assigned to Jeb Stuart and the cavalry. "Our attack on the left was repulsed with considerable loss to us, though we gained the outer works," said the topographer Jed Hotchkiss. Hays and his Louisianans had a rough time on the slopes of Cemetery Hill when they encountered enemy rifle pits backed up by entrenched artillery pieces. By taking advantage of approaching darkness and smoke from the battle, Hays and Avery managed to elude their tormentors. "Our exact locality could not be discovered by the enemy gunners, and we thus escaped what in the full light of day could have been nothing else than horrific slaughter."

On they went after breaking through a second line hidden behind a stone wall until they reached the summit and "captured a number of pieces of artillery, four stand of colors, and a number of prisoners." And, Hays continues, "every piece of artillery which had been firing upon us was silenced." But Ewell's men were unable to sustain their triumph gained at considerable loss in the July darkness; they were obliged to abandon the high ground, Early noted, when support from Rodes failed to materialize. Little wonder that C. D. Grace, a participant in the struggle, was moved to write: "Had we occupied Cemetery Ridge, as was in our power to do [on July 1], in the opinion of the writer, victory would have crowned our banners."[32]

Meanwhile, Allegheny Johnson's men, crouching behind Rock Creek, could hear Hays and Avery struggling to reach the crest of Cemetery Hill. The attack ordered by Ewell got under way around 7:45 in near darkness and long after Longstreet had called off the main fight to gain Little Round Top and thus destroy Meade's right. Unlike Early and his compeers, Johnson charged ahead with his entire division. In obedience to Ewell's directions, Johnson wrote, "I then advanced my infantry to the assault of the enemy's strong position—a rugged and rocky mountain, heavily timbered and difficult to ascend—a natural fortification, rendered more formidable by deep entrenchments and thick abatis—Jones' brigade in advance, followed by Nicholls' and Steuart's." Later in the evening, after some difficulty on the far left, James A. "Stonewall Jim" Walker and the Stonewall Brigade joined the division. Unfortunately, Johnson's four brigades confronted crusty Brigadier General George S. "Pop" Greene, probably the oldest soldier in either army at Gettysburg. The sixty-three-year-old native of Warwick, Rhode Island, had graduated from West Point in the class of 1823, seventeen years before Ewell. "Pop Greene outlived many of these soldiers who thought a bullet would hurry to get him before his normal time ran out; he died in his ninety-eighth year and retained the West Point longevity record until 1958."[33]

Although Meade hurried reinforcements under Henry W. Slocum and Abner Doubleday, Greene not only fought alone but also with a bulldog ferocity that insured Johnson's failure to secure the height. Finally, George "Maryland" Steuart, with the First Maryland, two North Carolina, and two Virginia regiments plus help from the Stonewall Brigade composed of all Virginia outfits, was able to break the Federal defenses at the base of Culp's Hill. In spite of Pop Greene's extra men, Steuart broke through his hastily drawn but formidable barriers. Johnson, who soon learned that he was within "musket shot" of the Baltimore Pike (Meade's lifeline), now had gained a toehold on the much sought-after hill. Rumors soon apprised Ewell of the breakthrough, and an effort was put in motion to have Extra Billy Smith, still on the York Road, seize the pike, which failed because "he lacked orientation" in the darkness. As night settled over the high ground, soldiers north and south bivouacked near a watering hole known locally as Spangler's Spring. According to historian Tucker: "Water details of both armies exchanged banter as if they were on a school picnic. Nobody wanted to deny anyone water, even if he had to be disemboweled the next morning." Ewell had again missed an opportunity to register a compelling blow for the Confederacy; the least additional effort (with assistance from A. P. Hill on his left side) would have broken a vital artery for Meade's army and warned the enemy general that his right wing was far from secure.[34]

With the coming dawn, in Ewell's own words: "I was ordered to renew the attack at daylight Friday morning, and as Johnson's position was the only one affording hopes of doing this to advantage he was re-enforced by Smith's brigade, of Early's division and Daniel's and Rodes' brigades of Rodes' division. . . . In Johnson's attack, the enemy abandoned a portion of their works in disorder, and as they ran across an open space to another work, were exposed to the fire of Daniel's brigade at 60 or 70 yards." No matter that Daniel slaughtered the Yankees on his front, "repeated reports that enemy cavalry was approaching at last caused [Johnson] about 1 p.m., to evacuate the works already gained," continues Ewell. The difficult terrain precluded the heavy use of artillery, according to Campbell Brown, and caused Johnson to inform Ewell that the "enemy had saved him the trouble of deciding whether to attack, by assaulting themselves the troops in the captured works." Despite efforts by Walker and the Stonewall Brigade to lend a hand, Johnson himself noted that "all had been done that it was possible to do." When Stonewall Jim failed to provide Johnson with the momentum to drive the enemy from Culp's Hill, it was over for Ewell and the Second Corps. There was nothing left to do but withdraw to the base of both heights and endure a withering skirmish fire from the entrenched foe throughout July 3. Lee's grand scheme to have Ewell open on the left to coincide with the main attack had come to naught.[35]

While Ewell was losing his precarious grip on Culp's Hill, Lee had been organizing the greatest artillery bombardment ever seen on this side of the Atlantic in preparation for his all-or-nothing thrust at Meade's center and right. Accounts vary about the number of guns used in the cannonade that lasted, in the words of Jed Hotchkiss, from sunrise until early afternoon. "We had 120 pieces of art. on one ridge [Seminary]," he wrote. "Fully 400 pieces were firing at the same time." Although the so-called softening up accomplished little, Brown is adamant that "we were to open also—& keep up our fire for an hour (if I mistake not), when it would cease and the assault take place." While Brown does not elaborate further, E. P. Alexander, Longstreet's artillery chief, pulls no punches: "Only one of Ewell's five fine battalions, & he had some of the very best in the army, & under officers second to none, participated in our bombardment at all. It only fired a few dozen shots, for, apparently it could not see what it was doing." And a critical Alexander added: "But every shot was smashing up something, & had it been increased & or kept up, it is hard to say what might have resulted."[36]

At some point before the grand assault following the cannonade— what history calls "Pickett's Charge"—Longstreet reportedly looked up at Cemetery Ridge and the Round Tops and told Lee: "I have been a soldier all my life. I have been with soldiers engaged in fights by couples, by squads, companies, regiments, divisions and armies, and should know as well as any one what soldiers can do. It is my opinion that no 15,000 men ever arrayed in battle can take that hill." Undeterred, Lee gave the go-ahead nod, after choosing to overlook the lessons of Fredericksburg when Ambrose Burnside's forces had been cut to pieces while charging the entrenched Confederates atop Marye's Heights. Pickett's Charge, the name taken from the prominent role played by George Pickett in organizing the attack (although he did not actually lead it), was composed of nearly fifteen thousand troops—some modern scholars find a lower figure—from several divisions and army corps. Isaac Trimble, Ewell's nemesis from the first and second days' fighting, who had been given Dorsey Pender's command just before the attack, advanced on the far left in support of James Johnston Pettigrew. Trimble was wounded in the charge and underwent a leg amputation by Dr. Hunter McGuire, the same surgeon who had attended Ewell. But Trimble was not the only casualty on that horrible July afternoon; in about the time it takes a man to walk a mile, Lee lost approximately ten thousand men, including several officers of general rank. The flower of Southern manhood had been spilled while an inert Ewell looked on from afar.[37]

Ewell and the Second Corps had become inconsequential after the abortive fighting on Culp's Hill during the morning of July 3 and took no part in the carnage belched out by Meade's guns along Cemetery Ridge. Modern historian Peter S. Carmichael offers the supposition that Ewell could well have altered the outcome of Pickett's Charge had he employed his batteries to bombard Meade's right while the infantry advanced. In the end, however, it made little difference as the tattered and decimated brigades fell back on Seminary Ridge and Lee made his preparations to head for the Potomac. In all, the Confederates had lost upward of thirty thousand men in Pennsylvania; the Gettysburg campaign was over. "Don't forget that you are from Old Virginia," Pickett had intoned his troopers at the start, and now the Army of Northern Virginia began its full retreat toward the Old Dominion, never again to advance into northern territory.[38]

The Second Corps remained in place throughout July 4 at the ready for any counterattack on "the very ground of the first day's fighting." Ewell and his men looked out at the horrors of war from their temporary bivouac before joining the southward trek. "Just in front of us lay the unburied Federals of that affair—in large numbers," observes Brown. "Corpses so monstrously swollen that the buttons were broken from the loose blouses & shirts, & the baggy pantaloons fitted like a skin so blackened—that the head looked like an immense cannonball, the features being nearly obliterated—& that the necks were almost indistinguishable, being marked only by a sharp line between head & body." Brown recalled that he saw heads actually forced from the torso from unchecked swelling. By Saturday morning, July 5, Ewell had his entire corps headed south toward the Potomac crossings, although, according to Sandie Pendleton, he was obliged to leave some of his wounded as well as a cache of captured arms and other supplies. Ewell had to fight at least two attacks on his rear guard before reaching the river.[39]

Lee assigned the Second Corps to bring up the rear during the retreat. Ewell reached Williamsport, Maryland, on the evening of July 14; here, opposite present Berkeley County, West Virginia, he learned that the pontoon bridges used by Longstreet and A. P. Hill were unavailable for most of his troops. Darkness and constant rain coupled with steep embankments offered a dismal prospect as Ewell had no choice but to order his men into the water. "Just before midnight, my advance (Rodes' division) commenced crossing," reads his official report. "By 8 o'clock my whole corps was over, all fording excepting Hays' brigade, which was sent with the artillery on the pontoons." John B. Gordon, who marched with Jubal Early's division, later wrote a somewhat comical account of the early morning return to Virginia. It seems the taller men, the six-footers, had a field day jousting with the shorter fellows, calling them "Lee's waders." "Run here, little boy, and get on my back, and I'll carry you over," shouted one stalwart, while another offered congratulations on this "opportunity for being washed, the first he has had, boys, for weeks and General Lee knows we need it."[40]

Ewell pushed south through Martinsburg to Darkesville, about twenty miles beyond the Potomac, where he went into camp with Rodes and Johnson; Early joined them on the sixteenth. The Second Corps was now back in Virginia, twenty-eight days after crossing into Maryland during mid-June. As Ewell's troopers rested from their ordeal, thousands of wounded and maimed greyclads shuttled past them to hospitals in Charlottesville and Staunton. After being wounded on July 2, one Confederate, R. J. Hancock, spent eighteen days in an army wagon before he reached a Staunton medical depot. While the parade of injured soldiers sped around the Second Corps, Ewell put Johnson's division to work destroying bridges and tracks along the Chesapeake and Ohio Railroad, still a crucial Federal link to the west. A Northern cavalry force under Benjamin F. Kelley, appeared opposite Back Creek, a northward-flowing stream through Berkeley County that reaches the Potomac northwest of Martinsburg. When "a brisk skirmish" with Rodes's men between Hedgesville and Martinsburg took place, Ewell sent Early in pursuit, but Kelley withdrew quickly before a fight could develop.[41]

Meade, meanwhile, passed down the eastern escarpment of the Blue Ridge, while Ewell proceeded southward through the Shenandoah Valley. After camping near Winchester, he wrote later: "On reaching Manassas Gap, found [A. R.] Wright's brigade of [R. H.] Anderson's division deployed to repel a large body of the enemy who were advancing through the gap." Ewell immediately ordered "some 250 sharpshooters" from Rodes's contingent to the aid of Wright. He was successful in driving out the interlopers, and with help from Allegheny Johnson, Ewell eluded the enemy near Front Royal before he proceeded up the Luray, or Page, Valley between Massanutten Mountain and the Blue Ridge. Next it was through Thornton's Gap and on to the Virginia Piedmont. At Ewell's command, Early and his division continued up the Shenandoah through Strasburg and New Market, where he turned eastward past the old battlegrounds at Cross Keys and Port Republic. Early continued through Conrad's Store to Swift Run Gap, and by July 24 the Second Corps—Ewell, Johnson, Rodes, and Early—were encamped around Madison Court House very near the Cedar Mountain battlefield. Meade also pressed his southern incursion and took up a position along the Rappahannock astraddle the Orange and Alexandria Railroad. When he sent cavalry "with supporting infantry" below the river by way of Rappahannock Station and Kelly's Ford, Lee summoned Ewell to abandon his bivouac at Madison Court House. By August 4 the entire Second Corps had moved to the Rapidan to hold the Yankees at bay.[42]

While Ewell's private life improved when his bride of two months soon joined him, he remained concerned about his command. He requested Early as well as Johnson and Rodes to advise him of vacancies "that have occurred in the late campaign," because there could be no doubt that Lee's divisions had suffered during the Gettysburg affair. "The army had received no accessions, but had been diminished by the march, from straggling, exhaustion, and sickness," Early noted. "My own division had been reduced from 7,226, its strength when it left Culpeper, to 5,611 when it crossed the Potomac, those numbers representing the strength in officers and men, and not muskets." Early's was not the only division in the Army of Northern Virginia to incur heavy, irreplaceable losses. Although Lee's official returns set Early's casualties slightly lower at 1,188, Rodes reported 2,853 and Johnson 1,873 in killed, wounded, and missing. In all, Ewell lost more than 5,800 men before his return to the Rapidan. And as he waited in camp until the scrap at Bristoe Station, Ewell's three divisions and artillery batteries reported 16,986 effectives, the largest contingent in Lee's aggregate of 53,286 at the close of the march into Pennsylvania.[43]

Chapter 12

"POOR EWELL—A CRIPPLE"

While the army remained inactive except for minor engagements at Bristoe Station, Rappahannock Station, and Mine Run until the Wilderness campaign opened in May 1864, Ewell was a man trapped in a paradox; he was basking in the joys of a new and successful marriage even as he suffered continued ill health in the aftermath of his amputation. And he had to contend with persistent whispers throughout the ranks that his performance at Gettysburg had been lacking. Mrs. Ewell and her nineteen-year-old daughter, Harriet (Hattie), joined him almost immediately after his encampment on the Rapidan, which evoked another outcry against him. When he needed rest from the rigors of command, he was expected to participate in a number of reviews that Lee staged during late 1863 to early 1864 as a means of reviving an esprit de corps among the Army of Northern Virginia as his troops gazed out at the gathering Federals beyond the river.

"I saw Ewell's whole corps under review the other day," Jeb Stuart told his wife in a September 11 letter. "Every Gen'l and Col. In the Infty appears to have his wife along." Stuart, of course, was lamenting that his duties with the cavalry kept his "Darling One" from his side, but he hit upon a pervasive ambience engulfing the army. The presence of numerous women in the Southern camp led to some high times before the next major campaign. "Mrs. Ewell looked very happy," Stuart added.[1]

After Gettysburg and the retreat into Virginia, Ewell was busy at his station near the Orange and Alexandria Railroad between Orange and Gordonsville during most of August. As early as August 1863 Lee asked him to visit his own headquarters to view "a medallion bust" of Jackson—

a sculptor wanted feedback from those who knew Stonewall intimately to comment on its features.[2] Ewell corresponded with Lee's son Custis about a change in cipher codes used by the high command; and the heavy toll in manpower during the Pennsylvania fighting led to many housekeeping chores in the weeks ahead. Ewell was forced to authorize confiscation of officers' horses by Rodes in order for him to picket roads around the Confederate encampments. Perhaps most telling of all about Gettysburg was when he ordered Early to cease elections for officers until sufficient recruits could be found to round out company rosters.[3]

Ewell's chief military concern lay beyond the Rapidan; while there was time for pleasant outings with the ladies—jaunts to the peak of nearby Clark's Mountain, today crested by a gigantic radio tower—a real threat loomed on the horizon. Across the Rapidan, General John Newton not only excluded all ladies from his camp but also crowed "in great glee over a tete-de-pont he had erected, and hoped to decoy some unfortunate rebels to within range of it." Then, continues Theodore Lyman, an aide to George Meade, when he arrived in early September: Newton "produced a huge variety of liquids which I had to refuse . . . even champagne!" The growing disparity between the two armies was already manifest when the Yankees sipped champagne and showed their colors far inside the Old Dominion at the same time Ewell was experiencing difficulty getting his brigades up to their pre-Gettysburg strength. In the period after September 14, when Longstreet departed for Tennessee with the First Corps, Ewell and A. P. Hill were obliged to play at blindman's bluff to keep the Yankees in check. "Troops moved to create an impression of activity and strength, army bands and trains came into Rapidan Station (supposedly filled with troops) to be greeted by cheering men," writes a campaign historian. But these ploys, reminiscent of John Bankhead Magruder in front of Richmond a year before, were in a sense too successful, because they prompted Meade to push forward several infantry corps instead of cavalry outfits opposite Ewell's encampments.[4]

Amid the watching and waiting the army was in a mood to play throughout August and September when Meade showed no inclination to challenge Lee in force. For G. Moxley Sorrel, an officer on James Longstreet's staff, these were "lovely days," when the houses of the region were "spacious, well fitted for dances and entertainments, and being crowded with joyous, happy Virginia girls there was no lack of fun and gaiety." Young officers in particular devoted themselves to a near-constant round of parties: "We got out our best, cleaned up, kept the barber busy, became very particular as to the shine of our boots . . . in honor of the lovely eyes and true Virginia hearts that were joyfully giving us welcome." Nor was the incessant partying by day and evening confined to the First Corps. Father James B. Sheeran, a Catholic priest and chaplain of the Fourteenth Louisiana Infantry, called on Ewell in early September and told him: "That for some weeks previous there has been nothing but parties and officers riding about with young ladies, whilst our poor men [are] confined to camp and living on short rations. I tell you, General, these parties had better be stopped or they will do much injury to your men. It is not the time for them." Two weeks later the priest again visited Ewell, who admonished him in turn to continue reproving the officers under his command. Although Ewell urged Sheeran to call on Mrs. Ewell, who was yet with him on September 12, the chaplain gives no hint that he took a hand in squelching his men.[5]

The halcyon times on the Rapidan began to wane, at least for a spell, on September 13 when Meade's cavalry under Judson Kilpatrick and John Buford crossed the Robertson River, temporarily overpowering Jeb Stuart. For the next two weeks, as the Northern horsemen sped farther into Madison, Greene, and Orange Counties, a series of running cavalry engagements took place south of Ewell's position. Upon his return to Meade's headquarters, Buford proclaimed his reconnaissance of Confederate forces south of the Rapidan "a triumph." Not only Federal officers but also Lee himself braced for a major assault by Meade on the Confederate left held by Ewell and A. P. Hill. But a stroke of good fortune—even providence—befell Ewell's corps for the present. "The disastrous military situation resulting from the Northern defeat at Chickamauga changed everything," notes historian William D. Henderson. "Washington intervened and Meade had to forget about a move against Lee's left." Within hours the Northern army commenced a withdrawal from the Culpeper sector as well as from the Shenandoah.[6]

As Lee watched the enemy leave his front and learned that two whole corps from Meade's army had been sent to Chattanooga, he resolved to take the initiative once more. As early as August 31 he had informed Longstreet that "I see nothing better to be done than to endeavor to bring General Meade out and use our efforts to crush his army." Although Longstreet, by his own account, attempted once more to sway Ewell and A. P. Hill to his position that the army should assume the defensive or let Meade attack them, he was now in the west, and Ewell, instead of lolling about the Rapidan with his new wife and stepdaughter, found himself preparing to take the field. For Lee the time for renewed action had arrived. In preparation Ewell joined Lee, Hill, and Early for a trek to the top of Clark's Mountain, once the scene of carefree outings with adoring ladies. The assembled horsemen had a wide vista that "took in most of Culpeper County along with parts of Madison, Rappahannock, and Fauquier as well." The Northern hordes were gone, and though Ewell did not file a battle report for his role in the subsequent fiasco at Bristoe Station, which resulted from Lee's determination to smite Meade, he did leave a detailed summary or "Diary of the Campaign," now housed among his papers in the Duke University Archive. The four-page piece was unquestionably written by Campbell Brown.[7]

"Doubtless, in making the present movement, Lee gathered in all available scraps, and added to Hill's and Ewell's corps; but that is all," Abraham Lincoln told Henry Halleck on the sixteenth. And Lee "made the movement in the belief that *four* corps had left Gen. Meade; and Gen. Meade's apparently avoiding a collision with him had confirmed him in that belief." Although Lincoln was correct that the completed campaign resulted in nothing but disaster, Ewell crossed the Rapidan on October 8 by the Somerville, Raccoon, and Morton's fords. Then it was on through Culpeper along present Route 229 to Rixeyville and Warrenton. A running skirmish developed around Jeffersonton that resulted in the capture of three hundred Yankee prisoners before Rodes and Johnson crossed the Rappahannock, while Early remained south of the river for the night of October 12. After the Jeffersonton fight, Ewell, with all three of his divisions, moved into Warrenton on the thirteenth, where he met up with A. P. Hill's corps. At their new camp, one and a half miles from the Fauquier County town, Ewell got word from Jeb Stuart at 4:00 A.M. on October 14 "that he was enclosed between two columns of the enemy going thro' Auburn & down the R.Rd. and we moved at once, Rodes, Early, & Johnson to his help." The Second Corps was about to make contact with Meade's withdrawing troops along the Orange and Alexandria tracks.[8]

A firefight at Auburn that resulted in driving the Unionists northward across Cedar Run delayed Ewell from reaching the railroad by four hours. From his Warrenton bivouac Ewell set out for Greenwich and Bristoe Station, while A. P. Hill took a more northerly route beyond Auburn. The route took Ewell past Stony Lonesome, which surely reminded him of happier times, although the press of the march probably hindered a tour of the old place until later. With Early in the van, A. A. Humphreys, a Northern writer, contends that Ewell left the road at Greenwich and "moved across the country through fields and woods, or by obscure farm roads, as it was a section of the country well known to him, or to those with him." Upon his arrival at the railroad, about three miles east of Stony Lonesome, reads his diary: ". . . found Hill engaged with the lead of Yankee column near Bristoe—Early formed on his right parallel to the R.Rd. & Gordon pushed ahead, but came across the only cav. Tho Hill had reported the enemy trying to turn to his right. Hill had stopped fighting before Early's line was formed—afterwards found he had lost 6 guns & Heth whipped."[9]

While Ewell reported his losses on October 14 at "only 15 men," it was a different story for A. P. Hill; his impetuous tangle with Meade's retreating veterans resulted in "a battering" of the brigades of John R. Cooke and William W. Kirkland of Heth's division. "The former lost 700 men, the later 602," reports Hill's biographer. "The 27th North Carolina which caught the full force of the enfilading fire suffered 290 casualties of 416 engaged—thirty-three of its thirty-six officers were killed, wounded, or captured. Hill's total losses were 1,378, or roughly one man lost every two seconds of the engagement."

After the fight, when the two soldiers rode over the field, Lee told a distraught Hill: "Well, well general, bury these poor fellows and lets say no more about it." Ewell had come on the scene about four o'clock in the afternoon, and though Early and Gordon managed to nip at the retreating Federals, there was nothing more to be done. The Second Corps went into camp "near a pine thicket not far west of Bristoe Astride the R.Rd." The affair at Bristoe Station was finished.[10]

"We remained near Bristoe two or three days, but were unable to supply our army in this position, and as the enemy had destroyed the bridge over the Rappahannock on his retreat, we crossed the river on a pontoon bridge," Jubal Early said as the Confederates abandoned their northward thrust. Bristoe Station was a good twenty miles north of the Rappahannock and thirty or more from the Rapidan, where Lee finally encamped on November 9 following the affrays at Rappahannock Station and Kelly's Ford. When Lee reached the Rappahannock, the Second Corps went into camp along the south bank around Brandy Station, a mile or so below the river. Rappahannock Station was immediately north and covered by a semicircle of rifle pits at the pontoon bridge. Although the army was delayed by its retrieving and bringing south several miles of Orange and Alexandria tracks, Ewell reached Brandy Station on October 18, four days after the Bristoe fight, and established his headquarters "at Fred W. Brown's house in a grove." During Ewell's two-week stay on the Rappahannock, Early

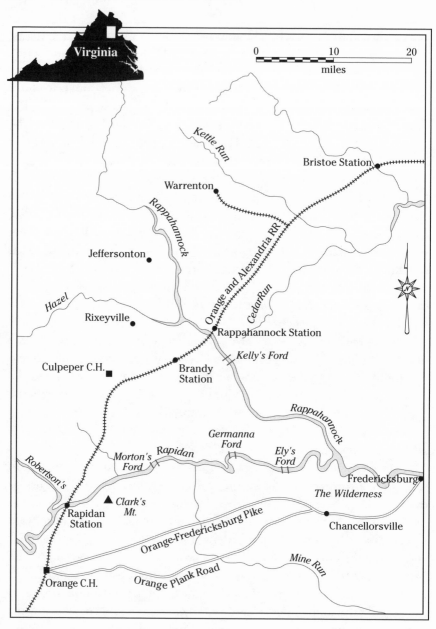

Bristoe to the Wilderness, 1864

established his encampment "to the rear" of Brandy Station, while Rodes positioned his division opposite Kelly's Ford about three miles downstream, with Allegheny Johnson between them; A. P. Hill's Third Corps was posted on Ewell's left extending upriver toward Jeffersonton.[11]

Campbell Brown wrote at least two letters to his mother and sister back in Charlottesville while Ewell was off fighting Meade; mostly the letters from Brandy Station discussed family chitchat and complained about the sameness of camp life. They also decried the lack of sociable society; apparently the company of gay young females had dried up. There was company to be enjoyed in Warrenton, Brown relayed, "but the Yankees are there." Dispatches flowed from Ewell's headquarters demanding that his division commanders arrange leaves of absence so that one officer could go home for every three remaining on duty, and there was an admonition that brigade leaders exert renewed efforts to conserve ammunition of all sizes. At this point the near daily flow of directives indicate that Ewell was in charge of his corps, but, suggests Clifford Dowdey, after Gettysburg "his course went steadily down hill militarily, though he continued personally in the high esteem of Lee and brother-officers." His health also became an increasing concern because of near-constant discomfort from his poorly healing stump.[12]

A weakened Ewell was forced once more to contend with Meade on the morning of November 7 when the bluecoats moved against his positions on the Rappahannock. Although Ewell himself joined Rodes's men at Kelly's Ford, most of the fighting was carried out by Early's division at Rappahannock Station, where north of the river a redoubt had been maintained on a rotating basis. First Early sent Hoke's brigade across the river to bolster Hays's Louisianans who were stationed in the rifle pits and ordered up the remainder of his men to the still-intact pontoon bridge. After an artillery duel for most of the day, Meade's generals decided to attack in force. The late-evening advance caught the Confederates off guard and resulted in a failure by Hoke and Hays (who was captured but managed to escape) to hold the enemy. As Lee and Early sat astride their mounts watching the river where the pontoon bridge was fired, "the assault was gallantly made, and its success was complete." Then, continues General Humphreys, "the redoubts with connecting rifle-pits, four pieces of artillery with caissons and ammunition, 103 commissioned officers, 1,200 enlisted men, 1,225 stands of small arms and seven battle-flags were captured." When Lee viewed the result he gave up any notion of holding the Federals at Kelly's Ford and ordered an immediate withdrawal. Two days later, on

November 7, Ewell, who came south with Rodes, was again bivouacked on the Rapidan.[13]

When he returned and took up residence at Morton's Hall near the Rapidan, Ewell was in decidedly poor health. Although he was relieved from duty on November 12 for a short stay in Charlottesville so that his ulcerated leg could be treated (there may have been blood poisoning), he remained in active command to the end. A directive to Rodes one day before he left admonished him to get his division in shape for a renewed campaign; and in departing Ewell told him to "instruct your quartermasters not to use harshness toward the people, but to purchase everything they have beyond what is needed for consumption." In another dispatch issued after his departure, Ewell asked Rodes for his views on conditions in the army that he might pass them to Lee. Immediately upon reaching Charlottesville with Lizinka and Harriet, Ewell rented a house for sixty dollars per month, although he had not drawn his pay since August 10. Besides paying for a servant's hire at ten dollars per month, he had apparently loaned differing sums to various officers and continued collecting payment from them throughout the year.[14]

During the sojourn in Charlottesville, Ewell wrote at least one letter to the Reverend Moses D. Hoge in Richmond; dated November 27, it thanked the parson for a Bible he had sent. "Please add to the value of the gift by joining in my prayers that I may be assisted in following the precepts therein laid down & that I may be guided by its wisdom." A penitent as well as eloquent Ewell made no mention of the intense revival sweeping his corps, especially Johnson's division. And he added one of his few self-references to his discomfort: "I am about starting for the army having been absent because of an injury to my leg." Jubal Early had been placed in temporary command of the Second Corps, with Harry T. Hays in command of Early's division and William Monagham over the Louisianans. Monagham, a native of Ireland and a New Orleans notary, was killed several months later during the Overland campaign.[15]

The date of Hoge's letter from Charlottesville makes it clear that Ewell was not present when Early and Hays spearheaded the Second Corps in the November 26 fight at Mine Run. Early, in fact, says bluntly that he did not rejoin the army "until a few days after our return from Mine Run . . . and I returned to my division, all remaining quiet on the Rapidan." In a December letter to Harriet, Campbell Brown sets Ewell's return to command as December 4, but Ewell was patently a sick man in spite of McGuire's efforts to effect a cure—in short, it was questionable if he was fit to lead his men. Hal W. Hanson, a young member of A. P. Hill's signal company atop Clark's Mountain, recalls that "Old Ewell, with his flea-bitten gray and crutches, was a frequent visitor" to the station as was Gordon, who "came up and showed us how to steady the eyes with the fingers so as to look a long time." "Poor Ewell—a cripple—is now laid up and not able to take the field," Lee's adjutant, Walter H. Taylor, wrote on November 15, two or three days after Ewell left the army for Charlottesville.[16]

Ewell had missed the Mine Run imbroglio when Meade forced the Germanna and Ely Fords on the Rapidan and moved westward toward the Confederate encampments around Orange Court House. The Second Corps, under Early's direction, was able to check the Federal onslaught along the banks of Mine Run, a northward-flowing tributary of the Rapidan on November 26–27, although Meade lingered a few days in cold, rainy weather before ordering a general withdrawal. Mine Run was situated within three or four miles of Morton's Hall, which became Ewell's home until the onset of the Wilderness scrap in May 1864. Even though Campbell Brown was seemingly living in the place during his recuperation in Charlottesville, Ewell instigated an immediate campaign to have Lizinka and Harriet rejoin him the minute he returned to the army. "[I]t has been a serious injury to me not to hear from you as I was imagining all sorts of terrible reasons," he wrote on December 13. Not only did Ewell tell his wife that he preferred a clerk to either Brown or Tom Turner, but he also indicated that the Morton family was living in the house with him and Brown. "I will not stop untill I make arrangements for your coming." Another letter before Christmas informed her that Morton and his wife were still there and that he would inform her by telegraph when to leave Charlottesville.[17]

Morton's Hall was located near the Rapidan about equidistant between the Raccoon and Somerville fords; it was eight or nine miles north of Orange Court House. Although Ewell himself said the house was "very cold without furniture and tolerably dull," young Sandie Pendleton, who kept an office in an unused room, was taken with the Morton's Hall library. In a letter written before her arrival, Ewell told Lizinka that he had been reading a copy of *Blackstone's Commentaries* found in the house. The home had no formal garden—only young trees and grass covered the lawn.[18]

Mrs. Ewell's residence at Morton's Hall caused a stir throughout the army—at least in some parts of it—and the young officers who later wrote caustic accounts of her presence may have been swept with jealousy at not having the general to themselves as before. The venerable Douglas Southall

Freeman attests that she was not liked in camp, and General James Conner was pointedly harsh: "Mrs. Ewell, with the best intentions in the world no doubt, has very seriously injured Ewell, and the very cleverness which would at other times be agreeable, has only tended to make her more unpopular," he told his mother in February 1864. "She manages everything from the General's affairs down to the courier who carries his dispatches."[19] Gossip soon raced through camp that it was under "petticoat government," and Conner allowed further that "Ewell [was] worse in love than any eighteen year old . . . you ever saw." It was during the Morton's Hall interlude that soft-spoken Sandie Pendleton became critical of Mrs. Ewell's presence.[20]

Although the famous diarist Mary Boykin Chesnut took a dim view of women at the front, Father Sheeran was favorably impressed with Lizinka. "Mrs. Ewell is a lady of more then ordinary intellectual powers, well educated and for one of her sex remarkably well posted on military and political matters," he noted after a February visit to Morton's Hall. "In religion she is a rigid Episcopalian, somewhat fond of discussing religious subjects, but very respectful when speaking of Catholic dogmas." Before his departure from the home, however, she told Sheeran: "A general in my opinion should keep himself as far as possible out of danger, but in such a position to see or hear of movements in battle, but there may arise circumstances which would require even a general to expose himself to every danger." The kindly priest thought from the drift of the conversation that she and her husband had been recently discussing the matter.[21]

Lizinka Ewell was unquestionably protective of her husband, and her prominence in the household can be explained not by her domineering posture but by Ewell's long-recognized dependency. Given his history of relying upon others when confronted with difficult choices, it was inevitable that he should put his trust in a strong but loving wife. Mrs. Ewell assumed her position for one simple reason: Lieutenant General Richard S. Ewell was proud of his wife and not only seized every opportunity to show her off but also allowed, even encouraged, her to take the forefront. As always, Ewell was more than willing to take a backseat when she arrived on the scene.

Ewell's deteriorating health continued to be a concern throughout late 1863 and into early 1864, with Lee formally relieving him from command in June. Lee in particular began to have doubts that Ewell was up to field duty. That Lee did not act sooner raises serious questions about his own ability as commanding general. When Richmond suggested that Ewell be sent as a replacement for Braxton Bragg, and later that he go to Tennessee in place of Longstreet, Lee squelched both schemes because of health considerations: "General Ewell's condition, I fear, is too feeble to undergo the fatigue and labor incident to the position." Compounding Ewell's difficulties was the severe weather that gripped northern Virginia for much of the winter; Jed Hotchkiss noted in his diary that ice had formed to a thickness of five inches along the Rapidan. "I was riding the gray mare I bot from your father a day or so ago, when the ground was slippery with snow," Ewell told Lizzie on January 18. "Down she went rolling over and leaving me pretty well buried on the ground."[22]

The very day Ewell accepted responsibility for his renewed injury while making light of the incident, Robert E. Lee sent him a letter in response to his own correspondence with the secretary of war regarding his ability to retain corps command. Instead of acting decisively to save himself more difficulty in the campaign that was sure to erupt, Lee waffled. His own resignation in the aftermath of Gettysburg on the pretext of diminished physical powers had been spurned by Jefferson Davis, and now he was thrusting the onus of leaving the army upon Ewell himself. "I do not know how much ought to be attributed to long absence from the field, general debility, or the result of your injury, but I was in constant fear during the last campaign that you sink under your duties or destroy yourself; in either event injury might have resulted," Lee proffered. "You now know from experience what you have to undergo, and [are the] best judge of your ability to endure it."[23]

With strong encouragement from his wife, Ewell resolved to keep his preeminent place in the Confederate scheme no matter the outcome. In early February he sent "a mutton" to Lee for his personal table, although the commanding general wrote in reply to ask the price of the forty-six-pound animal that he might reimburse Rodes's commissary. Small scraps of correspondence in numerous archival collections indicate that Ewell was very much in command in the weeks leading to the Overland march. When Lee left the Rapidan on February 22 to consult with the president in Richmond, Colonel Robert H. Chilton, who remained at headquarters, was told to consult with Ewell "on all matters of importance connected with the army." Beyond that his instructions read: "Gen. Lee desires you either to move up to Orange C.H. or remove the office to your quarters as you may think proper." Interspersed with the duties of command, there was also time for relaxation and play. An eighteen-inch snow blanketed Ewell's encampment on the night of March 22, and, comments Father Sheeran, eight thousand men from Johnson's and Rodes's divisions "fought a regular scientific battle with snow balls." The Louisiana boys—laughing so hard they could barely maneuver—drove Rodes's contingent "more than a mile" through the camp. While he says nothing about Ewell during the hoopla, Sheeran comments: "This was the first battle I ever witnessed with pleasure," and "our boys came home [from pelting Rodes's men] as proud as if they had gained a victory over Yankees."[24]

Amid the winter high jinks all was not well in the Second Corps, as a terse entry in Jed Hotchkiss's diary for April 26 relates: "Gen. Early arrested by Gen. Ewell." Although Freeman speculates that Mrs. Ewell had a hand in the affair—that she did not like Early and saw him as a threat—the whole business has remained cloaked in mystery. Lee, who would tolerate no animosity among the officer corps, apparently demanded Early's immediate release and squelched the entire matter. Outwardly, the two men maintained a certain civility, but hard feelings between them continued for some time. Early's recent biographer theorizes that Old Jube made disparaging remarks about Lizinka's influence over military affairs, and that "a man in love is seldom inclined to tolerate criticism of his beloved." Major General Jubal Early was still a subordinate, even though an opinionated one given to forceful, profane outbursts. He had led the corps though the Mine Run fracas, and rumors were rife that an obviously ailing Ewell might precipitate his recall to corps command in the near future. Ewell, in fact, may have brought some of the difficulty on himself by making Early spokesman for the Second Corps and by regularly pushing him to the forefront. Later in the summer, when Lee finally removed Ewell from command because of his health and Early took the corps down the Shenandoah Valley to Washington itself, Campbell Brown told his stepfather that his old headquarters staff was bitterly unhappy. "Everybody is disgusted," Brown said. "Old Early did not ask me how you were, but I made my speech so that he will hear it before four or five—it was outrageous treatment."[25]

In February Ewell had complained about the poor food in camp and asked his brother Ben to send his shotgun so that he might kill "a few birds" to liven his fare. But events in Washington soon altered the entire course of the war when President Lincoln tapped Ulysses S. Grant to become lieutenant general and commander of the Federal armies. From the moment Grant arrived in Washington from the west to assume command in March, there would be no relief from the Yankee onslaught. Always before Lee and his men had a respite following a major campaign as faltering Union generals withdrew to rest and replenish themselves. Now Grant would keep coming until the final collapse of the Army of Northern Virginia in April 1865. His plan called for Meade to attack from the north (with Grant at his side), Franz Sigel in the Shenandoah Valley, Benjamin F. Butler from the south, from the Bermuda Hundred; Phil Sheridan and his cavalry would wreak havoc across northern Virginia that eventually led to the death of Jeb Stuart at Yellow Tavern, and Ewell's old pal William Tecumseh Sherman would continue tramping through the Southern heartland. Richmond, and indeed the Confederacy, was doomed once Grant set his scheme into motion. Although their old adversary George Gordon Meade remained in nominal command of the Army of the Potomac, it was Grant who led the charge against Lee, Ewell, A. P. Hill, Jeb Stuart, Longstreet, Richard H. Anderson, and the rest. In response to frantic signalmen atop Clark's Mountain, Lee, Ewell, and Longstreet (who was newly returned from Tennessee), and A. P. Hill rode to the crest on May 2 and gazed out beyond the river to sight the feverishly stirring Yankees.[26]

The next morning, May 3, Lee "sent an order to Lieutenant General Ewell to break his winter camp along the Rapidan," writes Clifford Dowdey. "There where the river runs almost due west before taking the southwestward swing beyond Orange Court House Ewell was to put the Second Corps immediately in motion towards the Wilderness." Ewell was still a sick man, and his indecisiveness on the battlefield would again disappoint a beleaguered Lee, but he was the commander chosen to take the van, just as Jackson had done in more vigorous times. On the very morning that Ewell headed east to open one of the bloodiest fights ever on this side of the Atlantic, Grant and Meade began to push their legions across the fords over the Rapidan. And, writes Grant's biographer, the "assaults of the two armies as each sought the other out in the maddening forest on May 5, 1864, can be plotted and described, but in truth there was no sense to the battle of the Wilderness."[27]

According to his own reckoning, Ewell had "about 3,500 effective infantry and 2,000 artillery" when he set out on the Orange-Fredericksburg Pike at noon on May 4. Two roadways pointed eastward from Orange Court House—the regular pike taken by the Second Corps and the Orange Plank Road. The latter, a turnpike specially constructed from split logs turned on their sides, part of a nineteenth-century phenomenon built by entrepreneurs (companies) to free travelers from the mud and mire, was transversed by A. P. Hill and the Third Corps as well as Longstreet. Generally, the turnpike proceeded north of (but parallel to) the Plank Road through Old Verdierville and Locust Grove past the Wilderness Tavern where the Brock Road intersects from the south—and where Stonewall Jackson turned eastward one year earlier during the march upon Joe Hooker's rear to seal the enormous Confederate victory at Chancellorsville. The two pathways came together for a short span at John Chancellor's old inn but parted again about two miles farther east at Salem Church and made their way separately into Fredericksburg. Through much of their eastward progress the roads bisected the renowned Wilderness—an area known for its cutover timber and matted undergrowth.[28]

Still broken into three divisions under Early, Johnson, and Rodes, Ewell's corps had several new brigade chieftains who had not been with him during the bloodletting at Gettysburg. John Pegram, who transferred from the west to court the vivacious Hetty Cary, had charge of Extra Billy Smith's brigade at Mine Run, but when Pegram was shot on May 5, Early replaced him with John Stringer Hoffman. A native of Virginia, Hoffman, "distinguished for his physique, his bachelorhood and his fondness for a game of euchre or whist," commanded five regiments through the Wilderness, Spotsylvania, and Cold Harbor. Also serving under Early was Brigadier General Robert Daniel Johnston, a North Carolina lawyer before and after the war, who led four regiments from the state until he was badly wounded on May 12. John B. Gordon, with six Georgia regiments, and Harry T. Hays, with his Louisiana Tigers, completed Early's division when the campaign commenced.[29]

The brigade of John M. Jones in Johnson's division was commanded by Colonel William Witcher after Jones was killed on the first day of the Wilderness "while trying to rally his men in the face of a Union onslaught." Witcher, who took his six Virginia regiments—Twenty-first, Twenty-fifth, Forty-second, Forty-fourth, Forty-eighth, and Fiftieth—was wounded at Spotsylvania, but he survived to resume his law practice and serve in the Virginia legislature before his death in 1888. Five infantry outfits from Louisiana—First, Second, Tenth, Fourteenth, and Fifteenth—were generaled by Leroy P. Stafford when Ewell marched from Orange Court House. When Stafford fell mortally wounded on May 5, his brigade passed to Zebulon York, a Louisiana planter who survived the war and lived another thirty-five years. Maryland Steuart's brigade—composed of Virginia and North Carolina regiments—and the famed Stonewall Brigade under James A. Walker, men who had toiled under Ewell in earlier campaigns—rounded out Allegheny Johnson's command. The slaughter that followed May 5 and the heavy consolidation and revamping of the army makes it difficult to follow the exact order of battle at any given point in the campaign.[30]

Robert E. Rodes, like Early and Johnson, marched for the Wilderness with a different brigade organization than he had utilized at Gettysburg. After Alfred Iverson quit the Army of Northern Virginia, his four North Carolina regiments—Fifth, Twelfth, Twentieth, and Twenty-third—were placed under Robert D. Johnston and assigned to Early. Rodes's five brigades in Pennsylvania had been cut to four at the beginning of the Wilderness tussle. Accordingly, the departure of E. A. O'Neal from Lee's command after his debacle at Gettysburg resulted in the elevation of Cullen A. Battle. At Gettysburg, Battle had detached his Third Alabama Infantry from O'Neal and joined Stephen D. Ramseur, "where he fought fiercely" throughout July 1. After receiving a glowing report and recommendation from Ramseur, who already enjoyed the ear of higher-ups, Battle, "a 38 year old lawyer and a politician but able and self taught in the art of war," was promoted to brigadier general in August 1863. Rodes's division also had brigades under Daniel, Ramseur, and Doles when the campaign opened.[31]

Grant began crossing the Rapidan by the Germanna and Ely fords on the morning of May 4 about three miles north of Ewell's line of march along the "Old Turnpike." The Second Corps was thus fated to make first contact with the carefully planned and executed Federal incursion. "Before nightfall all the troops, and by the evening of the 5th the trains of more than four thousand wagons, were safely on the south side of the river," Grant wrote later. His was the third Northern thrust into the Wilderness within fifteen months, so his generals had an excellent grasp of the terrain and difficulties before them. "The result of all their careful preparations was that within 18 hours after they started 120,000 men, with their artillery and fighting trains, had made a march of 20 miles & put themselves in selected positions, crossing a river on five pontoon bridges of their building, & all in the face of the enemy without mishap or interruption," observes artillerist E. P. Alexander. "They might easily have made five or six miles more, but purposely encamped the night of the 4th in close order for the 9th Corps & the great bulk of their subsistence & ordnance trains to close up."[32]

Ewell too had his orders not to advance without support from other Confederate units. May 4 was obviously a critical day in the entire campaign, and though Lee was well aware that Grant was on the move, he made no serious effort to contest the Rapidan crossings. Even Grant argued that Lee did not grasp the exact route of his army until "one o'clock in the afternoon," when Ewell first encountered the enemy four miles from the old battlefield at Chancellorsville. Yet Ewell and Porter Alexander are in slight disagreement about events: The latter says Ewell was ordered to coordinate his movements with those of A. P. Hill throughout the fourth and for this reason went into camp at Locust Grove to wait for the Third Corps to close up. But in his battle report, Ewell notes it was not until he advanced, on May 5, that Lee instructed him "to regulate my march by General A. P. Hill, whose progress down the Plank Road I could tell by the firing at the head of his column and informed me that he preferred not to bring on a general engagement before General Longstreet came up." The Second Corps bivouacked for the night of May 4 around Locust Grove, a stage layover about midway between Orange Court House and Chancellorsville. Although some brigades encamped near Mine Run where it crossed the turnpike, most of Ewell's men stayed near Locust Grove, "which was about the centre of the Federal line & three miles from his battlefield of the next day." Edward Johnson and Lieutenant Colonel William Nelson's three artillery batteries camped two miles south, with Rodes's division slightly behind or west of them. Early's division remained on the roadway at Locust Grove with the artillery units of Carter M. Braxton, Richard C. M. Page, Wilfred E. Cutshaw, and Robert A. Hardaway. The artillery was now under the command of General Armistead L. Long, who became a biographer and apologist for Robert E. Lee after the war. "Ramseur's brigade of Rodes' division, with three regiments from each of the other divisions, was left on picket."[33]

When the mapmaker Hotchkiss reached Locust Grove at 3:30 on the morning of May 5, Ewell had already left for the front. Although he should probably have been in bed nursing his wounds and shepherding his strength, he was upbeat and ready for the enemy. An adjutant with one of the artillery battalions, Robert Augustus Stiles, a Kentuckian educated at Yale and the University of Virginia, who happened upon Ewell, found him "'thin and pale . . . but bright-eyed and alert.'" He even invited the young gunnery officer to join him for a cup of early morning coffee. "As they chatted, Major Stiles diplomatically asked Lieutenant General Ewell 'if he had any objections to telling me his orders,'" records historian Noah Trudeau. "Ewell's response was brisk. 'Just the orders I like,' he piped, 'to go right down the road and strike the enemy wherever I find him.'"[34]

Ewell may have started early, but the heavily forested countryside, laden with smoke from several thousand campfires belonging to both armies, demanded caution. One of Richard H. Anderson's brigade commanders, Nathaniel H. Harris, who marched along the plank road parallel to Ewell's route, noted that the "density of the woods" made it almost impossible to detect enemy movements or to readily tell friend from foe. Nor was Ewell as enthusiastic to meet the onslaught as Stiles recollected. Advancing with John Marshall Jones's brigade of Johnson's division in the lead, Ewell, by his own account, not only moved slowly, but he did not make contact with the Federals under Gouverneur K. Warren until 11:00 A.M. Although Jed Hotchkiss told his wife two days later that Lee "praises the commander of our corps much," Ewell, anxious to heed Lee's admonition to move cautiously—and, one might add, to avoid a head-on collision with Grant's legions—did not move in a headlong manner. And his hesitation soon infected others, with Allegheny Johnson riding among remaining parts of his division, imploring them to be wary and not rush to the front. An inevitable clash of arms occurred when Ewell "came in sight of a column of the enemy crossing the pike from Germanna Ford toward the Plank road." During the early afternoon, Jubal Early later wrote, "there was heavy skirmishing all along the line" as the opposing forces became locked in deadly combat resulting in some of the worst slaughter of the entire war.[35]

Early might have added that on Ewell's left the fighting reached almost to the Rapidan itself. Although the main battle took place in something called Saunder's Field across Ewell's center, James A. Walker had been sent toward the ford with the Stonewall Brigade upon first sighting the enemy. Ewell's battle report says Walker got within one and a half miles of the river and that his brigade became heavily engaged almost immediately. While attempting to plug a gap on his right that existed between him and Leroy Stafford's brigade, the Federals struck with full fury. "Before the Rebels could turn to meet the onslaught, they received a point-blank volley." Stonewall's veterans did all they knew to do as they mounted a handsome defense, and, James Robertson continues: "In the next few minutes no less than eight attempts were made to crack the Confederate positions." Men and officers fell left and right in the maddening struggle until Ewell ordered Hays and the Louisianans to stabilize his left flank and to strengthen Walker's overtaxed men as darkness interceded to halt the mayhem. With less than a hundred men engaged, Walker's losses reached a staggering but unverified amount with the Fourth Virginia Infantry alone, reporting five killed and forty-five wounded. Casualties of that magnitude "all along the line" could not be sustained by Lee for long without any foreseeable replacements.[36]

Meanwhile, Ewell ran into a hornet's nest along his direct front when he halted to give A. P. Hill an opportunity to close up on the Plank Road.

Although Hotchkiss and Early were correct that fighting was heavy from the Rapidan to the Plank Road and beyond, near disaster struck around one o'clock when "the Union Fifth Corps surprised Jones' brigade with a well-directed attack against the Confederate flank." Then, Peter Carmichael elaborates: "The Virginians panicked and collapsed upon Cullen A. Battle's brigade resting a few hundred yards to the rear." Confusion reigned supreme when one officer yelled out a command to fall back on Mine Run. Unquestionably, there was a prevailing opinion among officers and men that Lee's order to withdraw slowly if pressed by the enemy meant to resume the old battlements and ramparts on the Mine Run battleground, though Lee said this was a misinterpretation of his plans. After pointing out that Jones and Battle were driven back "200 or 300 yards only," and that was shortly regained, Campbell Brown notes further: "I don't believe these brigades wd so easily have been broken, had it not been for the general understanding that we were to retire to Mine Run if attacked in force." Although Jones, an 1841 graduate of West Point and a career officer before the war, fell dead along with Early's nephew, Captain Robert D. Early, his aide, in the vicious fray, Ewell inadvertently became the hero of the day and with dispatch ordered up reinforcements to check his faltering line.[37]

Actually, Jones was conferring with Ewell, Early, and Rodes on horseback in Saunder's clearing when he galloped forward to oversee the fighting. Some differences exist as to what happened next—whether Early or Ewell had the presence of mind to summon the intrepid Gordon and his six Georgia regiments as reinforcements. "After planting a Confederate flag firmly in the roadway, Ewell, Early, and their staff officers labored to rally stragglers back to the fray," notes Gordon Rhea. This scenario had Early turning to his aide, Major John W. Daniel, and bidding him to find Gordon at the double-quick. John Brown Gordon, however, offers an entirely different story, although in fairness Rhea points out the disparity. After noting that virtually no resistance was being mounted against the on-rushing bluecoats, Gordon offers a compelling recollection of what happened next:

> At that moment of dire extremity I saw General Ewell, who was still a superb horseman, notwithstanding the loss of his leg, riding in furious gallop towards me, his thoroughbred charger bounding like a deer through the dense undergrowth. With a quick jerk of his bridle-rein just as his wooden leg was about to come into unwelcome collision with my knee, he

checked his horse and rapped out his few words with characteristic impetuosity. He did not stop to explain the situation; there
was no need of explanation. . . . The rapid words he did utter
were electric and charged with tremendous significance: "General Gordon, the fate of the day depends on you sir," he said.

The Georgia boys and Gordon responded without delay, and Gordon continues: "[T]hat glorious brigade rushed upon the hitherto advancing enemy, and by the shock of their furious onset shattered into fragments
all that portion of the compact Union line which confronted my troops."
Although no mention of Early appears, it could well have been that Major
Daniel reached Gordon first and that Ewell appeared in short order to
speed him forward. Early says only that his "division was ordered up. In
conjunction with Daniel's, Doles,' and Ramseur's brigades, of Rodes' division, it drove the enemy back with heavy loss, capturing several hundred
prisoners, and gaining a commanding position on the right." In his official
report, Ewell paid tribute to the other units, but for him it was certainly
Gordon who "captured by a dashing charge several hundred prisoners [note
he uses the same phrase as Early] and relieved Doles, who, though hard
pressed, had held his ground."[38]

A late-evening assault on Ewell's left north of the turnpike by Horatio
Wright resulted in the serious wounding of John Pegram and the death of
Leroy Stafford. When darkness fell, Ewell had the Second Corps aligned at
right angles to the turnpike, with the right of Maryland Steuart's brigade
and the left of Battle's actually resting on the road. South of the turnpike,
Battle, Doles, and Daniel composed Ewell's right flank. Although Lee specifically requested Ramseur's brigade for another assignment, it was placed
on the extreme right toward A. P. Hill's command on the morning of May
6 when it returned from picket duty. North of the turnpike stretching
almost to the Rapidan were the brigades of Steuart, Stafford, Walker, Hays,
and Pegram, with Gordon bent slightly to the rear of the line behind Doles,
who also shifted to the left later in the evening. After his spectacular performance in the early afternoon, Gordon had been given the task of bol-
stering Ewell's left flank. A quick glance at detailed drawings in the *Official
Atlas* shows unmistakably that Ewell's positions shifted just slightly to the
left, or north, during the fighting on the following day.[39]

Ewell unquestionably adhered to Lee's instructions on May 5 and
directed his corps with decisiveness. He had maintained the army's left
flank against overwhelming odds, and he had removed himself from the

equally uneven struggles of Lee and A. P. Hill south of his lines. But the general commanding renewed an old bugaboo in his dealings with Ewell when he dispatched discretionary orders to Second Corps headquarters. Two communiqués were sent with Lieutenant Colonel Charles Marshall's signature—one at 6:00 P.M. and the other an hour later. In both, Marshall, Lee's aide-de-camp, emphasized that Longstreet was expected to arrive in the morning (May 6), that the battle still raged on the Orange Plank Road, and that the Federals on Lee's front were concentrated around the Wilderness Tavern Ridge about one mile beyond Ewell's position. "The general suggests to you the practicability of moving over and taking that ridge, thus severing the enemy from his base, but if this cannot be done without too great a sacrifice, you must be prepared to reinforce our right and make your arrangements accordingly," reads the first message that may have gotten to Ewell later in the evening. Instead of heeding Lee's wishes, however, Ewell put his troopers to work chopping abatis and digging trenches in front of his existing position. Ewell would remain where he was—making a decision without a specific order was as alien to his nature as it had ever been. "He saw to it that his strongly fortified and well-aligned lines were ready to receive the enemy the next day," writes campaign historian Clifford Dowdey. "By this action, Lieutenant General Ewell divorced his corps from the plans of the army and settled down to continue his separate battle."[40]

When Friday, May 6, dawned over the smoke-laden Wilderness, where smoldering swatches from riflemen in both armies had ignited the all-pervasive undergrowth, Lee resolved to continue his bold strategy that had threatened and confused a determined Grant. As on the previous day, most of the fighting took place to Ewell's south on A. P. Hill's front. "Lee slept on the field, taking his headquarters a few hundred yards from the line of battle for the day," writes Colonel Charles S. Venable. "It was his intention to relieve Hill's two divisions with Longstreet's, and throw them further to the left to fill up a part of the great unoccupied interval between the plank road and Ewell's right, near the old turnpike, or use them on his right as the occasion might demand." Although Ewell's disregard for the mile-wide gap greatly influenced the ensuing clash, Longstreet's arrival on the field resulted in near disaster: he was shot through the neck and shoulder while urging his men forward and was replaced by Richard Herron Anderson, a man as yet untried at corps command. At first Lee attempted to lead Longstreet's veterans into battle, but John Gregg's Texans refused to follow, yelling, "General Lee to the rear" before they would advance. Throughout

May 6, A. P. Hill was sick with a high fever and an apparent urinary complaint that led to his dismissal from duty and his replacement by Jubal Early before the next scrap at Spotsylvania Court House. That was a mere five days before Lee was forced to make additional changes in his command structure when word arrived from Yellow Tavern, a few miles north of Richmond on the Telegraph Road, that Jeb Stuart had fallen with a Yankee bullet in his liver.[41]

According to Ewell's official report, the early hours of May 6 were "occupied in partial assaults on my line (now greatly strengthened), which were promptly checked." Ewell had in fact improved his artillery emplacements through the night, and with the dawn his batteries opened a blistering cannonade against Grant's right. The Federals under Truman Seymour—6th Maryland; 110th, 122nd, 126th Ohio; as well as the 67th and 138th Pennsylvania—of John Sedgwick's Sixth Army Corps had remained in position opposite Ewell's flank north of the turnpike. Sedgwick ordered a renewed attack against John Pegram's brigade, now commanded by Colonel John S. Hoffman after Pegram's disabling wound the previous evening. The brigade had a field day joking and shooting down scores, if not hundreds, of Yankees as they charged into their abatis-encrusted positions. "The killing continued even after Seymour's Federals withdrew," writes Gordon Rhea. "Enticed by fat knapsacks and haversacks on dead Yankees, hungry Confederates darted into the no-man's land between the lines" only to be shot down by enemy snipers. General Alexander Shaler, who led his tiny brigade of New York and Pennsylvania troops into the fray on the extreme Union right, grew furious as his unit was cut to pieces without hope of reinforcements. Even Seymour had to admit that his instructions "to lay up log shelters . . . was effected except on the extreme right of General Shaler's line, where contact was so close and exposure so great as to forbid this work by day." Jubal Early wrote later that the Federal thrust at Hoffman's six regiments of Virginians was "handsomely repulsed."[42]

Seymour's rout opposite the Confederate left gave Ewell's men a respite from the battle raging to the south, but the troublesome gap with A. P. Hill, and now Longstreet, was not only a problem, but it was also partially Ewell's making. During the night of May 5, Henry Heth and Cadmus Wilcox pleaded with Hill to plug the open space, but the ailing corps commander refused, saying that he did not want to hear "any more about it." The mass shuffling of troops under existing conditions, Hill retorted, would certainly attract notice from the ever-present Yankees. Matters worsened dramatically at 6:30 A.M. on May 6, when Ambrose Burnside, commanding the Federal Ninth Army Corps, found the gap and launched a drive to split the Army of Northern Virginia in two. Ewell, who was locked in an ongoing tiff with Early and Gordon over initiating a new, more aggressive assault on the Federal right, not only paid little attention to his exposed left, but he also ignored the role of Rodes and Stephen Dodson Ramseur in the fighting that followed. Nor does Ramseur mention Ewell in his reports, positing only that his division chief, Robert E. Rodes, ordered him "to form on Brigadier General Daniel's right and to push back Burnside's advance." Thereupon, he asserts, "moving at the double-quick, I arrived just in time to check a large flanking party of the enemy, and by strengthening and extending my skirmish line half a mile to the right of my line I turned the enemy's line, and by a dashing charge, under the gallant Major [Edward A.] Osborne of the Fourth North Carolina Regiment, drove not only the enemy's skirmishers, but his line of battle, back fully a mile, capturing some prisoners and the knapsacks and shelter-tents of an entire regiment." Shortly after Ramseur single-handedly stopped the attack, the gap was plugged at last by the guns of William R. J. "Willie" Pegram as well as the infantry brigades of James H. Lane, Samuel McGowan, and Abner M. Perrin, all from A. P. Hill's command. "Burnside's attack never got off the ground, however, and the threat had passed by 8:30 in the morning," writes Willie Pegram's biographer.[43]

Ewell, meanwhile, was preoccupied with events on his far left totally removed from Ramseur's thrust. Although Pegram's brigade under Hoffman had repelled the troops of Shaler and Seymour on the fifth, Gordon had ridden along the far left of the Confederate line and had determined that Shaler's position was "in the air," despite the previous fighting. Neither Ewell nor Early had made a personal reconnaissance, but Gordon was convinced that an assault around Meade's right would be successful and that it might even "roll up" the entire Federal army. Gordon's scheme was straightforward: "He would place his brigade with whatever others could be spared, in line squarely on the flank and rear of the VI Corps." And, continues Gordon's biographer, "as he hit the flank, the Federals would inevitably be compelled to withdraw, and as they fell back they could easily be captured by the Confederates rapidly moving into their rear." Hopefully, additional manpower would be available to strike the front of Seymour's line. Ewell says only that he first learned of Gordon's plan "about 9 a.m.," but, wishy-washy as usual, he deferred to Early. According to Charles Osborne, Old Jube "rejected it instantly, on the grounds that Federal troops were threatening the army's flank, and that a reserve Union Corps under Ambrose

Burnside was poised close behind the Union right; this force, Early asserted, was capable of not only thwarting Gordon's plan but of menacing the entire Confederate position." If Gordon should fail and Burnside succeed, this reasoning went, Ewell would have no reserve troops to save himself from disaster.[44]

Here the matter rested for several hours. Although Ewell says "a personal inspection" was made, it is not clear from his battle summary if he or someone else actually rode along and around the Federal right. Furthermore, Ewell received intelligence from his cavalry that Meade was removing his pontoon bridge at Germanna Ford, redirecting his troops north of the Rapidan toward Ely Ford, thus making a move toward the south, which left his extreme right in a vulnerable position. In the early afternoon Robert E. Lee himself encountered a lull in the fighting near the Plank Road and rode to the Second Corps to ascertain the reasons for Ewell's inactivity on the Confederate left. In other words, Lee wanted a movement that would give the First and Third Corps a breather. Ewell is silent about Lee's presence and says only, "I ordered the attack, and placed Robert D. Johnston's brigade of Rodes' division to support Gordon."

Others, however, offer a different scenario for Lee's visit. As had been the case nearly a year before Gettysburg, "a dismal conference, which included Gordon and Jubal Early, revealed that Old Bald Head had suffered a paralysis of the will at the necessity of making a decision." Then, continues Clifford Dowdey, "Once again Lee listened with little comment, as it was learned that Ewell had heeded Early and overridden Gordon's importunities to attack the enemy's flank. At the end, Lee simply ordered Ewell to send Gordon on the attack, as late as it was." Confederate master Douglas Southall Freeman concludes his chapter on the Wilderness with a terse observation that Dowdey echoes: "Ewell seemed unable to make a decision."[45]

In an 1868 letter Lee stressed to Gordon that "he may have confounded our conversation subsequent to your attack with my visit to General Ewell before it took place." And in Lee's celebrated 1868 interview with William Allan at Washington College, he seemed to suggest that Ewell was "urged to make the flank attack." Although Campbell Brown later argued that Ewell favored Gordon's scheme from the start but "begged out" because of Early's objections, Allan noted further: "He (Lee) intended it to be a full attack in flank & intended to support it with all of Ewell's Corps and others if necessary, and to rout the enemy. Early, Lee thinks, kept Ewell from pushing this matter, until very late. When Gordon did go, it was too late in the day, and he was not supported with sufficient force to accomplish anything decisive."[46]

Lee was correct—Ewell's hesitancy to issue prompt orders for Gordon to move out meant the poorly coordinated assault did not begin until very late in the evening. It created a good amount of confusion, briefly rolled up the Federal right, and even culminated in the capture of Generals Shaler and Seymour. Ewell, willing to put an acceptable face on an impossible situation, said later that "Gordon attacked vehemently, and when checked by darkness had captured, with slight loss, a mile of works held by the Sixth Corps, 600 prisoners, and 2 brigadier generals." But Ewell did not tell the whole story; Sedgwick promptly halted Gordon's drive by drawing in and reorganizing his remaining troops into a "defensive perimeter." When Gordon and Johnston were obliged to withdraw into their own defensive works, concludes historian Noah Trudeau, "the Battle of the Wilderness was over." And Gordon wrote in 1903: "As soon as all the facts in regard to the situation were fully confirmed, I formed and submitted the plan which, if promptly adopted and vigorously followed, I then believed and still believe would have resulted in the crushing defeat of General Grant's army."[47]

In his unparalleled war memoir, Ulysses S. Grant noted that "as we stood at the close, the two armies were relatively in about the same position to each other as when the river divided them." By most accounts Union losses exceeded those of Lee by several thousand, but they were losses the South could ill afford. Something new to the fighting in Virginia occurred after the bloodletting of May 5–6, when Grant, instead of drawing back, pushed onward toward Spotsylvania Court House and ultimately the Confederate bastion at Richmond. Ewell had been prominent in the maneuvering south of the Rapidan, but he was still a sick man depleted by the demands of the field, and within three weeks he would be relieved of command. His decision to remain aloof from A. P. Hill and Longstreet along the Plank Road did not earn him many friends among the officer corps, nor did it serve to endear him with the general commanding. More importantly, his failure through dalliance and indecision to push Gordon forward at the critical juncture undoubtedly prevented Lee from inflicting a heavier toll on the Yankee colossus now confronting the Southland. "In the evening [of May 6] the enemy gained an advantage; but it was speedily repulsed," none other than Grant himself wrote.[48]

Chapter 13

"LAID ON THE SHELF"

Although Ulysses S. Grant labeled May 5 and 6, 1864, the worst fighting ever in the Americas, he remained possessed with the capture of Richmond and the destruction of Lee's army. By his own account he disengaged from the Wilderness for two reasons: He was fearful lest Lee would somehow crush the force under Massachusetts politician-turned-general Benjamin F. Butler before he could succor him from the north. As part of Grant's multipronged push, Butler commanded a sizeable army in the Bermuda Hundred—that region south and slightly east of Richmond bounded by the Appomattox and James Rivers. Butler offered no immediate threat to the capital because of a blockading force led by P. G. T. Beauregard along his front that had him "like a cork in a bottle." Grant also "wanted to get between [Lee's] army and Richmond if possible; to draw him into the open field." After a day of relative inactivity for the bulk of Lee's men, including the Second Corps, the entire Army of Northern Virginia erupted into a beehive of alert endeavor once Lee determined that Grant was not withdrawing toward Fredericksburg but was heading farther south—deeper into the Confederate heartland. His famous "sidling" maneuvers by the left flank, designed to keep Lee from attacking to the east, had begun, "which were to take him from the Rapidan to the James across that river, clear around to the south of Petersburg and on to Appomattox Court House—eleven months later." Grant, after all, had promised Lincoln that "whatever happens, there will be no turning back."[1]

"When Grant commenced his change of base and turning operation on the evening of the 7th," proclaimed C. S. Venable in 1873, "General Lee, with the firm reliance in the ability of a small body of his troops to hold heavy odds in check until he could bring assistance, sent Anderson, who had been promoted to the command of Longstreet's two divisions to confront the enemy's columns at Spotsylvania Court House." The same communiqué, dated 7:00 P.M., that put Richard H. Anderson in motion also directed Ewell and the Second Corps to head south in his support. On what proved an exhausting march through burning, smoke-laden woods, Ewell led his men toward Spotsylvania on May 8. As the Second Corps rank and file toiled along hot, disagreeable roads past a junction on the Plank Road known as Parker's Store, where Lee spent the night of May 7, Ewell got word that his command would be significantly reorganized. Jubal Early was summoned to take charge of the Third Corps after A. P. Hill reported himself too "indisposed" to remain in the field. Additional changes occurred when Gordon was ordered to take over Early's division "as a reward for his services in the Wilderness fighting." And, continues historian William D. Matter: "Brig. Gen. Harry T. Hays and his brigade of Louisiana troops were transferred from Early's to [Allegheny] Johnson's division and combined with the Second Louisiana Brigade, whose commander, Leroy A. Stafford, had been killed in the Wilderness. To maintain a semblance of parity, the brigade of Brig. Gen. Robert D. Johnston was transferred officially from Rodes' to Gordon's (formerly Early's) division with whom it had been serving since joining the army on 6 May."

Ewell, who marched on the far right, did not reach Spotsylvania until five o'clock on May 8. Since Grant and the Yankees had possession of the well-manicured Brock Road—used by Stonewall Jackson a year earlier for his march to Joe Hooker's rear at Chancellorsville—Ewell was obliged to tramp across open ground until he reached the Catharpin Road leading past the Shady Grove Church to Spotsylvania from the west.

Like the corps of Hill and Anderson, Ewell's new line of march was influenced by Lee's troop dispositions at the close of fighting on May 6. With the Second Corps astride the turnpike and Hill and Anderson south of it, Anderson, followed by Hill (Early), took the direct route south, while Ewell, forming the left and center of the army on the sixth, proceeded farther west on Lee's extreme right. When Ewell began his trek after 8:00 A.M., Rodes was in the lead, with Johnson and Gordon bringing up the rear. Although Ewell's official report says he reached Spotsylvania around 5:00 P.M., some of his men encamped for the night at the Shady Grove Church a mile or so short of the courthouse.[2]

Anderson, who arrived first, encountered some enemy cavalry already occupying the town but succeeded in driving them off without difficulty.

Meade, however, anxious to secure the new position, launched an attack under Gouverneur K. Warren to check Anderson's entrenchments. When word went out for Ewell to join the melee from the Shady Grove Church Road, he hurried Battle and Ramseur of Rodes's division forward. Battle's Alabama and Ramseur's boys, followed by lead elements of Allegheny Johnson's division, went into action around 6:30 P.M. to reinforce Joseph B. Kershaw's brigade that held Anderson's right flank. Although Rodes's men were nearly spent from the painfully difficult march from the Wilderness and Cullen Battle received a crippling wound in the fracas, Ewell was able to halt the Federal onslaught.

"May 8 was thus a Sabbath of dashed hopes for the Federals," notes campaign authority Gordon Rhea. Ewell appears to have weathered the unbearably warm trek and late-evening collision without trouble, as Rhea had him bivouacking for the night at the Block House a few miles west of Spotsylvania with Lee and Early. The Confederate chieftains had every reason to be pleased with themselves, as the day ended with their forces pointing north between Grant's army and Richmond. Amid the jovial camaraderie Ewell found time to calm down and reminisce with Colonel William C. Talley, a captured Federal officer, about several acquaintances from Carlisle Barracks.[3]

When darkness halted the fighting on May 8, Ewell's three divisions were posted almost due north of Spotsylvania Court House; Johnson held the right, with Rodes on the left and Gordon in reserve slightly behind the other two. The First Corps, under Richard H. Anderson, was on Ewell's left, and Cadmus Wilcox of Early/Hill's corps was on his right. Johnson and Rodes were situated in a northward-pointing alignment to each other, with the former in an awkward position out of step with the remainder of Lee's rapidly developing fortifications. "The ridge Johnson was fortifying did not follow the curve of the entrenchments to his left. Instead it jutted forward, creating a huge bulge, or salient, in the Confederate position," observes Noah Trudeau.

A disagreement erupted among the rebel generals as to whether to strengthen Johnson's position or draw him back in order to straighten the entire line. Although many took a dim view about holding the projection, Ewell sided with his division commander in the face of engineers who argued that a salient was vulnerable to attack on its sides as well as its front. Ewell held that if the position were abandoned, "the Yankees would have the high ground in front of them." Fighting men north and south, Ewell among them, were becoming adherents of modern warfare

x = McCoull House   ⌢⌣⌢ = Mule Shoe   R, F and P RR = Richmond, Fredericksburg
and Potomac Railroad

Spotsylvania, May 1864

in which one rifleman behind a strong embattlement was worth three in
the open.[4]

Despite Lee's experience at Gettysburg when he hurled Pickett against
a strongly held position, the commanding general did not think much of
the salient built on May 9, 10, and 11 to house Ewell's Second Corps. The
salient, or "Mule Shoe," as it was dubbed by the men who had been put to
work digging and cutting timber along the front, was part of a three-mile-
long entrenched line. Without interruption the Confederate trenches and
abatis extended from one-half mile south of Spotsylvania Court House
northward to the Mule Shoe and then westward almost to the Shady Grove
Church. But it was the northernmost apex of Lee's great semicircle of men

and guns occupied by Ewell that held the attention of Grant and Meade. It was here that Lee would be broken or his army would live to fight another day. Brigadier General Martin Luther Smith, a native New Yorker who had married a Georgia belle and had been named chief engineer for the Army of Northern Virginia, agreed with Ewell that the high ground should be defended at all costs. It was Smith who enthusiastically oversaw not only construction of the salient but its gun emplacements as well.

When completed, according to Gordon, the Mule Shoe "was a long stretch of breastworks forming almost a complete semicircle"; it was actually a semicircle within a larger semicircle—the uppermost bulge about one-half mile across the base, with cleared forest and entrenchments along its faces. Although generals then and scholars today speculate on why Grant and Meade unexplainably allowed its construction to go unchallenged, it was a formidable military array when the fighting resumed on May 10. Ewell too labored with Smith to get the guns into position, and he personally oversaw the placement of men within the salient, with Rodes along the left leg and Johnson along the right or westernmost projection. Gordon's division was placed behind another string of fortifications across the salient base. In a sense the entrenchments had been constructed around Ewell's existing troop dispositions.[5]

Intermittent work on the Southern defenses continued until the great bloodbath on May 12. Though little combat occurred on May 9, sharpshooters and snipers were busy throughout the day on both sides. In one incident Major General John Sedgwick, commanding Grant's Sixth Army Corps, was felled by a Confederate bullet—struck in the left eye just minutes after boasting "they couldn't hit an elephant at this distance." Some skirmishing took place as the "entrenchments were perfected," and there was even a plan floated for Johnson to attack before the enemy got the jump, but it failed to materialize. During the afternoon an assault in some force was launched against Charles W. Field's brigade of Anderson's division on Ewell's left flank. The 148th Pennsylvania suffered one officer killed and eleven men wounded after it waded the four-foot-deep Po River to get at Field's men. After the attackers were driven off, William "Little Billy" Mahone's division was rushed to the left of Anderson's corps to guard the Shady Grove Church Road. May 9 was exactly one week after Ewell and his fellow generals met atop Clark's Mountain on the Rapidan to map their strategy; and although the army had been in constant maneuver for days, he appeared to be holding up under the strain of battle. "No time to write more now—All safe—will not telegraph unless something happens to one of us," Campbell Brown added in a May 9 (10:00 P.M.) postscript to a letter started earlier to his mother.[6]

The next day, May 10, Grant decided to probe the Mule Shoe in force by sending "twelve selected northern regiments" under Colonel Emory Upton against the northwest corner held by Johnson and Rodes. His assault was partially successful when it broke through the salient, capturing some three hundred prisoners. Grant and Meade were able to take advantage of what Lee feared most—they found the susceptibility of the entire line when they secreted their men in a nearby forest before the attack. Yet the Second Corps put up a spirited defense. "Gen. Ewell & staff & part of Gen. Lee's went in to rally our men & bring up reinforcements," Brown told Lizinka the following day. "We were under a hot fire for a time—say three quarters of an hour." From his headquarters at the Harris House, located near the base of the salient, Ewell had galloped to the flash point, summoning what troops he could from the brigades of Maryland Steuart, James A. Walker, Ramseur, Daniel, Battle, Gordon, Doles, and R. D. Johnston. "Ewell seemed to be everywhere. He rode up in a spar of dust to Daniel's brigade that adjoined Doles' lower flank," writes Gordon Rhea. "Halting behind the 45th North Carolina, he shouted, 'Don't run boys.' I will have enough men to eat up every damn one of them." A few moments later, he had seemingly forgotten his promises to the Reverend Hoge and Lizzie when in the heat of battle he yelled out to R. D. Johnston: "Charge 'em, general. Damn 'em, charge 'em."

"In a short time the enemy were driven from our works, leaving 100 dead within them and a large number in front," reads Ewell's battle report. "Our loss, as near as I can tell, was 650, of whom 350 were prisoners," he added. Yes, the salient had been secured, but it had also been breached—a fact that was not lost on the ever-perceptive Grant. According to Brown, the break had occurred because "Gen. Doles had no skirmishers out, which was the cause of the stampede (for it was nothing else)." Ewell's future son-in-law, Captain Thomas T. Turner, was among the wounded—shot in both legs, although Dr. McGuire told Brown he did not think an amputation was necessary. In a brief postscript to his mother, Brown added: "Gen. E's health is excellent."[7]

Rain fell throughout Wednesday, May 11, so no fighting took place, although Lee had his men digging ever longer trenches. Both armies were more than willing to enjoy a respite from the killing. "In the reconnaissance made by [Gershom] Mott on the 11th, a salient was discovered at the right center." And, continues Ulysses S. Grant, "I determined that an assault should be made at that point." Emboldened by the breakthrough the day before, the Yankee general resolved to ram the Mule Shoe for the second time. While Grant was preparing Winfield S. Hancock's Second Army Corps for his main thrust and Ambrose Burnside (Ninth Army Corps) to assail Lee's right, Lee decided the Federals would not renew the fight and accordingly ordered Ewell to remove his field pieces from the salient. "Late in the afternoon I received orders to have the artillery which was difficult of access removed from the lines before dark, and was informed that it was desirable that everything should be in readiness to move during the night; that the enemy was believed to be moving from our front," reports A. L. Long, Ewell's chief of artillery. "I immediately ordered all the artillery on Johnson's front, except two batteries of [Major Wilfred E.] Cutshaw's battalion to be withdrawn."[8]

When Johnson's men holding the center and northeast corner of the salient heard Hancock's stirrings along their front, all realized that a great blunder had been committed with departure of the cannon. Campbell Brown scrawled across the bottom of Long's report filed in late November: "By Gen. Ewell's direction I wrote to Gen. Long immediately upon receipt of this, asking him to specify *from whom* came the order for the withdrawal of the guns from Gen. Johnson's lines. No answer ever rec'd. Wrote a second time—with the same result." Brown added a terse remark that he had personally heard Lee issue the command to Long and that Ewell was also present. Whoever formulated the directive, it was soon recognized that additional artillery was needed back on the line. "At 3:30 a.m. on the 12th I received a note from General Johnson endorsed by General Ewell, directing me to replace immediately the artillery that had been withdrawn the evening before—that the enemy was preparing to attack," Long wrote afterward.

Just as Hancock was moving through a heavy fog to strike Johnson's "Bloody Angle," Richard C. Page's battery arrived as well as some guns under Cutshaw. The resultant bloodletting was so complete that Allegheny Johnson himself was captured along with General George H. "Maryland" Steuart and nearly all of the guns. Captain William Montgomery managed to retrieve two pieces, but, writes General Long: "The enemy thus captured twenty-guns—twelve from Page and eight from Cutshaw." Although Long and others, including Ewell, later insisted the lost artillery would have made a difference, perhaps even altering the outcome at Spotsylvania, historian Clifford Dowdey is probably correct that "the fact of the guns has been overemphasized." For one thing, the "obscuring ground fog" would no doubt have hindered their effectiveness. The Federal assault was so complete that no one had an opportunity to fight back—several infantry regiments merely broke and ran without offering any kind of resistance. In addition to the twenty guns, Ewell's losses, which would go higher as the day progressed, reached nearly four thousand in the initial surge.[9]

Not only a lack of cannon but rain-soaked musket powder also thwarted the Confederate response; men grappled desperately in the muddy salient to hold their line—often becoming so intertwined that opposing battle flags were frequently seen on the same rampart. In one famous episode, "an oak twenty-inches in diameter was chopped down solely by musket balls and crashed into the works of the nearby First Carolina." James A. Walker, asleep when the early morning firestorm hit, watched helplessly as his brigade was decimated. This brigade had been Stonewall Jackson's own from the beginning at Harpers Ferry, and it had fought through every Virginia campaign and now held "the western works closest to the toe." In spite of a heroic effort by Walker to steady his men before he was forced from the field with a horrible arm wound, they could not withstand the fury. "Near 6 a.m., droves of Federals struck the Old Brigade in front, flank, and rear," notes James Robertson. "The Fourth, Fifth, Twenty-seventh, and Thirty-third Regiments were trapped almost to the man." Those who managed to escape did so by fleeing the melee. What was left of the once-proud Stonewall Brigade was soon merged with other units for the remainder of the war.[10]

Although Ewell later thought a break in William Witcher's ranks adjacent to Walker's command caused the worst trouble, Brown noted after the war: "Next morning (May 12) just at daybreak, I was awakened by Gen. Ewell's calling for his horse & by a sharp fire on Johnson's line." Then Ewell rushed forward to the sound of gunfire from his Harris House headquarters and immediately ran into trouble with Lee, who also had sped to the uproar. Brown suggests that Ewell remained near his headquarters and sent him to "rally the debris of Johnson's division," while others say he was nearer the fighting. Some contend that what transpired influenced Lee's decision to remove him from command within the fortnight. Ewell had employed strong language two days earlier, but now he became so agitated that one of his aides, Colonel William Allan, says candidly, "he lost his head in the severity of the fight." General Lee joined him at the front, or very near it, but Ewell, with sword in hand, began whacking fleeing troopers on their backsides and yelling at the top of his voice for their return.

While Lee implored the men in "the calmest manner," Ewell seemingly forgot the Third Commandment as he excitedly chided the panicking men with "run, run, the Yankees will catch you; that's right, go as fast as you can." And, continues historian Robert Krick, "not surprisingly, all that Gen. Lee addressed at once halted and returned . . . all that Gen. Ewell angrily reproached continued their flight to the rear." Lee, very near the front, was taken to the rear by Gordon and one of his aides, who grabbed Lee's horse, Traveller, by his bit. The commanding general told Ewell before he departed: "You must restrain yourself; how can you expect to control these men when you have lost control of yourself. If you cannot repress your excitement, you had better retire."[11]

Ewell must have collected himself somewhat before reinforcements under General Abner Perrin began to arrive at the front. Perrin, who had been given Cadmus Wilcox's regiment of Alabamians after the latter's promotion to division command, was killed during the counterattack at the Bloody Angle when "he was struck by seven bullets."[12] Alfred Lewis Scott, one of Perrin's Alabama soldiers, who observed Ewell at close quarters on May 12, later composed a telling memoir of the encounter:

> The line was halted for something, I never knew what, and we were ordered to lie down for better protection while waiting. A group of generals collected at the point in the line occupied by my company, and engaged in an earnest and animated discussion. They were Ewell, Gordon, Rhodes [*sic*], and a general officer of Lee's staff and General Perrin, our brigadier. Things looked desperate, and there was a considerable show of excitement. Our Division commander was not present. Perrin was looking from one to the other as if at a loss for his orders. Gordon was talking rapidly and literally foaming at the mouth. I was leaning on my elbow, looking up, and heard all they were saying. Ewell's horse was standing almost over my feet. Looking down and seeing our line lying down he exclaimed, "Oh, boys, for God's sake don't lie down—it don't look well in a soldier to lie down in the presence of the enemy." Being right under his eyes as he spoke, I felt there was almost a flavor of personality in his words, and though realizing their absurdity under the circumstances, and that they meant nothing but flurry, I sprang to my feet at once saying, as I stood erect, "We were ordered to lie down, General." He replied, "Oh, well, if you were ordered to

lie down that's all right." I replied, "No, General, I don't want to do anything that looks badly in a soldier," and remained standing. He repeated, "That is all right, Lie down if that was the order." I suppose the gallant old fellow realized at once that in the excitement, he had "talked through his hat." The rest of the boys well knowing they were at their proper duty had all remained as they were and were smiling at the situation.[13]

When Johnson's line collapsed, Lee either had to find a means to check the Federal drive or abandon his entire position.[14] He turned not to Ewell but to John B. Gordon at the pregnant juncture. Before Perrin arrived to take part in the counterattack, Gordon sped into the Yankees with "a gallant furry." "[O]nward [my men] swept, pouring their rapid volleys into Hancock's confused ranks, and swelling the din of battle with their piercing shouts," Gordon observed. "Like the debris in the track of a storm, the dead and dying of both armies were left in the wake of this Confederate charge." Gordon's new thrust at Lee's behest cleared the east side of the salient but stalled near the apex or Bloody Angle. A major factor in the successful retaking of the Mule Shoe was the simple fact that too many Federals had rushed inside the works, and their disorganized regiments and brigades found themselves unable to combat the smaller, more compact rebel outfits.[15]

Although Ewell reported his force at "barely 8,000 with 1,500 reinforcements" after Allegheny Johnson's debacle, it was nonetheless true that the Second Corps had regained the salient. The Yankee foray, Ewell noted, "was met only by my corps, and three brigades [Abner Perrin, Samuel McGowan, and Nathaniel H. Harris] sent to my aid, and after lasting with unintermitted vigor from 4:40 a.m., till 4 p.m. of May 12, ceased by degrees, leaving us in possession of two-thirds of the works first taken from us and four of the captured guns that the enemy was unable to haul off." According to the later assessment of Major R. C. Page, detailed by Ewell to look for the "four brass guns," only caissons and not the pieces themselves were ever located. Both Sergeant S. S. Green, who accompanied Page on his late-evening quest for the missing armament, and A. L. Long wrote letters in support of Page, who became angered at Ewell's published reports suggesting that he had not gone after the guns but had merely sent his "orderly sergeant."[16]

Meanwhile, Stephen D. Ramseur brought his brigade on line at the direction of Rodes; then, with Ewell and Rodes present and watching, Ramseur formed his brigade toward the northwest corner of the Mule Shoe:

"On the right, 30th North Carolina, Colonel Parker; right center, Second North Carolina, Colonel Cox; left center, Fourth North Carolina, Colonel Grimes." The brigade was dressed "under a severe fire," Ramseur added. It was hard going, with infantrymen resorting to the bayonet and clubs, to regain this part of the salient. A sergeant was yanked by the hair from inside the works and made a Federal prisoner. Nathaniel H. Harris's Mississippi brigade from Little Billy Mahone's division was ordered to shore up Ramseur's right as the slaughter raged along the western face.[17]

Ramseur was beside himself when he wrote to his wife on June 4: "For the work of my brigade that day, May 12, I was thanked on the field by Maj. Gen. Rodes and Lt. Gen. Ewell." Like most of the Second Corps, Ramseur saw the day's fighting at close quarters because there was no way to avoid it; not only was he shot in the arm, but his "overcoat was pierced by four bullets, the pommel of his saddle struck, and even his pony was slightly wounded." But he appeared proudest that Ewell had publicly called him the "hero of the day."[18]

Although Ewell had managed to regain control of the Mule Shoe, he had done so at a terrible cost. The Confederate medical director officially cited his losses at 4,453 men killed and wounded during the month of May—men whom Ewell and the Confederacy could ill afford to lose. As the horrible mayhem of May 12 unfolded, Lee, realizing that the army could not stay where it was, sanctioned construction of a new defensive line across the base of the salient. Work on the revamped fortifications continued for several hours, partially under Ewell's direction, indicating that he had weathered the storm in reasonably good health. John O. Casler, author of the invaluable *Four Years in the Stonewall Brigade,* recalled, "General Lee and Ewell walked up and down the line all night encouraging the men to work, and telling them that 'the fate of the army depended upon having it done by daylight, and I knew by the way they acted it was a critical time.'" Sometime after midnight Ewell quietly repositioned his brigades behind the rebuilt works without notice of exhausted Federals beyond the Mule Shoe. "May 12 was the date of one of the most fearful combats, which along one limited line, and in one spot, lasted more than fourteen hours, without cessation," Meade's aide, Theodore Lyman, wrote later. "I fancy this war had furnished no parallel to the desperation shown here by both parties. It must be called, I suppose, the taking of the salient." Another staff officer on the Confederate side, Campbell Brown, "never imagined such a struggle was possible." He had "seen Gaines Mill and Gettysburg," Brown added.[19]

When the great fight ceased, both armies were in a state of depletion. Heavy rains swept the region, soaking Lee and Grant "in knee-deep mud" as both commanders continued to entrench and prepare to fight another day. After abandonment of the Mule Shoe, Ewell continued to occupy Lee's extreme left, or northernmost, position, with Early—still in charge of A. P. Hill's corps—in the center and Richard Anderson on the right, or southern, flank. The entire Confederate line was shaped like an inverted "L," reaching to the Po River along with the Ny, To, and Mat, tributaries of the Mattapony. "We have not had any fight since [May 12]—only a little skirmishing," Jed Hotchkiss told his wife on May 15. "The enemy has fallen from our left & we drove them on our right—he is still lying between us and the river—not daring to attack & unwilling to leave."[20]

On May 16, as Ewell remained in the trenches with his men across the base of the Mule Shoe, he took time for a brief note to Lizinka, assuring his wife that her "son had seen action but was safe." He also included a platitude about finding a Yankee horse and nursing it back to health, but no war news that sparkled in Hotchkiss's missives. A letter during the same respite from Campbell Brown to his mother indicated the army was in good shape except for Allegheny Johnson's division. Ulysses S. Grant, Brown told Lizinka, had not beaten the Confederates but had merely gone around them, with terrific losses. There can be no doubt that Ewell remained near his men in the afterglow of Spotsylvania. A few days later, on the nineteenth, Hotchkiss told his wife: "Gen. Ewell sleeps and stays in the trenches, but he will not let any of his staff stay where there is any danger if he can help it—sending them off as soon as they have done any duty he may require—he is so kind."[21]

Until the Second Corps moved toward the enemy on May 19, Ewell was primarily taken with minor skirmishing, as Jed Hotchkiss and Jubal Early indicate. On the fourteenth, Grant withdrew Wright and Warren from his extreme right to reinforce his left opposite Early. A feint at Ewell's line led his infantry to unleash a sharp firefight, but the fighting tapered off when Lee resolved not to reinforce Ewell's left flank. More skirmishing developed on May 15, and by Monday, the sixteenth, Grant had determined that a stab at Ewell, still entrenched along the base of the once-fortified Mule Shoe, by Wright, Hancock, and Burnside could well throw the entire Confederate line into disarray. Ewell's veterans had some advance warning that the Yankees were coming, and several regiments erupted with shouts of joy when they looked out at the tightly packed Federals coming at their entrenchments. The one-sided contest had ended by 8:30

or 9:00 in the morning when Grant issued orders for Burnside and others to fall back. The troopers under Ewell not only fired a parting volley, but they also taunted their hapless foes to return for more. "Ewell's skirmishers pursued the Federals to the McCoull house [in the old salient] tarrying to scoop up prisoners and loot," observes historian Gordon Rhea. "The carnage wrought by the artillery shocked even these combat-hardened veterans."[22]

Ever fearful that Grant would once more "sidle" to his left, Lee wanted to reconnoiter to his own right. Since Ewell still held the Confederate left, or northernmost, flank, he was ordered to move around Warren's men and cross the Ny toward the Fredericksburg Road leading north from Spotsylvania Court House. "Dick Ewell going along personally, acted with poor judgment and lost even his skill in fundamental tactics," notes Clifford Dowdey. "Going with only six guns he managed to get a division entangled with a sizeable body of the enemy, who were aching for such a crack at some of Lee's soldiers outside their works." Many, and Lee in particular, began to suspect that Ewell was simply no longer fit for field command. With help from William Pegram and John B. Gordon, Stephen D. Ramseur moved to the front around 3:00 P.M. after Ewell had crossed the Ny. The affair was bungled from the inception, although Lee was able to learn that Grant indeed still had a potent fighting force in the Spotsylvania sector.[23]

Ramseur said it was the steady conduct of his brigade that saved Ewell from disaster, and Ewell, in paying his respects to Ramseur as well as to Pegram, said the two "held their ground so firmly that I maintained my position till night fall and then withdrew unmolested." The timely arrival of Wade Hampton's cavalry and horse artillery helped Ewell extricate himself from the escapade. Even so, the heavily entrenched Federals inflicted a crippling loss on the six thousand effectives remaining in the Second Corps. As Ramseur's biographer points out, Ewell's reconnaissance cost him one-sixth of his fighting strength. "Gen. Ewell had his horse shot under him" in the fray, according to Campbell Brown, who wrote to his mother the next day so that she would not learn about the incident from newspaper accounts. And he confirmed Jed Hotchkiss's assertion that Ewell was not taking undue chances at the front by needlessly exposing himself or his staff. Brown likewise continued his one-man crusade to assure his mother, or anyone who would listen, that Ewell was performing his duties: "So far the Gen's health is excellent & he has done more than any man in the army, I think, since commencement of this affair two weeks ago."[24]

Lee, however, entertained other notions about Ewell's fitness for command, because sometime during the next two weeks the decision was made to send him down. As had been the case earlier, Lee, with Ewell in the van, crossed the North Anna on May 22, one day ahead of Grant. The steep banks of the stream, a headwater of the Pamunkey, afforded Lee's command a formidable defensive barrier. When completed the new Confederate line resembled an inverted "V" that ran from Hanover Junction northwestward to the river at Ox Ford and then veered to the southwest toward the Virginia Central Railroad. Ewell had marched farthest south and held Lee's right flank around the tiny hamlet clustered about the Virginia Central where it intersected with the Richmond, Fredericksburg, and Potomac coming north from the capital. Richard Anderson held the center, and A. P. Hill, newly returned to command, occupied the northernmost, or left, of the line. Here, a mere twenty miles north of the Confederate citadel, Lee received his first reinforcements since the beginning of the campaign when the commands of Robert F. Hoke, George Pickett, and John C. Breckinridge reached the army. Although the new troops only amounted to between eight thousand and nine thousand effectives, the coming of Breckinridge, fresh from his defeat of Franz Sigel at New Market in the Shenandoah, was a boost to morale. The popular Kentuckian, who led the pro-slavery forces against Abraham Lincoln in the election of 1860, though not a military man except for a brief service in the Mexican War, had proven himself an able campaigner under the Confederate banner. Breckinridge had been James Buchanan's vice president during 1857–1861, and when Campbell Brown wrote his mother from Hanover Junction, he told her that the soldier "looked as fine as when he was Vice President."[25]

The recovery and subsequent return of A. P. Hill meant that Jubal Early returned to Ewell's command as the army marched south from Spotsylvania. Since the Mule Shoe fiasco Ewell had been operating with two divisions, but now at Lee's insistence Gordon was appointed major general and put at the head of one division at the same time Early and Rodes retained their own. Thus, notes Gordon Rhea, Ewell had "three strong subordinates." Upon reaching the North Anna, or Hanover Junction (another name for the same operation), Ewell, who held the far right, arranged his divisions, with Early supported by Breckinridge on his own right; Rodes with Daniel, Battle, Doles, and Ramseur on his left adjacent to Charles W. Fields's division of Anderson's corps. Gordon held the rear position similar to that in the Mule Shoe behind Early and Breckinridge. In his postwar memoirs Early avows flatly that his division was not engaged at Hanover Junction, and Ewell comments briefly in his official report that "after some days skirmishing we marched toward the Totopotomy." Although A. P. Hill got into a fight with Warren at Jericho Mills north of Hanover Junction, the two armies did little more than stare at each other during May 23–26.

Lee and Ewell both contracted an intestinal disorder that swept the ranks and hindered the Confederates from taking advantage of Grant's blunder in dividing his army on two sides of the North Anna with Lee's "V" in between. Ewell reportedly told someone during the "stalemate on the North Anna" that Grant was like a "measuring worm, and the time to strike him is when he has just lengthened out his line." Anderson was new at his job, A. P. Hill was still recovering from his recent indisposition, and Ewell—nearing exhaustion, contrary to Brown's assertions—left Lee yearning for the glory days of 1862–1863 when Jackson and Longstreet could and did seize the initiative. As the army awaited its next move, Ewell jotted a note to Lizinka, at home in Tennessee, saying he was sick but that the ailment was unrelated to his amputation. It had "just occurred" to him that it was their first anniversary, and in a philosophical temper he lamented that the army was being forced back to Richmond. But Ewell did not think "there was much danger that the Yankees would actually enter the capital," even though he told his wife that additional men were needed for the ranks.[26]

As Lee and Grant headed down the two arms of the Anna before they join to form the Pamunkey, both armies met a countryside covered with lush vegetation. Bruce Catton describes the scene: "The land was featureless, with sluggish little rivers looping across flatlands that could turn into swamps when the rains came . . . there was no such thing as a straight road." Once more, Lee, although still ailing, was able to reach the next natural barrier astride the Totopotomy very near the old Seven Days battlefield on the evening of May 28, two days ahead of his adversaries. He was obliged to pause and establish a temporary headquarters at Atlee, a stop on the Virginia Central Railroad a mere six miles from Richmond. "As he lay prostrated by his sickness, he would often repeat: 'We must strike them a blow—we must never let them pass again—we must strike them again.'" His aide, Colonel Charles Venable, points out additionally that Lee in his tent was not Lee at the head of his troops, yet he "still received reports of operations in the field constantly brought to him." At Atlee Lee learned that Ewell too was incapacitated and unable to perform his duties. Ewell told him he was suffering from diarrhea, proceeding in an ambulance, and that he had turned command of the corps over to Early. Although he emphasized that Early's elevation was temporary, it was soon apparent that Lee would seize the opportunity to expel Ewell from the Second Corps.[27]

When Ewell filed his battle report for the Overland campaign ten months later while serving as commander of the capital garrison, he took considerable pains to say he was still fit for duty after Lee removed him. "I rode in an ambulance to Mechanicsville, remaining in my tent Saturday and Sunday, May 28 and 29." According to Ewell, he sent word to both Lee and Hunter McGuire that he would resume command of his corps on Tuesday, May 31: "I reported for duty on Tuesday, four days after my attack, and remained over a week with the army, wishing to place the question of health beyond a doubt, but the change in commanders was made permanent." A remarkable collection of letters and notes in the New York Historical Society between Ewell, Lee, Dr. McGuire, Walter H. Taylor, and Jubal Early enables the modern scholar to trace in close detail the sequence of events as well as Lee's adamant refusal to consider Ewell for further command. Responding to a note from Campbell Brown on the twenty-eighth asking if Ewell might ride a horse into Richmond, apparently from Totopotomy Creek, which the army had reached on the same day, McGuire told him: "If you are suffering any pain or uneasiness of diarrhea, I think it would be very imprudent to attempt to ride on horseback. You will certainly make yourself quite sick by attempting it." In an effort at diplomacy, McGuire added his opinion that if Ewell watched his diet he could take the field on May 29. Although Brown and Ewell forwarded McGuire's note to headquarters, Lee remained fixed in his course.[28]

Instead of taking the field, Ewell remained indisposed throughout the twenty-ninth as Walter Taylor cut a formal order releasing him from command and placing Early in charge. "In the temporary absence of Lt. Gen. Ewell caused by sickness Maj. Gen. Early is assigned to the command of the 2nd Corps," reads Taylor's unnumbered edict, which suggests that Lee had also been consulting with McGuire. "Permission is granted to Gen. Ewell to retire from the field that he might have the benefit of Medical treatment." And in an effort to salve Ewell's self-esteem, Lee wrote a direct note and "assured" him of his "deep concern."[29]

Ewell surely spent a fitful night, because with the dawn of June 1 he initiated a letter-writing campaign in the forlorn hope that he might retain his place. "The opinion of my medical attendant Dr. McGuire & that of myself is that I am as fit for duty today as at any time since the campaign commenced," a disenchanted Ewell fired back to Taylor, though Lee surely saw the letter. "I am unwilling to be idle at this crisis, and with the permission of the Com'dy Gen. I would prefer to remain with this army until circumstances may admit of my being replaced in command of my Corps." Not content, and boiling inside, Ewell wrote another pointed note to Taylor (not Lee) also on June 1: "I would be obliged to you for a copy of the order relieving me from command of the 2nd Corps & assigning General Early to the position." Ewell came close to insubordination when he continued: "The only authority I have is S.O. of the 29th ulto which contemplates my temporary absence caused by sickness. This now—having reported for duty does not cover the case." Taylor and Lee, unquestionably tiring of the affair, lost no time in responding: "The Gen. Com'dy directs me to say that the order you quote is the only one issued as yet." With a terse codicil, Taylor added: "You are at liberty to act under that however & should any other be issued you will of course be furnished a copy."[30]

Ewell had written an upbeat letter to his wife on May 29 while recuperating in his tent but obviously before receiving word of his expulsion from command. After bragging about leading the army on the march through Hanover Junction, he asked Lizinka to send his "flannel shirts—not knit that are worn when amongst the troops." A follow-up missive hinted that all was not well with headquarters. Although Ewell had commented in the previous letter that he and Campbell were in "capital health," his note of June 1 told a different tale: "I reported myself recovered yesterday & rec'd a letter last night that the troops being in line of battle no change was deemed advantageous at this time—but the Gen'l recommended that as soon as I could move with safety that I retire to some place untill the impending battle is over to recuperate my health & restore my strength for future service." In a brief postscript Ewell whined that Early was being promoted to lieutenant general and that he was without influence but wanted to be prepared if it meant that he would be harmed in any way. Early's promotion dated from May 31, one day before Ewell told his wife that he was without pull in Richmond and that "you should have thought about this before we were married."[31]

When Lee got the letter of protest, he responded with another personal note reemphasizing what had already been said—that the troops were engaged and he would make no changes. He had acted under a recent law enacted by the Confederate congress that enabled him to appoint Early "to the command of your corps for the present & Ramseur to the command of Early's division." Lee added, "it would be better for you to take command of all the troops in Richmond than for me to disturb the present arrangement." After another sleepless night, Ewell sent a long missive to Lizinka on June 2; while Campbell Brown was livid that his stepfather should have been shelved, Ewell informed her that Lee would make no changes in the foreseeable future. He also warned his wife that she needed to stop treating him like an invalid—that he was sick for two days only and had recovered, though Lee remained fixed that Early should retain corps command. Lee had even put it in writing, Ewell announced, as he added: "I pray for protection to you and all that interests you."[32]

Lizinka Brown Ewell was not a woman to let sleeping dogs lie; she had married her husband hoping for a stellar place in the Confederate social hierarchy, and now she embarked upon her own campaign to salvage the family "interests." In a forceful letter to his brother Ben on June 8, she said Ewell had been attacked by "something of the nature of scurvy, consequent to living on salt meat, and terrible exertions of the 28th when he reported sick." After reciting the recent chain of events for Ben's benefit, Lizinka said Early's appointment to command had greatly annoyed her husband until June 7, when he called on the president, no doubt at his wife's instigation. That visit may have been a mistake, as Jefferson Davis had been with the army almost daily as Grant drove ever closer to Richmond; and he knew firsthand about Ewell's deteriorating condition as well as Lee's growing lack of faith in his ability to handle troops. Davis, unwilling or unable to dispute with his old friend, simply passed the buck. "He was assured on the contrary," and according to Lizinka's account: "General Ewell then asked if he could not be placed in command of his corps (division?). The President replied that his rank was too high. General Ewell offered to resign and let the President appoint him Major General. The President told him no—he needed him at the head of his corps, and advised him to report again to General Lee [now] that his health was recovered."[33]

When Ewell called at Lee's tent on June 8, the army was holding its own after Grant's all-out thrust five days earlier. After the Yankee advance from the North Anna, two parallel defensive lines about six miles in length had been established around Cold Harbor stretching from Totopotomy Creek to the Chickahominy. As Ewell fumed in camp, Early had the Second Corps arrayed on the Confederate north, or left, facing Grant's entrenchments to the east. Apparently wishing to assist Abraham Lincoln's reelection campaign in the north, Grant, after some hesitation, ordered a general assault for the small hours of June 3. The 4:30 A.M. charge lasted no more than fifteen minutes when units under Burnside, Warren, Smith,

Wright, and Hancock confronted the rebel divisions on their immediate fronts. With Early calling the shots, Rodes and Gordon were tenacious in turning back Ambrose Burnside before Grant summoned Meade to halt the one-sided killing. The heavily entrenched Confederates inflicted losses approaching ten thousand in killed, wounded, and missing to about fifteen hundred for themselves. "I have always regretted that the last assault at Cold Harbor was ever made," Grant was moved to write in his postwar memoir. After a hassle over removing dead and wounded from the battleground, Grant once more "sidled" to the Confederate right and continued his press toward Richmond. He did not order the advance until June 12–13 several days after Ewell's discussion with Lee, when he again refused to reinstate his ailing corps commander.[34]

After Ewell presented his case to Lee on June 8—this time in person—the conversation was transcribed by Lizinka and hurried to Ben the same day. It covered essentially the same ground already hashed out in correspondence between the two warriors, with Ewell offering to resign and accept a lesser role with the army, while Lee would have none of it. Lee thought Ewell might collapse at a critical moment in the ongoing campaign, and Ewell sought to convince him that he was perfectly fit. When the question of Early's command arose, Lee responded that he did not prefer Old Jube but considered him stronger—more able to command. The public interest, Lee asserted, was paramount to every consideration, and for that reason alone he thought others better suited to lead. Ewell got off a parting shot that his health was now recovered but that he would "go somewhere to be out of the way." As the affair ended, Lee admonished him: "[Y]ou are not in the way, but you had better take care of yourself."[35]

"Ewell's corps now under my command, by reason of General Ewell's sickness" is the only reference to the power shift in Early's 1912 memoir of the war years. In 1864, however, conscious of criticism from Campbell Brown and other members of Ewell's staff, Early wrote a long letter to his old chief as the Second Corps marched from the North Anna. "All operations are now so intimately connected with what precedes that I think Gen. Lee does not wish to change commanders & because at any moment we may expect a decisive conflict & a change in commanders might result in mistakes," Early wrote on June 5, three days before Ewell's session with Lee. After informing him that he had had no previous communication with headquarters before taking over, Early added: "I am satisfied this is Gen. Lee's view & the present arrangement does not result from any dissatisfaction with yourself. I assure you that I would regret exceedingly that any misunderstanding between ourselves should result from it & I further assure you that I entertain no unpleasant feelings on account of the little affair at the Rapidan, but hope that cordial & friendly relations which have always existed between us shall continue in the future." Still, Early apologized for not visiting him in person before leading the Second Corps south; he had been "incessantly engaged all of the time."[36]

Although Lee was obviously in charge to call the shots, he took time to write two letters on June 12 concerning Ewell. Once he resolved to order Early and the Second Corps into the Shenandoah as well as toward Washington itself "to divert Federal strength from his own front," Lee inadvertently fueled a debate swirling through the army over Ewell's removal— Was it due to his health, a loss of confidence in his ability to command, or a combination of both? After telling Ewell that "it has been determined to detach your corps on a distant expedition," Lee resorted to the old canard that in his opinion he was not up to its demands. And, Lee continued: "In order, however, that your services may not be lost to the country at this critical period, I enclose herewith a letter to the Adj. & Ins. of the army recommending if circumstances permit that you be placed in charge of the defenses of Richmond." Lee's June 12 letter to Samuel Cooper played on Ewell's health one more time, but it carried a strong second for the position unless, he said, there might be conditions that he was unaware to hinder the nomination. A month or so later Ewell wrote to Lizinka expressing the hope that Early "would draw off some of the Yankee troops from the James River." One day before a contingent of Pennsylvania coal miners exploded the famous mine under the Confederate entrenchments at Petersburg, Ewell told his wife that he had been given the job of protecting the capital. Lee had kept his word, but it was not a temporary appointment, as he stressed to Cooper; Ewell would remain at the new post until the final Confederate collapse.[37]

Ewell and his wife made a determined effort to escape the Richmond job by seeking to find a post with Joseph E. Johnston in the west. Johnston apparently acquiesced and agreed to take him, but the prospect failed when Johnston himself was replaced by John Bell Hood as the Army of Tennessee fell back on Atlanta. "I would be a captain under Johnston if he were the Colonel of a regiment," Ewell told his brother on July 20. "He was my only hope of remaining in command." Johnston, however, may not have entirely wanted him. The army was in turmoil, with Grant pressing toward Richmond and Sherman threatening Atlanta, yet Lizinka on her own sought out Braxton Bragg, an advisor to Jefferson Davis in Richmond since February, to advance her husband's cause.

"She learned that the authorities declined to make the transfer," Ewell said. "I regretted her going very much, as I wanted the chance to give the authorities a plain statement of my case, and if developments authorized it, to hand in my resignation. I would have telegraphed to General Johnston for a command upon being relieved, . . . of course it was too late." Ewell informed Ben further that his position in Richmond was one "without troops, merely a polite way of being laid on the shelf."[38]

Lee was the man in charge and he clearly demanded a new corps commander. Ewell and Lizinka could protest only to a point. Repeated concern for Ewell's health may have presented Lee with a convenient vehicle for removal when he had actually lost faith in him at Gettysburg and had never regained it. The protracted struggle with Ewell's recalcitrance to forge ahead on the battlefield had not only exasperated Lee but also spotlighted a fundamental flaw in his own makeup. Lee placed undue confidence in seasoned West Point soldiers with long experience in command who were themselves lacking in fighting tenacity when originality was called for; in short, Lee relied upon subordinates who were afraid, or at least reticent, to gamble on a throw of the dice without direct orders. Ewell's stepdaughter had been correct that no one could replace Jackson, but— politics aside—there were soldiers in the Confederate service who would have made aggressive warriors. Changes were rampant during the Overland campaign—Richard Anderson was brought forward to replace Longstreet, A. P. Hill left the army and returned to command, Gordon had been elevated in rank, Jeb Stuart's death had necessitated changes in the cavalry—but Lee would not lift a finger for the return of Ewell to the Second Corps, because he wanted to be done with him. Lee at last realized that Ewell would not or could not do what was required in the field.

Although Ewell, abetted by Campbell Brown and Lizinka, strove mightily to present himself physically equipped for corps command, Harriet Stoddert Turner would write later: "The month of battles and malaria of the Chickahominy swamps broke down General Ewell's health and he was assigned to the Department of Henrico defending Richmond." This frank assessment of Ewell's condition was echoed three months later after he assumed command in the capital; when he visited St. Paul's Church on October 2, to receive confirmation, a fellow parishioner reported him "so maimed and hurt that he could hardly stand." Yet Jed Hotchkiss called on him in late October and found him strong enough to ride among the city's outer defenses. "I don't know what disposition has been made of Genl. Ewell," wrote J. H. Woodruff, a member of Rodes's staff, on June 7. "His physical condition unfitted him for command I suppose." And, Woodruff added: "I think highly of the old fellow though. His gallantry and bravery are unquestioned."[39]

Chapter 14

THE LAST MARCH

When forty-seven-year-old Lieutenant General Richard Stoddert Ewell took over the defense of Richmond in mid-June 1864, he found not only a city crumbling from four years of constant warfare but also a national capital facing a worsening military situation. Since the summer of 1861, Abraham Lincoln's war machine had targeted Richmond for capture and destruction. This jewel of the Southland had become—at least in the Northern psyche—the great symbol of Southern nationhood, and now with Grant's armies poised within sight of city spires, Ewell was summoned to save it from annihilation. Although Lee had intended Richmond as a place of withdrawal and rest for his onetime corps leader, Ewell found himself almost immediately confronted with a renewed need for command, but this time he had almost no troops or war materials at his disposal other than a conglomeration of civilian clerks and mechanics employed by sundry governmental offices and bureaus. When the first big test came in late September, Ewell was able to muster just two thousand men at a place known as Fort Gilmer, situated a scant six miles from Capitol Square—the only troops, as it turned out, that stood between Richmond and capture.

Three defensive shields had been constructed around Richmond prior to Ewell's assignment to command, some of them dating from the Peninsula campaign of 1862. Almost within the city proper was the interior line that encircled the capital and Manchester beyond the Mayo Bridge south of the James River. This part of the fortifications was strengthened by the gun emplacements of Charles E. Lightfoot and James M. Howard, although both were later moved south of the city. The formidable intermediate barrier extended from Chaffin's Bluff/Farm on the James due north to Richmond and arced around it to the river again; it also enclosed the interior line at its farthest reaches. At the southern extremes of this defensive fortification were Forts Gilmer and Harrison overlooking the James River bottoms and standing guard over the southern approaches to the city. A mile or so east was the exterior line that connected at Fort Harrison and ran northeastward to the Chickahominy at Mrs. Price's place on the Nine Mile Road. There were other ancillary lines branching from the major barriers as well as an arcing line that stretched across the New Market Heights and then north to the famed White Oak Creek. This latter line, manned by Brigadier General John Gregg's Texans, was directly opposite Deep Bottom on the James.[1]

From his first arrival on the Richmond ramparts, Ewell made his bivouac at Chaffin's Farm, very near the juncture of the two main defensive lines;[2] nor was he far from Lee's headquarters at Howlett's place on the south shore of the river. With pitifully few men to execute his duties north of the James while Lee was preoccupied with the Petersburg defenses, Ewell seemed unduly concerned with the several hundred civilian employees who made up a significant part of his force. John Beauchamp Jones, a fifty-six-year-old war department clerk, noted in his diary for July 28 that Ewell called out the clerks "to occupy the Darby Town, New Bridge, and Williamsburg Roads, for the enemy's cavalry were working around to our left." Two days later Ewell was rebuked for his impromptu action by Jefferson Davis himself. "The President directed the secretary of war to inform General Ewell that he misapprehended the character of these troops," Jones continues. Ewell later agreed to "employ them exclusively on city fortifications and only in times of extreme peril." Although Ewell thought an emergency existed in late July when Yankee cavalry patrols were spotted between the defensive lines and Richmond, the clerks were summoned en masse for the defense of Fort Gilmer a month later. Before that fight, however, the adjutant general issued an order demanding "workmen at arsenals and ordnance depots under charge of the Ordnance Bureau not be called from their work for military purposes except on orders from the War Department or the general commanding the department in which the arsenal or depot is situated." While officers of lesser rank were prohibited from tapping the reserve forces, Ewell could still call them out in a crisis. The war office again demanded that all workmen, clerks, and mechanics be returned to their posts as soon as any military contingency had faded.[3]

In late September Ewell called his brother Colonel Benjamin S. Ewell to join his personal staff as assistant adjutant general. Campbell Brown had remained with the Second Corps and had marched for the Shenandoah with Jubal Early, which meant that Ewell wanted another loyalist he could trust at his new headquarters. Brigadier General Robert Ransom, who had held the Richmond post immediately prior to Ewell, also went to the Shenandoah as commander of Early's cavalry. Following service in southwestern Virginia and East Tennessee, Ransom had been sent back to Richmond for duty under Beauregard at Drewry's Bluff and Bermuda Hundred. "Black-bearded Robert Ransom, who could not get along with anybody, was shunted off once more, making a place for the broken lieutenant general," observes Clifford Dowdey.[4]

There can be no doubt that Lee, with the second of President Davis, had manipulated the army to afford Ewell a respectable place. John Clifford Pemberton, who had resigned from high command after the Vicksburg fiasco, also found himself in Richmond looking for a position in the summer of 1864; he too was a friend of the president and ended up serving under Ewell "as a volunteer lieutenant colonel of a battalion of stationary artillery." It was likewise certain that Ewell was an energetic superintendent over his defensive lines, perhaps seeking to dispel Lee's earlier rejection on medical grounds. From his perch at Chaffin's Farm he was constantly along the fortifications while maintaining a regular communication with Lee.[5]

With the Federal hordes pressing ever closer, Richmond was in a state of flux, its residents were afraid, and Ewell, with his reputation for indecisive command, was not the man to inspire their confidence. "Idle rumors" were rampant, and though it occurred beyond the limits of Ewell's command, writes John B. Jones, the "reported rapes by negro soldiers on young ladies in Westmoreland County" threw the city into a panic during late June. Ewell's occasional calls on government workers to man the barricades south of the city did not help matters, with significant numbers of black troops known to be with Grant beyond the James. But as Ewell stayed close to the trenches around Chaffin's, it is questionable if he commanded anything in spite of Lee's admonition to smite the enemy "if practicable." "I found upon the north side of the James, permanently stationed there, an artillery force of many guns at Chaffin's Bluff, the Richmond City battalion, and a Tennessee brigade [Johnson's] all under the nominal command of Lieutenant General Ewell," Major General C. W. Field wrote about his arrival in late July. "I say nominal because, though General Ewell commanded the Department of Richmond, which embraced these troops, and everything which might be located there, in fact I commanded, and made dispositions without consulting him, and received no orders from him."[6]

Even before Grant decided to push north of the river in late September, Lee, who "could not deprive the old soldier of his own departmental sector," had not assigned all troops in the area to Ewell. In spite of limited resources at hand, "nearly 2900 men on the New Market line reported to [John] Gregg, an officer of the Army of Northern Virginia . . . In an emergency the lieutenant general could of course issue orders to the Texan, but he normally did not command the junior officer." And, notes R. J. Sommers, foremost authority on Richmond fighting, "Ewell and Gregg operated independently of each other, each concerned with defending his own front." Throughout June, July, and August, Ewell, at Chaffin's, held the keep nearest the serpentine James, and it was from this vantage point that Lee called on him for assistance south of the river. Lee sent an appeal for him "to see what can be done about stopping the digging at the Dutch Gap Canal," a short way downstream from Chaffin's Bluff. When George Pickett got into trouble below the river, Lee also asked him to detach one of his brigades to provide reinforcements. The heavy buildup by Lee and Grant opposite Petersburg became a race for mastery of the campaign, and Ewell could hardly escape the set-to, although his forces for the most part remained on the Richmond side of the river. At Pemberton's urging, Ewell did send a number of "howitzers and mortars" to be employed by Colonel J. M. Maury against the Federal pontoon bridge at Deep Bottom in anticipation of Grant's foray across the James in September.[7]

G. W. Custis Lee, the commanding general's eldest son, was assigned to Ewell's department in mid-August, ostensibly to train local defense forces but more likely as a steadying influence. Ewell made other additions to his staff during August when Captain F. T. Forbes was recruited as his "commissary of subsistence" for not only his troops but also for the city. Likewise, Major Legh R. Page came on board as another adjutant general to assist Ben; after the war, Page, a lawyer, remained in Richmond as city attorney before his death in 1893. The South Carolina cavalryman Wade Hampton, seemingly unbeknownst to Ewell, wrote to Adjutant General Samuel Cooper on August 13 advocating creation of a "bureau of cavalry" and suggested that "someone who has had experience in this branch of the service be assigned to duty as chief of the new bureau." But Hampton had surely talked the prospect over with Lee in advance. "I think that R. S. Ewell is the officer best qualified by experience and information and service for the position of chief," Lee wrote to Richmond and noted perfunctorily: "Besides possessing great merit he has great claims." The proposition to remove Ewell farther from the fighting languished until December 8 when Cooper "respectfully referred" it to Ewell along with Lee's endorsement. It fell by the wayside when he "respectfully returned" the overture with the codicil that he had been in field command for twenty-five years and had no desire to be "a bureau officer."[8]

Meanwhile, Ulysses S. Grant instructed Edward O. C. Ord, commanding the Eighteenth Corps, and William Birney with the Tenth, to cross the James on the night of September 28; the order was implemented, Grant said, "to retain Lee in his position." "An effort was made to surprise the enemy," but Grant admitted that his men failed miserably in that venture and that the "enemy's lines were very strong and very intricate." The Yankee assault called for Ord to span the James with four thousand men under George J. Stannard and Charles A. Heckman "by a ponton [sic] bridge to be established during the early part of the night at Aikens, two miles below Dutch Gap, where the Varina Road abutted on the river." Both Ord and Birney were supported by cavalry units under August V. Kautz, a German-born graduate of West Point, class of 1843. Varina Road, Ord's pathway north, not only intersected with the New Market Road leading directly into the capital, but it also passed very near Ewell's bivouac at Mrs. Chaffin's as well as Forts Harrison and Gilmer. While Ord's troops came from the Bermuda Hundred, Birney commanded ten thousand troopers gathered from the Petersburg entrenchments. Birney crossed at Deep Bottom by the upper pontoon bridge about one mile downstream from Ord. "General Ord," writes A. A. Humphreys, "was to engage the enemy in his works at or near the river at Chapin's Bluff, and prevent reinforcements being sent from the south side against Birney's column."[9]

By daybreak Grant was driving toward Richmond with fourteen thousand men, but Ewell and the Confederate high command knew that Ord and Birney were across the river almost immediately; the Federals had forfeited the element of surprise before their crossings were complete. Twenty-eight-year-old Colonel Robert B. Snowden, a New Yorker and longtime associate of Major General Bushrod Johnson, rushed to the James upon receiving word from junior officers that Grant was on the prowl. After a personal inspection of the area, he raised the alarm, according to General Marcus J. Wright, by hurrying couriers "to General Gregg, and also to General Ewell in Richmond." Ewell, however, was not in Richmond but at Chaffin's Farm, where he got the word along with Gregg. Both soldiers alerted Lee, south of the James, who immediately set in motion a scheme to rush additional troops north of the river. Attuned to the danger, Ewell ordered the mobilization of all local forces around Richmond, and fifteen minutes later, at 7:45 A.M., he asked for naval support from Confederate gunboats lurking in the James.[10]

"To brace Ewell for the imminent battle, Lee urged him 'to take the field with all you have. Encourage your men to fight boldly.'" Ewell needed men, not admonition, as Ord and Birney pressed onward, and, writes Captain C. T. Allen, who was present, "There were almost no troops between us and Richmond." Ewell needed time to gather his disparate forces, and he was able to do so because Allen, a few hundred yards down the line at Fort Maury, "about half way between Fort Harrison and the river, rallied some seventy-five to one hundred men and held the fort until Pickett came to our relief about midday." Back in Richmond great confusion reigned when suitable officers could not be found to lead the two thousand or so clerks and mechanics called to arms. Robert Ransom, who had defended the city previously, flatly refused the job, and Lee suggested that Ewell step aside in support of Richard H. Anderson, but that plea was conveniently ignored as Secretary of War James A. Seddon asked General James Lawson Kemper to marshal the civilian troops. Although Ewell went briefly to Fort Harrison, he spent most of his effort at Fort Gilmer, the closest fortified position to the capital, as he awaited his men.[11]

Benjamin F. Butler, the infamous "Beast" of New Orleans, who had designed the Yankee advance by Ord and Stannard, watched through a telescope from City Point as the initial assault was made against Fort Harrison, three-quarters of a mile south of Ewell at Fort Gilmer. "Possession of Fort Harrison did not give possession of the defenses at Chapin's Bluff," Humphreys noted, "but possession of Fort Gilmer would give it." The Federals understandably wanted to reduce Gilmer as the key to speeding into Richmond and also capturing the formidable Confederate batteries at Chaffin's Bluff. With Grant himself looking on, his lead units encountered "a big oblong on a hill, with stout ramparts, good trenches on either side, anchoring it firmly to the rest of the Confederate system."

Then, continues Bruce Catton, "Ord's soldiers crossed the open fields, halted close to the fort to reform, and then went down into the ditch and up over the ramparts, storming into the fort and driving out its last defenders." When Ord sought to extend his line westward to the James, the attackers not only fell short of their goal of Chaffin's Bluff, but Ord himself fell with a horrendous arm wound. Although the Confederates gathered enough men to deny the enemy access to the river, the capture of Fort Harrison was complete by six o'clock in the moring.[12]

According to one of his men, Ewell met the forces led by Birney, son of the abolitionist James G. Birney, and Heckman, who had taken charge of Ord's Eighteenth Corps, "with cool courage and presence wherever the fight was hottest, [and] contributed as much to victory as any one man could have done." While the fight to retain Fort Harrison still raged, Ewell had assembled at best a polyglot force to meet the charge against Fort Gilmer. Charles Johnston, "a private soldier in Huff's, afterwards Griffin's battery," recounted Ewell's force twelve years later:

> About two thousand (2000) men consisting of what re-
> mained of Bushrod Johnson's Tennessee brigade (300 strong),
> commanded by a Colonel whose name I think was Johnson;[13]
> the Texas brigade, also commanded by a Colonel whose name I
> do not remember;[14] clerks and attaches of different departments
> of the Government; [Martin W.] Gary's brigade of cavalry, the
> Louisiana Guard Artillery, [Robert A.] Hardaway's battalion,
> consisting of four batteries, four guns each; the Rockbridge Ar-
> tillery, Captain [Archibald] Graham; Third Company, Rich-
> mond Howitzers, Lieutenant Carter; the Powhatan Artillery,
> Captain [Willis J.] Dance, and the Salem Artillery, Captain
> [Charles B.] Griggin.[15]

Ewell, Johnston recalled in 1876, was "constantly on the skirmish line" at Fort Gilmer, situated "on a hill, with quite an extensive flat in front from which the trees had been cut, and most of the trees were lying on the ground with their limbs still attached." Two redoubts on either side of the fort were manned by the "Louisiana Guard Artillery and the Salem Artil-lery," which offered a lethal enfilading fire upon any attackers. After an initial thrust,, the enemy fell back to regroup, and there followed one of the war's more questionable episodes. Ewell's cannoneers had loaded with canister when the Federals began to rush Gilmer with a brigade of black soldiers, and, Johnston continues, "the way those negroes fell before it was very gratifying on our side of the works." A ten-foot-deep by twelve-foot-wide ditch surrounded the fortress, and it was here that many of the black troopers were killed. More than a few attempted to span the moat by climb-ing on each other's shoulders. "No great number of negroes," Private Johnston recollected, "and the rest of the attacking column having no shelter from the fire of both artillery and infantry were forced to give way and retire."[16]

The killing stopped instantly when Ewell received firsthand reports about the slaughter of Birney's black infantrymen—that those men were now U.S. Army soldiers and enjoyed the same status accorded all combatants. G. Moxley Sorrel, Longstreet's trusted adjutant, labeled the killing an ugly affair. Without condoning the slaughter, the biographer of 135 years later can speculate that the Confederate grunts on the front line had had enough of the abolitionist surge to alter their way of life, and the Negro, in their minds, was at the very core of the Northern war effort. General Humphreys sets the number of black soldiers killed at 434. At the close of September 29 Ewell had not only foiled the stabs by Birney and Heckman to capture Fort Gilmer, but he had also halted Yankee attempts to extend their lines to the James, thereby threatening Chaffin's Bluff. At 3:00 P.M. Ewell telegraphed Braxton Bragg, with a copy to Seddon in Richmond, saying that "the attack on Fort Gilmer was repulsed by Generals Field and Gregg handsomely."[17] And, he added: "We will take the offensive as soon as the troops come up." Although he did not undertake further action, Ewell's stepdaughter later wrote that he considered September 29 "his best achievement of the war." Fort Harrison was lost until the final surrender, but there can be no doubt that Ewell, with less than fifty men at Fort Gilmer, had blunted the bluecoated drive against the capital. "Acting in the face of imminent disaster to forge and sustain a continuous line from Fort Gilmer to the James that bade fair to contain the Federal breakthrough and save Richmond was the greatest contribution Ewell ever rendered to the Confederate cause," writes Richard Sommers, the campaign's major chronicler.[18]

New difficulties started for Ewell when Robert E. Lee sped to the Confederate defenses north of the river and commenced ordering up reinforcements from the Petersburg line. He also asked Ewell to launch an assault on Fort Harrison before Grant had an opportunity to fortify his newly won position. Field was anxious to charge down the Varina Road while the iron was hot, but even with the afterglow of success, Ewell had not changed from his earlier reticence—once more he held back. Perhaps conditions were not favorable for a late-evening charge, but other, less reticent officers would have taken the bit in hand. Although he had made known his intention to attack to Braxton Bragg, confidant to President Davis and to the secretary of war, he could not make himself commit to action; to compound matters, he suffered a bothersome spill while riding along his positions with Lee, Richard Anderson, and several other officers.

In a widely cited account of the incident, Moxley Sorrel relates what happened:

> [Ewell] was so good a horseman that his one leg was equal to most riders' two, but his horse stumbling, down came both— an awful cropper. I made sure the General's head and neck were not cracked. He was picked up, no bones broken, but [had] an "object" about the head; scratched, bruised, torn, and bloody. Lee instantly ordered him back to Richmond and to stay there until completely well.
>
> In two or three hours he was again on the lines! Painfully comical it was. He had gone to the hospital, where the bald head and face were dressed. He returned swathed in bandages from crown of head to shoulders. The little apertures for his piercing eyes and two small breathing spaces were all that was left open for the Lieutenant General. Quite indifferent, however, to such mishaps, he was sharp about his work and lisping out directions as usual.[19]

Ewell left the front for Richmond when Richard Anderson marshaled an attack on Fort Harrison that ended in utter failure. A day or so later, on Sunday, October 2, he presented himself before Bishop John Johns for formal confirmation into St. Paul's Episcopal Church. Fellow communicants noted Ewell's banged-up condition, described earlier by Colonel Sorrel— that he could hardly maneuver during the service. Confirmation in mid-nineteenth-century Virginia would have been a perfunctory ceremony that conferred full church participation, including communion. The rite was normally performed by the presiding bishop whenever a number of candidates had gathered for the purpose. Five others—Colonel Virginius Groner, Sixty-first Virginia; Davis S. Forbes; John R. Thomas, First Maryland Artillery; Mrs. Juliet T. Burton; and Miss Mary M. Ray were confirmed at the same time as Ewell.[20]

Three days later Ewell unwittingly opened a Pandora's box when he sanctioned the transfer of eighty-four United States Colored Troops from Libby Prison in Richmond to work on a new set of defensive lines in the aftermath of Fort Harrison. Some of these men had been captured during the Federal assault on Fort Gilmer. Ewell and Confederates generally did not distinguish between freedmen and runaway slaves, and in fact slave owners had been encouraged to inspect the captives in search of their property after the recent fighting. Although some black troopers sought release from imprisonment to work in the open, most did not, and a real question arose about their status as prisoners of war when they were put to work under a Federal fire directed at the rebel construction. Major General Benjamin F. Butler, a unique Northern officer who was more interested in winning civil rights than winning the Civil War, not only waged a violent protest but also quickly engaged in acts of retaliation. Eighty-seven Confederate prisoners of war were sent to the Dutch Gap project and placed where Ewell's guns, as well as others clustered about Chaffin's and Drewry's Bluffs, would strike them.

The Dutch Gap Canal, Butler's brainchild, had been under construction since August 10. Because of heavy Confederate bombardment of the James at Chaffin's Bluff, the Union high command resolved to dig a channel across a 174-yard oxbow, or loop, in the river. It would shorten the water voyage into Richmond by nearly five miles and require the removal of sixty-seven thousand cubic yards of sediment. Although black laborers did most of the digging, steam-powered dredges and a liberal use of explosives were also employed. "While no serious civil-engineering difficulties occurred, the troops employed were constantly subjected to a severe and continuous fire, first of heavy rifled guns and afterwards of mortars," observes General P. S. Michie, who was superintendent of the project. "The casualties were continuous throughout, on one occasion resulting in twelve killed and forty wounded; in addition, great losses in mules, horses, and carts were sustained."

When Lee learned that Ewell and Porter Alexander were firing on some of his own men, he reportedly recoiled in horror; he even ordered construction of a special cage in front of his cannon to house Federal prisoners as a deterrent to Butler's attempts to silence his artillery. After a direct appeal to Grant, the standoff ended on October 20—two weeks after Ewell called out the United States Colored prisoners—when the Yankee commander summoned Butler to remove all Confederate hostages from the diggings. Lee likewise implemented a new policy: Federal prisoners of war would no longer be used as laborers. The Dutch Gap Canal was completed on January 1, 1865, when a roaring blast dislodged the remaining bulkhead containing six thousand cubic yards of dirt. Wartime Richmond reeled from the downriver explosion, although the new waterway was not opened to traffic until several months after Appomattox.[21]

Following the last Confederate charge to regain Fort Harrison and Jubal Early's setback on the nineteenth at Cedar Creek in the Shenandoah, the Virginia fighting tapered off until the next spring except for sporadic forays. On the very day that Early was pounded by Phil Sheridan, Ewell received a new boss when James Longstreet returned to active command several months after his neck and shoulder wound in the Wilderness. Lee assigned Longstreet to lead troops north of the James, including those under Ewell. Although he made occasional jaunts into the city, Ewell remained close to his bivouac at Mrs. Chaffin's, as his numerous communications with Colonel Osmun Latrobe plainly indicate. Latrobe, a Marylander who became a devoted Confederate, was the son of John H. B. Latrobe, "an attorney, inventor, author, and public servant." The twenty-nine-year-old officer, grandson of architect Benjamin H. Latrobe, had been a valued adjutant on Longstreet's staff for several months.[22]

Richmond and the Confederacy continued to ebb away through the fall and early winter of 1864–1865. Lee's Army of Northern Virginia was heavily burdened by the desire, if not urgency, to defend this gem of the Southland. He simply could not maneuver or take the offensive with Grant tearing at the city gates. The reelection of Abraham Lincoln in the first week of November brought the war home to Ewell and his compeers. Now there would be no accommodation with the Yankee colossus threatening the Confederacy—from here on out it was surrender or annihilation. Ewell's requests for additional troops to man the Richmond defenses met with constant rebuff from Longstreet, because there were no reinforcements available.

As the specter of defeat and ruin engulfed the city, Ewell was constantly concerned about the quality of his fighting effectiveness. On November 8 he informed Walter H. Taylor that between four and five thousand troops were available around Richmond when fully mobilized, but, he added: "For the most part [these troops] are inexperienced both as regards officers and men. Very few of them have made any combined movements, and in case of necessity to use them in more than one Battalion neither officers or men would know what to do." While critical of most officers in his charge, Ewell thought himself fortunate to have General G. W. Custis Lee in command of his Richmond troops. This eldest son of Robert E. Lee, graduate of West Point, class of 1854, had trained and now led the "Troops for Local Defense, composed of the 2nd regiment, Colonel D. E. Scraggs; 3rd Regiment, Colonel John McAnerney; 1st Battalion, Major Thomas H. Ayres; 4th Battalion, Major Martin W. Curtin; and, 5th Battalion, Lieutenant Colonel Phillip J. Ennis." Custis Lee, who followed Ewell to the surrender at Sailor's Creek, later assumed the presidency of Washington and Lee University upon his father's death.[23]

Ewell had returned to Richmond briefly on December 3, where he proclaimed a Federal raid against the Weldon Railroad at Stony Creek "threatening." Although consumed with the ramparts at Petersburg, south of Ewell's command, Lee struggled mightily to keep this lifeline open to the Carolinas for supplying his own troops as well as those in Richmond. "While the enemy was well fed, well clothed, and well manned, with recruits filling the ranks, the Southerners knew only shortages," notes Jeffry Wert. "For hundreds in Lee's army the suffering and specter of final defeat proved too much. Soldiers disappeared every night, never to return to their regiments." Ewell's command was no exception—they too were suffering great deprivation as Christmas and the end of 1864 approached. Yet he was often called to repel the enemy. "General Pickett reports that the enemy are crossing at Cox's Landing. They have driven in our pickets and are now laying pontoons," Latrobe telegraphed on December 7. "Will you see if the lower batteries can be brought to bear on the bridge they are laying? If so, open fire." There is no response from Ewell in the *Official Records,* but Porter Alexander, who received the same request, personally climbed a tall pine and reported that he could not see the bridge.

When Ewell asked for more troops to defend the Fort Gilmer-James River line, Latrobe responded on December 21 that General Joseph B. Kershaw would be ordered up on his right with "two small regiments." And one day before Christmas, when Ewell told Longstreet that his lines were too thin, Latrobe again answered: Longstreet, he said, agreed with him—"that nearly one-half of his force on this side of the river has been taken away during the past week, and that should the enemy make an attack he will have to fight him with a line about as thin as the one you complain of." Desertions and total lack of replacements played havoc with Ewell's command as they did with other parts of the Army of Northern Virginia. At year's end, in addition to Custis Lee's local defense forces and fixed batteries near the river, Ewell reported present three brigades commanded by Colonel John M. Hughes, Colonel M. Lewis, and Major Edward M. Boykin, the last a small cavalry outfit. Rounding out his contingent was the First Virginia Reserves, composed primarily of invalids and convalescents from Richmond hospitals. The reserves were now headed by General Patrick T. Moore, a native of Ireland, who was not confirmed to general rank until January 1865.[24]

In the face of a disintegrating Confederacy, Ewell and his wife began to take a pragmatic view of her property and their life together after the war. As early as their marriage in May 1863 Ewell had asked for legal advice on how Lizinka's extensive holdings might escape seizure in the event of a Yankee victory. It is difficult to fathom his concern as a Confederate corps commander if he had full confidence that Southern independence would become a battlefield reality. In the months preceding the final Confederate collapse as Lizinka left Richmond to see after her western properties, some of Ewell's activities came close to treason. Ulysses S. Grant records a conversation in his famed memoirs with a Dr. Smith, a distant relative of Ewell and a regimental surgeon, who had remained in the Federal army. The Grant-Smith meeting took place on the road to Appomattox after Ewell's capture at Sailor's Creek in April 1865. Smith relayed an earlier conversation with his kinsman in which "he said that when we [the Yankees] got across the James River he knew their cause was lost." The bluecoats had been south of the river since June 14–16, 1864, which meant Ewell had been harboring a defeatist mindset for the last ten months of the war.

While Grant does not record when the conversation between Smith and Ewell occurred, he does say that Ewell felt "it was the duty of their authorities to make the best terms they could while they had a right to claim concessions." According to Grant and Smith, when the Richmond caciques waited too long to make any negotiated demands on the Lincoln government, Ewell thought "that for every man killed after this in the war somebody is responsible and that it would be very little better than murder." As the end approached, Ewell even speculated that Lee would never surrender the army without prior consultation with President Davis. In January 1865, however, he believed Richmond should be defended at all costs. According to his brother Benjamin S. Ewell, he said, "if it was given up our fortunes will be rendered well-nigh desperate."[25]

The defeatism that gripped Ewell and his wife in late 1864–early 1865 resulted in her leaving Richmond for St. Louis in an effort to salvage her property, some of which had been confiscated. In a letter dated April 9 from Missouri, Lizinka indicated that she had approached a daughter of Vice President Johnson, whom she insisted on calling "governor." She had enjoyed "a long acquaintance" with the irascible politico, and she was not hesitant about seeking help for herself and her husband, although she was rebuffed in the initial attempt. "I should like very much to get acquainted with Gov. Johnson's family but could not of course call on them unless they either called on me first or intimated in some way that a call from me would be acceptable to them," she wrote to David T. Patterson, Johnson's son-in-law and a Tennessee circuit judge who later represented the state in the United States Senate. "The desire I really had to obtain an acct-book from the drawer of one of the book cases gave me a fair excuse to offer to make the acquaintance of Miss Johnson and Mrs. Patterson but the offer was decidedly & repeatedly declined." However, Lizinka would soon have an opportunity to contact Johnson on another occasion.[26]

Presumably, Mrs. Ewell had made her overture to the Johnsons when she and her daughter, Harriet, passed through Washington on her flight from Richmond.[27] Harriet's account of their journey posits that Lee knew about the trip and gave his personal nod for Campbell Brown to leave his post to assist his mother and sister. One wonders if Lee realized the wife of one of his most trusted lieutenants was also on a mission to contact the vice president of the United States—ostensibly to save her property. Was she also on a mission to seek accommodation in the days leading up to Appomattox? There is apparently no genuine answer other than that she sought to establish contact with Andrew Johnson.

After a two-day buggy ride from Ashland, north of Richmond, "with starved horses," the tiny party reached the house of Dr. Richard Stuart in King George County. They lingered here on the southern shore of the Potomac for ten days awaiting a dark night suitable for crossing to the Maryland shore in a "row boat manned by two blockade runners." Nearly run down by an excursion steamer—they were close enough to hear a band playing for dancing couples—Ewell's wife and stepdaughter made it to Port Tobacco, roughly twenty-five miles southeast of Washington. "Our luggage consisted of one carpetbag, and my mother had her diamonds and money sewed up in her dress," writes Harriet Turner. Mother and daughter hiked through the night to a crossroads inn, where they found lodging and a hearty breakfast. "The next day we took the stage, and entering Washington that night, we went in a street-car to Georgetown, not having been challenged or asked for our passports."[28]

Meanwhile, the worsening military situation, which resulted in thousands of blacks, prisoners of war, and stragglers from various commands wandering around Richmond and the adjacent countryside, precipitated a renewed drive to find additional manpower for the army. The only conceivable source of significant numbers of recruits for the Confederate war effort was Virginia blacks, whether freed or slave. It was a thorny question that had been around from the beginning and that struck at the heart of Southern nationhood. When the notion of slaves serving in the army was first broached by General Patrick Cleburn, fighting with the Army of Tennessee, it received a divided reception. Although the governor of Texas rejected the concept out of hand, as did most other chief executives, Jefferson Davis finally embraced the concept, as did manpower-starved commanders in Virginia and elsewhere. By February 17 Longstreet asked Ewell, whose wife was maneuvering in enemy territory, to "send the company of Negroes he understands has been raised in the city of Richmond down to his line to be tested." It is unclear if Ewell complied with Longstreet's wish "to overcome a prejudice existing in the minds of many adverse to their employment as troops."[29]

"For my own gratification, as well as those who are taking great interest, with regard to the using of slaves of the Confederacy as an assistant element to us, in defending our houses, firesides and homes. . . . I caused the hired male slaves at [Jackson] hospital to be convened," Dr. F. W. Hancock informed Ewell on February 11. "[S]ixty out of seventy two responded they would willingly go to the trenches and fight the enemy to the bitter end." While Ewell may have been lukewarm toward the use of willing blacks as troops, Lee and Longstreet were not. When Ewell informed Lee on March 29 that numerous slave owners would not release their bondsmen for army service, Charles Marshall, one of Lee's adjutants, fired off a rapid reply: "General Lee deems it of concern that some of this force should be put in the field as soon as possible, believing that they will remove all doubts as to the [?] of the measure." A few days earlier Ewell had informed Secretary of War Breckinridge that a number of "negroes at the hospitals wish to join this force" of local defense troops and by implication that he was willing to employ them. Since he remained at Chaffin's Bluff until the final Confederate withdrawal, he no doubt relied upon Hancock's assessment.[30]

Although the Confederate congress narrowly blocked legislation that would have permitted blacks to enlist, at Lee's urging the Virginia legislature enacted suitable laws to permit their service. With less than two weeks before evacuation of the capital, Jefferson Davis and the war office issued General Order Number 14 calling for the recruitment of blacks into the army, thereby settling the long-standing debate over the feasibility of arming the nation's blacks who wanted to serve. Earlier, on March 15, Ewell had directed two members of his staff, James West Pegram and Thomas T. Turner, to begin recruiting and organizing two black companies. Within a couple of days General William R. J. Pegram wrote to congratulate his brother on creating the "Corps D' Afrique." Some of the blacks in Pegram's

outfit were immediately "marched through Richmond to the entrenchments." At least one scholar of note argues that none of the black troopers
"ever saw action," but there appears little argument that some of them, if
led by other officers, were observed guarding Ewell's wagon trains during
the march for Sailor's Creek. As startled onlookers commented on the presence of blacks among Ewell's fleeing forces, one of their officers identified
them as "the only company of colored troops in the Confederate service."[31]

"About the middle of February," reads Ewell's report, he received a
direct order from Lee to burn all tobacco and cotton in the city to keep
them from enemy hands. This widely available report, in several archival
collections as well as the *Southern Historical Papers* and the *Official Records,*
not only set the tone for Ewell's movements until the final pullout but also
presents the modern reader with a firsthand account of his decisions. Lee
later moderated his ironclad edict to say that "tobacco and cotton must be
moved, and in case of necessity, burned." This was serious stuff—Lee clearly
began to anticipate the loss of Richmond, the capital he had striven for
nearly three years to maintain. "My correspondence with the [War] Department will show the extreme difficulties under which we have labored
during the past year to keep this army furnished with necessary supplies,"
Lee informed Secretary Breckinridge on March 9 when he presented his
overall assessment of the army. One month before his surrender, Lee continued: "The difficulty is increased, and it seems almost impossible to
maintain our present position with the means at the disposal of the government." Amid the growing alarm, Ewell, who became increasingly concerned that firing Richmond warehouses to keep government supplies from
the Yankees might lead to a disastrous conflagration, told Breckinridge
two weeks earlier that "including the negroes at the hospitals," he could
muster just one thousand men "within an hour's notice to defend the city."[32]

The glory days of 1861–1863, until the failure at Gettysburg, were
long gone. Plans to abandon the beloved Richmond spelled an end to the
great work Robert E. Lee and Stonewall Jackson had done in holding back
the flood tide through the early months of the war. The abolitionist juggernaut could not be halted or diverted by Lee's desertion-infested regiments. Although many have fostered the notion that the Confederate
enterprise "did not will hard enough and long enough to win," and though
many were leaving the army nightly, and not only in Virginia, the Army of
Northern Virginia was overwhelmed by the raw brute force of the enemy.
Ironically, Ewell, whose rise to corps command came on Jackson's demise,
had spent most of his tenure at Lee's side during the era of decline; and

now, with thousands of men readying themselves for the last march, Ewell had his wife on an errand to secure their personal wealth. Others would live out their days in virtual poverty—his fellow corps leader, Richard H. Anderson, was even reduced to day labor during Reconstruction—but not so Ewell.[33]

Ere that, Ewell, according to his own account, was preoccupied during February and March with Lee's instruction for his eventual departure; interestingly, his final report was written by his stepson nine months after the cessation of hostilities. Upon getting Lee's mandate, Ewell wrote, "I immediately sent Major Brown of my staff, to Mayor [John] Mayo with the document, and requested him to call a meeting of the common council to give their opinion as to the measures proper to be taken." Almost from the beginning, voices were raised against the burning out for fear that a general inferno might engulf the capital. Ewell, who had gained some of his old vitality, went about the city "piping in his thin voice and giving orders with the quaint gestures that won him the sobriquet 'the woodcock.'" In rapid order he issued at least two circulars addressed to the "merchants and owners of cotton and tobacco" as he rode through Richmond accompanied by a tobacco wholesaler who was likewise a member of the city council. After a personal examination of all facilities, Ewell informed Secretary Breckinridge on February 26 that "the warehouses where leaf tobacco is stored" could be burned without difficulty. Those with "manufactured tobacco will require preparation and some days to collect it." Ewell rejected an offer from the ordnance authorities to furnish a quantity of turpentine to assist the fire—too volatile, he said.[34]

As Ewell prepared a return to his Chaffin's Bluff headquarters, he drafted a requisition for horses and new buggy; he likewise drew an order on government stores to supply Mrs. Susan Hoge, wife of the Episcopal minister, and her family with "a barrel of flour and potatoes." Even the departmental commander, however, could not secure anything "in the shape of horse flesh" for her to escape the city. But the watching and waiting came to a close when Ewell's old subordinate John Brown Gordon spearheaded an attack on Fort Stedman at the northernmost reaches of Lee's lines opposite the Federal entrenchments. President Davis insisted upon one last offensive in hope that Grant's advance might be checked, or at least slowed down. After an initial success, a Yankee counterattack under John F. Hartranft, later governor of Pennsylvania, drove Gordon and his men from the field with considerable loss. General Humphreys put the causalities at: Federals, two thousand; Confederate, four thousand. Worse still, on the following morning, March 26, Lee sent an urgent communiqué to Jefferson Davis: it was time to consider the abandonment of Richmond.[35]

The next attempt to check the onslaught came at the westernmost extent of the opposing lines at a place forever inscribed on the American psyche called Five Forks—the last significant battle of the Civil War. Phil Sheridan had returned from the Shenandoah two days after the fiasco at Fort Stedman to reinforce Grant along the Petersburg entrenchments. Although George Pickett, commanding about nineteen thousand around Five Forks, attempted to move on Dinwiddie Court House as a foil to Sheridan on the night of March 31, he was driven back. A combined assault by Sheridan, Gouverneur K. Warren, and Ranald S. Mackenzie on April 1 caused the entire Confederate right to collapse, with the loss of four thousand prisoners. Ewell, at Chaffin's, received quick orders to gather his local troops and to march down the Charles City Road for a linkup with Longstreet. Additional Federal assaults east of Five Forks in the early hours of April 2 by Ord, Wright, and Humphreys not only led to the death of A. P. Hill but also drove many Confederates back on Petersburg itself. And though Longstreet managed to hold two small forts—Gregg and Whitworth—Lee was obliged to send his famous message to the president: "I think it is absolutely necessary that we should abandon our position tonight. I have given all the necessary orders on the subject to the troops, and the operation, though difficult, will be performed successfully." He sent an equally poignant appeal to Secretary Breckinridge at 10:40 A.M.: "I see no prospect of doing more than holding our position here till night. I am not certain that I can do that."[36]

At ten o'clock on that fateful Sunday morning Ewell received an urgent message from one of his staff officers: Please return to the city! That was about the time the Reverend Charles Minningrode's sermon was interrupted at St. Paul's Episcopal Church by the arrival of Lee's notice. "I happened to sit in the rear of the president's pew so near that I plainly saw the sort of gray pallor that came upon his face as he read a scrap of paper thrust into his hand by a messenger hurrying up the middle aisle," recalled Mrs. Burton Harrison, wife of Jefferson Davis's secretary. "With stern lips and his usual quick military tread, he left the church, a number of people rising in their seats and hastening after him, those who were left swept by a universal tremor of alarm." Instant pandemonium gripped the metropolis. Another lady, Mrs. Fannie Miller, "a copyist" in the war office, observed citizens of every station and gender rushing about the streets grabbing what provender they could for the coming invasion. "Delicately raised ladies were seen with sheets and shawls filled with, Provisions, etc., even boxes of tobacco," she wrote after the war. "I remember one lady showing as many as one dozen boxes of tobacco, a foot or more square, she had carried from some factory on Cary Street to her home on Franklin, and she was a delicate woman." Accounts abound that Richmond erupted in an orgy of looting and mayhem when word got out that Lee's Petersburg defenses could not long contain the enemy. "Before dismissing his congregation the rector announced that General Ewell had summoned the local forces to meet for defense of the city at three in the afternoon," Mrs. Harrison added. "We knew then that Longstreet's regulars must have been suddenly called away, and a sick apprehension filled our hearts."[37]

By the time Ewell arrived from Mrs. Chaffin's, chaos had taken control of the once-dignified capital of the Southern Confederacy. Ewell must have shared Mrs. Harrison's fears, because he quickly summoned Joseph Brevard Kershaw to move his division into the city from Fort Gilmer. The question arises: Did Ewell give the order to fire the tobacco and cotton warehouses, creating an inferno that destroyed much of Richmond, or were the flames ignited by unchecked mobs rampaging through city streets? In an 1871 letter Benjamin S. Ewell told his brother to take the stance that the Confederate government had sanctioned the burnings. During the crisis of April 1865, when all kinds of people, including Josiah Gorgas and Mayor Mayo, objected to setting the warehouses on fire, Secretary Breckinridge reportedly told one delegation to his office he "didn't give a damn if every house in Richmond was consumed, the warehouses must be burned." Although the decision to destroy four storage facilities stood— "the Public Warehouse near the Petersburg railroad depot, Shockoe Warehouse in the center of the business district close to the Gallego flour mills, and Mayo and Dibrell's warehouses on Cary Street"—at least two modern scholars, Emory Thomas and Rembert W. Patrick, argue persuasively that no one can assign "responsibility for burning the stores."[38]

When Ewell filed his official report several months after the war and the possibility of legal action loomed on the horizon, he was circumspect in his choice of words: "A mob of both sexes, and colors soon collected and about 3 A.M., set fire to some of the buildings on Cary Street and began to plunder the city." "By daylight, Ewell continues, "the riot was subdued, but many buildings which I carefully directed should be spared, had been fired by the mob." His willingness to pass the blame upon a nebulous rabble was supported by Kershaw, who posted his own report in October 1865, two months before Ewell: "I detached two battalions to suppress the mob engaged in sacking the city." Before Kershaw's arrival on the scene, Captain Clement Sulivane notes that his local defense forces, "numbered fewer than 200 men," primarily from desertion, tried to control the surging crowds. Although neither Ewell nor Brown came right out and said that he gave the go-ahead to fire the commodity storehouses, another modern scholar, Ervin Jordan, suggests that some of the black troops "received orders to burn military warehouses in Richmond to prevent their falling into the hands of the enemy." General Godfrey Weitzel, one of the first Federal officers to enter the city, said it was his understanding that the great burning spread from warehouses ignited on Ewell's specific orders. "Weitzel's intelligence agrees with the account of Emmie Sublett, a thirteen-year-old girl who lived close enough to the area of the fire to know of its origin," posits historian Emory Thomas. "She wrote to a friend that the fire began about three or a little earlier and raged furiously; you know the warehouses and some of the public buildings were set on fire, from which the others caught."[39]

The last Confederates sped across the remaining open roadway, the Mayo Bridge, which was fired by tar barrels surrounded by pine knots on the morning of April 3 to cover their exodus. Ewell avows that all rebel troops had departed by 7:00 A.M. Eleven days later, when he was in Washington on his way to a Northern prison with Ewell, Campbell Brown wrote a brief account about the events of April. As Ewell sat with some of his staff above the James at Manchester watching the consuming inferno, he called out in the hearing of all: "I recommended to the Sec. Of War not to have the tobacco in the city fired. If I could have had my way it never would have been done." Later, according to Brown, "he mentioned that he had prevailed so far as to keep the Tredegar Works from being burned." In a brief postscript, Brown added that the mob had set the arsenal aflame and that most of the fire had spread from it.[40]

Benjamin S. Ewell entered the fray with a letter to the *Richmond Whig* dated April 1865 in which he maintained that his brother had no discretion in the burnings—that he was merely acting on orders from the government. He was yet using the same argument in 1871 shortly before his brother's death. Six years after the war Benjamin warned Ewell that it was "quixotic folly for you to be willing to submit to the odium of what I knew you disapproved, and what was foolish, outrageous, and in the bargain, very unnecessary." When Ewell continued his silence about his role in the withdrawal, Ben told him further: "I can and will testify if you do not, but I can't give so direct a story." In 1865, however, Lizzie

Ewell wrote to her favorite uncle, assuring him that by April 14 the Yankees had reestablished order throughout Richmond in a quiet and orderly fashion.[41]

After his short pause on the high ground at Manchester, Ewell led his
small band south toward Chesterfield; Custis Lee, who joined his chief on
April 3, crossed the James by a pontoon bridge at Drewry's Bluff. From the
Mayo Bridge Ewell's troops advanced southeast on Hull Street (present
Route 360), which crosses the state to Danville on the North Carolina
border after passing through Amelia Court House and Burkeville. After
veering off the main road for the linkup with Lee, Ewell marched straight
toward Amelia Court House and by nightfall had reached the Tomahawk
Church on the Genito Road (present Virginia 10) about ten miles from
the capital. Other parts of the army were also closing on the projected
rendezvous at Amelia Court House: "Little Billy" Mahone, who had been
on station opposite the Bermuda Hundred, was south of Ewell. Gordon,
who brought up the rear, and Longstreet were fresh from the defenses at
Petersburg, and like Ewell, they proceeded north of the Appomattox River.
The Third Corps, under Richard Anderson, stayed south of the river until
April 4 when it spanned the High Bridge near Farmville.[42]

Ewell spent April 4 pushing his troops and wagon trains farther west
on the Genito Road, but, finding the Appomattox River flooded, he was
forced to turn south to the railroad bridge at Mattoax. "When Ewell's column reached the Genito Bridge and found it out, they sent the wagons
accompanying them . . . to Powhatan to join the main train to Paineville,"
writes C. M. Calkins. The train from Richmond under Ewell's charge had
been following a more northerly route along the Midland Trail (present
U.S. 60). After covering the Mattoax Bridge on the Richmond and Danville
Railroad with planking, Ewell was able to cross the river and go into camp
a few miles short of Amelia Court House. Most of April 5 was taken with
attempts to replenish not only Ewell's command but also the remainder of
Lee's dwindling force, which had combined for the trek to join Joseph E.
Johnston in North Carolina. Poor staff work coupled with rain-clogged
roads had rendered the Army of Northern Virginia without provisions and
obliged Lee to call upon local citizenry for the barest supplies. With his
troops and supporting wagons, Ewell wrote in his December missive to
Lee, he left Amelia Court House around 5:00 P.M. and marched "all that
night, but owing to the slow progress of the trains and troops in front, had
only reached Amelia Springs, seven miles off, by 8 a.m." Throughout April 6
heavy cavalry forays by the Federals impeded the advance from 11:00 A.M. to

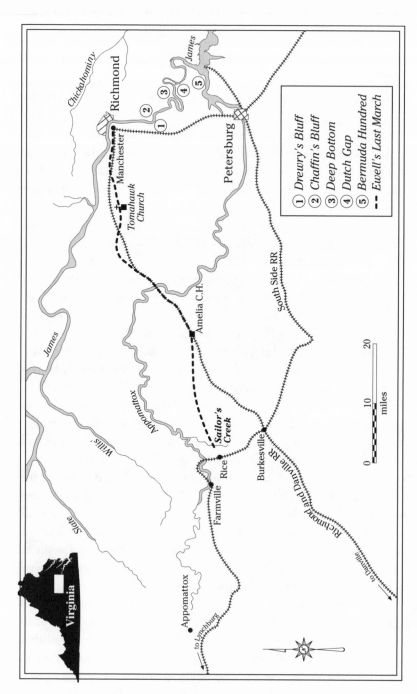

The Road to Sailor's Creek, March-April 1865

Legend:
1 Drewry's Bluff
2 Chaffin's Bluff
3 Deep Bottom
4 Dutch Gap
5 Bermuda Hundred
- - Ewell's Last March

2:00 P.M., although Ewell was able to fall in behind Anderson and travel toward Farmville, with Gordon still bringing up the rear.[43]

Upon reaching the nondescript stream known as Sailor's Creek, which flows northward into the Appomattox, Ewell encountered his final enemy.[44] The last order he ever received from Lee directed him to follow Anderson's corps and to protect the trains as far as possible. Sheridan's cavalry had continually crowded Ewell and Gordon since Amelia Springs, and Ewell's devotion to his supply wagons unquestionably contributed to his slow progress during much of the sixth. "Later in the day I got to the ground overlooking Sailor's Creek where there was a block owing to the convergence of trains and a narrow passage over the creek on a rickety bridge," F. M. Colston noted later. "General Ewell was there and told me to make the wagons double up, saying, 'if we don't get away from here they will all be captured.'" When Colston glanced back down the hill, he "saw the enemy setting fire to our wagons."[45]

Ewell reached the crest beyond the creek, now a Virginia state park, without his trains and no artillery. And he was left to face the enemy alone when Gordon, still in the rear, at the last moment decided not to follow him across the creek but to march to his right and head for Farmville. "This sudden change of direction on his part as soon as his column passed, turned the enemy in at once on Ewell's rear, and there was some fighting around the Hillsman House before the crossing of the creek was successfully completed," noted a battle participant. The Hillsman home, dating from the eighteenth century and now a visitor's center maintained by the state of Virginia, dominated the battleground on the eastern side of the creek; it shortly became a field hospital for the Federals. Gordon admits in his postwar memoir that a gap opened between himself and Ewell that the enemy was quick to exploit. "The overpowering Yankee force," he allows, "soon surrounded the command of that brave old, one-legged hero and forced him to surrender." First, Ewell was subjected to a horrendous bombardment from enemy guns arrayed in front of the Hillsman place about eight-tenths of a mile from his hastily drawn position beyond Sailor's Creek. "My line ran across a little ravine which leads nearly at right angles towards Sailor's Creek," Ewell wrote in his report. "General G. W. C. Lee was on the left, with the naval battalion under Commodore [John R.] Tucker behind his right." Joseph Kershaw's brigade held Ewell's right flank. Richard Anderson, at the crest of the slope, attempted to assist, but his feeble countercharge was broken in moments without success.[46]

Gordon and Anderson managed to escape Grant's noose, although

Ewell's thirty-five hundred men, overwhelmed by more than thirty thousand Federals, were able to put up a stiff resistance. W. L. Timberlake, one of his troopers, recalled that Ewell nearly rode over him "as I was lying down in the grass sharpshooting at the Yankees across the creek." The marksman had a "splendid blue-barreled Enfield rifle and plenty of the best English ammunition." Some of Ewell's men threw up a crude rail barrier in front of their positions, but a number of participants attest to the quickness of his rout. Ewell's contingent of the once proud Army of Northern Virginia, now numbering a total thirty thousand men to withstand Grant's more than one hundred thousand, was nearly starved as well as hopelessly outnumbered. "On riding past my left I came suddenly upon a strong line of the enemy's skirmishers advancing upon my left rear," Ewell wrote. "This closed the only avenue of escape, as shells and even bullets were crossing each other from front and rear over my troops and my right was completely enveloped."[47]

Ewell realized that events had reached a climax. He located a Federal cavalry officer, according to Brown's version of events, and surrendered "to prevent the useless loss of life." The actual capitulation took place near a private home on the road to Rice Station. Although Ewell said later that he gave himself up to a Northern officer, park ranger Christopher M. Calkins has studied the Sailor's Creek affray in a careful detail and offers a different account: "Some of the Federals who were receiving Kershaw's surrender did not stop there. Members of the 5th Wisconsin skirmish line advanced to the main Confederate element, and, reaching the vicinity of Swep Marshall's house, made prisoners of General Ewell and part of his staff. Sergeant Angus Cameron of Company A, 5th Wisconsin, was given credit along with five others for capturing the famous general 'Baldy Dick' Ewell." Nearby, Custis Lee was also taken prisoner by two privates from the 121st New York and 37th Massachusetts. Out of 6,000 troops at the time he left Richmond, Ewell avowed, 2,800 were taken prisoner, and about 150 killed and wounded: "The difference of over 3,000 was caused mainly by the fatigued days' and nights' of almost constant marching, the last two days with nothing to eat. Before our capture I saw men eating raw fresh meat as they marched in the ranks." Douglas Southall Freeman estimates Gordon's losses at 1,700, with the combined total for Anderson and Ewell at 6,000. "With the killed and wounded counted in, the day had cost Lee not less than 7,000 and perhaps 8,000 men."[48]

The disaster at Sailor's Creek that wreaked havoc on roughly one-fifth of the army had been caused in part by the wagon trains left in Ewell's charge. Although Freeman, dean of Confederate historians, offers the observation that the trains hampered Ewell's progress, "as there was no way to be rid of the wagons because the roads were so few," several Northern writers contend otherwise. The Maine schoolman and Yankee hero at Gettysburg, Joshua Chamberlain, argues that Lee showed poor generalship on April 6 by insisting the trains be salvaged—that had he not done so "he might have been able to move rapidly enough to make a junction with Johnston at Danville, or at least, to reach the mountains of Lynchburg." At Rice Station, almost within sight of the Sailor's Creek battleground, Longstreet did nothing to help Ewell as he waited in place throughout the sixth for "Anderson, Ewell, and Gordon to unite with him." "They were covering the trains, but notwithstanding their efforts, the greater part of them were destroyed," General Humphreys continues. "Ewell's whole force was lost together with nearly half of Gordon's, all in an useless effort to save the trains." His men were exhausted and starving as he sought to comply with Lee's last order regarding the trains and their supplies. Attentive though he was during his last campaign of the war, Ewell was unable to comply with the commanding general's wishes.[49]

Chapter 15

"NOT MY WILL, BUT THINE BE DONE"

When Ewell was captured at Sailor's Creek along with six other general officers—J. B. Kershaw, G. W. Custis Lee, Eppa Hunton, Seth W. Barton, Dudley M. DuBose, and Montgomery D. Corse—as well as Commodore John Randolph Tucker, he was taken to Grant's headquarters. General Gouverneur K. Warren told him that his force had been surrounded by thirty thousand Federals, which served to bolster his spirits—he had been right in his decision to surrender his hopelessly outnumbered contingent. After a miserable, snowy night near the battlefield, Ewell and his compeers caught up with Grant "at Nottoway Junction—the junction of the Richmond and Danville and Norfolk and Western Roads." It was near the area where, thirty-four years earlier, Nat Turner had unleashed his bloody revolt that put the fear of black insurrection into the souls of white Southerners. "We were conducted to a big log fire at General Grant's headquarters," remembered Eppa Hunton, who grew hostile toward Ewell in the days following Sailor's Creek. "Grant was at the front, but quite a few of his staff officers were present. We had not been there long before hot whiskey punch was handed around. At night a residence in the little village was taken by one of Grant's staff officers and all of the captured generals were sent to this house for the night." In spite of Grant's later assertion that Ewell thought the war was over before Sailor's Creek, there is no indication of a meeting between the two antagonists. Moreover, Ewell had lost all contact with Lee, who was pushing the sad remnants of his army toward the rendezvous at Appomattox.[1]

Isolated as he was, Ewell remained the senior prisoner of war when the party left on April 8. General officers were allowed to travel in ambu-

338

lances, although several fit members of the group traded off walking so that junior officers and disabled men might ride for brief interludes. "It must have taken us three or four days to make the march of fifty miles to Petersburg," writes McHenry Howard, a Marylander accompanying Ewell and the rest. "The day before we got there, some Union general met us on the road (I think it was Major-General Hartranft) and taking General Custis Lee aside, had a conversation with him." While the young Lee was asked if he knew his invalid mother had died, Eppa Hunton employs a different remembrance of events: "[T]he officer said, 'General Lee, I am directed to inform [you] that your mother is dying in Richmond; I have brought your parole, and you are ordered to mount this horse and go to her immediately.'"[2]

Hunton avows the encounter took place in Petersburg, while Howard says it was a during the march. "Custis Lee was unselfish and generous hearted," Hunton continues. "He said he could not leave his fellow prisoners, but must share the hardships of their prison life with them. We said to him at once, 'General, don't hesitate to leave us. Go to your ill mother.' He finally mounted the horse and went to his mother, saying that he would join us as soon as his mother got better." Outwardly Ewell exhibited no ill will toward Custis Lee, who lived until 1913 (his mother died in 1873), because of the plot "on the part of his old army friends and West Point classmates to avoid sending him to prison." In his final report to Robert E. Lee after the war, he went to extraordinary lengths to paint his son in a favorable light. "I deem it proper to remark that the discipline preserved in camp and on the march by General G. W. C. Lee and the manner in which he handled his troops in action, fully justified the request I had made for his promotion."[3]

Ewell learned about Lee's surrender at Appomattox on April 9 as he made his way toward Petersburg on the first leg of his journey to incarceration at historic Fort Warren in Boston Harbor. He also learned that Grant's liberal stance toward the defeated army—officers and men were paroled to return to their homes, commissioned officers could keep their sidearms, and all men could retain privately owned horses and mules—did not apply to himself or Campbell Brown. As a Yankee prisoner who had the misfortune to capitulate hours before the generous provisions extended to Lee's troopers, he found himself beyond the pale. Early on, Lee recognized the difficulties imposed on those not covered by the Federal blanket, and as early as April 25 he made a personal appeal to Grant. After asking that men captured on the march from Petersburg be offered "the same terms" as those who surrendered at Appomattox, he continued: "I see no benefit that will result by retaining them in prison; but, on the contrary, think that good may be accomplished by returning them to their homes. Indeed, if all now held prisoners of war were liberated in the same manner I think it would be advantageous. Should there, however, be objections to this course, I would ask that exceptions be made in favor of invalid officers and men." Lee singled out Ewell as an officer in need of relief, but the latter was still a prisoner and would remain in Federal custody for several weeks, even months, after the war. Although Grant later corresponded with Lee to clarify the terms given at Appomattox, he did not respond to the specific request that men taken before April 9 be paroled.[4]

If Eppa Hunton is to be believed, Ewell did not ingratiate himself with his fellow Confederates on the northward trek. Hunton, a Virginia lawyer, who had been wounded during Pickett's Charge at Gettysburg and who served in both the U.S. House of Representatives and Senate after the war, was in Ewell's company throughout his imprisonment. On the next leg, which took them to City Point on the James, Ewell encountered several of his West Point classmates, and "he seemed bent on making himself popular with them," Hunton writes. "He told the officer he was talking with that our troops had devastated Yankee territory more than the Yankees had devastated ours. I said, 'General Ewell, you know that is not true. Will you tell me that what Yankee territory we devastated more than the Valley of Virginia was devastated by the Federal forces?'" According to Hunton, Ewell broke off the conversation without an answer.

> The next squad we met General Ewell told them that he admitted that our government had been cruel to the Yankee prisoners. I told him that he knew that was not true; that while Yankees had fared very badly at our hands, they fared just as well as our own soldiers. That we had called upon the Federal Government over and over again to exchange them. The fact that they were prisoners on our hands was due to the refusal of the Federal Government to exchange prisoners. It was Grant's policy to keep out of the Confederate army all the men he could.

Hunton appeared particularly miffed that Ewell had armed himself with "500–600 dollars" before his capture. Although Ewell's boyhood friend was sick with an open fistula, Ewell refused to offer Hunton any help whatsoever in the way of food or room accommodations. George Armstrong Custer, who had been instrumental in the capture of both men, intervened when Ewell declined to assist his comrade. Hunton speculates that Ewell "was thoroughly whipped and seemed to be dreadfully demoralized."[5]

Ewell's sister Rebecca, who died in 1867 at age sixty, had possession of several papers belonging to Lizinka in Washington/Georgetown and told her not to worry—that she was "carrying them in her pocket." Toiling to retain control of her property in St. Louis and Nashville, Lizinka was understandably anxious for news about her husband and son. Ewell's capture with the other generals had been widely reported in the newspapers, but detailed, personal information was lacking. On the eighteenth, Thomas T. Gantt, her attorney in St. Louis and her kinsman through marriage, wrote to report: "From the information just recd, we feel perfectly certain that both Campbell and Tom Turner were taken with Dick Ewell and they are with him still. As to the duration of their confinement it is useless to hazard a conjecture." Gantt felt the assassination of Abraham Lincoln was sure to "complicate matters." Two days later Lizinka got word from Harriet through others that Campbell Brown was all right when they saw him in Washington and that "Cousin Richard looked well but thin." Rebecca was able, Harriet said, to get them "clothes and refreshments."[6]

As Ewell made his way toward imprisonment, Lizzie wrote on the thirteenth confirming that the family knew he was all right and that he was accompanied by Campbell Brown and Tom Turner; she also sent the hope that his "captivity may not be of long duration." When Ewell's party reached City Point at the mouth of the Appomattox, many of the common soldiers and lesser officers, including Tom Turner, were separated from the generals. A good many of these men, several black troopers among them, were paroled and sent home. From the James, Ewell was placed aboard a steamer that sailed out into Chesapeake Bay and up the Potomac to Washington. "In the afternoon of Good Friday, April 14, we left the steamboat and marched to the Provost Marshall's [sic] office on Pennsylvania Avenue, where I suppose our sorts and conditions were noted down," reads the account of McHenry Howard. Although Campbell Brown was able to break away for a visit with Rebecca Ewell, Ewell himself remained close to the other officers on Pennsylvania Avenue. Members of the family around Washington and Georgetown could do little to help or pay visits because of the shortness of their stay. After less than a day in Washington, Ewell, Brown, and twelve other general officers were placed aboard a northward-bound train.[7]

"We left for Fort Warren, Boston harbor, that night at dusk, and Lincoln was assassinated that same night at half-past nine o'clock," notes

Eppa Hunton. The unsettling events in Ford's Theater as the triumphant president watched a play called "Our American Cousin" not only altered the course of American history but also made an impact on Ewell's journey. Emotions ran high throughout the country, and nowhere more than among antislavery strongholds in New York and New England—the very countryside that lay between Washington and Massachusetts. After a night ride from the capital and a hearty breakfast in New York, throngs of riled-up loyalists met Ewell and his companions at every depot with threats of mayhem. "One man jumped on the train, and rode sixty miles, just to jump out at every station and cry 'Hang Them.'" It made no difference that Ewell was one of the first Confederates to speak out against the president's murder—the threats continued. When the train rolled into Providence, Rhode Island, "'three groans for Ewell' were called for and men armed themselves with stones to stone the car in which he was sitting," writes his stepdaughter. "General Kershaw and my brother called the attention of the conductor to this, and to save life he called to the crowd that they were nothing but blockade runners and started the car ahead of schedule and thus got to Fort Warren in safety." The Boston authorities in charge of Ewell, afraid of more trouble, "telegraphed ahead to order conveyances held in readiness," Hunton says, "and we were rushed into the hacks and driven at full speed to the wharf." The boat ride across the bay went off without incident.[8]

Like all prisons, Fort Warren was not an inviting place, although the officers in charge struggled to accommodate its inmates within the parameters of confinement. It was situated on George's Island, one of several islands that dot Boston Harbor. Nearby is Governor's Island, which had been the home of John Winthrop before his death in 1649. Fort Warren was a massive stone structure about seven miles from the city of Boston, with a damp, forbidding aspect. Constructed during 1833 as part of the coastal defenses, it had been converted to a prisoner-of-war facility at the outbreak of hostilities and received its first Confederate detainees in October 1861. Among the rebels incarcerated there had been sixty-one-year-old Isaac Trimble, Ewell's nemesis at Gettysburg, before he was exchanged in 1864. James M. Mason and John Slidell, Confederate envoys to England and France, were also made prisoners there after the so-called *Trent* affair following their capture aboard a mail packet carrying them to Europe. Confederate Vice President Alexander H. Stephens, who commented upon Ewell's arrival and conditions at the prison, was imprisoned there after his arrest at his Crawford, Georgia, home, as was John H. Reagan.

The Texan Reagan, postmaster general of the Confederacy, had a difficult time at Fort Warren being kept in solitary confinement for several weeks. Ewell had a better time of it when he was assigned to a cell with six messmates: Joseph B. Kershaw, Montgomery D. Corse, Seth M. Barton, Eppa Hunton, and Dudley M. DuBose; several others, including Commodore Tucker and William L. Cabell of Arkansas were housed nearby and enjoyed regular access to his room.[9]

"Major Brown is confined in a different part of the Fort, and though I see him daily no intercourse is allowed," Ewell wrote to Rebecca immediately upon his arrival. "It would be better for both of us, were we together, but there is no authority here." Rebecca quickly transcribed the missive for Lizinka on April 18 and hurried it off to St. Louis. The letter also demonstrated that Ewell was mightily agitated about two issues that had plagued him during the journey to Fort Warren: his role in the burning of Richmond and a fear that Lincoln's assassination would cause hard feelings toward him and his fellow prisoners. About the former, he told Becca, "I am abused for burning Richmond. It was burned by the mob." And he elaborated on his previous arguments advanced by Campbell Brown. "There were no troops to keep order. I had told the principal citizens monthly before what would happen and urged them to have a constabulary force to keep order, but they would not . . . I had taken every precaution possible and the people must blame themselves."[10]

Ewell expounded further upon "the performance of that wretch Booth," in an April 16 letter to Ulysses S. Grant. The oft-cited missive, written soon after Ewell was sent to George's Island, originated from his fear of retribution. Before sending it to Grant, Ewell had gathered a number of officers to ponder their positions. "One day when I was asleep on my bed in my room, I was aroused by an unusual commotion, and found that twelve Confederate officers were holding a meeting," says Eppa Hunton. "I inquired what it meant and was surprised and indignant to learn it was a meeting called by General Ewell to declare by resolution that they had no complicity in the assassination of Abraham Lincoln and deplored the act." Hunton, by his own admission, was not only irate but also launched an outburst toward Ewell for introducing such a document—that officers of the Confederacy would stoop to murder. He even asked if Ewell knew where his leg had been buried and, upon getting a negative response, crowed that he "wished to pay honor to that leg, for I had none to pay for the rest of his body."[11]

Undeterred by Hunton's tirade, Ewell kept to his agenda of courting any and all Federal authorities within reach. "[O]f all the misfortunes which could befall the Southern people, or any Southern man, by far the greatest, in my judgment, would be the prevalence of the idea that they could entertain any other feeling than one of unqualified abhorrence and indignation for the assassination of the President of the United States, and the attempt to assassinate the Secretary of State," Ewell wrote in his April 16 appeal to Grant. "No language can adequately express the shock produced upon myself, in common with all the other generals confined here with me, by the appearance of this appalling crime, and by the seeming tendency in the public mind to connect the South and Southern men with it." Ewell concluded his epistle by telling Grant that officers imprisoned at Fort Warren were not "assassins." Although Hunton declares the proclamation was defeated, Ewell informed Grant that fifteen officers, including Hunton, concurred with his letter.[12]

As Ewell, with Campbell Brown's help, was writing letters to gain his release on parole through the summer, Lizinka waged a collateral effort to gain their freedom. Mrs. Ewell indeed was a burdened woman through the spring and summer of 1865; not only was she seeking aid for her husband and son, but she also learned that the amnesty conferred on her by Abraham Lincoln on March 23 had been rescinded for all practical purposes. She had been arrested on April 22 by order of Secretary of War Edwin M. Stanton, her property seized, and was escorted from Nashville to Missouri by a young staff officer belonging to General J. H. Thomas. Upon arriving in St. Louis, Lizinka moved into the home of Thomas T. Gantt until her departure for the east in June. Through the auspices of Gantt, Ewell and his wife were able to establish communications with Missouri politicians Francis P. Blair Jr. and his brother, Montgomery Blair, the latter being Lincoln's postmaster general during much of the war. Their father, Francis Preston Blair, publisher of the influential *Congressional Globe,* had known Lincoln from the 1830s, and during Reconstruction both his sons allied themselves with the new president, Andrew Johnson, because of his lenient stance toward the South. Montgomery Blair quickly joined Gantt in counseling against Lizinka's notion that she and Ewell should go abroad until the political dust settled following Lincoln's assassination. In late May he spoke with Grant, who had given his pledge to speak with President Johnson about a parole for Ewell.[13]

On the very day that Blair worked out a deal with Grant, an anxious Lizinka wrote on her own to the Federal commander, saying that General Ewell's "health is very delicate and the loss of his leg makes his confinement very painful" and unabashedly asking for his release. Ewell and Brown, whose letters goaded his mother to greater exertions, were still separated in late April because of prison regulations to keep general officers apart. "[I]f I could be allowed to be with Gen. Ewell I would be very contented, but I have not seen him in three days," Brown had written on April 13. "His comparative helplessness and the fact that all the Genls confined with him smoke tobacco, which is poison to him, make his case exceptional." Brown announced that no matter the inconvenience he would not leave Fort Warren without his stepfather. That was after Ewell told Becca on May 8: "Campbell and myself are finally in the same part of the Fort and are in a mess with several officers."[14]

The post commandant, Major H. A. Allen, was a North Carolina native who had remained in the Union army and thus incurred the wrath of many Southern prisoners. He and a Lieutenant Woodman, who dealt with Ewell on a daily basis, tried to make his internment as easy as possible, but prisoner Ewell still found himself in want. He was even obliged to ask Becca for a Bible as well as additional clothing and vegetables to augment his diet of "meat and bread." Nevertheless, through it all Ewell was able to retain his "sense of humor." A. H. Stephens, also a prisoner at Fort Warren, noted in his diary for June 14: "Saw General Ewell on his crutches. He was walking on the parapet. I remarked that I thought Ewell had an artificial leg; wonder why he did not use it. Lieut. W[oodman] replied that Ewell said he was waiting to see if the authorities were going to hang him. . . . He intended to wait and make out on his crutches until that matter was decided." Ewell was hesitant, he said, to spend money on a new limb if he was going to be executed.[15]

Matters quickened on May 29 when Andrew Johnson issued his initial amnesty proclamation; he used the pardoning power of the president for individual Southerners. The chief executive, who harbored a deeply held resentment toward the aristocratic Southern "slavocracy" at the same time he rejected civil rights for freedmen, interjected a number of exemptions into his document. Among those denied amnesty and restitution of property were Confederate officers above the rank of colonel as well as all who had resigned as "congressmen, federal judges, or military officers to join the rebellion." Also excluded were "all persons owning taxable property with an estimated value of more than $20,000," which was Johnson's way of humbling purse-proud aristocrats. The category may not technically have applied to Ewell, but it certainly did to his wife. Undaunted, on May 30 Ewell hurried a letter to the president requesting permission to take an oath of allegiance when word of the proclamation percolated through the country. "I am excluded," he said in the brief missive, "as having been educated at the U.S. Military Academy, on account of my rank as lieutenant-general in the Confederate service, and as being now a prisoner of war, and on no other grounds."[16]

When no reply was forthcoming, Brown told his sister, "someone has to go see the President because letter writing won't work." Ewell himself informed Lizinka on June 8 that he was weary of talk about oaths, and even Ben wrote to say he was going to Francis H. Pierpont, Reconstruction governor of Virginia, for help. Finally, in mid-month Ewell had Brown draft an oath, which he sent to Washington on the sixteenth: "I, Richard Ewell do solemnly swear in the presence of Almighty God that I will henceforth faithfully obey the Constitution of the United and the Union of States thereunder." The accompanying letter to the president, similar to the one sent earlier, was extremely short; in it he reiterated that he was in the excepted classes as a West Point graduate and had "resigned an appointment in the U.S. Army."[17]

Lizinka, meanwhile, was pressing her own agenda; convinced that nothing should be done that might upset President Johnson, she felt that Ewell had blundered when he responded to an enlisted man in Minnesota who had served in one of his prewar companies in the west. The fellow had written to encourage him while in prison, but Ewell seized the opportunity to broadcast his reasons for joining the Confederacy in 1861. Ewell's letter, given to the press by its recipient in an effort to help him, roused some negative comment when the *New York Herald* headlined his rejoinder as "Ewell's Reasons for Leaving the Old Flag." Lizinka, still in St. Louis under house arrest, appealed to General John Pope—Ewell's onetime adversary at Groveton when he lost his leg—for permission to visit Washington and the east. Pope, commanding at St. Louis, responded that he had no authority to alter a war department decree, but he forwarded her request and offered to help in any way he might. Growing anxious and apparently acting on her own, on June 20 Lizinka dispatched a letter directly to the White House, despite a warning from Benjamin Ewell that it was unwise to pester Johnson. After rehashing Ewell's poor health and diet, she told the president: "I am too restless and miserable to be quiet, and I appeal to you as a weak woman to a strong man, and entreat you by all that makes life dear to give me back my husband and child." Her desperation was evident when she added that she would hate him "if Richard dies in Fort Warren." Whether it was happenstance, Pope's intervention, or her hasty letter to the White House, Lizinka received the following telegram: "The President is willing for Mrs. Ewell to visit Washington or go further North or wherever she pleases except the State of Tennessee."[18]

Lizinka at last had her meeting with Andrew Johnson on June 28 after a hurried train ride across the country. Harriet Turner's charming account of the encounter for a national magazine has it taking place in the presidential bedroom. Johnson, who pleaded an indisposition, asked her about Campbell Brown and other family members but refused to release her husband. Permission to visit Fort Warren was also denied. Lizinka and her daughter thought the president was recovering from one of his well-publicized drinking bouts—in short, that he was suffering from a hangover. Following a less-than-tasty lunch with Johnson, she "went to see General Grant, whose office was nearby on Seventeenth Street."[19]

Grant was able to give his consent for Lizinka to visit Fort Warren and authorized Brown's release, but he was unable to help with Ewell, although he spent an hour with Johnson arguing for his parole. Lizinka and Harriet traveled north to Wakefield, Rhode Island, but a letter from Ewell dated July 1 told her that she would not enjoy a visit to the island fortress. The rules governing prisoners were just as strict as during the war, he said—boats from the mainland remained only "a few minutes and the meetings were hurried." A recent fall had apparently caused Ewell no discomfort, even though Brown confirmed that his stepfather was suffering from a bout of diarrhea. Brown also warned his mother to do absolutely nothing to compromise the amnesty of March 28 issued by President Lincoln as she sped back to Baltimore and Washington. Harriet, who remained in Wakefield, told her brother that Lizinka was "so sanguine of success that I am almost afraid she will meet with some disappointment." However, the soon-to-be bride of Tom Turner, imprisoned at Johnson's Island, Ohio, was "having a grand time" bathing and taking in the sights. If her mother were successful in Washington, she would come "straight to Boston and bring you both back here," she said. "There is excellent boating and fishing and we can get horses & wagons and drive all over the country."[20]

The good times lay in the future as Ewell wrote to Rebecca on June 28 from Fort Warren asking for foodstuffs, including canned tomatoes and white sugar as well as a length of telegraph wire to make "a gridiron" for his stove. Ewell was still a prisoner of the Federal government, and though he perked up when George A. Trenholm, Confederate secretary of the treasury, was released, he had to wait until July 19 for his own freedom. Meanwhile, Lizinka wrote on the fourteenth to say that she had posted bond for both of them in Washington and playfully added that both husband and son "would have to toe the line when I am your jailer." Then, in quick order, Andrew Johnson gave consent for her to repossess her Nashville property on July 17 and agreed to Ewell's parole two days later to reside in Maryland and Virginia. The formal document, in which Ewell swore to uphold the "Constitution and Government of the United States," was executed on July 19, 1865, before William H. Jeffery, the post adjutant at Fort Warren. It also listed Ewell's personal characteristics: "Light complexion, brown hair, and grey eyes; and he is 5 feet 8 inches high." Strangely, the document, which is still wonderfully preserved in the Library of Congress, says nothing about his age, weight, or physical condition, which was far from good. Nor did it mention his leg amputation. "Walked out as usual," Vice President Stephens jotted on July 19: "Lt. W[oodman] told me he had sent off General Ewell and Major Brown, of Ewell's staff today. Right glad I am that the General, lame as he is, had been discharged."[21]

Lizinka was not ungrateful when she fired off a thank-you note to Johnson for the release of her husband and son, although she "begged" him to free all Confederate prisoners. With Ewell's freedom the reunited family traveled first to Stony Lonesome and then to nearby Warrenton for the marriage of Harriet and Tom Turner in October. All the while Lizinka called on Attorney General James Speed, brother of Joshua Fry Speed, Abraham Lincoln's boyhood chum, as well as others to secure the unfettered return of her properties in Missouri and Tennessee. Thomas Gantt, who pressed her interests in Missouri, was finally able to apprise her that for the payment of $409.85 in court costs the case against her St. Louis property would be dropped. The house in Nashville and her farm in Maury County, Tennessee, were handed back to her later in the year.[22]

Ewell had been correct to worry about the status of her assets before their marriage, and as late as Sailor's Creek, Eppa Hunton thought he was more concerned about "Mrs. Brown's property than the welfare of his officers and men." After considerable discussion among family members, Ewell and his wife resolved to settle on her extensive farmlands near Spring Hill, about thirty miles south of Nashville. "We are packed away like herrings in a barrel, but talk of building a new house," he notified Ben on January 7. Ewell's efforts to employ blacks—whom he insisted on calling "darkies"—on the farm was a far cry from his prewar experiences at Stony Lonesome and, indeed, in the west. "The fact is they are crazy half the time and constantly apparently trying to see if they are really free." Lizinka, he said, had made herself ill trying to persuade "the darkies to do half a day's work" in return for a full wage. Ewell and his wife regained ownership of her property, but they were also confronted with the realities of a changed South.[23]

At first Ewell had misgivings about his new life; nor was he enthusiastic about his neighbors. "I suppose you know we are not in very brilliant society out here," he wrote to Lizzie after the new year. "In fact, there is very little society. The few people seem torpid from the war—except for drinking whiskey, don't do much. I am sick of it—don't see much in the future." But Lizinka and the Browns had a long connection with Spring Hill and Maury County—the second county south of Davidson and the capital at Nashville. She and her first husband, James Percy Brown, had been considered "early settlers in the area," which was located in the very northern reaches of the county. At the outbreak of war in 1861, Lizinka Brown, a widow for seventeen years, had personally "uniformed the Brown guards," a companion company to the "Maury Grays," who saw heavy combat in the Kentucky and Tennessee fighting as well as in the Georgia campaign. After 1865–1866 Lizinka and Ewell, in spite of himself, found many friends and gracious contacts across central Tennessee.[24]

Ewell in effect was a kept man after the war, and, though he did good work in improving her Spring Hill property during 1866–1868, other than suggestions on family matters he found Lizinka and Campbell Brown in charge. And work he did at making the farm a showplace as well as a profitable operation. "I am very busy planting for cotton, but there is no fencing hardly or scarcely any implements of any kind; it is like opening an entirely new farm," he apprised Ben at the end of January. Although he was optimistic that petroleum deposits might be found on the property, Ewell relayed to his brother that he was searching for other moneymaking crops and livestock. Sheep flocks were introduced to the farm along with a string of thoroughbred horses, several of the latter eventually becoming well known across the racing South. "A noted stallion, Brown Hal, and many other famous animals," writes a local historian, sprang from Ewell's efforts. "We are farming with the complaints; cut worms destroyed all of the corn, and the cotton has come up badly, etc., etc.," he observed. And, he added in an April note to Lizzie, "[I] have a good deal of disagreeable feelings at times, stretchy and nervous, that makes me disinclined to do anything." Sick and disenchanted though Ewell and Lizinka were, all was not drudgery; during late 1866 the couple traveled to New Orleans, where they attended banquets and cavorted with a number of prominent Confederates, including Generals Richard Taylor, John Bell Hood, John Brown Gordon, and their wives.[25]

Back at Spring Hill, Ewell wrote to Robert E. Lee, at Lexington, Virginia, endorsing several Tennessee lads for study at venerable old Washington College, now Washington and Lee University. Earlier he had contributed a significant sum to the college, with the stipulation that it be used to supplement Lee's salary as president of the nearly broke institution. Though Lee rejected the scheme out of hand, Ewell kept a lively interest in education throughout the postwar era. He became associated with the Columbia Female Institute, an Episcopal establishment in the Maury County seat at Columbia, from 1866 until his death, at one time serving as president of the school's board of trustees. The girls' academy had been organized in 1835 by two clergymen, the Reverend Leonidas K. Polk and Bishop James H. Otey. President James K. Polk had been an early supporter of the institution, and Leonidas Polk, later Episcopal bishop of Louisiana and Civil War commander, served as its first principal. Some of the school's buildings had burned during the war while it served as a Federal hospital, and in 1866 when a drive was initiated to revive it Lizinka became an early subscriber. The reopened main building resembled an English castle "with a front of 120 feet, three stories high with impressive turrets and windows. It still stands [1955] among fine forest trees on a four-acre elevated lot, an ornament to the whole city."[26]

In September Campbell Brown was married to nineteen-year-old Susan Rebecca Polk after a courtship of several months. Her father, Lucius J. Polk, not to be confused with Confederate General Lucius E. Polk (1833–1893), was another founding member of the Columbia Female Institute and a prominent Episcopalian. Perhaps it was Ewell and Lizinka's connection with the Institute that quickened the union, although Polks had been prominent in Maury County since the 1840s. Like the families of Andrew Jackson and Andrew Johnson, they had crossed the mountains from North Carolina with William Polk (1758–1834), who became a major land speculator and owner in middle Tennessee. The Brown-Polk marriage was a happy occasion for the family, and the new bride, who lived until 1922, was universally described as a gracious, accomplished lady. Brown and his wife named their first child, born in 1867, Lucius after her father, but the second, who arrived in 1870, was christened Richard Ewell Brown. More children followed after Brown moved his fledgling family into an adjoining farm of seven hundred acres purchased in 1871. After a stint in the Tennessee House of Representatives (1877–1879) and service with several community organizations, Campbell Brown died in July 1893 at age fifty-three.[27]

While Ewell labored to improve the farm throughout 1867, he received some spirit-lifting news in a letter from Ben, who was going around the country soliciting funds for the rebuilding of the College of William and Mary. The old institution, like the Columbia Female Institute, had suffered heavily during the conflict, and, due to the uncertainties of Reconstruction, had few students. Although Ben had difficulty getting money out of the "gothamites," he found New York full of pretty girls who thought he was General Richard S. Ewell—he even attempted "to walk a little lame" in order to "take advantage of the mistake." Best of all, he told Ewell, he enjoyed a kindly reputation among New Yorkers as a "galant." Another letter from Williamsburg was neither playful nor uplifting. It brought word that Becca had passed away on August 9 "after an illness of over a week." Rebecca Lowndes Ewell, born in 1810, the eldest of Ewell's brothers and sisters, had been his lifelong friend and confidant. He agreed with Ben that "another old link is broken, who was a true relative that cared more for us than she did for herself."[28]

In spite of his toil, which led to eventual success of the Spring Hill property, 1867 was not a good year for Ewell. Campbell Brown, traveling in the east, advised Lizinka that she should invest at least forty thousand dollars in European stocks and to sell off some of her unproductive lands; the latter scheme, he argued, "would be much less expense on the farms." Ewell was pleased to learn that Lizzie was returning with him for a stay at Spring Hill and to plan her forthcoming marriage to a young Virginian named Beverly S. Scott. That the family had money was obvious when Brown informed his mother that he was going to Williamsburg from Charlottesville, where he had been a student at the University of Virginia Law School shortly after the war. All the time, he was staying in the very best accommodations. Brown's party, he wrote, "would probably go straight on to Canada from Balto, & do our visiting on return—coming on to Balto—thence to Charleston by steamer, on to Louisville by rail."[29]

The continued outlay of money likewise interfered with Ewell's hope that he could move back to Virginia. When Ben sounded him out about acquiring a tract of land in the Tidewater, he responded bluntly and with an aura of resigned disappointment: "The truth is Mrs. Ewell has made such large expenditures this year—$25,000 to Harriet & 15,000 that she owes Campbell that funds are not on hand." Lizinka was apparently concerned if Tom Turner could "be trusted" within the family so that funds directed to Harriet were intended "to buy out" her share in the Mississippi property at Melrose Plantation. "This place [Spring Hill] has required large expenditures in its development that have hardly begun to give returns." Ewell confessed a fondness for the Peninsula of Virginia and told Ben at year's end that if he could get "this place" on a sound footing, he would "use his money to purchase a tidewater farm."[30]

Robert E. Lee, still overseeing "his boys" in Lexington, sent a note of good cheer in early 1868, which undoubtedly heartened Ewell. But his Tennessee affairs continued to flag. Although details are sketchy from the archival record, Tom Turner and Harriet did not approve of Brown's handling of Lizinka's fiscal affairs. When Lizinka left Spring Hill for a visit to the Turner home in St. Louis, Ewell found himself alone and brooding at the farm. Brown, then residing in Nashville, visited Ewell several times during 1868 and promptly wrote to his mother behind Ewell's back: "I have just come from Spring Hill—and having while there been a good deal bothered by the contumacy of your better half." Ewell, he told Lizinka, talked incessantly of moving to Virginia—he did not want to live in Tennessee. "I would not be here one minute if it were not for your mother," Ewell had informed him, and asked Brown to move to the farm and assume its daily operations. Brown told him he might be able to spare three days a week from his chores in Nashville, but when the scheme was rejected, Brown carped to Lizinka that he was going to take his "wife and child" and leave the state.[31]

The family rift had not disappeared three weeks later when Brown relayed news of a renewed encounter at Spring Hill. Ewell, deprived of Lizinka's company as well as Campbell Brown's, had reached the boiling point:

> On talking . . . to the Gen'l about the plan of moving to Va., he expressed a good deal of irritation at my idea that his wishes should be consulted in the matter at all—saying that the project of moving was entirely mine—was revived by me—and used the expression "that the dearest wish of his heart" two years ago was to settle in Va., but that you would not hear of it—and that he wanted one thing settled, and he *would have* understood—that the project must not be attributed to any wish to please him—that his wishes were not *then* consulted, and he would not have them *now* consulted, & he would not now make them an ostensible reason.

And Brown added: "The amount of the matter is that he is full of pain at his position—that I think he holds me as to some extent to blame for the present talk of moving." According to Brown, Ewell decided against a solitary return to Stony Lonesome and Virginia because the harvest season was approaching and it would be imprudent for him to leave. Brown, however, made another trip east to check out his prospects in Richmond, and by late summer he and "Sussie" had traveled to Cobb's Island, a resort off the Atlantic coast of the Delmarva Peninsula, where he wrote to his mother: "You and Gen'l Ewell would spend a week or ten days very pleasantly here."[32]

Instead of going to Virginia, Ewell remained at Spring Hill and turned his attention to Washington County, Mississippi, where he leased a plantation of several hundred acres along the Mississippi River from a man named Robert M. Carter. Lizinka and her son had had a long association with the area, and Brown himself, after helping refurbish his mother's Tennessee property, farmed "Melrose" in neighboring Bolivar County, a few miles north of Ewell's rented place at Tarpley. Their Mississippi agent, Charles I. Field, who presumably facilitated Ewell's initial interest in the new cotton venture, had been an associate of James Percy Brown (1812–1844) before the war. The elder Brown—Lizinka's first husband and father of Campbell Brown—and Field served together on the Bolivar County Levee Board prior to the former's death at age thirty-two; later, Field was a longtime chairman of the board, charged with laying taxes for upkeep of Mississippi River levees, as well as chairman of the county police board. Washington and Bolivar Counties abutted the river, with its myriad oxbows and channels, midway between Memphis and Vicksburg. The Washington County seat at Greenville, across the river from Chicot County, Arkansas, was very near Ewell's new farming operations and the center of his and Campbell Brown's lives for much of 1869–1870. Melrose, cultivated by Brown, had been inherited from his father, although a parcel of the land had been sold to a man named Alexander Yerger, whose wife was Elizabeth Brown Rucks, a distant relative. During the war, much of the plantation had been ravaged by Union forces, including destruction of the cotton gin and several buildings.[33]

The whole purpose of Ewell's Mississippi project was the production of cotton as a moneymaking operation. At the same time he left for Mississippi, Brown helped him introduce several prime Kentucky sheep onto the Spring Hill farm. For the time being Ewell's focus was on Tarpley and not Tennessee. He did not return home for Christmas but found himself in Jackson, Mississippi, ninety-five miles southeast of Greenville, on his way to New Orleans. His journey was designed to raise cotton money for Tarpley, although he had dispatched $350 of his own funds to the manager at Melrose to "keep it running" before his departure. A December letter to Brown, with whom the old differences had been patched over, complained about the difficulty of hiring field hands to work his cotton. Brown, who was in Nashville but preparing to move his family to Mississippi, received a bit of advice from the Confederate general-turned-cotton farmer: "If you raise 50 bales you will be forced to have a gin & if you fail to raise any a gin will make the place easier to rent or sell. I think under any point of view I would put up the gin as soon as convenient & not as proposed to wait to see [if] the crop is in."[34]

Ewell sent an undated letter to Brown from the packet *Mary Houston* during his return from New Orleans; he had enjoyed a lengthy conversation with General Peter B. Starke, also aboard the packet, about farming, although Ewell was mostly concerned with renewing his lease on Tarpley with a five-thousand-dollar loan he had secured in Louisiana. However, if the owners refused to repair the levees, he was planning to "decline the whole business & work in Tenn." Ewell was optimistic that his 1870 crop would fetch ten thousand dollars when picked and sold. Upon his return to Mississippi after the New Year, he was obviously near Brown at Melrose, and his correspondence for this period is rushed and seldom dated other than the day of the week. The two planters were within a day's journey of each other.

Many of their letters were sent back and forth by hired hands, although Ewell found one man, who went by the name "Mines," so "dull" that he was hesitant to use him as a courier—he did not trust him to transport mules or correspondence. Another hand, "Charley," who lived with him at Tarpley, lost several letters written by Brown. Since 1865 Bolivar and Washington Counties had been under black domination, and though he encountered constant problems in securing adequate manpower to pick and work his cotton, Ewell does not appear to have experienced difficulty with local authorities. He told Brown that he preferred living on the riverbank instead of taking hotel accommodations in Greenville. After years in the field and in the saddle, Ewell was not cramped by the rustic living at Tarpley, and in fact he rather enjoyed his open-air life with Charley. "His tent is comfortable & commands a beautiful view of the river," Brown informed Lizinka after a visit. "Being a bend where the river runs directly *north*, the sun *rises* across it from him, & the sunrise I saw there was one of the finest I ever looked at."[35]

Throughout his cotton operations Ewell made frequent, even extended visits to Spring Hill, especially after Lizinka complained "to dear Richard" about her loneliness without him: "Still our room is status Quo & I go there sometimes to be quiet." General Cadmus Wilcox, a West Point contemporary of Stonewall Jackson, touring the Hermitage in Nashville, came for a visit in 1870 during one of Ewell's interludes at home. Wilcox was researching his classic *History of the Mexican War,* published in 1892, and wanted to discuss their young army life together beyond the Rio Grande. Although Ewell spent considerable time at Tarpley during 1870 after his lease had been renewed, most of 1871 was devoted to overseeing the Spring Hill operations. While a good part of his effort was taken with serving as chairman of the Maury County Farmer's Club, he found time to correspond with old acquaintances and to vacation without Lizinka. "Gen. Ewell, Maj. Brown, Col. Martin Cheairs, Col. Wm. Pointer, and others have been absent for more than a week down on the Buffalo, fishing, and hunting," reported the *Columbia Herald* on August 8. He also wrote a note to A. J. Hoarsley, the *Herald's* editor, complaining that the paper had misrepresented an agenda for a farmer's meeting. The group did not discuss "the cutting of Wheat," he said, but "The Best Kind of Wheat and Mode of Cultivation." On another occasion, Ewell chaired a club discussion on "Fruit Culture and the Blight Upon Fruit Trees," with an emphasis on apples and pears.[36]

Ewell's affiliation with the organization hurled him briefly into the political arena during the summer of 1871, when widespread dissatisfaction with the Grant administration led to an insurgency among some Republicans to his renomination for a second term. *New York Tribune* editor Horace Greeley, an old antislavery crusader but a friend of the South after Appomattox, Carl Schurz of Missouri, and others, became champions of the movement to displace Grant that later evolved into the Liberal Republican Party of 1872. With the endorsement of the national Democratic Party, which declined to name a presidential candidate, Greeley carried the banner against Grant in the next election eleven months after Ewell's death. In 1871, Greeley, who had just written the book *What I Know About Farming,* left New York for a visit to Texas in search of support for the forthcoming presidential canvass. When Ewell's group learned about Greeley's southern trip, the body extended a formal invitation for him to stop in Columbia: "Dear Sir—At a recent meeting of the Maury County Farmer's Club, your tour through a portion of our Southern States was mentioned, and your friendly views towards our country gratefully dwelt upon, and a resolution was offered and unanimously adopted, that the undersigned be appointed a committee to invite you to visit our town, and address our farmers upon the subject of agriculture: We hereby extend you a cordial and hearty request to come among us." As chairman, Ewell signed the appeal first, followed by the signatures of four others: J. M. Williams, L. D. Myers, Andrew J. Hoarsley, and J. H. Dew. Greeley passed up the opportunity in spite of his well-known "itch for office," and though Ewell passed away before the 1872 elections, Ben issued a strong endorsement of Grant before the election but several months after his brother's death. Although Ben thought Grant had accomplished a great good for Virginia, and indeed the whole South, interestingly, Tennessee and Maury County voted for Greeley and the Liberal Republicans.[37]

All the while, Ewell worked to make Spring Hill into a showplace. By May 1871, writes A. J. Hoarsley, he had "one of the largest and finest farms in our county, containing in one body of land, over 3000 acres of land, besides one or two other tracts in the neighborhood—in all nearly 4000 acres of land." Hoarsley, who became a confidant of Ewell after assuming control of the *Columbia Herald,* continued his tribute: "It requires talents, of the highest executive order, to manage and control such a farm. To say the General's management is a success is but simple justice, whether viewed as a question of profit and loss, or viewed as a question of progress and improvement." Although the paper said nothing about Lizinka's ownership, it did announce that Ewell had 1,200 sheep in his flock of Cotswolds and Merinos. The farm had 250 head of cattle as well as a "large number of hogs and mules." Ewell remained an enthusiastic sheepherder until the very end. "My specialty is sheep," he told his old West Point messmate Robert Hall Chilton later in the year. "I have tried different kinds of stock & settled upon them as the most profitable." He hoped, he said, to have a flock numbering 5,000 in the near future.[38]

"I am farming here but don't make anything unless it is on sheep," he told General John R. Cooke later in the year. He wanted Cooke to come out to Maury County and take over one of his farms—a "worn out place three miles from here," which Ewell proposed should be renamed "Breckinridge." "I occasionally find solace in ale or Catawba wine," he relayed to Cooke as well as the fact that he had sheared nine hundred sheep for the season. And he warned his former comrade that if he did come, he should know that life moved at a simple pace. "People here are not very elegant or refined—but clever & kind & very fond of swapping horses. When the harvest is over & cotton laid by there is any amount of Baptist,

Methodist, & Presbyterian preaching." It was the very sentiment he conveyed to Lizzie in 1866 after they had first arrived in Tennessee four years earlier.[39]

Although the *Herald* noted during the autumn that "Gen. Ewell and Maj. Brown are planting extensively in the rich cotton lands of Mississippi, and their crops this season are said to be very good," Ewell was clearly finished with his Tarpley enterprise. Brown remained at Melrose through much of 1871 without his stepfather but told his mother that things were not going well in Bolivar County. In fact, he was convinced that both plantations were losing propositions. As Brown mentioned that he was engrossed with one of Benjamin Disraeli's novels when not tending his crops, Ewell wrote to him effectively abandoning his Mississippi venture after the new year. He had asked his agent "to sell out" if he could and not rent the place. "If you want any of my means [at Tarpley] to carry on your projected improvements at Melrose, you are welcome to them." Writing again to Brown, in what was probably one of his last, if not the last, letter ever written by Ewell, he bowed out entirely: "I am rather tired of Miss & cotton & [have] made up my mind to quit & don't care to recommence." He told Brown that he needed to retain his funds "to run this place" (Spring Hill), although he thought Tarpley would be worth forty thousand dollars within two years.[40]

Brown persevered in Mississippi for several years and later took over the family farming operations at Spring Hill, but according to his biographer, Terry L. Jones, he possessed a lifelong fear of losing his fortune. Once free of his mother's steadying influence as well as that of Ewell, he became increasingly unstable. After several lawsuits with his sister Harriet and Tom Turner, he was in and out of sanitariums until he became obsessed with how the economic downturn of 1892 might devastate the family wealth. Attracted to Christian Science teachings, he entered a church-related sanitarium at Battle Creek, Michigan, in search of professional help. Here, his adult manias came crushing down. "On August 30, 1893," Jones continues, "apparently overwhelmed with guilt and the thought of economic ruin, Campbell walked into a quiet field near Grand Rapids, put a pistol to his head and committed suicide." His father, James Percy Brown, had likewise died by his own hand in 1844, which conjures up the stigma of family instability. Harriet also experienced mental difficulties but seems to have recovered after a divorce from Tom Turner. In retrospect it is easy to speculate that the close association between Ewell and his stepson during the war and afterward was prompted by a dependency of the latter and not the former. Perhaps Ewell's inherent inclination to draw back at critical junctures helped seal an obvious bond between the two men.[41]

Within days of abandoning Tarpley in 1872, Ewell, then fifty-four years of age, without warning fell desperately ill. News reports of the day indicate he suffered a "violent attack of pneumonia," a potentially catastrophic disease in the days before the ready availability of antibiotics and related substances. "At one time his life was despaired of, but by the assiduous and skillful attention of Dr. A. C. White, he is, somewhat improved, and hopes are now entertained for his recovery," declared the *Columbia Herald* on January 19. White had been summoned after the Reverend William Stoddert (Ewell), living and working in Nashville, arrived at Spring Hill on January 8 and found his brother "lying on the floor before the fire wrapped in an old blanket, in the midst of a chill." Ewell's early biographer, Percy Gatling Hamlin, himself an army physician of long standing, suggests that he had developed "a violent influenza," because the disease spread rapidly throughout the household. The problem did not subside, which prompted White to wire a Dr. Maddin from Nashville, who arrived "on the first train." In spite of their efforts, a Nashville paper reported on January 23 that Ewell "still lies in a critical condition, with the chances of recovery against him." Death came, wrote his new friend A. J. Hoarsley, "at half past twelve o'clock, on last Wednesday [January 25] night."[42]

In a twist of fate that would strain an adept novelist, his beloved Lizinka had also fallen sick with the same disease. After lingering "only a few days," she succumbed "at her residence near Spring Hill, Maury County, about noon yesterday [January 22]." "It is said he loved her when she was a young girl, and being unsuccessful in his devotions, remained a soldier and bachelor . . . since he did not hope to find her equal in all the noble qualities of person, head, and heart which were required by his exacting ideal," commented Hoarsley. While Ewell clung to life in the same house, his doctors thought the fateful news should be kept from him. On the day of her burial, his priest, the Reverend Dr. Beckett, told him that his wife of ten years was dead. "No emotion was visible in the expression on his face, or his pulse, for some time, but he seemed to be in silent mediation," said the *Herald*. "Finally, he requested them to bring her remains, and after gazing upon them for some time, he expressed himself in audible prayer as ready and willing to die, and added 'not my will, but Thine be done.'"[43]

At the first signs of difficulty, wires were dispatched to Campbell Brown at Melrose. Unfortunately, his Mississippi location had no direct telegraphic connection, so his arrival at Spring Hill was delayed by several days. When he got there on January 22, four hours before his mother's death, he not only encountered Ewell struggling for life but also learned that his wife, Susan, as well as one of Harriet's daughters were dangerously ill. Several newspapers also reported that Drs. White and Maddin, who attended Ewell throughout, had developed "typhoid pneumonia" themselves. Lizinka's services took place in Nashville's Christ Church, where "the beautiful and impressive funeral rites of the Episcopal Church were conducted by the Rev. Dr. Ellis of Edgefield and the Rev. Dr. Beckett of Columbia." Interment followed in the Campbell family plot beside her mother and father in Nashville's City Cemetery.[44]

Ewell's own funeral was held two days later in the same place after his body was transported to Nashville by a special car. An impressive roster of pallbearers accompanied the casket from the train to Christ Church: "Gov. John C. Brown; Gen. L. E. Polk of Maury; Gen. R. D. Lilley of Virginia; Gens. B. R. Johnson, E. Kirby Smith, S. R. Anderson, W. B. Bate, W. H. Jackson, and Col. Thomas Claiborne" of Nashville. The church ceremony was led by the Reverend William Graham and Tennessee bishop Charles T. Quintard, who also assisted at the graveside with several other clergymen. At the cemetery, reported a Nashville paper, "The solemn silence that pervaded was more impressive of the profound sorrow and keen anguish of friends than could have been the martial music so often proclaiming the death of the great and the good." When Ewell had made his will and the disposition of his assets, he made it clear to his executors that he wanted only a simple inscription on his crypt, with nothing negative toward the United States government or its leaders. "Gen. Ewell had been in the habit of wearing a pair of blue infantry pantaloons, which he had purchased subsequent to the war. Upon one occasion, not long before his death, and when he could speak only with the greatest difficulty, he said of them, 'After fighting against the United States for so long, it is strange that an old pair of infantry pantaloons should kill me at last.'" And, continued the *New York Times* vignette, "He attributed his death to having put them on during cold weather after having worn a much warmer pair." The old trooper, for all his faults as a corps commander in the Army of Northern Virginia and despite his inherent difficulties with life itself, was able to face death with a smile on his lips.[45]

NOTES

Care has been exercised to present multiple sources within a single endnote in their order of appearance in the material cited.

Abbreviations:

ALUV	Alderman Library, University of Virginia, Charlottesville, Virginia
B-EPFCL	Brown-Ewell Papers, Filson Club Library, Louisville, Kentucky
B-EPTSL	Brown-Ewell Papers, Tennessee State Library and Archives, Nashville, Tennessee
BSE	Benjamin Stoddert Ewell
CHS	Chicago Historical Society
EPWM	Ewell Papers, Swem Library, College of William and Mary, Williamsburg, Virginia
HL	Huntington Library, San Marino, California
JEJ	Joseph Eggleston Johnston
LC	Library of Congress, Washington, DC
NA	National Archives, Washington, DC
NCSA	North Carolina State Archives, Raleigh, North Carolina
MOC	Museum of the Confederacy, Richmond, Virginia
NYHS	New York Historical Society, New York
PBEP	Polk, Brown, Ewell Papers, Southern Historical Collection, University of North Carolina, Chapel Hill
PLDU	Perkins Library, Duke University, Durham, North Carolina
REL	Robert E. Lee
RSE	Richard Stoddert Ewell
SHC	Southern Historical Collection, University of North Carolina, Chapel Hill, North Carolina
TJJ	Thomas Jonathan "Stonewall" Jackson
USMA	U.S. Military Academy, West Point, New York
VHS	Virginia Historical Society, Richmond, Virginia

Chapter 1: Beginnings

1. Richard B. McCaslin, *Lee in the Shadow of Washington* (Baton Rouge: Louisiana State UP, 2001), 144; Percy Gatling Hamlin, *"Old Bald Head": General R. S. Ewell* (Strasburg, VA: Shenandoah Publishing, 1940), passim.

2. Robert Selph Henry, *The Story of the Confederacy* (New York: Bobbs-Merrill, 1936), 270; John W. Thomason, *JEB Stuart* (New York: Charles Scribner's Sons, reprint, 1958), 390ff.; James Longstreet, *From Manassas to Appomattox: Memoirs of the Civil War in America* (New York: Da Capo Press, reprint, 1992), 332; William Allan, "Conversations with R. E. Lee" (typescript), William Allan Papers, SHC; Gary W. Gallagher, ed., *Lee: The Soldier* (Lincoln: U of Nebraska P, 1996), 11.

3. Terry L. Jones, ed., *Campbell Brown's Civil War: With Ewell and the Army of Northern Virginia* (Baton Rouge: Louisiana State UP, 2002), 28–29, 255, 278–79, and passim; Douglas Southall Freeman, *Lee's Lieutenants: A Study in Command* (New York: Charles Scribner's Sons, 1943), 3: 187; Edwin B. Coddington, *The Gettysburg Campaign: A Study in Command* (New York: Charles Scribner's Sons, reprint, 1979), 710–11; Peter S. Carmichael, "Escaping the Shadow of Gettysburg: Richard S. Ewell and Ambrose Powell Hill at the Wilderness," in Gary W. Gallagher, ed., *The Wilderness Campaign* (Chapel Hill: U of North Carolina P, 1997), 136; Edward J. Stackpole, *They Met at Gettysburg* (Harrisburg, PA: Stackpole Books, reprint, 1996), 148; Clifford Dowdey, *Lee and His Men at Gettysburg: Death of a Nation* (Lincoln: U of Nebraska P, reprint, 1999), 335; James M. McPherson, *Battle Cry of Freedom: The Civil War Era* (New York: Ballantine, reprint, 1989), 656–60; *Nashville Union and American*, January 27, 1872.

4. Harriet Stoddert Turner, "The Ewells of Virginia: Especially of Stony Lonesome" (typescript), EPWM, 5; BSE, "Fragments of an Autobiography," EPWM; Eleanor M. Ewell and Alice Maude Ewell, "History of the Ewell Family" (typescript), Jesse Ewell Papers, Center for the Study of American History, University of Texas, Austin, 1.

5. Anne West Chapman, "Benjamin Stoddert Ewell: A Biography" (PhD dissertation, College of William and Mary, 1984), 11. Dr. Chapman's work contains an excellent survey of the Ewells and should be consulted by anyone seeking detailed information. Prince William County Historical Commission, *Homeplace: Prince William County* (Woodbridge, VA: Minute Man Press, 1986), 77; Ewell and Ewell, "History of the Ewell Family," 3; Fairfax Harrison, *Landmarks of Old Prince William: A Study of Origins in Northern Virginia* (Berryville, VA: Chesapeake Book, reprint, 1964), 258, 427, 435.

6. James T. Flexner, *George Washington: The Forge of Experience, 1732–1775* (Boston: Little, Brown, 1965), 10–11; BSE, "Fragments of an Autobiography"; Alice Maude Ewell, *A Virginia Scene; or, Life in Old Prince William* (Lynchburg, VA: J. Bell, 1931), 15.

7. Jesse Ewell, "Richard Stoddert Ewell" (unidentified newspaper clipping), Ewell Papers, ALUV; Chapman, "Ewell: A Biography," 11–12.

8. J. Ewell, "Richard Stoddert Ewell"; Hamlin, *"Old Bald Head,"* 4; Prince William County Historical Commission, *Homeplace,* 77.

9. Chapman, "Ewell: A Biography," 12–15; J. Ewell, "Richard Stoddert Ewell"; Thomas Ewell to Jesse Ewell, December 20, 1802, Jesse Ewell Papers, Center for the Study of American History, University of Texas, Austin.

10. J. Ewell, "Richard Stoddert Ewell"; Jesse Ewell, "A History of the Medical Profession in Virginia" (typescript), Ewell Papers, ALUV.

11. Stoddert Family Genealogy, B-EPTSL; Dumas Malone, ed., *The Dictionary of American Biography,* (New York: Charles Scribner's Sons, 1936), 18: 62–63.

12. Michael A. Palmer, *Stoddert's War: Naval Operations During the Quasi-War with France, 1798–1801* (Columbia: U of South Carolina P, 1987), 10–11; Malone, ed., *Dictionary of American Biography,* 18: 63; BSE, "Fragments of an Autobiography."

13. Malone, ed., *Dictionary of American Biography,* 18: 63; Weymouth T. Jordan, "Diary of George Washington Campbell: Minister to Russia, 1818–1820," *Tennessee Historical Quarterly* 7 (June 1948): 152ff.; Palmer, *Stoddert's War,* 6–12; Stephen G. Kurtz, *The Presidency of John Adams: The Collapse of Federalism, 1795–1800* (Philadelphia: U of Pennsylvania P, 1957), 322–24; Page Smith, *John Adams, 1784–1826* (New York: Doubleday, 1962), 967; Chapman, "Ewell: A Biography," 10–11.

14. J. Ewell, "Richard Stoddert Ewell"; Ewell Family Genealogy, Ewell Papers, ALUV; Turner, "Ewells of Virginia," 13; Flexner, *Washington: The Forge of Experience,* 357; William E. S. Flory, "Parson Weems: Marketer," in *A Collection of Articles about Dumfries and Prince William County* (n.p., 1990), unpaged; McCaslin, *Lee in the Shadow,* 12, and passim.

15. J. Ewell, "Richard Stoddert Ewell"; Turner, "Ewells of Virginia," 12; Chapman, "Ewell: A Biography," 18–21; Ewell Family Genealogy, B-EPTSL.

16. Malone, ed., *Dictionary of American Biography,* 8: 189–90; U.S. Congress, *Biographical Directory of the American Congress, 1774–1961* (Washington, DC: Government Printing Office, 1961), 1140; Irving Brant, *James Madison: Commander-in-Chief* (Indianapolis: Bobbs-Merrill Company, 1961), 126–28, 164; J. Ewell, "Richard Stoddert Ewell"; Chapman, "Ewell: A Biography," 17–18.

17. Turner, "Ewells of Virginia," 18–19; Mark M. Boatner, *The Civil War Dictionary* (New York: David M. McKay, 1959), 780; U.S. Congress, *Biographical Directory,* 1161, 1600. "Other residents were Elihu Root, Secretary of War under Theodore Roosevelt, and publisher William Randolph Hearst. The building was razed in 1930 and replaced by the Brookings Institution. That building was razed in 1963 when the Kennedy administration decided to restore the historic character of the square." Brookings Institution pamphlet, n.d.

18. Works Project Administration, *Prince William: The Story of Its People and Its Places* (Manassas, VA: Bethlehem, Good Housekeeping, reprint, 1961), 150–51; Anonymous, "Biographical Sketch of Richard Stoddert Ewell," EPWM; Turner, "Ewells of Virginia," 26–27; Hamlin, *"Old Bald Head,"* 4–6.

19. Academy records consistently give Ewell's age on admission as nineteen years, nine months. Born in February 1817, he would have been nineteen years and four months on July 1, 1836.

20. Fourth Class Roll, 1837, Register of Merit, Personal Records—Records Relating to Cadets, Records of the USMA, Record Group 404, NA Records on Deposit at the USMA; U.S. Congress, *Biographical Directory,* 654; Donald C. Pfanz, *Richard S. Ewell: A Soldier's Life* (Chapel Hill: U of North Carolina P, 1998), 13–14; Hamlin, *"Old Bald Head,"* 7.

21. Douglas Southall Freeman, *R. E. Lee: A Biography* (New York: Charles Scribner's Sons, 1937–1940), 1: 43; Fitzhugh Lee, *General Lee* (New York: D. Appleton, 1894), 22; Robert V. Remini, *Andrew Jackson and the Course of American Empire, 1767–1821* (New York: History Book Club, reprint, 1998), 117; Robert V. Remini, *Andrew Jackson and the Course of American Freedom, 1822-1832* (New York: History Book Club, reprint, 1998), 108, 409; Gerard A. Patterson, *Rebels from West Point* (New York: Doubleday, 1987), 158–60.

22. Anonymous, "Biographical Sketch of Richard Stoddert Ewell"; Henry H. Simms, *A Decade of Sectional Controversy, 1851–1861* (Chapel Hill: U of North Carolina P, 1942), 49; Turner, "Ewells of Virginia," 27; Richard O'Connor, *Thomas: The Rock of Chicamauga* (New York: Prentice Hall, 1948), 63.

23. Cadet Application Papers, 1805–1868, USMA, NA Record Group 94, microfilm reel 688.

24. Stanley Hirshson, *The White Tecumseh: A Biography of General William T. Sherman* (New York: John Wiley, 1999), 10–11; Bernarr Cresap, *Appomattox Commander: The Story of General E. O. C. Ord* (San Diego, CA: A. S. Barnes, 1981), 13; USMA, *Register of Graduates of the United States Military Academy, West Point, New York: Class of 2000 Centennial Edition* (West Point, NY: USMA, 2000), 1080–1081.

25. Stephen E. Ambrose, *Duty, Honor, Country: A History of West Point* (Baltimore: Johns Hopkins UP, 1966), 282–83; RSE to Dear Becca, August 29, 1846, RSE Papers, USMA; BSE to George Washington Cullum, February 6, 1850, BSE Papers, USMA; Percy Gatling Hamlin, *The Making of a Soldier: Letters of General R. S. Ewell* (Richmond, VA: Whittet and Shepperson, 1935), 21–23.

26. Thomas J. Fleming, *West Point: The Men and Times of the United States Military Academy* (New York: William Morrow), 55–47; Ambrose, *Duty, Honor, Country,* 60–72; USMA, "Conduct Roll, 1837," Register of Merit, Personal Records, Record Group 404, NA Records on Deposit at USMA; USMA, "Record of Delinquencies," Department of Tactics, Record Group 404, NA Records on Deposit at USMA.

27. Albert Ensign Church, *Personal Reminiscences of the Military Academy from 1824 to 1831* (West Point, NY: USMA Press, 1879), 45–46; Hamlin, *Making of a Soldier,* 21; Hirshson, *White Tecumseh,* 10; James L. Morrison, "The Best School in the World": *West Point; The Pre–Civil War Years, 1833–1866* (Kent State UP, 1986), 15-20.

28. USMA, "Third Class Roll, 1838"; USMA, "Conduct Roll, 1838"; USMA, "Record of Delinquencies, 1837–1838"; Church, *Personal Reminiscences,* 25–26, and passim; Hirshson, *White Tecumseh,* 10–11.

29. T. Michael Parrish, ed., *Reminiscences of the War in Virginia by David French Boyd* (Austin, TX: Jenkins Publishing, 1989), 21–23; Stephen B. Oates, "Texas Under the Secessionists," *Southwestern Historical Quarterly* 47 (October 1963): 195; USMA, "Third Class Roll, 1838"; Hamlin, *Making of a Soldier,* 23–25.

30. RSE to Dear Mother, October 3, 1839, Ewell Papers, LC; Hamlin, *Making of a Soldier,* 26–27. Almost without exception the original correspondence in Hamlin can be found in the Library of Congress collection of Ewell papers.

31. USMA, "Second Class Roll, 1839"; USMA, "Conduct Roll, 1839"; USMA, "Record of Delinquencies, 1838–1839": Grady McWhiney, *Braxton Bragg and Confederate Defeat: Field Command* (Columbia: U of South Carolina P, 1969), 21; Stephen W. Sears, *George B. McClellan: The Young Napoleon* (New York: Ticknor and Fields, 1988), 9–10.

32. USMA, "West Point Library Catalog, 2002"; Boatner, *Civil War Dictionary,* 501; Ambrose, *Duty, Honor, Country,* 100; Sears, *George B. McClellan,* 9; McWhiney, *Braxton Bragg and Confederate Defeat,* 17.

33. The O'Connor translation of Gay de Vernon, which was intended as the first textbook specifically for West Point use, can also be found in the Preston Library, Virginia Military Institute, Lexington. Other works by Gay de Vernon in the original French can be secured in the Library of Congress, Washington, DC.

34. USMA, "West Point Library Lending Records, February 1840"; Ambrose, *Duty, Honor, Country,* 54.

35. RSE to BSE, March 29, 1840, Ewell Papers, LC; Hamlin, *Making of a Soldier,* 33; James W. Pohl, "The Influence of Henri de Jomini on Winfield Scott's Campaign in the Mexican War," *Southwestern Historical Quarterly* 77 (July 1973), 86–88; Ambrose, *Duty, Honor, Country,* 98–101.

36. USMA, *Register of Graduates: Class of 2000,* 1082–1083; Boatner, *Civil War Dictionary,* 500; *Third Annual Reunion of the Association of Graduates of the United States Military Academy at West Point, New York, June 14, 1872* (New York: Crocker and Company, 1872), 44–45.

37. USMA, *Cadets Arranged in Order of Merit in Their Respective Classes as Determined at the General Examination in June 1840* (West Point, NY: USMA, 1840), 9; USMA, "Conduct Roll, 1840"; USMA, "Record of Delinquencies, 1840"; RSE to BSE, March 29, 1840, Ewell Papers, LC; Hamlin, *Making of a Soldier,* 33–34; Church, *Personal Reminiscences,* 25.

38. Frederick Rudolph, *The American College and University: A History* (New York: Vantage Press, 1962), 118–20; Ellsworth Eliot Jr., *West Point in the Confederacy* (New York: G. A. Baker, 1941), xii-xix.

Chapter 2: Dragoon

1. Carlisle Barracks, "Returns from U.S. Military Posts, 1800–1916," NA Publication M-91, reel 183; RSE to BSE, October 21, 1840, and RSE to Dear Becca, November 12, 1840, Ewell Papers, LC.

2. Robert B. Roberts, *Encyclopedia of Historic Forts: The Military, Pioneer, and Trading Posts of the United States* (New York: Macmillan, 1988), 64–65; "Returns from Regular Cavalry Regiments," NA Publication M-744, reel 1; Fort Gibson, "Returns from U.S. Military Posts," reel 404; Mrs. James Edmondson, "Maysville Reports on Big Spring," *Benton County Pioneer* 10 (1967): 69; Hamlin, *Making of a Soldier,* 39.

3. Hamlin, *Making of a Soldier,* 38–39.

4. "Returns from Regular Cavalry Regiments," reel 1; Thomas H. S. Hamersly, *Complete Army and Navy Register of the United States from 1787 to 1887* (New York: T. H. S. Hamersly, 1888), 357, 759; Francis B. Heitman, *Historical Register and Directory of the United States Army, 1783–1903* (Washington, DC: Government Printing Office, 1903), 1: 299, 889; Boatner, *Civil War Dictionary,* 154; Hamlin, *Making of a Soldier,* 39–40.

5. RSE to Dear Becca, November 13, 1841, Ewell Papers, LC; Hamlin, *Making of a Soldier,* 38–40; Otis K. Rice, *West Virginia: A History* (Lexington: UP of Kentucky, 1985), 67; Wilbur H. Clamblet, *The Christian Church (Disciples of Christ) in West Virginia: A History of its Cooperative Work* (St. Louis, MO: Bethany Press, 1971), 1–44.

6. RSE to Dear Becca, April 10, 1842, Ewell Papers, LC; R. Roberts, *Encyclopedia of Historic Forts,* 30; "Returns from Regular Cavalry Regiments," reel 1; Fort Gibson, "Returns from U.S. Military Posts," reel 404.

7. RSE to Dear Becca, April 10, 1842, Ewell Papers, LC.

8. Hamilton Gardner, "The March of the First Dragoons from Jefferson Barracks to Fort Gibson in 1833–1834," *Chronicles of Oklahoma* 31 (spring 1953), 22–23; Arkansas Sesquicentennial Commission, *Sessie Facts* (Siloam Springs, AR: Simon Sager Press, 1985), 3: 7; R. Roberts, *Encyclopedia of Historic Forts,* 65; Boatner, *Civil War Dictionary,* 895.

9. Louise Barry, "The Fort Leavenworth-Fort Gibson Military Road and the Founding of Fort Scott," *Kansas Historical Quarterly* 11 (May 1942): 128–29; Ralph Richards, *Headquarters House* (Fort Scott, KS: *Fort Scott Tribune,* 1954), 2–5; Dudley T. Cornish, "Historical Significance of Fort Scott, Kansas" (typescript), Pittsburg, Kansas, n.d.), 2–4.

10. Barry, "Leavenworth-Fort Gibson Military Road," 127; "Returns from

Regular Cavalry Regiments," reel 1; U.S. Army, *Field Staff and Officers of the First Regiment of Cavalry from March 4, 1833, to June 1, 1900* (Fort Meade, SD, n.p., 1900), unpaged.

11. "Returns from Regular Cavalry Regiments," reel 1; Ralph Richards, *The Forts of Fort Scott and the Fateful Borderland* (Kansas City, MO: Lowell Press, 1976), 21; Hamlin, *Making of a Soldier,* 44–45; Seymour V. Connor and Jimmy M. Skaggs, *Broadcloth and Britches: The Santa Fe Trade* (College Station: Texas A&M UP, 1977), 50–51.

12. Henry Inman, *The Old Santa Fe Trail: The Story of a Great Highway* (Topeka, KS: Crane and Company, 1916), 28; Walter P. Webb, ed., *The Handbook of Texas* (Austin: Texas State Historical Association, 1952), 2: 570.

13. Hamlin, *Making of a Soldier,* 44; R. L. Duffus, *The Santa Fe Trail* (New York: David M. McKay, 1958), 186; Connor and Skaggs, *Broadcloth and Britches,* 112; Richards, *Headquarters House,* 570.

14. "Returns from Regular Cavalry Regiments," reel 1; Richards, *Forts of Fort Scott,* 23; Hamersly, *Complete Army and Navy Register,* 802. For a detailed account of the Cooke expedition, see Otis E. Young, *The West of Philip St. George Cooke, 1809–1895* (Glendale, CA: Arthur C. Clark, 1955), 109ff.

15. RSE to Dear Becca, March 2, 1844, Ewell Papers, LC; Richards, *Headquarters House,* 5.

16. Thomas Ewell to Dear Sir, April 13, 1842, and James K. Polk to Thomas Ewell, February 1, 1844, Ewell Papers, LC; Charles Sellers, *James K. Polk: Jacksonian, 1795-1843* (Princeton, NJ: Princeton UP, 1957), 461–62.

17. RSE to Dear Becca, July 30, October 25, 1844, Ewell Papers, LC; Jefferson Barracks, "Returns from U.S. Military Posts," reel 546.

18. Hamlin, *Making of a Soldier,* 54–55; William Garrett Piston, *Lee's Tarnished Lieutenant: James Longstreet and His Place in Southern History* (Athens: U of Georgia P, 1987), 3–4; RSE to Dear Becca, October 25, 1844, Ewell Papers, LC.

19. R. Roberts, *Encyclopedia of Historic Forts,* 459; Jefferson Barracks, "Returns from U.S. Military Posts," reel 546; Emory M. Thomas, *Robert E. Lee: A Biography* (New York: W. W. Norton, 1995), 90–100; Stella M. Drumm, "Robert E. Lee and the Improvements of the Mississippi River," *Missouri Historical Review* 6 (February 1929): 157–65; RSE to BSE, October 15, 1844, Ewell Papers, LC.

20. Hamlin, *Making of a Soldier,* 59; Heitman, *Historical Register,* 1: 308; Robert V. Remini, *Henry Clay: Statesman for the Union* (New York: W. W. Norton, 1991), 684.

21. David L. Chandler, *The Binghams of Louisville: The Dark History Behind One of America's Great Fortunes* (New York: Crown, 1987), 48–49; Isabel M. McMeekin, *Louisville: The Gateway City* (New York: J. Messner, 1945), 201–04; Allan W. Eckert, *That Dark and Bloody River: Chronicles of the Ohio River Valley* (New York: Bantam, 1995), 250ff.

22. RSE to Dear Becca, January 14, 1845, Ewell Papers, LC.

23. William T. Sherman, *Memoirs of General W. T. Sherman* (New York: Library of America, reprint, 1990), 36–37; Lloyd Lewis, *Sherman: Fighting Prophet* (New York: Harcourt, Brace, 1932), 75; Zachary Taylor's Order Number 83, July 7, 1846, "Orders of General Zachary Taylor to the Army of Occupation in the Mexican War, 1845–1847," NA Publication M-29, reel 1; Paul D. Casdorph, *Prince John Magruder: His Life and Campaigns* (New York: John Wiley, 1996), 61–63.

24. "Returns from Regular Cavalry Regiments," reel 2; Malone, ed., *Dictionary of American Biography*, 10: 271–72.

25. Justin H. Smith, *The War with Mexico* (New York: Macmillan, 1919), 2: 77, 346; Adjutant General to William Eustis, September 4, 1847, "Letters Sent by the Office of the Adjutant General, 1800–1890," NA Publication M-565, reel 15; T. Harry Williams, *The History of American Wars, from 1745 to 1918* (New York: Knopf, 1981), 161–64.

26. David M. Potter, *The Impending Crisis, 1848–1861* (New York: Harper and Row, 1976), 21–25; John Edward Weems, *To Conquer a Peace: The War Between the United States and Mexico* (Garden City, NY: Doubleday, 1974), 8–10; Seymour V. Connor and Odie B. Faulk, *North America Divided: The Mexican War, 1846–1848* (New York: Oxford UP, 1971), 28–29.

27. Joseph M. Nance, *After San Jacinto: The Texas-Mexican Frontier, 1836–1841* (Austin: U of Texas P, 1963), 227–30; Holman Hamilton, *Zachary Taylor: Soldier of the Republic* (Hamden, CT: Archon Books, reprint, 1966), 173ff.; John S. D. Eisenhower, *So Far from God: The U.S. War with Mexico, 1846–1848* (New York: Random House, 1989), xix.

28. Jack Bauer, *Zachary Taylor: Soldier, Planter, Statesman of the Old South* (Baton Rouge: Louisiana State UP, 1985), 160–79; Charles A. McCoy, *Polk and the Presidency* (Austin: U of Texas P, 1960), 94–95; War Proclamation, May 13, 1846, Copy in "Letters Received by the Office of the Adjutant General, 1801–1880," NA Publication M-567, reel 321.

29. Hamilton, *Taylor: Soldier of the Republic*, 79; James I. Robertson Jr., *General A. P. Hill: The Story of a Confederate Warrior* (New York: Random House, 1987), 18; Malone, ed., *Dictionary of American Biography*, 20: 537.

30. Vincent J. Esposito, *West Point Atlas of American Wars, 1689–1900* (New York: Praeger, 1959), 14; Robert W. Johannsen, *To the Halls of the Montezumas: The Mexican War in the American Imagination* (New York: Oxford UP, 1985), 91; Thomas Ewell to Dear Mother, February 12, 1847, Ewell Papers, LC.

31. "Returns from Regular Cavalry Regiments," reel 2; J. Smith, *War with Mexico*, 2: 77, 333; U.S. Congress, *House Executive Document 60*, Thirtieth Congress—First Session, 1848 (Washington, DC: Wendell and Benthuysen, 1848), 921.

32. Alfred Hoyt Bill, *Rehearsal for Conflict: The War with Mexico, 1846–1848* (New York: Knopf, 1947), 204–14; A. L. Long, *The Memoirs of Robert E. Lee: His Military and Personal History* (Secaucus, NJ: Blue and Grey Press, reprint,

1983), 51–52; Hamlin, *Making of a Soldier,* 66; "Returns from Regular Cavalry Regiments," reel 2.

33. Robert Selph Henry, *The Story of the Mexican War* (Indianapolis: Bobbs-Merrill, 1950), 278ff.; Ulysses S. Grant, *Personal Memoirs of U. S. Grant* (New York: Da Capo Press, reprint, 1982), 61; Paul D. Casdorph, *Lee and Jackson: Confederate Chieftains* (New York: Paragon House, 1992), 78–79.

34. Henry, *Story of the Mexican War,* 286; William Starr Myers, ed., *The Mexican War Diary of George B. McClellan* (Princeton, NJ: Princeton UP, 1917), 91; RSE to Dear Mother, April 22, 1847, Ewell Papers, LC.

35. RSE to BSE, May 3, 1847, Ewell Papers, LC; U.S. Congress, *Senate Executive Document 1,* Thirtieth Congress—First Session (Washington, DC: Wendell and Benthuysen, 1848) 266, 276, 282–83, hereafter cited as *Senate 1848.*

36. RSE to BSE, May 3, 1847, Ewell Papers, LC; Bill, *Rehearsal for Conflict,* 257–59; William L. Haskin, *History of the First Regiment of Artillery from Its Organization in 1821 to January 1, 1876* (Portland, ME: B. Thurston, 1879), 98–101.

37. "Returns from Regular Cavalry Regiments," reel 2; Arthur D. H. Smith, *Old Fuss and Feathers: The Life and Exploits of Lt. General Winfield Scott* (New York: Greystone Press, 1937), 278; Eisenhower, *So Far from God,* 202–03; Bill, *Rehearsal for Conflict,* 258; Cadmus Wilcox, *History of the Mexican War* (Washington, DC: Church News Publishing, 1892), 349–54.

38. *Senate 1848,* 304; Esposito, *West Point Atlas of American Wars,* 15–16; Eisenhower, *So Far from God,* 316.

39. *Senate 1848,* Appendix, 37; RSE to Dear Mother, September 1, 1847, Ewell Papers, LC.

40. *Senate 1848,* 346, and Appendix, 36; Casdorph, *Prince John Magruder,* 75; Frank E. Vandiver, *Mighty Stonewall* (New York: McGraw-Hill, 1957), 34–36.

41. *Senate 1848,* 313, 347, and Appendix, 36–37; "Extract from Report of Colonel William S. Harney to Major General Scott, August 24, 1847," RSE to Dear Mother, September 1, 1847, and Jefferson Davis to William Smith, February 19, 1855, Ewell Papers, LC.

42. Henry, *Story of the Mexican War,* 348–50; Weems, *To Conquer a Peace,* 514–16; RSE to Dear Mother, September 1, 1847, Ewell Papers, LC; Henry Alexander White, *Robert E. Lee and the Southern Confederacy, 1807–1870* (New York: G. P. Putnam's Sons, 1910), 42–45.

43. Esposito, *West Point Atlas of American Wars,* 16; Emma J. Blackwood, ed., *To Mexico with Scott: Letters of Captain E. Kirby Smith to His Wife* (Cambridge, MA: Harvard College Press, 1917), 217; W. A. Croffut, ed., *Fifty Years in Camp and Field: The Diary of Major General Ethan Allen Hitchcock, USA* (New York: G. P. Putnam's Sons, 1909), 397; Jeffry D. Wert, *General James Longstreet: The Confederacy's Most Controversial Soldier, A Biography* (New York: Simon and Schuster, 1993), 45.

44. Clifford Dowdey, *Lee* (Boston: Little, Brown, 1965), 93–94; Hamlin,

Making of a Soldier, 69; Heitman, *Historical Register,* 1: 44; Stoddert Genealogical Chart, B-EPTSL; RSE to BSE, September 25, 1847, Ewell Papers, LC.

45. Otis A. Singletary, *The Mexican War* (Chicago: U of Chicago P, 1960), 96; Edward G. Longacre, *Pickett, Leader of the Charge: A Biography of General George E. Pickett, C.S.A.* (Shippensburg, PA: White Mane, 1995), 26; Winfield Scott, *Memoirs of Lieutenant General Scott: Written by Himself* (New York: Sheldon, 1864), 2: 520–22.

46. Henry, *Story of the Mexican War,* 368–69; Military Society of the Mexican War, *Constitution of the Aztec Club of 1847 and List of its Members, 1928* (n.p., 1928), 9, 29; John Esten Cooke, *Stonewall Jackson: A Military Biography* (New York: D. Appleton, 1866), 14–15; Alexander Watkins Terrell, *From Texas to Mexico and the Court of Maximilian in 1865* (Dallas: Book Club of Texas, reprint, 1933), 58.

47. RSE to BSE, November 25, 1847, and Unsigned to BSE, May 14, 1848, Ewell Papers, LC; "Returns from Regular Cavalry Regiments," reel 2.

Chapter 3: Indian Fighter

1. James S. Hutchins, "'Bald Head' Ewell: Frontier Dragoon," *Arizonian* 3 (spring 1962): 21; T. Harry Williams, "General Ewell to High Private in the Rear," *Virginia Historical Magazine* 54 (1946): 217; W. Webb, ed., *Handbook of Texas,* 1: 652; Marshall Trimble, *Arizona: A Panoramic History of a Frontier State* (New York: Doubleday, 1977), 156–57; Henry A. Chambers Diary, June 21, 1862, Henry A. Chambers Papers, NCSA.

2. "Returns from Regular Cavalry Regiments," reels 2 and 3; Adjutant General to RSE, January 8, 1849, "Letters Sent by the Office of the Adjutant General," reel 17.

3. BSE to Joseph Henry, January 8, 1849, William J. Rhees Papers, HL; RSE to Phil Kearny, March 7, 1849, John L. Graham Papers, HL; RSE to BSE, March 13, 1849, Ewell Papers, LC; Heitman, *Historical Register,* 1: 863; Hamersly, *Complete Army and Navy Register,* 752.

4. RSE to BSE, April 9, 1848, Ewell Papers, LC.

5. Lorenzo Thomas to RSE, July 13, 19, 1850, "Letters Sent by the Office of the Adjutant General," reel 17; RSE to BSE, June 7, 1849, and RSE to Dear Becca, April 24, 1840, Ewell Papers, LC; Boatner, *Civil War Dictionary,* 446. For William's name change, see also Ewell and Ewell, "History of the Ewell Family," 9.

6. RSE to BSE, June 7, 1849, Ewell Papers, LC; Edward M. Coffman, *The Old Army: A Portrait of the American Army in Peacetime, 1784–1898* (New York: Oxford UP, 1986), 147.

7. RSE to Dear Becca, February 25, April 24, June 26, 1850, Ewell Papers, LC; Robert E. Lee Jr., *Recollections and Letters of General Robert E. Lee* (Garden City, NY: Garden City Publishing, 1903), 10–11; Freeman, *R. E. Lee: A Biography,* 1: 301–03.

8. RSE to BSE, August 10, 1850, Ewell Papers, LC; RSE to Benjamin L. Towson, August 6, 1850, George A. Zabriski Papers, VHS; Adjutant General to RSE, September 5, 1850, "Letters Sent by the Office of the Adjutant General," reel 17.

9. Paul Horgan, *The Great River: The Rio Grande in North American History* (New York: Rinehart, 1954), 2: 732; Erna Fergusson, *New Mexico: A Pageant of Three Peoples* (New York: Knopf, 1971), 253–55; William A. Keleher, *Turmoil in New Mexico, 1846–1868* (Santa Fe, NM: Rydal Press), 36ff.

10. Warren A. Beck, *New Mexico: A History of Four Centuries* (Norman: U of Oklahoma P, 1962), 115–23.

11. Averam B. Bender, "Military Transportation in the Southwest, 1848–1860," *New Mexico Historical Review* 32 (April 1957): 127–29; Robert M. Utley, *Frontiersmen in Blue: The United States Army and the Indian, 1848–1865* (New York: Macmillan, 1967), 142–43.

12. Richard Taylor, *Deconstruction and Reconstruction: Personal Experiences of the Late War* (New York: D. Appleton, 1879), 37; R. Roberts, *Encyclopedia of Historic Forts,* 28; James H. Carleton, "Map of the Military Department of New Mexico, 1864," folio copy in back of Lawrence C. Kelly, *Navajo Roundup: Selected Correspondence of Kit Carson's Expedition Against the Navajo, 1863–1865* (Boulder, CO: Pruett Press, 1978).

13. Fort Defiance, "Returns from U.S. Military Posts, 1800–1916," reel 301; R. Roberts, *Encyclopedia of Historic Forts,* 37; Frank McNitt, *Navajo Wars: Military Campaigns, Slave Raids, and Reprisals* (Albuquerque: U of New Mexico P, 1972), 198–99, 203–05.

14. RSE to H. K. Craig, January 1, 1852, Lee Family Collection, Jesse Ball du Pont Library, Stratford, Virginia; R. Roberts, *Encyclopedia of Historic Forts,* 526; RSE to BSE, July 21, 1852, Ewell Papers, LC.

15. RSE to L. D. Sturgis, May 24, 1853, RSE to Samuel Cooper, August 21, 1853; "Letters Received by the Office of the Adjutant General, 1822–1860," reel 480.

16. RSE to Dear Becca, October 28, 1853, and RSE to BSE, December 23, 1853, Ewell Papers, LC.

17. McNitt, *Navajo Wars,* 218ff.; Dan L. Thrapp, ed., *Encyclopedia of Frontier Biography* (Spokane, WA: Arthur H. Clark, 1988–1994), 4: 144.

18. McNitt, *Navajo Wars,* 228–36; Ruth M. Underhill, *The Navahos* (Norman: U of Oklahoma P, 1956), 112ff.

19. RSE to Dear Becca, January 28, 1854, Ewell Papers, LC; Robert Lewis Reiter, "The History of Fort Union, New Mexico" (MA thesis, University of California, Berkeley, 1950), 57–61.

20. RSE to Dear Becca, January 28, 1854, Ewell Papers, LC; Hamlin, *Making of a Soldier, 78;* Noel B. Gerson, *Kit Carson: Folk Hero and Man* (New York: Doubleday, 1964), 171–79; Stanley Vestal, *Kit Carson: The Happy Warrior of the Old West, A Biography* (Boston: Houghton Mifflin, 1928), 269.

21. Stoddert Family Genealogy, B-EPTSL; RSE to Dear Becca, January 28, 1854, Ewell Papers, LC.

22. Hamlin, *Making of a Soldier,* 78; Winfield Scott to BSE, December 16, 1854, NA Record Group 107, "Applications for Leave," reel 37; BSE to Jefferson Davis, January 11, 1855, BSE to James Mason, February 28, 1855, "Applications for Leave," reel 37.

23. Albuquerque, "Returns from U.S. Army Posts," reel 125; "Returns from Regular Cavalry Regiments," reel 4; Beck, *New Mexico,* 151.

24. Keleher, *Turmoil in New Mexico,* 76–77; *National Cyclopaedia of American Biography* (New York: James T. White, 1892–1894), 12: 219.

25. W. Webb, ed., *Handbook of Texas,* 2: 55; Keleher, *Turmoil in New Mexico,* 81; C. L. Sonnichsen, *The Mescalero Apaches* (Norman: U of Oklahoma P, 1958), 73–75.

26. RSE to W. A. Nichols, February 10, 1855, William J. Ritch Papers, HL; Clinton E. Brooks and Frank D. Reeve, *Forts and Forays: A Dragoon in New Mexico, 1850–1856; James A. Bennett* (Albuquerque: U of New Mexico P, 1996), 59–61; Sonnichsen, *Mescalero Apaches,* 74–79.

27. Sonnichsen, *Mescalero Apaches,* 80–81; John Garland to Lorenzo Thomas, February 28, 1855, William J. Ritch Papers, HL.

28. "Returns from Regular Cavalry Regiments," reel 4; Brooks and Reeve, *Forts and Forays,* 64–66.

29. RSE to Dear Becca, July 1, 1855, Ewell Papers, LC.

30. McNitt, *Navajo Wars,* 256–67; Brooks and Reeve, *Forts and Forays,* 68.

31. RSE to Adjutant General, November 21, 1855, NA Record Group 94; "RSE Application for Leave with Attached Memos from Winfield Scott, Samuel Cooper, and Jefferson Davis, November 21, 1855," NA Record Group 94.

32. RSE to Dear Elizabeth, January 16, March 5, 1856, and RSE to BSE, March 25, 1856, Ewell Papers, LC.

Chapter 4: Fort Buchanan

1. Adjutant General to RSE, March 6, 11, Adjutant General to H. K. Craig, March 6, Jefferson Davis to David Meriwether, March 7, Adjutant General to John Garland, March 17, 1856, "Letters Sent by the Office of the Adjutant General," reel 18.

2. RSE to Jefferson Davis, February 12; Jefferson Davis to RSE, February 16; Mrs. Rebecca Hubbard to Jefferson Davis, September 15; Lizinka C. Brown to Jefferson Davis, September 15; Jefferson Davis to Dear Madam (Rebecca Hubbard), September 25; Lizinka C. Brown to Jefferson Davis, October 4; C. J. Brown to Jefferson Davis, October 4; Aaron V. Brown to Jefferson Davis, October 4; BSE to Jefferson Davis, December 4, 1856—all in NA Record Group 94; see also BSE to James M. Mason, December 4, 1856, NA Record Group 94.

3. T. T. Gantt to Lizinka C. Brown, March 14, 1856, B-EPTSL; RSE to Dear Elizabeth, March 21, and RSE to BSE, March 26, 1856, Ewell Papers, LC; Lizinka C. Brown to RSE, July 1, 1856, PBEP.

4. McNitt, *Navajo Wars,* 282; RSE to Dear Elizabeth, July 28, 1856, PBEP; "Returns from Regular Cavalry Regiments," reel 4.

5. Paul Neff Garber, *The Gadsden Treaty* (Philadelphia: Press of the University of Pennsylvania, 1923), 3–4, 184; Potter, *Impending Crisis,* 182–83; Simms, *Decade of Sectional Controversy, 1851–1861,* 63.

6. R. Roberts, *Encyclopedia of Historic Forts,* 38; Ray Brandes, *Frontier Military Posts of Arizona* (Globe, AZ: D. S. King, 1960), 23; B. L. E. Bonneville to Adjutant General, July 15, 1859, in *Senate Executive Document,* Thirty-sixth Congress, First Session, 1859–1860 (Washington, DC: George W. Bowman, 1860), 306; RSE to Dear Elizabeth, December 27, 1856, in Percy Gatling Hamlin, ed., "An Arizona Letter of R. S. Ewell," *Journal of Arizona History* 7 (spring 1966): 25; see also Benjamin Sacks, "The Origins of Fort Buchanan: Myth and Fact," *Arizona and the West* 7 (1965): 207–225.

7. "Returns from Regular Cavalry Regiments," reel 4; Thrapp, ed., *Encyclopedia of Frontier Biography,* 136–37; Utley, *Frontiersmen in Blue,* 145-55.

8. Utley, *Frontiersmen in Blue,* 155; RSE to W. A. Nichols, June 8, 1857 (Ewell's Report), and B. L. E. Bonneville to W. A. Nichols, June 8, 1857, both in NA (Records of U.S. Army Continental Commands, 1820-1920), entry #3156.

9. Hamlin, *Making of a Soldier,* 81–83.

10. Utley, *Frontiersmen in Blue,* 156–57; Frank C. Lockwood, *The Apache Indians* (New York: Macmillan, 1938), 95–98; Constance Wynn Altshuler, *Cavalry Yellow and Infantry Blue: Army Officers in Arizona Between 1851 and 1886* (Tucson: Arizona Historical Society, 1991), 125.

11. *Florence Weekly Enterprise,* January 17, 1891; *Tombstone Prospector,* January 8, 1915.

12. Lizinka C. Brown to RSE, July 1, 1857, PBEP.

13. Georgia Wehrman, "Harshaw: Mining Camp of the Patagonias," *Journal of Arizona History* 6 (spring 1965): 22–24; Bert M. Fireman, *Arizona: Historic Land* (New York: Knopf, 1982), 88–92; *Tucson Arizona Daily Star,* July 5, 1879.

14. *San Francisco Daily Bulletin,* May 14, 1859; Hamlin, *Making of a Soldier,* 85–86; RSE to Dear Lizzie, August 17, 1859, Ewell Papers, LC; Wehrman, "Mining Camp of the Patagonias," 24–25.

15. Hamlin, *Making of a Soldier,* 83–84; W. Webb, ed., *Handbook of Texas,* 1: 258; *San Francisco Golden Era,* October 18, 1857.

16. RSE to Dear Lizzie, May 16, 1858, Ewell Papers, LC; John Garland to Lorenzo Thomas, September 5, 1858, in U.S. Congress, *Senate Executive Document,* Thirty-fifth Congress, Second Session (Washington, DC: William A. Harris, 1859), 299; Ewell Family Genealogy, B-EPTSL.

17. John Garland to Lorenzo Thomas, May 1, 1858, in U.S. Congress,

Senate Executive Document, Thirty-fifth Congress, Second Session, 288; Edwin R. Sweeney, *Cochise: Chiricahua Chief* (Norman: U of Oklahoma P, 1991), 118ff.; Odie B. Faulk, *Crimson Desert: Indian Wars of the American Southwest* (New York: Oxford UP, 1974), 150–53.

18. Sweeney, *Cochise,* 118ff.; "Cochise," in Thrapp, ed., *Encyclopedia of Frontier Biography,* 1: 290–91; Fireman, *Arizona,* 104.

19. Sweeney, *Cochise,* 184ff.; John A. Spring, "The Ordeal of Mrs. Page," *Wide World Magazine* 15 (February 1912): 362–63; *San Francisco Daily Bulletin,* November 5, 27, 1858; RSE to Dear Lizzie, November 14, 1858, Ewell Papers, LC.

20. Utley, *Frontiersmen in Blue,* 157–60; Lockwood, *Apache Indians,* 98–99; *Tubac Weekly Arizonian,* May 3, 31, 1859; *San Francisco Evening Bulletin,* March 22, 1859.

21. *Tucson Arizona Daily Citizen,* January 19, 1895.

22. Ewell Family Genealogy, B-EPTSL; RSE to Dear Bettie, May 19, 1858, Ewell Papers, LC.

23. Joseph Fish, "Fish Manuscript" (unpublished typescript), Snowflake, Arizona, 1906, copy in Department of Library, Archives, and Public Records, Phoenix, 2: 2–3; Samuel W. Cozzens, *The Marvelous Country; or, Three Years in Arizona and New Mexico, the Apache's Home* (Minneapolis: Ross and Haines, reprint, 1967), 115; *Tubac Weekly Arizonian,* May 3, July 14, 1859; "Returns from Regular Cavalry Regiments," reel 5.

24. RSE to Dear Lizzie, September 22, RSE to Dear Becca, September 27, and RSE to Dear Bettie, October 10, 1859, Ewell Papers, LC; Hamlin, *Making of a Soldier,* 89–93.

25. Adjutant General to Commanding Officer, Fort Buchanan, October 10, 1859, "Letters Sent by the Office of the Adjutant General," reel 19; *San Francisco Evening Bulletin,* November 2, 1859; *Tubac Weekly Arizonian,* November 3, 1859.

26. *San Francisco Evening Bulletin,* November 25, December 13, 1859; Samuel A. Cooper to RSE, February 6, 1859, Samuel Cooper to I. V. D. Reeve, November 11, 1859, "Letters Sent by the Office of the Adjutant General," reel 19.

27. Constance Wynn Altshuler, *Chains of Command: Arizona and the Army, 1856–1875* (Tucson: Arizona Historical Society, 1981), 11–12; Utley, *Frontiersmen in Blue,* 15; U.S. Congress, *Senate Executive Document,* Thirty-sixth Congress, Second Session (Washington, DC: George W. Bowman, 1861), 199–200.

28. RSE to Dear Becca, January 10, 1860, Ewell Papers, LC; Altshuler, *Chains of Command,* 11; "Returns from Regular Cavalry Regiments," reel 5.

29. *San Francisco Evening Bulletin,* February 24, March 26, 1860; Byrd Howell Granger, *Arizona Place Names (X Marks the Spot)* (Tucson, AZ: Falconer, 1983), 232.

30. Various accounts give different ages for the child.

31. Virginia Culin Roberts, *With Their Own Blood: A Saga of Southwestern Pioneers* (Fort Worth: Texas Christian UP, 1992), 3ff.; Altshuler, *Chains of Command,* 11–12; Spring, "Ordeal of Mrs. Page," 363–64; see also Constance Wynn Altshuler, *Latest from Arizona! The Hesperian Letters, 1859–1861* (Tucson: Arizona Pioneers Historical Society, 1969).

32. *San Francisco Evening Bulletin,* April 4, 11, 1860; V. Roberts, *With Their Own Blood,* 33–96; Spring, "Ordeal of Mrs. Page," passim; Thrapp, ed., *Encyclopedia of Frontier Biography,* 3: 1104.

33. *San Francisco Evening Bulletin,* April 16, 1860; Altshuler, *Chains of Command,* 12; Spring, "Ordeal of Mrs. Page," 366.

34. Hamlin, *Making of a Soldier,* 95; L. Boyd Finch, *Confederate Pathway to the Pacific: Major Sherod Hunter and the Arizona Territory, C.S.A.* (Tucson: Arizona Historical Society, 1996), 38–39; Odie B. Faulk, *Arizona: A Short History* (Norman: U of Oklahoma P, 1970), 100–01.

35. Frank C. Lockwood, *Life in Old Tucson, 1854–1864, as Remembered by the Little Maid* (Los Angeles: Ward Richie Press, 1943), 176–78; Keleher, *Turmoil in New Mexico,* 144, 393; Secretary of War, *The War of the Rebellion: A Compilation of the Official Records of the Union and Confederate Armies* (Washington, DC: Government Printing Office, 188ff.), vol. 50, 637, hereafter cited as O.R.; all references to the O.R. hereafter are from series 1 unless otherwise indicated; see also Robert Stephen Milota, "John Bankhead Magruder: The California Years" (MA thesis, University of San Diego, 1990), passim.

36. Benjamin Sacks, *Be It Enacted: The Creation of the Arizona Territory* (Tempe: Arizona Historical Foundation, 1964), 137–51; Henry Walker and Don Bufkin, *Historical Atlas of Arizona* (Norman: U of Oklahoma P, 1979), 26–29; Odie B. Faulk, *Land of Many Frontiers: A History of the American Southwest* (New York: Oxford UP, 1968), 185–86.

37. Sweeney, *Cochise,* 136–37; *San Francisco Evening Bulletin,* July 14, 1860.

38. "Andrew Talcott Diary, June 20, 21, 1860," Talcott Family Papers, VHS; Casdorph, *Lee and Jackson,* 167–70; George G. Shackleford, "Lieutenant Lee Reports to Captain Talcott on Fort Calhoun's Construction on the Rip Raps," *Virginia Magazine of History and Biography* 60 (April 1952): 458–87.

39. Sweeney, *Cochise,* 137–39; *San Francisco Evening Bulletin,* July 20, 1860; Lockwood, *Apache Indians,* 100–30.

40. Hamlin, *Making of a Soldier,* 97–98; "Returns from Regular Cavalry Regiments," reel 5; RSE to Dear Becca, July 29, 1860, B-EPTSL; Altshuler, *Chains of Command,* 13.

Chapter 5: The Lost Order

1. Hamlin, *Making of a Soldier,* 97–98; David Herbert Donald, *Lincoln* (London: Jonathan Cape, 1995), 207–11; Potter, *Impending Crisis,* 405ff.

2. Carl Coke Rister, *Robert E. Lee in Texas* (Norman: U of Oklahoma P, 1946), 146–55; Williams, "General Ewell to High Private," 159; Wert, *General James Longstreet*, 51–53; Oates, "Texas Under the Secessionists," 195–98. The best source for creation of the Confederate government is William C. Davis, *"A Government of Our Own": The Making of the Confederacy* (New York: Free Press, 1994).

3. Williams, "High Private in the Rear," 158–59. See also P. G. Hamlin to Andrew Wallace, September 2, 1965, Richard S. Ewell Biographical File, Arizona Historical Society, Tucson. This source has an attached copy of Ewell's letter as printed in the *New Orleans Times*, date not given.

4. Charles H. Ambler and Festus P. Summers, *West Virginia: The Mountain State* (Englewood Cliffs, NJ: Prentice-Hall, 1951), 190–94; Simms, *Decade of Sectional Controversy, 1951–1961*, 233–34; Oliver Chitwood, *John Tyler: Champion of the Old South* (New York: Russell and Russell, reprint, 1964), 436–38.

5. Vandiver, *Mighty Stonewall*, 136; Freeman, *Lee's Lieutenants*, 1: 721; Dowdey, *Lee*, 145, 173.

6. O.R., vol. 2, 835; Heitman, *Historical Register*, 410; William T. Poague, *A Gunner with Stonewall: Reminiscences of William Thomas Poague*, ed., Monroe F. Cockrell (Jackson, TN: McCowat-Mercer Press, reprint, 1957), 5.

7. James N. Bosang, *Memoirs of a Pulaski Veteran* (Pulaski, VA: privately printed, 1930), 4–5; C. G. Chamberlayne, *Ham Chamberlayne, Virginian: Letters and Papers of an Artillery Officer in the War for Southern Independence* (Richmond, VA: Dietz, 1932), 117; O.R., vol. 2, 364; William Snow, *Lee and His Generals* (New York: Fairfax Press, reprint, 1982), 346.

8. Henry, *Story of the Confederacy*, 50–53; Boatner, *Civil War Dictionary*, 531; Esposito, *West Point Atlas of American Wars*, 18; Edwin S. Barrett, *What I Saw at Bull Run* (Boston: Beacon Press, 1886), 11–13.

9. William C. Davis, *Battle at Bull Run: A History of the First Major Battle of the Civil War* (Baton Rouge: Louisiana State UP, reprint, 1981), 50–51; Kenneth P. Williams, *Lincoln Finds a General: A Military Study of the Civil War* (New York: Macmillan, 1964), 1: 60; O.R., vol. 2, 894; see also James B. Fry, *McDowell and Tyler in the Campaign of Bull Run, 1861* (New York: D. Van Nostrand, 1884), passim.

10. "From Fairfax C. H. to Richmond" (unsigned, unpaged memoir), PBEP; Campbell Brown, "Reminiscences" (handwritten memoir), B-EPTSL.

11. Tompkins himself reported fifty cavalrymen under his command, while General Irvin McDowell set the number at seventy-five. See O.R., vol. 2, 59–62.

12. "From Fairfax C. H. to Richmond"; Mrs. M. R. Barlow, "History of the Prince William Cavalry," *Confederate Veteran* 15 (August 1907): 353–54; O.R., vol. 2, 59.

13. In his official report Ewell says it was the Germantown Road; Campbell Brown has it as the Centreville Road.

14. "From Fairfax C. H. to Richmond"; O.R., vol. 2, 59–63; Dowdey, *Lee*, 153ff.

15. "From Fairfax C. H. to Richmond"; Snow, *Lee and His Generals*, 363; Mary A. R. Lee to Mildred C. Lee, June 17, 1863, Lee Family Papers, VHS.

16. "From Fairfax C. H. to Richmond"; "Gen. and Gov. William Smith," *Confederate Veteran* 8 (1900): 161; "Memoirs of S. W. Ferguson," Samuel Wragg Ferguson Papers, PLDU; Richard N. Current, ed., *Encyclopedia of the Confederacy* (New York: Simon and Schuster, 1993), 2: 570.

17. Maxey Gregg to RSE, June 31, 1861, Maxey Gregg Papers, VHS; Marcus J. Wright, *General Offices of the Confederate Army, of the Executive Departments of the Confederate States, Members of the Confederate Congress by States* (New York: Neale Publishing, 1911), 51–54; RSE to M. L. Bonham, June 21, 1861, Milledge L. Bonham Papers, University of South Carolina Library, Columbia.

18. P. G. T. Beauregard to RSE, July 18, 1861, P. G. T. Beauregard Papers, CHS; T. Harry Williams, *P. G. T. Beauregard: Napoleon in Gray* (Baton Rouge: Louisiana State UP, 1954), 67; Boatner, *Civil War Dictionary*, 54–55; O.R., vol. 2, 507; C. Vann Woodward and Elisabeth Muhlenfeld, eds., *The Private Mary Chesnut: The Unpublished Civil War Diaries* (New York: Oxford UP, 1984), 97.

19. M. L. Bonham to P. G. T. Beauregard, August 28, 1877, and RSE to M. L. Bonham, July 21, 1861, Bonham Papers; Robert M. Johnston, *Bull Run: Its Strategy and Tactics* (Boston: Houghton Mifflin, 1913), 159–61; Jubal A. Early, *Lieutenant General Jubal Anderson Early C.S.A.: Autobiographical Sketch and Narrative of the War Between the States* (New York: Konecky and Konecky, reprint, 1994), 4–5.

20. Davis, *Battle at Bull Run*, 102–05; Louis A. Sigaud, "Mrs. Greenhow and the Confederate Spy Ring," *Maryland Historical Magazine* 41 (September 1946): 173–75; O.R., vol. 2, 504; M. L. Bonham to P. G. T. Beauregard, August 25, 1877, Bonham Papers.

21. Davis, *Battle at Bull Run*, 109; O.R., vol. 2, 460; RSE, "Report of Brigadier General Richard Ewell, Commanding Second Brigade, First Corps" (handwritten report), PBEP.

22. Davis, *Battle at Bull Run*, 125–31; O.R., vol. 2, 444, 467; James Franklin, "Incidents at First Manassas Battle," *Confederate Veteran* 2 (1894): 292; Wert, *General James Longstreet*, 71; Daniel Tyler, *Autobiography and War Record* (New Haven, CT: privately printed, 1883), 53–55.

23. Gary W. Gallagher, ed., *Fighting for the Confederacy: The Personal Recollections of Edward Porter Alexander* (Chapel Hill: U of North Carolina P, 1989), 47; James I. Robertson Jr., *The Stonewall Brigade* (Baton Rouge: Louisiana State UP, 1963), 36–37; S. D. Buck, "Personal Memoirs," Samuel D. Buck Papers, PLDU; D. B. Conrad, "History of the First Battle of Manassas and the Organization of the Stonewall Brigade," *Southern Historical Society Papers* 20 (1892): 27.

24. Casdorph, *Lee and Jackson*, 204-06; George Cary Eggleston, *The History of the Confederate War: Its Causes and Conduct; A Narrative and Critical His-*

tory (New York: Sturgis and Walton, 1910), 224; Vandiver, *Mighty Stonewall,* 161; W. H. C. Whiting to R. L. Dabney, November 30, 1863, W. C. Dabney Papers, SHC.

25. O.R., vol. 2, 498; P. G. T. Beauregard, "The Battle of Bull Run," *Century Magazine* 28 (November 1884): 93; Gallagher, ed., *Fighting for the Confederacy,* 49.

26. Beauregard, "Battle of Bull Run," 101–02; Carmichael, "Escaping the Shadow," 137, 156.

27. Woodward and Muhlenfeld, eds., *Private Mary Chesnut,* 64, 107; Hamlin, *Making of a Soldier,* 107.

28. Brown, "Reminiscences"; Ewell's "handwritten report"; O.R., vol. 2, 536–37; RSE to P. G. T. Beauregard, July 25, 1861, PBEP.

29. RSE to JEJ, July 25, 1861, PBEP; J. A. Early to Harriet Stoddert Turner, Jubal A. Early Papers, December 4, 1884, PLDU; Campbell Brown, "General Ewell at First Manassas," *Southern Historical Society Papers* 13 (January 1885), 41–46; George F. Harrison, "Ewell at First Manassas," *Southern Historical Society Papers* 14 (1886), 356–58; see also "Memoranda of the Civil War: General R. S. Ewell at Bull Run," *Century Magazine* 29 (January 1885): 777–79.

30. Hamlin, *Making of a Soldier,* 106; James A. Kegel, *North with Lee and Jackson* (Mechanicsville, PA: Stackpole Books, 1996), 31; Henry, *Story of the Confederacy,* 60–61; O.R., vol. 2, 539.

31. Here Campbell Brown seems unintentionally misleading. Henry Thompson Hays was a Tennessean who became a New Orleans lawyer by way of Baltimore. Following service in the Mexican War, he became colonel of the Seventh Louisiana Infantry during 1861. Richard Griffith had been born in Pennsylvania but moved to Vicksburg, Mississippi, after 1837, where he became a schoolteacher until the Mexican War, when he enlisted in Jefferson Davis's First Mississippi Rifles. At the outbreak of Civil War he was made colonel of the Twelfth Mississippi Infantry. He was later elevated to general rank. Robert Emmett Rodes was a Virginian through and through, a graduate of VMI, who was working as an engineer in Alabama and became colonel of the Fifth Alabama Infantry. Rodes also attained general rank as well as becoming "one of the most popular and respected general officers in Robert E. Lee's army." See, Current, ed., *Encyclopedia of the Confederacy,* 2: 717–18, 753, 3: 1344–45.

32. O.R., vol. 2, 779; J. A. Gardner to Amanda Gardner, July 27, 1861, Amanda Gardner Papers, PLDU; Campbell Brown to Mrs. G. C. Hubbard, August 20, 1861, PBEP.

33. The Confederate Army of the Potomac should not be confused with the more widely known Union force of the same name. The former was organized when Beauregard took charge of the Alexandria Line, and the army in the Manassas sector continued under the designation until Robert E. Lee took command on June 1, 1862, when it was changed to the Army of Northern Virginia, see Boatner, *Civil War Dictionary,* 664.

34. O.R., vol. 5. 249, 913, 935, 939, 944, 1049; Julien Harrison to RSE, September 14, 1861, Julien Harrison Papers, ALUV; Brown, "Reminiscences"; J. A. Early to Joseph D. Balfour, October 14, 1861, Jubal A. Early Papers, VHS; see also RSE to J .A. Washington, October 10, 1861, James W. Eldridge Papers, HL.

35. Brown, "Reminiscences"; James I. Robertson Jr., *Stonewall Jackson: The Man, the Soldier, the Legend* (New York: Macmillan, 1997), 683; Mary Anna Jackson, "With Stonewall Jackson in Camp: More Confederate Memories," *Hearst Magazine* 34 (1913): 392-94; Mary Anna Jackson, *Memoirs of Stonewall Jackson By His Widow* (Louisville, KY: Prentice Press, 1895), 449–56.

36. J. Pelot to Lalla Pelot, September 5, 1861, Joseph Pelot Papers, PLDU; M. Wright, *General Officers of the Confederate Army*, 24–25; Brown, "Reminiscences."

37. Sears, *George B. McClellan*, 140, 160; Craig L. Symonds, *Joseph E. Johnston: A Civil War Biography* (New York: W. W. Norton, 1992), 145–46; O.R., vol. 5, 526.

38. T. Michael Parrish, *Richard Taylor: Soldier Prince of Dixie* (Chapel Hill: U of North Carolina P, 1992), 141; Brown, "Reminiscences"; Terry L. Jones, *Lee's Tigers: The Louisiana Infantry in the Army of Northern Virginia* (Baton Rouge: Louisiana State UP, 1987), 127–30; R. Taylor, *Deconstruction and Reconstruction*, 37–38.

39. "During his West Point Years [Elzey] dropped his last name (Jones) and used his middle name, that of his paternal grandmother," Boatner, *Civil War Dictionary*, 264.

40. Brown, "Reminiscences"; O.R., vol. 5, 1030; Paul D. Casdorph, *Republicans, Negroes, and Progressives in the South, 1912–1916* (University: U of Alabama P, 1981), 28; Robert G. Tanner, *Stonewall in the Valley: Thomas J. "Stonewall" Jackson's Shenandoah Valley Campaign, Spring 1862* (Garden City, NY: Doubleday, 1974), 173.

41. Brown, "Reminiscences"; Early, *Autobiographical Sketch*, 56.

Chapter 6: "All Running—All Yelling"

1. Brown, "Reminiscences"; RSE to Dear Lizinka, March 5, 1862, Ewell Papers, MOC; RSE to Dear Lizinka, February 20, March 7, 1862, Ewell Papers, LC.

2. RSE to Dear Lizinka, March 15, 1862, Ewell Papers, MOC; RSE to Dear Lizinka, March 16, 1862, LC; Bruce Catton, *Grant Moves South* (Boston: Little, Brown, 1960), 186–87; Henry, *Story of the Confederacy*, 86.

3. James M. McPherson, *Ordeal By Fire: The Civil War and Reconstruction* (New York: Knopf, 1983), 151; Hans L. Trefousse, *Andrew Johnson: A Biography* (New York: W. W. Norton, 1989), 20–23, 154-57; RSE to Dear Lizinka, March 16, 1862, Ewell Papers, LC; RSE to Dear Lizinka, March 23, 1862, Ewell Papers, MOC.

4. Brown, "Reminiscences"; O.R., vol. 11, pt. 3, 404, 495, 501; Symonds, *Joseph E. Johnston,* 152; Robertson, *General A. P. Hill,* 59–60; see also C. W. Field to RSE, April 20, 1862, War, 1861–1865, Letters (E, Box 3), NYHS.

5. RSE to JEJ, April 8, 1862, Ewell Papers, PLDU; Hamlin, *"Old Bald Head,"* 80–83; John H. Worsham, "Jackson's Valley Campaign," *Southern Historical Society Papers* 38 (1910): 327.

6. R. Taylor, *Deconstruction and Reconstruction,* 35–38; Parrish, *Richard Taylor,* 146; J. C. Haskell, "Memoirs" (typescript), John C. Haskell Papers, PLDU.

7. RSE to JEJ, April 16, 1862, JEJ Papers, HL; TJJ to RSE, April 10, 1862, PBEP; Brown, "Reminiscences"; TJJ to RSE, April 10, 1862, Whitwell Autograph File, Massachusetts Historical Society, Boston; see also TJJ to RSE, April 11, 12, 13, 14, 16, 17 (three letters), and 18 (three letters), 1862, B-EPTSL.

8. JEJ to RSE, April 17, 1872, B-EPTSL.

9. Robert K. Krick, *Conquering the Valley: Stonewall Jackson at Port Republic* (New York: William Morrow, 1996), 5; Burke Davis, *They Called Him Stonewall: A Life of Lt. General T. J. Jackson, C.S.A.* (New York: Fairfax Press, reprint, 1988), 18–20; O.R., vol. 11, pt. 3, 445.

10. Henry Kyd Douglas, *I Rode with Stonewall* (Chapel Hill: U of North Carolina P, reprint, 1984), 41–45; Vandiver, *Mighty Stonewall,* 221–23. For a different assessment of Douglas, see, Robertson, *Stonewall Jackson,* 853.

11. Lieutenant Keith Boswell, later Jackson's chief engineer, was an Alabama boy who became a valued member of Jackson's staff. He was apparently sent to Ewell at Brandy Station before Douglas.

12. This route crossed the Blue Ridge through Swift Gap. Jackson had abandoned the Fisher's Gap idea after his own fallback around the southern spur of the Massanutten to Conrad's Store in the Luray, or Page, Valley.

13. O.R., vol. 12, pt. 3, 858; Vandiver, *Mighty Stonewall,* 513; Tanner, *Stonewall in the Valley,* 145; Brown, "Reminiscences"; see note 7 above for mss. relating to Jackson's changing instructions.

14. Brown, "Reminiscences"; R. Taylor, *Deconstruction and Reconstruction,* 42; TJJ to RSE, April 20, 1862, B-EPTSL. The original in Jackson's own hand is in the T. J. Jackson Papers, CHS; the copy in the B-EPTSL is by one of Ewell's aides, probably Campbell Brown.

15. John H. Worsham, *One of Jackson's Foot Cavalry* (Jackson, TN: McCowat-Mercer Press, reprint, 1964), 25–27; Millard K. Bushong, "Jackson in the Shenandoah," *West Virginia History* 27 (January 1966): 88–89; William L. Wessels, *Born to Be a Soldier: The Military Career of William Wing Loring of St. Augustine, Florida* (Fort Worth: Texas Christian UP, 1971), 60–61; John Esten Cooke, *Stonewall Jackson: A Military Biography* (New York: D. Appleton, 1866), 97.

16. Vandiver, *Mighty Stonewall,* 205–24; Robertson, *Stonewall Jackson,* 357; Esposito, *West Point Atlas of American Wars,* 50.

17. O.R., vol. 12, pt. 3, 872, 876; Brown, "Reminiscences"; TJJ to RSE,

April 30, 1862, Rives Family Papers, ALUV; J. A. Harman to Dear Brother, April 29, 1862, John A. Harman Papers, LC.

18. William C. Davis, *Jefferson Davis: The Man and His Hour* (New York: HarperCollins, reprint, 1992), 388; Parrish, ed., *Reminiscences of the War,* 8–10.

19. Brown, "Reminiscences"; RSE to Samuel Cooper, Ewell Log Book, May 14, 1862, Ewell Papers, PLDU.

20. O.R., vol. 12, pt. 3, 878; TJJ to RSE, May 3, 1862, TJJ Papers, Maine Historical Society, Augusta.

21. O.R., vol. 12, pt. 3, 879; TJJ to RSE, TJJ Papers, VHS.

22. Columbia Bridge was a major crossing on the South Fork of the Shenandoah; it was in the Luray, or Page, Valley roughly ten miles north of Conrad's Store.

23. James I. Robertson, "Stonewall in the Shenandoah," *Civil War Times Illustrated* 2 (May 1963): 20; John W. Fravel, "Jackson's Valley Campaign," *Confederate Veteran* 27 (1898): 418; John W. Schildt, *Stonewall Jackson Day by Day* (Chewsville, MD: Antietam Publications, 1980), 50–51; TJJ to RSE, May 6, 1862 (two letters), B-EPTSL.

24. RSE to REL, May 8, 1872, JEJ Papers, HL; REL to TJJ, May 8, 1862, TJJ Papers, SHC; TJJ to RSE, May 8, 1862, Western Manuscript Collection, Ellis Library, University of Missouri, Columbia.

25. Campbell Brown to My Dear Mother, March 9, 1862, B-EPTSL; O.R., vol. 12, pt. 3, 137–40.

26. Robert L. Dabney, *Life and Campaigns of Lieut. Gen. Thomas J. Jackson* (New York: Blelock and Company, 1866), 353; Boatner, *Civil War Dictionary,* 532; O.R., vol. 12, pt. 1, 470–74; see also Richard L. Armstrong, *The Battle of McDowell, March 11-May 18, 1862* (Lynchburg, VA: H. E. Howard, 1990).

27. Franklin M. Myers, *The Comanches: A History of White's Brigade, Virginia Cavalry* (Marietta, GA: Continental Book, reprint, 1956), 38–39; John E. Divine, *35th Battalion Virginia Cavalry* (Lynchburg, VA: H. E. Howard, 1985), 5–6; D. Pfanz, *Richard S. Ewell,* 168.

28. Thomas T. Munford, "Reminiscences of Jackson's Valley Campaign," *Southern Historical Society Papers* 7 (1879): 526; Brown, "Reminiscences"; M. Wright, *General Officers of the Confederate Army,* 150.

29. Current, ed., *Encyclopedia of the Confederacy,* 7: 1671; Casdorph, *Republicans, Negroes, and Progressives, 28*; A. L. Long, "Reminiscences of the Army of Northern Virginia," *Southern Historical Society Papers* 9 (July 1881); 346; Munford, "Reminiscences," 530. Both Long and Munford offer additional vignettes about Ewell during the war.

30. James Dabney McCabe, *The Life of Thomas J. Jackson; By an Ex-Cadet* (Richmond, VA: James E. Goode, 1864), 66–68; O.R., vol. 12, pt. 3, 890–96; Hamlin, *Making of a Soldier,* 107–08.

31. TJJ to RSE, May 13, 1862, Richmond Autograph Collection, Massa-

chusetts Historical Society, Boston; JEJ to RSE, May 13, 1862, James W. Eldridge Papers, HL; RSE to TJJ, May 13, 1862, HL; RSE to TJJ, May 13, 1862, Charles W. Dabney Papers, SHC; William W. Kirkland to Turner Ashby, May 13, 1862, Ashby Family Papers, ALUV; RSE to REL, May 13, 1862, Heatt-Wilson Papers, SHC; RSE to TJJ, May 13, 1862, George and Katherine Davis Collection, Tulane University, New Orleans.

32. Vandiver, *Mighty Stonewall*, 234; O.R., vol. 12, pt. 3, 896; Clifford Dowdey, *The Seven Days: The Emergence of Lee* (Boston: Little, Brown, 1964), 73–75; see also J. L. Power to Dear Sister, May 19, 1862, James L. Power Papers, VHS.

33. Tanner, *Stonewall in the Valley*, 195; M. Jackson, *Memoirs of Stonewall Jackson*, 259.

34. Brown, "Reminiscences"; Tanner, *Stonewall in the Valley*, 364–65; John W. Wayland, *Stonewall Jackson's Way: Route, Method, Achievement* (Staunton, VA: McClure, 1940), 202–05; see also R. L. Dabney to RSE, May 20, 1862, War, 1861–1865, Letters (E, Box 3), NYHS.

35. Robertson, "Stonewall in the Shenandoah," 28; Brown, "Reminiscences"; R. Taylor, *Deconstruction and Reconstruction*, 50–53; Louis Sigaud, *Belle Boyd: Confederate Spy* (Richmond, VA: Dietz, 1944), 45–49; see also Douglas, *I Rode with Stonewall*, 52, and Parrish, *Richard Taylor*, 164–68.

36. Brown, "Reminiscences"; O.R., vol. 12, pt. 1, 565, 778; RSE to Dear Becca, May 23, 1862, B-EPTSL.

37. O.R., vol. 12, pt. 1, 704, 709; Henry, *Story of the Confederacy*, 146; William Allan, *History of the Campaign of Gen. T. J. (Stonewall) Jackson in the Shenandoah Valley of Virginia* (Dayton, OH: Morningside Book Shop, reprint, 1974), 182ff.; R. Taylor, *Deconstruction and Reconstruction*, 55; see also R. L. Dabney to RSE, March 27, 1862, BPEP.

38. O.R., vol. 12, pt. 1, 732, 779; Current, ed., *Encyclopedia of the Confederacy*, 4: 1732; Campbell Brown, "Notes on Ewell's Division in the Campaign of 1862," *Southern Historical Society Papers* 10 (1882): 256; Gary Schreckengost, "Stonewall's Triumphant Return to Winchester," *America's Civil War* 13 (July 2000): 27–32.

39. O.R., vol. 12, pt.1, 706–10; Campbell Brown to Dear Mother, May 31, 1862, PBEP; TJJ to RSE, May 31, 1862, TJJ Papers, SHC; Brown, "Notes on Ewell's Division in 1862," 256–57.

40. Roy P. Basler, ed., *Collected Works: The Abraham Lincoln Association, Springfield, Illinois* (New Brunswick, NJ: Rutgers UP, 1953), 5, 230–32, 246; O.R., vol. 12, pt. 1, 13–14, 817; RSE to JEJ, April 12, 1866, JEJ Papers, HL.

41. Tanner, *Stonewall in the Valley*, 238–40; William H. Condon, *The Life of Major General James Shields* (Chicago: Blakely Printing, 1900), 227–28; RSE to JEJ, April 12, 1866, JEJ Papers, HL; Robertson, *Stonewall Brigade*, 103.

42. James H. Lane, "History of Lane's Brigade," *Southern Historical Society Papers* 10 (1882): 257; Munford, "Reminiscences," 529; M. Jackson, *Memoirs of Stonewall Jackson*, 261; RSE to JEJ, April 12, 1862, JEJ Papers, HL; Clarence

Thomas, *General Turner Ashby: The Centaur of the South* (Winchester, VA: Eddy Press, 1907), 155; James B. Avirett, *The Memoirs of General Turner Ashby and His Compeers* (Baltimore: Selby and Dulany, 1867), 221–24.

43. Dabney, *Life and Campaigns of Jackson,* 153–56; Allan Nevins, *Frémont: The West's Greatest Adventurer* (New York: Harper and Brothers, 1928), 2: 636–37; Esposito, *West Point Atlas of American Wars,* 53; Current, ed., *Encyclopedia of the Confederacy,* 4: 431.

44. RSE to JEJ, April 16, 1866, JEJ Papers, HL; Campbell Brown to Dear Mother, June 17, 1862, PBEP; Allan, *Jackson in the Shenandoah,* 156; see also T. T. Munford to R. L. Dabney, December 12, 1865, and RSE to R. L. Dabney, October 1, 1863, Charles W. Dabney Papers, SHC.

45. Poague, *Gunner with Stonewall,* 26–28; John O. Casler, *Four Years in the Stonewall Brigade* (Marietta, GA: Continental Book, reprint, 1951), 86; Esposito, *West Point Atlas of American Wars,* 53.

46. Robertson, *Stonewall Brigade,* 110; Campbell Brown to Dear Mother, June 17, 1862, PBEP; O.R., vol. 12, pt. 1, 798–802; Tanner, *Stonewall in the Valley,* 286–89.

47. O.R., vol. 12, pt. 1, 781–87; Krick, *Conquering the Valley,* 394–95; Campbell Brown to Dear Mother, June 17, 1862, PBEP.

Chapter 7: In Front of Richmond

1. Schildt, *Stonewall Jackson Day by Day,* 62; R. Taylor, *Deconstruction and Reconstruction,* 72–79; Campbell Brown to Dear Mother, June 17, 1862, PBEP; Divine, *35th Battalion Virginia Cavalry,* 6.

2. Samuel J. Martin, "Ewell at Gaines Mill," KEPI 3 (April-May 1985): 10–11; R. Dabney, *Life and Campaigns of Jackson,* 434; Vandiver, *Mighty Stonewall,* 288–92.

3. D. H. Hill, "The Battle of Gaines Mill: Including a Sketch of Jackson's March by Major R. L. Dabney," *Century Illustrated Magazine* 10 (1885): 295; H. K. Douglas, *I Rode with Stonewall,* 101; Casdorph, *Lee and Jackson,* 243; W. Webb, ed., *Handbook of Texas,* 1: 452; see also Thomas Cary Johnson, *The Life and Letters of Robert Lewis Dabney* (Richmond, VA: Presbyterian Committee on Publication, 1903), 269–71.

4. S. Martin, "Ewell at Gaines Mill," 11; Hill, "Battle of Gaines Mill," 295–97; Edward A. Moore, *The Story of a Cannoneer under Stonewall Jackson* (Lynchburg, VA: J. P. Bell, 1910), 83.

5. For a second view, see, Gallagher, ed., *Lee: The Soldier,* 322, 329.

6. O.R., vol. 11, pt. 3, 872; Dabney, *Campaigns of Jackson,* 431; John B. Hood, *Advance and Retreat: Personal Experiences in the United States and Confederate States Armies* (New Orleans: P. G. T. Beauregard, 1880), 23–25; Dowdey, *Seven Days,* 115–22.

7. O.R., vol. 11, pt. 3, 589; Dabney, *Campaigns of Jackson*, 435.

8. Brown, "Reminiscences"; Hamlin, *"Old Bald Head,"* 107–08; Louisa H. A. Minor "Diary," Minor Family Papers, ALUV; S. Martin, "Ewell at Gaines Mill," 11.

9. O.R., vol. 11, pt. 2, 612; Stephen W. Sears, *To the Gates of Richmond: The Peninsula Campaign* (New York: Ticknor and Fields, 1992), 385; Robert K. Krick, *Lee's Colonels: A Biographical Register of the Field Officers of the Army of Northern Virginia* (Dayton, OH: Morningside Book Shop, 1979), 77, 97.

10. Esposito, *West Point Atlas of American Wars*, 43; Charles Royster, *The Destructive War: William Tecumseh Sherman, Stonewall Jackson, and the Americans* (New York: Knopf, 1991), 42–43; Lee's Order Number 75, copy in John Bankhead Magruder Papers, MOC; Casdorph, *Prince John Magruder*, 169–70.

11. For a detailed map of the Jackson/Ewell line of march, see Dabney, *Campaigns of Jackson*, 437; a map of the fracas at Hundley's Corner can be found in Dowdey, *Seven Days*, 195.

12. Brown, "Reminiscences"; O.R., vol. 11, pt. 2, 882; Longstreet, *From Appomattox to Manassas*, 122–23; Schildt, *Stonewall Jackson Day by Day*, 64.

13. Eggleston, *History of the Confederate War*, 400; Poague, *Gunner with Stonewall*, 29; Dowdey, *Seven Days*, 193–95; Robertson, *General A. P. Hill*, 74–75.

14. Dabney, *Campaigns of Jackson*, 442; O.R., vol. 11, pt. 2, 223, 605, 621.

15. Esposito, *West Point Atlas of American Wars*, 45; Sears, *To the Gates of Richmond*, 231; Sears, *George B. McClellan*, 209–13.

16. See Sears, *To the Gates of Richmond*, 220, for a detailed map showing Ewell's line of march.

17. O.R., vol. 11, pt. 2, 621; Brown, "Reminiscences"; Hal Bridges, *Lee's Maverick General: Daniel Harvey Hill* (Lincoln: U of Nebraska P, reprint, 1991), 69–70; B. Davis, *They Called Him Stonewall*, 222–23.

18. O.R., vol. 11, pt. 2, 606; Robertson, *General A. P. Hill*, 81; Long, *Memoirs of Robert E. Lee*, 172; Alexander S. Webb, *The Peninsula: McClellan's Campaign of 1862* (New York: Jack Brussell, reprint, 1959), 131.

19. O.R., vol. 11, pt. 2, 605; Sears, *To the Gates of Richmond*, 231, 238.

20. O.R., vol. 11, pt. 2, 605–06; Emory M. Thomas, *Richmond: The Peninsula Campaign* (Harrisburg, PA: Eastern Alcorn Press, 1985), 36–37; Sears, *To the Gates of Richmond*, 230; Krick, *Lee's Colonel's*, 313; William M'Comb, "The Battles in Front of Richmond," *Confederate Veteran* 23 (1915): 161.

21. O.R., vol. 11, pt. 2, 606; Hamlin, *"Old Bald Head,"* 110–11; S. Martin, "Ewell at Gaines Mill," 11; Brown, "Reminiscences."

22. Gallagher, ed., *Fighting for the Confederacy*, 105; George B. McClellan, *Report on the Organization and Campaigns of the Army of the Potomac* (Freeport, NY: Books for Libraries, reprint, 1970), 353–55; Dowdey, *Lee*, 261–63. The spelling of Despatch Station varies; it is often presented as Dispatch Station.

23. Thomason, *JEB Stuart*, 114–15; A. Webb, *The Peninsula*, 136–37; O.R., vol. 11, pt. 2, 607; Hamlin, *"Old Bald Head,"* 112; William W. Goldsborough,

The Maryland Line in the Confederate Army, 1861–1865 (Gaithersburg, MD: Olde Soldier's Books, reprint, 1987), 59–63.

24. R. Taylor, *Deconstruction and Reconstruction,* 89.

25. D. Pfanz, *Richard S. Ewell,* 229; Hamlin, *"Old Bald Head,"* 113; Hill, "Battle of Gaines Mill," 298; O.R., vol. 11, pt. 2, 608; R. Taylor, *Deconstruction and Reconstruction,* 89.

26. Long, *Memoirs of Robert E. Lee,* 235–36; Robertson, *General A. P. Hill,* 86–87; Wert, *General James Longstreet,* 140–41.

27. Casdorph, *Prince John Magruder,* 179; D. Augustus Dickert, *History of Kershaw's Brigade* (Dayton, OH: Morningside Book Shop, reprint, 1976), 129–30; Longstreet, *From Manassas to Appomattox,* 132; K. Williams, *Lincoln Finds a General,* 1: 235–37; R. Taylor, *Deconstruction and Reconstruction,* 90.

28. See Robertson, *Stonewall Jackson,* 878, for a discussion of whether the site should be called "Frayser's Farm" or "Glendale."

29. Esposito, *West Point Atlas of American Wars,* 49; Schildt, *Stonewall Jackson Day by Day,* 64–65; O.R., vol. 11, pt. 2, 495; William Swinton, *Campaigns of the Army of the Potomac* (New York: Charles Scribner's Sons, 1882), 152–57; F. Lee, *General Lee,* 154–56.

30. Swinton, *Campaigns of the Army of the Potomac,* 159; O.R., vol. 11, pt. 2, 561, 613; Parrish, *Richard Taylor,* 235–37; Gallagher, ed., *Fighting for the Confederacy,* 108–09.

31. Hunter H. McGuire, *The Confederate Cause and Conduct in the War Between the States* (Richmond, VA: L. H. Jenkins, 1907), 200–01; Robertson, *Stonewall Brigade,* 120; Gallagher, ed., *Fighting for the Confederacy,* 108; Freeman, *Lee's Lieutenants,* 1: 587; J. E. Phillips, "Memoirs of the War" (handwritten manuscript), James E. Phillips Papers, VHS; Robertson, *Stonewall Jackson,* 497.

32. Stewart Sifakis, *Who Was Who in the Confederacy* (New York: Facts on File, 1988), 85; M. Wright, *General Officers of the Confederate Army,* 19; Robertson, *General A. P. Hill,* 270.

33. Early, *Autobiographical Sketch,* 77–78; Millard K. Bushong, *Old Jube: A Biography of General Jubal A. Early* (Shippensburg, PA: White Mane, 1955), 60.

34. Secretary of War, *Atlas to Accompany the Official Records of the Union and Confederate Armies* (New York: Thomas Yoseloff, reprint, 1958), 21; Jennings C. Wise, *The Long Arm of Lee: The History of the Artillery of the Army of Northern Virginia* (New York: Oxford UP, reprint, 1959), 56; Eggleston, *History of the Confederate War,* 412; Freeman, *Lee's Lieutenants,* 1: 593; McPherson, *Battle Cry of Freedom,* 470.

35. A. Webb, *The Peninsula,* 152–53; Vandiver, *Mighty Stonewall,* 318; Early, *Autobiographical Sketch,* 79.

36. O.R., vol. 11, pt. 2, 618–19; Goldsborough, *Maryland Line,* 64; Freeman, *Lee's Lieutenants,* 1: 603; E. Thomas, *Richmond: The Peninsula Campaign,* 46–47.

37. Early, *Autobiographical Sketch,* 79–82; O.R., vol. 11, pt. 2, 611–13; Bridges, *Lee's Maverick General,* 81–83.

38. Goldsborough, *Maryland Line,* 64; E. Thomas, *Richmond: The Peninsula Campaign,* 47–48; see also Joseph P. Cullen, *The Peninsula Campaign, 1862: McClellan and Lee Struggle for Richmond* (Harrisburg, PA: Stackpole Books, 1973), passim.

39. Brown, "Reminiscences"; Fitz-John Porter, "The Last of the Seven Days Battle," *Century Illustrated Monthly Magazine* 34 (1889): 629–31; Campbell Brown to My Dear Mother, July 3, 1862, PBEP; Thomas T. Munford to W. T. Poague, November 6, 1863, Munford-Ellis Papers, PLDU.

40. Freeman, *Lee's Lieutenants,* 1: 655.

Chapter 8: Jackson's Man

1. Boatner, *Civil War Dictionary,* 659; John Codman Ropes, *The Army Under Pope* (New York: Charles Scribner's Sons, 1881), 173–75; John Pope, "To Gain Time . . . The Second Battle of Bull Run," in Ned Bradford, ed., *Battles and Leaders of the Civil War* (New York: Appleton-Century-Crofts, 1956), 209–10.

2. Sears, *George B. McClellan,* 246–47; Edward J. Stackpole, *From Cedar Mountain to Antietam* (Harrisburg, PA: Stackpole Books, 1993), 22–23; Ropes, *Army Under Pope,* 173–76.

3. O.R., vol. 12, pt. 3, 919; Stackpole, *From Cedar Mountain to Antietam,* 25; W. C. Davis, *Jefferson Davis,* 458.

4. Hamlin, *"Old Bald Head,"* 117; Henry, *Story of the Confederacy,* 175; Ropes, *Army Under Pope,* 177; Patterson, *Rebels from West Point,* 159–60.

5. Thomason, *JEB Stuart,* 204–05; Emory M. Thomas, *Bold Dragoon: The Life of J. E. B. Stuart* (Norman: U of Oklahoma P, reprint, 1999), 136–37; Schildt, *Stonewall Jackson Day by Day,* 65–66; Brown, "Reminiscences."

6. Secretary of War, *Atlas to Accompany the Official Records,* 42; Goldsborough, *Maryland Line,* 64; H. K. Douglas, *I Rode with Stonewall,* 117.

7. Brown, "Reminiscences"; Robertson, *Stonewall Jackson,* 510; R. Taylor, *Deconstruction and Reconstruction,* 31–34; O.R., vol. 12, pt. 3, 918–19.

8. "Civil War Note Book of Washington Hands" (handwritten manuscript), Washington Hands Papers, ALUV; John J. Hennessy, *Return to Bull Run: The Battle and Campaign of Second Manassas* (Norman: U of Oklahoma P, reprint, 1999), 564; Krick, *Lee's Colonels,* 60.

9. O.R., vol. 12, pt. 2, 227, pt. 3, 964–65; H. K. Douglas, *I Rode with Stonewall,* 118; E. F. Paxton to RSE, August 16, 1862, Elisha Franklin Paxton Papers, CHS; A. S. Pendleton to RSE, August 7, 1862, Alexander S. Pendleton Papers, CHS; Sifakis, *Who Was Who in the Confederacy,* 218.

10. Ewell's artillery consisted of Balthis's Battery, Staunton Virginia; Brown's Battery, Chesapeake, Maryland; D'Aquin's Battery, New Orleans; John R. Johnson's

Virginia Battery; Dement's Maryland Battery; and Latimer's Battery, Courtney, Virginia; see, Hennessey, *Return to Bull Run*, 566.

11. Early, *Autobiographical Sketch*, 92; Brown, "Reminiscences"; J. Gay Seabourne, "The Battle of Cedar Mountain," *Civil War Times Illustrated* 5 (December 1966): 29; I. G. Bradwell, "From Cold Harbor to Cedar Mountain," *Confederate Veteran* 29 (1921): 224.

12. RSE to Dear Lizzie, July 20, 1862, Ewell Papers, LC; Hamlin, *Making of a Soldier*, 111–13; "H. J. Mugler Memoir" (handwritten manuscript), West Virginia University Library, Morgantown.

13. "War Memoirs of S. D. Buck" (typescript), Samuel D. Buck Papers, PLDU; Charles J. Faulkner to RSE, undated, War, 1861–1865, Letters (E, Box 3) NYHS; "Washington Hands Note Book"; Hennessy, *Return to Bull Run*, 566; RSE to George W. Randolph, August 15, 1862, Ewell Papers, MOC; M. Wright, *General Officers of the Confederate Army*, 143.

14. V. D. Groner to RSE, July 17, 1862, James W. Eldridge Papers, HL; Krick, *Lee's Colonels*, 227–28, 337; RSE to I. R. Trimble, July 30, 1862 (Misc. Mss.), Isaac Ridgeway Trimble Papers, NYHS.

15. Frederic Denison, *The Battle of Cedar Mountain: A Personal View* (Providence, RI: N. B. Williams, 1881), 6–7; James T. Lyon, *War Sketches: From Cedar Mountain to Bull Run* (Buffalo, NY: Young, Lockwood, 1882), 10–13; Ropes, *Army Under Pope*, 8–9.

16. Robert K. Krick, *Stonewall Jackson at Cedar Mountain* (Chapel Hill: U of North Carolina P, 1990), 14–15; Freeman, *Lee's Lieutenants*, 2: 8–10; Robert K Krick, "The Army of Northern Virginia's Most Notorious Court-Martial," *Blue and Gray* 3 (June-July 1986), passim; Stackpole, *From Cedar Mountain to Antietam*, 46–54.

17. O.R., vol. 12, pt. 2, 214, pt. 3, 926; Secretary of War, *Atlas to Accompany the Official Records*, 85; Brown, "Reminiscences"; Early, *Autobiographical Sketch*, 92; John Selby, *Stonewall Jackson as Military Commander* (London: B. T. Batsford, 1968), 125–27.

18. O.R., vol. 12, pt. 2, 215; Robertson, *General A. P. Hill*, 100; R. Dabney, *Life and Campaigns of Jackson*, 492–94.

19. Robertson, *General A. P. Hill*, 102; Rev. Mr. Hullihen, "Stonewall Jackson at Prayer," *Southern Historical Society Papers* 19 (1891): 111–13; Gary W. Gallagher, *Lee and His Generals in War and Memory* (Baton Rouge: Louisiana State UP, 1998), 93; Stackpole, From *Cedar Mountain to Antietam*, 44–45; Campbell Brown, "Cedar Run Mountain" (handwritten memoir), B-EPTSL; O.R., vol. 12, pt. 2, 226–27; Brown, "Reminiscences."

20. Krick, *Stonewall Jackson at Cedar Mountain*, 30–31; Casler, *Four Years in the Stonewall Brigade*, 103; Vandiver, *Mighty Stonewall*, 335–37; Early, *Autobiographical Sketch*, 93.

21. H. T. Childs, "Cedar Mountain as I Saw It," *Confederate Veteran* 28 (1920): 24; Stackpole, From *Cedar Mountain to Antietam*, 45–46; Denison, *Battle of Cedar Mountain*, 11–12.

22. O.R, vol. 12, pt. 2, 226, 237; Secretary of War, *Atlas to Accompany the Official Records,* 42; Brown, "Reminiscences."

23. Sifakis, *Who Was Who in the Confederacy,* 165; O.R., vol. 12, pt. 2, 227; Edward Porter Alexander, "The Battle of Fredericksburg—Paper No. 2," *Southern Historical Society Papers* 10 (1882): 446; William Woods Hassler, *Colonel John Pelham: Lee's Boy Artillerist* (Richmond, VA: Garrett and Massie, 1960), 144–49.

24. O.R., vol. 12, pt. 2, 238; Seabourne, "Battle of Cedar Mountain," 43; Brown, "Reminiscences"; Bradwell, "From Cold Harbor to Cedar Mountain," 224.

25. John Esten Cooke, *Stonewall Jackson and the Old Stonewall Brigade* (Charlottesville: UP of Virginia, 1954), 30; Bradwell, "Cold Harbor to Cedar Mountain," 224; Casdorph, *Lee and Jackson,* 290–91; Robertson, *General A. P. Hill,* 99–107; Hamlin, *"Old Bald Head,"* 118–20.

26. Stackpole, From *Cedar Mountain to Antietam,* 73; Krick, *Stonewall Jackson at Cedar Mountain,* 286.

27. O.R., vol. 12, pt. 2, 226, 236; Krick, *Stonewall Jackson at Cedar Mountain,* 286.

28. Brown, "Cedar Run Mountain"; John Blue, "Reminiscences of the Civil War," *Civil War Times Illustrated* Collection, U.S. Army Military History Institute, Carlisle Barracks, Pennsylvania (unpublished manuscript); Boatner, *Civil War Dictionary,* 23.

29. Brown, "Reminiscences"; O.R., vol. 12, pt. 2, 704; A. S. Pendleton to RSE, August 10, 11, 1892, Alexander S. Pendleton Papers, CHS; W. L. Jackson to RSE, August 11, 1862, William L. Jackson Papers, CHS; Freeman, *R. E. Lee: A Biography,* 2: 288–90.

30. Esposito, *West Point Atlas of American Wars,* 54; Stephen E. Ambrose, *Halleck: Lincoln's Chief of Staff* (Baton Rouge: Louisiana State UP, 1962), 65–69; RSE to Dear Lizzie, August 14, 1862, Ewell Papers, LC; Hamlin, *Making of a Soldier,* 114.

31. Hamlin, *"Old Bald Head,"* 121.

32. Hennessy, *Return to Bull Run,* 29, 38; O.R., vol. 12, pt. 2, 235; H. K. Douglas to RSE, August 15, 1862, Henry Kyd Douglas Papers, CHS; TJJ to RSE, August 14, 1862, Ewell Papers, PLDU; RSE "Letter Book," August 14, 1862, PLDU; Brown, "Reminiscences."

33. Esposito, *West Point Atlas of American Wars,* 57; Brown, "Reminiscences"; Longstreet, *From Manassas to Appomattox,* 162–63; Early, *Autobiographical Sketch,* 106; Hennessy, *Return to Bull Run,* 56–59.

34. G. J. Fiebeger, *Campaigns of the American Civil War* (West Point, NY: USMA Printing Office, 1914), 56–58, Ropes, *Army Under Pope,* 43–44; E. Thomas, *Bold Dragoon,* 151; John Esten Cooke, *A Life of General Robert E. Lee* (New York: D. Appleton, 1871), 115.

35. Early, *Autobiographical Sketch,* 114; RSE to Henry Forno, August 24, 25, 1862; RSE to Henry Forno, August 24, 25, 1862, James W. Eldridge Papers, HL; Ropes, *Army Under Pope,* 44–45.

36. Early, *Autobiographical Sketch,* 114; Brown, "Reminiscences"; Esposito, *West Point Atlas of American Wars,* 58.

37. O.R., vol. 12, pt. 2, 720; Early, *Autobiographical Sketch,* 114–15; Esposito, *West Point Atlas of American Wars,* 58.

38. O.R., vol. 12, pt. 2, 721, 723; E. Thomas, *Bold Dragoon,* 152–54; Thomason, *JEB Stuart,* 239–40; Krick, *Lee's Colonels,* 132, 142.

39. Hennessy, *Return to Bull Run,* 130–34; Gallagher, ed., *Fighting for the Confederacy,* 131; O.R., vol. 12, pt. 2, 708–09, 717; Robert C. Cheeks, "Ewell's Flawless Performance at Kettle Run," *America's Civil War* 13 (September 2000): 50–56.

Chapter 9: "What! Old Ewell Going to Marry That Pretty Woman"

1. Stackpole, *From Cedar Mountain to Antietam,* 169; K. Williams, *Lincoln Finds a General,* 1: 318–21; Ropes, *Army Under Pope,* 59–63; Brown, "Reminiscences."

2. Esposito, *West Point Atlas of American War,* 60; Brown, "Reminiscences"; W. W. Blackford, *War Years with Jeb Stuart* (New York: Charles Scribner's Sons, 1945), 117–21.

3. Walter H. Taylor, *General Lee: His Campaigns in Virginia, 1861–1865* (Norfolk, VA: Nusbaum Book and News, 1906), 102; Brown, "Reminiscences"; John J. Hennessy, *Second Manassas Battlefield Map Study* (Lynchburg, VA: H. E. Howard, 1991), 31, and Map No. 1. The latter work in two parts, text and maps, should be consulted by anyone seeking information about the Second Manassas; its trove of detail is unsurpassed.

4. Hennessy, *Return to Bull Run,* 554; Boatner, *Civil War Dictionary,* 427; Stephen W. Sears, *Landscape Turned Red: The Battle of Antietam* (New York: Ticknor and Fields, 1983), 193; Hennessy, *Second Manassas Map Study,* 55–56, and Map No. 2.

5. O.R., vol. 12, pt. 2, 555–59, 645; REL to Jefferson Davis, September 3, 1862, REL Papers, Washington and Lee University, Lexington, Virginia.

6. Jeb Stuart to My Dear Darling, January 24, September 4, 1862, James Ewell Brown Stuart Papers, VHS; O.R., vol. 12, pt. 2, 735, 740.

7. Brown, "Reminiscences"; Robert E. L. Krick, "The Wounding of General Richard Stoddert Ewell" (typescript, n.d.), Manassas National Battlefield Park; Robert H. Fowler, "How Ewell Lost His Leg," *Civil War Times Illustrated* 4 (June 1965): 17; Hunter H. McGuire, "Clinical Remarks on Gun-Shot Wounds of the Joints, Delivered January 10, 1866, at Howard's Grove Hospital," *Richmond Medical Journal* 1(March 1866): 262. Both Krick and Fowler offer detailed maps fixing the spot where Ewell fell.

8. William Starr Myers, "The Civil War Diary of General Isaac Ridgeway Trimble," *Maryland Historical Magazine* 17 (March 1922): 1–7; Isaac R. Trimble,

"The Campaign and Battle of Gettysburg," *Confederate Veteran* 25 (1917): 209; Sifakis, *Who Was Who in the Confederacy,* 284; Dowdey, *Lee and His Men,* 343–44.

9. Early, *Autobiographical Sketch,* 121; Brown, "Reminiscences"; Hennessy, *Return to Bull Run,* 182; Turner, "Ewells of Virginia," 34. The typescript cover says "Harriet"; the inside text says "Harriot." Although other writings have her name as "Harriot" also, the current writer has chosen "Harriet" hereafter.

10. McGuire, "Clinical Remarks on Gun-Shot Wounds," 263; Vandiver, *Mighty Stonewall,* 218; "Dr. McGuire Narrative" (handwritten memoir), Charles W. Dabney Papers, SHC; R. Dabney, *Life and Campaigns of Jackson,* 691–96; see also McGuire, *Confederate Cause and Conduct.*

11. For a map showing the location of Auburn and its relation to Groveton and Sudley Springs, see Vandiver, *Mighty Stonewall,* 363.

12. McGuire, "Clinical Remarks on Gun-Shot Wounds," 262; Brown, "Reminiscences"; Turner, "Ewells of Virginia," 34–35.

13. Dunblane in 1862 was owned by Dr. Jesse Ewell (or Jesse III, 1802–1897), whose wife was Ellen McGregor, 1800–1890. Five children were born to the union, the eldest of whom was John Smith Magruder Ewell; his third child was a daughter, Eleanor Mildred Beale Ewell, 1832–1916, a lifelong resident of Dunblane. Alice Maude Ewell was a daughter of John Smith Magruder Ewell and his second wife, Alice Taylor.

14. A. Ewell, *Virginia Scene,* 52–53; Emily G. Ramey and John K. Gott, *The Years of Anguish: Fauquier County, Virginia, 1861–1865* (Warrenton, VA: *Fauquier Democrat,* 1965), 23.

15. Ewell and Ewell, "History of the Ewell Family," 14–16; Brown, "Reminiscences"; J. Ewell, "History of the Medical Profession," 50, 57; A. Ewell, *Virginia Scene,* 63.

16. "When Richmond fell, [Friday] was at Jackson Hospital and went with a doctor to North Carolina. He was never heard from again." Turner, "Ewells of Virginia," 35.

17. Jackson Morton served in the United States Senate and later in the Confederate Congress, 1862–1865. His brother Jeremiah Morton was a Virginia congressman, 1849–1851, and made his home at Morton Hall in Orange County. See U.S. Congress, *Biographical Directory,* 1365.

18. A. Ewell, *Virginia Scene,* 64; Campbell Brown to Dear Mother, September 18, 1862, BPEP; Turner, "Ewells of Virginia," 35.

19. Clifford Dowdey, ed., *The Wartime Papers of Robert E. Lee* (Boston: Little, Brown, 1961), 298; Sears, *Landscape Turned Red,* 181–87; Vandiver, *Mighty Stonewall,* 399; Casdorph, *Lee and Jackson,* 391.

20. Brown, "Reminiscences," A. Ewell, *Virginia Scene,* 68–69.

21. Brown, "Reminiscences"; McGuire, "Clinical Remarks on Gun-Shot Wounds," 262; Esposito, *West Point Atlas of American Wars,* 18; Oren F. Morton, *Annals of Bath County* (Staunton, VA: McClure, 1917), 49; Joseph T. McAlister,

Historical Sketches of Virginia Hot Springs, Warm Sulphur Springs, and Bath County, Virginia (Salem, VA: Salem Printing, 1908), 37–39.

22. M. D. Hoge to My Dear Lizzie, September 4, 1862, Ewell Papers, LC; Campbell Brown to Dear Mother, September 18, 1862, BPEP; Jean Graham McAlister, *A Brief History of Bath County, Virginia* (Warm Springs, VA: Bath County School Board, 1920), 6–7; Brown, "Reminiscences."

23. Hamlin, *"Old Bald Head,"* 130; Marie Beach, ed., *The Only Complete Guide to Richmond* (Midlothian, VA: Guide to Richmond Press, 1979), 41, 99.

24. Hamlin, *"Old Bald Head,"* 121; BSE to Dear Lizzie, January 22, 1963, Ewell Papers, LC; McGuire, "Clinical Remarks on Gun-Shot Wounds," 262.

25. McGuire, "Clinical Remarks on Gun-Shot Wounds," 262; Turner, "Ewells of Virginia," 36; T. H. Carter, "Letter of Colonel Thomas H. Carter," *Southern Historical Society Papers* 39 (1914): 6–7; J. H. Claiborne to Dear Wife, July 21, 1864, John H. Claiborne Papers, ALUV. For correspondence about Ewell's artificial leg and special shoes, see Landon B. Edwards, M.D. to Dr. Jesse Ewell, May 12, 1900, Ewell Papers, ALUV; [?] Sharples [Nashville shoemaker] to RSE, January 8, 1872, B-EPTSL; G. Peyton to Dr. [?] LaFar, August 14, 1864, Ewell Papers, PLDU. LaFar was in charge of the South Carolina Hospital, Charlottesville, during the war.

26. Kenneth G. Swan and Roy C. Swan, *Gunshot Wounds: Pathophysiology and Management* (Chicago: Year Book Medical Publishers, 1989), 1–6.

27. Conversation with S. Murthy, M.D., December 20, 1999, Charleston, WV; Sikhar Nath Banerjee, ed., *Rehabilitation and Management of Amputees* (Baltimore: Williams and Wilkins, 1982), 416.

28. RSE to J. A. Early, March 8, 1863, Jubal A. Early Papers, LC; Hamlin, *Making of a Soldier,* 19.

29. Banerjee, ed., *Rehabilitation and Management of Amputees,* 416; RSE to J. A. Early, January 7, 1863, Jubal A. Early Papers, LC; Hamlin, *"Old Bald Head,"* 135.

30. Hamlin, *"Old Bald Head,"* 137; M. C. Fitzpatrick, "The Psychological Assessment and Psychosocial Recovery of the Patient with an Amputation," *Clinical Orthopedics* 361 (April 1999): 98–107; R. G. Frank, et al., "Psychological Response to Amputation as a Function of Age and Time Since the Amputation," *British Journal of Psychiatry* 144 (May 1984): 493–94; Paul E Steiner, *Medical-Military Portraits of Union and Confederate Generals* (Philadelphia: Whitmore Publishing, 1968), 137.

31. Current, ed., *Encyclopedia of the Confederacy,* 2: 789–91; Steiner, *Medical-Military Portraits,* 215–33; Richard M. McMurry, *John Bell Hood and the War for Southern Independence* (Lexington: UP of Kentucky, 1982), 216.

32. Tanner, *Stonewall in the Valley,* 182; Emory M. Thomas, *The Confederate Nation, 1861–1865* (New York: Harper and Row, 1979), 21–24; Gary W. Gallagher, *The Confederate War* (Cambridge, MA: Harvard UP, 1997), 50–51.

33. Hennessy, *Return to Bull Run*, 566; William W. Bennett, *Narrative of the Great Revival which Prevailed in the Southern Armies During the Late Civil War Between the States of the Federal Union* (Philadelphia: Claxton, Remsen, and Haffelfinger, 1877), 207–08.

34. Royster, *Destructive War*, 51–53; Bennett, *Narrative of the Great Revival*, 333, 351; J. William Jones, *Christ in the Camp; or, Religion in Lee's Army* (Richmond, VA: B. F. Johnson, 1887), 96–97; Thomas B. Buell, *The Warrior Generals: Combat Leadership in the Civil War* (New York: Crown, 1997), 221.

35. *Richmond Enquirer*, May 13, 1862; Turner, "Ewells of Virginia," 36.

36. Turner, "Ewells of Virginia," 35–36; Henry, *Story of the Confederacy*, 270; Longstreet, *From Manassas to Appomattox*, 332; Bridges, *Lee's Maverick General*, 183–86.

37. For another view, see Robertson, *Stonewall Jackson*, 757. Other writers skirt the issue of whether Ewell actually walked in the procession.

38. H. K. Douglas, *I Rode with Stonewall*, 229; *Richmond Enquirer*, May 12, 1863; *Richmond Examiner*, May 19, 1863.

39. H. K. Douglas, *I Rode with Stonewall*, 325; Mrs. Burton Harrison, *Reflections, Grave and Gay* (New York: Charles Scribner's Sons, 1916), 110–11; Walter S. Griggs, *General John Pegram, C.S.A.* (Lynchburg, VA: H. E. Howard, 1993), 39–40, 117-20; W. C. Davis, *Jefferson Davis*, 420ff.; Mary Boykin Chesnut, *A Diary from Dixie*, Ben Ames Williams, ed. (Boston, MA: Harvard UP, reprint, 1980), 311; Louise (Wigfall) Wright, *A Southern Girl in '61: The Wartime Memories of a Confederate Senator's Daughter* (New York: Doubleday, Page, 1905), 119–20.

40. Mary A. R. Lee to Mildred C. Lee, June 7, 1863, Lee Family Papers, VHS; Elizabeth Wright Weddell, *St. Paul's Church, Richmond: Its Historic Years and Memorials* (Richmond, VA: William Byrd Press, 1931), 1: 53, 206; Turner, "Ewells of Virginia," 37–38.

41. RSE to James Lyons, May 25, 1863, James Lyons Papers, HL; Current, ed., *Encyclopedia of the Confederacy*, 3: 964–65; "Campbell Family Genealogy," E-BPTSL. A detailed description of most of Lizinka Brown's landholdings can be found in D. Pfanz, *Richard S. Ewell*, 508–11.

42. Harriet S. Turner, "Reflections on Andrew Johnson," *Harper's Monthly Magazine* 120 (January 1910): 175–76; Edwin M. Staunton to Mrs. R. S. Ewell, April 24, 1865, and George H. Thomas to Mrs. R. S. Ewell, April 23, 1865, Ewell Papers, LC; Lizinka C. Ewell to Thomas T. Gantt, March 16, 1865, and Thomas T. Gantt to Lizinka C. Ewell, September 4, 1865, E-BPTSL.

Chapter 10: The March North

1. McPherson, *Battle Cry of Freedom*, 646; Michael A. Palmer, *Lee Moves North: Robert E. Lee on the Offensive* (New York: John Wiley, 1998), 52; Stackpole, *They Met at Gettysburg*, 2–4.

2. Kegel, *North with Lee and Jackson,* 50–54; Henry, *Story of the Confederacy,* 266; Joseph T. Glatthaar, "The Common Soldier's Gettysburg Campaign," in Gabor S. Borritt, ed., *The Gettysburg Nobody Knows* (New York: Oxford UP, 1997), 4–5.

3. Henry, *Story of the Confederacy,* 220; M. Wright, *General Officers of the Confederate Army,* 16; Robertson, *General A. P. Hill,* 213, 225; Longstreet, *From Manassas to Appomattox,* 332.

4. Kegel, *North with Lee and Jackson,* 239; Brown, "Reminiscences."

5. Coddington, *Gettysburg Campaign,* 12; O.R., vol. 25, pt. 2, 830, 840; Freeman, *Lee's Lieutenants,* 2: 696.

6. RSE, "1863" [only title given] (handwritten manuscript), PBEP, hereafter cited as "Gettysburg Report"; Long, *Memoirs of Robert E. Lee,* 265; Thomason, *JEB Stuart,* 395ff.

7. Freeman, *Lee's Lieutenants,* 2: 696; O.R., vol. 25, pt. 2, 840; W. C. Davis, *Jefferson Davis,* 505–06.

8. Early, *Autobiographical Sketch,* 238; Glenn Tucker, *Lee and Longstreet at Gettysburg* (Indianapolis: Bobbs-Merrill, 1968), 236.

9. Summarized biographical information for Hays and Gordon as well as those brigadiers that follow can be found in: Boatner, *Civil War Dictionary,* Sifakis, *Who Was Who in the Confederacy,* and Current, ed., *Encyclopedia of the Confederacy;* H. K. Douglas, *I Rode with Stonewall,* 234.

10. U.S. Congress, *Biographical Directory,* 1625; T. Jones, *Lee's Tigers,* 172; Early, *Autobiographical Sketch,* 273.

11. Gallagher, ed., *Fighting for the Confederacy,* 114; Freeman, *Lee's Lieutenants,* 2: xliv; William Couper, *One Hundred Years at VMI* (Richmond, VA: Garrett and Massie 1939), 171; Vandiver, *Mighty Stonewall,* 474.

12. RSE, "Gettysburg Report"; Freeman, *Lee's Lieutenants,* 2: 81; Gallagher, ed., *Fighting for the Confederacy,* 385; Vandiver, *Mighty Stonewall,* 473; Current, ed., *Encyclopedia of the Confederacy,* 2: 490.

13. Vandiver, *Mighty Stonewall,* 473; Boatner, *Civil War Dictionary,* 429; O.R., vol. 27, pt. 2, 287.

14. J. B. Magruder to S. D. Ramseur, April 16, 1862, John Bankhead Magruder Papers, MOC; W. Taylor, *General Lee: His Campaigns,* 114–17; M. Wright, *General Officers of the Confederate Army,* 43, 95; Gary W. Gallagher, *Stephen Dodson Ramseur: Lee's Gallant General* (Chapel Hill: U of North Carolina P, 1984), passim.

15. M. Wright, *General Officers of the Confederate Army,* 106; Coddington, *Gettysburg Campaign,* 289; Sifakis, *Who Was Who in the Confederacy,* 212.

16. Casdorph, *Lee and Jackson,* 236–37; O.R., vol. 27, pt. 2, 454; M. Wright, *General Officers of the Confederate Army,* 33.

17. Ewell, "Gettysburg Report"; Allan, *History of the Campaign,* 115–17; R. Dabney, *Life and Campaigns of Jackson,* 384; Boatner, *Civil War Dictionary,* 796.

18. Casdorph, *Republicans, Negroes, and Progressives,* 28; Current, ed., *Encyclopedia of the Confederacy,* 4: 1676–77; Willie Walker Caldwell, *Stonewall Jim: A Biography of General James A. Walker, C.S.A.* (Elliston, VA: Northcross House, 1990), passim.

19. Robertson, *Stonewall Brigade,* 158; Boatner, *Civil War Dictionary,* 442.

20. M. Wright, *General Officers of the Confederate Army,* 29, T. Jones, *Lee's Tigers,* 176, 235; Sifakis, *Who Was Who in the Confederacy,* 306.

21. A. S. Pendleton to Dear Mother, May 24, and A. S. Pendleton to Dear Mary, May 26, 1863, William Nelson Pendleton Papers, SHC; W. G. Bean, *Stonewall's Man: Sandie Pendleton* (Chapel Hill: U of North Carolina P, 1959), 128–29; Marietta M. Andrews, *Scraps of Papers* (New York: E. P. Dutton, 1929), 111.

22. Mary Conner Moffett, *Letters of General James Conner, C.S.A.* (Columbia, SC: R. L. Ryan, 1950), 110–11.

23. Bean, *Stonewall's Man,* 152–53, "Jackson's Staff" (handwritten list), Jedediah Hotchkiss Papers, LC, reel 39.

24. Samuel A. Marsteller to RSE, June 29, 1863, Minor Family Papers, VHS.

25. H. H. McGuire to Charles J. Faulkner, April 25, 1866, Hunter H. McGuire Papers, VHS; Robertson, *Stonewall Jackson,* 641; U.S. Congress, *Biographical Directory,* 877–78.

26. Bean, *Stonewall's Man,* 130; B. T. Lacy to Lieut. J. P. Smith, June 2, 1863, Beverly T. Lacy Papers, VHS; Brown, "Reminiscences"; O.R., vol. 27, pt. 2, 452.

27. Dowdey, *Lee and His Men,* 39; H. K. Douglas, *I Rode with Stonewall,* 244; O.R., vol. 27, pt. 2, 440.

28. Thomason, *JEB Stuart,* 408; Henry, *Story of the Confederacy,* 271; O.R., vol. 27, pt. 2, 546; Brown, "Reminiscences"; Current, ed., *Encyclopedia of the Confederacy,* 1: 211.

29. Brown, "Reminiscences"; U.S. Congress, *Biographical Directory,* 575; Rice, *West Virginia: A History,* 98–99.

30. O.R., vol. 27, pt. 2, 440, 449; Chamberlayne, *Ham Chamberlayne—Virginian,* 187; W. G. Bean, *The Liberty Hall Volunteers: Stonewall's College Boys* (Charlottesville: U of Virginia P, 1965), 145; Early, *Autobiographical Sketch,* 238–40.

31. Edward G. Longacre, "Target: Winchester, Virginia," *Civil War Times Illustrated* 15 (June 1976): 23–25; Michelle Lee Stewart, "Robert E. Rodes: Lee's Forgotten General" (MA thesis, University of Southwestern Louisiana, 1997): 78; Clifford Dowdey, "Richard S. Ewell: Virginian," *Virginia Record* 5 (May 1959): 8; Charles Grunder and Brandon H. Beck, *The Second Battle of Winchester, June 12–15, 1863* (Lynchburg, VA: H. E. Howard, 1989), 39, and passim.

32. Bushong, *Old Jube,* 193-96; Brown, "Reminiscences"; T. Jones, *Lee's Tigers,* 160.

33. Hamlin, "*Old Bald Head,*" 137–39; Early, *Autobiographical Sketch,* 248; T. Jones, *Lee's Tigers,* 161; Freeman, *Lee's Lieutenants,* 3: 23.

34. Robertson, *Stonewall Brigade,* 200; Brown, "Reminiscences"; Grunder and Beck, *Second Battle of Winchester,* 63–65; O.R., vol. 25, pt. 2, 442; Susan Leigh Blackford (comp.), *Letters from Lee's Army; or, Memoirs of Life In and Out of the Army in Virginia During the War Between the States* (New York: Charles Scribner's Sons, 1947), 179; see also William Woods Hassler, *The General to His Lady: The Civil War Letters of William Dorsey Pender to Fanny Pender* (Chapel Hill: U of North Carolina P, 1965), 251.

35. RSE' s General Orders, Number 43, June 11, 1863, Jubal A. Early Papers, LC; O.R., vol. 25, pt. 2, 453.

36. REL's General Order Number 72, June 2, 1863, (printed broadside), PBEP; *Harrisburg (PA) Weekly Patriot and Union,* July 2, 1863. "Whether or not [Lee's] order was printed before the army reached Chambersburg I cannot say, but on Wednesday following, along with an order issued by Lieutenant-General Ewell, which along with other papers, was printed at one of the printing establishments in Chambersburg, it was freely distributed upon slips among the people," Jacob Hoke, *The Great Invasion of 1863; or, General Lee in Pennsylvania* (Dayton, OH: W. J. Shuey, 1887), 122.

37. O.R., vol. 25, pt. 2, 503; Casdorph, *Lee and Jackson,* 337–38; Edmund Stephens to Dear Parents, June 20, 1863, Paul Stephens Collection, Northwestern State University of Louisiana, Natchitoches; Charles Batchelor to Dear Father, October 18, 1863, Charles Batchelor Papers, Louisiana State University Library, Baton Rouge.

38. H. K. Douglas, *I Rode with Stonewall,* 244; Dowdey, *Lee and His Men,* 41.

39. Owen E. Adams Jr., "Confederate General Robert E. Rodes: A Civil War Biography" (MA thesis, University of Southern Mississippi, 1995), 71; Hoke, *Great Invasion,* 114–15; Early, *Autobiographical Sketch,* 253–54; Coddington, *Gettysburg Campaign,* 175; Longstreet, *From Manassas to Appomattox,* 344–45.

40. Daniel Butterfield to Alfred Pleasanton, June 17, 1863, Charles Venable Papers, SHC; REL to Jeb Stuart, June 22, 23, 1863, James Ewell Brown Stuart Papers, VHS; Randolph H. McKim, "The Gettysburg Campaign," *Southern Historical Society Papers* 40 (1915): 258–59.

41. E. Thomas, *Bold Dragoon,* 240–47; Thomason, *JEB Stuart,* 412ff.; Longstreet, *Manassas to Appomattox,* 343.

42. O.R., vol. 27, pt. 2, 465.

43. Campbell Brown to Dear Sister and Mother, June 22, 1863, B-EPFCL; Campbell Brown to Dear Sister and Mother, June 25, 1863, PBEP; Hoke, *Great Invasion,* 125–36. This work contains a valuable collection of detailed information about Ewell and the Second Corps during the entire operation in Pennsylvania.

44. *Carlisle American,* August 5, 1863; Hamlin, *Making of a Soldier,* 121; Campbell Brown to Dear Sister and Mother, June 25, 1863, PBEP; John B. Gor-

don to My Own Precious Wife, July 7, 1863, John Brown Gordon Papers, University of Georgia Library, Athens; *Carlisle Herald,* July 10, 1863.

45. *Carlisle Herald,* July 10, 1863; Jed Hotchkiss, "Diary," July 1, 1863, copy in Robert L. Blake Collection, U.S. Army Military History Institute, Carlisle Barracks, Pennsylvania; O.R., vol. 27, pt. 2, 443.

46. O.R., vol. 25, pt. 2, 443, 467, 552; Stackpole, *They Met at Gettysburg,* 100; Adams, "Confederate Major General Rodes," 73; Coddington, *Gettysburg Campaign,* 186–89. This source contains a chapter entitled, "The Confederates Plunder Pennsylvania," which, among other things, contains an excellent account of the motives of Lee and Ewell for the Harrisburg operation.

Chapter 11: Paralyzed with Indecision

1. *Harrisburg Patriot and Union,* July 10, 1863; Dowdey, *Lee and His Men,* 125–27; O.R., vol. 27, pt. 3, 943–44.

2. Wert, *General James Longstreet,* 254–55; Hoke, *Great Invasion,* 220; Jed Hotchkiss, "Diary," July 1, 1863, Jedediah Hotchkiss Papers, LC; Stackpole, *They Met at Gettysburg,* 80–81.

3. J. B. Gordon to My Own Precious Wife, July 7, 1863, John Brown Gordon Papers, University of Georgia Library, Athens; Hoke, *Great Invasion,* 221; *Carlisle Herald,* July 10, 1863.

4. Secretary of War, *Atlas to Accompany the Official Records,* 40; O.R., vol. 27, pt. 2, 444, 607; Brown, "Reminiscences"; Peter S. Carmichael, *Lee's Young Artillerist: William R. J. Pegram* (Charlottesville: UP of Virginia, reprint, 1998), 96–97; Robertson, *General A. P. Hill,* 207–08.

5. O.R., vol. 27, pt. 2, 443, 552; Freeman, *Lee's Lieutenants,* 3: 90–95; Trimble, "Campaign and Battle of Gettysburg," 211; Adams, "Confederate General Robert E. Rodes," 74–75.

6. M. Wright, *General Officers of the Confederate Army,* 63; Harry W. Pfanz, *Gettysburg: Culp's Hill and Cemetery Hill* (Chapel Hill: U of North Carolina P, 1993), 35–37, 401; Krick, *Lee's Colonels,* 196; Early, *Autobiographical Sketch,* 267; Esposito, *West Point Atlas of American Wars,* 96.

7. Although Early never married, he fathered four children between 1850 and 1864, the last of whom was christened "Jubal." A woman named Julia McNealey, who later married and bore a second family, was the mother; see Charles C. Osborne, *Jubal: The Life and Times of General Jubal A. Early, C.S.A., Defender of the Lost Cause* (Chapel Hill, NC: Algonquin Books, 1992), 485.

8. Dowdey, *Lee and His Men at Gettysburg,* 133–34; Brown, "Reminiscences."

9. O.R., vol. 27, pt. 2, 553–54; Abner Doubleday, *Chancellorsville and Gettysburg* (New York: Charles Scribner's Sons, 1908), 173.

10. Doubleday, *Chancellorsville and Gettysburg,* 173; Freeman, *Lee's Lieutenants,* 3: 86; O.R., vol. 27, pt. 2, 444–45, 554; Current, ed., *Encyclopedia of the Confederacy,* 2: 826.

11. Coddington, *Gettysburg Campaign*, 289–99; Gallagher, *Stephen Dodson Ramseur*, 70–75, 171; Edward J. Stackpole and Wilbur S. Nye, *The Battle of Gettysburg: A Guided Tour* (Mechanicsville, PA: Stackpole Books, reprint, 1998), 58; O.R., vol. 27, pt. 2, 554, 556.

12. O.R., vol. 27, pt. 2, 486; John B. Gordon, *Reminiscences of the Civil War* (Baton Rouge: Louisiana State UP, reprint, 1993), 151; Ralph Lowell Eckert, *John Brown Gordon: Soldier, Southerner, American* (Baton Rouge: Louisiana State UP, reprint, 1989), 254; W. J. Seymour, "Diary" (handwritten memoir), William J. Seymour Papers, University of Michigan Library, Ann Arbor.

13. Trimble, "Campaign and Battle of Gettysburg," 211; Gordon, *Reminiscences of the Civil War*, 157.

14. Stackpole and Nye, *Battle of Gettysburg*, 63; Trimble, "Campaign and Battle of Gettysburg," 211; Dowdey, *Lee and His Men*, 152; Freeman, *Lee's Lieutenants*, 3: 90ff.; Brown, "Reminiscences."

15. For an up-to-date evaluation of Early's relationship to Lee and the Confederate crusade, see chapter 10, "Jubal A. Early, the Lost Cause, and Civil War History," in Gallagher, *Lee and His Generals*, 199–226.

16. Brown, "Reminiscences"; Alan T. Nolan, "R. E. Lee and July 1 at Gettysburg," in Gallagher, ed., *Lee: The Soldier*, 494.

17. McKim, "Gettysburg Campaign," 273; Trimble, "Campaign and Battle of Gettysburg," 211–12; Samuel J. Martin, "Did 'Baldy' Ewell Lose Gettysburg?" *America's Civil War* 10 (July 1997): 39.

18. McKim, "Gettysburg Campaign," 273; Isaac R. Trimble, "The Battle and Campaign of Gettysburg," *Southern Historical Society Papers* 26 (1898): 123; E. C. Cordon, "Controversy about Gettysburg," *Confederate Veteran* 28 (1920): 456.

19. Robert E. Rodes, "General R. E. Rodes' Report of the Battle of Gettysburg," *Southern Historical Society Papers* 5 (1877): 149–50; C. D. Grace, "Rodes' Division at Gettysburg," *Confederate Veteran* 5 (1897): 615; Adams, "Major General Rodes," 70–80; O.R., vol. 27, pt. 2, 582.

20. Winfield Hancock, "Letter from General Winfield Hancock," *Southern Historical Society Papers* 3 (1878): 172; John B. Bachelder, "Letter from John B. Bachelder, Esq.," *Southern Historical Society Papers* 6 (1878), 172–73; T. Jones, *Lee's Tigers*, 169; John F. Gruber to D. F. Boyd, August 23, 1863, David French Boyd Civil War Papers, Louisiana State University Library, Baton Rouge.

21. H. K. Douglas, *I Rode with Stonewall*, 247; Bean, *Stonewall's Man*, 139; Henry Kyd Douglas, "Lee and Ewell at Gettysburg," *The Nation* 54 (1892): 87; Henry Kyd Douglas, "The Bottom Facts about Gettysburg" (unidentified newspaper clipping), 49, C. E. Jones Scrapbook, Charles E. Jones Papers, PLDU.

22. A. S. Pendleton, "Battle of Gettysburg, July 1st & 2nd, 1863" (handwritten memoir/letter), n.d., William Nelson Pendleton Papers, SHC; Peter S. Carmichael, "'Oh! For the Presence and Inspiration of Old Jack': A Lost Cause

Plea for Stonewall Jackson at Gettysburg," *Civil War History* 41 (June 1995): 166–67. This superb evaluation reproduces Pendleton's memoir/letter in full; Carmichael offers an excellent overview of "what if Jackson had been there."

23. Parrish, *Richard Taylor,* 105, 138–39; Parrish, ed., *Reminiscences of the War,* 22; William Preston Johnston, "Memorandum of Conversation with General R. E. Lee," in Gallagher, ed., *Lee: The Soldier,* 29.

24. H. Pfanz, *Culp's Hill and Cemetery Hill,* 318; O.R., vol. 27, pt. 2, 318; Freeman, *Lee's Lieutenants,* 3: 97; Walter H. Taylor, *Four Years with General Lee* (New York: D. Appleton, 1877), 95; Hoke, *Great Invasion,* 284–85.

25. Gary W. Gallagher, "In the Shadow of Stonewall Jackson: Richard S. Ewell at Gettysburg," *Virginia Country's Civil War* 5 (1986): 57; H. Pfanz, *Culp's Hill and Cemetery Hill,* 419; Brown, "Reminiscences"; Harriet S. Turner to J. A. Early, March 29, 1878, Ewell Papers, VHS.

26. Gallagher, "In the Shadow of Stonewall," 59.

27. Osborne, *Jubal,* 195; Harry W. Pfanz, "Old Jack Is Not Here," in Borritt, *Gettysburg Nobody Knows,* 64; Early, *Autobiographical Sketch,* 271.

28. Harriet Turner, "Copy of a Portion of Capt. Turner's Memoranda relating to Gettysburg written before Capt. Walter Taylor's Book—written in either 76 or 77" (handwritten manuscript), Jubal A. Early Papers, VHS.

29. G. W. Peterkin to Joshua Peterkin, July 7, 1863, George W. Peterkin Papers, West Virginia State Archives, Charleston; Paul D. Casdorph, "Future Bishop Gives Account of the Civil War," *West Virginia Then and Now* 27 (October 1985): 9–11; Susan P. Lee, *Memoirs of William Nelson Pendleton, D.D.* (Philadelphia: J. B. Lippincott, 1883), 292; Osborne, *Jubal,* 195–96; Turner, "Copy of Capt. Turner's Memoranda."

30. Piston, *Lee's Tarnished Lieutenant,* 56-58; Wert, *General James Longstreet,* 268; Gallagher, ed., *Fighting for the Confederacy,* 237.

31. Stackpole and Nye, *Battle of Gettysburg,* 89; Glenn Tucker, *High Tide at Gettysburg: The Campaign in Pennsylvania* (Indianapolis: Bobbs-Merrill, 1958), 301; O.R., vol. 27, pt. 2, 446.

32. Harry W. Pfanz, *Gettysburg: The Second Day* (Chapel Hill: U of North Carolina P, reprint, 1987), xv, 111; Jed Hotchkiss, "Diary," July 2, 1863, Jedediah Hotchkiss Papers, U.S. Military History Institute, Carlisle Barracks, Pennsylvania; Osborne, *Jubal,* 198–200; Trimble, "Battle and Campaign of Gettysburg," 125; O.R., vol. 27, pt. 2, 480; Grace, "Rodes' Division at Gettysburg," 615.

33. Stackpole, *They Met at Gettysburg,* 214–15; O.R., vol. 27, pt. 2, 504; Tucker, *High Tide at Gettysburg,* 302.

34. Coddington, *Gettysburg Campaign,* 468–72; H. Pfanz, *Gettysburg: The Second Day,* 640; Robertson, *Stonewall Brigade,* 204; Tucker, *High Tide at Gettysburg,* 304–05.

35. O.R., vol. 27, pt. 2, 448, 505; Brown, "Reminiscences"; Robertson, *Stonewall Brigade,* 206; Dowdey, *Lee and His Men,* 260–62; Isaac R. Trimble to J.

B. Bachelder, July 8, 1863, John Bachelder Papers, New Hampshire Historical Society, Concord.

36. Jed Hotchkiss, "Diary," July 3, 1863; Brown, "Reminiscences"; Gallagher, ed., *Fighting for the Confederacy,* 251.

37. Carol Reardon, *Pickett's Charge in History and Memory* (Chapel Hill: U of North Carolina P, 1997), 85; Boatner, *Civil War Dictionary,* 331–39; W. Myers, ed., "Civil War Diary of General Isaac Ridgeway Trimble," 12; see also, Carol Reardon, "I Think the Union Army Had Something to Do with It," in Borritt, *Gettysburg Nobody Knows,* 127.

38. Dowdey, *Lee and His Men,* 302; Peter S. Carmichael, "Who Is to Blame for the Confederate Loss at Gettysburg?" *Civil War Times Illustrated* 37 (August 1998): 56; Frank A. Haskell, *The Battle of Gettysburg,* Bruce Catton, ed., (Boston: Houghton Mifflin Company, 1958), 96ff.; J. G. Randall, *Civil War and Reconstruction* (Boston: D. C. Heath, 1953), 523.

39. Brown, "Reminiscences"; Pendleton, "Battle of Gettysburg"; O.R., vol. 27, pt. 2, 448.

40. O.R., vol. 27, pt. 2, 449; Gordon, *Reminiscences of the Civil War,* 172–73.

41. Early, *Autobiographical Sketch,* 282; A. S. Pendleton, "Circular" (printed broadside), July 14, 1863, James W. Eldridge Papers, HL; R. J. Hancock to Walter Stewart, April 19, 1908, William and Walter Stewart Papers, Louisiana State University Library, Baton Rouge; O.R., vol. 27, pt. 2, 281, 448.

42. O.R., vol. 27, pt. 2, 324; Secretary of War, *Atlas to Accompany the Official Records,* 43.

43. Early, *Autobiographical Sketch,* 277, A. S. Pendleton, "Circular"; O.R., vol. 27, pt. 3, 340–42, pt. 3, 1065.

Chapter 12: "Poor Ewell—A Cripple"

1. Carmichael, "Escaping the Shadow," 136ff.; Jeb Stuart to My Darling One, September 11, 1863, James Ewell Brown Stuart Papers, VHS.

2. The artist was Alexander Galt (1827–1863), who died from smallpox later in the year. Galt made several drawings of Jackson in late 1862 in addition to his work with the Confederate Engineer Bureau.

3. William D. Henderson, *The Road to Bristoe Station, Campaigning with Lee and Meade, August 1-October 20, 1863* (Lynchburg, VA: H. E. Howard, 1987), 27; Campbell Brown (RSE) to H. T. Hays, August 12, 13, 1863, Campbell Brown (RSE) to R. E. Rodes, August 14, 1863, James R. Smith (RSE) to J. A. Early, August 17, 1863, and A. S. Pendleton (RSE) to J. A. Early, August 18, 1863, James W. Eldridge Papers, HL; REL to RSE, August 19, 1863, Ewell Papers, MOC; G. W. C. Lee to BSE, August 6, 1863, JEJ Papers, HL.

4. Theodore Lyman, *With Grant and Meade from the Wilderness to Appomattox,* ed. George R. Agassiz (Lincoln: U of Nebraska P, reprint, 1994),

9; Piston, *Lee's Tarnished Lieutenant,* 67–68; Henderson, *Road to Bristoe Station,* 49.

5. Wert, *General James Longstreet,* 299; G. Moxley Sorrel, *Reflections of a Confederate Staff Officer* (New York: Neale, 1905), 179–80; Joseph T. Durkin, ed., *Confederate Chaplain: A War Journal of Rev. James B Sheeran, c.ss.r. 14th Louisiana, C.S.A.* (Milwaukee: Bruce, 1960), 54–56.

6. Freeman, *Lee's Lieutenants,* 3: 352–53; Henderson, *Road to Bristoe Station,* 49, 63; Thomason, *JEB Stuart,* 263–64; E. Thomas, *Bold Dragoon,* 460–63.

7. Longstreet, *From Manassas to Appomattox,* 435; Henderson, *Road to Bristoe Station,* 69; P. W. Hairston to Dear Fanny, October 5, 1863, Peter W. Hairston Papers, SHC; "Diary of the Campaign," unsigned memoir, Ewell Papers, PLDU.

8. Basler, ed., *Collected Works of Abraham Lincoln,* 6: 518; "Diary of the Campaign"; Palmer, *Lee Moves North,* 106–07.

9. A. A. Humphreys, *From Gettysburg to the Rapidan: The Army of the Potomac, July 1863 to April 1864* (New York: Charles Scribner's Sons, 1883), 28; "Diary of the Campaign"; H. A. Wagstaff, ed., "The James A. Graham Papers," *James Sprunt Historical Studies* (Chapel Hill: U of North Carolina, 1928), vol. 20, 157.

10. Osborne, *Jubal,* 485; L. Van Loan Naiswald, "The Battle of Bristoe Station," *Virginia Cavalcade* 18 (autumn 1964), 44; Robertson, *General A. P. Hill,* 239.

11. Early, *Autobiographical Sketch,* 20; "Diary of the Campaign"; A. S. Pendleton to R. E. Rodes, October 18, 1863, Ewell Papers, MOC.

12. Early, *Autobiographical Sketch,* 307ff.; Campbell Brown to My Dear Sister, October 19, 1863, PBEP; Campbell Brown to My Dear Sister, October 26, 1863, B-EPFCL; RSE to R. E. Rodes, October 22, 1863, Ewell Papers, MOC; Campbell Brown to J. A. Early, October 22, 1863, James W. Eldridge Papers, HL; A. S. Pendleton to R. E. Rodes, October 18, 19, 1963, Ewell Papers, MOC; Dowdey, "Richard S. Ewell," 8.

13. Early, *Autobiographical Sketch,* 307; Campbell Brown to J. A. Early, October 22, 1863, James W. Eldridge Papers, HL; Humphreys, *Road to Bristoe Station,* 43–47; Gordon, *Reminiscences of the Civil War,* 189–93. For Ewell and Rodes at Kelly's Ford, see O.R., vol. 29, pt. 1, 618.

14. Hamlin, *"Old Bald Head,"* 163; A. S. Pendleton to R. E. Rodes, November 11, 1863, Ewell Papers, MOC; "Account Sheet" (ledger in Ewell's own handwriting), Ewell Papers, PLDU.

15. RSE to Moses D. Hoge, November 27, 1863, Ewell Papers, MOC; Terry L. Jones, ed., *The Civil War Memoirs of Captain William J. Seymour: Reminiscences of a Louisiana Tiger* (Baton Rouge: Louisiana State UP, 1991), 98; Krick, *Lee's Colonels,* 252–53.

16. Campbell Brown to My Dear Sister, December 5, 1863, B-EPFCL; H. W. Hanson, "A. P. Hill's Signal Corps," *Confederate Veteran* 2 (1894): 12; R.

Lockwood Tower, ed., *Lee's Adjutant: The Wartime Letters of Colonel Walter Herron Taylor, 1862–1865* (Columbia: U of South Carolina P, 1995), 88.

17. Boatner, *Civil War Dictionary,* 352; Freeman, *Lee's Lieutenants,* 3: 270ff.; RSE to Dear Lizinka, December 12, 20, 1863, PBEP; see also Martin F. Graham and George F. Skoch, *Mine Run: A Campaign of Lost Opportunities, October 21, 1863-May 1, 1864* (Lynchburg, VA: H. E. Howard, 1987).

18. Hamlin, *Making of a Soldier,* 125; Bean, *Stonewall's Man,* 154-55.

19. Freeman, *Lee's Lieutenants,* 3: 331; Moffett, *Letters of General James Conner,* 115.

20. Moffett, ed., *Letters of General James Conner,* 115; Bean, *Stonewall's Man,* 154–55.

21. M. Chesnut, *Diary from Dixie,* 300–01; Durkin, ed., *Confederate Chaplain,* 74–75.

22. Freeman, *Lee's Lieutenants,* 3: 329–33; Archie McDonald, *Make Me a Map of the Valley: The Civil War Journal of Stonewall Jackson's Topographer* (Dallas: Southern Methodist UP, 1973), 192; RSE to Dear Lizzie, January 18, 1864, Ewell Papers, LC; Hamlin, *Making of a Soldier,* 123.

23. O.R., vol. 33, 1096; Marshall W. Fishwick, *Lee After the War* (New York: Dodd, Meade, 1963), 209; J. William Jones, *Life and Letters of Robert Edward Lee: Soldier and Man* (New York: Neale, 1906), 280–81.

24. REL to RSE, February 18, 1864, War, 1861–1865, Letters (L, Box 5), NYHS; B. C. Adams to Samuel Cooper, February 10, 1864, Moses G. Peyton Letters, VHS; A. S. Venable to RSE, February 22, 1864, PBEP; Durkin, ed., *Confederate Chaplain,* 78–79.

25. Freeman, *Lee's Lieutenants,* 3: 330; McDonald, *Make Me a Map of the Valley,* 200; Osborne, *Jubal,* 338; Campbell Brown to RSE, June 13, 1864, BPEP; see also D. S. Freeman to P. G. Hamlin, June 10, 1943, and P. G. Hamlin to D. F. Freeman, July 3, 1943, Douglas Southall Freeman Papers, ALUV.

26. Casdorph, *Lee and Jackson,* 397–98; Henry, *Story of the Confederacy,* 355; J. F. C. Fuller, *Grant and Lee: A Study in Personality and Generalship* (Bloomington: Indiana UP, reprint, 1957), 200–10; Clifford Dowdey, *Lee's Last Campaign: The Story of Lee and His Men Against Grant, 1864* (Boston: Little, Brown, 1960), 3.

27. Dowdey, *Lee's Last Campaign,* 35; William S. McFeely, *Grant: A Biography* (New York: W. W. Norton, reprint, 1982), 166.

28. Secretary of War, *Atlas to Accompany the Official Records,* 55. This source maps the extent of the Wilderness in some detail. Esposito, *West Point Atlas of American Wars,* 121; O.R., vol. 36, pt. 1, 1070.

29. Gordon C. Rhea, *The Battles for Spotsylvania Court House and the Road to Yellow Tavern, May 7–12, 1864* (Baton Rouge: Louisiana State UP, 1997), appendix; Sifakis, *Who Was Who in the Confederacy,* 152, 219; Carmichael, *Lee's Young Artillerist,* 115; Krick, *Lee's Colonels,* 177.

30. Sifakis, *Who Was Who in the Confederacy,* 377; M. Wright, *General Officers of the Confederate Army,* 114, 142; William D. Matter, *If It Takes All Summer: The Battle of Spotsylvania* (Chapel Hill: U of North Carolina P, 1988), 362.

31. Rhea, *Battles for Spotsylvania,* appendix; Freeman, *Lee's Lieutenants,* 3: 119; Adams, "Confederate General Robert E. Rodes," 87; H. Pfanz, *Culp's Hill and Cemetery Hill,* 407.

32. Grant, *Personal Memoirs,* 401; Gallagher, ed., *Fighting for the Confederacy,* 351.

33. O.R., vol. 36, pt. 1, 1070; Gallagher, ed., *Fighting for the Confederacy,* 351; W. S. Shockley to Dear Eliza, August 16, 1864, William S. Shockley Papers, PLDU.

34. Jed Hotchkiss, "Diary," May 5, 1865, Jedediah Hotchkiss Papers, LC; Noah Andre Trudeau, *Bloody Roads South: The Wilderness to Cold Harbor, May–June, 1864* (Boston: Little, Brown, 1989), 41; Krick, *Lee's Colonels,* 334. According to Krick, Stiles was not promoted to major until January 1865.

35. N. H. Harris to William Mahone, August 2, 1866, William Mahone Papers, PLDU; Jed Hotchkiss to Dear Sara, May 7, 1864, Jedediah Hotchkiss Papers, LC; Early, *Autobiographical Sketch,* 347.

36. O.R., vol. 36, pt. 1, 1070; Early, *Autobiographical Sketch,* 346; Robertson, *Stonewall Brigade,* 219–20.

37. Jed Hotchkiss to Dear Sara, May 11, 1864, Jedediah Hotchkiss Papers, LC; C. S. Venable, "The Campaign from the Wilderness to Petersburg," *Southern Historical Society Papers* 14 (1886): 525; Sifakis, *Who Was Who in the Confederacy,* 154; Carmichael, "Escaping the Shadow," 148; Campbell Brown, "Memoranda— Campaign of 1864" (handwritten memoir), B-EPTSL.

38. Gordon C. Rhea, *The Battle of the Wilderness, May 5–6, 1864* (Baton Rouge: Louisiana State UP, 1994), 159; Gordon, *Reminiscences of the Civil War,* 238–39; Early, *Autobiographical Sketch,* 346; Trudeau, *Bloody Roads South,* 58; O.R., vol. 36, pt. 1, 1070.

39. Early, *Autobiographical Sketch,* 346; Adams, "Confederate General Robert E. Rodes," 89–90; O.R., vol. 36, pt. 1, 1070; Gallagher, *Stephen Dodson Ramseur,* 95–101; Secretary of War, *Atlas to Accompany the Official Records,* 83.

40. O.R., vol. 36, pt.1, 1070, pt. 2, 969–70; Dowdey, *Lee's Last Campaign,* 101; J. E. Phillips, "Civil War Memoir" (typescript), James E. Phillips Papers, VHS, 42.

41. Venable, "Campaign from the Wilderness to Petersburg," 524; Edward Steere, *The Wilderness Campaign* (Harrisburg, PA: Stackpole Books, 1960), 403-05; Burke Davis, *The Gray Fox: Robert E. Lee and the Civil War* (New York: Fairfax Press, reprint, 1988), 281–82; REL to RSE, May 8, 1864, B-EPTSL; E. Thomas, *Bold Dragoon,* 290–91.

42. Early, *Autobiographical Sketch,* 347; REL to A. P. Hill, May 6, 1864, Lee Family Papers, VHS; Rhea, *Battle of the Wilderness,* 323; Trudeau, *Bloody Roads South,* 106; O.R., vol. 36, pt. 1, 729.

43. A. S. Pendleton to J. B. Gordon, May 6, 1864, B-EPTSL; W. H. Taylor to RSE, May 7, 1864, PBEP; Robertson, *General A. P. Hill*, 261; O.R., vol. 36, pt.1, 1081; Carmichael, *Lee's Young Artillerist*, 114–16.

44. R. Eckert, *John Brown Gordon*, 65; O.R., vol. 36, pt. 1, 1071; Osborne, *Jubal*, 234–45.

45. O.R., vol. 36, pt. 1, 1071; W. H. Cheek to RSE, May 6, 1864, B-EPTSL. Cheek was lieutenant colonel of the First North Carolina Cavalry on outpost duty along the Rapidan as the Wilderness fighting unfolded; a copy of the communiqué can be found in PEBP; Dowdey, *Lee's Last Campaign*, 170; R. Eckert, *John Brown Gordon*, 65; Freeman, *Lee's Lieutenants*, 3: 375.

46. Rhea, *Battle of the Wilderness*, 412; Ewell, "Letterbook," 45, E-BPTSL. In this source Campbell Brown reproduces a letter "in Gordon's handwriting" and then adds a commentary of his own. "Memoranda of Conversations with Robert E. Lee" (handwritten transcripts), William Allan Papers, SHC. For a complete annotated transcript of the postwar conversations, see Gallagher, ed., *Lee: The Soldier*, 7–24. Brown noted further in the "Letterbook": "But the delay, occasioned was considerable, as Genl Early found Genl Ewell just summoned to Genl Lee & he had to delay the investigation until his return. Yet Early arrogates almost the whole credit to himself. Oh, Jubal!"

47. Rhea, *Battle of the Wilderness*, 412–16; O.R., vol. 36, pt. 1, 1071; Gordon, *Reminiscences of the Civil War*, 245–61; Trudeau, *Bloody Roads South*, 113.

48. Grant, *Personal Memoirs*, 408–09.

Chapter 13: "Laid on the Shelf"

1. Grant, *Personal Memoirs*, 408–12; Francis A. Boyle, "Diary," May 7, 1864, Francis A. Boyle Papers, SHC; Henry, *Story of the Confederacy*, 355; James M. McPherson, *The Civil War and Reconstruction* (New York: Knopf, 1982), 416–22.

2. Matter, *If It Takes All Summer*, 76; G. Moxley Sorrel, "Diary," May 8, 1864, G. Moxley Sorrel Papers, MOC; "Spotsylvania Court House" (unsigned memoir), PBEP; Henry Heth, "The Battle of the Wilderness," in *Broadfoot's Supplement to the Official Records of the Union and Confederate Armies*, vol. 36, no. 67–68: 206; Richard S. Ewell, "From the Rapidan to Spotsylvania Court House," *Southern Historical Society Papers* 13 (1885): 231, also a handwritten copy in B-EPTSL.

3. O.R., vol. 36, pt. 1, 1073; Gallagher, *Stephen Dodson Ramseur*, 104–05; Rhea, *Battles for Spotsylvania*, 86–88.

4. A. L. Long, "Report on Spotsylvania," PBEP; Esposito, *West Point Atlas of American Wars*, 127; Trudeau, *Bloody Roads South*, 144; Westwood Todd, "Reminiscences of the Civil War" (typescript), 197–98, Westwood Todd Papers, SHC.

5. Gordon, *Reminiscences of the Civil War*, 272; Rhea, *Battles for Spotsylvania*, 89–91; Dowdey, *Lee's Last Campaign*, 195–98.

6. Boyle, "Diary," May 9, 1864, (typescript), Boyle Papers, p. 1, J. E. Phillips, "Memoirs of the Civil War" (typescript), James E. Phillips Papers, VHS; Trudeau, *Bloody Roads South,* 146; Sorrel, "Diary," May 8–9, 1864, Sorrel Papers, MOC; Campbell Brown to Dear Mother, May 8, 1864, PBEP.

7. O.R., vol. 36, pt. 1, 1072; Gallagher, *Stephen Dodson Ramseur,* 105; Gordon, *Reminiscences of the Civil War,* 272–73; David F. Riggs, "Richard S. Ewell: Lee's Maligned Lieutenant," *Confederate Historical Institute Journal* 1 (summer 1980): 48; Rhea, *Battles for Spotsylvania,* 174–75; Campbell Brown to My Dear Mother, May 11, 1864, PBEP; Jed Hotchkiss to My Dear Wife, May 11, 1864, Jedediah Hotchkiss Papers, LC.

8. O.R., vol. 36, pt. 1, 1086; Matter, *If It Takes All Summer,* 183–85; Sorrel, "Diary," May 11, 1864, Sorrel Papers, MOC.

9. O.R., vol. 36, pt. 1, 1083; Long, "Report on Spotsylvania"; Long, *Memoirs of Robert E. Lee,* 339–40; Dowdey, *Lee's Last Campaign,* 203; Robert K. Krick, "An Insurmountable Barrier Between the Army and Ruin: The Confederate Experience at Spotsylvania's Bloody Angle," in Gallagher, ed., *Wilderness Campaign,* 86–87. This source contains a detailed analysis of the cannon and their importance.

10. Krick, "Insurmountable Barrier," 87; Robertson, *Stonewall Brigade,* 225; Bruce Catton, *Grant Takes Command* (Edison, NJ: Castle Books, reprint, 2000), 224–25.

11. Brown, "Memoranda—Campaign of 1864"; Krick, "Insurmountable Barrier," 90; Rhea, *Battles for Spotsylvania,* 256; J. Catlett Gibson and William W. Smith, "The Battle of Spotsylvania Court House, May 12, 1864," *Southern Historical Society Papers* 32 (1904): 200–01.

12. Sifakis, *Who Was Who in the Confederacy,* 223; Rhea, *Battles for Spotsylvania,* appendix.

13. A. L. Scott, "Memoir of Service in the Confederate Army" (typescript), Alfred Lewis Scott Papers, VHS, 19–20; A. L. Scott to S. T. L. Anderson, February 22, 1910, Alfred Lewis Scott Papers.

14. Theodore Lyman, Meade's staff officer, has left an account of Edward Johnson and Maryland Steuart immediately after their capture: "Johnson was a powerfully built man of a stern and rather bad face, and was dressed in a double-breasted blue-gray coat, high riding boots and a very bad felt hat. He was most horrified at being taken, and kept coughing to hide his emotion. Generals Grant and Meade shook hands with him, and good General Williams bore him off to breakfast. His demeanor was dignified and proper. Not so little a creature as General Steuart, who insulted everybody who came near him and was rewarded by being sent on foot to Fredericksburg where there was plenty of mud and one stream up to his waist." Lyman, *With Grant and Meade,* 111.

15. Trudeau, *Bloody Roads South,* 176–78; Gordon, *Reminiscences of the Civil War,* 280; Gibson and Smith, "Battle of Spotsylvania," 203–04.

16. O.R., vol. 36, pt. 1, 1073; R. C. M. Page, "The Captured Guns at

Spotsylvania Courthouse, May 12, 1864," *Southern Historical Society Papers* 7 (1879): 535–39.

17. Gallagher, *Stephen Dodson Ramseur,* 109–11; O.R., vol. 36, pt. 1, 1083; N. H. Harris to Charles J. Lewis, March 22, 1899, Nathaniel H. Harris Papers, SHC; R. A. Hardaway to REL, May 12, 1864, James W. Eldridge Papers, HL; Sorrel, Diary, May 12, 1864, Sorrel Papers, MOC.

18. S. D. Ramseur to My Darling Wife, June 4, 1864, Stephen Dodson Ramseur Papers, SHC.

19. Trudeau, *Bloody Roads South,* 185 (Casler quote); O.R., vol. 36, pt. 1, 1073–75; Lyman, *Grant and Meade,* 161; Brown, "Memoranda—Campaign of 1864."

20. Esposito, *West Point Atlas of American Wars,* 132; Early, *Autobiographical Sketch,* 357; Jed Hotchkiss to My Dear Wife, Jedediah Hotchkiss Papers, LC. Civil War–era documents refer to the river as "Ny," but contemporary usage has it as "Ni."

21. RSE to Dear Lizinka, May 16, 1864, and Campbell Brown to My Dear Mother, May 15, 1864, B-EPFCL; Gordon C. Rhea, *To the North Anna River: Grant and Lee, May 13–25, 1864* (Baton Rouge: Louisiana State UP, 2000), 150; Jed Hotchkiss to My Dear Wife, May 19, 1864, Jedediah Hotchkiss Papers, LC.

22. Esposito, *West Point Atlas of American Wars,* 132; Rhea, *To the North Anna River,* 152.

23. R. Eckert, *John Brown Gordon,* 81; Dowdey, *Lee's Last Campaign,* 225; O.R., vol. 36, pt. 1, 1083.

24. O.R., vol. 36, pt. 1, 1083; Gallagher, *Stephen Dodson Ramseur,* 114; Campbell Brown to My Dear Mother and Sister, May 20, 1864, PBEP.

25. Esposito, *West Point Atlas of American Wars,* 135; Rhea, *To the North Anna River,* 195; Campbell Brown to My Dear Mother and Sister, May 25, 1864, B-EPFCL.

26. O.R., vol. 36, pt. 1, 1074; Early, *Autobiographical Sketch,* 359–60; Henry, *Story of the Confederacy,* 361; Rhea, *To the North Anna River,* 253; RSE to Dear Lizinka, May 26, 1864, B-EPFCL.

27. Catton, *Grant Takes Command,* 256; Venable, "Campaign from the Wilderness to Petersburg," 535; Dowdey, *Lee's Last Campaign,* 269.

28. O.R., vol. 36, pt. 1, 1074; Campbell Brown to H. H. McGuire, May 28, 1864, and H.H. McGuire to RSE, May 28, 1864, War, 1861–1865, Letters (L, Box 5), NYHS.

29. REL to RSE, May 29, 1864, W. H. Taylor, Special Order (unnumbered), May 29, 1864, War, 1861–1865, Letters (L, Box 5), NYHS. There is also a copy of Taylor's order in PEBP.

30. RSE to W. H. Taylor, June 1, 1864 (two letters), and W. H. Taylor to RSE, June 1, 1864, War, 1861–1865, Letters (L, Box 5), NYHS.

31. M. Wright, *General Officers of the Confederate Army,* 19; RSE to Dear Lizinka, May 31, June 1, 1864, PBEP.

32. REL to RSE, June 1, 1864, War, 1861–1865, Letters (L, Box 5), NYHS; RSE to Dear Lizinka, June 2, 1864, PBEP.

33. Hamlin, *Making of a Soldier*, 126–28; W. C. Davis, *Jefferson Davis*, 559.

34. Early, *Autobiographical Sketch*, 363; Grant, *Personal Memoirs*, 445, 452; McFeely, *Grant: A Biography*, 367; Dowdey, *Lee's Last Campaign*, 284–91; Current, ed., *Encyclopedia of the Confederacy*, 1: 366–67.

35. Hamlin, *Making of a Soldier*, 128–30, includes a verbatim transcript of the Lee-Ewell meeting as does D. Pfanz, *Richard S. Ewell*, 400–01.

36. Early, *Autobiographical Sketch*, 361; J. A. Early to RSE, June 5, 1864, War, 1861–1865, Letters (L, Box 5), NYHS.

37. REL to RSE, June 12, 1864, War, 1861–1865, Letters (L, Box 5), NYHS; REL to Samuel Cooper, June 12, 1864, PBEP; RSE to Dear Lizinka, July 29, 1864, B-EPFCL; Boatner, *Civil War Dictionary*, 255–57; Frank E. Vandiver, *Jubal's Raid: General Early's Famous Attack on Washington in 1864* (Lincoln: U of Nebraska P, reprint, 1992), passim.

38. Robert M. Hughes, *General Johnston* (New York: D. Appleton, 1893), 246–47; Davis, *Jefferson Davis*, 541; Hamlin, *Making of a Soldier*, 130–31.

39. "Bessie" to Katherine Bastable, October 3, 1864 (letter is dated September 30, with postscript), Thornton Family Papers, VHS; Turner, "Ewells of Virginia," 43; Jed Hotchkiss, "Diary," October 26, 1864, Jedediah Hotchkiss Papers, LC; J. H. Woodruff to Dear Dave, June 7, 1864, Talcott Family Papers, VHS; Dowdey, "Richard S. Ewell," 8.

Chapter 14: The Last March

1. Richard J. Sommers, *Richmond Redeemed: The Siege of Petersburg* (Garden City, NY: Doubleday, 1981), 22; A. A. Humphreys, *The Virginia Campaigns of 1864 and 1865* (New York: Da Capo Press, reprint, 1995), appendix; Esposito, *West Point Atlas of American Wars*, 136.

2. Union General A. A. Humphreys consistently refers to this place (as well as nearby Chaffin's Bluff) as "Chapin's."

3. John B. Jones, *A Rebel War Clerk's War Diary* (Philadelphia: J. B. Lippincott, 1886), 2: 257; O.R., vol. 42, pt. 2, 1293.

4. O.R., vol. 42, pt. 2, 1293; Early, *Autobiographical Sketch*, 380; J. B. Jones, *Rebel War Clerk's Diary*, 2: 243; Sifakis, *Who Was Who in the Confederacy*, 239; Dowdey, *Lee's Last Campaign*, 269–70.

5. Dowdey, *Lee's Last Campaign*, 270; REL to RSE, August 10, 1864, Gunter Family Papers, CHS; REL to RSE, August 19, 1864, REL Papers, CHS; RSE to REL, September 22, 1864, Civil War Collection, HL.

6. J. B. Jones, *Rebel War Clerk's Diary*, 2: 236; Marie Tyler-McGraw, *At the Falls: Richmond, Virginia, and its People* (Chapel Hill: U of North Carolina P, 1994), 157; REL to RSE, n.d., F. W. Smith Papers, VHS; C. W. Field, "Campaign of 1864 and 1865," *Southern Historical Society Papers* 14 (1886): 550.

7. O.R., vol. 42, pt. 2, 1173, 1178; "Application for Medical Leave for

Lieutenant J. Watkins," signed by RSE, July 20, 1864, John Gratton Cabell Papers, VHS.

8. "Necrology, Legh R. Page," *Virginia Magazine of History and Biography* 1 (1894): 336; O.R., vol. 42, pt. 2, 1173–74; Freeman, *Lee's Lieutenants*, 3: 552; Hamlin, *Making of a Soldier*, 131–32.

9. Grant, *Personal Memoirs*, 476–77; Humphreys, *Virginia Campaigns of 1864 and 1865*, 284–85.

10. Krick, *Lee's Colonels*, 545; Marcus J. Wright, "Bushrod Johnson's Men at Fort Harrison," *Confederate Veteran* 14 (1906): 545; Sommers, *Richmond Redeemed*, 28.

11. C. T. Allen, "The Fight at Chaffin's Farm and Fort Harrison," *Confederate Veteran* 13 (1905): 418; Sommers, *Richmond Redeemed*, 28, 109–11.

12. Humphreys, *Virginia Campaigns of 1864 and 1865*, 286–87; Ernest B. Furgurson, *Ashes of Glory: Richmond at War* (New York: Knopf, 1996), 279–80; Catton, *Grant Takes Command*, 366; J. H. Martin, "Forts Gilmer and Harrison Forces," *Confederate Veteran* 14 (1906): 409.

13. Robert Bogardus Snowden, a former student of Bushrod Johnson at a Tennessee military school, had charge of Johnson's brigade; see, Krick, *Lee's Colonels*, 329, and Wright, "Bushrod Johnson's Men at Fort Harrison," 545.

14. The leader of the Texas brigade was Brigadier General John Gregg; after his death one month later, Gregg County, Texas, was named for him. See Boatner, *Civil War Dictionary*, 357, and W. Webb, ed., *Handbook of Texas*, 1: 733–34.

15. Charles Johnston, "Attack on Fort Gilmer, September 29, 1864," *Southern Historical Society Papers* 1 (1876): 438–39; see also Sommers, *Richmond Redeemed*, 470–61; O.R., vol. 42, pt. 2, 1221. According to the latter, Captain Benjamin H. Smith commanded the Third Company, Richmond Howitzers.

16. C. Johnston, "Attack on Fort Gilmer," 439–41; Humphreys, *Virginia Campaigns of 1864 and 1865*, 287–88; J. Martin, "Forts Gilmer and Harrison," 409; Ewell, "Letterbook," PLDU.

17. J. H. Martin maintains that the Fort Gilmer fighting did not end until 4:00 P.M.

18. D. Pfanz, *Richard S. Ewell*, 417–18; O.R., vol. 42, pt. 1, 937; Turner, "Ewells of Virginia," 47; Sommers, *Richmond Redeemed*, 63.

19. Humphreys, *Virginia Campaigns of 1864 and 1865*, 288–89; Sorrel, *Reflections of a Confederate Staff Officer*, 259–60; Sommers, *Richmond Redeemed*, 133.

20. Weddell, *St. Paul's Church*, 2: 229; "Bessie" to Katherine Bastable, October 3, 1864, Thornton Family Papers, VHS; Conversation with Rev. Dr. Robert Hall, Charleston, West Virginia, July 19, 2000.

21. Richard J. Sommers, "'The Dutch Gap Affair': Military Atrocities and the Rights of Negro Soldiers," *Civil War History* 21 (March 1975): 51–64; P. S. Michie, "Account of the Dutch Gap Canal," in Robert U. Johnson and Clarence C. Buell, eds., *Battles and Leaders of the Civil War* (New York: Thomas Yoseloff,

reprint, 1950), 4: 575; Gallagher, ed., *Fighting for the Confederacy,* 487–88; Furgurson, *Ashes of Glory,* 289–90.

22. Humphreys, *Virginia Campaigns of 1864 and 1865,* 308; Emory M. Thomas, *The Confederate State of Richmond: A Biography of the Capital* (Austin: U of Texas P, 1971), 176–77, Freeman, *Lee's Lieutenants,* 3: 593; O.R., vol. 42, pt. 1, 871; Wert, *General James Longstreet,* 211.

23. RSE to Walter H. Taylor, November 8, 1864, Ewell Papers, PLDU; Walter H. Taylor, General Order Number 316, Lee Family Papers, VHS; O.R., vol. 42, pt. 3, 1370; Boatner, *Civil War Dictionary,* 475–76.

24. O.R., vol. 42, pt. 3, 1288, 1301, 1307; Gallagher, ed., *Fighting for the Confederacy,* 528; M. Wright, *General Officers of the Confederate Army,* 122.

25. Samuel J. Martin, *The Road to Glory* (Indianapolis: Guild Press of Indiana, 1991), 343; Grant, *Personal Memoirs,* 550; Burke Davis, *To Appomattox: Nine Days in April 1865,* (New York: Rinehart, 1959), 295; BSE to Dear Sir, January 30, 1865, PBEP.

26. Lizinka Ewell to Hon. D. T. Patterson, April 9, 1865, PBEP; U.S. Congress, *Biographical Directory,* 1430; Hans L. Trefousse, *Impeachment of a President: Andrew Johnson, the Blacks, and Reconstruction* (Knoxville: U of Tennessee P), 152.

27. The published version of her encounter with Andrew Johnson has her name as "Harriot."

28. Harriet S. Turner, "Recollections of Andrew Johnson," *Harper's Monthly Magazine* 122 (June 1910): 173.

29. [Unidentified] to Dear Marshall, March 30, 1865, PBEP; E. Thomas, *Confederate Nation,* 262–64; F. R. Lubbock to J. B. Magruder, July 16, August 29, 1863, Francis R. Lubbock Records, Texas State Archives, Austin; J. B. Magruder, Broadside, June 15, 1863, John Bankhead Magruder Papers, Rosenberg Library, Galveston, Texas; O.R., vol. 46, pt. 2, 1237–38.

30. F. W. Hancock to RSE, February 11, 1865, George L. Christian Papers, VHS; Charles Marshall to RSE, March 30, 1865, Ewell Papers, LC; O.R., vol. 46, pt. 2., 1259; Gordon, *Reminiscences of the Civil War,* 383–84; J. S. Hunter, "To Whom It May Concern," March 24, 1865, Approved by RSE, Joshua S. Hunter Papers, Virginia State Library, Richmond.

31. E. Thomas, *Confederate Nation,* 296–97; O.R., vol. 46, pt. 2, 1318; Carmichael, *Lee's Young Artillerist,* 158; McPherson, *Battle Cry of Freedom,* 837; Ervin L. Jordan, *Black Confederates and Afro-Yankees in Civil War Virginia* (Charlottesville: U of Virginia P, reprint, 1999), 250–51.

32. RSE, "Evacuation of Richmond" (handwritten report by Campbell Brown), copies in B-EPSTL, PBEB, SHC; *Southern Historical Society Papers* 13 (1885): 247–52, and O.R., vol. 46, pt. 1, 1292–95; William C. Davis, *An Honorable Defeat: The Last Days of the Confederate Government* (New York: Harcourt, 2001), 247–52; O.R., vol. 46, pt. 2, 1259–60, 1297.

33. E. Merton Coulter, *The Confederate States of America, 1861–1865* (Baton Rouge: Louisiana State UP, 1950), 566; Freeman, *Lee's Lieutenants,* 3: 769–71.

34. E. Thomas, *Confederate Nation,* 196; J. B. Jones, *Rebel War Clerk's Diary,* 2: 434–35; B. Davis, *To Appomattox,* 39; O.R., vol. 46, pt. 1, 1292-93, pt. 2, 1260–61.

35. RSE, requisition, March 8, 1865, Ewell Papers, PLDU; Susan Hoge to Moses D. Hoge, March 19, 1865, Hoge Family Papers, VHS; Humphreys, *Virginia Campaigns of 1864 and 1865,* 318–21; Robertson, *General A. P. Hill,* 312; Freeman, *Lee's Lieutenants,* 3: 655.

36. Esposito, *West Point Atlas of American Wars,* 143–44; Freeman, *Lee's Lieutenants,* 3: 657ff.; O.R., vol. 46, pt. 3, 1378.

37. Mrs. Burton Harrison, *Recollections, Grave and Gay,* 207; Mrs. Fannie Walker Miller, "The Fall of Richmond," *Confederate Veteran* 13 (1905): 305; W. C. Davis, *An Honorable Defeat,* 56–67; A. J. Hanna, *Flight into Oblivion* (Richmond, VA: Johnson Publishing, 1938), 3–5.

38. Joseph B. Kershaw, "Report of General J. B. Kershaw," *Southern Historical Society Papers* 13 (1885): 252; BSE to RSE, May 2, 1871, B-EPTSL; E. Thomas, *Confederate State of Richmond,* 199; Rembert W. Patrick, *The Fall of Richmond* (Baton Rouge: Louisiana State UP, 1960), 42–44.

39. RSE, "Evacuation of Richmond," 249; Kershaw, "Report of General J. B. Kershaw," 252; Clement Sulivane, "The Fall of Richmond," in Robert U. Johnson and Clarence C. Buell, eds., *Battle and Leaders of the Civil War* (New York: Thomas Yoseloff, reprint, 1950), 4: 725–26; Jordan, *Black Confederates,* 250; Thomas, *Confederate State of Richmond,* 196.

40. E. T. Watehall, "The Fall of Richmond, April 3, 1865," *Confederate Veteran* 17 (1909): 215; Clement Sulivane, "Last Soldiers to Leave Richmond," *Confederate Veteran* 17 (1909): 602; Edward M. Boykin, *The Falling Flag: Evacuation of Richmond, Retreat and Surrender at Appomattox* (New York: E. J. Hale, 1874), unpaged; Brown, "Memorandum—April 14, 1865"; "Letterbook" (handwritten manuscript), PLDU, 25ff.

41. BSE to Editor, *Richmond Whig* (Edward H. Ripley), April (no day), 1865, Ewell Papers, PLDU; BSE to RSE, April 6, 1871, and Lizzie Ewell to RSE, April 14, 1865, B-EPTSL; BSE, "Magruder-Ewell Camp" (typescript), Ewell Papers, LC.

42. O.R., vol. 46, pt. 1, 1296; Christopher M. Calkins, *From Petersburg to Appomattox, April 1865* (Farmville, VA: *Farmville Herald,* 1983), 14; Christopher M. Calkins, *Thirty-six Hours Before Appomattox* (Farmville, VA: *Farmville Herald,* 1980), unpaged; Esposito, *West Point Atlas of American Wars,* 144.

43. O.R., vol. 46, pt. 1, 1294; Calkins, *From Petersburg to Appomattox,* 14; Freeman, *R. E. Lee: A Biography,* 4: 62.

44. Earlier the stream was known as Saylor's Creek, after a local family, but

it evolved quickly into the more widely proclaimed Sailor's Creek. When the writer visited the tree-lined waterway in August 2001, it could be crossed with a step or two, but accounts of April 1865 have it waist-deep.

45. REL to RSE, April 2, 1865, James W. Eldridge Papers, HL; REL to RSE, April 3, 1865, B-EPTSL; W. L. Timberlake, "Last Days in Front of Richmond," *Confederate Veteran* 20 (1912): 144; Frederick M. Colston, "Recollections of the Last Months in the Army of Northern Virginia," *Southern Historical Society Papers* 38 (1910): 10.

46. W. L. Timberlake, "The Retreat from Richmond in 1865," *Confederate Veteran* 22 (1914), 455; W. C. Watson, "Saylor's Creek," *Southern Historical Society Papers* 42 (1917): 144; Gordon, *Reminiscences of the Civil War,* 429; O.R., vol. 46, pt. 1, 1295.

47. "Proceedings," *Virginia Magazine of History and Biography* 1 (1894): xxxv; E. P. Reeve, "Diary," Edward Payson Reeve Papers, SHC; W. Todd, "Todd Reminiscences" (typescript), Westwood Todd Papers, SHC; J. McAnerney, "Account of the Civil War" (handwritten memoir), John McAnerney Papers, VHS, 43; Thomas B. Blake, "Retreat from Richmond," *Southern Historical Society Papers* 25 (1897): 140. This account contains a listing of all officers captured at Sailor's Creek. O.R., vol. 46, pt. 1, 1295.

48. Calkins, *Thirty-six Hours Before Appomattox,* unpaged; O.R., vol. 46, pt. 1, 1299; Freeman, *R. E. Lee: A Biography,* 4: 93.

49. Freeman, *R. E. Lee: A Biography,* 4: 79; Joshua Lawrence Chamberlain, *The Passing of the Armies: An Account of the Final Campaign of the Army of the Potomac* (New York: Bantam, reprint, 1993), 163; Humphreys, *Virginia Campaigns of 1864 and 1865,* 385.

Chapter 15: "Not My Will, But Thine Be Done"

1. O.R., vol. 46, pt. 1, 1295; Eppa Hunton, *The Autobiography of Eppa Hunton* (Richmond, VA: William Byrd Press, 1933), 124–25; Noah Andre Trudeau, "A Mere Question of Time: Robert E. Lee from the Wilderness to Appomattox," in Gallagher, ed., *Lee: The Soldier,* 549; Christopher M. Calkins, *The Final Bivouac: The Surrender Parade at Appomattox and the Disbanding of the Armies* (Lynchburg, VA: H. E. Howard, 1988), 192–94.

2. McHenry Howard, *The Recollections of a Maryland Confederate Soldier and Staff Officer Under Johnston, Jackson, and Lee* (Dayton, OH: Morningside Book Shop, reprint, 1975), 392; Hunton, *Autobiography,* 125.

3. Hunton, *Autobiography,* 128; B. Davis, *To Appomattox,* 180–286; Paul C. Nagel, *The Lees of Virginia: Seven Generations of an American Family* (New York: Oxford UP, 1990), 300; O.R., vol. 46, pt. 1, 1295.

4. Randall, *Civil War and Reconstruction,* 679–80; O.R., vol. 46, pt. 3, 1013; Jonathan Truman Dorris, *Pardon and Amnesty Under Lincoln and Johnson:*

The Restoration of the Confederates to Their Rights and Privileges, 1861-1898 (Chapel Hill: U of North Carolina P, 1953), 161.

5. Hunton, *Autobiography,* 125–26; Virginius Dabney, *Virginia: The New Dominion* (Garden City, NY: Doubleday, 1971), 428–29; U.S. Congress, *Biographical Directory,* 1100.

6. Rebecca L. Ewell to Dear Lizinka, April 11, 1865, PBEP; T. T. Gantt to My Dear Lizinka, April 18, 1865, PBEP; Campbell Brown to My Dear Mother, April 20, 1865 (two letters), B-EPFCL.

7. Lizzie Ewell to RSE, April 13, 1865, PBEP; Howard, *Recollections of a Maryland Confederate Soldier,* 393; Jordan, *Black Confederates,* 251; Hunton, *Autobiography,* 136.

8. Turner, "Ewells of Virginia," 47; Hunton, *Autobiography,* 130.

9. Minor H. McLain, "The Military Prison at Fort Warren," *Civil War History* 8 (1982): 136–37; Edward R. Snow, *The Islands of Boston Harbor* (Andover, MA: Frontier Press, 1953), 17–18; Ben Procter, *Not Without Honor: The Life of John H. Reagan* (Austin: U of Texas P, 1962), 169-71; Hunton, *Autobiography,* 381.

10. Rebecca L. Ewell to Dear Sister (Lizinka Ewell), April 18, 1865, Ewell Papers, LC.

11. Hunton, *Autobiography,* 137–38.

12. O.R., vol. 46, pt. 3, 787; Hunton, *Autobiography,* 137; Turner, "Ewells of Virginia," 48–49. The generals in Ewell's letter were: "Maj. Gens. Ed. Johnson of Virginia and Kershaw of South Carolina; Brigadier-Generals Barton, Corse, Hunton, and Jones of Virginia; DuBose, Simms, and H. R. Jackson of Georgia; Frazer of Alabama; Smith and Gordon of Tennessee; Cabell of Arkansas, and Marmaduke of Missouri; and Commodore Tucker of Virginia."

13. Basler, ed., *Collected Works of Abraham Lincoln,* 1: 38; Donald, *Lincoln,* 247; T. T. Gantt to Lizinka Ewell, April 18, 1865, Ewell Papers, LC; Montgomery Blair to RSE, May 17, 1865, B-EPFCL; Montgomery Blair to Lizinka Ewell, May 28, 1865, Ewell Papers, LC.

14. Lizinka Ewell to Ulysses S. Grant, May 29, 1865, B-EPFCL; Campbell Brown to Harriet S. Brown, April 23, 1865, PBEP; Campbell Brown to Harriet S. Brown, May 17, 1865, B-EPFCL; RSE to Rebecca L. Ewell, May 8, 1865, Ewell Papers, LC; Hamlin, *Making of a Soldier,* 134–35.

15. RSE to Rebecca L. Ewell, May 8, 1865, Ewell Papers, LC; Hunton, *Autobiography,* 139; Alexander H. Stephens, *Recollections of Alexander H. Stephens: His Diary Kept When a Prisoner at Fort Warren, Boston Harbor, 1865* (Baton Rouge: Louisiana State UP, reprint, 1998), 220; Edward R. Snow, *Historic Fort Warren* (Boston: Yankee Publishing, 1941), 52.

16. Eric L. McKitrick, *Andrew Johnson and Reconstruction* (Chicago: U of Chicago P, reprint, 1960), 7; McPherson, *Ordeal by Fire,* 498; Eric Foner, *Reconstruction: America's Unfinished Revolution* (New York: Harper and Row, reprint, 1988), 182–83; O.R., ser. 2, vol. 8, 852.

17. Campbell Brown to Harriet S. Brown, June 6, 1865, RSE to Lizinka Ewell, June 8, 1865, and BSE to RSE, June 16, 1865, B-EPFCL; RSE to Andrew Johnson, June 16, 1865, Ewell Papers, LC.

18. Williams, "General Ewell to High Private," 160–61; Dorris, *Pardon and Amnesty,* 145; Joseph Lewis to RSE, June 20, 1865, Lizinka Ewell to John Pope, June 19, 1865, and John Pope to Lizinka Ewell, June 19, 1865, B-EPFCL; Turner, "Recollections of Andrew Johnson," 175–76.

19. Turner, "Recollections of Andrew Johnson," 175; Martin, *The Road to Glory,* 388-89.

20. Turner, "Recollections of Andrew Johnson," 176; RSE to Lizinka Ewell, July 1, 1865, and Campbell Brown to Lizinka Ewell, July 14, 1865, B-EPTSL; Harriet S. Brown to Campbell Brown, undated, PEBP, Chapel Hill.

21. Hamlin, *Making of a Soldier,* 141–43; RSE to Rebecca L. Ewell, June 28, 1865, Ewell Papers, LC; Lizinka Ewell to RSE, July 14, 1865, B-EPFCL; Ewell Parole (legal document), July 19, 1865, Ewell Papers, LC; Stephens, *Recollections,* 365.

22. Lizinka Ewell to Andrew Johnson, July 21, 1865, B-EPFCL; RSE to BSE, September 19, 1865, Ewell Papers, LC; Lizinka Ewell to James Speed, August 18, 1865, Lizinka Ewell Legal Document, September 15, 1865, and T. T. Gantt to Lizinka Ewell, September 4, 1865, B-EPTSL; Turner, "Recollections of Andrew Johnson," 176.

23. Hunton, *Autobiography,* 129; Hamlin, *Making of a Soldier,* 147.

24. Hamlin, *Making of a Soldier,* 147; Jil K. Garret, *Maury County, Tennessee: Historical Sketches* (n.p., n.d.), 177.

25. Hamlin, *Making of a Soldier,* 197; William Bruce Turner, *History of Maury County, Tennessee* (Nashville, TN: Parthenon Press, 1955), 86–88; Mayor and Aldermen of Columbia, *Century Review, 1805–1902: Maury County, Tennessee* (n.p., 1905), 128; RSE to Dear Lizzie, April 22, 1866, Ewell Papers, LC; Hamlin, *"Old Bald Head,"* 192.

26. Freeman, *R. E. Lee: A Biography,* 4, 275, 468; *Columbia Herald,* February 2, 1872; W. Turner, *History of Maury County,* 131–32; Hamlin, *Making of a Soldier,* 148.

27. Campbell Family Genealogy; "G. Campbell Brown: Outline Biography" (typescript), B-EPTSL; *Columbia Herald,* November 3, 1871; Malone, ed., *Dictionary of American Biography,* 8: 44.

28. BSE to RSE, May 23, 1867, and BSE to RSE, August 9, 1867, B-EPTSL; BSE to Richard Taylor, April 2, 1867, L. M. Barlow Papers, HL.

29. Hamlin, *Making of a Soldier,* 152–53; Campbell Brown to My Dear Mother, October 1, 1867, PBEP.

30. RSE to BSE, December 8, 1867, Ewell Papers, Maine Historical Society, Augusta.

31. Freeman, *R. E. Lee: A Biography,* 4: 363; T. T. Turner to Campbell Brown, July 12, 1868, and Campbell Brown to My Dear Mother, May 26, 1868, B-EPTSL.

32. Campbell Brown to My Dear Mother, June 10, July 21, 1868.

33. BSE to RSE, June 10, 1869, B-EPTSL; D. Pfanz, *Richard S. Ewell*, 481; Florence Warfield Sillers, *History of Bolivar County, Mississippi* (Jackson, MS: Hederman Brothers, 1948), 18, 48, 83–84, 322, 581–82.

34. A. P. Alexander to RSE, December 3, 1869, Campbell Brown to RSE, December 6, 1869, and RSE to Campbell Brown, December 30, 1869, B-EPTSL.

35. Sillers, *History of Bolivar County*, 165; RSE to Campbell Brown, Saturday 5, 1870 (otherwise undated), B-EPTSL.

36. Lizinka Ewell to RSE, December 15, 1870, and Cadmus M. Wilcox, to RSE, April 18, 1870, B-EPTSL; *Columbia Herald*, July 7, August 8, 1871.

37. Earle D. Ross, *The Liberal Republican Movement* (New York: AMS Press, reprint, 1971), 46–48; Paul D. Casdorph, "Texas Delegations to Republican National Conventions, 1860–1896" (MA thesis, University of Texas, 1961), 24–32; Harlan H. Horner, *Lincoln and Greeley* (Urbana: U of Illinois P, 1953), 401; Henry L. Stoddard, *Horace Greeley: Printer, Editor, Crusader* (New York: G. P. Putnam's Sons, 1946), 266, 299; *Columbia Herald*, June 2, 1871; BSE, "The South and General Grant," May 18, 1872, Broadside, J. K. Hall Papers, SHC.

38. *Columbia Herald*, May 17, 1871; RSE to R. H. Chilton, January 3, 1871, Ewell Papers, MOC.

39. RSE to John R. Cooke, June 21, 1871, Cooke Family Papers, Virginia State Library, Richmond.

40. *Columbia Herald*, November 3, 1871; RSE to Campbell Brown, Saturday 25, 1871 (otherwise undated), January 2, 7, 1872, B-EPTSL.

41. T. Jones, ed., *Campbell Brown's Civil War*, 2, 350–54.

42. *Columbia Herald*, January 19, 26, 1872; Hamlin, *"Old Bald Head,"* 193; *Nashville Union and American*, January 23, 1872.

43. *Nashville Union and American*, January 23, 1872; *Columbia Herald*, January 26, 1872.

44. T. Jones, *Campbell Brown's Civil War*, 342–43; *Columbia Herald*, January 26, 1872; *Nashville Union and American*, January 25, 1872.

45. *Columbia Herald*, February 2, 1872; *Nashville Republican Banner*, January 27, 1872; *Nashville Union and American*, January 27, 1872; *New York Times*, January 29, 1872.

BIBLIOGRAPHY

Manuscripts

William Allan Papers, SHC, Chapel Hill, North Carolina

Ashby Family Papers, VHS, Richmond, Viriginia

John B. Bachelder Papers, New Hampshire Historical Society, Concord, New Hampshire

L. M. Barlow Papers, HL, San Marino, California

Albert Batchelor Papers, Louisiana and Lower Mississippi Valley Collections, LSU Libraries, Baton Rouge, Louisiana

P. G. T. Beauregard Papers, CHS, Chicago, Illinois

Robert Blake Collection, U.S. Military History Institute, Carlisle Barracks, Pennsylvania

Milledge L. Bonham Papers, University of South Carolina Library, Columbia, South Carolina

David French Boyd Civil War Papers, Louisiana and Lower Mississippi Valley Collections, LSU Libraries, Baton Rouge, Louisiana

Francis A. Boyle Papers, SHC, Chapel Hill, North Carolina

Brown-Ewell Papers, Filson Club Library, Louisville, Kentucky

Brown-Ewell Papers, Tennessee State Library and Archives, Nashville, Tennessee

Samuel D. Buck Papers, PLDU, Durham, North Carolina

John Gratton Cabell Papers, VHS, Richmond, Virginia

Henry A. Chambers Papers, NCSA, Raleigh, North Carolina

George L. Christian Papers, VHS, Richmond, Virginia

Civil War Collection, HL, San Marino, California

Civil War Times Illustrated Collection, U.S. Army Military History Institute, Carlisle Barracks, Pennsylvania

John Claibourne Papers, (#3633), ALUV, Charlottesville, Virginia

Cooke Family Papers, Virginia State Library, Richmond, Virginia

Charles W. Dabney Papers, SHC, Chapel Hill, North Carolina

George and Catherine Davis Collection, Tulane University Library, New Orleans, Louisiana

415

Henry Kyd Douglas Papers, CHS, Chicago, Illinois
Jubal Anderson Early Papers, PLDU, Durham, North Carolina
Jubal Anderson Early Papers, LC, Washington, DC
Jubal Anderson Early Papers, VHS, Richmond, Virginia
James W. Eldridge Papers, HL, San Marino, California
Benjamin Stoddert Ewell Papers, Swem Library, College of William and Mary,
    Williamsburg, Virginia
Benjamin Stoddert Ewell Papers, U.S. Military Academy, West Point, New York
Jesse Ewell Papers, Center for the Study of American History, University of Texas,
    Austin, Texas
Richard Stoddert Ewell Biographical File, Arizona Historical Society, Tucson,
    Arizona
Richard Stoddert Ewell Papers, PLDU, Durham, North Carolina
Richard Stoddert Ewell Papers, LC, Washington, DC
Richard Stoddert Ewell Papers, Maine Historical Society, Augusta, Maine
Richard Stoddert Ewell Papers, Brockenbrough Library, MOC, Richmond, Virginia
Richard Stoddert Ewell Papers, Microfilm copies on deposit, ALUV, Charlottesville,
    Virginia
Richard Stoddert Ewell Papers, U.S. Military Academy, West Point, New York
Richard Stoddert Ewell Papers, VHS, Richmond
Samuel Wagg Ferguson Papers, PLDU, Durham, North Carolina
Joseph Fish Papers, Arizona Department of Library, Archives, and Public Records,
    Phoenix, Arizona
Douglas Southall Freeman Papers, (#9535-B), ALUV, Charlottesville, Virginia
Amanda Gardner Papers, PLDU, Durham, North Carolina
John Brown Gordon Papers, University of Georgia Library, Athens, Georgia
John L. Graham Papers, HL, San Marino, California
Maxey Gregg Papers, VHS, Richmond, Virginia
Gunter Family Papers, CHS, Chicago, Illinois
J. K. Hall Papers, SHC, Chapel Hill, North Carolina
Washington Hands Papers, (#10361), ALUV, Charlottesville, Virginia
Peter W. Hairston Papers, SHC, Chapel Hill, North Carolina
John A. Harman Papers, LC, Washington, DC
Nathaniel H. Harris Papers, SHC, Chapel Hill, North Carolina
Julien Harrison Papers, (#7128-A), ALUV, Charlottesville, Virginia
John C. Haskell Papers, PLDU, Durham, North Carolina
Heatt-Wilson Papers, SHC, Chapel Hill, North Carolina
J. H. Henry Papers, VHS, Richmond, Virginia
Hoge Family Papers, VHS, Richmond, Virginia
Jedediah Hotchkiss Papers, U.S. Army Military History Institute, Carlisle Bar-
    racks, Pennsylvania
Jedediah Hotchkiss Papers, LC, Washington, DC

Joshua S. Hunter Papers, Virginia State Library, Richmond, Virginia
Thomas J. Jackson Papers, CHS, Chicago, Illinois
Thomas J. Jackson Papers, Maine Historical Society, Augusta, Maine
Thomas J. Jackson Papers, Massachusetts Historical Society, Boston, Massachusetts
Thomas J. Jackson Papers SHC, Chapel Hill, North Carolina
William L. Jackson Papers, CHS, Chicago, Illinois
Joseph E. Johnston Papers, HL, San Marino, California
C. E. Jones Papers, PLDU, Durham, North Carolina
Beverly T. Lacy Papers, VHS, Richmond, Virginia
Robert E. Lee Papers, HL, San Marino, California
Robert E. Lee Papers, Washington and Lee University Library, Lexington, Virginia
Lee Family Papers, VHS, Richmond, Virginia
Lee Family Papers, (#4236), ALUV, Charlottesville, Virginia
Lee Family Papers, NA, Washington, DC
Lee Family Collection, Jesse Ball du Pont Library, Stratford, Virginia
Francis R. Lubbock Records, Texas State Archives, Austin, Texas
James Lyons Papers, HL, San Marino, California
John Bankhead Magruder Papers, MOC, Richmond, Virginia
John Bankhead Magruder Papers, Rosenberg Library, Galveston, Texas
William Mahone Papers, PLDU, Durham, North Carolina
John McAnerney Papers, VHS, Richmond, Virginia
Hunter H. McGuire Papers, VHS, Richmond, Virginia
Minor Family Papers, (#10685), ALUV, Charlottesville, Virginia
Minor Family Papers, VHS, Richmond, Virginia
Henri Jean Mugler Diary and Memoir, West Virginia University Library, Morgantown, West Virginia
Munford-Ellis Papers, PLDU, Durham, North Carolina
Elisha Franklin Paxton Papers, CHS, Chicago, Illinois
Edward Reeve Payton Papers, SHC, Chapel Hill, North Carolina
Joseph Pelot Papers, PLDU, Durham, North Carolina
Alexander S. "Sandie" Pendleton Papers, CHS Chicago, Illinois
William Nelson Pendleton Papers, SHC, Chapel Hill, North Carolina
George W. Peterkin Papers, West Virginia State Archives, Charleston, West Virginia
Moses G. Peyton Papers, VHS, Richmond, Virginia
James E. Phillips Papers, VHS, Richmond, Virginia
Polk-Brown-Ewell Papers, SHC, Chapel Hill, North Carolina
James L. Power Papers, VHS, Richmond, Virginia
Stephen Dodson Ramseur Papers, SHC, Chapel Hill, North Carolina
William J. Rhees Papers, HL, San Marino, California
Carleton R. Richmond Autograph File, Massachusetts Historical Society, Boston, Massachusetts

William J. Ritch Papers, HL, San Marino, California
Rives Family Papers, (#2532), ALUV, Charlottesville, Virginia
Alfred Lewis Scott Papers, VHS, Richmond, Virginia
William J. Seymour Papers, University of Michigan Library, Ann Arbor, Michigan
William S. Shockley Papers, PLDU, Durham, North Carolina
F. W. Smith Papers, VHS, Richmond, Virginia
G. Moxley Sorrel Papers, MOC, Richmond, Virginia
Paul Stephens Papers, Watson Memorial Library, Cammie G. Henry Research Cen-
    ter, Northwestern State University of Louisiana, Natchitoches, Louisiana
William and Walter Stewart Papers, Louisiana and Lower Mississippi Valley Col-
    lections, LSU Libraries, Baton Rouge, Louisiana
J. E. B. Stuart Papers, VHS, Richmond, Virginia
Talcott Family Papers, VHS, Richmond, Virginia
Thornton Family Papers, VHS, Richmond, Virginia
Westwood Todd Papers, SHC, Chapel Hill, North Carolina
Isaac Ridgeway Trimble Papers, (Misc. Mss.), New York Historical Society, New York
Charles Venable Papers, SHC, Chapel Hill, North Carolina
War, 1861–1865, Letters, New York Historical Society, New York
Western Manuscript Collection, Ellis Library, University of Missouri, Columbia,
    Missouri
Whitwell Autograph Collection, Massachusetts Historical Society, Boston,
    Massachusetts
George A. Zabriski Papers, VHS, Richmond, Virginia

Newspapers

Carlisle (Pennsylvania) *American,* 1863
Carlisle (Pennsylvania) *Herald,* 1863
Columbia (Tennessee) *Herald,* 1872
Florence (Arizona) *Weekly Arizona Enterprise,* 1891
Harrisburg (Pennsylvania) *Patriot and Union,* 1863
Harrisburg (Pennsylvania) *Weekly Patriot,* 1863
Nashville Republican Banner, 1872
Nashville Union and American, 1872
New York Times, 1872
Richmond Enquirer, 1862, 1863
Richmond Examiner, 1863
San Francisco Evening Bulletin, 1858, 1859, 1860
San Francisco Golden Era, 1857
Tombstone (Arizona) *Prospector,* 1915
Tubac Weekly Arizonian, 1859
Tucson Arizona Daily Star, 1879

Government Publications

"Application for Leave—U.S. Army," NA Record Group 107.

"Letters Received by the Adjutant General, 1822–1860," NA Publication M-567.

"Letters Sent by the Office of the Adjutant General, 1800–1890," NA Publication M-565.

"Letters Sent by the Secretary of War, 1801–1900," NA Record Group 092.

"Orders and Endorsements Sent by the Secretary of War, 1846–1870," NA Publication M-444.

"Orders of General Zachary Taylor to the Army of Occupation in the Mexican War, 1845–1847," NA Publication M-29.

"Records of the U.S. Army Continental Commands, 1820–1920," NA Publication M-746.

"Returns from U.S. Military Posts, 1800–1916," NA Publication M-91.

"Returns from Regular Cavalry Regiments," NA Publication M-744.

Secretary of War, *Atlas to Accompany the Official Records of the Union and Confederate Armies* (New York: Thomas Yoseloff, reprint, 1958).

Secretary of War, *The War of the Rebellion: A Compilation of the Official Records of the Union and Confederate Armies* (Washington, DC: Government Printing Office, 1880ff.).

U.S. Congress, *Biographical Directory of the American Congress, 1774–1961* (Washington, DC: Government Printing Office, 1961).

U.S. Congress, House Executive Document 60, Thirtieth Congress—First Session (Washington, DC: Wendell and Benthuysen, 1848).

U.S. Congress, Senate Executive Document 1, Thirtieth Congress—First Session (Washington, DC: Wendell and Benthuysen, 1848).

U.S. Congress, Senate Executive Document, Thirty-fifth Congress—Second Session (Washington, DC: William A. Harris, 1859).

U.S. Congress, Senate Executive Document, Thirty-sixth Congress—First Session (Washington, DC: George W. Bowman, 1860).

U.S. Congress, Senate Executive Document, Thirty-sixth Congress—Second Session (Washington, DC: George W. Bowman, 1861).

U.S. Military Academy, "Cadet Application Papers, 1805–1888," NA Record Group 94.

U.S. Military Academy, *Cadets Arranged in Order of Merit in Their Respective Classes as Determined at the General Examination in June 1840* (West Point, NY: USMA, 1840).

U.S. Military Academy, "Fourth Class Roll, 1837; Third Class Roll, 1838; Second Class Roll, 1839." Personal Records, West Point, NA Record Group 404.

U.S. Military Academy, "Conduct Roll, 1837, 1838, 1839, 1840." Register of Merit, Personal Records, NA Record Group 404. (Also USMA printed records).

U.S. Military Academy, "Record of Delinquencies" (handwritten ledger), Department of Tactics, West Point, NA Record Group 404.
U.S. Military Academy, *Register of Graduates of the United States Military Academy, West Point, New York: Class of 2000 Centennial Edition* (West Point, NY: USMA, 2000).
U.S. Military Academy, "West Point Library Catalog, 2002."
U.S. Military Academy, "West Point Library Lending Records, 1836–1840" (handwritten ledger), West Point Archives.
War Department Collection of Confederate Records, NA Record Group 109, Washington, DC.

Books

Allan, William. *History of the Campaign of Gen. T. J. (Stonewall) Jackson in the Shenandoah Valley of Virginia*. Dayton, OH: Morningside Book Shop, reprint, 1974.
Altshuler, Constance Wynn. *Cavalry Yellow and Infantry Blue: Army Officers in Arizona Between 1851 and 1886*. Tucson, AZ: Arizona Historical Society, 1991.
———. *Chains of Command: Arizona and the Army, 1856–1875*. Tucson, AZ: Arizona Historical Society, 1981.
———, ed. *Latest from Arizona! The Hesperian Letters, 1859–1861*. Tucson: Arizona Pioneers Historical Society, 1969.
Ambler, Charles H., and Festus P. Summers. *West Virginia: The Mountain State*. Englewood Cliffs, NJ: Prentice-Hall, 1951.
Ambrose, Stephen E. *Duty, Honor, Country: A History of West Point*. Baltimore: Johns Hopkins UP, 1966.
———. *Halleck: Lincoln's Chief of Staff*. Baton Rouge: Louisiana State UP, 1962.
Andrews, Marietta M. *Scraps of Paper*. New York: E. P. Dutton, 1929.
Arkansas Sesquicentennial Commission. *Sessie Facts*. Siloam Springs, AR: Simon Sager Press, 1985.
Armstrong, Richard L. *Jackson's Valley Campaign: The Battle of McDowell, March 11-May 18, 1862*. Lynchburg, VA: H. E. Howard, 1990.
Avirett, James B. *The Memoirs of General Turner Ashby and His Compeers*. Baltimore: Selby and Dulany, 1867.
Banerjee, Sikhar Nath, ed. *Rehabilitation and Management of Amputees*. Baltimore: Williams and Wilkins, 1982.
Barrett, Edwin S. *What I Saw at Bull Run*. Boston: Beacon Press, 1886.
Basler, Roy P., ed. *The Collected Works of Abraham Lincoln:* The Abraham Lincoln Association, Springfield, Illinois. New Brunswick, NJ: Rutgers UP, 1953–1955.
Bauer, Jack. *Zachary Taylor: Soldier, Planter, Statesman of the Old South*. Baton Rouge: Louisiana State UP, 1985.

Beach, Marie. *The Only Complete Guide to Richmond.* Midlothian, VA: Guide to Richmond Press, 1979.

Bean, W. G. *The Liberty Hall Volunteers: Stonewall's College Boys.* UP of Virginia, 1964.

———. *Stonewall's Man: Sandie Pendleton.* Chapel Hill: U of North Carolina P, 1959.

Beck, Warren A. *New Mexico: A History of Four Centuries.* Norman: U of Oklahoma P, 1962.

Bennett, William W. *A Narrative of the Great Revival which Prevailed in the Southern Armies During the Late Civil War Between the States of the Federal Union.* Philadelphia: Claxton, Remsen, and Haffelfinger, 1877.

Bill, Alfred Hoyt. *Rehearsal for Conflict: The War with Mexico, 1846–1848.* New York: Knopf, 1947.

Blackford, Susan Leigh. *Letters from Lee's Army; or, Memoirs of Life In and Out of the Army in Virginia During the War Between the States.* New York: Charles Scribner's Sons, 1947.

Blackford, W. W. *War Years with JEB Stuart.* New York: Charles Scribner's Sons, 1945.

Blackwood, Emma J., ed. *To Mexico with Scott: Letters of Captain E. Kirby Smith to His Wife.* Cambridge, MA: Harvard College Press, 1917.

Boatner, Mark M. *The Civil War Dictionary.* New York: David M. McKay, 1959.

Bosang, James N. *Memoirs of a Pulaski Veteran.* Pulaski, VA: privately printed, 1912.

Boykin, Edward M. *The Falling Flag: Evacuation of Richmond, Retreat and Surrender at Appomattox.* New York: E. J. Hale, 1874.

Brandes, Ray. *Frontier Military Posts of Arizona.* Globe, AZ: D. S. King, 1960.

Brant, Irving. *James Madison.* Indianapolis: Bobbs-Merrill, 1941–1961.

Bridges, Hal. *Lee's Maverick General: Daniel Harvey Hill.* Lincoln: U of Nebraska P, reprint, 1991.

Brooks, Clinton E., and Frank D. Reeve, eds. *Forts and Forays: A Dragoon in New Mexico, 1850–1856; James A. Bennett.* Albuquerque: U of New Mexico P, 1996.

Buell, Thomas B. *The Warrior Generals: Combat Leadership in the Civil War.* New York: Crown, 1997.

Bushong, Millard K. *Old Jube: A Biography of General Jubal A. Early.* Shippensburg, PA: White Mane, 1955.

Caldwell, Willie Walker. *Stonewall Jim: A Biography of James A. Walker, C.S.A.* Elliston, VA: Northcross House, 1990.

Calkins, Christopher M. *The Final Bivouac: The Surrender Parade at Appomattox and the Disbanding of the Armies.* Lynchburg, VA: H. E. Howard, 1988.

———. *From Petersburg to Appomattox.* Farmville, VA: *Farmville Herald,* 1983.

———. *Thirty-six Hours Before Appomattox.* Farmville, VA: *Farmville Herald,* 1980.

Carmichael, Peter S. *Lee's Young Artillerist: William R. J. Pegram.* Charlottesville: UP of Virginia, 1987.

Casdorph, Paul D. *Lee and Jackson: Confederate Chieftains.* New York: Paragon House, 1991.

———. *Prince John Magruder: His Life and Campaigns.* New York: John Wiley, 1996.

———. *Republicans, Negroes, and Progressives in the South, 1912–1916.* University: U of Alabama P, 1981.

Casler, John O. *Four Years in the Stonewall Brigade.* Marietta, GA: Continental Book, reprint, 1951.

Catton, Bruce. *Grant Moves South.* Boston: Little, Brown, 1960.

———. *Grant Takes Command.* Edison, NJ: Castle Books, reprint, 2000.

Chamberlain, Joshua Lawrence. *The Passing of the Armies: An Account of the Final Campaign of the Army of the Potomac.* New York: Bantam, reprint, 1993.

Chamberlayne, C. G. *Ham Chamberlayne, Virginian: Letters and Papers of an Artillery Officer in the War for Southern Independence.* Richmond, VA: Dietz, 1932.

Chandler, David L. *The Binghams of Louisville: The Dark History Behind One of America's Great Fortunes.* New York: Crown, 1987.

Chesnut, Mary Boykin. *A Diary from Dixie.* Ben Ames Williams, ed. Cambridge, MA: Harvard UP, reprint, 1980.

Chitwood, Oliver P. *John Tyler: Champion of the Old South.* New York: Russell and Russell, reprint, 1964.

Church, Albert Ensign. *Personal Reminiscences of the Military Academy from 1824 to 1831.* West Point, NY: USMA, 1879.

Clamblet, Wilbur H. *The Christian Church (Disciples of Christ) in West Virginia: A History of its Cooperative Work.* St. Louis, MO: Bethany Press, 1971.

Coddington, Edwin B. *The Gettysburg Campaign: A Study in Command.* New York: Charles Scribner's Sons, reprint, 1979.

Coffman, Edward M. *The Old Army: A Portrait of the American Army in Peacetime, 1784–1898.* New York: Oxford UP, 1986.

Condon, William H. *The Life of Major General James Shields.* Chicago: Blakely Printing, 1900.

Connor, Seymour V., and Odie B. Faulk. *North America Divided: The Mexican War, 1846–1848.* New York: Oxford UP, 1971.

Connor, Seymour V., and Jimmy M. Skaggs. *Broadcloth and Britches: The Santa Fe Trade.* College Station: Texas A&M UP, 1977.

Cooke, John Esten. *A Life of General Robert E. Lee.* New York: D. Appleton, 1871.

———. *Stonewall Jackson: A Military Biography.* New York: D. Appleton, 1866.

———. *Stonewall Jackson and the Old Stonewall Brigade.* Charlottesville: UP of Virginia, 1954.

Cornish, Dudley T. *Historical Significance of Fort Scott, Kansas.* Pittsburg, KS: n.p., n.d.

Coulter, E. Merton. *The Confederate States of America, 1861–1865.* Baton Rouge: Louisiana State UP, 1950.

Couper, William. *One Hundred Years at VMI.* Richmond, VA: Garrett and Massie, 1939.

Cozzens, Samuel W. *The Marvelous Country; or, Three Years in Arizona and New Mexico, the Apache's Home.* Minneapolis: Ross and Haines, reprint, 1967.

Cresap, Bernarr. *Appomattox Commander: The Story of General E. O. C. Ord.* San Diego, CA: A. S. Barnes, 1981.

Croffut, W. A., ed. *Fifty Years in Camp and Field: The Diary of Major General Ethan Allen Hitchcock, USA.* New York: G. P. Putnam's Sons, 1909.

Cullen, Joseph P. *The Peninsula Campaign, 1862: McClellan and Lee Struggle for Richmond.* Harrisburg, PA: Stackpole Books, 1973.

Current, Richard N., ed. *Encyclopedia of the Confederacy.* New York: Simon and Schuster, 1993.

Dabney, Robert L. *Life and Campaigns of Lieut. Gen. Thomas J. Jackson.* New York: Blelock and Company, 1866.

Dabney, Virginius. *Virginia: The New Dominion.* Garden City, NY: Doubleday, 1971.

Davis, Burke. *The Gray Fox: Robert E. Lee and the Civil War.* New York: Fairfax Press, reprint, 1988.

———. *They Called Him Stonewall: A Life of Lt. General T. J. Jackson, C.S.A.* New York: Fairfax Press, reprint, 1988.

———. *To Appomattox: Nine Days in April 1865.* New York: Rinehart, 1959.

Davis, William C. *Battle at Bull Run: A History of the First Major Battle of the Civil War.* Baton Rouge: Louisiana State UP, reprint, 1981.

———. *A Government of Our Own: The Making of the Confederacy.* New York: Free Press, 1994.

———. *An Honorable Defeat: The Last Days of the Confederate Government.* New York: Harcourt, 2001.

———. *Jefferson Davis: The Man and His Hour.* New York: HarperCollins, reprint, 1992.

Denison, Frederick. *The Battle of Cedar Mountain: A Personal View, August 9, 1862.* Providence, RI: N. B. Williams, 1881.

Dickert, D. Augustus. *History of Kershaw's Brigade.* Dayton, OH: Morningside Book Shop, reprint, 1976.

Divine, John E. *35th Battalion Virginia Cavalry.* Lynchburg, VA: H. E. Howard, 1985.

Donald, David Herbert. *Lincoln.* London: Jonathan Cape, 1995.

Dorris, Jonathan T. *Pardon and Amnesty Under Lincoln and Johnson: The Restoration of the Confederates to Their Rights and Privileges, 1861-1898.* Chapel Hill: U of North Carolina P, 1953.

Doubleday, Abner. *Chancellorsville and Gettysburg.* New York: Charles Scribner's Sons, 1908.

Douglas, Henry Kyd. *I Rode with Stonewall: Being Chiefly the War Experiences of the Youngest Member of Jackson's Staff from the John Brown Raid to the Hanging of Mrs. Surratt.* Chapel Hill: U of North Carolina P, reprint, 1984.

Dowdey, Clifford. *Lee.* Boston: Little, Brown, 1965.

———. *Lee's Last Campaign: The Story of Lee and His Men Against Grant, 1864.* Boston: Little, Brown, 1960.

———. *Lee and His Men at Gettysburg: The Death of a Nation.* [1958] Lincoln: U of Nebraska P, reprint, 1999.

———. *The Seven Days: The Emergence of Lee.* Boston: Little, Brown, 1964.

———, ed. *The Wartime Papers of R. E. Lee.* Boston: Little, Brown, 1961.

Duffus, R. L. *The Santa Fe Trail.* New York: David M. McKay, 1958.

Durkin, Joseph T., ed. *Confederate Chaplain: A War Journal of Rev. James B. Sheeran, c.ss.r. 14th Louisiana, C.S.A.* Milwaukee: Bruce, 1960.

Early, Jubal A. *Lieutenant General Jubal Anderson Early C.S.A.: Autobiographical Sketch and Narrative of the War Between the States.* New York: Konecky and Konecky, reprint, 1994.

Eckert, Allan W. *That Dark and Bloody River: Chronicles of the Ohio River Valley.* New York: Bantam, 1995.

Eckert, Ralph Lowell. *John Brown Gordon: Soldier, Southerner, American.* Baton Rouge: Louisiana State UP, 1989.

Eggleston, George Cary. *The History of the Confederate War: Its Causes and Conduct; A Narrative and Critical History.* New York: Sturgis and Walton, 1910.

Eisenhower, John S. D. *So Far from God: The U.S. War with Mexico, 1846–1848.* New York: Random House, 1989.

Eliot, Ellsworth, Jr. *West Point in the Confederacy.* New York: G. A. Baker, 1941.

Esposito, Vincent J. *West Point Atlas of American Wars, 1689–1900.* New York: Praeger, 1959.

Ewell, Alice Maude. *A Virginia Scene; or, Life in Old Prince William.* Lynchburg, VA: J. P. Bell, 1931.

Faulk, Odie B. *Arizona: A Short History.* Norman: U of Oklahoma P, 1970.

———. *Crimson Desert: Indian Wars of the American Southwest.* New York: Oxford UP, 1974.

———. *Land of Many Frontiers: A History of the American Southwest.* New York: Oxford UP, 1968.

Fergusson, Erna. *Mew Mexico: A Pageant of Three Peoples.* New York: Knopf, 1971.

Fiebeger, G. J. *Campaigns of the American Civil War.* West Point, NY: USMA Printing Office, 1914.

Finch, L. Boyd. *Confederate Pathway to the Pacific: Major Sherod Hunter and Arizona Territory, C.S.A.* Tucson, AZ: Arizona Historical Society, 1996.

Fireman, Bert M. *Arizona: Historic Land.* New York: Knopf, 1982.

Fishwick, Marshall W. *Lee After the War.* New York: Dodd, Meade, 1963.

Fleming, Thomas J. *West Point: The Men and Times of the United States Military Academy.* New York: William Morrow, 1969.

Flexner, James T. *George Washington: The Forge of Experience, 1732–1775.* Boston: Little, Brown, 1965.

Foner, Eric. *Reconstruction: America's Unfinished Revolution.* New York: Harper and Row, reprint, 1988.

Freeman, Douglas Southall. *R. E. Lee: A Biography.* New York: Charles Scribner's Sons, 1937–1940.

———. *Lee's Lieutenants: A Study in Command.* New York: Charles Scribner's Sons, 1942–1944.

Fry, James B. *McDowell and Tyler in the Campaign of Bull Run, 1861.* New York: D. Van Nostrand, 1884.

Fuller, J. F. C. *Grant and Lee: A Study in Personality and Generalship.* Bloomington: Indiana UP, reprint, 1957.

Furgurson, Ernest B. *Ashes of Glory: Richmond at War.* New York: Knopf, 1996.

Gallagher, Gary W. *The Confederate War.* Cambridge, MA: Harvard UP, 1997.

———, ed. *Fighting for the Confederacy: The Personal Recollections of Edward Porter Alexander.* Chapel Hill: U of North Carolina P, 1989.

———. *Lee and His Generals in War and Memory.* Baton Rouge: Louisiana State UP, 1998.

———, ed. *Lee: The Soldier.* Lincoln: U of Nebraska P, 1996.

———, ed. *The Richmond Campaign of 1862: The Peninsula and the Seven Days.* Chapel Hill: U of North Carolina P, 2000.

———. *Stephen Dodson Ramseur: Lee's Gallant General.* Chapel Hill: U of North Carolina P, 1985.

———, ed. *The Wilderness Campaign.* Chapel Hill: U of North Carolina P, 1997.

Garber, Paul Neff. *The Gadsden Treaty.* Philadelphia: Press of the U of Pennsylvania, 1923.

Garret, Jil K. *Maury County, Tennessee: Historical Sketches,* n.p., n.d.

Gerson, Noel B. *Kit Carson: Folk Hero and Man.* Garden City, NY: Doubleday, 1964.

Goldsborough, William W. *The Maryland Line in the Confederate Army, 1861–1865.* Gaithersburg, MD: Olde Soldier's Books, reprint, 1987.

Gordon, John B. *Reminiscences of the Civil War.* Baton Rouge: Louisiana State UP, reprint, 1993.

Graham, Martin F., and George F. Skoch. *Mine Run: A Campaign of Lost Opportunities, October 21, 1863-May 1, 1864.* Lynchburg, VA: H. E. Howard, 1987.

Granger, Byrd Howell. *Arizona Place Names (X Marks the Spot).* Tucson, AZ: Falconer, 1983.

Grant, Ulysses S. *Personal Memoirs of U. S. Grant,* ed. E. B. Long. New York: Da Capo Press, reprint, 1982.

Griggs, Walter S. *General John Pegram, C.S.A.* Lynchburg, VA: H. E. Howard, 1993.

Grunder, Charles S., and Brandon H. Beck. *The Second Battle of Winchester, June 12–15, 1863.* Lynchburg, VA: H. E. Howard, 1989.

Hamersly, Thomas H. S. *Complete Army and Navy Register of the United States from 1787 to 1887.* New York: T. H. S. Hamersly, 1888.

Hamilton, Holman, *Zachary Taylor: Soldier of the Republic.* Hamden, CT: Archon Books, reprint, 1966.

Hamlin, Percy Gatling. *The Making of a Soldier: Letters of General R .S. Ewell.* Richmond, VA: Whittet and Shepperson, 1935.

———. *"Old Bald Head": General R. S. Ewell.* Strasburg, VA: Shenandoah Publishing House, 1940.

Hanna, A. J. *Flight into Oblivion.* Richmond, VA: Johnson Publishing, 1938.

Harrison, Mrs. Burton, *Reflections, Grave and Gay.* New York: Charles Scribner's Sons, 1916.

Harrison, Fairfax. *Landmarks of Old Prince William: A Study of Origins in Northern Virginia.* Berryville, VA: Chesapeake Book Company, reprint 1964.

Haskell, Frank A. *The Battle of Gettysburg,* ed. Bruce Catton. Boston: Houghton Mifflin, 1958.

Haskin, William L. *History of the First Regiment of Artillery from Its Organization in 1821 to January 1, 1876.* Portland, ME: B. Thurston, 1879.

Hassler, William Woods. *Colonel John Pelham: Lee's Boy Artillerist.* Richmond, VA: Garrett and Massie, 1960.

———. *The General to His Lady: The Civil War Letters of William Dorsey Pender to Fanny Pender.* Chapel Hill: U of North Carolina P, 1965.

Heitman, Francis B. *Historical Register and Directory of the United States Army, 1783–1903.* Washington, DC: U.S. Government Printing Office, 1903.

Henderson, William D. *The Road to Bristoe Station; Campaigning with Lee and Meade, August 1-October 20, 1863.* Lynchburg, VA: H. E. Howard, 1987.

Hennessy, John J. *Return to Bull Run: The Battle and Campaign of Second Manassas.* Norman: U of Oklahoma P, reprint, 1999.

———. *Second Manassas Battlefield Map Study.* Lynchburg, VA: H. E. Howard, 1991.

Henry, Robert Selph. *The Story of the Confederacy.* New York: Bobbs-Merrill, 1936.

———. *The Story of the Mexican War.* Indianapolis: Bobbs-Merrill, 1950.

Hirshson, Stanley P. *The White Tecumseh: A Biography of William T. Sherman.* New York: John Wiley, 1997.

Hoke, Jacob. *The Great Invasion of 1863; or, General Lee in Pennsylvania.* Dayton, OH: W. J. Shuey, 1887.

Hood, John B. *Advance and Retreat: Personal Experiences in the United States and Confederate States Armies.* New Orleans: P. G. T. Beauregard, 1880.

Horgan, Paul. *The Great River: The Rio Grande in North American History.* New York: Rinehart, 1954.

Horner, Harlan H. *Lincoln and Greeley.* Urbana: U of Illinois P, 1953.

Howard, McHenry H. *The Recollections of a Maryland Confederate Soldier and Staff Officer Under Johnston, Jackson, and Lee.* Dayton, OH: Morningside Book Shop, reprint, 1975.

Hughes, Robert M. *General Johnston.* New York: D. Appleton, 1893.

Humphreys, A. A. *From Gettysburg to the Rapidan: The Army of the Potomac, July 1863 to April 1864.* New York: Charles Scribner's Sons, 1883.

———. *The Virginia Campaigns of 1864 and 1865.* New York: Da Capo Press, reprint, 1995.

Hunton, Eppa. *Autobiography of Eppa Hunton.* Richmond, VA: William Byrd Press, 1933.

Inman, Henry. *The Old Santa Fe Trail: The Story of a Great Highway.* Topeka, KS: Crane and Company, 1916.

Jackson, Mary Anna. *Memoirs of Stonewall Jackson by His Widow.* Louisville, KY: Prentice Press, 1895.

Johannsen, Robert W. *To the Halls of the Montezumas: The Mexican War in the American Imagination.* New York: Oxford UP, 1985.

Johnson, Thomas Cary. *The Life and Letters of Robert Lewis Dabney.* Richmond, VA: Presbyterian Committee on Publication, 1903.

Johnston, Robert Matteson. *Bull Run: Its Strategy and Tactics.* Boston: Houghton Mifflin, 1913.

Jones, J. William. *Christ in the Camp; or, Religion in Lee's Army.* Richmond, VA: B. F. Johnson, 1887.

———. *Life and Letters of Robert Edward Lee: Soldier and Man.* New York: Neale, 1906.

Jones, John B. *A Rebel War Clerk's Diary at the Confederate States Capital.* Philadelphia: J. B. Lippincott, 1866.

Jones, Terry L. *Campbell Brown's Civil War: With Ewell and the Army of Northern Virginia.* Baton Rouge: Louisiana State UP, 2001.

———, ed. *The Civil War Memoirs of William J. Seymour: Reminiscences of a Louisiana Tiger.* Baton Rouge: Louisiana State UP, 1991.

———. *Lee's Tigers: The Louisiana Infantry in the Army of Northern Virginia.* Baton Rouge: Louisiana State UP, 1987.

Jordan, Ervin L. *Black Confederates and Afro-Yankees in Civil War Virginia.* Charlottesville: UP of Virginia, reprint, 1999.

Kegel, James A. *North with Lee and Jackson.* Mechanicsville, PA: Stackpole Books, 1996.

Keleher, William A. *Turmoil in New Mexico, 1846–1868.* Santa Fe, NM: Rydal Press, 1952.

Kelly, Lawrence C. *Navajo Roundup: Selected Correspondence of Kit Carson's Expedition Against the Navajos, 1863–1865.* Boulder, CO: Pruett Press, 1978.

Krick, Robert K. *Conquering the Valley: Stonewall Jackson at Port Republic.* New York: William Morrow, 1996.

————. *Lee's Colonels: A Biographical Register of the Field Officers of the Army of Northern Virginia.* Dayton, OH: Morningside Book Shop, 1979.

————. *Stonewall Jackson at Cedar Mountain.* Chapel Hill: U of North Carolina P, 1990.

Kurtz, Stephen G. *The Presidency of John Adams: The Collapse of Federalism, 1795–1800.* Philadelphia: U of Pennsylvania P, 1957.

Lee, Fitzhugh. *General Lee.* New York: D. Appleton, 1894.

Lee, Robert E., Jr. *Recollections and Letters of General Robert E. Lee.* Garden City, NY: Garden City Publishing, 1934.

Lee, Susan P. *Memoirs of William Nelson Pendleton, D.D.* Philadelphia: J. B. Lippincott, 1883.

Lewis, Lloyd. *Sherman: Fighting Prophet.* New York: Harcourt, Brace, 1932.

Lockwood, Frank C. *The Apache Indians.* New York: Macmillan, 1938.

————. *Life in Old Tucson, 1854–1864, as Remembered by the Little Maid.* Los Angeles: Ward Ritchie Press, 1943.

Long, A. L. *The Memoirs of Robert E. Lee: His Military and Personal History.* Secaucus, NJ: Blue and Grey Press, reprint, 1983.

Longacre, Edward G. *Pickett, Leader of the Charge: A Biography of General George E. Pickett, C.S.A.* Shippensburg, PA: White Mane, 1995.

Longstreet, James. *From Manassas to Appomattox: Memoirs of the Civil War in America.* New York: Da Capo Press, reprint, 1992.

Lyman, Theodore. *With Grant and Meade from the Wilderness to Appomattox,* ed. George R. Agassiz. Lincoln: U of Nebraska P, reprint, 1994.

Lyons, James T. *War Sketches: From Cedar Mountain to Bull Run.* Buffalo, NY: Young, Lockwood, 1882.

Malone, Dumas S., ed., *The Dictionary of American Biography.* New York: Charles Scribner's Sons, 1936.

Martin, Samuel J. *The Road to Glory: Confederate General Richard S. Ewell.* Indianapolis: Guild Press of Indiana, 1991.

Matter, William D. *If It Takes All Summer: The Battle of Spotsylvania.* Chapel Hill: U of North Carolina P, 1988.

Mayor and Aldermen of Columbia. *Century Revue, 1805–1902: Maury County, Tennessee.* n.p., 1905.

McAlister, Jean Graham. *A Brief History of Bath County, Virginia.* Warm Springs, VA: Bath County School Board, 1920.

McAllister, Joseph Thompson. *Historical Sketches of Virginia Hot Springs, Warm Sulphur Springs, and Bath County.* Salem, VA: Salem Printing, 1908.

McCabe, James Dabney. *The Life of Thomas J. Jackson; By an Ex-Cadet.* Richmond, VA: James E. Goode, 1864.

McCaslin, Richard B. *Lee in the Shadow of Washington.* Baton Rouge: Louisiana State UP, 2001.

McClellan, George B. *Report on the Organization and Campaigns of the Army of the Potomac.* Freeport, NY: Books for Libraries, reprint, 1970.

McCoy, Charles A. *Polk and the Presidency.* Austin: U of Texas P, 1968.

McDonald, Archie P., ed. *Make Me a Map of the Valley: The Civil War Journal of Stonewall Jackson's Topographer.* Dallas: Southern Methodist UP, 1973.

McFeely, William S. *Grant: A Biography.* New York: W. W. Norton, 1981.

McGuire, Hunter H. *The Confederate Cause and Conduct in the War Between the States.* Richmond, VA: L. H. Jenkins, 1907.

McKitrick, Eric L. *Andrew Johnson and Reconstruction.* Chicago: U of Chicago P, 1960.

McMeekin, Isabel M. *Louisville: The Gateway City.* New York: J. Messner, 1946.

McMurry, Richard M. *John Bell Hood and the War for Southern Independence.* Lexington: UP of Kentucky, 1982.

McNitt, Frank, *Navajo Wars: Military Campaigns, Slave Raids, and Reprisals.* Albuquerque: U of New Mexico P, 1972.

McPherson, James M. *Battle Cry of Freedom: The Civil War Era.* New York: Ballantine, reprint, 1989.

———. *Ordeal by Fire: The Civil War and Reconstruction.* New York: Knopf, 1983.

McWhiney, Grady. *Braxton Bragg and Confederate Defeat: Field Command.* New York: Columbia UP, 1969.

Military Society of the Mexican War. *Constitution of the Aztec Club of 1847 and List of Its Members, 1928.* n.p., 1928.

Moffett, Mary Conner. *Letters of General James Conner, C.S.A.* Columbia, SC: R. L. Ryan, 1950.

Moore, Edward A. *The Story of a Cannoneer under Stonewall Jackson.* Lynchburg, VA: J. P. Bell, 1910.

Morrison, James L. "The Best School in the World": *West Point; The Pre–Civil War Years, 1833–1866.* Kent, OH: Kent State UP, 1986.

Morton, Oren F. *Annals of Bath County.* Staunton, VA: McClure, 1917.

Myers, Franklin M. *The Comanches: A History of White's Brigade, Virginia Cavalry.* Marietta, GA: Continental Book, reprint, 1956.

Myers, William Starr, ed. *The Mexican War Diary of George B. McClellan.* Princeton, NJ: Princeton UP, 1917.

Nagel, Paul C. *The Lee's of Virginia: Seven Generations of an American Family.* New York: Oxford UP, 1990.

Nance, Joseph M. *After San Jacinto: The Texas-Mexican Frontier, 1836–1841.* Austin: U of Texas P, 1963.

National Cyclopaedia of American Biography. New York: James T. White, 1892–1894.

Nevins, Allan. *Frémont: The West's Greatest Adventurer.* New York: Harper and Brothers, 1928.

O'Connor, Richard. *Thomas: The Rock of Chicamauga.* New York: Prentice-Hall, 1948.

Osborne, Charles C. *Jubal: The Life and Times of General Jubal A. Early, C.S.A., Defender of the Lost Cause.* Chapel Hill, NC: Algonquin Books, 1992.

Palmer, Michael A. *Lee Moves North: Robert E. Lee on the Offensive.* New York: John Wiley, 1998.

———. *Stoddert's War: Naval Operations During the Quasi-War with France, 1798–1801.* Columbia: U of South Carolina P, 1987.

Parrish, T. Michael. *Reminiscences of the War in Virginia by David Boyd French.* Austin, TX: Jenkins Publishing, 1989.

———. *Richard Taylor: Soldier Prince of Dixie.* Chapel Hill: U of North Carolina P, 1992.

Patrick, Rembert W. *The Fall of Richmond.* Baton Rouge: Louisiana State UP, 1960.

Patterson, Gerard A. *Rebels from West Point.* New York: Doubleday, 1987.

Pfanz, Donald C. *Richard S. Ewell: A Soldier's Life.* Chapel Hill: U of North Carolina P, 1998.

Pfanz, Harry W. *Gettysburg: Culp's Hill and Cemetery Hill.* Chapel Hill: U of North Carolina P, 1993.

———. *Gettysburg: The Second Day.* Chapel Hill: U of North Carolina P, 1987.

Piston, William Garrett. *Lee's Tarnished Lieutenant: James Longstreet and His Place in Southern History.* Athens: U of Georgia P, 1987.

Poague, William T. *Gunner with Stonewall: Reminiscences of William Thomas Poague,* ed., Monroe F. Cockrell. Jackson, TN: McCowat-Mercer Press, 1957.

Potter, David M. *The Impending Crisis, 1848–1861.* New York: Harper and Row, 1976.

Prince William Historical Commission. *Homeplace: Prince William County.* Woodbridge, VA: Minute Man Press, 1986.

Procter, Ben H. *Not Without Honor: The Life of John H. Reagan.* Austin: U of Texas P, 1962.

Randall, J. G. *Civil War and Reconstruction.* Boston: D.C. Heath, 1953.

Ramey, Emily, and John K. Gott. *Years of Anguish: Fauquier County, Virginia, 1861–1865.* Warrenton, VA: *Fauquier Democrat,* 1965.

Reardon, Carol. *Pickett's Charge in History and Memory.* Chapel Hill: U of North Carolina P, 1997.

Remini, Robert V. *Andrew Jackson and the Course of American Empire, 1767–1821.* New York: History Book Club, reprint, 1998.

———. *Andrew Jackson and the Course of American Freedom, 1822-1832.* New York: History Book Club, reprint, 1988.

———. *Henry Clay: Statesman for the Union.* New York: W. W. Norton, 1991.

Rhea, Gordon C. *The Battle of the Wilderness, May 5–6, 1864.* Baton Rouge: Louisiana State UP, 1994.

———. *The Battles for Spotsylvania Court House and the Road to Yellow Tavern, May 7–12, 1864.* Baton Rouge: Louisiana State UP, 1997.

———. *To the North Anna River: Grant and Lee, May 13–25, 1864.* Baton Rouge: Louisiana State UP, 2000.

Rice, Otis K. *West Virginia: A History.* Lexington: UP of Kentucky, 1985.

Richards, Ralph. *The Forts of Fort Scott and the Fateful Borderland.* Kansas City: Lowell Press, 1976.

———. *Headquarters House.* Fort Scott, KS: *Fort Scott Tribune,* 1954.

Rister, Carl Coke. *Robert E. Lee in Texas.* Norman: U of Oklahoma P, 1946.

Roberts, Robert B. *Encyclopedia of Historic Forts: The Military, Pioneer, and Trading Posts of the United States.* New York: Macmillan, 1988.

Roberts, Virginia Culin. *With Their Own Blood: A Saga of Southwestern Pioneers.* Fort Worth: Texas Christian UP, 1992.

Robertson, James I., Jr. *General A. P. Hill: The Story of a Confederate Warrior.* New York: Random House, 1987.

———. *The Stonewall Brigade.* Baton Rouge: Louisiana State UP, 1963.

———. *Stonewall Jackson: The Man, the Soldier, the Legend.* New York: Macmillan, 1997.

Ropes, John Codman. *The Army Under Pope.* New York: Charles Scribner's Sons, 1881.

Ross, Earle D. *The Liberal Republican Movement.* New York: AMS Press, reprint, 1971.

Royster, Charles. *The Destructive War: William Tecumseh Sherman, Stonewall Jackson, and the Americans.* New York: Knopf, 1991.

Rudolph, Frederick. *The American College and University: A History.* New York: Vantage Press, 1962.

Sacks, Benjamin. *Be It Enacted: The Creation of the Arizona Territory.* Phoenix: Arizona Historical Foundation, 1964.

Schildt, John W. *Stonewall Jackson Day By Day.* Chewsville, MD: Antietam Publications, 1980.

Scott, Winfield. *Memoirs of Lieutenant General Scott: Written by Himself.* New York: Sheldon, 1864.

Sears, Stephen W. *George B. McClellan: The Young Napoleon.* New York: Ticknor and Fields, 1988.

———. *Landscape Turned Red: The Battle of Antietam.* New York: Ticknor and Fields, 1983.

———. *To the Gates of Richmond: The Peninsula Campaign.* New York: Ticknor and Fields, 1992.

Selby, John. *Stonewall Jackson as Military Commander.* London: B. T. Batsford, 1968.

Sellers, Charles. *James K. Polk: Jacksonian, 1795-1843.* Princeton, NJ: Princeton UP, 1957.

Sherman, William T. *Memoirs of General W. T. Sherman.* New York: Library of America, reprint, 1990.

Sifakis, Stewart. *Who Was Who in the Confederacy.* New York: Facts on File, 1988.

Sigaud, Louis: *Belle Boyd: Confederate Spy.* Richmond, VA: Dietz Press, 1944.

Sillers, Florence Warfield. *History of Bolivar County, Mississippi.* Jackson, MS: Hederman Brothers, 1948.

Simms, Henry H. *A Decade of Sectional Controversy, 1851-1861.* Chapel Hill: U of North Carolina P, 1942.

Singletary, Otis A. *The Mexican War.* Chicago: U of Chicago P, 1960.

Smith, Arthur D. S. *Old Fuss and Feathers: The Life and the Exploits of Lt. General Winfield Scott.* New York: Greystone Press, 1937.

Smith, Justin H. *The War with Mexico.* New York: Macmillan, 1919.

Smith, Page. *John Adams,* vol. 2: 1784–1826. New York: Doubleday, 1962.

Snow, Edward R. *Historic Fort Warren.* Boston: Yankee Publishing, 1941.

———. *The Islands of Boston Harbor.* Andover, MA: Frontier Press, 1953.

Snow, William P. *Lee and His Generals.* New York: Fairfax Press, reprint, 1982.

Sommers, Richard J. *Richmond Redeemed: The Siege at Petersburg.* Garden City, NY: Doubleday, 1981.

Sonnichsen, C. L. *The Mescalero Apaches.* Norman: U of Oklahoma P, 1958.

Sorrel, G. Moxley. *Reflections of a Confederate Staff Officer.* New York: Neale, 1905.

Stackpole, Edward J. *From Cedar Mountain to Antietam.* Harrisburg, PA: Stackpole Books, 1993.

———. *They Met at Gettysburg.* Harrisburg, PA: Stackpole Books, 1996.

Stackpole, Edward J., and Wilbur S. Nye. *The Battle of Gettysburg: A Guided Tour.* Mechanicsville, PA: Stackpole Books, 1998.

Steere, Edward. *The Wilderness Campaign.* Harrisburg, PA: Stackpole Books, 1960.

Steiner, Paul E. *Medical-Military Portraits of Union and Confederate Generals.* Philadelphia: Whitmore, 1968.

Stephens, Alexander H. *Recollections of Alexander H. Stephens: His Diary Kept When a Prisoner at Fort Warren, Boston Harbor, 1865.* Baton Rouge: Louisiana State UP, reprint, 1998.

Stoddard, Henry L. *Horace Greeley: Printer, Editor, Crusader.* New York: G. P. Putnam's Sons, 1946.

Swan, Kenneth G., and Roy C. Swan. *Gunshot Wounds: Pathophysiology and Management.* 2nd ed. Chicago: Year Book Medical Publishers, 1989.

Sweeney, Edwin R. *Cochise: Chiricahua Chief.* Norman: U of Oklahoma P, 1991

Swinton, William. *Campaigns of the Army of the Potomac.* New York: Charles Scribner's Sons, 1882.

Symonds, Craig L. *Joseph E. Johnston: A Civil War Biography.* W. W. Norton, 1992.

Tanner, Robert G. *Stonewall in the Valley: Thomas J. "Stonewall" Jackson's Shenandoah Valley Campaign, Spring 1862.* New York: Doubleday, 1976.

Taylor, Richard. *Deconstruction and Reconstruction: Personal Experiences of the Late War.* New York: D. Appleton, 1879.

Taylor, Walter H. *Four Years with General Lee.* New York: D. Appleton, 1877.

———. *General Lee: His Campaigns in Virginia, 1861–1865.* Norfolk, VA: Nusbaum Book and News, 1906.

Terrell, Alexander Watkins. *From Texas to Mexico and the Court of Maximilian in 1865.* Dallas: Book Club of Texas, 1933.

Third Annual Reunion of the Association of Graduates of the United States Military Academy at West Point, New York, June 14, 1872. New York: Crocker and Company, 1872.

Thomas, Clarence. *General Turner Ashby: The Centaur of the South.* Winchester, VA: Eddy Press, 1907.

Thomas, Emory M. *Bold Dragoon: The Life of J. E. B. Stuart.* Norman: U of Oklahoma P, reprint, 1999.

————. *The Confederate Nation, 1861–1865.* New York: Harper and Row, 1979.

————. *The Confederate State of Richmond: A Biography of the Capital.* Austin: U of Texas P, 1971.

————. *Richmond: The Peninsula Campaign.* Harrisburg, PA: Eastern Alcorn Press, 1985.

————. *Robert E. Lee: A Biography.* New York: W. W. Norton, 1995.

Thomason, John W. *JEB Stuart.* New York: Charles Scribner's Sons, reprint, 1958.

Thrapp, Dan L., ed. *Encyclopedia of Frontier Biography.* Glendale, CA: Arthur H. Clark, 1988–1994.

Tower, R. Lockwood, ed. *Lee's Adjutant: The Wartime Papers of Colonel Walter Herron Taylor, 1862–1865.* Columbia: U of South Carolina P, 1995.

Trefousse, Hans L. *Andrew Johnson: A Biography.* New York: W. W. Norton, 1989.

————. *Impeachment of a President: Andrew Johnson, the Blacks, and Reconstruction.* Knoxville: U of Tennessee P, 1975.

Trimble, Marshall. *Arizona: A Panoramic History of a Frontier State.* Garden City, NY: Doubleday, 1977.

Trudeau, Noah Andre. *Bloody Roads South: The Wilderness to Cold Harbor, May–June 1864.* Boston: Little, Brown, 1989.

Tucker, Glenn. *High Tide at Gettysburg: The Campaign in Pennsylvania.* Indianapolis: Bobbs-Merrill, 1958.

————. *Lee and Longstreet at Gettysburg.* Indianapolis: Bobbs-Merrill, 1968.

Turner, William Bruce. *History of Maury County, Tennessee.* Nashville, TN: Parthenon Press, 1955.

Tyler, Daniel, *Autobiography and War Record.* New Haven, CT: privately printed, 1883.

Tyler-McGraw, Marie. *At the Falls: Richmond, Virginia, and Its People.* Chapel Hill: U of North Carolina P, 1994.

Underhill, Ruth M. *The Navajos.* Norman: U of Oklahoma P, 1956.

U. S. Army, Field Staff and Officers of the First Regiment of Cavalry from March 4, 1833, to June 1, 1900. Fort Meade, SD: n.p., 1900.

Utley, Robert M. *Frontiersmen in Blue: The United States Army and the Indian, 1848–1865.* New York: Macmillan, 1967.

Vandiver, Frank E. *Jubal's Raid: General Early's Famous Attack on Washington in 1864.* Lincoln: U of Nebraska P, 1992.

————. *Mighty Stonewall.* New York: McGraw-Hill, 1957.

Vestal, Stanley, *Kit Carson: The Happy Warrior of the Old West, A Biography.* Boston: Houghton Mifflin, 1928.

Walker, Henry P., and Don Bufkin. *Historical Atlas of Arizona.* Norman: U of Oklahoma P, 1979.

Wayland, John W. *Stonewall Jackson's Way: Route, Method, Achievement.* Staunton, VA: McClure, 1940.

Webb, Alexander Stewart. *The Peninsula: McClellan's Campaign of 1862.* New York: Jack Brussell, reprint, 1955.

Webb, Walter P., ed. *The Handbook of Texas.* Austin: Texas State Historical Association, 1952.

Weddell, Elizabeth Wright. *St. Paul's Church, Richmond: Its Historic Years and Memorials.* Richmond, VA: William Byrd Press, 1931.

Weems, John Edward. *To Conquer a Peace: The War Between the United States and Mexico.* New York: Doubleday, 1974.

Wert, Jeffry D. *General James Longstreet: The Confederacy's Most Controversial Soldier, A Biography.* New York: Simon and Schuster, 1993.

Wessels, William L. *Born to Be a Soldier: The Military Career of William Wing Loring of St. Augustine, Florida.* Fort Worth: Texas Christian UP, 1971.

White, Henry Alexander. *Robert E. Lee and the Southern Confederacy, 1807–1870.* New York: G. P. Putnam's Sons, 1902.

Wilcox, Cadmus. *History of the Mexican War.* Washington, DC: Church News Publishing, 1892.

Williams, Ben Ames, ed. *A Diary from Dixie: By Mary Boykin Chesnut.* Cambridge: Harvard UP, reprint, 1980.

Williams, Kenneth P. *Lincoln Finds a General: A Military Study of the Civil War.* New York: Macmillan, 1964.

Williams, T. Harry. *P. G. T. Beauregard: Napoleon in Gray.* Baton Rouge: Louisiana State UP, 1954.

———. *The History of American Wars, from 1745 to 1918.* New York: Knopf, 1981.

Wise, Jennings C. *The Long Arm of Lee: The History of the Artillery of the Army of Northern Virginia.* New York: Oxford UP, reprint, 1959.

Woodward, C. Vann, and Elisabeth Muhlenfeld, eds. *The Private Mary Chesnut: The Unpublished Civil War Diaries.* New York: Oxford UP, 1984.

Works Progress Administration. *Prince William: The Story of Its Places and Its People.* Manassas, VA: Bethlehem, Good House Keeping, reprint, 1961.

Worsham, John H. *One of Jackson's Foot Cavalry.* Jackson, TN: McCowat-Mercer Press, reprint, 1964.

Wright, Louise (Wigfall). *A Southern Girl in '61: The Wartime Memories of a Confederate Senator's Daughter.* New York: Doubleday, Page, 1905.

Wright, Marcus J. *General Officers of the Confederate Army, of the Executive Departments of the Confederate States, Members of the Confederate Congress by States.* New York: Neale Publishing, 1911.

Young, Otis E. *The West of Philip St. George Cooke, 1809–1895.* Glendale, CA: A.C. Clark, 1955.

Articles

Alexander, Edward Porter. "The Battle of Fredericksburg—Paper No. 2." *Southern Historical Society Papers* 10 (1882).

Allen, C. T. "The Fight at Chaffin's Farm and Fort Harrison." *Confederate Veteran* 13 (1905).

Bachelder, John B. "Letter from John B. Bachelder, Esq." *Southern Historical Society Papers* 6 (1878).

Barlow, Mrs. M. R. "History of the Prince William Cavalry." *Confederate Veteran* 15 (August 1907).

Barry, Louise. "The Fort Leavenworth-Fort Gibson Military Road and the Founding of Fort Scott." *Kansas Historical Quarterly* 11 (May 1942).

Beauregard, P. G. T. "The Battle of Bull Run." *Century Magazine* 28 (November 1884).

Bender, Averam B. "Military Transportation in the Southwest, 1848–1868." *New Mexico Historical Review* 32 (April 1957).

Blake, Thomas B. "Retreat from Richmond." *Southern Historical Society Papers* 25 (1897).

Bradwell, I. G. "From Cold Harbor to Cedar Mountain." *Confederate Veteran* 29 (1921).

Brown, Campbell. "General Ewell at First Manassas." *Southern Historical Society Papers* 13 (January 1885).

———. "Note on Ewell's Division in the Campaign of 1862." *Southern Historical Society Papers* 10 (1882).

Bushong, Millard K. "Jackson in the Shenandoah." *West Virginia History* 27 (January 1966).

Carmichael, Peter S. "Escaping the Shadow of Gettysburg: Richard S. Ewell and Ambrose Powell Hill at the Wilderness." In Gary W. Gallagher, ed., *The Wilderness Campaign* (Chapel Hill: U of North Carolina P, 1997).

———. "'Oh! For the Presence and Inspiration of Old Jack': A Lost Cause Plea for Stonewall Jackson at Gettysburg." *Civil War History* 41 (June 1995).

———. " Who Is to Blame for the Confederate Loss at Gettysburg?" *Civil War Times Illustrated* 37 (August 1998).

Carter, Thomas H. "Letter of Colonel Thomas H. Carter." *Southern Historical Society Papers* 39 (1914).

Casdorph, Paul D. "Future Bishop Gives Account of the Civil War." *West Virginia Then and Now* 27 (October 1985).

Cheeks, Robert C. "Ewell's Flawless Performance at Kettle Run." *America's Civil War* 13 (September 2000).

Childs, H. T. "Cedar Mountain as I Saw It." *Confederate Veteran* 28 (1920).

Colston, Frederick M. "Recollections of the Last Months in the Army of Northern Virginia." *Southern Historical Society Papers* 38 (1910).

Conrad, D. B. "History of the First Battle of Manassas and the Organization of the Stonewall Brigade." *Southern Historical Society Papers* 20 (1892).

Cordon, E. C. "Controversy about Gettysburg." *Confederate Veteran* 28 (1920).

Douglas, Henry Kyd. "Lee and Ewell at Gettysburg." *The Nation* 54 (1892).

Dowdey, Clifford. "Richard S. Ewell, Virginian." *Virginia Record* 5 (May 1959).

Drumm, Stella M. "Robert E. Lee and the Improvements of the Mississippi River." *Missouri Historical Review* 6 (February 1929).

Edmondson, Mrs. James. "Maysville Reports on Big Spring." *Benton County Pioneer* 10 (1967).

Ewell, Richard S. "From the Rapidan to Spotsylvania Court House." *Southern Historical Society Papers* 13 (1885).

Field, C. W. "Campaigns of 1864 and 1865." *Southern Historical Society Papers* 14 (1886).

Fitzpatrick, M. C. "The Psychological Assessment and Psychosocial Recovery of the Patient with an Amputation." *Clinical Orthopedics* 361 (April 1999).

Flory, William E. S. "Parson Weems: Marketer." In Prince William Historical Commission, *Dumfries, Virginia: A Collection of Articles about Dumfries and Prince William County.* n.p., n.d.

Fowler, Robert H. "How Ewell Lost His Leg." *Civil War Times Illustrated* 4 (June 1965).

Frank, R. G., et al. "Psychological Response to Amputation as a Function of Age and Time Since the Amputation." *British Journal of Psychiatry* 144 (May 1984).

Franklin, James. "Incidents at First Manassas Battle." *Confederate Veteran* 2 (1894).

Fravel, John W. "Jackson's Valley Campaign," *Confederate Veteran* 7 (1898).

Gallagher, Gary W. "In the Shadow of Stonewall Jackson: Richard S. Ewell at Gettysburg." *Virginia Country's Civil War* 5 (1986).

Gardner, Hamilton. "The March of the First Dragoons from Jefferson Barracks to Fort Gibson in 1833–1834." *Chronicles of Oklahoma* 31 (1953).

Gibson, J. Catlett, and William W. Smith. "The Battle of Spotsylvania Court House, May 12, 1864." *Southern Historical Society Papers* 32 (1904).

Glatthaar, Joseph T. "The Common Soldier's Gettysburg Campaign." In Gabor S. Borritt, *The Gettysburg Nobody Knows* (New York: Oxford UP, 1997).

Grace, C. D. "Rodes' Division At Gettysburg." *Confederate Veteran* 5 (1897).

Hamlin, Percy Gatling, ed., "An Arizona Letter of R. S. Ewell." *Journal of Arizona History* 7 (1966).

Hancock, Winfield. "Letter from General Winfield Hancock." *Southern Historical Society Papers* 3 (1878)

Hanson, H. W. "A. P. Hill's Signal Corps." *Confederate Veteran* 2 (1894).

Harrison, George F. "Ewell at First Manassas." *Southern Historical Society Papers* 14 (1886).

Heth, Henry. "The Battle of the Wilderness." In Janet B. Hewett, et al., ed., *Broadfoot's Supplement to the Official Records of the Union and Confederate Armies*, 36, no. 67–68 (1994–1998).

Hill, D. H. "The Battle of Gaines Mill: Including a Sketch of Jackson's March by Major R. L. Dabney." *Century Illustrated Magazine* 30 (1885).

Hullihen, Rev. Mr. "Stonewall Jackson at Prayer." *Southern Historical Society Papers* 19 (1891).

Hutchins, James S. "Bald Head Ewell: Frontier Dragoon." *Arizonian* 3 (1962).

Jackson, Mary Anna. "With Stonewall Jackson in Camp: More Confederate Memories." *Hearst Magazine* 34 (1913).

Johnston, Charles. "Attack on Fort Gilmer, September 29, 1864." *Southern Historical Society Papers* 1 (1876).

Johnston, William Preston, "Memorandum of Conversation with General R. E. Lee." In Gary W. Gallagher, ed., *Lee: The Soldier* (Lincoln: U of Nebraska P, 1998).

Jordan, Weymouth T. "Diary of George Washington Campbell: Minister to Russia, 1818-1820." *Tennessee Historical Quarterly* 7 (1948).

Kershaw, Joseph B. "Report of General J. B. Kershaw." *Southern Historical Society Papers* 13 (1885).

Krick, Robert K. "The Army of Northern Virginia's Most Notorious Court-Martial." *Blue and Grey* 3 (June-July 1986).

———. "An Insurmountable Barrier Between the Army and Ruin: The Confederate Experience at Spotsylvania's Bloody Angle." In Gary W. Gallagher, ed., *The Wilderness Campaign* (Chapel Hill: U of North Carolina P, 1998).

Lane, James H. "History of Lane's Brigade." *Southern Historical Society Papers* 10 (1882).

Long, A. L. "Reminiscences of the Army of Northern Virginia." *Southern Historical Society Papers* 9 (1881).

Longacre, Edward G. "Target: Winchester, Virginia." *Civil War Times Illustrated* 15 (June 1976).

M'Comb, William. "The Battles in Front of Richmond." *Confederate Veteran* 23 (1915).

McGuire, Hunter H. "Clinical Remarks on Gun-Shot Wounds of the Joints, Delivered January 10, 1866, at Howard's Grove Hospital." *Richmond Medical Journal* 1 (March 1866).

McKim, Randolph H. "The Gettysburg Campaign." *Southern Historical Society Papers* 40 (1915).

McLain, Minor H. "The Military Prison at Fort Warren." *Civil War History* 8 (1982).

Martin, J. H. "Forts Gilmer and Harrison Forces." *Confederate Veteran* 14 (1906).

Martin, Samuel J. "Did Baldy Ewell Lose Gettysburg?" *America's Civil War* 10 (July 1997).

———. "Ewell at Gaines Mill." *KEPI* 3 (April-May 1985).

"Memoranda of the Civil War: General R. S. Ewell at First Manassas." *Century Magazine* 29 (January 1885).

Michie, P. S. "Account of the Dutch Canal." In Robert U. Johnson and Clarence C. Buell, eds., *Battles and Leaders of the Civil War.* (New York: Thomas Yoseloff, reprint, 1950).

Miller, Mrs. Fannie Walker. "The Fall of Richmond." *Confederate Veteran* 13 (1905).

Munford, Thomas T. "Reminiscences of Jackson's Valley Campaign." *Southern Historical Society Papers* 7 (1879).

Myers, William Starr "The Civil War Diary of General Isaac Ridgeway Trimble." *Maryland Historical Magazine* 17 (March 1922).

Naiswald, L. Van Loan, "The Battle of Bristoe Station." *Virginia Cavalcade* 18 (autumn 1964).

"Necrology, Legh R. Page." *Virginia Magazine of History and Biography* 1(1894).

Nolan, Alan T. "R. E. Lee and July 1 at Gettysburg." In Gary W. Gallagher, ed. *Lee: The Soldier* (Lincoln: U of Nebraska Press, 1996).

Oates, Stephen B. "Texas Under the Secessionists." *Southwestern Historical Quarterly* 47 (1963).

Page, R. C. M. "The Captured Guns at Spotsylvania Court House." *Southern Historical Society Papers* 7 (1879)

Pfanz, Harry W. "Old Jack Is Not Here." In Gabor S. Boritt, ed., *The Gettysburg Nobody Knows* (New York: Oxford UP, 1997).

Pohl, James W. "The Influence of Henri de Jomini on Winfield Scott's Campaign in the Mexican War." *Southwestern Historical Quarterly* 77 (1973).

Pope, John. "To Gain Time . . . The Second Battle of Bull Run." In Ned Bradford, ed., *Battles and Leaders of the Civil War* (New York: Appleton-Century-Crofts, 1956).

Porter, Fitz-John. "The Last of the Seven Days Battles." *Century Illustrated Monthly Magazine* 34 (1889).

"Proceedings." *Virginia Magazine of History and Biography* 1(1894).

Reardon, Carol. "I Think the Union Army Had Something to Do with It." In Gabor S. Borritt, ed., *The Gettysburg Nobody Knows* (New York: Oxford UP, 1997).

Riggs, David F. "Richard S. Ewell: Lee's Maligned Lieutenant." *Confederate Historical Institute Journal* 1 (summer 1980).

Robertson, James I. "Stonewall in the Shenandoah." *Civil War Times Illustrated* 2 (May 1963).

Rodes, Robert E. "General R. E. Rodes' Report on the Battle of Gettysburg." *Southern Historical Society Papers* 5 (1877).

Sacks, Benjamin. "The Origins of Fort Buchanan: Myth and Fact." *Arizona and the West* 7 (1965).

Schreckengost, Gary. "Stonewall's Triumphant Return to Winchester." *America's Civil War* 13 (July 2000).

Seabourne, J. Gay. "The Battle of Cedar Mountain." *Civil War Times Illustrated* 5 (December 1966).

Shackleford, George G. "Lieutenant Lee Reports to Captain Talcott on Fort Calhoun's Construction on the Rip Raps." *Virginia Magazine of History and Biography* 60 (April 1952).

Sigaud, Louis A. "Mrs. Greenhow and the Confederate Spy Ring." *Maryland Historical Magazine* 41 (September 1946).

———. "Gen. and Gov. William Smith." *Confederate Veteran* 8 (1900).

Sommers, Richard J. "The Dutch Gap Affair: Military Atrocities and the Rights of Negro Soldiers." *Civil War History* 21 (1975).

Spring, John A. "The Ordeal of Mrs. Page." *Wide World Magazine* 15 (February 1912).

Sulivane, Clement. "The Fall of Richmond." In Robert U. Johnson and Clarence C. Buell, eds., *Battles and Leaders of the Civil War* (New York: Thomas Yoseloff, reprint, 1950).

———. "Last Soldiers to Leave Richmond." *Confederate Veteran* 17 (1909).

Timberlake, W. L. "Last Days in Front of Richmond." *Confederate Veteran* 20 (1912).

———. "The Retreat from Richmond." *Confederate Veteran* 22 (1914).

Trimble, Isaac Ridgeway. "The Battle and Campaign of Gettysburg." *Southern Historical Society Papers* 26 (1898).

———. "The Campaign and Battle of Gettysburg." *Confederate Veteran* 25 (1917).

Trudeau, Noah Andrea. "A Mere Question of Time: Robert E. Lee from the Wilderness to Appomattox." In Gary W. Gallagher, ed., *Lee: The Soldier* (Lincoln: U of Nebraska P, 1996).

Turner, Harriet S. "Reflections of Andrew Johnson." *Harper's Monthly Magazine* 120 (January 1910).

Venable, C. S. "The Campaign from the Wilderness to Petersburg." *Confederate Veteran* 14 (1886).

Wagstaff, H. A., ed., "The James A. Graham Papers." *James Sprunt Historical Studies,* (Chapel Hill: U of North Carolina, 1928).

Watehall, E. T. "The Fall of Richmond, April 3, 1865." *Confederate Veteran* 17 (1909).

Watson, W. C. "Saylor's Creek." *Southern Historical Papers* 42 (1917).

Wehrman, Georgia. "Harshaw: Mining Camp of the Patagonias." *Journal of Arizona History* 6 (spring 1965).

Williams, T. Harry. "General Ewell to High Private in the Rear." *Virginia Historical Magazine* 54 (1946).

Worsham, John H. "Jackson's Valley Campaign." *Southern Historical Society Papers* 38 (1910).

Wright, Marcus J. "Bushrod Johnson's Men at Fort Harrison." *Confederate Veteran* 14 (1906).

Dissertations and Theses

Adams, Owen E., Jr. "Confederate General Robert E. Rodes: A Civil War Biography." (MA thesis, University of Southern Mississippi, 1995).

Casdorph, Paul D. "Texas Delegations to Republican National Conventions, 1860–1896." (MA thesis, University of Texas, 1961).

Chapman, Anne West. "Benjamin Stoddert Ewell: A Biography." (PhD dissertation, College of William and Mary, 1984).

Milota, Robert Stephen. "John Bankhead Magruder: The California Years." (MA thesis, University of San Diego, 1990).

Reiter, Robert Lewis. "The History of Fort Union, New Mexico." (MA thesis, University of California, Berkeley, 1950).

Stewart, Michelle Lee. "Robert E. Rodes: Lee's Forgotten General." (MA thesis, University of Southwestern Louisiana, 1997).

Miscellaneous

Brookings Institution. Descriptive Pamphlet, Washington, DC [an online publication, 2001].

Krick, Robert E. L. "The Wounding of Richard Stoddert Ewell" (typescript, n.d.), Manassas National Battlefield Park.

INDEX

Abbreviations are as follows: LB, Lizinka Brown; RSE, Richard Stoddert Ewell; TJJ, Thomas Jonathan "Stonewall" Jackson; REL, Robert E. Lee.